MAKING IT HAPPEN

From Interactive to Participatory Language Teaching:

Evolving Theory and Practice

FOURTH EDITION

PEARSON
Longman

Patricia A. Richard-Amato

To Jay

Making It Happen
From Interactive to Participatory Language Teaching:
Evolving Theory and Practice
Fourth Edition

Pearson Education, 10 Bank Street, White Plains, NY 10606

Staff credits: The people who made up the ***Making It Happen,*** **Fourth Edition**
team, representing editorial, production, design, and manufacturing are: Pietro Alongi,
Rhea Banker, Christine Edmonds, Pam Fishman, Nancy Flaggman, Ann France, Jaime
Lieber, Lise Minovitz, Linda Moser, and Jennifer Stem.
Cover photo: © Eric Meola/Getty Images
Text composition: S4Carlisle Publishing Services
Text font: 10.5/12.5 Garamond Book
Text credits: see pp. xiv–xv.

Library of Congress Cataloging-in-Publication Data

Richard-Amato, Patricia A.
   Making it happen: from interactive to participatory language teaching
: evolving theory and practice/Patricia A. Richard-Amato.—4th ed.
        p. cm.
   Includes bibliographical references and index.
   ISBN-13: 978-0-13-236137-8
   ISBN-10: 0-13-236137-X
  1. Language and languages—Study and teaching. 2. Second language
acquisition. 3. English language—Study and teaching—Foreign speakers.
I. Title.
   P53.R49 2010
   418′.007—dc22

                                                              2009007267

ISBN-10: 0-13-236137-X
ISBN-13: 978-0-13-236137-8

Printed in the United States of America
1 2 3 4 5 6 7 8 9 10—DHN—15 14 13 12 11 10

CONTENTS

PREFACE

Making It Happen itself is still evolving and has been since it was first published in 1988. The book began with a fervent belief that learners do best in situations that empower them and make them respected partners in the learning process. The ideas of Freire and Vygotsky found expression in that first volume and in subsequent editions that over time have become more and more deeply rooted in the sociocultural aspects of language development. Freire has taught us how important it is to look at learners as vital sources of knowledge and experience rather than as passive receptacles for knowledge. Vygotsky has impressed upon us the importance of the teacher, peers, and other facilitators in the learning process to help students "stretch" to higher levels of operation through mediation.

Although *Making It Happen* was originally developed for use with language learners in the United States and other western countries, it has been adapted for use in other cultures where at least portions of it have been deemed appropriate to the local situation.[1] However, the overall content is not, nor has it ever been, intended for universal application.

One constant since the book was first published has been its focus on interactive teaching as opposed to grammar-based teaching. However, explicit instruction in grammar and the various skill areas and the timing of that instruction have become increasingly important with each new edition. *Participatory language teaching*[2] when it was first introduced in the third edition seemed a natural outgrowth of the movement toward the sociocultural aspects of the learning process. It is neither a method nor an approach—it transcends both in that it gets to the very heart of the teacher–student relationship. Through participatory language teaching, individuals can eventually become active members of the sociocultural group to which they desire membership. Through dialogical processes they can identify what gives meaning to their lives; negotiate curriculum; explore issues comprising those things that often keep them marginalized; participate in collaborative learning; and critically analyze, deconstruct on their own terms, and draw from those ideas to which they are exposed.

Our increasing realization of the impact of sociocultural forces and the integral role they play in situated language learning has been greatly influenced by the postmodern movement which has caused us to question the supremacy of the native-speaker model and to become aware of the dangers of western hegemony[3] to our students and the rest of the world.

---

[1] See especially Nelson (2005) and Watanabe (1992).

[2] Please note that when I use the term *participatory language teaching* throughout the book, I am not excluding *participatory learning*, nor do I intend for *teaching* and *learning* to be synonymous; for they are not. I only mean to suggest that they are so closely related that to talk about one brings to mind the other.

[3] Hegemony involves supporting certain social practices to keep one's power over others, not by force but by the consent of the persons/groups with less influence. Unfortunately, those with less influence do not always realize that they are cooperating in a system that perpetuates their marginalization.

Besides bringing awareness to the sociocultural forces driving language learning, postmodernism has caused us to question positivistic thinking and its attempt to find definitive answers through traditional experimental research. Not that experimental research has no value in our field. Indeed it does. What we can look forward to now, perhaps, is an integration of the best of sociocultural and cognitive perspectives into a *sociocultural/cognitive synthesis,* at the same time recognizing what might remain irreconcilable. We may also be able to anticipate the development of a broader, more inclusive paradigm acknowledging the importance of the localization of knowledge and the inclusion of both western and nonwestern perspectives.

In response to the current realization of the importance of sociocultural contexts and affective factors, we are now beginning to witness a strong movement toward ethnographic and discourse-driven research in which context is not just another variable but instead is an integral part of the inquiry. This research, however relative and context-bound, may become instrumental to our knowledge of how language is learned and used in local situations, how our classrooms and the environments surrounding them are organized socially, and how identities are established within them. Although our own experiences as language students and language teachers are critical to our development, we need to take full advantage of what others have to offer. We owe it to ourselves and to our students to keep abreast of what is happening in our field and in closely related fields so that we do not stagnate.

This book is an attempt to present, for your critical consideration, some of the important theoretical concepts and research, limited as they may be, supporting interaction in language classrooms and to examine where we might go from here. The term *interaction* as used in this volume does not refer to the mechanistic definition given to it in many scientific paradigms in which the entities that come together remain unchanged as a result of their contact (see also Rosenblatt, 1985). Rather, interaction as I have defined it incorporates elements of a *transactional* nature. In other words, *the entities doing the interacting are affected and often changed by the contact and by the total social situation surrounding it*. This definition has important implications for what goes on in classrooms and why interaction, as defined here, does not occur as often as we might like it to. Without it, language learners are likely to play only passive or superficial roles in the classroom.

Central to this book is a description of *emergent participatory language teaching* and how it might evolve. I say "emergent" because participatory teaching is never a fixed end point but remains elusive and dynamic as it moves in and out of existence. In order for transactional elements to be fully realized, a *classroom community* needs to develop within the context of the larger world. In a classroom community, teaching goes beyond organizing a curriculum, deciding on an overall pedagogical strategy, and executing a program. It means facilitating learning and seeking student input into the decision-making process. It means forming dialectical relationships with students in which teachers and students are partners. It means accommodating students linguistically and culturally, having high expectations of them, and believing that they are intelligent human beings who can achieve academically. And it means involving parents and others in the school environment and the outside community in the learning/teaching process.

The information presented in this edition, as in those before it, is not intended to be the final word on second and foreign language teaching, nor is it intended to be prescriptive. Every teacher needs to develop his or her own philosophical foundation and ways of doing things. This book is simply a resource from which to draw. Authors, like all people, have their own cultural frameworks and biases from which they operate. Therefore, readers are invited to make their own judgments as they deconstruct the material presented here.

Patricia Abbott Richard-Amato
Professor Emeritus
California State University, Los Angeles

ACKNOWLEDGMENTS

I must first thank the English learners and colleagues with whom I have worked over the years. Many of them have been very influential in my own development as a teacher, from my first teaching position at Pueblo High School in Tucson, Arizona, to my later experiences at the university level as a graduate student and professor. I am most grateful to all those who learned with me and challenged me to do better.

John Oller, Jr., was particularly influential as my graduate committee chair at the University of New Mexico, Albuquerque. Although we didn't always agree when coauthoring the first edition of *Methods that Work*, his seminal ideas about naturalness in language testing and episodic structure made a huge impact on me and my later work.

Appreciation also goes to the many people with whom I exchanged ideas and developed friendships while teaching at several TESOL Institutes; at the Mediterranean Institute in Barcelona, Spain in 1994; and at two TESOL Academies. Many a fleeting notion became fleshed out through lengthy discussions in the classroom and out.

Although he probably doesn't remember me, I owe much to James Banks, who several years ago spoke to our faculty at California State University, Los Angeles, and whose book *Multiethnic Education* became a text for a course I taught there. His perspective helped me more fully realize what it might be like for language minority learners enrolled in institutions that do not value diversity.

There are many other authors to whom I am indebted for their influence on this and/or previous editions: Paulo Friere and Lev Vygotsky (see Preface), Gordon Wells, Sonia Nieto, and Leo van Lier. Freire's *Pedagogy of the Oppressed* and his discussion with me and other faculty members at California State University, Los Angeles, made lasting impressions. Wells's *Learning Through Interaction* influenced my thinking early on, but his later book *Dialogic Inquiry* both surprised and delighted me. Many of his interpretations, applications, and extensions of Vygotsky were similar to my own, although he described them much more eloquently than I. Nieto's book *The Light In Their Eyes* reinforced what Banks and Friere had taught me and presented a rich account of teachers' experiences from their own perspectives. Leo van Lier's *Interaction in the Language Curriculum* gave me greater insight into the language learning process and helped me clarify my own thinking. Of course I cannot forget Alastair Pennycook and Elsa Auerbach for their influence on my ideas about participatory language teaching, which changed the focus of the book beginning with the third edition.

In this new edition I want to add Suresh Canagarajah and James Lantolf to the list of authors to whom I am indebted. Canagarajah's substantial writings have made me more aware of the importance of local cultural identities and situations and their impact upon teaching decisions and pedagogical practice. Lantolf's volume *Sociocultural Theory and Second Language Learning* and its many contributors offered their own interpretations of Vygotsky's theories and brought to light the many paths that Vygotskian thought has taken in recent years. Their voices helped me render what I hope is a more nuanced treatment of Vygotsky than I was able to present in earlier editions.

I also am immensely grateful to Lyle F. Bachman (University of California, Los Angeles) and Elsa Auerbach (University of Massachusetts, Boston) whose careful reading and attention to detail helped me flesh out my views on language assessment and emergent participatory language teaching, respectively. I also owe many thanks to Neil Anderson (Brigham Young University, Provo, Utah), Mary McGroarty (Northern Arizona University, Flagstaff), Robert Oprandy (University of the Pacific, Stockton, California), Rachel Hayes-Harb (University of Utah, Salt Lake City), Fabiola Ehlers-Zavala (Colorado State University, Fort Collins), and Kerry Purmensky (University of Central Florida, Orlando). Although not all of these teacher educators and scholars will agree with every one of my interpretations and conclusions, their comments and suggestions were instrumental in helping me clarify my perspectives in the areas in which they have expertise.

In addition, I owe a debt of gratitude to Cathrene Connery (Ithaca College, New York) for her invaluable feedback on Chapter 5 and for her contribution of Case Study 1: "Motivating Beto," and to Lía Kamhi-Stein (California State University, Los Angeles) who shared with me her innovative ideas for additions to the book. Both Cathrene and Lía, long-time users of the text in their graduate courses—both as students and later as professors—have witnessed its change and development right from the beginning.

A special thanks to Christine Sims of the Pueblo of Acoma and the University of New Mexico, Albuquerque. I indeed feel honored to have been able to include her description of the Keres heritage language program written for this edition. Thanks also to Paula Kristmanson (University of New Brunswick), Michael Brunn (University of Colorado, Colorado Springs), and one anonymous reader for their helpful input this time around. In addition, appreciation goes to Margo Gottlieb (Illinois Resource Center) who shared with me her insights into language proficiency standards.

I am also grateful to Longman editor Lise Minovitz, who offered many creative suggestions, skillfully shepherded the book through the publication process, and was instrumental in arranging for several of the expert readers. In addition, I owe a debt of gratitude to my development editor, Julia Hough. Her clear focus and conscientious attention to form and organization were invaluable during the process. Thanks also to production editor Jaime Lieber whose expertise and diligence were critical during the final stages of publication; to copyeditor Kari Lucke, who carefully and consistently applied her skills from cover to cover; to Donna Wright and Amy Kefauver, who proofread the pages meticulously; and to Bernice Eisen, who once again prepared a very complete and functional index. In addition, I owe many thanks to Caroline Gloodt who left no stone unturned when tracking down sources and securing permissions.

Thanks also to my former editors Ginny Blanford, Eleanor Barnes, Louisa Hellegers, and the many others whose encouragement and advice were very important to me over the years; and to Joanne Dresner, who first published my work and has been a great inspiration ever since.

Of course I cannot forget those people in our field who contributed so much to past editions: Leslie Jo Adams, Kathleen Bailey, Mary Ann Christison, Alan Crawford, Marty Furch, José Galván, Barbara Kroll, Ruth Larimer, Diane Larsen-Freeman, Carolyn Madden, Holbrook Mahn, Mary McGroarty, John Oller, Jr., Linda Sasser, Ann Snow, Fred Tarpley, Kathy Weed, and many, many more.

In addition, I want to express my appreciation to the following publishing companies and individuals for permission to reprint or adapt materials for which they own copyrights:

American Council on the Teaching of Foreign Languages, p. 9 in *Standards for Foreign Language Learning in the 21st Century*. ©2006 American Council on the Teaching of Foreign Languages. Used by permission from ACTFL and the Standards for Foreign Language Learning in the 21st Century Project. (Figure 7.9, page 203 in this volume)

Bonne, Rose. Excerpt from "There Was an Old Lady Who Swallowed a Fly," illustrated by Pam Adams. Copyright ©1973 Michael Twinn, Child's Play Ltd. Reprinted by permission of Michael Twinn, Child's Play (International) Ltd. (Page 275)

Christison, Mary Ann. Adapted illustration by Kathleen Peterson from *English Through Poetry*, p. 29, 1982. Reprinted by permission of Alemany Press/Janus Book Publishers, Inc., Haywood, California. (Figure 10.1, page 268)

Ellis, Rod. From "Theories of Second Language Acquisition" in *Understanding Second Language Acquisition*, p. 266. © 1985 Oxford University Press. (Figure 3.4, page 77)

Evans, Joy, and Moore, Jo Ellen. Adapted illustration from p. 80 in *Art Moves the Basics Along: Animal Units*. ©1979. Used by permission of Evan-Moor, Carmel, California. (Figure 12.4, page 297)

Evans, Joy, and Moore, Jo Ellen. Adaptation of illustration, p. 64, from *Art Moves the Basics Along: Units About Children*, 2nd ed. © 1990. Reprinted by permission of Evan-Moor, Carmel, California. (Figure 11.1, page 286)

Krashen, Stephen. Figure 2, "The Relationship between Affective Factors and Language Acquisition," p. 110 in *Second Language Acquisition and Second Language Learning*; ©1981 Stephen Krashen. Reprinted by permission of the author. (Figure 3.2, page 75)

Krashen, Stephen. Figure from "Immersion: Why it Works and What it Taught Us," in *Language and Society, 12* (Winter 1984), p. 63. ©1981 Stephen Krashen. Reprinted by permission of the Office of Official Language, Ontario, Canada, and the Minister of Supply and Services, Canada. (Figure 17.2, page 430)

Krashen, Stephen. Figure 2.1 from *Principles and Practice in Second Language Acquisition*. ©1982 Stephen Krashen. Reprinted by permission of the author. (Figure 3.3, page 75)

Krashen, Stephen, and Terrell, T. From *The Natural Approach*, pp. 67–70. ©1983. Reprinted by permission of Alemany Press/Janus Book Publishers, Inc. Haywood, California. (Pages 227–231)

Prelutsky, Jack. "The Creature in the Classroom," from *The Baby Uggs are Hatching*, by Jack Prelutsky. ©2002 Jack Prelutsky. Used by permission of Harper Collins Publishers. (Page 267)

Shulman, Judith H., and Amalia Mesa-Bains, eds. "My Good Year Explodes: A Confrontation with Parents," pp. 85–86 in *Diversity in the Classroom: A Casebook for Teachers and Teacher Educators*. ©1993 Taylor & Francis Group LLC-Books. Reproduced with permission of Taylor & Francis Group LLC-Books in the format Textbook via Copyright Clearance Center. (Page 529)

Shulman, Judith H., and Amalia Mesa-Bains, eds. "Please, Not Another ESL Student," pp. 37–39 in *Diversity in the Classroom: A Casebook for Teachers and Teacher Educators*. ©1993 Taylor & Francis Group LLC-Books. Reproduced with permission of Taylor & Francis Group LLC-Books in the format Textbook via Copyright Clearance Center. (Page 531)

TESOL, p. 25 in *PreK–12 English Language Proficiency Standards.* ©2006 Teachers of English to Speakers of Other Languages. Reproduced with permission of TESOL in the format Textbook via Copyright Clearance Center. (Figure 7.5, page 197)

TESOL, pp. 39, 58–59, and 92–93 in *PreK–12 English Language Proficiency Standards.*©2006 Teachers of English to Speakers of Other Languages. Reproduced with permission of TESOL in the format Textbook via Copyright Clearance Center. (Figures 7.6, 7.7, 7.8; pages 198, 199, and 200)

TESOL, p. 8 in *TESOL Technology Standards Framework.* © 2008 Teachers of English to Speakers of Other Languages. Reproduced with permission of TESOL in the format Textbook via Copyright Clearance Center. (Figure 16.2, page 408)

Whitecloud, Thomas. Excerpt from "Blue Winds Dancing." Reprinted with the permission of Scribner, an imprint of Simon and Schuster Adult Publishing Group from *Scribner's Magazine*, vol. 103, February 1938. ©1938 Charles Scribner's Sons; copyright renewed © 1966. All rights reserved. (Page 280)

I thank also the following individuals whose programs are featured in Part IV: Programs in Action: Christine Schulze, Denise Phillippe, and Donna Clementi (Concordia Language Villages, Bemidji, Minnesota); Marguerite Straus and Good Jean Lau (Public School No. 1, Manhattan); Lydia Vogt and Sarah Clayton (Valley Center School District, Valley Center, California); Sally Cummings and Carolyn Duffy (Saint Michael's College, Colchester, Vermont); Blanca Arazi (Instituto Cultural Argentina Norteamericano, Buenos Aires); Ann Snow and Janet Tricamo (California State University, Los Angeles); Linda Sasser (Alhambra School District, Alhambra, California); Pamela Branch and Christina Rivera (ABC Unified School District, Cerritos, California); Christine Sims (Pueblo of Acoma); Sandra Brown (North Hollywood Adult Learning Center, North Hollywood, California); Brandon Zaslow and Beverly McNeilly (Los Angeles Unified School District; Los Angeles, California); and Ken Cressman (Lakehead Board of Education, Thunder Bay, Ontario, Canada).

And last to my husband, Jay. His patience, love, and good advice over the years remain a source of strength for me.

Introduction

CHANGE AND CHANGING[1]

Change is inevitable. We have come to expect it. It has brought new ways of looking at learning/teaching and the teacher's role in these processes. Sometimes we resist new ways of looking—at least at first. If we discover some truth in them based on our own experience, we are more likely to give them serious consideration, to talk (perhaps argue) about them with colleagues and other associates, and, eventually, to take action and incorporate from them what makes sense to us and disregard the rest. We have learned through our own experience that innovations in thought and action can make a big difference, not only for us personally but for our language learners. The innovations we often find most acceptable and enduring are those that do not bluntly tear down what already exists. Advocates of change would be wise to find its roots, not only in the present but also in history, and approach mainstream thought gingerly, realizing that others have also had their truths.

Unfortunately, those promoting change sometimes inadvertently fall into that great abyss—dichotomous thinking. To them every controversy involves an either/or situation—a cognitive perspective to language acquisition *or* a sociocultural one; transformational education *or* transmission education; a grammar-based syllabus *or* no grammar focus at all; whole language strategies *or* phonics instruction; a methods-based pedagogy *or* one without explicit recourse to methods; and the list goes on.

Try to imagine what these opposites might look like at the ends of a continuum or in a dialectical relationship to one another, rather than in a dichotomy. What if instructors in teacher preparation programs wanted to make teachers aware of the insights of both cognitive and sociocultural perspectives while, at the same time, recognizing that sociocultural factors are most likely to be determinant? What if language teachers wanted to help second language learners better their lives through critical-thinking processes and, at the same time, help them master some of the disciplinary knowledge required to meet immediate needs through transmission? What if teachers used whole-language strategies as a starting point because they knew that they could focus their students on sound-word correspondences when appropriate? What if they interjected grammar rules as needed because research told them that these rules would benefit language learners, but at the same time believed (again because of research) that other rules would be best learned through actual *use* of language? And what if in teacher preparation programs, participants realized that they just might want to experiment, both as learners and teachers, with various methods, not because they slavishly plan to follow their tenets and practices, but because they can be important sources from which to draw? When involved in real classrooms, teachers become pragmatic. They realize that the distinctions are not so clear-cut after all.

---

[1] Some of the ideas and the words here first appeared in a plenary I gave at the California TESOL State Conference, April 20, 2001, in Ontario and in an article I wrote for *ESL Magazine*, January/February 2002, pp. 16–18. The article was adapted in part from the manuscript for the third edition of this book.

This new edition of *Making It Happen*, like those before it, is based on the premise that teachers are pragmatic beings. In their efforts to be effective in classrooms, they will pick and choose whatever strategies are needed at the moment, depending on the situation and the participants involved—their histories, their preferred modes of learning, their personal, social, and political concerns, and their immediate as well as long-term goals.

Making It Happen draws from a synthesis of two major sources: psychology and sociology. A study of both is essential to understanding how humans learn language. From psychology, we take a close look at the *psycholinguistic* focus in second language acquisition theory and research based on modernism. From sociology we examine Vygotskian thought in addition to the renewed belief in the *sociocultural* focus on critical pedagogy[2] found in postmodernism. Because Vygotsky's ideas about learning are discussed in depth in Chapter 3, they are not included in this analysis.

SECOND LANGUAGE ACQUISITION THEORY/RESEARCH BASED ON MODERNISM

Modern psycholinguists view language acquisition as a developmental process. Second language learners move from little knowledge of the target language to fuller knowledge of it in somewhat nebulous stages.[3] Modern psycholinguists have assumed that the learner's goal is to communicate like a native speaker. This assumption alone raises the ire of critical pedagogists. To them, the concept "native speaker" brings with it certain baggage (i.e., a wish to divide the world into a colonial "us and them" dichotomy; see Brutt-Griffler & Samimy, 1999; Kachru, 1994; Sridhar, 1994). Although I do not feel the conscious motivation of most of these linguists has been to colonize others, some of the terminology they use such as *interlanguage* and *fossilization*, does lend itself to that interpretation. Although I have used such terms in my own writing, I must admit that I never felt entirely comfortable with them but was not consciously aware of why. Fortunately, we now recognize that many Englishes are spoken by millions of people around the world. The native-speaker standard is no longer the only model for English learners, nor should it be.[4] Not that we should do away with having a goal. We still need a target language, however fluid and hybrid it might be. The target language can and

---

[2] Critical pedagogy grew out of ideas of liberation made popular mainly by educator Paulo Freire of Brazil. It describes a transformation in the relationship between teacher and student (see Chapters 3 and 4) that empowers both and addresses oppression based on socioeconomic class, culture, and other factors.

[3] The progression of learning is now seen by many psycholinguists as continuous, not as an ordered set of stages (Sharwood-Smith & Truscott, 2005).

[4] Widdowson (1996) argued that there is still just one "standard" model and that the other models of English are nonstandard dialects that coexist with standard English and have their own appropriate smaller domains of use. He went on to say that there are good reasons for teaching standard English to those who want membership in the wider community of English speakers.

should be the *language of proficient second language users in whatever environment we find them*. In this context, the terms *interlanguage* and *fossilization* (*premature stabilization* is now the more preferred term)[5] are still useful to a large extent and lose some of their negative overtones. Not only is the more loosely defined target language less condescending, but it presents a more realistic goal for language learners, although many of them do approximate native-like proficiency under the right conditions (see Flege & Liu, 2001; Klein, 1995; Marinova-Todd, Marshal, & C. Snow, 2000). Moreover, this new definition recognizes that multilingual minds differ from monolingual minds (see Cook, 1999) and that it cannot be expected that both will come up with exactly the same end product. However, both can and should be considered proficient speakers of the language. As Cook reminded us, second language speakers should not be treated as failed native speakers.

Second language acquisition (SLA) based on modernism has come under recent criticism from the critical pedagogists for other reasons as well. Some say that it relies too heavily on a western view of applied linguistics. SLA does not appear to consider nonwestern experiences, and, if it does, it sees them through a western lens (see Makoni, 2005; Pakir, 2005). Some say it downplays sociocultural factors too much in favor of rationalist, cognitive ones (see especially M. Gebhard, 1999). Others criticize SLA's current tendencies toward positivism (looking for definitive answers and solutions) rather than toward the relativism associated with a more sociocultural perspective (see Block, 1996; Zuengler & Miller, 2006). Block even went so far as to accuse psycholinguists of "science envy" in their attempt to find answers that can be applied universally. Others claim that SLA has overemphasized developmental stages and end points, rather than viewing language development as fluid and largely influenced by social circumstances (see Genishi, 1999). Still others argue that it maintains an unhealthy reliance on "experts" and divorces itself too readily from pedagogy, focusing instead on how languages are learned rather than how they are taught (see Thomas, 1998).

As a former ESL teacher myself, one additional failure of SLA based on modernism, as I see it, is its failure to meaningfully explore the importance of the learning environment and the power relationship between language learner and teacher and between peer and peer. Are these relationships and environments mostly accepting, positive, and encouraging? Or do they tend to be judgmental, negative, and uncompromising? To language and cultural minorities, this issue is especially critical, for it can determine how well these language learners do in our classrooms.

However, in spite of the apparent shortcomings of the current SLA perspective based on modernism, it has indeed presented us with valuable psycholinguistic knowledge to help us understand more about how languages are learned. Its insights should not be given short shrift in our teacher preparation programs, as long as its limitations are fully acknowledged and discussed.

---

[5] See Long (2003).

CRITICAL PEDAGOGY AND POSTMODERNISM

One of the most interesting and, at the same time, controversial movements in second language teaching is the contemporary treatment of Paulo Freire's critical pedagogy. Freire (1970a, 1970b, 1985) believed that learners should not be considered empty heads waiting to be filled with information through transmission; rather, they should be considered valuable sources of knowledge, instrumental to their own learning and empowerment[6] (see Chapters 3 and 4).

Critical pedagogy considers itself postmodern. It goes beyond modern humanistic education, which assumes that individuals have the freedom to rise above their circumstances. Instead, critical pedagogy is based on the premise that such freedom may or may not exist and that powerful forces are determined to hold cultural minorities or persons with diminished influence in a state of oppression. For example, Pennycook (1999) pointed to the deterministic thinking often found in our classrooms and the literature of our discipline, in which different cultures are given distinctive labels and treated as the "exotic other" so typical of colonial discourse (see also Kubota, 1999, 2001, 2004a).

Unfortunately, English teachers in particular sometimes view their students' languages and cultures negatively and treat them as deficits. Some teachers feel that complete assimilation or acculturation is necessary to access the new societies in which minority language learners find themselves. Although the teachers' intentions may be good, the message learners often receive is that their first languages and cultures are inferior, perhaps even dysfunctional. As Gee (1994) reminded us, "Like it or not, English teachers stand at the very heart of the most crucial educational, cultural, and political issues of our time" (p. 190). All teachers need to gain as much knowledge as they can about today's relevant issues and learn to overcome whatever prejudices they may harbor. They need to show respect for their students' first languages and cultures and realize that political empowerment in a global society comes from being able to establish one's identity[7] and to develop the ability to function in more than one cultural environment (see also Canagarajah, 2006).

Critical pedagogists showcase Foucault (1980), who claimed early on that politics is the main factor influencing *all* social interaction, inside the classroom and out. They are convinced that teaching English as a second language is in itself a political act, and is not neutral (see Cox & Assis-Peterson, 1999). They believe that teaching English (or any second language, for that matter) is fraught with arbitrary implications about power and who has it and who does not, based on the values of the most influential in society.

---

[6] *Empowerment* is inner strength and confidence coming from feelings of pride in one's own social and cultural background and one's own knowledge and abilities. It involves a willingness to selectively question social practices or effect change.

[7] According to Norton (1997), *identity* encompasses the relationship of the individual to the world, is developed across time and space, and includes the way in which people see their future possibilities. Identity is situated, multiple, and socially constructed and reconstructed (Carbaugh, 1996; Norton, 2000; Weedon, 1987).

Critical pedagogy aims to take language learners beyond a modernistic awareness about what oppresses them and keeps them marginalized. Its goal is and always has been to encourage critical engagement, problem posing, and the kind of action that leads to political/personal empowerment through participation and action. The issues critical to the language learners' own lives become focal points of learning and teaching. Language learners and teachers together identify and pursue the areas of knowledge relevant to them. Thus the learners can gain perspective on those societal forces that help to shape their lives.

However, critical pedagogy also has its critics. One bone of contention concerns power and how it is perceived. For example, Gore (1992) concluded that critical pedagogists consider power a *product* that teachers have that can be "bestowed" upon learners. Even the very words *empowerment* and *transformation* carry a modicum of colonial baggage. Bill Johnston (1999), while emphasizing that power is not a commodity to be given away, argued that it is a *process* to be negotiated and that the teacher in the classroom will, in the end, always be the authority. He was convinced that teaching is neither about power nor politics; rather it is about a moral relationship between student and teacher.

A second criticism has to do with the claim made by the critical pedagogists that teaching English is a political act and is not neutral. Ghim-Lian Chew (1999) argued that learning English can indeed be neutral to many who use it around the world (see also Kachru, 2005). Ghim-Lian Chew pointed to Nigeria, where English now has a pragmatic function in the society, and to Singapore, where the speakers have accepted the English language but not its cultural values. She believes that bilingualism does not have to be accompanied by biculturalism. Byram clarified this point in 1998 by distinguishing between *biculturalism* and *interculturalism*. *Biculturalism*, according to him, implies that the learner identifies with the new culture and accepts it. *Interculturalism,* on the other hand, implies that the learner may know about the new culture but does not accept it or internalize it. One can be bilingual without being bicultural. Sandra McKay (2000) took the argument even further. She claimed that in English as an international language, the language belongs to its users and that interculturalism rather than biculturalism should be the goal. She suggested that, instead of choosing materials reflecting mainly American or British culture, we choose ones that reflect the *source culture*; in other words, the culture of the country in which English is being learned. Another alternative is to choose and/or create materials that incorporate the cultures of many countries around the world.

A third criticism of critical pedagogy concerns its stand on genre theory and its attitude toward "expertness" and authority opinion. It argues that a study of the conventional genres and how they are constructed perpetuates and reinforces structures of inequity (Luke, 1996). However, the fact that many language learners want (and even need) to know the literary conventions of a given society needs to be recognized. Such knowledge provides access to that society, making critical analysis and transformation possible (see especially Chapter 5). Because learners understand and use the constructs of a given genre does not mean that it has to control them; and just because they seek out the opinions of "experts" does not mean they need to accept what these "experts" say. Learners need to know that they have the same freedoms we do—to deconstruct what they read and hear, accept what makes sense, and reject the rest. This is, in part, what empowerment is all about.

We *can* share power in the classroom with our language learners and establish a more dialectical relationship with them. We *can* respect their first languages and cultures by learning about them and using them to inform our own teaching. We *can* realize that the language we are teaching is greatly influenced by social factors involving gender, race, religion, privilege, sexual orientation, and other such factors and study these influences. We *can* explore how discourse and language are influenced by power relationships and struggles for justice and equality, and we *can* encourage learners to consider the viewpoints of others, reflect on them, and be transformed by them, even if only in small ways.

WORLD ENGLISHES

Although World Englishes (e.g., Brazilian English, Nigerian English, Korean English, and so forth) and the localized varieties where they exist have already been mentioned briefly, the topic deserves a section of its own in this introduction because of its importance to English learners and their teachers everywhere. English speakers from around the world, including the varieties of English as a *lingua franca*,[8] now greatly outnumber those in English-dominant countries such as England, the United States, Canada, Australia, and other countries in Kachru's inner circle (see the distinctions he has drawn on pp. 355–356). Many recent books and dictionaries have documented versions of the English spoken outside the inner circle and have found them different linguistically in many ways from the English versions spoken by native speakers. These World Englishes often include utterances such as "He like the cake she give him," or "Omar has much informations to tell us," which sound ungrammatical to the ears of native speakers who have a strong sense of ownership of the language. Unfortunately, Englishes containing such forms and the people who speak them are frequently thought to be inferior, even though the English each speaks may be the only version they know and need to know. According to Jenkins (2006),

> attempts to label the English of whole speech communities as deficient and fossilized are thus unjustifiable because these labels ignore the local Englishes' sociohistorical development and sociocultural context. (p. 167)

Such labels have often been the result of *linguistic imperialism* (Phillipson, 1992) that more often than not can be extremely detrimental to speakers in many parts of the world and should be resisted (Canagarajah, 1999). Speakers need to be able to speak the language (the norm) of the local community in which they participate or the communities (international or otherwise) in which they want to more fully participate.

---

[8] A version of English used by speakers for communication across language borders.

At the international level of participation, controversy surrounds what should constitute *World Standard English*. Native speakers in inner-circle countries, including teachers and others in the educational community, generally like to think of British English and the North American standard as two acceptable varieties of the "world standard." Many nonnative speakers appear to perpetuate this assumption as well and often hire "native speakers" even over their often better-educated and more experienced peers (see also the discussion on p. 11). Not only can this practice cause hard feelings, it can be a serious threat to learners' identities and cultural sensitivities. Which version of English they are taught should depend on the learners' aspirations, goals, and current needs.

Testing is another area in which changes in attitude need to take place as we begin to see the importance of accommodating the different varieties of English and respecting the people who speak them. One means of testing and one standard for evaluation will not work for all learners as a measure of proficiency. Testing, like teaching, needs to be situated and relevant to the learners' needs. See Chapter 7 for various alternatives in language testing.

TEACHER EDUCATION: WHAT ARE THE POSSIBILITIES?

Today, teacher education itself has changed. Much greater emphasis is now placed on participants' experience, collaboration, reflection, and development than in the past.[9] Critical exploration, decision making, question posing, problem solving, and strategy modification have been brought into clearer focus.

Now we appear to be moving toward an exploration of the driving force provided by the sociocultural aspects of language learning (see especially Chapters 3, 4, and 6). However, the contributions of cognitive theorists and researchers is still valuable to teachers as long as they know the limitations of the research and the theories that have grown out of it. In developing their own principles of second language teaching in whatever contexts they find themselves, teachers draw from numerous sources. Most teachers do not want to be spoon-fed someone else's set of principles; nor do they want to simply be left to "discover" for themselves the theories and research that have taken decades to develop. Although teachers feel a need for bottom-up approaches arising from their own actions and reflection, they also know that they can benefit greatly from certain aspects of top-down learning, realizing that they have the freedom to be selective and take only what is relevant to their local situations (see also Richard-Amato, 1996a, 2003). From the interaction of teachers' values, what they are currently learning and experiencing, and their prior knowledge, a set of principles begins to take shape, which then evolves throughout a lifetime of teaching. The teachers, too, experience and benefit from transformational processes.

---

[9] See Richards (1991, 1998); Prabhu (1990); Freeman (1991, 1992); Fanselow (1992); Richards and Lockhart (1996); J. Gebhard and Oprandy (1999); Canagarajah (2006); K. E. Johnson (2006); and many more.

HAVE WE REACHED A POSTMETHOD CONDITION?

One concept of *method* involved looking for the best "one-size-fits-all" magical formula. It was this concept of method that many applied linguists severely criticized and rightly so (see especially Clarke, 1994; Kumarvadivelu, 1994, 1999, 2001, 2006; Pennycook, 1989). If this concept of method has actually been the prevailing one, then we have indeed reached a postmethod condition.

However, there exists another concept of method that has also been recognized by teachers and many others in the field, and that is the concept of *method as resource* (Richard-Amato, 1996a, 2003). All one has to do is go into the teachers' lounge of almost any school across the United States and elsewhere to hear spontaneous talk about the "how" of teachers' practices, particularly among those in similar fields. Teachers want to know what others are doing, not to mindlessly imitate them but rather to learn from them. There is nothing inherently wrong with an examination of methods with their supporting theories, strategies, best practices, and procedures, whether such methods have been prepackaged for consumption or not. According to Bartolomé (2003), "it is important that educators not blindly reject teaching methods across the board, but that they reject uncritical appropriation of methods, materials, curricula, etc." (p. 412).

In the context of this book, methods receive a treatment much different from the one-size-fits-all conceptualization. In this book, methods are considered dynamic, sensitive to local factors, and shaped by the teacher's own developing philosophy (see pp. 20-21, item 7 on pp. 206-207, and item 4 on p. 442). At the same time, methods are likely to contribute to that philosophy. A few of the more highly developed methods have made important contributions to current practice. Participants' exposure to methods does not preclude their own generation of methods and strategies; indeed they may even stimulate such generation. If teacher education is to be transformative, participants need to have access to information about methods and the different ways in which they have been viewed. It is important for programs to encourage participants to explore together the information they consider valuable.

AN INTERACTIVE CONCEPTUALIZATION
FOR SECOND LANGUAGE TEACHER EDUCATION

The rudimentary conceptualization I present in Figure I.1 has been evolving since the last edition of *Making It Happen*. The conceptualization comprises three basic components: The *affective base*, the *disciplinary knowledge base*, and the *experience/ research base*.

Each component consists of at least the items enumerated within the boxes. The details vary depending on the program and the sociocultural and political environment in which it is situated and how this environment has evolved over time. Related factors include the personal qualities of the individual: openness to others, creativity, flexibility, intelligence, ability to empathize with learners, and ability to make decisions (with learner input). The relationships between the components are *symbiotic*. The components are

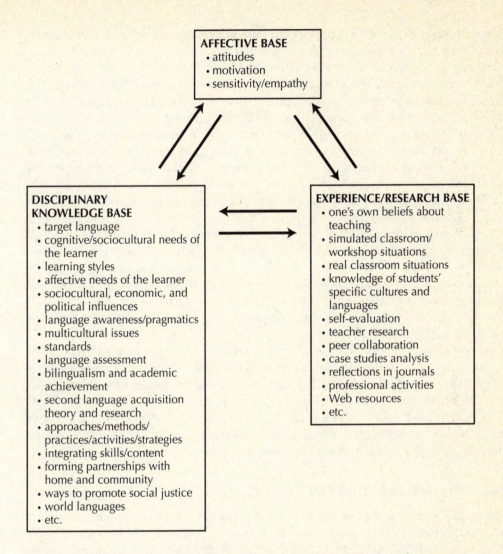

AFFECTIVE BASE
- attitudes
- motivation
- sensitivity/empathy

DISCIPLINARY KNOWLEDGE BASE
- target language
- cognitive/sociocultural needs of the learner
- learning styles
- affective needs of the learner
- sociocultural, economic, and political influences
- language awareness/pragmatics
- multicultural issues
- standards
- language assessment
- bilingualism and academic achievement
- second language acquisition theory and research
- approaches/methods/practices/activities/strategies
- integrating skills/content
- forming partnerships with home and community
- ways to promote social justice
- world languages
- etc.

EXPERIENCE/RESEARCH BASE
- one's own beliefs about teaching
- simulated classroom/workshop situations
- real classroom situations
- knowledge of students' specific cultures and languages
- self-evaluation
- teacher research
- peer collaboration
- case studies analysis
- reflections in journals
- professional activities
- Web resources
- etc.

Figure I.1 An Interactive Conceptualization for Second Language Teacher Education

interdependent and *interactive* in that the influences are two-way (notice the arrows). Each component informs and validates the others. Another feature is that the conceptualization is independent of any specific method or methodology.

It would be a mistake to think that the items in the disciplinary knowledge base are fixed and can be taught only through transmission. Rather these items are ever-changing and should be examined and reexamined by both teachers in preparation and their facilitators, each bringing to the table whatever knowledge and experience they have. *Making It Happen* provides a disciplinary knowledge base with which to begin.

Through further exploration, experience, and self-reflection, second and foreign language[10] teachers in preparation are expected to develop their own informed critical perspective. In addition, teachers are encouraged throughout the book to examine what is here and integrate what they accept with what they already know and believe about second language learning and teaching. Teachers are asked to keep professional-development journals mainly for this purpose (see item 3 on p. 37).

The text also encourages simulated experience in supportive environments. Teachers in preparation are asked to try out their own adaptations of various methods and activities, learn from them, critically analyze them with the help of peers, reflect on their use, and take from them what they want. Simulated experience can be particularly valuable early on in such an investigation. Moreover, during simulated phases teachers are often exposed to a target language with which they are not familiar and are asked to reflect on that experience. Thus they become *learners* themselves and are asked to respond to each other from a *learner's point of view*. Too often, this component is missing from teacher education programs. Another aspect that is often missing in teacher education programs is computer-mediated communication. Teachers can benefit from collaborating and discussing what they are learning in their teacher education programs and what they are actually doing or plan to do in their own classrooms (see Kamhi-Stein, 2000b, 2000c).

However, a teacher's knowledge of current practice, no matter how extensive, will not mean much if the school environment does not foster respect and mutual understanding. If the atmosphere is one of hostility (even though subtle), if minority language learners are expected to do all the accommodation and have little power in the decision-making process, and if they are not made to feel capable of academic work, then little that teachers do to teach the subject matter will be of consequence. Only when all learners are valued for who they are can learning be maximally successful.

PARTICIPATORY TEACHER EDUCATION

Just as language learners are not empty heads waiting to be filled with information, neither are their teachers. Even before entering education programs, teachers know what they value, what their political and cultural concerns are, and what they already know. Teacher educators would be wise to tap into this resource and encourage participants in their programs to reflect on what they are learning and deconstruct it on their own terms.

In addition, teachers in preparation often need and want assistance deciding which direction to take and/or which questions about their teaching to address. They often want advice and "expert" input from a supervisor who is generally more experienced

---

[10] *Second language teaching* occurs in programs in which the target language is the dominant language for communication in the area or domain in which it is being taught. *Foreign language teaching* occurs in programs in which the target language is *not* the dominant language in the area or domain in which it is being taught. However, now that English has become global, the distinctions are not so clear. See pp. 355–358 for the teaching implications related to each type. Note that often the terms are used when contrasting "first language acquisition" and "second language acquisition." In this case, "second" usually refers to any language that is not the first one learned.

and may have critical information to share. At the same time, supervisors should avoid authoritarian approaches, no matter how practical or expedient they appear. Active collaboration between teachers and their supervisors, each showing respect for the other's viewpoint and expertise, usually brings about the best results.

NONNATIVE SPEAKERS IN TEACHER EDUCATION PROGRAMS

Nonnative-speaking teachers need to be welcomed with open arms into teacher education programs. They make excellent role models for second and foreign language learners. Many have already successfully gone through some sort of acculturation process (see Chapter 6), and most have attained or are close to attaining proficient second language use. Because of their experience learning another language, they are generally more aware of helpful strategies, pitfalls to avoid, language learning difficulties, and the personal and social needs of learners.

Brutt-Griffler and Samimy (1999, p. 428) suggested that we take a close look at the concerns of nonnative-speaking teachers who are in these programs. Among their suggestions are the reexamination of nonnative speakers' experiences through self-representation, including goals and values; incorporation of discursive practices[11] which downplay the native/nonnative dichotomy; and a broadening of program goals to reflect the diversity of experience from both second and foreign language contexts (see also Kamhi-Stein, 2000a; Nemtchinova, 2005).

Participatory teacher education, where it is practiced, can provide the access nonnative speakers need to realize their full potential within teacher education programs. However, the educational institutions that do the hiring also need to become aware of the strengths that nonnative-speaking teachers can bring to their schools, especially to those programs designed for language minority learners.

DIRECTIONS IN RESEARCH

Research over the years has included both quantitative and qualitative designs. *Quantitative* research generally looks for definitive answers and universal applications. It tends to use statistical data including measurements as they relate to hypothesis testing and statistical analysis based on pre- and posttesting data. In much of this research the sociocultural and affective aspects of learning are not considered relevant, perhaps because data relating to these aspects cannot easily be measured. *Qualitative* research, on the other hand, most often does not seek definitive answers; instead it looks at all research as relative and situated locally. It prefers to look at and describe language behaviors as they relate to context, relationships, identity development and change, societal expectations, personality characteristics, motivation, and the like. Both kinds of research have made important contributions to the field of second language learning and teaching.

---

[11] Discursive practices are practices that adhere to certain cultural rules that govern what is acceptable and what is not in discourse and determine whose voice has authority and whose voice has no or little influence.

Interestingly, Vygotskian scholars and other socioculturalists have brought together both kinds of research in their efforts to study cognitive and social change. John-Steiner and Mahn (1996) put it this way:

> Sociocultural researchers emphasize methods that document cognitive and social changes. Rather than seeing a dichotomy between quantitative and qualitative research, approaches are chosen that emphasize process, development, and the multiple ways in which both can be revealed. (p. 198)

Sociocultural researchers are generally pragmatic in their approach to research. They have used description, ethnography, narration (including first-person accounts),[12] and discourse analysis—whatever appeared to work best at the time. They have studied collaboration by looking at interactional patterns, strategies, the needs and values of participants, and so forth, using many means and combinations of means, usually qualitative but sometimes with quantitative components.

Researchers today are beginning to show greater interest in collaborative research and in the possibilities of bringing together rich data bases provided by autobiographical accounts and other sources. These may include journals and diaries, interviews, questionnaires, context analysis and comparison, case studies, researcher observations, studies of actual discourse, protocol analyses (both think-aloud strategizing and stimulated recall),[13] timelines, and so on. Ethnography, qualitative/quantitative longitudinal designs (as opposed to cross-sectional designs),[14] and ecologically-based research (see later in this section) are being used for more nuanced and complete analyses by individual researchers, often through collaborations. One relatively recent study combines the use of a self-report questionnaire and a real-time classroom observation tool to see if teachers' motivational strategies are connected to increased levels of motivated learning behaviors and motivational states (see Guilloteaux & Dörnyei, 2008). Another combines hypothesis testing with qualitative description to see if positive feedback to second language utterances corresponds with improvement in interlanguage level (see Reigel, 2008).

Discourse analysis is of particular interest in that it enables us to explore what goes on in classrooms in real time through the use of transcriptions. It makes it possible for us to analyze the co-construction of ideas through dialogic inquiry[15] and to examine the language used to carry out such collaboration. Through it researchers can examine the

---

[12] See especially Pavlenko and Lantolf (2000) for examples of effective use of first-person narratives.

[13] *Think-aloud protocols* encourage students to think out loud about their strategies as they are actually doing an assignment, often involving composition (usually this type of private speech is recorded for later analysis); *recall protocols* require students to think back on the strategies they used after completing an assignment. Wigglesworth (2005) cautioned us, however, that the usefulness and validity of think-aloud protocols may vary depending on who is thinking aloud (that person's cultural and social perspective), the audience of the think-aloud, and the type of task.

[14] *Longitudinal* research looks at one or more individuals over time to examine long-term effects and development; *cross-sectional* research, on the other hand, measures what many individuals can do at a specified point in time.

[15] *Dialogic inquiry* is inquiry that is arrived at through dialogue during which participants collaborate with one another to bring about mutual understanding.

appropriation of language including the very words, syntactic structures, and intonation that is often taken from "other people's mouths" (Bakhtin, 1981) and used to express one's own thoughts and viewpoints and establish individual identities and bond with others (see also Toohey, 2000; Zuengler & Miller, 2006).

Corpus analysis is finding its legitimate place as an important branch of research in linguistics (O'Keeffe, McCarthy, & Carter, 2007). Corpora or electronic data collections can be found on Web sites such as the Bank of English or the Michigan Corpus of Spoken Academic English. Such data bases can be used to study collocational patterns (words together with the words that typically accompany them), idioms, or discourse itself (turn taking, and so on). They have also been used to study the effects of priming specific grammatical structures and lexical items through interaction. However, all such analyses require interpretation by humans (see especially Conrad, 2005). Researchers, teachers, and their students are able to examine natural oral and written language to discover target language features, patterns, and frequency of use in multiple environments. Corpora have been used to familiarize students with various registers[16] and teach the vocabulary and structures associated with many career choices including business, science, math, and so forth. Analyses of corpora relevant to each person's needs can promote student-driven research and the formation and testing of hypotheses under the guidance of a knowledgeable teacher. Corpora, appropriately applied, can inform pedagogy and research as well as textbook, dictionary, and materials development. Longitudinally collected corpora are of special interest to applied linguists in that they allow them to study various interlanguage constructions and how they develop in specific situations over time.

Longitudinal research, in general, has gained popularity in recent years. Descriptive/ quantitative longitudinal research (using both description and simple mathematical calculations involving proportions, frequencies, percentages, rankings, as well as statistical analysis) allows us to look at program effectiveness and make instructional comparisons (see especially Ortega & Byrnes, 2008; Ortega & Iberri-Shea, 2005).

In the case of studying language acquisition in its totality, Atkinson (2002) suggested that qualitative research approaches "attempt to honor the profound wholeness and situatedness of social scenes and individuals-in-the-world" (p. 539). "In-the-world" in this sense can refer to the classroom. Van Lier (2000) recommended an ecological approach that examines the social environment to see what relational linguistic affordances are available to learners. He believes that active, participating learners have many opportunities in the social environments in which they find themselves. He summed up such an approach this way:

> By studying the interaction in its totality, the researcher must attempt to show the emergence of learning, the location of learning opportunities, the pedagogical value of various interactional contexts and processes, and the effectiveness of pedagogical strategies. (p. 250)

---

[16] *Register* refers to the distinguishable varieties of a language as determined by context. For example, a person writing a laboratory report in science will probably use the specialized vocabulary and structures typical of such reports. A person talking to other members of a group with similar careers or educational backgrounds will use registers typical of those groups. A mother talking to her child will often use a register called *motherese*, a teacher will use "teacher talk," and so forth.

Van Lier, however, admitted that we are just beginning to move toward an ecological approach to research. It will be interesting to see what the future holds for this branch of investigation (see also Kramsch, 2002).

Teacher research itself has become a much talked-about subject in the more recent literature (see pp. 437–439 in this volume). Teachers are in need of data to help them explore their own teaching. The exploration may involve real-time observation by peers and/or videotaping for later self and peer analysis; collecting student evaluations, student products, test scores; and keeping teacher journals and other written records (see also J. Gebhard & Oprandy, 1999). Important questions are addressed: Are my students learning what I think they are from my instructional practices? Why or why not? How can I do better? Am I being sensitive enough to the social and cultural influences on learners?

Teachers themselves have become the subjects of descriptive research. This research looks at who teachers are, how they manage their daily work, and how they learn to teach (see especially K. E. Johnson, 2006). It explores questions about their values, beliefs about teaching, concerns, goals, strategies, to what extent they incorporate what they have learned from outside sources, how they go about developing their practices, and so on.

Advocates of critical pedagogy such as Canagarajah (2005) argue that "all research is situated and that it is important to appreciate the particularity of each study in order to realistically assess the relativity of one's findings and generalize more cautiously," (p. 944). Canagarajah mentioned a few critical research approaches that appear to be emerging: *critical ethnography* (examines culture and the ways in which it influences pedagogy), *action research* (helps teachers to reflect on their experience in the classroom), *participant action research* (gives students greater input into research designs), *self-reflexive studies* (encourages the subject to become the researcher of his or her own learning and teaching), and *critical language socialization* (looks at second language acquisition in sociopolitical contexts).

The many research types discussed here can complement one another and work together to help us learn about all sides of the second language learning and teaching experience. The research that is relative and context driven can be particularly revealing in that it brings in the sociocultural and affective factors so crucial to second language learning yet so often ignored. These aspects are key, especially to our understanding of our own teaching situations and how we and our students function within them.

OVERVIEW

In this edition of *Making It Happen*, as in the others, I have responded to the feedback and suggestions of many teacher educators and students who have used the book in the past or are currently using it. In addition to updating the supporting research, I have added the following:

- *new sections on World Englishes and Directions in Research* (Introduction)
- *a new section on the contributions to current practice of communicative language teaching (CLT), Curran's community language learning*

(counseling-learning), Gattegno's silent way, and Lozanov's suggestopedia (Chapter 1)
- *the following modified chapters with new titles:*
  Chapter 2: The Process of Learning a Second Language in the Classroom: A Cognitive View
  Chapter 3: Toward a Sociocultural/Cognitive Model (includes a proposed dialogical model for second language acquisition)
  Chapter 5: Developing Skills: Implicit and Explicit Teaching Strategies (includes listening, speaking/pronunciation, reading/vocabulary development, and writing)
- *the interactive approach and Long's Focus on Form vs. Focus on FormS* (Chapter 2)
- *new sections on "Test Evaluation, Selection, and Development" based on the work of Bachman, Palmer, and others; "Identifying and Assessing Learner Outcomes"; and on "A Dialogical Approach to Assessment"* (Chapter 7)
- *a new section on "Modifying and Enhancing Instruction in the Language Classroom"* (Chapter 9)
- *a revised section on "Working with Large and Mixed-Level Classes"* (Chapter 15)
- *a revised section on "Professional Development" that includes a summary of the Sheltered Instruction Observation Protocol (SIOP) model for teacher observation* (Chapter 17)
- *a new program in action*—the Acoma (Keres) heritage language program of New Mexico (Chapter 20), written by Christine Sims
- *one new case study, "Motivating Beto (Kindergarten)"* contributed by Cathrene Connery for reflection and discussion (Part VI).

This edition of *Making It Happen*, like the ones before it, concentrates on ways of providing opportunities for learning both language and content, but it goes far beyond that to address not only the academic but the cultural and sociopolitical needs of students in emergent participatory classroom environments.

Part I presents a theoretical orientation to the remaining chapters. It begins in Chapter 1 with a brief summary and analysis of the grammar-based methods of the past, Chomsky's contributions to language teaching, and connectionism. It then goes on to trace the development of communicative approaches, including glimpses of what the future may hold for language teaching. Chapter 2 explores notions about how errors can be dealt with most effectively and the supporting research. It discusses ways in which grammar instruction can best fit into the language learning process. Chapter 3 presents a synthesis of sociocultural and cognitive perspectives. This chapter includes a comparison of first and second language acquisition, information-processing models, Vygotsky's view of learning and its ramifications, and a proposed dialogical model for second language learning. Chapter 4 examines emergent participatory language teaching and how it might be realized in the language classroom. A working description of participatory language teaching is provided, and several practices promoting it are described.

The chapter then looks at how students can be enabled through the power provided by strategic learning. Strategies for teaching listening, speaking/pronunciation, reading/vocabulary development, and writing along with the related research are featured in Chapter 5 as well as sections on skills integration and critical literacy. Chapter 6 examines the crucial role played by the affective domain in second language learning in the classroom and includes a discussion of attitudes, motivation, level of anxiety, and related factors and how they influence second language learning. It also considers ways of creating a supportive environment both in the school and in the community. Chapter 7 on language assessment and standards discusses topics such as appropriate placement within a program, making testing an integral part of instruction, identifying and assessing outcomes, and dialogical testing. It also talks about the use and misuse of standards and large-scale testing. Highlighted briefly in this chapter are Bachman and Palmer's six qualities of test usefulness and their assessment use argument (AUA) framework.

Part II features several methods and activities that can be, for the most part, compatible with interactional/participatory teaching. The Introduction to Part II defines the terms used and stresses that many of the activities described can be considered prototypes in that they can be modified to meet different objectives, proficiency levels, and age levels. Chapter 8 focuses on early physical involvement in the language learning process and takes a look at the total physical response (along with total physical response storytelling) and the audio-motor unit. Interactive language teaching is the subject of Chapter 9, which revisits the natural approach and offers strategies to modify and enhance instruction. Chapter 10 talks about the use of chants, music, and poetry and their importance to the internalization of routines and patterns. Chapter 11 presents storytelling, role play, and drama as vehicles leading to and enhancing second language acquisition. Nonverbal, word-focus, and other kinds of games used to reinforce concepts and link students to other cultures are the subjects of Chapter 12; Chapter 13 considers many ways to promote literacy in a new language including the language experience approach, a literature-based curriculum, and writing workshops. It also discusses advanced academic literacy and how it can be achieved. Chapter 14 offers affective activities related to what learners value in their lives and how clarifying their values helps to shape their identities.

Part III discusses several considerations that should be taken into account when one is developing and implementing programs. In the Introduction to Part III we learn about the different types of programs and the implications that each type of program has for teaching. Chapter 15 zeros in on such issues as devising a flexible curriculum, structuring lessons, investigative inquiry, standards, determining the focus of the instruction (proficiencies, tasks, or content), preparing peer facilitators and lay assistants, using cooperative learning, and working with large and mixed-level classes. The selection and use of tools such textbooks, computer programs, and videos for teaching languages is the subject of Chapter 16. Chapter 17 outlines the various program designs, including those used for bilingual education, and talks about their political implications. In this chapter we also learn about teacher research and teacher observation and evaluation through the Sheltered Instruction Observation Protocol (SIOP). Both are important to professional development.

Part IV describes programs in action. Chapter 18 (ESL Programs) discusses a college English language program at Saint Michael's College in Colchester, Vermont; a university support program at California State University, Los Angeles; a life-skills adult basic education program at the North Hollywood Adult Learning Center in North Hollywood, California; a secondary sheltered English program at Artesia High School in Artesia, California; an elementary district-wide program in the Alhambra School District in Alhambra, California; and a kindergarten ESL program within a Spanish bilingual school at Loma Vista Elementary in Maywood, California. Chapter 19 (Foreign Language Programs) describes a village immersion program for global understanding near Bemidji, Minnesota; a French immersion program for elementary language learners in Thunder Bay, Ontario, Canada; a bicultural institute for children, adolescents, and adults at the Instituto Cultural Argentine Norteamericano (ICANA) in Buenos Aires, Argentina; a middle school Spanish language program at Millikan Junior High School in Los Angeles; and a high school Spanish program at Artesia High School in Artesia, California. Chapter 20 (Two-Way Bilingual and Heritage Language Programs) presents a Spanish/English language program in Valley Center, California; a Cantonese/English language program in Lower Manhattan; and the Acoma tribal language program of New Mexico (written by Christine Sims). All these programs were selected because of the quality of their more salient features. However, they are not meant to be representative of all the programs available.

Part V presents five case studies for reflection and discussion. Each pertains to a different age group: kindergarten, elementary, middle school, high school, and college/university.

PART I

Theoretical Considerations

The selected theories and hypotheses presented here are intended to serve as a foundation for the methods, activities, and strategies presented in the remainder of the book. However, the intent is not to divorce the theoretical from the practical. Rather, readers are encouraged to explore these ideas with a critical mind and to create praxis—a blending of reflection and action—at every possible juncture. This section is intended to be representative, not all-inclusive. Research and scholarship in interactive language teaching that may lead to emergent participatory teaching has expanded to the point where no single volume can reflect it all.

Because learning another language is so complex and involves sociocultural as well as cognitive factors, no two learners will get there by exactly the same route. In spite of the variations, we can describe some of the processes that seem to be common to large numbers of people struggling with a new language and, in many cases, a new culture. Most people agree that simple exposure to the new language and/or culture is not enough. By understanding more about the processes that many language learners seem to share, we can be in a better position to develop our own language teaching principles and to make possible classroom experiences that are appropriate locally and that will lead to personal and collective empowerment. Thus we can continue to develop means by which language, culture, and influence are made more accessible to students while at the same time help them maintain their first languages and cultures to the greatest extent possible.

Part I will contribute to the reservoir—which also includes your own beliefs, experiences, and prior knowledge.

EXPLORING YOUR CURRENT BELIEFS ABOUT LEARNING AND TEACHING LANGUAGES

A. Before reading further in this book, think about the following questions and discuss them with a partner.

What role should a teacher play in the language classroom?
What should the role of the student be?
How does a teacher know when he or she is teaching effectively?
Think about the best teacher you have ever had. What qualities made that teacher so good?
What kind of language teacher are you or do you want to be?
In what ways can you examine the effectiveness of your own teaching?

B. Read the statements below and place a number in front of each one to indicate the extent to which you agree or disagree.

1 = strongly agree
2 = somewhat agree
3 = somewhat disagree
4 = strongly disagree

_____ If students learn some basic vocabulary words and most of the rules governing the grammar and use of a language, they should be able to communicate reasonably well.
_____ Anyone who can function cognitively, no matter what his or her age, can learn to speak another language.
_____ Learning a second language is almost identical to learning a first language.
_____ Peers should not be teaching peers because they do not have the knowledge or experience necessary.
_____ A positive attitude and high motivation are very beneficial, if not essential, to learning another language.
_____ Much of language is learned by incorporating what others say.
_____ Because language teachers are the authorities and have the most knowledge, the students should not try to change what is on the syllabus or the events of the classroom.
_____ The standardized test scores of students should be used to evaluate their teachers.
_____ One goal of teachers should be to help students become independent learners.
_____ Students should practice with the sounds of the new language and learn sound/letter correspondences before trying to communicate orally or read and write.
_____ Vocabulary lists should be displayed and the meanings studied for periodic tests on the words.

_____ Singing and chanting in the new language is silly and a waste of time, especially for adults.

_____ Participating in situations in which students express their opinions helps them to become fluent in the language they are learning.

_____ Learning to read in another language can be facilitated by learning to write in it.

_____ Students should not be allowed to make mistakes in the new language without immediate correction.

_____ Teachers need to accommodate students from other cultures and always show respect for their first languages.

_____ One thing language teachers should not have to worry about is the students' self-esteem; that should be left up to trained counselors.

_____ If students try not to use their first languages or adhere to the customs of the countries from which they came, they will adjust to the new culture much more quickly.

_____ Students will usually misbehave if they are seated in a circle and allowed to talk to one another.

_____ It is important for teachers to use strategies associated with just one method so the students do not become confused.

_____ The teacher should always find out what the needs of the students are before trying to teach them.

_____ Teachers need to continually examine their own teaching.

_____ Computers can make the language teachers' role obsolete if the programs are well designed.

_____ Grammar rules do not need to be taught because students can learn the new language just by having plenty of opportunities to use it.

_____ Students should not discuss issues that affect their lives negatively because doing so will depress them.

As you continue to read the book, periodically return to this section to see if any of your beliefs have changed.

CHAPTER 1

From Grammar-Based to Communicative Approaches: A Historical Perspective

Not to let a word get in the way of its sentence
Nor to let a sentence get in the way of its intention,
But to send your mind out to meet the intention as a guest;
That is understanding.

Chinese proverb,
Fourth Century B.C.
(Wells, 1981)

QUESTIONS TO THINK ABOUT

1. How do humans learn language? Are we born with something that helps us learn language?

2. With what approaches to second language teaching[1] are you already familiar? Are these primarily grammar-based? Do you know of any other approaches to second language teaching?

3. How would you envision an effective communicative approach? How might it differ from other approaches with which you are familiar?

---

[1] Note that the generic definition of *second language* learning and teaching is often used in this volume and refers to any language that is not the first or native language (see footnote 10 on p. 10). Depending on the context, "second language" can also include "foreign language."

GRAMMAR-BASED APPROACHES

Grammar-based approaches advocate *language structure* as the main content for study in language learning. They generally expose students to isolated aspects of the grammar system consecutively—present tense before past, comparative before superlative, first-person singular before third-person singular, and so forth. These approaches include

- grammar translation
- audiolingualism
- the direct method
- cognitive code

The characteristic features of each of these approaches are presented below, but many variations exist that are not included in this brief analysis.

Grammar Translation

Grammar translation, also known as the Prussian method, was popular in Europe and America from about the mid-nineteenth to the mid-twentieth century. Versions of it are still popular today in many countries around the world, especially in English as a foreign language classes and other foreign language teaching situations (Fotos, 2005). The aim of this approach is to produce students who can read and write in the target language by focusing on rules and their applications.

A typical grammar-translation lesson begins with a reading followed by the grammar rule it illustrates. Often several strings of unrelated sentences are given to demonstrate how the rule works. New words are presented in a list, along with definitions in the first language (L1). These new words are also included in the reading, which, more often than not, is syntactically[2] and semantically[3] far above the learner's level of proficiency. Students are asked to translate the readings into their first language. Lessons are grammatically sequenced, and learners are expected to produce errorless translations from the beginning. Little attempt is made to communicate orally in the target language. Directions and lengthy explanations are given in the learner's first language.

Audiolingualism

Audiolingualism, an oral method based on behaviorism (Skinner, 1957), adhered to the theory that language is acquired through habit formation and stimulus/response association. Learning another language was thought to be a matter of fighting off the habits of the first language. Introduced as a component of the "Army Method" used by the U.S. government during World War II, audiolingualism was developed to replace or enhance grammar translation. Leonard Bloomfield had developed an earlier version for linguists to use when studying languages. This approach was labeled the "audiolingual method" when it began to gain favor in teaching English as a foreign language and English as a second language in the 1950s. In the United States, the rise of audiolingual instruction was

---

[2] Related to the word *syntax*, which means the way words are arranged to form phrases or sentences.

[3] Related to the word *semantics*, which refers to meaning.

closely related to scholarship on structural linguistics and contrastive analysis[4] (see Fries, 1945; Lado, 1977).

In the audiolingual method, grammatical structures of the target language were carefully ordered and dialogues repeated in an attempt to develop correct habits of speaking. Sentences in substitution activities, mim–mem (mimic and memorize), and other drills were usually related only syntactically ("I go to the store," "You go to the store," "He goes to the store") and had nothing to do with actual events or narrative. Sometimes, however, these sentences did resemble real communication in that the situational scenarios to be memorized included greetings and idiomatic expressions. Rules were presented but often not formally explained, and activities such as minimal pairs (seat–sit, yellow–Jell-O, and so on) were commonly used in an effort to overcome the negative transfer (interference) of first language sounds. Listening and speaking skills took precedence over reading and writing skills. However, in most of the applications, there was very little use of creative language,[5] and a great deal of attention was paid to correct pronunciation. Often practice sessions took place in fully equipped language laboratories.

The Direct Method

Also known today as Berlitz, this approach was based on the very early work of Montaigne in the sixteenth century. The direct method was derived from the natural method developed by Sauveur in the mid-nineteenth century and later applied by de Sauzé. It is natural in the sense that it makes an effort to "immerse" students in the target language. Teacher monologues, formal questions and answers, and direct repetitions of the input were frequent. Correct pronunciation was stressed; vocabulary was taught not in lists but through context; and there was no translation used. In fact, the first language was avoided as much as possible.

Although the discourse used today in Berlitz schools is often structured temporally, the topic for discussion is usually the grammar itself. The students inductively discover the rules of the language. Books based on the direct method often move students so quickly through new syntactic structures that their internalization becomes very difficult.

Cognitive-Code Approaches

Cognitive-code approaches, most evident since the 1960s, are described rather vaguely in the literature. According to Richards and Rodgers (2001), the term *cognitive code* refers to any attempt to rely consciously on a syllabus based on grammar but at the same

---

[4] *Structural linguistics* is a grammatical system whereby the elements and rules of a language are listed and described. Phonemes (sounds), morphemes (words or parts of words), phrases, and sentences are ordered linearly and are learned orally as a set of habits. *Contrastive analysis*, emphasizing the differences between the student's first language and the target language, was relied on in an effort to create exercises contrasting the two. The first language was thought of chiefly as an interference, hindering the successful mastery of the second.

[5] One exception was Fries's own language program at the University of Michigan. According to Morley, Robinett, Selinker, and Woods (1984), Fries utilized a two-part approach: One part focused on the structural points being drilled and the second part on automatic use through meaning. The "personalized" elements that were considered vital to the program somehow became lost in most of its adaptations.

time allows for the practice and use of language in meaningful ways. It was thought that subskills in listening, speaking, reading, and writing such as sound discrimination, pronunciation of specific elements, distinguishing between letters that are similar in appearance, and so on needed to be mastered before the student could participate in real communication activities. Phonemes needed to be learned before words, words before phrases and sentences, simple sentences before more complicated ones, and so forth.

Lessons are highly structured through a deductive process, and the "rule of the day" is practiced. Although creative language is used at later levels during the practice, learners generally need to produce correctly from the start. A great deal of time is devoted to temporally related but often unmotivated (contextually unjustified) discourse (see Chapter 16).

Analysis

Although grammar-based methods varied, they all adhered to the same central principle: Grammar is the foundation on which language should be taught. Even as early as 1904, Otto Jespersen saw the artificiality inherent in this principle. He criticized the French texts of his era, saying,

> The reader often gets the impression that Frenchmen must be strictly systematical beings who one day speak merely in futures, another day in passé définis and who say the most disconnected things only for the sake of being able to use all the persons in the tense which for the time being happens to be the subject for conversation while they carefully postpone the use of the subjunctive until next year. (p. 17; also in Oller & Obrecht, 1969, p. 119)

Advocates of cognitive-code approaches are particularly interesting with respect to their interpretation of Chomsky's *transformational grammar*,[6] a complex description of the language system in which Chomsky claims that sentences are "transformed" within the brain to other sentences by the application of what he calls *phrase structure rules*. For example, a phrase structure rule known as *extraposition* applied to the sentence "That summer follows spring is a known fact" transforms it into "It is a known fact that summer follows spring." The first sentence is what is called the "deep structure" (also referred to as a *kernel sentence* by some cognitive-code advocates). The sentence into which it is transformed is called the "surface form." An appropriate context in which these sentences might be found was not provided, leaving the learner without a clue about their use.

Some applications of cognitive-code approaches began instruction with the translation of kernel sentences. Chomsky felt that kernel sentences of different languages would probably be very similar and that positive transfer would then occur between languages.

---

[6] Chomsky argued that within the *idealized speaker* in a homogeneous speech community there is a finite system of rules that make it possible for the speaker to comprehend an infinite number of sentences. Chomsky set out to describe this deep underlying system that he referred to as the speaker's *competence* (as opposed to the speaker's actual *performance*).

Second language (L2) teachers who used cognitive-code approaches often taught sentences that were neither temporally sequenced nor logically motivated. Instead, their main reason for existence seemed to be to demonstrate the use of a particular grammatical structure to aid the development of linguistic competence. These teachers were disappointed to find that Chomsky himself did not advocate such a method—or any specific method for that matter. In his address to the 1965 Northeast Conference on the Teaching of Foreign Languages, Chomsky stated that neither the linguist nor the psychologist had enough knowledge about the process of language learning to provide a basis for methodology.

> I am, frankly, rather skeptical about the significance, for the teaching of languages, of such insights and understanding as have been attained in linguistics and psychology. . . . I should like to make it clear from the outset that I am participating in this conference not as an expert on any aspect of the teaching of languages, but rather as someone whose primary concern is with the structure of language and, more generally, the nature of cognitive processes. (Allen & Van Buren, 1971, p. 152)

Chomsky cautioned teachers against passively accepting theory on the grounds of authority, real or presumed.

CHOMSKY'S CONTRIBUTIONS

Inferences drawn from Chomsky's innatist theory are perhaps more important to second language teaching than any of the applications of transformational grammar. He argued that language development is too complicated a phenomenon to be explained on the basis of behaviorism alone (Chomsky, 1959). That children seem to have mastered the structure of their first language by the age of five or earlier suggests that at least some aspects of language are innate or inborn.

Chomsky (1980) opposed the idea that the mind is simply a *tabula rasa*, or a blank slate, on which to store impressions. He refused to believe that grammar is simply an output based on a record of data. However, he did not deny that the mind is capable of the abilities attributed to it by behaviorism. He reminded us that language is not made by us but rather develops as a result of the way we are constituted when we are placed in the "appropriate external environment" (p. 11). For Chomsky, the jury is still out concerning how much of language is shaped by experience and how much is intrinsically determined (see discussion of connectionism later in this chapter).

Support for the idea that certain aspects of language are innate first came from early psycholinguistic research. Roger Brown (1973) discovered universal trends in language acquisition after studying the speech of several children in natural situations over a period of years. Slobin (1971) and others added to this body of research. They found that children across languages use similar linguistic structures in their language development and that they make the same kinds of errors. In addition, they concluded that linguistic structures are learned in the same order.

These findings led many researchers to agree with Chomsky that the brain is not a blank slate but rather contains highly complex structures that seem to come into operation through an interactional process. To house these complex structures of the brain, Chomsky proposed the notion of a "language organ" which he called the *language acquisition device*. Critics over the years have ridiculed the possibility that such an "organ" could magically appear, but Pinker (1994) argued that such a device or networking might have evolved through natural selection.

The Language Acquisition Device

To Chomsky, the language acquisition device is associated with all that is universal in human languages. Its structures (or networking of structures) are activated when we are exposed to natural language. To help clarify what happens during the process of activation, Chomsky compared the language acquisition device to a computer (see Gliedman, 1983) that contains a series of preprogrammed subsystems responsible for meaning, syntax, relationships among various types of words, and their functions. Within each subsystem, the individual, through experience, makes subconscious choices from a linguistic menu.

For the purpose of much simplified illustration, consider a task that asks students to choose the correct word order in a sentence that has a direct object. Perhaps the choices consist of something like this: subject–verb–object (SVO), verb–subject–object (VSO), subject–object–verb (SOV), and object–subject–verb (OSV). Children born into Spanish, Chinese, and English environments, for example, subconsciously select SVO; a child born into an Arabic environment, VSO; one born into a Korean environment, SOV; and so forth. Other choices might be available for varying degrees of inflection, dropping pronouns under certain conditions, and so on. Depending on the language environment in which it finds itself, the brain selects items appropriate to the specific language to which it is exposed. All humanly possible options are included in this computer within the brain.

Universal Grammar

Another related perspective explored by Chomsky is *universal grammar,* the embodiment of the basic principles shared by all languages. Because all humans are born with this set of principles, they are able to acquire something as complex as the structure of their first language at a very early age.

The shared principles can vary along certain parameters, which, in newborn children, are called *unmarked* (that setting which is most common and most restrictive to all languages). As the child is exposed to the language of the environment, the initial settings are reset to *marked* forms, reflecting the less common features of a particular language.

To return to our example, let's say that the parameter for using an object is first set to SVO (assuming that SVO is the unmarked setting). The brain of a child born into an Arabic environment would then quickly reset this parameter to VSO, because that is the order to which he or she has been exposed through input from the community. Some rules of language are thought to be so marked that they can be acquired only through experience because they are not parameterized (Larsen-Freeman & Long, 1991, p. 231).

Implications for Second Language Acquisition

Some linguists believe that the brain *resets* parameters only when it is exposed to a language that deviates from the parameters set for the first language (see especially White, 1989, 1990). White maintained that universal grammar is indeed available to second language learners (see also Gass, 2003; Sorace, 2003). If it were not, the learner would have to depend wholly on input and the cognitive domain to acquire another language. White and many others argued that the learner would not be able to acquire the more abstract and complex knowledge necessary to learn another language without having access to universal grammar (see also Flynn, 1987, 1990; Hulk, 1991). However, considerable controversy exists concerning whether the brain can reset parameters as easily as it did originally, considering that second language learners are usually older when exposed to their second language. Perhaps a *critical period* (an optimal time) exists for the resetting of parameters (see especially J. Johnson, 1992; Schachter, 1990). Such speculation, however, does not negate the possibility that the brain may indeed be capable of resetting parameters for another language (see also Felix, 1988; Tomaselli & Schwartz, 1990).

Although some innatists feel that simple exposure is enough to trigger the appropriate settings, at least for children learning a first language, many others take an interactionist point of view and insist that, for normal development to occur, the individual must receive input tailored to his or her developing proficiency. In other words, the child needs to receive *motherese* or *caretaker* speech, if not from parents then from siblings or others in the environment willing to give it. Motherese consists of generally shorter utterances, the use of high-frequency vocabulary, a slower rate, some exaggeration in expression, redundancy, frequent explanations, repetitions, and the like. Furthermore, the topics are usually about the *here and now* rather than about something removed in time and space from the immediate environment. Interestingly, the speech addressed to second language learners by fluent speakers of the target language often contains many of the same modifications in the input (see Chapters 2 and 3).

Although the theories of universal grammar based on Chomskyan thought are highly abstract, they may well give us clues about what could possibly be happening in the brain when we acquire language—either first or second.

THE CONNECTIONISTS

Other theories abound in the more recent literature. Of particular interest is the *connectionist approach* to how language develops. Connectionism considers the brain a *neural network of networks* consisting of nodes that operate in nonlinear ways when stimulated. Patterns and sequences begin to take shape from the input. Atkinson (2002), who believes that connectionism has the potential to tie together cognitive and social aspects of language use and acquisition, is among those who are critical of Chomksy's reductionist model:

> By reducing the social out of language, he [Chomsky] was able to produce an idealized pseudolanguage about which some "facts" could be explained using the tools of logic and calculus. Yes, speakers of English certainly do use question transformations . . . but

to base a whole linguistic theory on a handful of such phenomena belies the reductiveness and abstractness of Chomsky's model of language. (p. 526)

Connectionism, however, is not necessarily an antinativist perspective (see especially Elman, Bates, M. H. Johnson, Karmiloff-Smith, Parisi, and Plunket, 1996). Whereas knowledge of language itself is not considered innate in Elman's view, the constraints that are imposed on that knowledge are. Connectionists believe that a structure of the networks in the brain controls and constrains the kinds of information that the brain can internalize, the tasks that it can perform, and the data that it can store. Elman and colleagues were looking for a unified theory that makes connectionism compatible with some form of innateness theory. Their hope was that a connectionist model would provide a framework for examining more closely what may or may not be innate. Because both theories view language competence itself as implicit and intuitive, their advocates eventually may be able to find common ground in some areas.

Although Deacon (1997) argued that the human brain is preequipped by evolutionary forces for dealing with the symbolic representation that distinguishes human languages, he believed that the language acquisition device does *not* contain a universal grammar and that Chomsky's computer analogy is incorrect—that the brain does not innately contain that kind of knowledge. However, he also did not think that learning alone could account for the complex phenomenon of human language. Deacon was convinced that the fact that children master a great deal of the grammatical system at an early age is due to the evolution of the language itself to fit the child's capacity for learning. The capacity to learn language also goes through evolutionary changes but very slowly. A language that does not evolve to fit the child's early learning biases, which are universal, will quickly disappear because it cannot be passed to the next generation of speakers through the process of socialization. To Deacon, this explains why languages independently resemble one another structurally. Children take many years to develop the vocabulary of a language, but they quickly master its grammatical system through trial and error by making "lucky" guesses due to their *innate biases*. Children who are isolated during their immature period—the so-called feral or wild children that we have read about—will not develop a full language system, for it is that very immaturity that allows them to minimize cognitive interference and develop the fundamentals of language.

> Being unable to remember the details of specific word associations, being slow to map words to objects that tend to co-occur in the same context, remembering only the most global structure–function relationships of utterances, and finding it difficult to hold more than a few words of an utterance in short-term memory at a time may all be advantages for language learning. . . . Precisely because of children's learning constraints, the relevant large-scale logic of language "pops out" of a background of other details too variable for them to follow, and paradoxically gives them a biased head start. Children cannot tell the trees apart at first, but they can see the forest and eventually the patterns of growth within it emerge. (Deacon, 1997, p. 135)

Thus the same limitations that make it difficult for children to learn other things make it possible for them to access something as complex as their first language.

The connectionists' theories offer yet another way to look at first language acquisition. What implications these theories may have for second language development remain somewhat unclear at present. Macaro (2003) concluded that, although innateness and connectionism appear irreconcilable, the two may be reconciled by the fact that the brain has a strong tendency to discover patterns and develop an "architecture of connections" used to sort out new linguistic information. However, this is probabilistic, not absolute. He argues:

> The theory is that it [the architecture of connections] arises through the strength of the connections not from a genetically transmitted cerebral structure based on universal language rules. Whether this theory will continue to hold sway, in SLA research, over universal grammar remains to be seen. (p. 253)

Although connectionism may not at present have much influence in classrooms, we are beginning to see in second language learning literature the buds of connectionist thought, especially as it relates to the language learning process (see N. Ellis, 1996, 1998, 2002, 2003, 2005, 2006). According to Ellis, connectionists are interested in "the representations that result when simple associative learning mechanisms are exposed to complex language evidence" (2006, p. 106). Researchers adhering to connectionism believe that it is the *frequency of items* used in the input that is essential to language learning. Thus connectionist explanations appear to support a natural route to second language acquisition (see especially N. Ellis, 1996, 2002). Connectionist accounts of second language learning so far appear to support the notion that networks of connections develop only when the learner is exposed over and over again to language in context. However, the role of explicit learning is also being explored in relation to implicit learning within a connectionist framework (N. Ellis, 2005). It will be interesting to see where further exploration in this area might lead.

COMMUNICATIVE APPROACHES

Chomsky drew criticism not only from the connectionists but from those who had pointed out much earlier that his basic linguistic model failed to adequately address the social aspects of language (e.g., Halliday, 1979; Hymes, 1970). Many agreed with the competence/performance distinction drawn by Chomsky but felt that competence should include not only grammatical sectors but also psycholinguistic, sociocultural, and *de facto* sectors (to use Hymes's terms). Halliday rejected the distinction between competence and performance altogether, calling it misleading or irrelevant. He felt that the more we are able to relate the grammar system to meaning in social contexts and behavioral settings, the more insight we will have into the language system. It was this basic idea that Wilkins (1979) used in constructing his notional–functional syllabus as a structure for input in the classroom.

The Notional-Functional Syllabus

Wilkins (1979) was concerned with helping the learner meet specific communication needs through input. The notional–functional framework he proposed organized input into a set of notional categories for the purpose of syllabus design. For example, a category may have included various ways to express probability: "I am *certain* this project will be finished by Friday," "*Maybe* it will be finished by Friday," "I *doubt* it will be finished by Friday," and so forth. Syllabi based on a notional approach often included such topics as accepting/rejecting invitations, requesting information, and expressing needs or emotions of various kinds.

Although Wilkins (1979) felt that this kind of notional syllabus was superior to a grammatical one, he was not yet ready to replace grammatically focused systems with functionally focused ones. He did, however, see a notional approach as providing another dimension to existing systems. It "can provide a way of developing communicatively what is already known, while at the same time enabling the teacher to fill the gaps in the learners' knowledge of the language" (p. 92).

Not everyone agreed with Wilkins. Henry Widdowson (1979), for example, warned that although some linguists might boast of ensuring communicative competence through the use of a notional syllabus, this approach did not necessarily ensure such competence as its result. For one thing, a notional syllabus isolates the components of communication. Widdowson argued:

> There is one rather crucial fact that such an inventory [typically included in a notional syllabus] does not, and cannot of its nature, take into account, which is that communication does not take place through the linguistic exponence of concepts and functions as self-contained units of meaning. It takes place as discourse, whereby meanings are negotiated through interaction. (p. 253)

Because a notional approach uses an artificial breakdown of communication into discrete functions, most of its applications lose their potential as providers of effective input. Activities based on a notional approach did not always involve real communication situations any more than repetitive dialogues or "structures for the day" did.

Consider the following excerpt from an early textbook employing a notional approach (Jones & von Baeyer, 1983):

> Here are some useful ways of requesting. They are marked with stars [in this case asterisks] according to how polite they are.
>
> *   Hey, I need some change. I'm all out of change.
> **   You don't have a quarter, do you? Have you got a quarter, by any chance? Could I borrow a quarter?
> *** You couldn't lend me a dollar, could you? Do you think you could lend me a dollar? I wonder if you could lend me a dollar.
> **** Would you mind lending me five dollars? If you could lend me five dollars, I'd be very grateful.
> ***** Could you possibly lend me your typewriter? Do you think you could possibly lend me your typewriter? I wonder if you could possibly lend me your typewriter.
> ****** I hope you don't mind my asking, but I wonder if it might be at all possible for you to lend me your car.
>
> Decide with your teacher when you would use these request forms. Can you add any more forms to the list?

Not only would such an analysis be superficial, but the subtleties involved would be very difficult for English learners, even at an advanced level. Native speakers also might have trouble determining the differences. For example, is "Would you mind lending me five dollars?" more or less polite than "Do you think you could lend me a dollar?" In addition to the activity's syntactic problems, semantic and situational differences are not at all clear. Asking someone for a car is certainly different from asking someone for a quarter. Important variables are missing, such as the positions, ages, and other characteristics of the interlocutors and their relationships to one another. Thus the activity lacks not only meaning but comprehensibility.

Note, however, that a function explicitly taught as a need for it arises in connection with a specific context can indeed have meaning and comprehensibility. For example, if the students are discussing a character's actions in a drama in which the character is misunderstood and thought to be rude, the teacher might want to explain how the character might have reworded his or her statement to make it more acceptable.

A basic question the reader might ask is what other kinds of activities and lessons are both meaningful and comprehensible. Although some organizing principles might lend themselves to effective communicative approaches more than others, the organizational principle is not what necessarily makes the difference. It is also not content. For some students and teachers, grammar itself *is* a stimulating topic (see especially Fotos & R. Ellis, 1991). A discussion of function, too, as mentioned in the example above, may both be of interest and raise pragmatic awareness in a given classroom. However, any discussion of a specific grammatical and/or functional item and its alternatives will probably be most effective if it grows out of a need that makes itself felt during the process of communication.

Breen and Candlin's View of an Effective Communicative Approach

Breen and Candlin (1979) characterized an effective communicative approach as one in which a shared knowledge is explored and then modified (see also Hatch, 1978; Pica, 1994). Such an approach implies a negotiation of "potential meanings in a new language," as well as a socialization process. Breen and Candlin rejected systems in which the learner is separated from that which is to be learned, as though the target language could be objectively broken down into isolated components. They argued further that:

> In a communicative methodology, content ceases to become some external control over learning–teaching procedures. Choosing directions becomes a part of the curriculum itself, and involves negotiation between learners and learners, learners and teachers, and learners and text. (1979, p. 104)

They felt that a *negotiation for meaning* in general was crucial to a successfully applied communicative methodology.[7] This idea seemed to suggest the need for greater

---

[7] That is not to say, however, that all attempts to negotiate meaning result in comprehensible language. What is important here is the intention to understand and to be understood.

interdependence and a greater flexibility on the parts of teachers and learners to allow the syllabus and its content to develop in ways that make learning of the target language most likely. What Breen and Candlin were talking about here seems to have provided an early glimpse of *emergent participatory language teaching* (see Chapter 4).

Communicative Language Teaching

Communicative language teaching (CLT) grew out a 1970s movement led by the Council of Europe. It was at first based on the notional–functional approach to learning languages. What functions did the learners need to be able to perform in relation to their goals? Needs assessments led to courses in language for specific purposes designed mainly for students in various technological fields and guest workers. Parallel movements in Europe and North America focused on language use (as opposed to language structure) and on the process of communication in the classroom. They gave birth to what came to be known as CLT.

In the United States, Savignon (1983, 1991, 1997, 2005) and other linguists considered CLT an approach rooted in *communicative competence*, a term first used by Hymes (1970). His goal was to move beyond Chomsky's focus on syntactic rules to a focus on the ability to use language in social settings. Savignon later described communicative competence as the ability to engage in the interpretation, expression, and negotiation of meaning. Her idea of CLT was contrary to what was going on in most classrooms of the 1970s and much of the 1980s, such as dialogue memorization, grammar tests, pattern practice, and so on. Out of her work, based on Halliday and Hasan (1976), Canale and Swain (1980), and Canale (1983), came a communicative classroom model that divided communicative competence into four interrelated competencies:

1. sociocultural
2. strategic
3. discourse
4. grammatical

Sociocultural competence stresses the social rules of language use and relies on the social context, including participants' roles, their shared knowledge, and the function of the interaction. *Strategic competence* consists of coping strategies for dealing with imperfect knowledge in all of these competencies. *Discourse competence* concerns itself with creating the overall meaning of interrelated speech and writing and is dependent on coherence and the structural links that make the discourse cohesive. *Grammatical competence* focuses on sentence-level grammatical structures and includes the recognition and use of the semantic, syntactic, morphological, and phonological features of the new language. Mastering such competencies did not require that the learner be able to state rules to provide evidence of competence but rather to *use* rules appropriately in context. However, as will soon be seen, there is considerable doubt about the appropriateness of CLT for universal application.

One likely drawback associated with CLT in foreign language environments is the fact that teachers may not be competent enough in the target language to flow within a communicative classroom. A second is that they may lack the appropriate preparation to use it effectively, and a third is that the surrounding community may not offer learners opportunities to use the target language outside the classroom. This leaves it up to the teacher to provide sufficient opportunities for communication within the classroom—a difficult challenge but not impossible. Yet another problem may be that students in foreign language situations are often expected to take exams based on grammar (not communicative) approaches to teaching (see Fotos, 2005).

Other drawbacks relate to sociocultural compatibility. Canagarajah (1999), a postmodernist, suggested that other cultures might find CLT incompatible with traditional learning styles and practice. Some might even consider it an attempt to force its commonly associated western teaching methods and thinking on the rest of the world. Knowing our students, their local situations, needs, issues of concern, interests, goals, and aspirations, is critical to making appropriate decisions about those strategies to which we might expose them. Sociocultural knowledge is important—indeed critical—to such decisions. Much depends on the situation and the individuals involved. Although one would not want to indoctrinate others, trying out something different might not be all that bad and might even be well accepted and preferred in other cultural environments. In fact, teachers often discover that introducing students to something new can be exciting for both teacher and students as they work together to accommodate cultural differences in a classroom where all can benefit. Stereotypical behaviors assigned to specific cultural groups are not set in stone. Even teaching styles within a single school can be quite different and still be within the range of acceptability.

In recent years communicative competence models in general have come under fire for several reasons other than cultural incompatibility. For example, M. Johnson (2004) argued that, even though models based on communicative competence may claim to be situated and communicative, in reality they are not. They are basically cognitive in nature and are not socioculturally oriented to the local situation, even though they may have sociolinguistic or sociocultural components. In her view, in practice there appears to be little need for the co-construction of knowledge or for dialogical negotiation based on a shared local reality (see Chapter 3). She went on to say that most of the communicative competence models emphasize the *ability to use* language in a universal way (to come as close as possible to Chomsky's "ideal"), which is not the same as *actual use* in dynamic and often unstable local situations in which identities, agency, and appropriation are important factors. Perhaps her most significant criticism of communicative competence models relates to the expectations of the learner. She fears that the learner will experience great disappointment when learning the four competencies mentioned above leads to something less than effective communication.

In spite of the criticism of the communicative competence models, one thought remains clear: Versions of CLT itself and the interactive methods, practices, and strategies that have grown out of them have freed teachers in many places in the western world in particular, from the grammar-based paradigms of the past (e.g., Krashen, 1981a, 1982, 1985; Richard-Amato, 1988; Rivers, 1987).

Over the years, teachers have drawn from several interactive methods that have made important contributions to current theory and practice. These include

- **community language learning:** This method was also known as *counseling learning*, the name given to it by its originator, Charles Curran (1972, 1976). It was a therapeutic, nonthreatening way to teach language using the teacher as the counselor. The students (clients) sat in a circle, and the teacher remained outside the circle and translated for the students what they revealed about themselves and their needs in their first language. In other versions of community language learning, students were given relevant topics to discuss. It was expected that the students would gradually become independent of the teacher over time.

  Contributions to current practice: the importance of setting up nonthreatening environments for language learning; using relevant topics for discussion; providing translations in first languages as needed; expecting the student to become less dependent on the teacher over time.

- **the silent way:** Using Caleb Gattegno's (1972) method, the teacher remained silent after modeling basic utterances using Cuisenaire rods of different sizes and colors. The students were expected to fill the silence. Holding up a red rod, the teacher might say, "a rod" in the target language. The teacher might then say "a red rod" again in the target language, then do the same for a white rod, and so forth. In addition to colors, the length of the rods; verbs such as *give, put, drop*; plurals; words and syntax used for comparisons; and so on were modeled. Little guidance was given during the silence that the students were to fill, and the students often felt under pressure and anxious in their struggle to come up with what the teacher expected.

  Contributions to current practice: the importance of using real objects and carefully controlling the input, especially at beginning levels.

- **suggestopedia:** Based on Soviet psychology, suggestopedia put learners in a relaxed state using Baroque music, controlled breathing, comfortable chairs, and the authoritative but soothing voice of the teacher. Some versions employed soft lighting and Yogic breathing; others used imagery, relaxation exercises, and a recall of pleasant early learning experiences accomplished in the first language for beginners or in the second language once the students had sufficient proficiency. Students using the original method (Georgi Lozanov, 1978) spent several hours relaxing and memorizing dialogues actively and passively. During part of the time the teacher read dialogues, using much contrasting emotion by varying the tone of voice. The method has been used for many purposes, including the memorization of whole dialogues, vocabulary items, chunks of language, and so on.

  Contributions to current practice: the importance of relaxation strategies when appropriate, especially the use of background music, imagery, and the recall of pleasant early learning experiences to help the students feel comfortable with the learning environment and open their minds to the target language.

Indeed teachers have much to learn from the many diverse practices falling under the communicative teaching umbrella, particularly teachers of beginning to intermediate language learners. To learn more about these and similar methods, see the cited sources above in addition to Oller and Richard-Amato (1983); Larsen-Freeman, (2000), and Richards and Rodgers (2001). The *total physical response* (Asher, 1972, 1993, 2000) and the *natural approach* (Krashen & Terrell, 1983; Terrell, 1983) are two additional versions of communicative language teaching that are discussed in some detail in Part II of this volume.

SUMMARY

Although methodologies have changed over the years, particularly in western cultures, the content of language teaching remained basically the same until the latter part of the 1980s. Until then, meaningful interaction critical to learning itself generally took a back seat to an analysis of language.

Chomsky's transformational grammar was mistakenly used to justify and perpetuate a focus on structure in language teaching whereas his real contributions to the field remained largely ignored until recent years. Although we currently appear to be moving in other directions (see especially the connectionists), Chomsky's concepts of a possible language acquisition device and universal grammar have had a profound influence on where we are today.

Along the way, Hymes, Halliday, Wilkins, Widdowson, and Breen and Candlin have added much to our knowledge, particularly concerning the sociocultural aspects in defining a language system, and Savignon and many others have been crucial to the development of approaches that involve students in meaningful experiences in their new language. Now we find ourselves moving toward participatory teaching and a greater emphasis on the sociocultural and situated aspects of language learning (see especially Chapters 3 and 4 in this volume).

Yet we have a long way to go in understanding the full impact of sociocultural and cognitive factors on both the first and the second language learning process. A synthesis of sociocultural and cognitive forces may be taking root (see Chapter 3) and may move us toward a new paradigm in language teaching. Compatible theories are beginning to evolve and are, in many cases, losing their "purist" origins. We will not want to miss examining their implications as they unfold in the years to come.

QUESTIONS AND PROJECTS FOR REFLECTION AND DISCUSSION

1. Many have speculated about the existence of Chomsky's language acquisition device, what it might contain, and how it might work. Both the computer analogy and the notion of parameter setting have been posited as possibilities. Discuss the feasibility of Chomsky's theories. Consider what you know about the views of the connectionists in your discussion. Also consider what you already know about a sociocultural perspective. Do you have any hypotheses of your own about how first languages may develop within the brain? What about second languages?

2. Widdowson, as early as 1978, argued that "we do not progress very far in our pedagogy by simply replacing abstract isolates of a linguistic kind by those of a cognitive or behavioral kind." Explain what you think he meant. Can you think of abstract isolates, other than those mentioned in this chapter, on which programs might attempt to focus?

3. ✎ **Journal Entry:** Begin a professional development journal. The main purpose of such a journal is to include your questions and reflections concerning the issues about which you will be reading. In your first entry reflect on the issues you found most important in Chapter 1. In this entry and the ones to follow, relate your response to the notions you already hold about language learning based on your prior knowledge and experience as well as what you know now. What ideas or concepts will you want to apply to your own teaching? At the ends of Chapters 2–17 you will find at least one question or task description that specifically suggests that you respond in your journal.

    Your professional development journal can go beyond the entries specifically suggested by this book. It can include many other issues about which you have interest and/or concerns. If you are currently teaching in a classroom, you can reflect in your journal on your own day-to-day practice and how it relates to what you are learning. From time to time, include answers to questions such as these: What strategies am I using that are different from what I used in the past? How well are they working? What alternative strategies might I try? What have I learned about language teaching from my experiences? What evidence do I see of my growth over time? Your journal need not end when your particular program of study is finished; instead it should be there for you to write in as you evolve as a teacher throughout your entire career.

    You may want to share some of your journal entries with a peer to get his or her response. If so, leave room for the response after each entry.

SUGGESTED READINGS AND REFERENCE MATERIALS

Brumfit, C. J., & Johnson, K. (Eds.). (1979). *The communicative approach to language teaching*. Oxford: Oxford University. This classic book presents an in-depth analysis of the fundamental arguments underlying communicative approaches. Included are key writings of Hymes, Halliday, Wilkins, Widdowson, and many others who have led the way to a new look at language teaching processes.

Chomsky, N. (1995). *The minimalist program*. Cambridge, MA: MIT Press. Chomsky reiterates his basic assumption that there is a component of the human brain whose functions (both cognitive and performance) are devoted solely to language and that this component interacts with other systems in ways that still remain a mystery. He speculates that this language faculty relies on a single computational system that limits what is possible in language syntactically and allows for limited lexical variation—thus making the word *minimalist* appropriate to his analysis.

Deacon, T. (1997). *The symbolic species: The co-evolution of language and the brain*. New York: Norton. As fascinating as it is controversial, this book takes a close look at the kind of symbolic thinking that distinguishes humans from other living things and at the role evolution has had in the process. The author's disagreements with Chomsky are discussed at length.

Elman, J., Bates, E., Johnson, M. H., Karmiloff-Smith, A., Parisi, D., & Plunkett, K. (1996). *Rethinking innateness: A connectionist perspective on development*. Cambridge, MA: MIT Press. A difficult but important book in the development of connectionist theory. It examines the origins of knowledge in the human brain and looks at the role played by the interaction of innateness, neurobiology, and learning in cognitive development.

Savignon, S. (2005). Communicative language teaching: Strategies and goals. In E. Hinkel (Ed.), *Handbook of research in second language teaching and learning* (pp. 635–651). Mahwah, NJ: Lawrence Erlbaum. Here Savignon discusses the theories on which community language is based and the way it has been practiced in a variety of global contexts. She puts it into perspective for us historically and then attempts to clear up any misunderstandings we may have about its use, stressing it as an approach to intercultural communicative competence.

CHAPTER 2

The Process of Learning a Second Language in the Classroom: A Cognitive View

A discernible trend, especially in the 1980s and 1990s, has been for increasing numbers of researchers and theorists, rationalists all, to focus their attention on SLA as an internal, individual, in part innately specified, cognitive process—one that takes place in a social setting, to be sure, and can be influenced by variation in that setting and by other interlocutors, ... but a psycholinguistic process, nonetheless, which ultimately resides in the mind-brain, where also lie its secrets.

M. Long and C. Doughty, 2003

QUESTIONS TO THINK ABOUT

1. Have you attempted to learn another language in a classroom setting? Did you eventually become fluent? If so, what kinds of experiences seemed necessary to your fluency?

2. Think about the times your use of language may have been corrected by a teacher. Were these experiences generally positive or negative? Were you ever embarrassed by the way a teacher corrected you? How should teachers handle error correction in their classrooms? Should it differ for oral and written work?

3. What role should formal grammar instruction play in the language classroom? Is it possible to become fluent in another language without it?

Since the early 1980s, many in the field of second language (L2) learning have supported, indeed made possible, the revolutionary movement taking us from grammar-based to interactive approaches grounded in social interaction. Although criticized by those coming from a sociocultural point of view for its reliance on hypothesis testing and its frequent insistence on the native-speaker model, the cognitive perspective[1] has helped to bring us to the crossroads where we now stand. One road leads to a continuation of the same or similar cognitive research and theory with some modification. Another road leads to sociocultural positions on both research and theory based on the establishment of identities in situated contexts and the development of dynamic classroom communities. A third road leads to a synthesis of cognitive and sociocultural viewpoints (see Chapter 3), and attempts to draw the best from each.

This chapter and part of the next explore the cognitive perspective of second language acquisition (SLA) and some of the more typical research on which it has been based to glean from it what we can accept for our own developing theories of practice.

THE INTERACTION APPROACH

Exposure to Language (Input)

Krashen (1982, 1985), one of the early key players in the discussion about the components of an interaction approach from a cognitive perspective, concentrated on his *input hypothesis* and the role input plays in the interactional process (see pp. 73 and 75 in this volume for a description of his complete model). According to him, the language input received through exposure should be relevant and/or interesting and it should approximate the $i + 1$. In other words, it should be comprehensible in that it is near what students already understand (i), but then it should stretch beyond that to include concepts and structures that the student has not yet acquired ($i + 1$). Free conversation with competent speakers does not generally produce input that can be comprehended unless the competent speakers are talking directly to the student and are aware of his or her needs; neither does TV nor radio ordinarily produce such input.

One important question teachers and researchers have asked is what kind of input given by teachers and peers is most conducive to forming generalizations about the language, thereby making learning possible. Long (1981, 1983a, 1983b) theorized that interactional modification is an important way to make input understood. He began with the idea that input can be made comprehensible through modification triggered by a lack of understanding on the part of one of the interlocutors. Both he and Krashen

---

[1] This term is intended to be a composite of the viewpoints that many variations of the cognitive perspective seem to share.

agreed that the student ideally needs to be in a situation in which all the interlocutors desire to understand and be understood. Through gestures, the context itself, and linguistic modifications in the input, new concepts become internalized. In other words, the student needs to receive *foreigner talk.*

The term *foreigner talk* was coined by Ferguson in 1975. He defined it as a simplified register or style of speech used when addressing people who are nonnative speakers. Foreigner talk in the classroom is generally well formed and includes exaggeration of pronunciation and facial expression; decreasing speech rate and increasing volume; frequent use of pauses, gestures, graphic illustrations, questions, and dramatization; sentence expansion, rephrasing, and simplification; prompting; and completing utterances begun by the student (Gaies, 1977; Henzl, 1973; Kleifgen, 1985; Richard-Amato, 1984; Wesche & Ready, 1985).[2]

A word of caution is in order here, however. Sometimes teachers, in their efforts to make their input comprehensible, simplify it to the extent that it loses the richness and variety that it might otherwise have (see also van Lier, 1996). Teachers also may slow down and overly enunciate the simplified input to the point that students perceive it as condescending. This kind of talk should be avoided.

Teachers involved in meaningful dialogue with their students often automatically adjust their input in an attempt to ensure understanding, but they keep the intonation natural so as not to be perceived as talking down. See the following example.

Two teachers are talking to a group of foreign students in the Intensive English Center at the University of New Mexico.

		Strategy Used
TEACHER 1:	Who's the man with the hood on his face?	Question
	(points to the word "executioner" on	Gesture
	the board)	Graphic aid
TEACHER 2:	Yeah. You've seen the pictures . . . they have	Decreased rate
	black hoods (she pantomimes as she crouches and	
	ominously pulls a pretend hood over her head) . . .	Dramatization
	with the eyes. (She uses her fingers to encircle her	Increased volume
	eyes to appear as though she is looking through a	Pausing
	mask. Teacher 1 does the same and they both scan the	Expansion
	group as if to frighten them.) You know . . . really	Dramatization
	creepy looking . . . scary . . . oh . . .	Simplification
	what is it called?	Expansion
		Question

(Richard-Amato, and Lucero, 1980, p. 6.)

---

[2] An important question here is how does foreigner talk differ from regular teacher talk in the classroom? Studies have been done in an attempt to at least partially answer this question (see Kleifgen, 1985; Richard-Amato, 1984; Wesche and Ready, 1985). Researchers have found that many of the same strategies are used by mainstream teachers but to a lesser degree.

One modification of written input that is especially useful to reading comprehension is *elaboration* (similar to the expansion strategy in the dialogue above). Oh (2001) investigated the effects of elaboration or expansion, as opposed to simplification, and found elaboration to be equal to or better than simplification in improving the comprehension of written texts at both high and low proficiency levels. Both elaboration and simplification improved performance on basic comprehension. However, elaboration, in particular, significantly improved the students' performance on inference items. It gave students more opportunities to understand the information provided in the text by using redundancy and clear signals concerning its meaning.

Accommodation through modified input is often motivated by the students themselves. In the western world in particular, beginners in the target language are often asked to perform beyond their levels of proficiency by the teacher. Then the teacher helps ensure success by offering the necessary accommodation during the performance (Ochs & Schiefflin, 1984; Poole, 1992; see especially Foster, 1998, for a detailed discussion of negotiation of meaning based on research).

Production of Language (Output)

Krashen seemed to downplay the importance of the full interactional process by focusing on *input* (the language to which students are exposed) and discrediting *output* (the production of language), and, although he stressed affective factors (e.g., motivation, attitude, anxiety), he all but ignored the social situation, cultural influences, and so forth (see Lantolf, 2005). Krashen claimed that language can be acquired simply by comprehending input. He argued particularly against the belief that output is used for *hypothesis testing*, a process by which the learner tries out new structures in discourse to see what does and does not work. He was convinced that second language learners test hypotheses not through the use of output but by subconsciously matching forms in the input to their own notions about the language. He did admit that full two-way communication results in more comprehensible input because it necessitates more negotiation of meaning.

Swain (1985, 1993, 1995, 2000, 2005) preferred to take a stronger stand for the importance of the role of output in her development of the *output hypothesis*. She argued that among other functions, output is a significant way to test hypotheses about the target language (also see Corder, 1967; Seliger, 1977). She concluded, on the basis of her study of English-speaking children in a French immersion program in Canada,

> Comprehensible output ... is a necessary mechanism of acquisition independent of the role of comprehensible input. Its role is, at minimum, to provide opportunities for contextualized, meaningful use, to test out hypotheses about the target language, and to move the learner from a purely semantic analysis of language to a syntactic analysis of it. (1985, p. 252)

Swain found that although the French immersion students comprehended what their teachers said and focused on meaning, they were still not fully acquiring the syntactic system of French. Swain suggested that this result may have been due to the fact that the students had not had enough opportunities to produce the language.[3] She agreed especially with those who had suggested that it is not only input that is important but that the input be part of negotiated interaction. Simply knowing that one will eventually be expected to produce may serve as an impetus to notice the way things are said.

Obviously, there is less chance to give output in subject-matter classes in which the teachers do most of the talking and students the listening. Output has a much greater role than simply to receive more comprehensible input. Swain was convinced that when, through interaction, the second language learner is given negative input (see the error correction section later in this chapter), he or she is given reason to seek alternative ways to get the meaning across. Just by noticing a gap between what they say and what others say helps language learners become aware of what some of their own structural and semantic problems are.

Once the meaning has been negotiated, according to Swain, students during similar future exchanges can go from semantic processing to syntactic processing. In other words, once meaning is understood, the learner is free to focus on form within the interactional situation. If Swain is right, then output is indeed critical to the acquisition process itself. See also Izumi and Bigelow (2000) and Izumi (2002), who came to similar conclusions based on research of English learners.

The Interactional Hypothesis

The *interactional hypothesis* (Long, 1981, 1983a, 1983b, 1996) argues that environmental contributions to the acquisition process are mediated by selective attention and the learner's processing capacity in the new language. Long pointed out that conversational modifications in the input encourage the noticing of some structures. Gass (1997) agreed. Both concluded that because negotiation involves learners in comprehensible language, it pushes students beyond current levels. However, Gass reminded us that the actual results of the negotiation may not be realized until much later in the language learning process. Earlier, Pica (1994) had found that premodified input tailored to the level of learners made negotiation less necessary in some situations. However, she (and others) had concluded that negotiation provides the learner with more chances to notice the features of the second language due to the frequent repetitions, modifications, and feedback (Gass & Varonis, 1994; Long, Inagaki, & Ortega, 1998; Mackey, 1999; Mackey, Gass, & McDonough, 2000; Mackey & Philp, 1998; Polio & Gass, 1998).[4] For extensive reviews of the literature on the effects on language learning of

---

[3] However, there may have been other reasons as well. One may have involved a lack of well-timed grammar instruction (see pp. 54–62) during the formative phases of the language acquisition process. Another may have been a lack of proficient linguistic models (all, except the teacher, were French language learners operating at similar levels). It is possible that the use of highly trained peer facilitators who were proficient speakers of French may have helped to provide the input and the appropriate negative feedback necessary to accuracy in the new language (see Chapter 15). On the other hand, the fact that the students were at similar levels in the target language could also have been an advantage if group work had been used more extensively to give students more opportunities to produce the language.

[4] Also see R. Ellis, Tanaka, and Yamazaki (1994) and de la Fuente (2002) who looked at the effects of negotiation on vocabulary comprehension, receptive and productive acquisition, and retention.

peer–peer dialogue and teacher–student interaction, in particular, see Swain, Brooks, and Tocalli-Beller (2002) and Hall and Walsh (2002), respectively.

Through negotiation of meaning, learners are pushed to make adjustments as needed in "linguistic form, conversational structure, message content, or all three, until an acceptable level of understanding is achieved" (Long, 1996, p. 418). Long (1983a) early on identified three mechanisms to ensure that an utterance during the negotiation for meaning has been understood: *confirmation checks*, *clarification requests*, and *comprehension checks*.

- A *confirmation check* is a restatement of the utterance. For example, if someone says, "I went to the movie with my cousin," the confirmation check might be "I see; you went with your cousin."
- A *clarification request* might be "You went with your cousin?" (emphasis on "cousin") followed by something like "Yes, my girlfriend didn't want to go."
- A *comprehension check* might be something like "Did you say you and your cousin went to the movie?"

Syntactic priming effects found in dialogues in which second language learners are participants also appear to have a significant influence on language development and have been a subject of much investigation since the mid-1980s. These investigations have looked at the penchant on the part of the learner to use structures that were presented earlier in the conversation. We could say that the earlier uses of a particular structure "prime" subsequent uses of that structure when the same or similar stimuli are present. However, the subsequent use may involve different lexical items. McDonough and Mackey (2008) indicated that syntactic priming may make the representations of knowledge that have already been stored in the brain stronger. In their study of intermediate Thai learners of English at a public university in Thailand, they discovered that those learners who had high levels of syntactic priming were the ones most likely to advance in the sequential development of question formation.

The effects of syntactic priming have been particularly well documented in the corpora studies of Szrecsanvi (2005) and Gries (2005), the McDonough and Mackey's study mentioned above, and many others. Branigan (2007), in her extensive review of the literature on priming, reported that the participants in interaction are usually not aware of the priming that is taking place. Interestingly, Hartsuiker, Pickering, and Veltkamp (2004) found that priming may exist to a similar extent across languages. For example, they showed that Spanish speakers tend to produce the passive voice in English after hearing the Spanish passive being used. Many facets of syntactic priming call for more research. Syntactic priming is a phenomenon that appears to have a substantial influence on second language development through interaction.

Thus many factors need to be considered when speaking of the interaction approach. Perhaps Gass and Mackey (2006) summed it up best:

In simple terms, the interaction approach considers *exposure to language (input)*, *production of language (output)*, and *feedback on production* (through interaction) as constructs that are important for understanding how second language learning takes place. (pp. 3–4)

THE PROCESS OF LEARNING A SECOND LANGUAGE

From a cognitive point of view, we need to examine the differences between *contrastive analysis* and *error analysis* (proposed by Corder in 1967) to get perspective on the mental process of learning a second language in general.

Contrastive Analysis

Contrastive analysis is based on *behaviorism.* It considers the first language (L1) mainly an interference to the mastery of the second language. To become proficient in the second language, the habits of the first language must first be "broken." The most well-known manifestation of contrastive analysis, audiolingualism (see Chapter 1), offers mim–mem drills and practice with minimal pairs such as *ch*ew and *sh*oe (for Spanish speakers), *gl*ass and *gr*ass (for Japanese speakers), and dialogues to be memorized so that students can avoid errors in the new language and take on its proper forms.

Cognitivists have a problem with this philosophy because contrastive analysis is generally not a good predictor of errors in the second language. The fact is that most of the errors students make in the second language cannot be traced to the differences between the first and second language.[5] In addition, regardless of the features of the students' first languages, many of them appear to go through a similar variable progression in the second language. For example, even if students' first language uses inversion to form questions (as does English), they still tend to experience the same process as other students when learning interrogatives in English. That is, they use intonation to mark a question ("He is going?") before they use inversion ("Is he going?").

Error Analysis

Error analysis is based on *developmentalism,* the idea that learning develops in a variable progression as learners interact with the environment. It considers the errors made by learners while they are learning and asks questions about them:

- Why are these errors being made?
- What do they suggest about the hypotheses being tested (generally subconsciously) by learners?
- Do the errors mean that the learners are doing something wrong? Or do they mean that the learners are in the process of acquiring a rule and are, in reality, progressing in the language?

Consider a student who has changed "went" to "goed" because the past tense "ed" has just been internalized. Error analysis looks at such errors positively and deems them necessary to the development of language (be it first or second). Used appropriately, then, error analysis does not pinpoint deficits in the student's use of the new language

---

[5] There may be exceptions. Some applied linguists believe that first language influence on errors can be important, especially when it interacts in combination with other factors to make certain ungrammatical forms more likely in the second language. If this is the case, then direct instruction for such forms may be necessary. See especially Doughty and Williams (1998).

but rather helps determine in what ways the student is progressing in the developmental process.

Overall, error analysis considers the first language beneficial to the development of the second language. At first, students rely heavily on first language structures and sometimes even vocabulary to get their meaning across. As the second language becomes internalized and students move toward proficiency, they rely less on the first language. Interestingly, the interim language that develops is neither the first nor the second language. It has some features of each but also has features that are not found in either language. This is called *interlanguage* (Selinker, 1972).

Interlanguage Development

The term *interlanguage* refers to the variable progression through which each language learner constructs a system of abstract linguistic rules (R. Ellis, 1997). This process reflects the systematic development of the syntax, semantics, and pragmatics of the second language and is very similar to the process followed by first language learners. Chunks of language not fully understood at first are stored and then analyzed later as the students become more proficient. Hypothesis testing occurs usually at the subconscious level, and predictable errors are made along the way, regardless of what first language the students speak (e.g., Butterworth & Hatch, 1978; Fuller & Gundel, 1987; Ravem, 1978).

The progression toward proficient second language use is not linear, and it does not have to be at the expense of the first language. Students move forward and back, from one language to the other, all the while stretching to increasingly more advanced levels. Thus the word *variable* is used to describe the progression of development. Although students regress frequently, the general movement is forward, toward the goal: that is, proficient second language use. We need considerably more research to understand this progression fully. We do have evidence about how students progress, particularly in the formation of negatives, interrogatives, and relative clauses. For example, Schumann (1980) looked at the speech of five Spanish speakers learning English and found that clauses are first used to modify objects: "Roberto has a book is about electricity." Notice that the relative pronoun is missing. This later becomes "Roberto has a book that is about electricity." In more recent years, Bardovi-Harlig (1992, 1995, 2000) conducted considerable research on the acquisition of several morpheme[6] and syntactic constructions and found, as did her predecessors, that these constructions emerge in a variable progression throughout the acquisition process. One of her findings concerning past-tense acquisition was that learners start with no explicit time reference other than chronological order, slowly begin to incorporate adverbials (*last week*, *then*, *after*, and so on), and gradually add verb endings that indicate past tense. Once the past tense has stabilized and students feel the need to communicate about what occurred prior to the main events about which they are speaking, they add past perfect forms.

---

[6] The smallest unit of meaning. It may be a word or a part of a word.

Premature Stabilization

Although the language acquisition progression is generally forward and structures eventually become stabilized, students sometimes reach a plateau before certain forms are fully developed. We say that at this point or for that particular structure (sometimes called a *pidginized form*) the student's interlanguage has *prematurely stabilized* or *fossilized*.[7] When pidginized forms become obligatory in the student's production, we say that fossilization has occurred. Interestingly, such fossilization is unique to second language learners and does not usually occur in first language learners (R. Ellis, 1997).

We know relatively little about what causes premature stabilization or fossilization in second language learners and what can be done to reverse their effects. We do know that many related factors deserve attention. Some of these are

- increased anxiety about the learning situation
- overemphasis on being "nativelike" (which for many is an unrealistic and inappropriate goal)
- lack of competent linguistic models
- insufficient amounts of *positive evidence* (input that serves as a model) and *corrective feedback* (see also Han & Selinker, 2005)
- not enough flexibility within the learner; a lack of tolerance for ambiguity[8]
- insufficient motivation (perhaps the learner is already able to communicate as effectively as deemed necessary)
- lack of well-timed instruction in grammar (see Chapter 3)
- maturation constraints and age of onset (see Dörnyei & Skehan, 2003; Han, 2004; Long, 2003)[9]
- possible first language interference (see Han, 2004)
- language aptitude (see especially Abrahamsson & Hyletnstam, 2008; Dörnyei, 2006; Dörnyei & Skehan, 2003; and p. 72 in this volume for a discussion of aptitude)

In some cases, the learner may have reached specific communicative goals and no longer feels the need to become more competent. The language of many adults tends to prematurely stabilize at some point in the interlanguage process, particularly in the area of pronunciation (see especially Mendes Figueiredo, 1991), but this is not a great cause for concern unless it interferes with communication. Han and Selinker (2005) suggested that longitudinal studies are necessary before premature stabilization can be identified in a given learner. However, the authors indicated that if it *can* be established, it will probably continue to persist even with attempts to remedy it.

---

[7] Long (2003) preferred the term *stabilization*. His basic arguments included the notion that *fossilization* implies a permanence, which is difficult if not impossible to substantiate. On the other hand, *stabilization* does indeed exist and can be tested empirically.

[8] A tolerance for ambiguity involves the acceptance of apparent contradictions and information that is not complete.

[9] For neurobiological perspectives on the issue of age, see especially Lenneberg (1967) and Scovel (1988).

Defining and Reaching a Goal

Adults have been known to acquire all aspects of a second language under the right conditions. Sorenson (1967) studied the Tukano tribes of South America who must, according to their culture, marry someone outside of their first language group. He found that adults in this situation do indeed learn second languages and reach high levels of proficiency, even in pronunciation. Incidentally, they were permitted a very long silent period (see pp. 70–71 in this volume). Ioup, Boustagui, El Tigi, and Moselle (1994) found that their subject, Julie from the United Kingdom, who appeared to have a high aptitude for language learning, gained nativelike proficiency in Egyptian Arabic (she was married to an Egyptian). In both studies, continual access to the language was available, and the intrinsic motivation to speak in nativelike ways seemed very high.[10] Although we obviously cannot provide students with access to a second language around the clock or heighten motivation to this level in our classrooms, we can do a great deal to prevent stabilization from occurring prematurely and maybe even keep fossilization from happening at all. Klein (1995), who saw the phenomenon from a psychosocial perspective, concluded that older learners who have sufficient access to input in the second language (see also Flege & Liu, 2001) and who have high motivation to speak it can, indeed, reach nativelike levels (see also Moyer, 2004). However, nativelike proficiency should clearly *not* be the goal for all second language learners (see Cook, 1999; M. Gebhard, 1999; Liu, 1999). A more realistic and appropriate goal is to be understood by the group of people with whom the second language learner needs to communicate. Now that English has become global, many Englishes have developed around the world, any one of which could become the target language for any given group of people (see also pp. 6–7 in this volume).

If lack of motivation is part of the problem, then bringing students into increased contact with competent speakers of the language, especially peers, may help. Such contact might involve

- setting up peer-facilitator situations (see Chapter 15)
- inviting fluent speakers of the target language to the classroom (including administrators, counselors, teachers, adults from the community, as well as peers and other second language users)
- providing opportunities for students to develop relationships with peers who are more advanced in the language (e.g., organizing pen-pal possibilities, arranging field trips and planning celebrations that involve people from outside the language classroom)

Situations such as these sometimes can provide enough motivation to prevent premature stabilization or, in some cases, get students moving again in the language development process. One thing is clear: Fossilized learners should not be labeled as such. Han (2004) stated,

---

[10] The researchers noted, in the case of Julie, that she seemed to be an outstanding language learner and paid close attention to form. Although the researchers appear to attribute most of her success to aptitude, without strong motivation in the first place, it is questionable whether she would have been able to achieve what she did in spite of her abilities as a language learner had she not married an Egyptian Arabic speaker.

> Labeling learners as fossilized or something of that kind does nothing but create stress and anxiety in learners that further inhibits their learning. Instead, a careful examination, in this case, would be beneficial to both teachers and learners, that seeks to understand, and subsequently combat, factors underlying the lack of progress. (p. 173)

Although error analysis is an important tool in studying interlanguage, it is clear that we need to move beyond it to include discourse and performance analyses as well as ethnography. We have much to learn about the total situations of second language users, the details of the interactional events, and the feelings, attitudes, political concerns, and motivational factors relevant to the process of learning another language in the classroom.

ERROR TREATMENT

Interestingly, direct corrections of ungrammatical forms in the output are seldom found in motherese, the simplified speech register used with children learning their first language. Krashen (1982) early on supported Roger Brown's conclusion that the caretaker seems to be more interested in the truth value of the utterance. As an example of this, he pointed to R. Brown, Cazden, and Bellugi (1973), who reported that "Her curl my hair" was not corrected in their study because the statement was true, whereas "Walt Disney comes on Tuesday" was corrected because in reality Walt Disney comes (on television) on Wednesday. Thus content, not form, is the emphasis.

It is interesting also that parents are usually thrilled by any effort at all that the child makes in forming utterances. For example, when the child says "Daddy home" for the first time, no one labels this a mistake or calls it substandard or even considers it an error at all. Instead it is thought to be ingenious and cute, and the child is hugged or rewarded verbally. The utterance is considered evidence that the child is indeed acquiring the language.

What if in the classroom the language teacher treated "errors" as being evidence that the language was being acquired and that generalizations (often overgeneralizations) were being formed by the student? How might that facilitate acquisition of the language? It is probable that in such an environment, the learner would be more willing to take the risk of being wrong and would be freer and more uninhibited in developing an interlanguage. The forms would thus, in many cases, become acquired, as they are in the first language, through extensive use of modified language in meaningful situations (Chaudron, 1985; Long, 1991; R. Ellis, 1985, 1997; Wagner-Gough & Hatch, 1975; Winitz, 1996).

Teachers are generally concerned both with the *accuracy* and *fluency* of the output. However, Sutherland (1979) pointed out early on that both goals "cannot realistically be achieved in the early stages of learning. Fortunately, and perhaps more importantly, they do not need to be achieved simultaneously in order to ultimately produce effective speakers" (p. 25). He further argued that learners in classrooms in which accuracy is the most important factor tend to develop very little proficiency in the target language. In such classrooms, the teachers often consider themselves "Guardians of the Linguistic Norm" and feel that their main reason for being there is to ensure correctness. Such teachers often think that if students are allowed to make mistakes at beginning levels, they are doomed to a lifetime of linguistic errors based on the bad habits they form. Sutherland would disagree. He stated that "since errors persist in learners anyway—no matter what method is employed—we certainly cannot look to methods to explain this phenomenon" (p. 27).

Early research done in the area of error correction appears to have supported Sutherland's idea that increased direct error correction does not lead to greater accuracy in the target language (e.g., Dvorak, 1977; Hendrickson, 1976; Semke, 1984). Moreover, it was found later that such emphasis on error correction can be overly directive and intimidating, and in some cases it can even lead to increased language anxiety (see Young, 1991).

Corrections, including those involving syntactic, semantic, and pronunciation errors, can be very direct (explicit) or indirect (implicit) or somewhere in between (see Figure 2.1 on p. 52). Because many experienced teachers of second languages intuitively are aware of the problems often associated with direct correction when interacting with students, they tend to use indirect mechanisms of correction during interaction. However, that does not mean they never use explicit correction, especially when the need for it is perceived. Explicit correction is often given in response to written work and even to oral production, especially if the student has requested it in one-to-one interaction. However, during communication itself, the most commonly used type of correction is indirect and is delivered in the form of a *recast* (Fanselow, 1977; Mackey, Gass, & McDonough, 2000).

A recast is usually indirect, implicit, negative feedback given by the teacher (or a peer) during which the error is corrected through reformulation. Often the recast is embedded in a confirmation check, a clarification request, or a comprehension check (see p. 44). For example, if the student says, "I buy my lunch yesterday," the teacher may reformulate it by replying "Oh, you bought your lunch yesterday." By using a recast embedded in a confirmation check, the teacher is able to correct the student indirectly while at the same time maintaining the flow of conversation.

If the teacher instead had corrected the error very directly by saying, "No, 'buy' is not correct. You need to use the past tense 'bought,'" the conversation would have been put on hold, which may have added to the student's anxiety. How direct the teacher can be with corrections during conversation often depends on a student's expectations, the purpose of the lesson, how sensitive the student is to being corrected in front of peers, and the kind of relationship that has been established between student and teacher and student and peers.

The recast has received support in many studies, though it may not always be recognized as error correction by the learner. Ishida (2004) in a longitudinal study of students learning Japanese found that the recast brought about both immediate and sustained benefits. This study supported the findings of Long (1996); Long, Inagaki, and Ortega (1998); Mackey and Philp (1998); Doughty (2001); Han (2002); Braidi (2002); Loewen (2005); and Ammar and Spada (2006), all of whom found that recasting promotes to one degree or another the acquisition of grammatical forms.

Sometimes a recast used for correction is more direct and focused than in the illustration above. For example, the teacher could have used exaggerated rising intonation to emphasize the error ("Oh, you BOUGHT your lunch yesterday," putting strong emphasis on "bought") or used the same words as the student but as a question ("I buy . . . ?"). Sometimes a teacher will use a paralinguistic clue to indicate an error, such as raising an eyebrow or pointing over the shoulder to indicate the past (Davies, 2006). Of course using paralinguistic clues assumes a certain amount of linguistic knowledge on the part of the student.

To complicate matters, any given recast may not be interpreted by the student as a correction at all but as positive evidence in the input in which a form has been modeled by the teacher. For example, if the student says, "I eating lunch with my friends," the teacher might respond with, "Yes, I see . . . you eat lunch with your friends, don't you?" "Don't you" is an added feature which the student may interpret as a form modeled for his or her benefit. Instead of focusing on the correction, the student might focus on the tag "don't you" and wish to incorporate it at a later time in a similar or a different context. The utterance in this sense has served the student as a type of scaffolding[11] on which to build as he or she stretches to higher levels. The correction in the recast may have been missed altogether in this case. Egi (2007) concluded based on a study of forty-nine learners of Japanese that the learners appeared to pay attention to a structural or lexical correction in a recast when the utterance was intended to serve a single function, when it was short, and when it closely mirrored the original wording. Similar conclusions were reached by Philp (2003); Loewen and Philp (2006); and Sheen (2006). Egi reported that:

> recasts are ambiguous in meaning-focused contexts in which recasts serve multiple functions. Learners' failure to interpret recasts as feedback was significantly related to features of the recasts. When recasts were long and different substantially from the trigger, the learners were likely to report interpreting them as responses to content. On the contrary, when recasts were short and closely resembled the trigger, learners were more likely to attend to the linguistic evidence provided in recasts. . . . In conclusion, recast length and number of changes might, in part, determine their explicitness as corrective feedback and thus influence the ways learners interpret recasts. (2007, p. 534)

In addition, Loewen and Philp as well as Sheen found that recasts with only one modification were very effective in bringing about uptake of the correction by the learner.

Long (1991, 1996) saw a negotiation of meaning as a process involving both positive and negative feedback. He affirmed that negative feedback is essential to making errors salient, causing the learner to focus on form without interrupting the flow of what might be generally considered a meaning-focused context. However, there are times when attention can be shifted even during conversation to language as an object. (See the discussion of an incidental focus on form on p. 60 in this chapter.) At these times, teachers can give mini-lessons involving a rule. Generally such a shift is triggered by a breakdown in communication or a problem with production (Long & Robinson, 1998).

---

[11]The term *scaffolding* is a metaphor used to describe assistance offered usually by giving an example or a prompt, coauthoring a product, or simply expressing an idea for someone to build on. It is often focused on reaching a specific task-based goal (Lantolf & Thorne, 2006) and may only incidentally further development.

Another kind of error correction is called a *prompt*. A prompt occurs during the communication process and falls somewhere between indirect error correction and direct error correction on the continuum (see Figure 2.1). It often involves a request for repetition or clarification. For example, in response to an error, the teacher might ask "When did that happen?" if prompting the use of the past tense, or "He did what?" if prompting the use of a more acceptable lexical term. The learner is expected to respond by restructuring the original utterance or at least part of it.

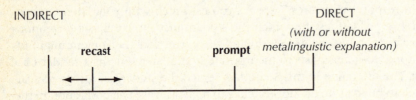

Figure 2.1 Type of Error Correction Continuum

Interestingly, a study of recasts and prompts by Ammar and Spada (2006) found that both prompts and recasts were effective corrective tools with high-proficiency learners and that prompts were more effective than recasts with low-proficiency learners. Another study looked at the results of prompts and recasts and explicit correction in French and Japanese immersion programs (Lyster & Mori, 2006). The researchers found that in the French immersion program, prompts resulted in the largest proportion of repairs, whereas recasts were more effective in the Japanese programs. Much depends on the communicative orientation of the instructional setting, the cultural background of the learner, the learner's developmental readiness, and how (and if) the learner perceives the correction.

Doubts among researchers about which correction practices or combination of practices are best to use in classrooms are very common, because we still know so little about the effects of various mechanisms of correction on different learners in different cultural settings. Peer-facilitating situations (see Chapter 15) might be the most conducive to the efficacy of prompts and recasts in the acquisition process because, in these settings, the corrections can be more intensive and focused in that the work is highly individualized.

Although recasts, both negative and positive, may appear intuitively to have the best potential for language development because they are both natural and ubiquitous, many researchers have insisted that form-focused techniques do a better job, particularly when it comes to accuracy. R. Ellis and Sheen (2006) summed up the controversy in these words:

> [W]hereas there is clear evidence that recasts can facilitate acquisition, we still do not really have a clear picture of when they will do so. Learner factors, the nature of the targeted features, and the characteristics of the recasts help to determine, in complex ways, when recasts work for acquisition and when they do not. If recasts are intensive, focused, and individualized (as has been the case in laboratory studies), they are likely to be effective; however, so are other form-focused techniques. (p. 595)

Because students learning a second language are often at an age when they are more developed cognitively, they are able to benefit greatly from form-focused techniques used during the communication process, especially at later phases of second language development. Such techniques were the subject of several studies in the 1990s and continue to be in this century. Many researchers have indicated possible advantages in providing direct, explicit correction in context, sometimes coupled with some sort of explanation or focus on a rule (see especially S. Carroll, 2001; S. Carroll & Swain, 1993; R. Ellis, Loewen, & Erlam, 2006; Lyster, 1998; Lyster & Ranta, 1997; White, Spada, Lightbown, & Ranta, 1991).

However, we want to be careful when interpreting studies of error correction practices—both direct and indirect practices. Several researchers, when investigating the effectiveness of recasts as opposed to more direct correction, have assumed that the recast has not worked if there is no evidence of immediate correction through *uptake* (see especially Panova & Lyster, 2002). However, Lightbown (1998) reminded us,

> The fact that the learner does not make an immediate behavioral change cannot be taken as evidence that there is no effect of the focus on form [referring to recasting]. Nor can a corrected response from the learner be taken as evidence that the more correct or advanced form has been integrated into the learner's interlanguage. Nevertheless, a reformulated utterance from the learner gives some reason to believe that the mismatch between learner utterance and target utterance has been noticed, a step at least toward acquisition. (p. 193)

Ohta (2000b) argued, too, that just because there is no immediate uptake does not mean that the recast has not been noticed and has not facilitated acquisition. Indeed, there may be other reasons for the lack of uptake. A restructuring by the learner may not have been considered appropriate at the moment, or there may not have been enough time for such restructuring. Moreover, the effects of recasts are often delayed (Mackey & Philp, 1998) and are acted on only after several recasts of a similar nature have been noticed over time. This is one reason longitudinal research is so important, particularly in studies of error correction.

Although researchers may label various teachers' corrective behaviors, they often do not provide adequate documentation or even descriptions of these behaviors, including how many times these behaviors were used, the learners' follow-up questions or practice, the pattern of behaviors, and so forth (see also Chaudron, 1991). More important, much of the research seems to involve short-term, experimental studies using pretest and posttest data rather than longitudinal data that employ both quantitative and qualitative data. It is almost impossible to learn what effect a treatment has had on the interlanguage process unless it is looked at over a long period of time. In addition, critical factors about learners seem not to be taken into account in most studies. Factors such as motivation, attitude, anxiety levels, willingness to take risks, age, cultural expectations concerning the language learning situation, relationship between teacher and student, and many others should not be ignored.

Yorio (1980), whose ideas can be applied to both writing and speaking, suggested early on that we keep careful note of the errors our students make to determine whether the errors are systematic (appear with regularity) or random (caused by memory lapse, inattention, not having acquired the rule, or overgeneralization). It is the systematic errors that should concern us:

- Are the errors increasing? (The student is regressing.)
- Are the errors decreasing? (The student is learning.)
- Are they stationary? (The student's language may be stabilizing prematurely or fossilizing.)

Of course, if the student appears to be regressing, we want to act before the forms have had a chance to prematurely stabilize or fossilize. However, Yorio warned that teachers should not inundate students' papers with red ink (in the case of written work) but rather should discuss errors in a meaningful way. It is important, too, that the student know that errors are being noticed only for pedagogical purposes and are not part of some overarching "deficit" approach (refer to p. 4 in this volume). The following were among Yorio's suggestions:

- Hold sessions at once with several students who seem to be making the same kinds of errors.
- Give students a chance to find their own errors and correct them.

(See suggestions pertaining specifically to written work in Chapters 5 and 13.)

Yorio noted that adults often want to know the nature of the errors they are making. Students who ask for explanations are probably motivated to learn that particular rule and are ready to incorporate it into their linguistic systems. However, if the student's goal is to understand and be understood in social and/or academic situations, then methods need to focus on real communication in those kinds of situations.

INSTRUCTED GRAMMAR

How necessary is instructed grammar to language acquisition? Consider the following constructed scenario, which illustrates the negotiation of meaning in a typical one-to-one communication. In this kind of collaboration, the "stretching" into the language of the teacher or more advanced peer becomes more obvious.

STUDENT: I throw it—box. [He points to a box on the floor.]
TEACHER: You threw the box.
STUDENT: No, I threw *in* the box.
TEACHER: What did you throw in the box?
STUDENT: My ... I paint ...
TEACHER: Your painting?
STUDENT: Painting?
TEACHER: You know ... painting. [The teacher makes painting movements on an imaginary paper.]
STUDENT: Yes, painting.
TEACHER: You threw your painting in the box.
STUDENT: Yes, I threw my painting in box.

The teacher's input is near the student's current level. It provides scaffolds on which the student can build. The conversation is about the immediate environment, the vocabulary is simple, repetitions are frequent, and acting out is used. The focus is on meaning as opposed to form. The student is acquiring correct forms not by the process of direct correction but through the content and the process of indirect correction and modeling. Notice that *throw* in the student's speech becomes *threw*, *in* is incorporated into the prepositional phrase, and the article *the* is picked up before *box* but then lost again. In this case it will probably take a lot more comprehensible input containing these forms before they become firmly established in the student's mind.

Thus grammar is acquired through the natural process of communication, without any conscious use of grammatical sequencing. Similar conclusions have been borne out by many others since the 1970s and beyond (d'Angeljan, 1978; Hammond, 1988; Hatch, 1983; Ioup, Boustagui, El Tigi, & Moselle, 1994; Krashen, 1982; Long, Adams, McLean, & Castanos, 1976; Long & Robinson, 1998; B. Taylor, 1983).

But is there a role for instructed grammar in the natural process? Let's take a look at what Rod Ellis (2006) had to say:

> Grammar teaching involves any instructional techniques that draw learners' attention to some specific grammatical form in such a way that it helps them either to understand it metalinguistically and/or process it in comprehension and/or production so that they can internalize it. (p. 84)

Rutherford and Sharwood-Smith (1988) theorized that instructed grammar can result in *consciousness raising* which they defined as "a deliberate attempt to draw the learner's attention specifically to the formal properties of the target language" (p. 107); see also R. Ellis (1994); Rosa and O'Neill (1999); and Schmidt (1994, 2001). By knowing certain rules, students may be more likely to "notice the gap" between their own output and the input they receive (N. Ellis, 1994; Schmidt, 1990, 1993, 2001). By noticing not only the gap between what they say and what they hear but also *how* things are said, learners can (when time allows) consciously plan their utterances. Fotos and R. Ellis (1991) hypothesized that these utterances can then serve as input on which learners can internalize grammar rules. In addition, Fotos and Ellis argued that knowing about a structure may make it more salient to begin with and therefore easier to internalize. There is evidence that a judicious use of instructed grammar is likely to be helpful and in some cases may even be necessary for some structures.

Many applied linguists over the years have insisted that to internalize acceptable forms of the target language, learners must focus first on instructed grammar rules and only second on communication.

Early researchers such as Higgs and Clifford (1982) claimed that students in communicative foreign language courses in which grammar is expected to be acquired inductively, through interactive processes, become victims of early fossilization from which they are unlikely to recover. However, this report lacked evidence to sufficiently support its conclusion, and, in addition, the courses on which the study was based were not described but rather only mentioned. Even more troublesome is that fossilization was not clearly defined.

We do know that students need to be moving through an interlanguage process, requiring interaction, before they can reach a plateau at which certain language structures may prematurely stabilize. Determining whether premature stabilization or even fossilization has indeed occurred requires longitudinal studies that cover several months or perhaps even years. Errors by themselves do not tell us much; it is the pattern of errors over time that is revealing.

Unfortunately, problems similar to those discovered in that early study by Higgs and Clifford in addition to other problems often can be found in SLA research: lack of adequate definition of one or more key concepts; basing the study on the acquisition of an artificial language rather than a natural language;[12] using cross-sectional research which measures what students can do at a specified point in time, instead of longitudinal research which reveals long-term effects and development; and a paucity of description and documentation of the instruction, communicative events, and/or discourse on which the studies are based. Moreover, many of the studies that compare an instructed-grammar environment with a naturalistic environment equate the first with classroom learning and the second with street learning. Of course, the classroom will usually come out best, because it is often very difficult to receive comprehensible input on the street, and the linguistic models there may not be competent speakers of the language. The common failure of street learning is often used, unfairly, to disparage naturalistic classrooms.

Instead, instructed classrooms need to be compared with naturalistic classrooms if one wants to make a true comparison. Even this would be a bit simplistic in that no one classroom would be or could be completely one or the other. Moreover, individual learners draw from a variety of sources of which neither the teacher nor the researcher may be aware. For example, a communicative event might be consciously analyzed by the learner for its grammatical qualities; an instructed grammar event might be of value only in that it presents comprehensible input. It may be of greater benefit to refine our studies by looking at various types of grammar instruction, the timing of the instruction, learner strategies, and so forth in relation to their effects on the interlanguage process. Studies of this type, although highly complex, would be far more valuable to informed decisions about using instructed grammar in the second language classroom.

In recent decades, instructed grammar has not generally been considered to be the most important contributor to interlanguage development, nor is the overall order of the development affected to any great extent by instructed grammar (R. Ellis, 1997; Lightbown, 1983; Pienemann, 1984; VanPatten, 1986). However, Doughty and Williams (1998) concluded based on research that although the order of development cannot be changed, the progress may be accelerated. Some researchers were convinced that instructed grammar does increase the rate of acquisition for some structures (Doughty, 1991; Gass, 1982; Weslander & Stephany, 1983). Pavesi (1984), R. Ellis (1990), and Bardovi-Harlig (1995) found that instructed learners seemed to reach higher levels of

---

[12] When learning an artificial language which has been created for the study, subjects do not have the same motivation to learn it as they would have if the target language were a natural one. The outcome therefore is suspect.

attainment in their second language than did the uninstructed learners. However, this finding was weakened by Pavesi's own conclusion that the results may have been due to the fact that the instructed learners had received more elaborated and richer input than did the uninstructed learners in the study.

Concerning foreign language teaching in particular, Winitz (1996) looked at college students who had completed one semester of college Spanish. Two groups of students each received one of two treatments: *explicit* instruction, in which students were exposed to a grammar-translation approach, and *implicit* instruction, in which students were focused on the comprehension of sentences in Spanish through the total physical response (see Chapter 8) and pictures. Both groups had to identify Spanish sentences that were well formed grammatically. He found that students who had had implicit instruction received significantly higher scores than those who had had explicit instruction.

Exposing students to less interaction and more instructed grammar may have been counterproductive, considering that the time spent in the foreign language classes is usually very limited. However, if instruction in grammar is well timed and based on individual needs (see Pienemann's hypothesis below), it can indeed benefit the acquisition process.

Perhaps some of the most exciting research in the area of instructed grammar that holds great possibilities for future study comes from Pienemann (1984, 1988), who developed the *learnability/teachability hypothesis*. This hypothesis states that instructed grammar may help the learner progress but only if the learner is developmentally ready to incorporate the structure(s) taught. He does not believe that we "squirrel away" rules only to pull them out and apply them later.

Evidence Supporting the Learnability/
Teachability Hypothesis

Pienemann (1984) found evidence supporting the learnability/teachability hypothesis in his study of five Italian children learning German as a second language. The children were instructed in the use of inversion. The two learners who were ready to incorporate inversion into their interlanguage did, in fact, learn it; the three who had not yet reached that point did not. In 1988 Pienemann replicated the study with twelve university students of German as a second language and found similar results: Those who were ready learned the structure. In addition, data gathered from the spontaneous language samples of three informants over the period of one year indicated that their interlanguage development did not coincide with the structures they were being taught in the German course they were taking (Pienemann, 1984). The conclusion was that because they were not developmentally ready for the structures when they were taught, the students did not incorporate them into their repertoire of language. R. Ellis (1993) went even further to say that practice with a rule that a student is not ready for can actually confuse rather than facilitate the acquisition of that rule.

On the other hand, Lightbown (1998) rightly suggested that working on some structures before the time is optimal may actually promote noticing and may push students toward readiness for incorporating those structures. This indeed may be the case for some structures and for some learners in certain situations.

Generally speaking, however, if direct instruction in grammar is to achieve the most benefits for a given structure, deciding *what* structures to teach and approximately *when* the time is right to teach them appears critical for any given individual learner. A knowledge of the process involved in acquiring some structures is certain to be of value to teachers making decisions about what the student may or may not be ready for. Although we do know something about the process involved with negation, question formation, relative clause formation, and past tense, we have much to learn about what happens during interlanguage development for each individual and the structures about which we can verbalize rules. It is important also not to try to zero in on exact phases of learner progression when trying to determine developmental readiness. The progression will always be continuous, variable, and difficult to define.

One strategy that currently holds some promise in identifying structures for which students may be ready is teacher-generated error analysis (see pp. 45–46). This focuses on what structures students already know something about and are trying to use in their written and oral output, as well as whether the mistakes made with these structures are still variable. In other words, they have at least partial knowledge of the structures but do not yet have control over their use. Lightbown (1998) pointed out that teachers generally are able to make reasonably accurate guesses about students' proficiency levels and can predict the types of errors their students will make and what structures they might be ready for. Sometimes work with specific forms that the students are actually trying to use will be enough to help us use appropriate instruction and give students considerable exposure to input containing these forms. Once the structures are identified and considered teachable, small groups of students can be formed to work explicitly with a particular rule, or the rules can be worked on by individuals.

Focus on FormS versus Focus on Form

Focus on formS and *focus on form* are terms used in the literature to distinguish two very different grammar treatments.

A *focus on formS* (see Figure 2.2) refers to explicitly teaching from a grammar-based syllabus (see examples in Chapter 1). Selected structures are taught additively, one-by-one, whether students are developmentally ready for them or not. The focus is intensive in that it generally involves one structure at a time or a contrasting of two structures in any given lesson or group of lessons before moving on to the next. It constitutes a *synthetic approach* in that it begins with discrete points of language and aims to bring them together or synthesize them into a whole (the conversation). The rules form declarative knowledge and, if practiced again and again, are thought to become proceduralized or automatic (see DeKeyser, 1998).[13]

On the other hand, a *focus on form* (see Figure 2.2) constitutes an *analytic approach* in that the learner begins with the whole (the interaction) and analyzes (or notices) its parts. It appears to be at least somewhat compatible with Pienemann's learnability/teachability

---

[13] It is interesting to note here that Hulstijn (2002) refuted DeKeyser's claim by saying that practice will speed up the procedures but does not make them automatic. This is an issue that will not be resolved quickly and may remain one about which we can only speculate.

Option	Approach	Syllabus	Type of Teaching Strategies	Teaching Strategies
Focus on FormS (separate from meaning-focused lessons)	*Synthetic* (parts or rules accumulate to form the whole structure of the second language)	*Grammar-Based* (see Ch. 1 for examples) *Intensive* (one rule at a time)	*Mainly Explicit* Not dependent on student's developmental readiness	-rules taught explicitly, one-by-one -rules practiced, one-by-one
Focus on Form (within meaning-focused lessons)	*Analytic* (moving from the second language system or the *whole* toward selective attention to parts or rules as needed)	*Content-Based and/or Task-Based* *Extensive* (multiple rules as they come up in the discourse in the case of an *incidental* focus) *Intensive* (one rule at a time in the case of a *planned* focus)	*Mainly Implicit* Usually dependent on student's developmental readiness	*Incidental Focus* (not predetermined) -rules learned mostly *indirectly* from positive evidence (modeling) and negative evidence (recasts) through negotiation of meaning -rules learned occasionally *directly* as needed during explicit "mini-lessons" interjected into meaning-focused discourse ***Planned Focus*** (predetermined) -rules learned *indirectly* and *directly* from meaning-focused content/tasks selected because of the structures inherent to the discourse typically used in them

Figure 2.2 Two Perspectives on Grammar Teaching

hypothesis in that the need for specific structural information becomes apparent at a time when the student is most likely to be ready for its internalization. Rules are learned implicitly from positive evidence (modeling) and negative evidence (mainly recasts) through a negotiation of meaning. See the interactive hypothesis described earlier in this chapter. Rules may also be learned explicitly and directly during mini-lessons interjected into meaning-focused dialogue at later levels of development.

There are two kinds of focus on form: incidental focus on form and planned focus on form.

Incidental Focus on Form

An incidental focus on form is the most common kind of focus on form. It is not pre-determined but rather occurs as a natural result of the communicative activity itself (see Long, 1991, 1996). An incidental focus on form is usually extensive in that several errors may be responded to during the course of a given meaning-based lesson. A specific form becomes the target when the learner makes an error with that form and/or asks a question about it. In other words, the focus is *learner driven* rather than *syllabus driven*. It is expected that many of the structures will be revisited repeatedly over time as the student needs them—usually when the student makes errors (see also Celce-Murcia, 2002). An incidental focus occurs when the teacher or more advanced peer reacts to an error, usually indirectly through negative evidence supplied most often in a recast. As mentioned earlier in this chapter, during the recast the utterance is repeated but with the appropriate correction embedded in it. Thus the learner's intended meaning is maintained. As Long and Robinson (1998) put it:

> Such feedback draws learners' attention to mismatches between input and output, that is, causes them to focus on form, and can induce noticing of the kinds of forms for which a pure diet of comprehensible input will not suffice. (p. 23)

The recast as we learned earlier normally does not interrupt the flow of conversation (Long, 1991) unless the learner stops to make the correction on the spot or asks a question about the error. Sometimes during the same interactional sequence, the learner will later use a similar utterance without the error (meaning that uptake may have occurred); other times the learner will store away the error for later analysis. It is possible, too, that the learner may not notice the correction at all. Noticing often depends on factors such as the clarity of the correction, the learner's developmental level and emotional state at the time. Explicit knowledge of the structure gained at an earlier time may help as well.

If the learner asks a question about an error noticed in a recast or if there has been a breakdown in the communication, then these become teachable moments during which the teacher can give a very brief mini-lesson explaining the error and perhaps teach a rule before going back to the conversation (see also Master, 1994. 1995). Such a time out promotes "an occasional shift of attention to linguistic code features—by the teacher and/or one or more students—triggered by perceived problems with comprehension or production" (Long & Robinson, 1998, p. 23).

Planned Focus on Form

A planned focus on form encourages the students to complete an assigned communicative task during which they will probably need some intensive work on a specific structure as predetermined by the teacher (see R. Ellis, 2006; Nobuyoshi & R. Ellis, 1996). A planned focus on form is usually intensive in that only one grammatical structure is emphasized—one for which the students have previously demonstrated a need or one that the teacher anticipates they will soon have a need for. The topic or task has been purposely chosen by the teacher mainly because discussing it will require considerable use of a particular structure. For example, in a task comparing two sports, the target structure might be "_____ is more fun than _____," or "_____ requires more athletic ability than _____." Usually the ensuing discourse is "flooded" with the target structure, which is highlighted or flagged in some way to call attention to it (Williams, 2005).

Larsen-Freeman's (2001) work on the teaching of grammar is of particular interest in that it also involves a type of planned focus on form approach. She proposed marrying form to both meaning and pragmatics and offered an array of communicative activities that can incorporate grammar practice. She pointed out that this approach differs from traditional grammar instruction in that it is the communication that generates work with given grammatical structures rather than a predetermined syllabus. The treatment involves planned activities such as highlighting the target structure in a given passage, figuring out a given rule from specific data, giving students only part of a rule and letting them learn the exceptions when they make overgeneralization errors and are corrected, and so forth. She reminded us that structures inherent in total physical response-type activities (the imperative), games such as twenty questions (*yes–no* questions), problem-solving activities (*wh-* questions), information-gap activities (using concepts and typical forms for giving directions), role playing (choosing pragmatically appropriate structures), and the like become salient during the interaction itself. She suggested that when the time is right, rules can be explicitly taught within a communicative framework such as in a content-based or task-based program (see Chapter 15 in this book).

Spada and Lightbown (2008) added yet another category to the focus on form approach to grammar instruction: *isolated form-focused instruction*. This category perhaps could be subsumed under the planned focus on form if the definition of "planned" were modified somewhat and extended to include instruction that follows a communicative activity. Isolated form-focused instruction comprises explicit lessons taught either *before* and *in preparation for* a communicative activity or *after* such an activity, in the case where problems with a particular structure have arisen. Isolated form-focused instruction has been thought to be very beneficial depending on the structure to be taught, the learning conditions, and the learner. Although some research has been accomplished on structures that may be best taught in isolation (e.g., plural *s*, structures influenced by misleading similarities between the first and second language, and so on), I hesitate to make recommendations here until sufficient research in all three areas has been completed.

Individual Grammar Profiles

We can be fairly certain at this time that it would be unwise in most situations for a language teacher to rely on the same rigid grammatical syllabus for everyone. What might be helpful instead is an individual grammar profile kept for each student that changes as the student changes. Which structures does the student seem to have already acquired? Which structures are those over which the student has only partial control? The grammar treatment could grow out of the perceived needs of each student and out of the communication activities themselves. The more explicit lessons may be mini-lessons interjected within the communicative activity or longer lessons given either before or after specific communicative events. They may involve individuals or small groups of students making similar errors. In addition, they may involve the use of lay assistants and peer facilitators operating under the teacher's supervision (see pp. 377–382 in this volume).

Indeed some students may need very little grammatical instruction; others may need and will be able to benefit from considerable work with rule application as new forms begin to emerge. In fact, adults (particularly those who are well educated and literate) are often used to learning rules that have been explicitly taught and then working with them deductively (see Celce-Murcia, 1993). In addition, many adults find that some structures require some intervention while developing an interlanguage. However, no matter which treatments are used, students at any age need to be spending much of their time in interactive activities where they are exposed to modeling and recasts within a rich, meaning-focused environment. No matter how well the rules are taught, they will not be relevant to the language acquisition process if students are not developing an interlanguage. To quote Lightbown (1998),

> a great deal of language acquisition will take place without focused instruction and feedback, when learners are exposed to comprehensible input and opportunities for meaningful interaction. However, some features of a language are very difficult—or perhaps impossible—to acquire in this way. Future research should focus not only on identifying such features but also on seeking to understand what makes them difficult or impossible to acquire without guidance. (p. 196)

Although we have made great strides in examining the cognitive aspects of language learning in the classroom, we clearly now should begin to turn to research that includes a component of a different kind. We need to know how sociocultural and affective factors come into play before we can make fully informed decisions, especially in the areas of error correction and instructed grammar and their roles in the language classroom.

Possibly the most critical questions we need to address deal with long-term effects of diverse teaching strategies on the language learning process in the classroom. Only by adding longitudinal, descriptive/naturalistic research components to our studies will we ever even come close to gaining insights into how best to help each individual language learner become more proficient.

SUMMARY

The cognitive theorists of the past few decades have been successful in helping to bring us to where we are today. Our field indeed owes much to them for their contributions in the past and for the cognitive research that continues to this day.

From a cognitive perspective, we have learned that second language acquisition appears to be dependent on an interactional process that involves recasts, prompts, modeling, and other strategies used in an attempt to negotiate meaning. We have learned that second language acquisition develops in a variable but continuous progression through an interlanguage process until the learner reaches proficient second language use. We have learned that a focus on form (vs. a focus on formS) seems to make the most sense as an approach to teaching grammar in that it includes explicit instruction but only as needed and mainly when the learner is perceived to be developmentally ready. We have learned that although the role of input in the interaction is important, that of output cannot be ignored. Output appears to play a substantial role in the acquisition process. It not only aids in receiving comprehensible input, it offers opportunities for practice and appears to be an important means for testing hypotheses and noticing the gaps. Also, even though the accuracy versus fluency debate continues to rage, most agree that it is the systematic (not random) errors that need attention and that there are ways to deal with them that can be very effective.

QUESTIONS AND PROJECTS FOR REFLECTION AND DISCUSSION

1. How might you define a "native speaker"? Do you think native-speaker language should be the goal for second language learners? Why or why not? Discuss the political ramifications of your answer. What influence do you think English as a global language should have on the issues involved here? You might want to refer back to the Introduction where this topic was first discussed.

2. Why do you think premature stabilization and fossilization are both unique to second language learners? Do you have any ideas about how a teacher might help second language learners overcome them and move forward again in the language development process?

3. Some people might argue that a discussion of the acquisition process is not relevant to the classroom because it is difficult, if not impossible, to make it happen there. What might be your stand on this issue? Base your answer on your own experience either as a language student or as a teacher.

4. In your opinion, how should student errors be handled in the classroom? Have your views changed in any way now that you have read this chapter? Consider the following:

   a. level of student proficiency in the target language
   b. the age of the student
   c. the relationship between student and teacher
   d. the relationship between student and peers
   e. systematic versus random errors
   f. correction of oral versus written output

Work out an error correction policy of your own, based on both your own experience and what you have learned. Share it with a small group to obtain feedback.

5. Visit a language classroom in the area where you live on two or more occasions. Describe how the teacher handles grammar instruction. Observe how the students respond to the instruction. Does the instruction appear to be well received? Do you think it is effective? Why or why not? Make sure to obtain the permission of the school administration and the teacher prior to your observations. Discuss your findings with a small group of peers. What did you learn about teaching from this experience?

6. What advantages does a focus on form appear to have over a focus on formS? Disadvantages? How is an isolated focus on form as defined by Spada and Lightbown (2008) different from a focus on formS? What factors might influence your choices about grammar instruction in your own classroom?

7. ✎ **Journal Entry:** If you have studied another language in a classroom setting, describe how your teacher treated error correction. How effective was this treatment for you personally in your efforts to learn the language? If you feel such treatment was ineffective, how could the teacher have improved it? If you have never studied another language, answer the same questions as they pertain to the furthering of the development of your first language in school. How might it differ were you to study a second language?

SUGGESTED READINGS AND REFERENCE MATERIALS

Cook, V. (1999). Going beyond the native speaker in language teaching. *TESOL Quarterly, 33*(2), 185–209. In this seminal article, Cook explains why the *native-speaker* goal creates unrealistic expectations and unnecessary frustration in second language learners for whom it may be unattainable.

Doughty, C., & Long, M. (Eds.) (2003). *The handbook of second language acquisition*. Malden, MA: Blackwell. This comprehensive anthology covers the many aspects of the study of second language acquisition as a cognitive science: its goals; the cognitive processing involved; the roles played by universal grammar, interaction, and the social environment; instructed second language acquisition; implicit and explicit learning; individual differences; cross-linguistic influences; second language acquisition research and theory; assessment; and several others. A variety of perspectives are presented in chapters contributed by a number of researchers, including Lydia White, Nick Ellis, Susan Gass, Robert DeKeyser, Jan Hulstijn, Zoltán Dörnyei, Peter Robinson, Manfred Pienemann, Craig Chaudron, and many more.

Larsen-Freeman, D. (2003). *Teaching language: From grammar to grammaring*. Boston: Thomson-Heinle. The term *grammaring* suggests a characterization of grammar as a dynamic process. Larsen-Freeman offers practical ideas on how to make teaching it interesting and challenging. She attempts to get us to reexamine the way we have looked at grammar in the past—as a static set of rules. She encourages us to teach students, not language as such.

Lightbown, P., & Spada, N. (2006). *How languages are learned* (3rd ed.). Oxford: Oxford University Press. This book presents a nicely developed, cognitively based discussion of topics such as first and second language learning, affective factors, interlanguage (learner language) development, instructed and natural environments, and common myths about language learning.

Long, M., & Robinson, P. (1998). Focus on form: Theory, research, and practice. In C. Doughty and J. Williams (Eds.), *Focus on form in classroom second language acquisition* (pp. 15–41). New York: Cambridge University Press. In this important article, the authors clearly distinguish the terms *focus on formS* and *focus on form* within a historical context. They argue against a focus on formS and in favor of a focus on form that provides room for brief instructional intervention as needed throughout the process.

CHAPTER 3

Toward a Sociocultural/ Cognitive Model

My numerous years as a language learner (and user) ... included rich and specific historical situatedness, webs of social interactivity, context contingent identity work ... These qualities of historical, contextual, and social situatedness are the "universals," in all their many forms, that need explicating in any account of the process of second language acquisition.

S. Thorne (2000)

QUESTIONS TO THINK ABOUT

1. In the quote above, what might Thorne have meant by "historical situatedness," "webs of social interactivity," and "context contingent identity work"? How might these terms be important to a sociocultural perspective of second language learning?

2. How is learning a second language like learning a first language? How is it different? How might such knowledge help you plan classroom experiences?

3. Is it possible to learn a second language by oneself? To what extent are teachers and peers necessary to the process?

4. Speculate about what a sociocultural/cognitive model of second language acquisition might look like. What kinds of factors would be important to consider in developing such a model?

According to Thorne (2000), language learning—first and second—involves a process by which cognitive activity within the individual (intrapsychological) and social activity between individuals (interpsychological) are tied to "environments with histories, and an ongoing negotiation of social identity" (p. 224). The intrapsychological and the interpsychological cannot be separated in an informed theory of learning. In spite of the differences between the cognitive and sociocultural approaches to learning, the work that grew out of each approach has much to teach us. The roots from which each approach grew may appear incompatible in several ways, as you will see. However, to keep them totally separated and in a dichotomous relationship seems foolish at best (see also Atkinson, 2002; Gee, 1990, 1992; Lave & Wenger, 1991; Rogoff, 1990). John-Steiner and Mahn (1996) reminded us that Vygotsky himself eschewed dichotomies as a way of viewing apparent opposites. They stated,

> Throughout his work Vygotsky used the dialectical method[1] to analyze, explain, and describe interrelationships fundamental to human development where others posed dichotomies. (p. 195)

Later in this chapter we discuss the Vygotskian perspective of learning, which is both sociocultural and cognitive. From this perspective, the social, the cultural, and the cognitive are not considered separate components but are instead interdependent and integral parts of the same phenomena. At the same time, we take a look at the implications and possible applications of Vygotskian concepts to second language learning in the classroom. The chapter ends with Marysia Johnson's proposed dialogically-based[2] model of second language acquisition.

Before we begin a discussion of sociocultural theory, a comparison of first language (L1) and second language (L2) acquisition is in order so that we might be in a better position to understand some of the cognitive work that has been accomplished over the past several decades. Then we examine a few of the information-processing models that grew out of the cognitive perspective to more fully appreciate the thinking that went into their development.

A COMPARISON OF L1 AND L2 ACQUISITION

Similarities

As early as 1974, Ervin-Tripp argued that if the human brain is equipped to handle language, then certainly this ability is not confined to L1 acquisition (see also O'Grady,

---

[1] The *dialectical method* looks at apparent opposites not in a dichotomy but intertwined in a relationship in which each entity is "interlaced" with the other. Sometimes one entity is dominant; at other times the other one is. The term *interlacement* used in this sense comes from John-Steiner and Souberman (1978).

[2] The meaning of *dialogically* or *dialogical* goes beyond the typical definition of *dialogue* and includes an interpretation that "constructs the self as it constructs the other" (Kramsch, 2000, p. 133; see also Bakhtin, 1981). A dialogically-based model assumes the presence of a space where different voices and discourses come together. Holquist (2002) described dialogism as "a way of looking at things that always insists on the presence of the other, on the inescapable necessity of outsideness and unfinalizability" (p. 195).

1999). To show that the brain uses many similar strategies for L2 acquisition, she pointed to her study of American children learning French in Geneva in which children used three sources for acquiring French:

1. peers (interaction in and out of the classroom)
2. school (content-area subject matter was taught in French)
3. home (exposure to parents who often spoke French to servants and to the mass media)

Generally speaking, "the conclusion is tenable that first and second language learning is similar in natural situations . . . the first hypothesis we might have is that in all second language learning we will find the same processes: overgeneralizations, production simplification, loss of sentence medial items, and so on" (Ervin-Tripp, 1974, p. 205).[3]

Evidence supporting the idea that similar mechanisms are involved in L1 and L2 acquisition comes also from connectionism (see description on pp. 28–30). N. Ellis (2003) stated:

> Given that connectionist models have been used to understand various aspects of child language acquisition, the successful application of connectionism to SLA [second language acquisition] suggests that similar mechanisms operate in children and adults, and that language acquisition, in its essence, is the distributional analysis of form-function mappings in a neural network. (p. 95)

Atkinson (2002), also a connectionist, took the argument even further when he examined the very heart of the process:

> One does not usually acquire a language *in order to* acquire it, or talk about it, or provide data for SLA researchers. One acquires a language in order to act, and by acting, in a world where language is performative. This is exactly why and how children learn their first language, and it accounts as well for most of the second/additional language going on in the world today. (p. 537)

Many in the field of applied linguistics have found much credible evidence early on that L2 learners use many strategies similar to those used for learning a first language. For example, Taylor (1980) looked at the use of overgeneralization and transfer made by elementary and intermediate students of English as a second language. By examining errors, he found that "reliance on overgeneralization is directly proportional to proficiency in the target language, and reliance on transfer is inversely proportional" (p. 146). In other words, learners may depend quite heavily on L1 knowledge to communicate in the target language at first, but they will begin to work within the framework of the target language—without harming the framework for the first language—once they are able to form hypotheses about the new language. Students will then make errors mainly due to overgeneralization of the newly acquired structures. For example, a student of English who has just hypothesized that past tense verbs end with "ed" may put "ed" on

---

[3] See Slobin (1973) for the "operating principles" associated with the acquisition of first languages.

everything that happens in the past. Thus "sat" (the correct form already picked up from the input) may become "sitted" or maybe even "satted." Taylor pointed out that overgeneralization (and transfer, too, for that matter) are the result of a necessity to reduce language to the simplest possible system. He referred to Jain's (1969) observation that this phenomenon represents an effort to lessen the cognitive burden involved in trying to master something as complex as language. The L2 learner, like the first, attempts to "regularize, analogize, and simplify" in an effort to communicate.

Both first and second languages appear to develop in predictable ways from a cognitive perspective. In reference to the natural order hypothesis, Krashen (1982) pointed to some striking similarities between L1 and L2 acquisition orders. If valid, these similarities may add credence to the argument that there are many parallels in cognitive strategies. He based his early conclusions on the following morpheme studies:

- Dulay and Burt (1974), who found what may be a universal order in L2 morpheme acquisition in children
- Bailey, Madden, and Krashen (1974), who found that adults and children followed a similar order in learning L2
- R. Brown (1973) and DeVilliers and DeVilliers (1973), who reached similar conclusions in their well-known findings on the L1 morpheme acquisition order

Krashen (1982) argued, "In general, the bound morphemes have the same relative order for first and second language acquisition (*ing, plural, ir past, reg past, third person singular*, and *possessive*) while the auxiliary and copula (*to be*) tend to be acquired later in first language acquisition than in second language acquisition" (p. 13). Larsen-Freeman (1978) found in her study that morpheme orders seem to reflect the frequency of certain morphemes in the input. She stressed the importance of carefully examining the input when investigating such orders.[4]

However, we should be cautious in interpreting the morpheme studies. Although the evidence appears impressive, equating accuracy order with acquisition order (as was done in the cross-sectional studies) is a questionable assumption at best. Structures are known to fluctuate within given speakers. Because the student uses "sat" at one point in time does not mean that it has been acquired. Recent thinking in this area emphasizes the inadequacy and inconsistency in the way in which the emergence of particular morphemes may have been determined. Pallotti (2007) called for more research to come up with and validate key operational definitions and to reach an agreement about how researchers can determine the *systematic emergence of a structure*.

More convincing early evidence supporting a similar process for first and second languages began with Cazden (1972) and others who based their conclusions on longitudinal studies. To illustrate, R. Ellis (1986) pointed out that the L1 orders

---

[4] Interestingly, the frequency effect has been looked at as a possible component of an informed model of L2 acquisition. See especially the N. Ellis (2002), Gass and Mackey (2002), Larsen-Freeman (2002), and Tarone (2002). Note also arguments questioning the importance of frequency in some situations. Harley (1998), for example, wondered why students of L2 French and L2 English have so many problems with article use if articles are so common in both languages. Obviously, other factors must be considered which may override frequency in the input.

Cazden noted in the acquisition of the transitional forms of negatives and interrogatives are very much like those of L2 acquisition. For example, negatives begin with the "no" attachment ("no can walk here") followed by "no" moving to an internal position ("Juan no can walk here"). Finally, "no" is part of the verb ("Juan can't walk here"). Concerning question formation, rising intonation is used to mark questions before the incorporation of *wh-* structures, and word-order inversion does not occur until later.

Similarity between speech addressed to children in their first language (motherese) and speech addressed to foreigners (foreigner talk) is evidence that others at least perceive the process of L1 and L2 acquisition to be alike in many ways. Shorter sentences, high-frequency vocabulary, "here and now" items (but to a lesser extent in the second language), indirect correction, frequent gesture, and lack of overt attention to form are among the many similarities observed in situations in which the interlocutors were involved in real communication (Freed, 1978; Hatch, Shapira, & Gough, 1978; Henzl, 1973; Long, 1981; Richard-Amato, 1984; Wesche & Ready, 1985).

Additional support for a similar process comes from Asher (1972): "[A] reasonable hypothesis is that the brain and nervous system are biologically programmed to acquire language, either the first or second, in a particular sequence and in a particular mode." He believed that both require a *silent period* (i.e., time to simply comprehend language without having to orally produce it). "If you want to learn a second language gracefully and with a minimum of stress, then invent a learning strategy that is in harmony with the biological system" (p. 134). The concept of the silent period which Asher proposed, and Krashen (1982, 1985) later incorporated, was a reaction to *being forced to speak* which so often happens to learners of second languages. It respected the right of the individual to remain silent mainly for cognitive and affective reasons.

We already know that children learning their first language require a fairly extensive silent period before they begin to produce utterances that are meaningful. Postovsky (1977) demonstrated the benefits of a silent period for L2 learners in a study of adult American students of Russian at the Defense Language Institute in Monterey, California. The students in the experimental group were asked to write their responses to input rather than speak. In contrast, the control group had to produce orally right from the beginning. The first group did better than the second, not only in syntactic control of the language but also in accuracy of pronunciation.

Gary's (1975) research also gave strength to arguments for a silent period. The study involved fifty American children learning Spanish. Half the students were allowed a silent period during which they could respond with nods, pointing, and other gestures. The other half had to respond orally using an audiolingual format. The experimental group outperformed the control group in both listening comprehension and speaking performance.

De Jong (2005) suggested that if L2 learners are required to produce language before they are ready, particularly during beginning levels of proficiency, they will be forced to rely on incomplete knowledge, their first language, or explicit knowledge. Thus their ability to acquire the structure of the second language could be greatly impeded.

Granger (2004) reminded us, however, that with L2 acquisition, the silent period is not required by everyone (as it is with L1 acquisition), nor is it uniform. She added a psychoanalytic view to Asher's original conception by stressing the importance of allowing learners to determine when they are ready to orally produce the second language in recognition of the "limbo" that often exists when they are moving between two languages and basically two selves.

Differences

Because learners are usually older when acquiring a second language,[5] they are more developed cognitively than L1 learners. (See especially Marinova-Todd, Marshall, & C. Snow, 2000, for a review of the literature on older learners.) Older learners appear to have distinct advantages in several areas:

- They tend to learn more quickly (although some processes may be more difficult).
- They have a greater knowledge of the world in general.
- They have more control over the input they receive (e.g., they are able to ask for repetitions, renegotiate meaning, change the topic, and so forth more readily).
- They are able to learn and apply rules that can aid in facilitating the acquisition process.
- They have a first language (and perhaps one or more second languages) from which they can transfer strategies and linguistic knowledge.
- They have one or more cultures that give them advanced information about expectations, discourse in general, and how to get things done with language. Of course, there will be many differences between the first language and culture and the second with which the learners eventually become familiar.

However, being older is not always advantageous in learning a second language. Indeed, being older often brings with it a loss of brain flexibility or plasticity. (See the universal grammar explanation in Chapter 1.) Learners may lose some of their earlier abilities as they gain others while they age. Lenneberg (1967) formulated the *critical period hypothesis* that claimed that, after puberty, language learners have a great deal of difficulty learning second languages—especially in the area of pronunciation. He indicated that this period coincides with the completion of lateralization of language to the left hemisphere of the brain; however, others insisted that such lateralization occurs much earlier, even before the age of five (Krashen, 1973). Nevertheless, debate concerning the critical period hypotheses still rages on, and the decision (if there ever is one) appears to be in doubt (see Birdsong, 1999, for analysis).

It does seem likely based on what we know now that older learners do have maturational constraints affecting ultimate attainment of the second language, but many

---

[5] An exception would be the *compound* or *simultaneous* bilingual acquirer, one who learns both languages from infancy.

of these constraints can be compensated for (see especially Hyltenstam & Abrahamsson, 2003). Adult speakers sometimes have trouble with grammaticality judgment tasks in their second language, although Birdsong (1992) found only a modicum of evidence supporting this conclusion. Pronunciation has also been found to be a problem for adult learners (Mendes Figueriedo, 1991; Moyer, 1999). However, several have found exceptions (see discussion of premature stabilization in Chapter 2). We must remember, too, that, some of these problems are associated with a concern about L2 learners becoming more "nativelike," which is no longer considered by many to be a desired goal, as discussed earlier. Becoming proficient in the target language, whatever it may be, however, *is* a goal desired and achieved by many.

Language aptitude, which is usually considered to be separate from general intelligence (Sheen, 2007), may play an important role, particularly for older learners who are learning in naturalistic settings. Abrahamsson and Hyltenstam (2008), DeKeyser (2000), Dörnyei and Skehan (2003), and Ioup (2005) stressed aptitude as an important predictive factor for adult language learners.[6] In her study of adults learning English, Sheen (2007) found a positive correlation between her subjects' aptitude for analyzing language and their ability to respond effectively to direct metalinguistic corrections in written feedback. However, considerable disagreement has occurred here among researchers and theorists. Whereas Robinson (2005), Reber, Walkenfeld, and Hernstadt (1991), and Krashen (1982) agreed that adult learners can be very different in their ability to acquire a second language and that this may affect ultimate attainment, they remained convinced that aptitude mainly affects explicit learning. Its positive effects on implicit learning were considered negligible or nonexistent. However, O'Brien, Segalowitz, Freed, and Collentine (2007) found that phonological memory in adults, or the aptitude for recognizing and remembering sounds and their order of occurrence, appeared to play an important role in L2 acquisition in natural situations. Abrahamsson and Hyltenstam (2008) stressed to an even greater extent the importance of language aptitude in naturalistic settings, especially for older learners. Thus the answers here are far from clear.

Other possible difficulties for older learners that may have a profound effect on L2 acquisition are found in the social situation and the affective realm (see Chapter 6). The social situation for older learners may not be conducive to L2 learning; positive relationships and group intersubjectivity within an accepting, encouraging environment may be missing. This in turn may add to the increased inhibitions and anxiety and other factors that older learners often must deal with (see MacIntyre & Charos, 1996). In such situations, older learners may find themselves afraid to make errors or to experiment with the new language. These fears may also be the result of an undue emphasis on form in their earlier experiences with language learning and on the pressure they may have felt to perform in nativelike ways. In addition, older learners may have poor attitudes

---

[6] Dörnyei (2006) believed that aptitude for mastering second languages is not a single factor but is a group or complex of very basic abilities related to such things as attentional control, memory, phonemic coding ability, grammatical sensitivity, inductive language learning ability, and so on (see also Ackerman, 2003; Robinson, 2001).

and a lack of motivation, as well as the absence of a nurturing environment (Bialystok & Hakuta, 1999). Much depends on their feelings about and the conditions under which they are learning the second language. Perhaps they are studying the language only because it is required in their program of study, or they find themselves in a country with a language and culture in which they have little interest. Although the influence of the first language is usually positive in learning the second one, interference may occur later on, particularly for items that are similar in the two languages either structurally or semantically (Newmark, 1983). Moreover, students may avoid using certain structures altogether because they are not part of their L1 (see Kleinmann, 1977; Schachter, 1974). We do know for certain that older learners demonstrate much greater variation in their rate of acquisition and in their degree of ultimate proficiency than do younger learners.

The chart in Figure 3.1 on p. 74 summarizes some of the typical characteristics of child L1 learners, child L2 learners, and adult L2 learners. Several have already been mentioned; others are discussed later. You may add yet other characteristics as you read further. Although little research has been accomplished on child L2 learning, the consensus appears to be that it is pretty much the same as learning a first language, except for older children who may have some of the same characteristics as adults but to a lesser extent.

In sum, important differences between L1 and L2 acquisition development that may present problems for adults appear to center on situational and affective factors as well as on language aptitude and loss of flexibility due to maturation. The similarities appear to lie mainly in the socialization process itself, although there are some differences here to look for as well. Future research on the human brain and how it functions in social situations and changes over time may shed light on this critical but little understood area.

INFORMATION-PROCESSING MODELS

Several cognitive information-processing models have been advanced in the past three or more decades. They include the monitor model (Krashen, 1981a, 1982) and the variable competence model (R. Ellis, 1986). The better known of these, the monitor model, is probably also the more controversial.

The Monitor Model

Krashen (1981a, 1982) distinguished between two different linguistic systems: *acquisition* and *learning*. Acquisition, he insisted, is *subconscious*, and learning is *conscious*; he considered them to be completely separate systems with no interface between the two.

Acquired items (Figure 3.2) are those that are able to pass through an "affective filter" of inhibitions, motivation, personality factors, and so on. The input then moves into the subconscious to become *intake*, a term proposed by Corder in 1967 to describe what is actually internalized. *Learned items* or rules, on the other hand, become part of a monitor (see Figure 3.3) and are used in production to ensure correctness but only if they are relatively simple, if the speaker is focused on form, and if there is time to apply them.

Typical Characteristics	Child L1 Learner	Child L2 Learner*	Adult L2 Learner
Is an active learner who tests and revises hypotheses	✓	✓	✓
Requires an interactional/socialization process	✓	✓	✓
Uses cognitive strategies (e.g., oversimplification)	✓	✓	✓
Is aided by modified input	✓	✓	✓
Develops language in flexible but fairly predictable ways	✓	✓	✓
Makes developmental errors	✓	✓	✓
Is helped by a nurturing environment	✓	✓	✓
Requires a silent period	✓		
Can benefit from a silent period		✓	✓
Has an L1 as a resource (unless compound learner)		✓	✓
Is likely to make transfer errors from the first language			✓
May experience aptitude as an important factor			✓
Is cognitively more highly developed and is able to organize information more efficiently			✓
Is likely to have a longer attention span and may have a better memory			✓
Generally has a greater knowledge of the world			✓
Can learn and apply rules and self-regulating strategies more readily			✓
Has greater control over the input			✓
Is more likely to be familiar with one or more other cultures			✓
Is more likely to have a problem with attitude and/or motivation			✓
Is more likely to be inhibited, anxious, and/or afraid of making errors			✓
Is more likely to have other second languages from which to draw			✓
Is likely to have some maturational constraints			✓

*Older child L2 learners may have some of the same characteristics typical of adults but probably to a lesser extent.

Figure 3.1 A Comparison of a Typical Child L1 Learner, Child L2 Learner, and Adult L2 Learner

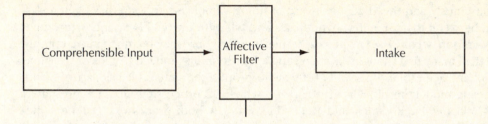

Figure 3.2 The Acquisition Process ©1981a by Stephen Krashen

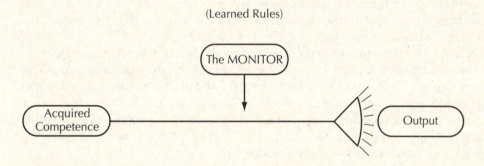

Figure 3.3 Performance Model © 1982 by Stephen Krashen

In the flow of normal discourse, the speaker does not have the opportunity to monitor the output to any great extent unless he or she is what Krashen called a "super monitor user"—in other words, one who is adept at applying rules and communicating simultaneously. Now and then a language learner appears not to monitor at all. Such learners make many errors in form; Krashen referred to them as "underusers." However, Krashen (1981a) also identified the "optimal user," one who applies the monitor appropriately. There are situations, he believed, in which the monitor can be maximally effective—for example, when the language learner is taking grammar tests, writing papers, or preparing planned speeches. Although items in the learning store do not directly become part of the acquisition store, according to Krashen, the rules of the target language do become acquired, but only by exposure to language that students can understand, in other words, by exposure to *comprehensible input*.

Criticism of the Monitor Model

Krashen's learning/acquisition and subconscious/conscious distinctions within the monitor model have been targets of considerable criticism over the years. Many have argued that it is possible for rules that have been consciously applied over and over in a variety of situations to become at least partially automatic (Bialystok & Fröhlich, 1977; DeKeyser, 1998; R. Ellis, 1986, 2006; Gregg, 1984; McLaughlin, 1978; Segalowitz, 2003; Sharwood-Smith, 1981; Stevick, 1980). Learners also seem continually to "monitor" subconsciously, and they become aware of doing so only when there has been a mismatch between their acquired hypotheses and what they would hear and/or produce (see Morrison & Low, 1983). Thus the issues involved here may be much more complicated than many first thought. Learning and acquisition may indeed be part of the same component. See especially Levelt (1989) who proposed a similar idea as part of his L1 processing model[7] and R. Ellis (1984, 1986) whose L2 processing model is presented below. McLaughlin, Rossman, and McLeod (1984) saw both processes as falling somewhere on a continuum between conscious and subconscious functioning.

Krashen's concept of the affective filter, although well-intentioned, has come under fire as well. It has often been called confusing and imprecise (see especially M. Johnson, 2004). Even though its operation is not clearly understood, most teachers do realize that affective factors are crucial and can negatively or positively affect one's ability to acquire another language.

In spite of the criticism, Krashen's monitor model has had an important impact on L2 classrooms across the United States and elsewhere. His model made sense to teachers, and through it he brought the point home that affective factors are important and that the classroom does not have to confine itself to formal instruction in the target language. Rather, it can provide input that better facilitates L2 learning—input that is, according to him, comprehensible, interesting, and/or relevant, not grammatically sequenced, and is present in sufficient quantity.

The Variable Competence Model

R. Ellis (1984, 1986) called his conceptualization of L2 processing the variable competence model. Whereas Krashen's monitor model emphasized the importance of providing comprehensible input, Ellis's (1984) model focused on a cognitive view of interaction. Ellis suggested that appropriate input is not enough but that a key factor in L2 acquisition is "the opportunity afforded the learner to *negotiate* meaning with an interlocutor, preferably one who has more linguistic resources than the learner and who is adept at 'foreigner/teacher talk'" (p. 184). Ellis recognized a *single* knowledge store containing variable transitional rules, some of which tend to be more automatic and others more analyzed.

The L2 learner demonstrates variation in the production of interlanguage forms (see also Larsen-Freeman, 1991). Sometimes the learner appears to have mastered a particular structure; other times he or she regresses to earlier forms. The variation, according to Ellis, is often the result of whether the process is a primary one (using automatic rules) in unplanned discourse or a secondary one (using analyzed rules) in planned discourse. (See Figure 3.4.)

---

[7] In his model, Levelt (1989) proposed a "conceptualizer" that is responsible for producing preverbal messages reflecting the speaker's intentions and for monitoring, using both controlled and automatic processing. This conceptualizer can monitor both internal speech and overt speech through what he referred to as the *perceptual loop theory of monitoring*. According to this model, monitoring is done during the planning stage of an utterance even before it leaves the conceptualizer. Then it is looped back to the conceptualizer for monitoring later when it is actually being produced.

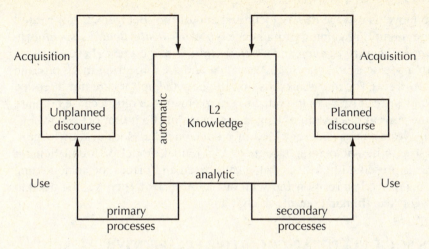

Figure 3.4 Variance Competence Model ©1985 Oxford University Press

According to this model, primary processes utilize and facilitate the *automatic system*, and secondary processes utilize and facilitate the *analytic system*. Both systems represent a continuum rather than a dichotomy. The rate of acquisition depends on the quantity and quality of the interaction in which the learner is involved. Ellis (1984) argued, "rapid development along the 'natural' route occurs when the learner has the chance to negotiate meaning in unplanned discourse" (p. 186). However, he reminded us that this process is influenced by such affective factors as motivation and personality (see Chapter 6).

WHERE DO WE GO FROM HERE?

Although we can learn much by reading about the information-processing models and other similar models,[8] most of them, including the Krashen and Ellis models described above, were intended to be universal models of L2 acquisition and did not acknowledge the importance of a sociocultural context to any great extent. Furthermore, they depended on technological metaphors referring to computers and databases. Consider for example these terms: *input*, *output*, *uptake*, *information processing*, *acquisition*, and other terms not usually associated with dynamic social situations. Such terminology still abounds in today's literature (see especially Thorne, 2000). Although such terminology remains useful to the field, a flow of metaphors related to dialogical thinking

---

[8] Other models have been proposed: VanPatten's (1996) input-processing model and Gass and Selinker's (2001) model of second language acquisition. Some cognitive models (the first two were mentioned in Chapter 1) focus on communicative competence rather than on information processing. They include Hymes's (1972) communicative competence model; Canale and Swain's (1980) communicative competence model; and Bachman's (1990) communicative language ability model.

is beginning to move us toward the sociocultural end of the spectrum. Terms related to a sense of community are gaining prominence—*historical situatedness*, *social context*, *appropriation*, *identity*, *agency*, and *participation*, to name a few. These terms are associated with a sociocultural view of L2 learning and are appearing more often in what we read. However, Thorne assured us that the new metaphors are not intended to replace the old; instead they are intended to complement the old, because both are important to any current discussion of language acquisition, be it first or second.

Now we move toward a different kind of model, one that does acknowledge—indeed emphasizes—the sociocultural context. A potential model or foundation for models to come is presented here. It is dialogically-based and places the sociocultural and cognitive in a dialectical relationship with one another. However, we first need to examine the Vygotskian thinking out of which it grew.

VYGOTSKY'S SOCIOCULTURAL/COGNITIVE PERSPECTIVE[9]

The *zone of proximal development* (Vygotsky, 1962, 1978) is a hypothesis that may help to explain some of the social/cognitive requirements necessary to learning in humans. Underlying the surface complexity of this concept are fundamentals that are extremely important to understanding not only how humans learn languages but how they develop higher-order mental processes. Although this hypothesis cannot account for the actual process of first or second language acquisition, it can teach us a lot about the social nature of this process as it relates to learning itself.

Although Vygotsky (1978), like Chomsky, did not speak directly to second language pedagogy to any great extent, he did formulate ideas concerning learning and development in children that have important implications for second language teaching. Before we proceed, a comparison of Vygotsky's and Piaget's views of the relationship of learning and development may be beneficial. Vygotsky and Piaget were both *constructivists*, meaning that they believed that knowledge itself is structured and developed from *within* the individual through active learning.[10] This is in sharp contrast to the *behaviorists*, who thought that knowledge was structured from *without* the individual and that all the teacher had to do was imprint this knowledge on the learner's mind.

---

[9] Just a brief word here about Lev Vygotsky's life: He was born in Orsha near Minsk in Byelorussia in 1896 and graduated from Moscow University. Later he taught literature and psychology in Gomel. He moved to Moscow in 1924 and began his work in psychology and pedagogy at the Institute of Psychology. His works were banned after his death from tuberculosis in 1934. Fortunately, his colleagues, former students, and other scholars brought his work (much of it unpublished) to light and continued his legacy after Stalin's death.

[10] Constructivism assumes that students are able to search for their own answers; that lessons can be built around concepts and ideas, not facts and skills; that student thinking can spearhead lessons, raise important questions, and change content; and that students can grapple with open-ended questions and elaborated responses and construct relationships, create metaphors, and build collaborative communities (see also Kaufman & Brooks, 1996). Although Vygotsky was considered a constructivist in the more general sense of the word, he differed from those constructivists who stressed individual development as independent of society (see especially Matusov, 1998; Piaget, 1979).

To Piaget (1979), the processes of learning and mental development are independent of each other. Learning utilizes development but does not shape its course. Piaget believed that maturation precedes learning. Educators who adhere to this idea emphasize the "readiness" principle. A student must be exposed primarily to input that can be handled without difficulty. In other words, the input must be at the student's actual level of development.

Vygotsky differed, in that he saw the individual as having two developmental levels that interact with learning from birth forward. Vygotsky argued that learning precedes maturation; it creates new mental structures within the brain. Through interaction, the individual progresses from what Vygotsky called an *actual* developmental level to a *potential* developmental level. Between these two levels is the zone of "proximal development," which Vygotsky (1978) defined as "the distance between the actual developmental level as determined by independent problem solving and the level of potential development as determined through problem solving under adult guidance of and in a collaboration with more capable peers" (p. 86). The potential level becomes the next actual level through learning that "presupposes a specific social nature and a process by which children grow into the intellectual life of those around them." Learning, then, should always be one step ahead of development. The zone of proximal development is a powerful concept that can indeed provide impetus for transforming the way we teach.

To illustrate how learning can occur in the classroom, a constructed dialogue is presented here, in which an English as a second language teacher during a literature lesson is helping the students stretch to a higher academic register. The students and their teacher are discussing the short story "Zelig" by Benjamin Rosenblatt. "Zelig" is the story of an immigrant man from Russia who has moved with his wife to the United States in order to be near his son. After his son's death, the man forces his wife and grandson to lead a life of deprivation so he can save up enough money to one day return with the family to his beloved Russia.

TEACHER: What did you think of the main character in the story?
STUDENT 1:   He was very . . . selfish.
TEACHER: Selfish? Maybe. Why do you say that, Pablo?
STUDENT 1:   Well, he made his grandson work until it made him sick. And what for?
TEACHER: I agree it did seem rather senseless since at the end they don't go back to Russia anyway. But why? What was his motive? Didn't the protagonist just want to pursue his dream? Didn't he have a good motive?
STUDENT 2:   He just wanted to get back to Russia. That was all he ever thought about. But was this fair? His . . . you say . . . motive . . . made him do bad things to his family.
TEACHER: Yes, Joe, I think you're right. Motives often make protagonists do bad things. But it can make them do good things too.
STUDENT 1:   Yeah, like that protaggg . . .
TEACHER: Protagonist.
STUDENT 1:   Yeah, protagonist . . . we read about last week. Gregory, or something like that. His motive ended up doing good things.

TEACHER: Yes, his motive did end up making him do good things. You can probably think of more protagonists from more than one story who did good things. Who were the protagonists we have read about who had motives that made them do good things? [Several hands fly up.] Okay, let's make a list. [The teacher draws rough columns on the board and labels the first column "protagonist," the second column "motive," and the third column "good results."]

Although this discussion is teacher initiated and led (typical of most classroom discourse), the students are being introduced to the terminology associated with an academic discussion about literature. Starting at what the teacher thinks is the students' level of development, she stretches them to a higher level by introducing them to the concepts "motive" and "protagonist." Through redundancy, the co-construction of ideas, and transitioning from the familiar to the unfamiliar, the teacher leads them to a reformulation of their utterances (see also Gibbons, 2003). Here language learning and content learning are linked. Through mediation, the teacher recasts what the students are saying using different language. We can see that the students are beginning to appropriate the new terminology into their own language systems.

As Wells (1999) noted based on his own interpretation of Vygotsky:

In the place of traditional transmissional teaching[11] on the one hand and unstructured discovery learning on the other, his [Vygotsky's] theory places the emphasis on the co-construction of knowledge by more mature and less mature participants engaging in activity together. . . . In the place of competitive individualism, his theory proposes a collaborative community in which, with the teacher as leader, all participants learn with and from each other as they engage together in dialogic inquiry. (p. xii)

Piaget stressed *biology* as the determiner in what he called the "universal" stages of development. Vygotsky did not emphasize universal stages; instead he stressed *society* as the determiner of development, although the resulting progression is similar. The progression is variable because each person's history and opportunity for interaction is different. Vygotsky emphasized a dialectical unity between biological foundations and dynamic social conditions. He was convinced that higher psychological functions entail new psychological systems; they are not simply superimposed over the more elementary processes, as Piaget believed.

In addition, Vygotsky placed a great deal of stress on children's play, which he saw as rule governed. Children, he argued, do not typically jump around aimlessly—or, at most, they do so for only brief periods of time. Rather, they invent rules to make the activity fun. Even pretending to be a mother requires rules. Play, like school, should create a zone of proximal development. Through it the "child always behaves beyond his average age, above his daily behavior; in play it is as though he were a head taller than himself" (Vygotsky, 1978, p. 102).

---

[11]*Transmissional teaching* is teaching whereby learners are expected to gain most of their knowledge by being fed information by the teacher (see discussion on page 95–96).

Three key concepts important to our understanding of Vygotskian thought and what has evolved from it are *mediation, internalization*, and *imitation*. A fourth concept, *activity theory*, is related but perhaps more peripherally.

Mediation uses signs (words, gestures, facial expressions, and so on) through which external societal activity on the outer plane eventually is reconstructed on the inner psychological plane. This process has become known as *internalization*. All successful language learners go through an internalization process. During this process, *external socially mediated speech* becomes *private speech*. Private speech can either be audible, uttered under one's breath, or accomplished silently. While engaging in private speech, learners may repeat over and over what they have heard, play with the words (most common in children), and/or rehearse conversations with others. They may use private speech to plan and practice what they want to say before saying it or respond to a recast with an off-the-record correction. However, one of private speech's most common functions for language learners and nonlearners alike is to self-regulate during activities by audibly thinking through part of a process as one experiences it. Private speech then moves to the inner plane to become *inner speech* where it is organized and becomes anchored in the individual's life experience. However, even on the inner plane, inner speech never forgets its "social roots" (Lantolf & Thorne, 2006). Inner speech is condensed and forms part of the center of thinking. During particularly difficult tasks or if destabilization has occurred due to mismatches in form or meaning, the process may reverse itself as learners seek additional assistance from mediation on the external social plane.[12]

Internalization involves *imitation* but not in the behaviorist sense which would involve parroting or repeating. The reconstructed activity on the inner plane is not an exact copy of that found on the outer plane (Strauss & Quinn, 1997). If it were, then it would not result in mental development (see also Lantolf & Thorne, 2006). Imitation is a matter of the learner's appropriating what others say and reconstructing it, usually over time. However, the learner can only imitate that which is within his or her level of development. Vygotsky (1978) used the following example to illustrate:

> if a child is having difficulty with a problem in arithmetic and the teacher solves it on the blackboard, the child may grasp the solution in an instant. But if the teacher were to solve a problem in higher mathematics, the child would not be able to understand the solution no matter how many times she imitated it. (p. 88)

Some aspects of performance need clarification later on, after they become internalized, and so the individual may once again require mediation through social activity or assistance through cultural artifacts such as books, dictionaries, the Internet, and so on. Once internalization of language itself has taken place, the signs, including words,

---

[12]Atkinson (2002), while discussing his ideas about the importance of the social in an evolving sociocognitive approach, disagreed with Vygotsky and the neo-Vysotskian second language acquisition researchers on their almost complete separation of the inner and outer planes. He argued that language at *all* levels of development integrates the social and the cognitive and that the development is always "mutually, simultaneously, and co-constitutively in the head and in the world" (p. 538).

gestures, and so forth, can be rearranged to create new meanings. Language internalized in this way can then be used as a semiotic tool to participate in the community and to pursue personal and societal goals.

The fourth key concept important to socioculturalism is *activity theory.* This theory is based on the notion that individuals, as agents,[13] are unique in that each possesses a set of motives, beliefs, sociocultural history, values, and capacities and that these shape their activity, as do the circumstances of the situation. Activity is mainly determined by an underlying motive about which the learner may not be consciously aware (see especially Leont'ev, 1981). Activity becomes what it is by those participating in it.[14] Often teachers and researchers ignore the complexity that each person brings to an assigned task (Coughlan & Duff, 1998; Roebuck, 2000). They often forget that each person is an intentional being whose intentions are realized in different ways. "What begins as one activity can reshape itself into another activity in the course of its unfolding" (Lantolf, 2000, p. 11).

The same task produces different activity on the part of each individual. For example, let's say a task in a Spanish class is to change a paragraph from the present to the past tense. The task seems simple enough. For a person with minimal interest in Spanish who is taking the course mainly to fulfill a requirement, the task may be accomplished quickly and independently just to get it over with. On the other hand, for a person whose motive is to communicate effectively in the language, the task may be much different. Such a motivated person may want to reshape the same task into an interactive activity with a partner with a similar motive. The two may decide, for example, to do the activity together and try to use only Spanish as they collaborate in the process of completing it. For them, focusing intently on the task at hand and actually using the language offers them the best chance for internalization.

Although learning and development are directly related, Vygotsky (1978) suggested that they do not increase in equal amounts or in parallel ways. "Development in children never follows school learning the way a shadow follows the object that casts it" (p. 91). The relationship between the two is extremely complex and uneven and cannot be reduced to an easy formula. Vygotsky was convinced that learning itself is a *dynamic social process* through which the teacher or a more advanced peer in a dialogue with a student can focus on emerging skills and abilities.

Based on his own perception of Vygotskian thought, Wells (1999) suggested that we

- engage *with* learners in challenging, personally significant activities
- observe what the students can do independently
- give them help and guidance in moving forward to solve problems, thereby forming a type of "cognitive apprenticeship" (see also Rogoff, 1990)

---

[13]Agents are learners and doers who are actively involved in negotiating the circumstances and means by which they learn and work. Their development is mediated and shaped by what is afforded within their environment and by the constraints under which they operate.

[14]What has grown out of earlier interpretations of activity theory is the concept of *collective activity theory* involving a community of participants with the same or similar motive or group goal (see especially Engeström, 2001). The work to be done is divided among the members of the group.

Through a cognitive apprenticeship, "knowledge is co-constructed, as students and teacher together make meaning on the basis of each others' experiences, supplemented by information from other sources beyond the classroom" (Wells, 1999, p. 160). Interestingly, Wells saw the zone of proximal development as operating not only within the student but also within a group or the class as a whole. He called this the *communal zone of proximal development,* for which he credits Hedegaard (1990).

Ohta (2000a), like Wells and many others, offered suggestions for the classroom based on her own applications of the zone of proximal development. In her discussion of assisted performance, she warns us that:

> development cannot occur if too much assistance is provided or if a task is too easy. Development is impeded both by helping the learner with what she or he is already able to do, and by not withdrawing assistance such that the learner develops the ability to work independently. (p. 52)

Ohta claimed that learners are able to provide *scaffolding*[15] of language (see p. 51) and ideas as they collaborate to assist each other (see also Donato, 1994). Through the process, both partners can end up operating at higher levels. However, the assistance must be timed well. Ohta's study exploring interactional cues found that developmentally appropriate assistance is dependent on the interlocutor's sensitivity to the partner's readiness for assistance (indicated by subtle cues) as well as on the interlocutor's ability to assist. She argued that scaffolding can indeed lead to language development, and, to the extent that mediation is involved, she considered both scaffolding and assisted performance to be compatible with the zone of proximal development.

Enlarging on ideas that are for the most part complementary to Vygotsky's, Freire (1970b) in *Pedagogy of the Oppressed* distinguished between two kinds of education: *banking* (transmissional) and *libertarian* (transformational). *Banking education* involves the act of depositing. The student is an empty depository, and the teacher is the depositor. The students "receive, memorize, and repeat." There is no real communication. The role of the student is passive—a sort of "disengaged brain." On the other hand, in *libertarian education* the teacher and students are partners. Meaning is inherent in the communication. Through it students are involved in acts of cognition and are not simply empty heads waiting to be filled with information. The process is *dialectical*. Sometimes the teacher is a student and the students are teachers in a dialogue through which all individuals can benefit (see Chapter 4).

This cooperative relationship is important to second language teaching. It leads to meaningful interaction about relevant content; through such interaction, the teacher is naturally attuned to the students' emerging skills and abilities. Without this cooperative relationship, meaningful communication cannot take place. If we consider "development" to include the students' actual levels with the target language and their potential levels, then Vygotsky's theory makes sense for students learning a second language at

---

[15]According to Wertsch (1979), scaffolding is a process by which knowledge that has been coproduced is internalized by learners. See also Bruner (1978).

any age, whether cognitive structures are already highly developed or not. Meaningful social interaction seems to be the key.

The Importance of Social Interaction

One early example of the importance of social interaction to language learning came from John-Steiner (1985), who referred to the study done with Finnish immigrant children entering Swedish schools. She reported that they experienced "severe difficulties in their academic and linguistic development" because they were at first placed in very structured classrooms where there was little chance for meaningful interaction. The teacher did most of the talking, and the activities were written.

John-Steiner also cited Wong-Fillmore's (1976) study of five new arrivals to the United States from Mexico. These children were paired with Anglo peers, and their communication was taped over the period of a school year. The children stretched their knowledge of the target language remarkably. Sometimes these extensions were inadequate in getting across intentions, but the peers were able to fill in the gaps.

Additional evidence of the importance of social interaction in second language teaching is found in an early study by Seliger (1977). He first became interested in social interaction as a phenomenon when he observed his own two-year-old child. She would

> often push her father's newspaper aside to get his attention and then direct a stream of gibberish at him mixed with a few hardly understood words. He, in turn, could discuss the weather, the stock market, her siblings, or American foreign policy with her. It didn't seem to matter what was said as long as some interaction was taking place. As long as the child was answered, she would continue the same for quite some time. (p. 269)

The question Seliger posed is why a child would participate in and prolong an activity without having much understanding of what was being said to her. He concluded that this phenomenon is actually rather typical behavior and that the strategy being used may be important to the learning process itself.

In his study, he argued that adults who successfully learn a second language use a similar strategy. Although his study was not without critics (see Day, 1984),[16] it was an important one. It attempted to measure not only a public willingness to interact in the classroom, but also a willingness to participate in private classroom interaction. His subjects had studied English as a foreign language and were enrolled in an upper-intermediate level class in the English Language Institute at Queens College in New York. Each student fell into one of two groups: the high input generator group at one end of an interaction continuum or the low input generator group at the other end. The members of the high input generator group interacted intensively, not only with the teacher but with each other. In addition, they initiated much of the interaction.

---

[16] One of Day's findings in his study of ESOL students in Honolulu was that there appeared to be no significant relationship between a measure of public exchanges (involving both responses to general solicits by the teacher and student self-initiated turns) and scores given on an oral interview and on a cloze test.

The low input generator group, on the other hand, either avoided interaction altogether or remained fairly passive in situations in which they could have interacted. They seemed more dependent on formal instruction.

Even though Seliger's subjects were few in number (only three in each category), the study nevertheless had interesting implications. Scores on pretests and posttests suggested that by receiving more focused input through interaction, the high input generators were able to "test more hypotheses about the shape and use of the second language thus accounting for increased success" (p. 273). Low input generators, on the other hand, were particularly dependent on the classroom environment to force interaction because they did not tend to initiate or allow themselves to become involved in it on their own.[17]

Bruner (1978), who believed strongly in the social nature of language learning, chastised those who were committed philosophically to the idea that language learning is reducible to a linking of simple forms, which thereby become complex forms. Of course, here he was referring to the behaviorists and the cognitive-code theorists (see Chapter 1). Bruner emphasized the fact that these people "failed to take into account the inherently social nature of what is learned when one learns language and, by the same token, to consider the essentially social way in which the acquisition of knowledge of language must occur" (p. 244).

A PROPOSED DIALOGICAL MODEL FOR SECOND LANGUAGE ACQUISITION

Marysia Johnson's (2004) dialogically-based model for second language acquisition uses her own interpretations of both Vygotsky's (1978) sociocultural theory and Mikhail Bakhtin's (1986) *dialogized heteroglossia*[18] on which to build. She felt that our field has focused too much on "language as a system of linguistic rules." According to her, it has given short shrift to important theorists such as Bakhtin, the twentieth-century Russian literary critic, linguist, and philosopher, whose ideas complement Vygotsky's work in many ways. Although Vygotsky's sociocultural theory stressed the importance of interaction, it did not take a close look at the specific characteristics of speech itself.

Bakhtin rejected Saussure's (1959) distinction between linguistic forms (*la langue*) and language use (*la parole*) and Chomsky's comparable language competence and language performance dichotomy. Bakhtin insisted that the two entities in each case must be synthesized into one. Bakhtin believed that language is the most

---

[17] At the end of the semester, Seliger gave a discrete point test of English structure (Lado-Fries) and an integrative test of aural comprehension (the Queens College English Language Institute Test of Aural Comprehension) in addition to a cloze test. He found that the scores on the pretests were not good predictors of scores on the posttests; however, measures of social interaction were. The amount of interaction accounted for 85 percent of the variance in the posttest scores on the discrete point test and 69 percent of the variance in the posttest scores on the aural comprehension test.

[18] *Heteroglossia* refers to the huge variety of social and discourse possibilities to which the learner is exposed in different contexts. Holquist (2002) calls it "a plurality of relations, not just a cacophony of different voices" (p. 89).

influential tool in the development of cognition. He considered the utterance (not the sentence) the most basic unit of communication in speech. Sentences require no context; utterances do. He used the term *speech genres* which are typical forms that utterances take in local contexts found in simple speech such as one finds in journals, letters, everyday conversation, and so on (primary genres) and those in complex speech such as one finds in novels, plays, academic reports, and writings of various kinds (secondary genres).

Bakhtin felt that we learn language mainly through exposure to diverse speech genres within the local environment, not by setting out to learn discrete elements of language such as vocabulary, grammar rules, and so on. We choose appropriate specific speech genres, depending on what we want to say at any given time. We take the many voices of others (heterglossia) and make them our own to express our own perspectives, intentions, thoughts, and feelings. Our voices are always in a dialogic relationship with the voices that have preceded ours. To illustrate this phenomenon, I quote Eva Hoffman, a Polish immigrant learning English in America:

> Since I lack a voice of my own, the voices of others invade me as if I were a silent ventriloquist. They ricochet within me, carrying on conversations, lending me their modulations, intonations, rhythms. I do not yet possess them; they possess me. But some of them satisfy a need; some of them stick to my ribs.... Eventually, the voices enter me; by assuming them, I gradually make them mine. (Hoffman, 1989, pp. 219–220; also in Pavlenko & Lantolf, 2000, p. 167)

All of what we hear or read is dependent on the speech genres that we have appropriated. Without them, comprehension of what others are saying would be impossible. Bakhtin felt that even what we say to ourselves is in dialogue form as though we were speaking with another individual or with a collective other. Thus we synthesize the internal and the external through a dialogic process that goes far beyond the input/output metaphor. This synthesis begins with other people on the social level and then moves inward to the psychological level within each individual.

Johnson's (2004) proposed model of second language learning is intended to "'heal' the schism that currently separates the learner's social environment from his or her mental functioning" (p. 170). Like Vygotsky, she sees opposites not as part of a dichotomy but in a dialectical relationship with one another. There is a dialectical interdependence between social and cognitive processes, just as there is between language competence and language performance and the external world and the internal world. We cannot disregard one when looking at the other. The second languages we acquire are all the results of the *appropriation* of the many voices or speech genres to which we are exposed in diverse contexts. Such appropriation gives us the ability to participate actively in the culture of the target language. Full participation does not mean learners need to forget what Johnson refers to as the "old" voices of the first language and first culture. The old and new voices need to become synthesized within each individual. The second language learner in Johnson's model is able to give attention to *form* and *meaning* simultaneously while appropriating speech genres (in this case "discursive practices") of the target language culture. Cognition and second language development are not considered separate entities but are merged within the learner. The goal is to become an active participant in the local sociocultural milieu.

Johnson's model considers the concept of the zone of proximal development essential to learning. Through mediation, including the process of arriving at shared understandings and the co-construction of knowledge, learners begin to internalize the second language. Interactive activities (see Part II of this book) can be accomplished with learners who are operating at similar or different levels of proficiency, depending on the activity itself and its participants. The learners can come from different language and cultural backgrounds or the same, again depending on the activity selected and what the participants want to accomplish.

Testing itself using this model could be revolutionary. The model would need to be dialogical and measure what the learner can do under guidance (potential level) instead of just the actual level, as we do now in our more traditional testing. Newman, Griffin, and Cole (1989) suggested that using such testing would require the learner to operate independently until he or she begins to have problems (actual level). At that point the tester steps in and the learner's performance begins to be co-constructed. The more help the learner requires to complete the task, the less advanced the learner is considered. Thus, the testing becomes highly meaningful. The results can add to the knowledge obtained by other means: traditional testing, portfolios, self-evaluation procedures, and the like (see Chapter 7). Johnson (2004) reminded us, however, that testing potential ability (which is socially-based) is not to be confused with testing aptitude, which has been traditionally defined as one's innate capacity to learn a language and is cognitively based. She stated:

> We have stayed for too long in the mind of the learner, and in the process we have neglected to recognize the forces that interact with the individual mind. We have created an illusion of the reality and promoted a false sense of security by claiming that the knowledge of a linguistic system, the mastery of the centripetal forces of language, will allow us to create one global community, one shared reality, one level of intersubjectivity. . . . In order for better mutual understanding to take place, we need to begin the process of real communication and engage in a true dialogue in which language is viewed not as an abstract object but as a *living* entity. The time has come to give new voices a chance. The time has come to give a dialogically-based approach to SLA serious consideration. (p. 189)

What can your own voice add to Johnson's perspective? Although her model appears to be an auspicious beginning in our quest to gain knowledge about second language learning and what it might comprise, we need to make our own voices heard based on what we have learned, what we value, and our own experience. We need to critically view all the reservoirs of knowledge to which we have been exposed so far, acknowledging that with which we agree and that with which we disagree and the various points in between. With new eyes we need to examine the work that has already been done and the various kinds of research described to see how we might view different reservoirs of knowledge in relation to Johnson's model.

We will no doubt want to revisit this discussion once we have considered implicit and explicit teaching strategies (Chapter 5), affective factors (Chapter 6), and language assessment and standards (Chapter 7) to see how the information there might relate as well.

Bridging the Gap between Cognitive and Sociocultural Perspectives

A well-informed, dialogically-based model eventually could evolve to the point at which it serves as a bridge between the cognitive and sociocultural work that has been accomplished thus far in our field. Such a bridge is possible and could lead to a blending of at least some aspects of cognitive and sociocultural views. However, this will never happen if sociocultural factors continue to be ignored. As Watson-Gegeo and Nielsen (2003) reminded us, "all cognitive development is constructed in and profoundly shaped by sociocultural contexts, whether they be home, community, or school" (p. 162). This point is crucial to our understanding of second language acquisition and must be built into the foundation of any bridge that is attempted between the two approaches.

Of course, any newly developed model would belong to and have the most meaning for the person(s) who create it, but others could learn from the many variables and levels of thinking that would be necessary to its development. If it is to be at all useful, such a model would no doubt need to be multitiered, multifaceted, and fluid, not fixed or static. Its creators would need a means for changing and modifying it as they themselves change over time and as new research and ideas emerge.

SUMMARY

Learning a first language and learning a second language are cognitively alike in many ways and different in others. The similarities can be found mainly in the process itself; the differences are in the areas of affect, maturational constraints, and language aptitude particularly.

Krashen's monitor model and Ellis's variable competence model were developed to help clarify the second language acquisition process in the classroom from a cognitive perspective. The first emphasized the importance of comprehensible input; the second emphasized interaction and negotiated meaning in a variety of situations. Other cognitive models mentioned in footnote 8, p. 77 in this volume, are worth looking at for those wanting to learn more about cognitive perspectives and how they have developed over recent decades.

Vygotsky's zone of proximal development offers insights into the essentially social nature of the language acquisition process, be it first or second. Contrary to Piaget, who proposed one level of cognitive development, Vygotsky described two levels: an actual level and a potential level. Although both were constructivists, Piaget emphasized the influence of biological maturation in learning and Vygotsky stressed social interaction. The pivotal role of social interaction in second language acquisition was supported early on by John-Steiner, Lilly Wong Fillmore, Seliger, and several others.

It is possible that many of the interactive theories can be merged, as long as we acknowledge what might be considered incompatible between cognitive and socio-cultural approaches and as long as the sociocultural aspects of learning remain essen-tial to whatever model we create. As a start, Johnson proposed a dialogically-based model that finds roots in her own interpretation of the works of Vygotsky and Bakhtin. Perhaps other similar models will be developed in the near future incorporating much of what we now know (or think we know) about learning another language, drawing from both sociocultural and cognitive perspectives.

QUESTIONS AND PROJECTS FOR REFLECTION AND DISCUSSION

1. Some applied linguists feel there are enough similarities between L1 and L2 acquisition to support a common theory; others argue vehemently against such a notion, focusing instead on the differences. Where do you stand on this issue? How might your stand affect your teaching and the kinds of content and activities in which you might involve your students?

2. How important do you think age is in learning another language? To what extent do affect, maturation, and language aptitude have roles to play? Relate your answer to your own experiences with language learning and/or to those of people you know. Discuss with a partner.

3. Considering Vygotsky's ideas with regard to learning and development, what might his reaction be to each of the following?

   a. homogeneous ability grouping for most activities
   b. a focus on audiolingual drill
   c. an individualized program approach in which an individual works alone at his or her own rate
   d. an interactive classroom in which heterogeneous grouping is the norm

4. According to Freire (1970b), the relationship between teacher and student should be dialectical. What kind of classroom environment might foster this relationship? What sorts of activities might take place in such a classroom? Can you envision yourself in a dialectical relationship with your students? Discuss with a small group.

5. Wells (1999) believed that teachers or other assistants working with students approximately within their zone of proximal development do not necessarily need to be human; they can also be books and other supplementary materials. They can even be works of art. To what extent can a work of art or

other nonhuman entity serve as a guide or assistant to help students stretch to higher levels?

6. Let us return to the challenge that ends this chapter: to create a model synthesizing the best of cognitive and sociocultural work to date while at the same time acknowledging what you may consider incompatible. Take into consideration your prior knowledge and experience and what you have learned about the other reservoirs of knowledge (e.g., error treatments, grammar instruction, the information-processing models).

   Describe and/or draw what your model might look like. You may want to describe and/or draw more than one model or create a multitiered, multifaceted model to represent the different levels of your thinking. Present your ideas to a small group of peers for their feedback. You may want to modify your first ideas based on what you learn from your peers, or you and your peers may decide to develop a group model incorporating all of your voices to present to the whole class and your instructor for their reaction.

7. ✎ **Journal Entry:** Reflect on the work you did for item 6 above. Did you enjoy doing it? Why or why not? What were some of the problems you encountered? Did what you come up with at first seem too simplistic? How did you try to build in or indicate some of the complexities? What did you learn from the experience? Write about what you learned from your peers and instructor during the process.

SUGGESTED READINGS AND REFERENCE MATERIALS

Atkinson, D. (2002). Toward a sociocognitive approach to second language acquisition. *The Modern Language Journal, 86*(4), 525–545. The author lays out a case for focusing on the social essentialness of both first and second language acquisition. He argues that we have had an obsession with the decontextualized, autonomous learner and that this obsession has kept us from looking at second language acquisition as "a situated, integrated sociocognitive process." He believes that a connectionist perspective puts us in a better position than other perspectives to account for the full integration of the social and the cognitive at all levels of social and mental activity.

Block, D. (2003). *The social turn in second language acquisition*. Edinburgh, England: Edinburgh University Press. The main thrust of this book is to challenge the theoretical foundation supporting the cognitivist input–interaction–output model. He maintains that theories of language acquisition must incorporate social aspects such as appropriation and participation, which, he feels, have been marginalized. He suggests that perhaps the cognitive and socialculturalists might find common ground in descriptive research.

Gibbons, P. (2003). Mediating language learning. *TESOL Quarterly, 37*(2), 247–273. In this important article, Gibbons presents the results of a discourse analysis involving teacher–student discussion of concepts in science. The excerpts presented give us a glimpse into how teachers are able to mediate between what students actually know and can describe in their own words and how, through reformulations, redundancy, and the co-construction of knowledge, they can begin to incorporate the same concepts and describe them using an academic register. Both teachers and researchers should find this information of great value.

Hall, J. K., Vitanova, G., & Marchenkova, L. (Eds.). (2005). *Dialogue with Bakhtin on second and foreign language learning: New perspectives.* Mahwah, NJ: Lawrence Erlbaum. Offered here are many insights into how Bakhtin's theories shed light on teaching and learning second and foreign languages. Scholarly explorations of several contexts of language learning allow us to take a closer look at topics of interest such as the acquisition of an academic voice through dialogue with teachers and peers, using semiotic tools to understand others and develop a sense of intersubjectivity, the influence of heteroglossic community discourse on students, and many other issues. Implications of Bakhtin for both theory and practice are examined.

Hinkel, E. (2005). *Handbook of research in second language teaching and learning.* Mahwah, NJ: Lawrence Erlbaum. Included in this very comprehensive and scholarly anthology are sections on the importance of social context to learning, teaching, and research; various research methods; second language process and development, methods, and curricula; testing and assessment; identity, culture, and critical pedagogy; language planning; and policy and language rights.

Johnson, M. (2004). *A philosophy of second language acquisition.* New Haven, CT: Yale University Press. In this book, Marysia Johnson critiques the cognitive, information-processing models of the past, and the theories and research on which they are based. She also lays out in detail her own sociocultural model of second language acquisition, grounded in her perspectives of the theories of Vygotsky and Bakhtin and her belief that both the external (social) and internal (mental) planes transform each other.

Lantolf, J. (Ed.). (2000). *Sociocultural theory and second language learning.* Oxford, England: Oxford University Press. Here Lantolf and his contributors address applications of Vygotskian concepts to the classroom, the language acquisition process itself, and ideas related either directly or indirectly to the zone of proximal development. The volume includes highly readable chapters by many respected theorists and researchers in the field of second language learning: Richard Donato, Amy Ohta, Merrill Swain, Claire Kramsch, Steven Thorne, Leo van Lier, and many others.

Vygotsky, L. (1978). *Mind in society.* Cambridge, MA: Harvard University Press. Editors M. Cole, V. John-Steiner, S. Scribner, and E. Souberman spent several years compiling this volume of manuscripts and letters that might otherwise have been lost to us. The collection highlights and clarifies Vygotsky's theories of the mind and its higher psychological functions.

Wells, G. (1999). *Dialogic inquiry: Toward a sociocultural practice and theory of education.* Cambridge, MA: Cambridge University Press. Wells's interpretations of Vygotsky and Halliday are described at length in this illuminating book. Examples and applications abound, making it a valuable resource for teachers across the content areas.

Wong, S. (2006). *Dialogic approaches to TESOL: Where the ginkgo tree grows.* Mahwah, NJ: Lawrence Erlbaum. The author, a very experienced teacher herself, brings her own unique perspective to dialogic pedagogy. She examines feminist contributions, the development of methods, classroom as community, and many other topics. She traces the origins of dialogic pedagogy and those of the ginkgo tree back to ancient China and uses the ginkgo tree as part of an extended analogy that runs throughout the book.

CHAPTER 4

Emergent Participatory Language Teaching

The dance of teachers and students as they negotiate their respective goals, expectations, and understandings is central.

Auerbach, 2000

QUESTIONS TO THINK ABOUT

1. Think about classrooms in which you were a student. How much input did you have into decisions about the content studied or the activities in which you participated? Did teachers consider you a person with important knowledge to share? How did their treatment of you make you feel?

2. What do you think *participatory teaching* means? Why do you think the word *emergent* is used to modify participatory teaching? What might be the effects of such teaching? How might it differ from other kinds of teaching?

3. From your experience and/or observation, what strategies do good language learners appear to use to become successful? To what extent might the establishment of a participatory classroom environment be dependent on students' being good strategic learners?

Although participatory language teaching involves the important aspects of interactive teaching and negotiation for meaning, it also reaches into the very core of the individual by concerning itself with that individual's place in society and with society in general. Participatory teaching finds its roots mainly in critical pedagogy and is based on Paulo Freire's assertion that teachers and students can establish dialectical relationships in which their roles are interlaced with one another (see Chapter 3). The shared power that results enables students to reach academic goals and enables both students and teachers to explore together issues that affect their lives (Norton & Toohey, 2004; Smoke, 1998). The collaboration found in interlacing roles is dialogic in nature in that it operates in conjunction with the perspectives and discourses of all participants.

Diane Larsen-Freeman's (1996) closing remarks summarizing what had been said at the 1996 World Congress of Applied Linguistics shed light on a *dialogic view of learning* (see also Chapter 3):

> The learner is not acted upon by some (hopefully) benevolent proficient user of the target language; instead the learner's individual competence is connected to, and partially constructed by, both those with whom the learner is interacting and the larger sociohistorical forces. Following from this reasoning, teaching is not transmission, but rather is providing the scaffolding through which input is not comprehensible, but participatable. Teaching is invited, not imposed. (p. 90)

Postmodernist Alastair Pennycook (1999) called participatory teaching the *pedagogy of engagement*. He stressed inclusivity and the discussion of relevant issues often having to do with matters of gender, race, privilege, and other issues that can make a difference in students' lives—in other words, issues in which students can be truly invested. Moreover, Pennycook argued that the pedagogy of engagement cannot be reduced to simply another teaching method, for it involves a fundamental change in our attitude toward the teaching act itself.

Participatory teaching, like other kinds of communicative teaching, considers language learning a social and cultural process. However, it is about more than incorporating relevant issues; it is also about the way in which teachers and students relate to one another, the way in which teachers perform their roles, and the way in which the whole classroom environment contributes to transformational processes and meets students' needs. At its best, it can free students from society's negative labels and empower them to assert more control over their own academic, social, political, and economic destinies.

EMPOWERMENT IN THE LANGUAGE CLASSROOM

Empowerment begins with the way teachers interact with students. Traditionally, interaction in the classroom has adhered to the initiation/response/feedback (IRF) paradigm (see Bellack, Kliebard, Hyman, & Smith, 1966; Mehan, 1979; Sinclair & Coulthard, 1975). The teacher asks a question (the initiation); the student gives the answer (the response);

the teacher, more often than not, then evaluates the answer (the feedback). The process may look something like this in a beginning second language class:

TEACHER: What is this? Do you remember? [points to a picture of a penguin]
STUDENT(S): A pen-guin.
TEACHER: Yes. Very good.

As van Lier (1996) reminded us, this kind of exchange turns almost every interaction into an examination of sorts. The interaction may require little of the student (a memorized answer), it may require a great deal of thought (the solution to a problem), or it may fall somewhere in between. Now if it is the student who asks the question and the teacher who gives the response, we have turned this typical interactive pattern on its head.

The IRF structure as used in the example above does have its place in the classroom for many learning situations, and it can be effective, depending on when, how, and with whom it is used. However, if such a pattern becomes the one most often relied on in the classroom, the critical pedagogists would probably object, and rightfully so (see also Walsh, 2002). To them, such a reliance would be far too controlling and manipulative. Their ideal exchange would more likely resemble natural dialogue outside the classroom, except that it would be *instructional*.[1] The following is a constructed dialogue illustrating such an exchange. It represents an attempt to meet academic goals in science:

[Students and the teacher are performing a physics experiment on pendulums.]

STUDENT 1: I wonder what would happen if we added weight to the pendulum bob?
STUDENT 2: It would swing slower because it's heavier.
TEACHER: Let's try it. Put on another weight and we'll time the swing.
STUDENT 1: Okay. I'm adding another half kilogram. You time the swing [refers to Student 2].
STUDENT 2: That's funny; the time didn't change.
TEACHER: So what did you learn?
STUDENT 1: Making it heavier didn't change it. Let's try making it lighter.
TEACHER: Yes, let's try that.

Notice that the IRF paradigm is still used, but the participants have changed roles. In the first line, Student 1 initiates and Student 2 responds. Lines 3 and 4 do not seem to follow the paradigm. Now look at the last three lines. The teacher provides the initiation and feedback, as is typical. However, the feedback is not an evaluation as we know it; instead it is an agreement to complete an action just suggested by Student 1. It is an affirmation, which in a sense may be considered evaluative, but it is accomplished in a different way. The dialogue adheres to Wells's (1999) ideas about the co-construction of knowledge which, he says "creates a social-intellectual climate that is both supportive and challenging" (p. 220). Learning opportunities such as the one presented in this dialogue are usually anticipated and planned by the teacher. They do not just happen by chance.

The above dialogue reflects a broader definition of participatory teaching than is assumed in many discussions of the concept. In this context, participatory teaching concerns itself not only with sociopolitical issues and goals but with academic issues and goals as well.

---

[1] Tharp and Gallimore (1988) referred to similar exchanges as *instructional conversations*.

Transformative versus Transmissive Classroom Discourse

The typical IRF structure with its traditional roles can be advantageous in many circumstances, particularly for beginning students; it allows for initial teacher-led practice and response and other teacher-fronted activities so essential to beginners. However, once students become more proficient and are able to apply strategies, especially metacognitive ones, they may require the complex interactions and role alternatives offered in transformative discourse. At this point, they may also have the abilities to operate independently and, at the same time, participate more fully in a classroom community.

What are some of the distinguishing characteristics of transformative and transmissive classroom discourse? Perhaps the two can best be seen on a continuum such as illustrated in Figure 4.1.

When critical pedagogist Paulo Freire argued convincingly against transmission education (see Chapter 3), he expressed the conviction that such education was a political strategy to keep those who are marginalized by society in their place. In his own teaching experience with Brazilian farm workers, he developed a dialogic, transformative orientation to their learning how to read. He felt that they, too, had knowledge to share and that learning should be a mutually beneficial activity. He argued that *praxis* (the combination of reflection and action) was needed for transformation to occur. Neither reflection nor action by themselves leads to empowerment. According to Freire and other critical pedagogists, teachers can help to make such praxis a reality and, at the same time, give their students greater input into what goes on in classrooms as their students begin to take full advantage of what a transformative education may have to offer.

Although teachers in emergent participatory classrooms are vitally interested in what students understand and what they are learning, they work to *transform the discourse* in all aspects of instruction. They encourage students to:

- initiate topics and questions that are relevant to their own learning
- move to other topics of interest or concern

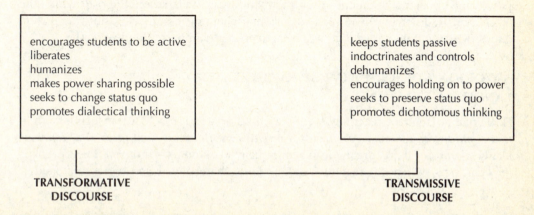

encourages students to be active
liberates
humanizes
makes power sharing possible
seeks to change status quo
promotes dialectical thinking

keeps students passive
indoctrinates and controls
dehumanizes
encourages holding on to power
seeks to preserve status quo
promotes dichotomous thinking

**TRANSFORMATIVE
DISCOURSE**

**TRANSMISSIVE
DISCOURSE**

Figure 4.1 Transformative/Transmissive Discourse Continuum

- investigate independently or with peers and/or the teacher
- reflect on what they are learning

Discourse in which students have a personal stake or investment and about which teacher and student have a mutual interest is at least part of what critical pedagogists intended. The knowledge that develops grows out of what the teacher and students contribute to the dialogue. One question or piece of knowledge builds or scaffolds on the next (see also Donato, 1994). An example of scaffolded dialogue leading to dialectical relationships can be found in the section below on teacher/student coauthored products. While working on coauthored products, teachers and students become integral parts of the composing process and together create a written piece by building on one another's ideas. Both form and meaning are negotiated through the interaction.

However, students may find it difficult to fully participate in the classroom in any language (be it first or second) if they have *only* been exposed to transmission education with all of its implications. For the students to become functioning members, they need to be given the chance early on to grapple with issues important to their lives and the lives of others. Of course, in the case of bilingual education, full participation[2] leading to emergent participatory teaching can be achieved right from the beginning in the primary language.

The Teacher's Role

Modifying the traditional teacher's role is essential to the implementation of participatory practices. Significant changes can be made in how the teacher operates, even though the teacher–student relationship will most likely always be considered unequal by society (i.e., the teacher is expected to have much more disciplinary and worldly knowledge). Students need increasingly greater responsibility for their own learning through planning, critical exploration, decision making, and reflective thinking. This does not mean that the teacher has to completely turn over the reins of power to students. On the contrary, the teacher can be very much involved and influential concerning what happens in the classroom. What it does mean is that the teacher shares power and encourages student input into many areas of classroom life over which the teacher has traditionally made all the decisions—planning lessons, choosing themes and issues, deciding how knowledge will be arrived at and imparted, and so forth.

A WORKING DESCRIPTION OF PARTICIPATORY LANGUAGE TEACHING

Participatory language teaching is not a method or an approach. It transcends both in that *it embraces the very essence of the relationship between student and teacher*. Manifestations of it are already in place in many classrooms—and have been perhaps for centuries—whenever teachers and students share power as they come together

---

[2]*Full participation* in the context of this book means being proficient and open enough to participate in interactions requiring high levels of negotiation for meaning and collaboration based on shared knowledge.

in dialogue and mutual respect. Current manifestations can be found in cooperative learning (pp. 382–385), the use of peer facilitators (pp. 377–382), applications of the language experience approach (pp. 303–306), theme cycles (a type of investigative inquiry discussed later), and many other practices discussed throughout this book. Manifestations of it can be found in full participation wherever it occurs, although full participation itself does not mean that participatory teaching will make itself felt. Participatory teaching also has important implications, not only for the relationship between student and teacher but for content. Perhaps one of its greatest strengths, as mentioned earlier, is that it brings to the fore the issues that touch students' lives and in which students have a personal investment.

Although participatory language teaching focuses on social/collective empowerment, it perhaps cannot be fully examined except as it interlaces with individual empowerment, for neither can exist without the other. Participatory language teaching can best be understood when viewed in a dialectical relationship, as Vygotsky might do, with concepts that come from individualistic theoretical underpinnings such as humanistic practices (personal development is the emphasis), strategic learning, and other learner-centered approaches to teaching (see later sections). At the same time, we must remember that some practices that fall under the umbrella of individualism may actually serve as tools to undermine participatory practices and should be avoided. For example, a teacher may decide to use humanistic activities to indoctrinate students in a specific way of thinking (see Chapter 14) or use other individualistic practices to confine students mostly to isolated seat work, depriving them of opportunities to collaborate with peers.

Participatory language teaching itself may find its seeds in the simple (often teacher-fronted) interactions at beginning levels. From there the interaction may gradually develop to encompass a sharing of teacher–student roles as learners become increasingly more able to communicate about the things that matter to them.[3] For example, beginning interactive (but teacher-fronted) lessons such as learning about going to the doctor (see Chapter 9) can serve as scaffolds for later lessons on everything from locating the best doctors in one's area to the social implications of the inability to afford basic dental care. Elements of participatory language teaching can appear whenever students engage in decision making along with their teacher in their second language, or (as mentioned earlier) they can become emergent right from the beginning in bilingual programs when the primary language is the medium for discussion and instruction.

Elsa Auerbach (2000) is convinced that "ideal participatory classrooms probably do not actually exist; they are always in the process of becoming" (p. 149). In other words, they are constantly emerging and never finished. She reminded us (as did Johnston, see p. 5) that teachers do have power and will always have power, no matter how much they try to give it away. The important thing, according to her, is that learning be collaborative and that students be given the chance to become informed about issues

---

[3] Lave and Wenger (1991) talked about moving from what they termed *legitimate peripheral participation* gradually toward full participation encompassing greater involvement and complexity in a type of apprenticeship. However, they did not consider language proficiency a factor influencing this process, probably because they were not relating their ideas to language learners.

that concern them and make reasonable choices based on a critical analysis of what is at stake for themselves and the world at large. Auerbach offered the following basic principles (pp. 147–148):

1. The starting point is the experience of the participants; their needs and concerns should be central to curriculum content.
2. Everyone teaches; everyone learns.
3. Classroom processes are dialogical and collaborative.
4. Individual experience is linked to social analysis.
5. The acquisition of skills and information is contextualized.
6. The content goes back to the social context.

Components of the Participatory Learning Experience

Following Elsa Auerbach's lead, I have developed the "Components of the Participatory Learning Experience" (see below). Here I add two factors that have been largely overlooked in current discussions of critical pedagogy:

- the student's *cognitive abilities*
- the student's *proficiency in the language*

Both determine the kinds of issues that each student is able to identify and deal with in a meaningful way.

1. **Identification** of students' interests, needs, problems, and concerns within the social context of the classroom and the outside world.
2. **Negotiation** of the curriculum. The curriculum grows out of the students' prior experience, hopes for the future, and present needs (academic, personal, and sociopolitical).
3. **Dialectical relationship formation** throughout the process between students and teachers. All participants are both learners and teachers. *All serve as sources of knowledge; their strengths are critical to their own learning and to that of others.*
4. **Skills development** occurring within the context of the tasks at hand.
5. **Exploration** of the issues important to students, leading to in-depth reading and research, composition, discussion, analysis, and reflection. Moreover, such exploration often leads to related issues of interest forming the pivot around which the next investigations are built. These explorations need to be generally appropriate to students' cognitive abilities and proficiency in the language that is to be the medium of discussion and instruction.
6. **Collaborative learning**, which is critical to the process.
7. **Critical analysis** during which students deconstruct what they read and hear, accept what makes sense to them, and reject the rest.

These components assume a broader context for participatory teaching than most other descriptions. In this context, participatory teaching concerns itself not only with sociopolitical issues and goals but with academic and personal issues and goals. Although sociopolitical needs often serve as pivots around which the other goals are accomplished, academic needs should be included to make education a meaningful and transformative experience for students.

Creating an Environment in Which an Emergent Participatory Classroom Can Become a Reality

Questionnaires can ascertain what topics interest students most, how students might rank common goals based on their aspirations, where they most need improvement, and the kinds of lessons they find most helpful and enjoyable.

Students can give feedback regularly by answering questions such as the following:

- What instructional activity did you participate in this week that helped you most? Why?
- Was there an activity you didn't like or didn't find helpful? Explain.
- What did the teacher do that helped you the most? the least?
- How might you change the class so it can better meet your needs?

In addition, students can rank specific activities from "most effective" to "least effective" and give brief comments explaining their decisions. Several specific participatory practices described later in this chapter can further goals of critical pedagogy and serve as catalysts to help transform the student–teacher relationship.

Not only can students provide input into the content of the classes, the nature of the classroom itself can be transformed. As Breen and Candlin (1979) explained several decades ago:

> It would not necessarily mean changing or disguising the classroom in the hope that it will momentarily serve as some kind of "communicative situation" resembling situations in the outside world. The classroom itself has a unique social environment with its own human activities and its own conventions governing these activities. (p. 90)

PARTICIPATORY PRACTICES

Strategies that engage students in dialogue and draw them into decision-making processes can elevate them to high levels of participation. Perhaps the best-known participatory practice is *problem posing* as developed by Freire and elaborated on by Nina Wallerstein and others. Other practices described here are *dialogical writing* and *theme cycles/investigative inquiry*.

Problem Posing

Wallerstein (1983) presented problem posing to develop critical thinking skills in students. The teacher listens to students to discover their important issues and then finds codifications (e.g., stories, photographs, pictures) to highlight those issues and tap into what is meaningful. For example, let's say the students in an advanced English as a second language class have recently been discussing the difficulties a person faces when first arriving in another country. As a codification, the teacher has selected a picture of a lone, obviously frustrated woman waiting with her suitcases near departing taxis at an international airport in the United States. She is dressed in native garments of India. The teacher asks inductive questions about the codification to pinpoint a problem as students see it:

> What is happening here? Is there a problem?
> Have you or someone you have known experienced a similar problem?
> To what causes can you attribute this problem?
> What can we do?

The students may decide that the woman speaks no English and has been forgotten by those who were to meet her. She must survive on her own, at least for a while. A discussion ensues about the students' own experiences in similar situations and about the possible causes of such dilemmas. They decide, as a group, that they can do something to help others who find themselves in similar predicaments. They decide to create helpful pamphlets for new arrivals and make them available at their local airport. First they obtain the support and input of airport officials. Next they outline steps for preparing the pamphlets in a variety of languages that will clearly provide and explain important information and procedures (a map of the airport that identifies restrooms, information desks, and security offices; explanations for converting money into dollars, using the telephone, finding a hotel or alternative lodging, taking a taxi or a shuttle bus; and so on). Once the pamphlets are completed and approved, the students distribute them at various locations throughout the airport. In addition to providing information for new arrivals at the airport, they develop a welcoming orientation for students and their families who are new to the school and community (see also Zacarian, 2007, for similar ideas).

The process of problem posing has three major components: listening, dialogue, and action. The focus is placed on only one problem at a time so issues do not become clouded, and teachers are advised to be careful to allow students to pinpoint the problem rather than lead them to a predetermined one. Issues can involve home, school, community, nation or state, and/or world. Actions can run the gamut from developing helpful information, to speaking frankly with those who are in charge at the local level, to writing letters to members of Congress or leaders of countries. The teacher and the students work to determine effective and appropriate actions in each situation. Problem posing often requires considerably more time than originally anticipated, but potential benefits can make the practice worthwhile. The results can include increased student interest and subsequent gains in language learning.

Problem posing is not, however, a one-approach-fits-all formula. It differs for different courses, students, and situations.

Dialogical Writing[4]

Dialogical writing has come into its own in many language classrooms as a legitimate way to ease students into the writing process. One aspect that makes dialogical writing

---

[4]Many of the ideas in this section were first presented in a keynote to the TESOL Summer Institute at Comenius University, Bratislava, Slovakia (Richard-Amato, 1992b).

unique is that the reader is immediately accessible. In most kinds of writing, the reader is only an abstract presence to the writer, who then needs to anticipate reader needs, prior knowledge, and possible reactions. Dialogue journals (see p. 324), in particular, can provide effective contexts for language development. Students write about what is important to them on any given day. The teacher and/or peers respond in writing.

Success with dialogue journals as effective transitions to other kinds of composition is possible with both native-language speakers and language minority students at all levels. A partial explanation for their effectiveness may be that legitimate communication is taking place in the written mode. The teacher acts as a real reader as opposed to a mistake detector, the traditional role often assumed by composition teachers. Moreover, through the dialogue, the student is encouraged to stretch cognitively to higher levels of meaning and expression. Because this process is a dialogical one, students can improve their writing skills and build confidence in their ability to anticipate reader needs.

Other dialogical writing practices include *reaction dialogues* and *teacher/student coauthored products*.

Reaction Dialogues

Reaction dialogues may have possible benefits similar to the dialogue journal. I have identified four types of reaction dialogues:

1. teacher-presented stimulus/student reaction
2. student-presented stimulus/student (peer) or teacher reaction
3. student product/teacher reaction
4. student product/student (peer) reaction

(Richard-Amato, 1992b)

In the first type of reaction dialogue, the stimulus can be almost anything—a story, picture, photo, poem, song, editorial, political cartoon—and student reactions can comprise writings of various kinds—a few sentences, a paragraph, several paragraphs in essay form, and so on. The key is that teacher and students discuss the possibilities for reaction. For example, with a story stimulus, students might agree or disagree with the characters' actions, critique the story, or describe similar experiences. With a visual stimulus, students might describe what is happening or will happen next in the picture, write a short scenario based on the picture, or simply write their opinions about the meaning the visual has for them. If students and teacher agree, the reaction does not have to be in writing at all, particularly at first; it might be a drawing, for example (drawings are especially appropriate for reluctant writers and nonliterates or preliterates).

In the second type of reaction dialogue, the student brings in the story, picture, poem, or other stimulus, and the other students and teacher react in writing. The classroom has now become more dialectical; students are now assuming a role that would traditionally belong to the teacher.

The last two types of reaction dialogues are self-explanatory. In each case, however, the process can be extended. For example, assigned expository readings can also serve as stimuli. Before class discussion of the reading, students may write a reaction relating the reading to their own life experiences and valuing systems. The teacher may respond by writing short messages and asking questions to extend and/or clarify the students' thoughts, and the student may respond to these messages with further writing. This way, the teacher can see how students are deconstructing each reading on their own terms. Through this process, teachers and students often find themselves communicating on a much deeper and more personal level than is usually possible during class discussions.

No matter who is responding, the teacher or a peer, that person is providing a written scaffold on which the student can build not only structurally but contextually. Like problem posing, reaction dialogues can lead to other lessons, compositions, projects of various kinds, and other topics of interest and concern.

Teacher–Student Coauthored Products

An application of the language experience approach (see pp. 303–306) that is particularly apropos to dialogical writing is the teacher–student coauthored product in which the teacher is a facilitator and coauthor rather than simply a recorder of what students say. As teacher and students compose together, the teacher records what is mutually agreed on on the board or on a transparency for all to see. The teacher guides students, bringing out their ideas and helping them shape their language through questions and meaning clarification. Material is deleted, rearranged, modified, or expanded as the product is created. (See the extended example on p. 305.) As students become more proficient, one or more may exchange places with the teacher and serve as facilitators themselves. This practice can begin at very early levels of proficiency and continue through the high intermediate levels and beyond.

Theme Cycles/Investigative Inquiry

Theme cycles, a type of investigative inquiry proposed by Harste, Short, and Burke (1988), actively involve students in research and in negotiating curriculum itself. First the teacher and students individually list topics they find important and interesting. The lists are then blended by mutual agreement. The resulting list provides possibilities for the next topic of research and discussion. Teacher and students then negotiate to select one topic from the list as a starting point. Let's say that the topic selected originally grew out of a student's misconception about American Indians. The students decide that they want to clear up the misunderstanding and learn more about American Indians. Using theme cycles, the class then generates a simple list of questions, including all the things students want to learn about them. A sample list for possible investigation might be:

> How did the American Indians live?
> How did their cultures differ from one another?
> What problems have the various tribes had to overcome in the past?
> What problems do they face now?
> What contributions have they made to our society?

Then students and the teacher together make a list of books to read, people to interview, places to visit, and so on. (See an additional example of investigative inquiry on pp. 369–370.) As the questions are explored, new questions arise and new discoveries are made, leading to further questions and research. Throughout the process, students and teacher share what they learn. The teacher is a facilitator as well as a participant, ensuring that the activity is carried out successfully. All the while, skills are integrated with the content and are taught as they are needed.

MEETING STANDARDS THROUGH PARTICIPATORY TEACHING

A central question often raised about participatory learning is its relationship to the current emphasis on standards: Can participatory learning prepare students to meet standards? The answer here, I believe, is a very definite yes.

Participatory teaching makes it likely students will be motivated to acquire necessary skills in the first place because such skills are taught at the very time they are most needed rather than according to the mandates of a highly specified curriculum (see also Chapters 7 and 15). Moreover, within a participatory framework, standards are *negotiated* whenever possible. This might sound like anathema to some, but not all students need or want to know the intricacies of parallel structure, for example, or how to use rhetorical questions to advantage in a composition. Much depends on their goals and aspirations. Learning in specific content areas can be part of the negotiated instruction designed to empower students individually and collectively to meet agreed-on goals.

COMMON MISUNDERSTANDINGS

Unfortunately, a few misconceptions about participatory teaching have arisen.

Myth #1: *The teacher must give up all traditional practices to establish a participatory environment.* This is simply not true. Many practices (including well-timed grammar instruction) can be effective, depending on the proficiency levels, age levels, needs, and cultural expectations of the students. In addition, basic interactive practices can serve as launching platforms for participatory practices. For example, at mid-beginning to intermediate levels, sentences to finish such as "I like to _____" can progress to "I wish I could _____," and eventually to more issue-oriented stems such as "If only _____."

What appears to be essential to the implementation of participatory practices is a modification of the traditional teacher's role at all levels. As students gain maturity and proficiency and become more accustomed to sharing power in the classroom, they are able to continually work toward becoming fully functioning members in the classroom community and effective communicators in the classroom and out.

Myth #2: *The teacher needs to turn over the reins of power to students.* On the contrary, Freire himself stressed that the teacher *can* and *should* be very much involved and influential concerning what happens in the classroom. The teacher still teaches, but so do the students. The students still learn, but so does the teacher. Each participant considers the other to be an important source of knowledge and skills. Although Wells (1999) did not talk about participatory teaching as such, he argued for a strong teacher role in a "community of inquiry." Also, although a dialectical relationship takes place in such a community, the dialogue is usually not between equals because of essential differences in status, education, and experience. The teacher's main role, according to Wells (1999), is to lead and to guide students through the curriculum. He argued that the teacher is still the chief initiator and decision maker. Although the teacher maintains a leadership role, the

> leadership does not have to be exercised in a directive manner, and although the teacher is ultimately responsible for the goals to which "action" is directed, and for monitoring the outcomes in terms of students' increasing mastery of valued cultural tools and practices, it is still possible for students to have a significant part in negotiating both these processes. (p. 243)

In emergent participatory classrooms, the learning becomes more and more collaborative as the students become informed about the issues that concern them and are able to express their opinions, explore options, and make reasonable choices based on a critical analysis of what's at stake for themselves and for the society in which they live.

ENABLING STUDENTS THROUGH STRATEGIC LEARNING

In conjuction with the collaborative learning so essential to participatory classrooms, self-directed learning can also lead to individual empowerment on the part of learners (see also Bartolomé, 2003). Although strategic learning and participatory learning appear oppositional in theory (strategic learning finds its roots in individualism, participatory learning in critical pedagogy and social collectivism), in many ways they are inseparable and perhaps can best be viewed in a dialectical relationship with one another rather than in a dichotomy. *In order to function in a collective sense, the individual needs to bring all of his or her individual attributes and skills that have been highly developed through social processes to the table.* Keep in mind, too, that strategic learning can be used with almost any orientation to teaching languages, not only participatory teaching.

Strategy training enables students in several areas of second language learning.[5] Dörnyei (1995) found that teaching topic avoidance strategies and fillers to gain more time for comprehension and response was very effective. Deep processing strategies (e.g., association, using context) have been found to facilitate vocabulary development (Nassaji, 2003; O'Malley & Chamot, 1990; Schmitt, 2000). Strategies to locate organizational markers have aided reading (Jung, 2003). Pretask planning strategies are useful in writing (R. Ellis & Yuan, 2004). In reading, the use of learning strategies was retained in students even five months after the instruction ended (Ikeda & Takeuchi, 2003). Research indicates that learners who are less successful do not seem to have a wide range of strategies available to them and tend to repeat the same strategies without realizing that they

---

[5] In the literature on learning strategies, some researchers distinguish between strategies and tactics (see especially Oxford & Cohen, 1992; Winne, 2001). Strategies are the more general category under which tactics (specific behaviors or devices) fall. For the purpose of this discussion, the word *strategies* refers to both general and specific behaviors.

are not working (see Anderson, 2005, and his sources). In addition, strategies cannot be judged as to their inherent effectiveness. Anderson made this clear when he said that there are no good or bad strategies, only good and bad *applications* of strategies. Based on his earlier research, Anderson (1991) found that both successful and not so successful second language learners had used similar strategies but that the difference is in "how the strategies are executed and orchestrated" (Anderson, 2005, p. 762).

During the process of learning, the strategies used are usually applied spontaneously, and they often (but not always) come to the individual naturally as the situation demands. However, frequently there are times when such strategies are applied methodically after having been learned from others (the teacher, a book, other language learners) or through deliberate trial and error. If used often enough, these strategies can become spontaneous.

Hedge (2000) asked a group of English language teachers from around the world to define what *self-directed learning* meant to them. From their reactions, she concluded that the teachers placed great importance on certain learning strategies used to enable students to define their objectives, build on what they have already learned, use materials to their advantage, and so on. Hedge suggested developing a facility where students have access to such resources as computers, devices for listening and recording, library materials, language games, and testing materials.

Bartolomé (2003) also placed great importance on certain learning strategies to help enable students. She suggested that various text structures be learned and reinforced through the use of frames and graphic organizers. The goal, according to her, is to help students become more independent and metacognitively aware. These strategies are intended to equalize power within the teacher–student relationship.

No matter what teachers deem important, the strategies the students choose to use are generally compatible with their learning styles and preferences,[6] personalities, and cultural backgrounds. For example, students who are high risk takers and for whom being assertive is acceptable culturally are more willing to use overt strategies such as seeking out people (even strangers) with whom they can interact; purposely steering the discourse in ways that are beneficial; asking questions, even though some sort of disapproval might result; and so forth (S. Wilke, personal communication). Although people may not be high risk takers, they may feel comfortable making friends with proficient speakers of the language, seeking a language helper, debriefing after participation in interactional situations, and/or keeping notes in a journal.

O'Malley and Chamot (1990) helped organize the myriad of strategies available to language learners by identifying and describing three major categories:

1. *Metacognitive strategies:* Self-regulatory strategies that help students to plan, monitor, and self-evaluate

---

[6]Learning styles and preferences relate closely to matters of culture and personality: high risk/low risk, cooperative/competitive, and so forth (see Chapter 6). They include sensory modality preferences (auditory, visual, tactile-kinesthetic), field-dependence/independence, and so on (see Scarcella, 1990). When we tie learning styles too tightly to a specific cultural group, however, we are in danger of stereotyping (see especially Hilliard, 1989; Parry, 1996).

2. *Cognitive strategies:* Task-appropriate strategies that help students to actively manipulate the content or skills they are learning
3. *Social and affective strategies:* Communicative and self-control strategies that help students interact with others to enhance learning or control their own affective states

A metacognitive strategy might be one that helps control one's own learning and/or evaluate one's own progress; a cognitive strategy might be to write down key ideas during a lecture; a social or affective strategy might be to use self-talk (silently giving oneself encouragement) to lower anxiety. Through direct instruction, students can use such strategies, maintain them over time, and transfer them to new tasks when it is beneficial to do so.

Chamot (1990, 2005a, 2005b) argued that students need to have experience with a variety of strategies in order to choose those that work best for them. She recommended that strategy instruction start at beginning levels by providing it in students' first languages and that it be integrated within the curriculum rather than taught as a separate entity. She also recommended that teachers identify the strategies by name, describe them, and model them. Students who are not living up to their own expectations in the language learning process can be assured that their lack of progress may well be due to a lack of appropriate strategy application and not to a deficiency in intelligence.

Oxford (1990) developed a strategy inventory for students learning English that may be useful to help identify areas needing focus. Similar inventories can be developed in any language and used in situations in which they are culturally appropriate. In Oxford's inventory, students tell how true specific statements are for them. For example:

I actively seek out opportunities to talk with native [I would say "proficient"] speakers of English.
I ask for help from English speakers.
I try to relax whenever I feel afraid of using English.
I look for opportunities to read as much as possible in English.
I try not to translate word for word.
I say or write new English words several times.

The simple act of completing the survey may be enough to make most students aware of many strategies that they can incorporate into their language learning practices. Other strategies may need to be expanded, modeled, and practiced before they can be incorporated.

Following is a list of strategies and helpful hints that I have shared with my own students. You may want to discuss these items, which are organized by skill area, with your students and even have some of them translated into your students' first languages so they can benefit early on. Ask students which ones they are already using and which they have found most helpful. Then ask them if there are any strategies they might add to each list.

LISTENING

- Focus attention as completely as possible on what is being said.
- Relax and let the ideas flow into your mind.
- Don't be upset if you don't understand everything.
- Try to connect what you hear to what you already know.
- Listen for key words and ideas.
- Listen for overall meaning.
- Ask the speaker to repeat or to speak more slowly, if necessary.
- Try not to be afraid to ask questions about meaning when it seems all right to do so.
- Make guesses about what is being said.
- In conversation, check out your understanding by using confirmation checks ("Is this what you are saying?").
- Whenever possible, pay attention to the forms fluent speakers are using (How are they different from the forms you use?).
- Write down what you have learned—key ideas, new words, meanings, concepts, structures, idioms—in a notebook.
- Find a buddy with whom you can compare lecture and discussion notes later to see if you missed any important points.
- Find opportunities to listen outside of class by watching television shows and movies, going to lectures, and so on.

SPEAKING

- Find fluent speakers of the language with whom you can talk.
- Think about what you are going to say.
- Think about the grammar you are using, but do not let it interfere with what you want to say.
- Do not be afraid to make mistakes (mistakes are normal as you are learning the language).
- Use repetition, gestures, similar words, definitions, examples, or acting out to help people understand you.
- Record and write down some of the conversations you have with fluent speakers (ask their permission, of course); afterwards, analyze them. (What was successful? Were there any breakdowns in communication? If so, what happened? Did you or your partner use any repair strategies to get back on track? Did you notice any errors?)[7] Ask your teacher or another student to help you analyze what was said.

---

[7] This idea was adapted from one that was described by Heidi Riggenbach during a presentation she gave at the Summer TESOL Institute in San Bernardino, California, 1993.

PRONUNCIATION

- Look for opportunities to talk to fluent speakers.
- Pay attention to the rhythm, intonation, and stress of fluent speakers.
- Realize that you will not always be understood (keep trying).
- Ask people to show you how to pronounce difficult words.
- Listen to your pronunciation, and correct yourself while you speak.
- Rehearse (make up a little song or chant—have fun with the language).
- Record yourself reading passages aloud from a book. Work with your teacher to decide what parts of the reading, if any, are hard to understand. Ask your teacher about appropriate software programs that may be available to give you additional feedback on your pronunciation.

Note: Not all students desire target-like pronunciation. Some will prefer to maintain certain prosodic elements of the first language in their speech, perhaps to retain identity with the first language (L1) culture (Morley, 1991) or for other reasons. What is important is that the student be understood.

READING

- Look for opportunities to read in the new language outside of class.
- See what the reading material is about before you start to read (look the text over; think about the title/subtitles; notice the pictures, figures, and charts—if there are any). Ask questions about them. Try to imagine what you might learn from the text.
- Read the introduction and conclusion first to help you predict what will be covered in the text and what its organizational structure might be.
- Notice how the reading selection is actually organized. (What does each paragraph do? Why do you think it is put together this way?) Ask questions about the way it is structured.
- While you read, relax and feel the words and sentences flow together.
- Question yourself as you read (What is the author trying to say here? How does it relate to what you already know? What does it have to do with what the author has just said? What might come next?).
- Mark the important ideas with a pencil, pen, or highlighter. You may want to return to them later.
- Do not stop reading each time you find an unfamiliar word or phrase (the meaning may come as you read further).

(Continued)

- If a word seems important but you still don't understand it even after you read further, check the glossary (if there is one) or look in a dictionary.
- Talk about a new idea or phrase with another student or with your teacher.
- Note any parts you do not understand and read them again later. (Are the parts you did not understand at first clearer to you now? If not, discuss them with a student or with your teacher.)
- Map out the ideas to show how they relate to one another, tell a partner about them, summarize them in writing, discuss the issues/themes the reading presents, write about the issues or themes from your own point of view, write a critique of the reading.

VOCABULARY DEVELOPMENT

- Create a word bank or keep a vocabulary notebook using only the words or word groupings that you think will be useful. You may want to create a computer database in which to store your words.
- At the beginning, try to learn new words as part of a story, part of a theme (fish, water, boat), or part of a word group (celery, carrot). Be careful not to make your group too large.[8]
- When you are more advanced, use word maps or clustering to show relationships and help you remember.
- Try to focus on groups of words (or chunks) rather than individual words.[9]
- Make yourself some flashcards and use them often to see if you can remember what the words mean. Write the definitions, draw pictures, and/or write sentences or phrases for the words on the backs of the flashcards.
- Research a corpora database to find the most frequent use of specific vocabulary items and the words they are most often used with. Ask your teacher for assistance. Include use and collocations in your word bank or dictionary.
- Use different dictionaries including learner dictionaries as well as bilingual ones.
- Use the new words or phrases in your own writing.

---

[8]Some of the research on vocabulary learning has produced contradictory results. Some research supports the idea that lexical sets interfere with memory (Tinkham, 1997; Waring, 1997); other research has concluded that lexical sets can help (Higa, 1963). See Nation (2000) for a summary of the studies accomplished in this area.

[9]See Lewis (1993).

WRITING

- Find out as much as you can about your topic using sources in the library and/or on the Internet. What do you already know about the subject?
- Brainstorm for ideas (discuss with other students, the teacher, family members, and others in the school or in your community).
- Consider whom you are writing for. Who is your audience?
- Make a plan; map out or cluster your ideas.
- Think about the grammatical structures you are using, but do not let such a focus interfere with what you want to write.
- Begin writing (do not worry about making mistakes at first); let your ideas flow.
- Use examples, facts, and other supporting details to develop your paragraphs.
- Rewrite, making whatever changes seem necessary.
- Think of writing as a process that develops slowly.
- Ask for advice from other students and/or your teacher as you are writing.
- Share your written products with others if you feel comfortable doing so.

Although these lists may be useful to many students, most strategies may be too complex to be reduced to lists. Furthermore, we cannot assume that our students are not metacognitively aware. All one has to do is listen to students' conversations about what they are doing to find that they, indeed, are aware. Even young children appear to have very complex ways of self-regulation that they can often verbalize. It may be wise to ask students to share with others some of the strategies they already use. In addition, a debriefing session can be valuable in focusing students on the strategies they have used to complete a task and in providing them with the opportunity to learn from each other. Questions, such as "What did you do to get started?" or "What helped you remember that?," can be used to stimulate discussion.

Practice and a focus on strategies need not be so extensive or intrusive as to interfere with learning. Sometimes too much emphasis on strategies causes students to lose the meaning of *what* they are learning if they become too focused on *how* they are learning it. Furthermore, practice with strategies that may be inappropriate culturally (see especially LoCastro, 1994) or that students may not be ready for or do not need could be a waste of precious time. On the other hand, instruction in strategies that are well timed and well suited to the needs of the students can make a noticeable difference in the way they approach learning a second language.

SUMMARY

Critical pedagogy, as Freire, Pennycook, Auerbach, and others described it, can take us beyond meaningful communication at a basic level to communication about what most deeply affects students' lives. Participatory language teaching may begin to appear in classrooms where students and teachers negotiate power as students become more involved in decision making when it matters and where students are respected both individually and collectively.

Participatory language teaching, although not considered a method or an approach, identifies and describes the dialectical relationship that can occur between students and their teachers if both are active and successful members in a classroom community.

Although strategic learning and participatory learning appear oppositional in theory, in many ways they are inseparable and perhaps can best be viewed in a dialectical relationship with one another. To function collectively, individuals need to bring to the table all their capabilities that have been highly developed through social processes. Success with strategy application begins with the realization that students can be in charge of their own learning and that teachers can provide an environment conducive to that end. Instruction in learning strategies can be beneficial if well timed, suited to the students' needs, and compatible with students' cognitive styles and cultural expectations.

QUESTIONS AND PROJECTS FOR REFLECTION AND DISCUSSION

1. What possibilities might participatory teaching have for your own classrooms based on what you have read and learned from others? What might be its advantages? disadvantages?

2. What has been your own experience with strategic learning? If you have attempted to learn another language, what were some strategies you used of which you were aware? Discuss with a small group.

3. Visit two or more language classrooms in your area. Describe the kind of interaction that seems to prevail in each classroom. To what extent do the students participate in the events of the classroom? To what extent do they appear to be part of the decision-making process? Make sure you obtain the permission of the school administration and the teacher prior to your observations. Discuss your findings with a small group of peers.

4. Considering the fact that traditional teaching relies mainly on transmission education, how wise is it for teachers to make their teaching more participatory? What might be some practical restraints? Do you feel there may be political dangers in store for teachers modifying their roles? If so, what might these dangers be, and how might teachers best deal with them?

5. Design a ten- to fifteen-minute lesson using an adaptation of one or a combination of the participatory practices described in this chapter. Make sure that it would be appropriate for a group of fellow classmates. After

presenting your lesson, ask your group in what ways it was effective and how it might be improved. Begin by sharing with them your own reactions to the lesson.

If you are currently teaching students, use what you have learned to try out an adaptation of a participatory practice with them. Make sure the lesson is relevant and appropriate to age level. If possible, have your lesson videotaped to analyze and discuss with peers. Reflect on its outcome and how you felt about doing it. Pay close attention to student response. Do you see any problems with your lesson? How might you improve it?

6. ✎ **Journal Entry:** Reflect on the lesson(s) you carried out in item 5 above. What strategies did you use? How comfortable did you feel with them? Did you think they were effective overall? Why or why not? What were some of the specific problems you encountered? How can they be overcome? Write about what you learned from your peers and your instructor during the process. What insights did you gain about learning and teaching from the experience? To what extent do you plan to incorporate participatory practices into your own teaching?

SUGGESTED READINGS AND REFERENCE MATERIALS

Auerbach, E. (2000). Creating participatory learning communities: Paradoxes and possibilities. In J. K. Hall & W. Eggington (Eds.), *The sociopolitics of English language teaching* (pp. 143-164). Clevedon, England: Multilingual Matters. This important contribution to the field defines and describes participatory learning and looks at some of the various contexts in which it may occur. The author's very pragmatic approach to the subject includes an exploration of ways to identify issues around which to build curriculum. At the same time, she addresses participatory learning's challenges and how they might be dealt with in a productive way.

Norton, B., & Toohey, K. (Eds.). (2004). *Critical pedagogies and language learning*. Cambridge, England: Cambridge University Press. In this seminal volume, Norton and Toohey discuss issues involving gender and sexuality, race, multiculturalism, social justice, critical pedagogical practices in a variety of contexts, teacher education, and so on as well as their relationship to the instruments of power and the promotion of equity in education. The views of Ryuko Kubota, Aneta Pavlenko, Elana Shohamy, Pippa Stein, and many others are represented.

Pennycook, A. (1999). Introduction: Critical approaches to TESOL. *TESOL Quarterly*, *33*(3), 329-348. This article serves as the introduction to the special issue of the *TESOL Quarterly* on the same topic. In it Pennycook discusses what it means to take a critical approach to TESOL, in what ways transformative pedagogy can change attitudes toward education, and why it might be important to consider TESOL a dynamic field subject to constant critical examination.

Smoke, T. (1998). *Adult ESL: Politics, pedagogy, and participation in classroom and community.* Mahwah, NJ: Lawrence Erlbaum. Pedagogical and personal/social issues and instructional and political strategies are addressed in this volume. It is argued that ESL courses help students become empowered in all ways, not only academic.

Walker, L. (2001). Negotiating syllabi in the adult ESL classroom. *CATESOL News, 32*(4), 5-7. This brief but pithy article offers numerous strategies for discovering what is important to students studying English. Through the use of questionnaires, Walker suggests that teachers explore the students' learning preferences and goals. She recommends that teachers ask students to rank commonly stated objectives in order of their importance. By this means, a curriculum can be developed which reflects student input. Although her ideas are intended for the teachers of adult learners, they can be applied to other levels as well.

CHAPTER 5

Developing Skills: Implicit and Explicit Teaching Strategies

For the Kashinawá, learning and teaching are experiential and as such have to occur while doing the activity to be learned....There is no moment for abstract theoretical learning followed by practice; the learning, the practice, and the activity are the same and simultaneous.

Lynn Mario T. Menezes
de Souza, 2005

QUESTIONS TO THINK ABOUT

1. What do you remember about learning such skills as reading and writing in your first language? Did your teachers intervene in some way to help you learn these skills? What kinds of intervention did you find most helpful? What kinds did you find least helpful, perhaps even detrimental to your development? How might learning how to read and write be different if you were studying another language? What kinds of intervention do you think you might require? What about listening and speaking?

2. Is there a "natural" way to teach skills? If so, what might such teaching entail? How might it be different from other kinds of teaching?

3. To what extent is it wise to integrate reading, writing, listening, and speaking in the language classroom? How might you go about it as a teacher of a second or foreign language?

For the Kashinawá culture in the upper Western Amazon region of Brazil, learning is both implicit and experiential. According to Menezes de Souza (2005), learning and teaching among the Kashinawá are experience based. There are no instructions or theoretical discussions followed by practice. Although *implicit* teaching strategies are primary to teaching skills across cultures, it is important to examine the role that *explicit* teaching strategies play, particularly when teaching skills to second language learners.

IMPLICIT AND EXPLICIT: WHAT'S THE DIFFERENCE?

Implicit teaching strategies are those actions that teachers take to encourage students to learn by doing, without overt instruction. Such strategies often expose students to materials and tasks[1] of their own choosing or to those selected by the teacher because of their high interest level and their abundant inclusion of whatever it is teachers think learners should know. Textbook writers can also encourage implicit learning (see especially Richard-Amato, 1990, 1993a, 1993b, 1998; Richard-Amato & Hansen, 1995). The textbook writer, like the teacher, often utilizes materials and tasks that have been purposefully selected (or created) to meet the perceived needs of learners. What is learned from exposure to such materials and tasks is generally below a conscious level of awareness, and the accessibility to it is thought to be fully automatic. Interestingly, implicit knowledge may partially surface from time to time, resulting in the gradual formation of a rule or strategy which can evolve into something quite explicit and sometimes capable of being verbalized. Thus, explicit knowledge may come from implicit knowledge via some kind of inductive process (see also De Jong, 2005).

Learners, through the materials and tasks themselves, are exposed to various grammatical structures, vocabulary items, spelling, punctuation conventions, organizational markers or transitions, input that illustrates the use of specific organizational patterns, and other conventions typically used in all modes of communication. Students are introduced to a variety of genres,[2] including narration, description, definition, classification, comparison, cause and effect analysis, illustration and example, and many other formats. The *recycling* of key concepts, grammatical structures, and vocabulary found throughout the materials and tasks can aid and may even be necessary to their becoming internalized.

Explicit teaching strategies, on the other hand, include those strategies used to overtly focus the students' attention on explanations, rules, steps to follow, direct

---

[1] The word *task* as used in this book generally is akin to the word *activity*. Bygate, Skehan, and Swain (2001) defined *task* as an activity requiring use of language and involving either short or extended teacher intervention (see also page 373).

[2] Genre are not just "text types," but they and the processes involved in reading and writing are situated and thus influenced to one extent or another by the cultural and social contexts and purposes out of which they grow and develop (see excellent discussion in Johns, 2003).

corrections, conventions, and so forth to help them become more proficient in the new language through a conscious application of declarative knowledge. Access to such knowledge usually is not automatic but instead requires at least some control and thinking ahead.[3] Explicit teaching strategies may come from the textbook, the teacher directly, or peers (see pp. 377–382). The strategies may include:

1. explaining a rule or learning strategy and providing practice using it
2. outlining a series of possible steps to follow in completing a process
3. providing word definitions; explaining the use of specific lexical items; presenting conclusions drawn from corpus data, collocations, and so on
4. pointing out how texts in different subject areas are organized; how organizational markers make the ideas flow smoothly from one to another; what rhetorical devices are typical of specific genres, spelling, and punctuation, and so forth

Explicit strategies may also come in the form of self-help features included in a textbook (see Richard-Amato, 1990, 1993a, 1993b, 1998; Richard-Amato & Hansen, 1995). They often include concise guides containing:

1. glossaries, cultural notes, and strategy suggestions found at the bottoms of pages or in the margins
2. questions and activities that aid comprehension and focus students on relevant skills such as
    a. making inferences
    b. determining the main idea or ideas
    c. summarizing
    d. relating to identity, cultural knowledge, and social issues
    e. predicting
    f. thinking critically
    g. finding support for conclusions
    h. distinguishing fact from opinion
    i. recognizing and being able to use literary devices such as symbolism, metaphor, and the like
    j. interpreting graphs, charts, and tables
    k. creating outlines and clustering devices to facilitate long-term memory
3. learning strategies and grammar rules to be applied as needed while students are communicating through various modes
4. critical analyses of rhetorical conventions, organizational patterns found in the typical genres of any given culture, organizational markers, and so forth

---

[3] Note that DeKeyser (2003) claimed the opposite—that explicit knowledge (declarative) can become automatic (procedural knowledge) through practice (the strong *interface* position; for the *noninterface* position, see Krashen's description as it relates to grammar, p. 73 and pp. 75–76 in this volume). However, Hulstijn (2002) had refuted DeKeyser's claim earlier, saying that practice will only speed up the procedures but that the knowledge itself will still remain basically different when it comes to accessibility. Bialstok (1994), too, had claimed even earlier that explicit knowledge with sufficient practice may become more accessible but that it is still represented as explicit knowledge.

Explicit teaching strategies are often used to enhance implicit learning by drawing attention to procedures, patterns of use, and specific lexical or syntactic items. Even though second language (L2) learners, like first language (L1) learners, are thought to acquire most of their language (especially grammar) by implicit means, they often depend on both explicit teaching and learning strategies (DeKeyser, 2003; N. Ellis, 2005; R. Ellis, 2004). Whether explicit or implicit strategies are used, the strategies should be appropriate. Following are some important considerations:

1. immediate needs of the learner
2. age and the learner's approximate cognitive development
3. proficiency level in the second language
4. interests, goals, and aspirations
5. communication needs
6. academic requirements

L2 learners are thought to be in need of explicit intervention to a greater extent than are L1 learners, and they may be able to profit from it more, because they are usually more developed cognitively at the time of initial exposure to their new language (see pp. 67–73). Interestingly, Celce-Murcia (1985) suggested, based on research, that younger learners and beginning language learners might do better with implicit instruction, and Lightbown and Spada (2006) concluded, also based on research, that explicit instruction is perhaps more beneficial to older, more proficient learners. However, it has been shown that in reading, for example, the more advanced learners are better able to benefit from at least one important implicit strategy (i.e., inferencing) than beginners because advanced learners are better at finding and understanding contextual clues to meaning (Carter, 2001). Thus the picture is far from clear.

Although valuable in many ways, the currently available research often adheres to the experimental tradition alone and thus generally ignores the effects of identity and relationships, the sociocultural situation in which the strategy is being used, and the strength of motivational factors and other affective influences on learning. In addition, much of the research fails to address the linguistic context in which the strategy is being applied and the nature of the strategy itself.

Furthermore, conclusions drawn from current research probably do not reflect the pure uses of either explicit or implicit strategies, especially if the studies have been accomplished in real classrooms as opposed to laboratory settings. In real classrooms, explicit and implicit teaching strategies become intertwined to the extent that research results are often difficult to attribute to one or the other. The very notions of *explicit* and *implicit* and their possible interface are extremely complex even as they apply to knowledge itself and the learning process. (See also Chapter 2.) Researchers, in particular, might want to see Isemonger (2007) and R. Ellis and Loewen (2007) for a debate about this and related research issues.

Another problem is that almost all of the studies to date are based on short-term results using pretest/posttest data. Even if implicit teaching could be isolated for classroom research purposes, sufficient time and many exposures to selected input in different situations may be required before students begin to demonstrate its effects on the interlanguage process. For example, it stands to reason that if a rule is taught followed by a direct test of that rule, the learner will probably get it right. Carefully designed longitudinal studies that include both quantitative and qualitative data may be our best bet for studying whatever lasting effects may be gained from the use of both implicit and explicit teaching strategies. Although many current studies employ delayed posttesting, they still cover a relatively short time period (R. Ellis, 2006).

One difficulty for teachers and their students may occur when teachers, in their effort to increase their use of explicit teaching strategies, find themselves relying too much on a "teaching point" approach to skills. Although it is helpful to give clear instructions and flexible guidelines before students embark on a writing project, for example, teaching points, especially those concerning grammar and usage (e.g., the intricacies of parallel structure, the multiple uses of transitions, or similar extended instruction) often can be a waste of time until the student is in the midst of the writing project itself and is struggling with such issues. Think about how much more meaningful explicit instruction might be if given in small doses and interjected as needed. Here I do not mean to imply that there is never any benefit to more lengthy instruction not tied to a specifically identified, immediate need. On the contrary, there may be benefits from such instruction, especially if students are convinced that they eventually will need the information for an upcoming task or project. Touted benefits of any research, however, should be applied with caution and may not be generalizable to all situations; as Han (2007) reminded us, pedagogy is largely local.

SKILLS INTEGRATION

Before launching into each of the separate skill areas, it is important to point out that many teachers of second language learners believe that, whenever possible, skills should be integrated within a communication-based program. Integrating the four skills—listening, speaking, reading, and writing—is not difficult.[4] It may come as naturally for the teacher as it does for the students. When we listen, opportunities for writing evolve. When we read, opportunities for speaking arise. Classrooms in which students are encouraged to flow with these opportunities tend to allow the skills to grow naturally; all the while explicit strategies can appropriately be interjected as needed.

Often, the impetus for skill development comes from a need of the moment. For example, students may need to write to fulfill immediate obligations. A foreign language student in the later elementary grades may need to respond to a letter from a pen pal. A second language student at the adult or secondary level may need to fill out a job application. In these situations, students often cannot wait until the later levels for language to emerge. The teacher and/or peers can aid students in fulfilling these

---

[4] The assumption is made here that the goal of any particular language program is to promote proficiency in all four skills. It should be noted, however, that not all language programs have this as a goal; some may be concerned with only one or two of the skills.

obligations. With guidance, students may frequently find themselves performing far above levels for which they are supposed to be "ready."

Integration of the four skills usually can take place from the beginning of study without causing cognitive overload. For example, even before students are ready to speak, literacy in the new language can be introduced to those who need to survive in school settings and on the street. Clear labels on the doors of various rooms throughout the school can help—especially the words designating male and female bathrooms and other critical locations. Words for the street are even more important: Words such as *stop*, *danger*, and *keep out* can be crucial for survival. In the foreign language classroom, teachers can label common objects around the room after students have acquired or partially acquired their oral forms.

Beginners at any age may be highly motivated by story experience (see Chapter 11), which often allows students to participate in a rich language environment even before they can utter a word in the target language. Later, students may be able to read simple stories with accompanying pictures in both second and foreign language classes. Speech development may be accelerated simply through involvement in a character's conflict. Natural curiosity may push students into more complex levels of communication, incorporating all the skills of which they are capable—listening, speaking, reading, and writing. If teachers are there to take advantage of these teachable moments, they can guide students in tasks sometimes far beyond what might have been considered possible in the traditional teacher-oriented, inflexibly structured classroom.

NEEDS ASSESSMENT: PRODUCT OR PROCESS ORIENTED?

Before embarking on a program involving any of the teaching strategies discussed in this chapter, a needs assessment can be completed for each learner and reexamined again periodically with student input. This does not mean that the assessment should be completely *product oriented* and approached one need at a time in a syllabus designed for that purpose. On the contrary, the needs can be addressed as they come up in the course of *process-oriented* classroom activities. In addition collecting objective data, teachers can elicit and consider students' perspectives. What do students perceive their needs to be? Academic, sociopolitical, cultural, and affective needs can be considered from their point of view in relation to their goals and aspirations, both in school and out. Consider the following questions.

1. What kinds of listening, speaking, reading, and writing tasks will the learner be expected to perform successfully, depending on his or her goals and aspirations? personal communicative tasks? academic tasks such as comprehending lectures or reading and writing complex materials in specific content areas? tasks associated with certain occupations and/or specialized domains of knowledge (e.g., technological or business-related fields, the arts)?
2. What specific knowledge and skills might the learner require for each kind of task? What knowledge and skills does the learner already have? still need?

Data for a needs assessment can come from a variety of sources: student surveys, observation, authority opinion, diagnostic assessment and evaluation, and so forth (see Chapter 7).

TEACHING STRATEGIES FOR LISTENING, SPEAKING, READING, AND WRITING

The main focus of this chapter is on teaching strategies, both explicit and implicit, as they pertain to skills development. Such strategies have already been discussed in relation to error correction and teaching grammar in Chapter 2. Some teaching strategies included in this chapter may be more appropriate for some groups, individuals, and local situations than others. Computer use is encouraged whenever it can be advantageous (see the discussion in Chapter 16). Much will depend on the teacher's preparation in classroom computer use and the students' access to computers.

Specific learning (as opposed to teaching) strategies were covered in Chapter 4. Many of the activities or projects in which the students are involved—be it listening to a lecture, participating in normal conversation, reading a chapter from a textbook, or writing a composition—can be followed by a learning strategies analysis and discussion.

Even before beginning an assignment, the teacher might ask the students to discuss how they plan to go about completing it. For example, if the assignment involves a composition, the teacher can encourage the students to consider the learning strategies they may have used in the past. Which strategies will they apply to this particular assignment? Then the teacher can refer students to the learning strategies dealing with writing (or whatever skill will be used) found on pp. 104–110. The teacher may want to have the students practice some of these learning strategies and others in mini-lessons.

A word of caution: It is important for the teacher to avoid establishing rigid strategy guidelines for any particular skill area. Individual students may already have their own personal strategy preferences (Yongqi Gu, 2003); so, although it is important to offer a variety of strategies, it is just as important not to impose them.

After an assignment is completed, the teacher might ask students to share what strategies worked for them. For example, if the students have just listened to a presentation, either live or prerecorded, they might talk about the strategies they used while trying to understand the presentation. Encourage the students to consider the metacognitive strategies they may have used as well as the cognitive and the social/affective strategies (see p. 106). Invite them to add their own strategies to the lists of learning strategies found in Chapter 4. Teachers may want students to keep a strategy journal in which they record and reflect on the strategies they use.

The utilization of a wide array of teaching strategies, including holding frequent discussions about learning strategies, can be very effective. Note that no attempt has been made here to separate the ideas for teaching into an explicit/implicit dichotomy, because most of the teaching we do involves elements of both.

In this chapter, notice that pronunciation is subsumed under speaking, and vocabulary is subsumed under reading, although vocabulary, in particular, can be developed across all the skill areas. The teaching strategies presented here are, in many cases, supported mainly by short-term research (see the sources cited in the text and the references). Please note, however, that the research referred to here, either directly or indirectly, is by no means all-inclusive. In addition, several of the strategies presented, whether supported by research or not, may be excellent candidates for future study.

Listening

Teaching listening no longer focuses mainly on sounds and words, recognizing where sentences begin and end, and so on. It includes helping students become familiar with the culturally determined schematic assumptions on which all discourse is based. Listening can be an important way to learn spoken language, both first and second. Prelistening, predicting, finding the overall meaning, making inferences, summarizing, and examining possible comprehension problems can involve both learning and teaching strategies that can be developed in relation to a specific context. Kasper (1984) discovered early on from think-aloud protocols that when listening, the student first develops a basic interpretation or a frame and then attempts to fit the stream of speech being heard into it, changing the initial frame as necessary. Modified and enriched content (see pp. 251–255) can be particularly beneficial at beginning and intermediate levels to help students increase their understanding of personal communication and academic discourse gradually over time. Students can further develop their academic listening skills by being exposed to lectures, oral readings, and the like and by taking notes on what they hear. After listening, they can often benefit from discussing with the teacher and peers the meaning they have created.

Rost (2005) reflected on three basic processing phases that occur simultaneously while one is listening:

1. decoding
2. comprehension
3. interpretation

Decoding allows learners to process and recognize parts of words, whole words, phrases, and partial meanings, which eventually result in *comprehension* and *interpretation*. Due to the limits of working memory, decoding often depends on the appropriate speed—not too fast or too slow—so that the memory can process what is being said. The input at first can be slowed down, preferably at natural breaks within and between sentences (here Rost cited Flowerdew, 1994). Decoding also requires that there not be too many new elements or unusual items in the input, such as idiomatic expressions or abstractions with which the learner is unfamiliar.

Comprehension involves a synthesis of knowing what is important, associating it with the relevant schema, making inferences, and constantly revising what one believes is being said. Often misinterpretations and inappropriate responses are the result when the listener applies a culturally determined schema different from the one in the mind of the presenter or interlocutor. Interpretation often requires cultural knowledge and perspective and leads to the fourth phase: *listener response*. According to Rost, listener response can be overt (e.g., giving feedback to the speaker) or covert (e.g., adjusting one's attitudes and beliefs). What is understood and the effectiveness of the communication often depends on the identities and relationships established through the interaction. This negotiation becomes part of what Rost (2005) referred to as the "situational status," which is

> co-constructed by both interlocutors in each encounter, and can shift over the course of the encounter. Research on cross-cultural encounters [here Rost referred to Linell (1995), among others] has shown that the way in which interlocutors define their status relative to the other will determine a great deal about how they will communicate with each other, their degree of affective involvement, and what they will understand. (p. 520)

Anxiety is often a critical factor in listening and can arise as a result of the interpretation of one's own social status as a listener in relation to the presenter/interlocutor. Yang (1993) studied Chinese English learners and found a strong negative correlation between level of anxiety and listening performance (referred to in Rost, 2005, p. 520). Teachers would be wise to discuss this issue with their students.

Fluency in listening can be achieved by presenting listening input that contains mainly familiar words in situations in which pressure is placed on learners to speed up the process somewhat (Nation, 2005). Nation suggested that a familiar story be retold several times at a slightly faster speed each time and that graded readers (leveled below what the students can normally handle) be read aloud at a normal speed to see if they are understood. He claimed that much repetition using gradually faster rates is necessary to achieve fluency over time.

Other Teaching Strategies to Help Facilitate the Listening Process for Students

Teachers of second language learners are invited to consider the following strategies.

A. Listening during conversations and discussions
1. Remind students to let the person with whom they are conversing know if they do not understand the meaning of what is being said.
2. Teach students strategies for negotiating meaning and clarifying whenever possible ("Is this what you are saying?" "Do you mean _____?"). See Lam and Wong (2000).
3. Engage students in one-to-one interaction with you (the teacher) whenever possible. Modify what you say as needed during a negotiation for meaning.
4. Set up a self-access/self-study listening resource center in which the student has control of interesting, relevant, and authentic conversational materials (Morley, 2001). Students should be able to stop and replay the selections. Organize the selections into self-study packets or modules for easy access.

B. Listening to academic lectures/presentations
   1. *Prelistening*
      a. Explore with the students their prior knowledge and experience concerning the content of what they will be listening to. Provide background information to fill in any gaps (Anderson, 1999; Chang & Read, 2006).
      b. Introduce advance organizers (see p. 252) to give students clues about what to listen for.
      c. Emphasize the importance of listening for organizational markers that indicate transitions from one idea to the next, clarify relationships among ideas, and assign the relative importance of ideas to the topic. Such markers can make listeners aware of the overall structure of the presentation, aid comprehension and effective note-taking, and help listeners recall the relevant information (see Jung, 2003).
      d. Demonstrate effective note-taking and then have students practice to encourage them to look for what is important.
      e. Develop a facility where students have access to technology that allows them to practice their listening skills and learn new ones.
   2. *During listening*
      a. Involve students in relevant listening to which they will be asked to respond and for which they have a purpose (Ur, 1984).
      b. Encourage students to let the speaker know, when appropriate, if they do not understand the meaning of a key vocabulary item or if they have questions.
      c. At first, select listening materials in which the input is enhanced and/or modified to meet the needs of the listeners.
      d. When presenting information to students during a lesson, use simplification, expansion of ideas, direct definition, and visuals and graphic displays to aid comprehension. Ask questions frequently to make sure the students are comprehending the main points. (See examples of all of these strategies in Chapter 17.)
      e. Do not be afraid to use *code switching* when students appear confused. If you know at least some of their first language, especially in foreign language teaching situations, switching to their first language can be a very useful strategy. According to Cleghorn and Rollnick (2002), code switching can "clarify linguistically-based confusion, render the culturally unfamiliar familiar, make the implicit explicit, and provide English [or any language] vocabulary needed for examination purposes, provide contextualization cues, and raise learners' metalinguistic awareness" (p. 360). Code switching is also a matter of self-perception in that it allows learners to reflect more than one cultural identity (Shin, 2005).
      f. Recycle key concepts over and over in many different contexts.
      g. Summarize and review frequently during presentations.
      h. If possible, enrich the input with examples of a particular syntactic structure that you want to either reinforce or teach by implicit means (see R. Ellis, 2003).
      i. Encourage students to take notes to aid comprehension and help them remember the important points.

    j. Involve students in "narrow listening" during which they listen to many brief and redundant texts on the same topic (Dupuy, 1999; Krashen, 1996) until they are ready for texts of greater length and variety.

    k. Record lectures and presentations so students can listen to them as many times as necessary to aid comprehension and interpretation. Repetition of the input can be very crucial to understanding (Chang & Read, 2006; Hatch, 1983).

    l. If a lecture is recorded, students can "shadow" short segments of the lecture; in other words they can be asked to either repeat or paraphrase what has just been said before moving on to the next segment (see Macaro, 2003; Rost, 2005). When the students are finished, ask them to listen to the whole recording at once to obtain a global understanding of its content and organization.

  3. *Postlistening*

    a. Ask students to write down what they understood from the presentation. Then have them make a list of questions they still have. These can be discussed with individuals or a group (Carrasquillo & Rodríguez, 2005, p. 443).

    b. Have students fill out the graphic organizers they were introduced to during the prelistening phase.

    c. Ask the students to reconstruct in small groups the important points of the lecture or presentation.

    d. Have the students compare their notes to those of a partner and revise their notes as they see fit.

    e. Pose questions for discussion about issues brought up in the lecture or presentation. Request that the students pose questions as well.

Speaking

Speaking generally requires attention to a great number of tasks simultaneously: what to say, how to say it, what words to use, what others have just said, what their reactions might be to what the teacher might say or has said, noticing and self-correcting errors to prevent misunderstandings, and so on. The speaker makes assumptions about what the listener already knows and the knowledge the two of them share. A cross-cultural negotiation of meaning is often the purpose. Issues involve one's identity and social standing as well as knowing how to get things done with language (make requests, ask for clarification of meaning, participate in bonding routines, say "no" politely). Explicit teaching of the pragmatics of language can often be interjected into communicative tasks as the need for such instruction arises. Practice with idioms, reduced speech forms, slang, intonation, and stress can help students to meet some of the more challenging aspects of oral communication in another language.

    Speaking can involve a number of different types of activities:

1. Everyday conversation
   - allows participants to exchange ideas; make plans; talk about present, past, and future events; solve problems; and so on
   - encourages social bonding

2. Discussions/dialogues
   - small group or whole-class discussion
   - panel discussion (set speeches by panel members, often followed by open discussion among panelists and/or with the audience)
   - give-and-take dialogical discourse organized by topics, questions about a single topic, and so forth, with or without audience participation
3. Formal, prepared speeches (informative, persuasive, argumentative)
   - often grow out of what students have read and/or experienced
   - are organized for best effect (introduction, body, and conclusion)
   - utilize transitions to connect the parts and let the listener know how important each part is in relation to the others
4. Interviews (job, media, surveys)
   - require an interviewer to ask relevant, interesting questions and to transition from topic to topic
   - require an interviewee to answer, sometimes with short answers (e.g., yes/no) but usually with some elaboration
5. Role play (see pp. 282–285)
   - lends itself very well to practice with typical speech acts such as making requests (a teenager requesting permission to use the family car), asking for clarification or repetition (a new arrival not understanding directions on how to get to the hotel), refusing an offer (a girl refusing a friend's invitation to a party and trying not to hurt her friend's feelings), and so on
   - offers the opportunity to try out common routines, solve problems, and so forth.

Teaching Strategies to Help Facilitate Speaking

Teachers of second language learners may want to consider the following strategies:

1. Teach students ways to take more control of interactional situations by asking for clarification, confirming meaning, using fillers to provide more time for comprehension and response, or steering the topic to more familiar ground. See Dörnyei (1995). Role play might be a good way to practice various means of control.
2. Use scaffolding to fill in gaps during teacher-fronted interaction but only as much as needed to prevent a breakdown in communication. Be careful not to usurp the student's turn or interfere with what the student wants to say (Walsh, 2002).
3. Should a breakdown in communication occur during peer-to-peer interactions, wait as long as possible before intervening so that students have time to make their own repairs. If this does not appear likely after a period of time has lapsed, intervene subtly by leading or nudging students toward a solution (T. Lynch, 1997).
4. During teacher-fronted interaction or discussion, provide modified language aimed at Wells's communal zone of proximal development (see p. 83),

negotiate for meaning, provide for sufficient turn length, and make room for the co-construction of ideas.

5. Avoid forcing students to speak, especially when new concepts have just been introduced. Allow students to volunteer when they are ready to contribute (Walsh, 2002; see similar strategies in Chapter 17). If you call on someone who has not volunteered, make sure it is someone who looks eager to speak and has indicated a willingness to do so through gesture or partial vocalization (Antòn, 1999).

6. Allow students adequate time to volunteer responses to your questions before calling on others or responding to them yourself. Rephrase the question and be supportive throughout the discourse. (See also Walsh, 2002.)

7. Give beginners to low-intermediate students many opportunities to dialogue in pairs with intermediate and advanced students so that they can modify their output to a greater extent and stretch to higher levels of thinking (Iwashita, 2001).

8. In general, encourage group work with individuals of varying proficiency levels. (See cooperative learning in Chapter 15; see grouping strategies discussion on pp. 218, 294–295, 316, and 342.)

9. Allow students to participate in conversation tasks for which minimally structured guidelines have been prepared. Less structured tasks usually generate longer turn lengths, more complexity of utterances (measured by verb phrases), and more shifts in verb than do highly structured information-gap tasks (Nakahama, Tyler, & van Lier, 2001).

10. Encourage students to engage in pretask planning. Several studies have indicated that students who have been given the opportunity to plan a narrative before presenting it demonstrated considerable gains in fluency measured by temporal factors (e.g., number of syllables per minute) or hesitation variables (e.g., measured by frequency of reformulations). Benefits leading to increased complexity were also found in these same studies (measured mainly by degree of subordination; see especially R. Ellis, 1987; Ortega, 1999; Yuan & R. Ellis, 2003). Note, however, that results were quite different when looking at accuracy (measured mainly by the percentage of error-free clauses; see the teaching strategy in item 11 below, which might lead to increased accuracy).

11. Give students ample time (unpressured) to present their narratives and encourage them to formulate their ideas; monitor their own output by focusing on form as they are speaking (Yuan & R. Ellis, 2003). When students do not feel time pressure, it is more likely that they will be able to attend to form while speaking.

12. Have students evaluate their own presentations first using teacher-prepared guidelines or ones they have developed themselves. Using similar guidelines, ask peers to summarize what the speaker has said (Lazaraton, 2001) and list strengths and areas for possible improvement.

13. Provide for peer facilitating and/or tutoring for students who want additional help in preparing and practicing oral presentations (see pp. 377–382).
14. Advocate multilingualism whenever possible. Students who can function on personal and academic levels in more than one language and culture can have many advantages in today's global world (see Chapter 17).
15. Develop a facility where students have access to technology that allows them to record and listen to their own prepared presentations. Help students analyze their presentations for strategy use, organization, choice of lexical items, clarity of ideas, and so on. Some students may want to listen to any samples they have recorded of their own interpersonal communication with others. Once students are fairly proficient in their new language, give them access to *corpus data* (see p. 407) that they can explore to find frequently used rhetorical structures and lexical items common to various types of communication situations and registers.[5]

Pronunciation

Pronunciation instruction in earlier decades generally focused on the student's ability to speak like a native speaker and was based on behaviorism (see p. 23). Today, instruction focuses more on being understood within the linguistic environment in which one finds oneself. Many teachers now realize that pronunciation reflects the identity their students want to project and the social groups with which they want to align themselves. What is intelligible in one environment may not be intelligible in another. Sounds, stress, intonation, pausing, and so on can be taught as needed within the context of meaningful communication. The models are not necessarily native speakers. In fact, in most cases around the world, the linguistic models come from communities of non-native English speakers. *Correctness* has become a very relative term and is defined by what is appropriate for the local situation. Students may also prefer to maintain certain prosodic elements of their first language in order to retain identity with the first language culture (Morley, 1991) or for other reasons.

Intonation is a very important component of pronunciation. Through it the speaker can express feelings and emotional states, indicate beginnings and endings of thoughts, stress key phrases and words, and convey the register associated with persons in multiple professions and roles: teachers, ministers, politicians, rap artists, newscasters, mothers talking to their babies, and so forth.

Teaching Strategies to Aid Students with Pronunciation

1. Help students to develop realistic goals concerning pronunciation based on current research whenever possible and avoid insisting that they be "nativelike."
2. Involve students in communication activities tied to meaningful subject-matter content so that they have multiple opportunities to modify their

---

[5] See footnote 16 on page 13.

pronunciation as required for intelligibility. This way, they can escape the embarrassment often associated with direct correction (Jenkins, 2000; Walker, 2005).

3. Sound distinctions (based on a comparison with the student's first language can be taught and learned as needed for intelligibility (e.g., /b/ versus /v/). The learner may not be able to readily reproduce the differences in his or her speech at first. It is possible, too, that even if the student does appear to correct the pronunciation of a word, the change may not last long or be used in actual communication (Derwing & Munro, 2005). Recycling target words with sufficient frequency may help over time.

4. Teach students to *hear* the differences in specific sounds as needed. Bradlow, Pisoni, Akahane-Yamado, and Tohkura (1997) found that Japanese English learners, when trained to perceive the difference between /r/ and /l/, were able to produce them intelligibly in their speech even though no training in producing the sounds had been used (Derwing & Munro, 2005).

5. Keep in mind that intelligibility is more than contrasting sounds when such a contrast will make a difference in meaning; it also involves suprasegmental features such as intonation, rhythm, and stress, which may be even more important to understanding. Knowing that English is considered a stress-timed language (only some syllables are stressed) as opposed to a syllable-timed language (syllables are stressed approximately equally) may help (Brinton, 2005).

6. When needed, pay special attention to primary stress (also referred to in the literature as *nuclear stress*). Hahn (2004) found in her study of Korean stress patterns that the group that recognized where the primary stress fell was able to understand a lecture significantly better than the group that lacked such recognition.

7. Give students simple rules when they are likely to help (Seidlhofer, 2005).

8. Avoid working on some sound distinctions, such as voicing variation of past-tense endings (e.g., /t/ and /d/) and of plural nouns and third-person singular verb endings (e.g., /s/ and /z/). Such allophonic distinctions tend to confuse students in streams of speech because assimilation rules take precedence over voicing; for example, "He talked on the phone" becomes "He talk don the phone" (Toth, 2005). However, students might benefit from becoming aware (through teaching "asides") of some reduced speech features due to vowel reduction, omission, and so on (Brinton, 2005).

9. Teach students how to use the pronunciation guides included in most dictionaries to which they have access (Seidlhofer, 2005).

10. Develop a facility where students have access to technology that allows them to listen to the pronunciation of a wide range of proficient speakers in varying contexts. Make it possible for them to record and listen to their own production and help them analyze it for intelligibility. Computer tools are now available that give automatic feedback and diagnosis and can be very useful if used appropriately (see especially Levis, 2007). Software programs

are also available that can aid English learners in internalizing suprasegmental patterns by helping them recognize meaningful distinctions (Pennington & N. Ellis, 2000).

Pronunciation is a crucial area of language learning and has, perhaps, not received as much attention as it should have in recent years. Language teachers would be wise to learn as much as they can about it in order to recognize *when* students need work on their pronunciation and *the kind of work* that might be beneficial. Much of pronunciation is acquired by having to adjust one's speech to be understood. When speaking about English as an international language, Jenkins (2000) concluded that language learners modify their speech, sometimes consciously and sometimes not, in a continuing effort to achieve effective communication.

Approaching Errors in Oral Production

During student conversations, indirect error treatment such as using recasts (see Chapter 2) may be preferable to direct, on-the-spot correction. This way, the teacher can avoid possible embarrassment on the part of the learner. Those of us who have worked extensively with adolescents in particular know how important this is. When students are giving speeches or other presentations, one or two corrections can be included on a written evaluation and given to the student later. During conversation and presentations of various kinds, the teacher may want to keep track of student errors and have students work on the errors individually or in small groups at a later time.

However, not all research supports an indirect error treatment. Explicit feedback is defined by DeKeyser (1995) as corrections that provide a rule or direct attention to a specific form and appears to be more effective in a number of short-term studies (see especially N. Ellis, 2005; R. Ellis, 2001; Norris & Ortega, 2000; Schmidt, 2001).

On the other hand, recasts providing implicit negative feedback (see examples on pp. 50–51) were found effective by Mackey and Philp (1998), Iwashita (2003), Leeman (2003), Long (2007), and others. Some researchers found that recasts become most effective when they are short and simple and are used with prosodic stress to indicate what needs to be corrected (Loewen & Philp, 2006; Lyster, 1998; Nicholas, Lightbown, & Spada, 2001; Roberts, 1995).

More research needs to be done that demonstrates the results of various error treatments over time. In addition, sociocultural and affective factors need to be considered. What kind of relationship has been established between the learner and other students in the class? between the learner and the teacher? Are such relationships mainly positive and built on trust? These questions and many more need to be addressed before deciding which error correction strategies produce the best results over time within any given learner in any given situation.

Reading

Sometimes research results on reading are used for political purposes to demonstrate that a particular method is superior to other methods. However, one needs to look closely at the details on which such studies are based. If the method requires smaller classes, more individualized work, and large amounts of time devoted to reading and being read to, then the results might be a reflection of these requirements rather than the use of one method or another per se. We want to be especially leery of study reports that are not found in reputable publications and that have not been subjected to peer review.

Developing literacy and other abilities in another language can involve students in very positive, highly motivating experiences. Students often run into difficulty when learning a language is equated with the mastery of separate sets of skills and subskills. Learning to read in a first or second language is not a matter of stringing phonemes (sounds) into words, and words into phrases and sentences. Rather, it is a matter of learning to understand meaningful print in order to participate more fully in a community of readers and writers through collaborative learning, inquiry, and analysis (see especially Lee & Smagorinsky, 2000).

A Natural Language Framework

A natural language framework is based on the notion that reading is a process based on an *innate motivation to understand*. Harste, Woodward, and Burke (1984) found that preschool children growing up with print ubiquitous in their environment figured out what much of it meant without formal instruction. A natural language framework, also referred to historically as the "whole language approach," assumed that learning to read in a first or second language was largely a matter of wanting to make sense of text. However, readers were still expected to develop phonemic awareness. In fact, phonemic awareness was considered essential to being able to read. The important question was *how* and *when* phonemic awareness came about.

Readers generally use both bottom-up strategies (decoding from the phoneme level to the sentence level to determine what the words, phrases, sentences are) and top-down strategies (applying the context and prior knowledge, including relevant sociocultural knowledge, also known as schema). Most often bottom-up and top-down strategies are used simultaneously (Eskey, 2005; Grabe, 1991). Therefore, it makes sense that they are learned together as well for the most part. Problems can arise when bottom-up strategies (i.e., phonics) are used in isolation from and at the expense of top-down strategies or vice versa.

Written language is more abstract than speech and therefore may require more complex brain connections that very young children develop gradually as they interact with their environment. Wells (1999), referring to Halliday and Vygotsky, pointed out that written language is really second-order symbolism in which symbols represent spoken words, which, in turn, represent ideas. Wells also said that the meaning of what we read and write must be determined through the written word alone, adding further complication to both processes. Although there may be pictures, charts, or diagrams, there are no gestures, intonation, or facial expressions to help convey meaning.

All four skills—listening, speaking, reading, and writing—are socially motivated, active, creative processes requiring a high degree of personal involvement. For this reason, it seems reasonable to teach all four within a natural language framework in which motivation is high. Explicit instruction is also important to the process and can be interjected as needed. However, it is important to remember that reading and writing, like listening and speaking, appear to be best learned when they are necessary *for* something.

Goodman (1986), along with many others, was instrumental in developing a natural language perspective. He described it as "the easy way to language development." To make his point, he contrasted what makes language learning easy with what makes it difficult. One might want to look at the following two columns as ends of a continuum rather than as a dichotomy.[6]

It's easy when:	It's hard when:
it's real and natural.	it's artificial.
it's whole.	it's broken into bits and pieces.
it's sensible.	it's nonsense.
it's interesting.	it's dull and uninteresting.
it's relevant.	it's irrelevant.
it belongs to the learner.	it belongs to someone else.
it's part of a real event.	it's out of context.
it has social utility.	it has no social value.
it has purpose for the learner.	it has no discernible purpose.
the learner chooses to use it.	it's imposed by someone else.
it's accessible to the learner.	it's inaccessible.
the learner has power to use it.	the learner is powerless.

The right-hand column is most often associated with bottom-up approaches (i.e., phonics). These approaches adhere to the idea that acquiring literacy in a language begins at the most abstract level: sound and letter correspondences, syllables, words, and phrases. Learners are expected to use these as building blocks to move gradually to what is more concrete and meaningful. Such approaches can be especially devastating for children who may not be ready yet to think metalinguistically. Bottom-up approaches can also be frustrating for older learners, who, although they are usually cognitively highly developed, have not had other means for accessing the written language such as books or other materials of interest.

The left-hand column, on the other hand, is associated with top-down approaches, applied in some combination with bottom-up. Here students are introduced right at the beginning to meaningful language rather than to abstract bits and pieces. It may be a wordless book for which the teacher helps the student write a story, using the student's own words (see the language experience approach on pp. 303–306.) It may be a short message addressed directly to the student. What child or adult can resist trying to figure out a message (with help) that has his or her own name on it? Through effective top-down approaches in combination with bottom-up ones, students generally internalize bits and pieces as they engage personally with the reading and writing process. The abstract bits and pieces are learned as they are needed, often with the help of the teacher.

---

[6] Goodman, 1986, p. 8.

Unfortunately, natural language advocates are often accused of being against bottom-up processing—an assumption that is unfounded and misleading. More typically, natural language advocates are against approaches that *focus* on bottom-up processing to the exclusion of meaningful literacy events. They generally recognize the interaction between top-down and bottom-up processing and the importance of that interaction (see also Anderson, 1999; Eskey, 2005). Edelsky, Altwerger, and Flores (1991) reminded us that while using a natural framework, "teachers *do* teach children how to spell words they are using, *do* teach appropriate punctuation for letters children are writing, *do* teach strategies for sounding out particular combinations of letters under particular circumstances" (p. 38). The same can be true for older learners. However, what is taught, and when it is taught, may be different for each reader depending on the task, the situation, and individual needs. Interestingly, many good readers are not good at skills exercises, and many poor readers are (see Altwerger & Resta, 1986). What is crucial here is that developing readers be involved in reading and writing activities that are meaningful. (See Chapter 13 for descriptions of such activities.) Edelsky and Johnson (2004) emphasized the importance of "critical whole language practice" during which topics come from the students' lived experience.

Learning to Read in the First Language

Learning to read in the first language can be particularly important for language minority children; we do not want their cognitive development to be arrested while they are trying to learn a new language system (Cummins, 1981b). Nonliterates in second language classes may need special attention at the beginning of the learning process. If possible, they should develop literacy in their primary languages (if their languages have written traditions) and then apply this knowledge to literacy development in the second language. (See especially Collier & Thomas, 1989; Ramírez, Yuen, & Ramey, 1991.) If learning to read in the first language is not possible, then the teacher can wait until the student is sufficiently proficient in the second language before beginning reading instruction. Generally, the more similar the first language and culture are to those of the target group, the more likely the positive transfer of specific as well as general reading skills and strategies will occur. For example, if the first language is a European language using the Roman alphabet and the second language is English, specific positive transfer will involve many similarities in sound combinations, written symbols, punctuation, the movement of the eyes from left to right while reading, and so forth. On the meaning level, specific transfer might involve cognates, organizational patterns, shared cultural knowledge, experiences, and expectations. Of course it stands to reason that the student needs to have a basic level of L2 competence in order for L1 reading skills to be maximally helpful (see Clarke's *short-circuit hypothesis*, 1980).

On the other hand, when the language and culture are very different, the positive transfer is likely to be more general. For example, if the first language is an Asian language using an ideographic writing system, the positive transfer might tend to be limited to more general elements such as sensory-motor skills; the symbolic nature of written language; attitudes toward reading (see Yamashita, 2007); and general comprehension skills such as predicting, inferencing, coming to conclusions, and so on (see also Thonis, 1984).

Any negative transfer effects may need to be compensated for through instructional strategies. For example, speakers of Arabic often have problems distinguishing vowels in written English words because there is a lack of short vowel information in written Arabic; therefore, they are not accustomed to paying attention to them (Hayes-Harb, 2006).

Keep in mind, however, that knowledge gained in the content areas is always transferable across languages, regardless of the languages involved. See especially Dressler and Kamil (2006) for a very complete analysis of transfer issues.

Nonliterates who cannot master literacy skills in the first language for whatever reason can be introduced to the written form of their second language in much the same way that the other students are introduced to it, although more preliminary work may be necessary.

Nonliterate learners can first focus on the symbolic nature of language through such activities as role play (see Chapter 11) or game playing (see Chapter 12). In these activities, objects can be made to represent people or things. The symbols are arbitrary, just as the words on the printed page are arbitrary representations of concepts. In addition, nonliterate students may need considerable exposure to multisensory input to develop a rich visual and kinesthetic representational system before they can be eased into literacy. Experience with real books, charts, pictures to be labeled, maps, graphs, and actions associated eventually with written words (such as one finds in the physical activities in Chapter 8) can form important preliminary steps leading into literacy at any age.

Vocabulary Development

Although vocabulary development could have been subsumed by any one of the main skill areas, I have included it with reading because it is through reading that students, particularly those in academic settings, are exposed to the largest number of new lexical items. The number of familiar words needed for listening and speaking is generally lower than the number needed for both reading and writing (Nation, 2005).

Vocabulary can be learned both by intention and incidentally.[7] A vocabulary item, especially one learned incidentally from the context, generally is learned over time. Teachers should avoid expecting students to understand a word or use it upon first exposure. Even rote learning (repetition and memorization of lists), although it may produce excellent immediate results in testing situations, usually requires time and multiple exposures in order for the lexical items to become internalized. Rote learning can be quite effective for some learners, especially for those accustomed to learning this way (Yongqi Gu, 2003). Beginning students, in particular, can benefit from rote learning, glossing,[8] and translating into their first languages. Advanced learners appear to benefit more from inferencing and other implicit means (Carter, 2001). Successful vocabulary learners are generally motivated learners who tend to utilize a wide variety of strategies (both implicit and explicit), depending on their proficiency levels, preferences, the

---

[7] Hulstijn (2003) defined *intentional learning* as learning that "involves a deliberate attempt to commit new information to memory"; whereas *incidental learning* is a type of implicit learning that happens while the mind is focusing on something else; however, the individual is still paying attention at some level.

[8] *Glossing* here refers to a definition or an explanation of a term used in a text. It is usually found at the bottom of the page or in the margin.

situation, and the lexical items being learned. However, most vocabulary learning in another language appears to be implicit just as it is with L1 acquisition. Carter (2001) stated:

> We have not been taught the majority of words which we know. Beyond a certain level of proficiency in learning a language—and a second or foreign language in particular—vocabulary development is more likely to be mainly implicit or incidental. (p. 44)

However, Carter recommended that we not discourage explicit learning and that, in general, various kinds of knowledge about words can be acquired by different means. Knowing a vocabulary item can involve much more than people might think. Nation (2001, 2005) identified several aspects of knowing a vocabulary item:

1. know its form (how it is spelled, how it sounds, and what its parts consist of)
2. know its meaning (link form and meaning; know the concept it represents, what it refers to, and the other words often associated with it)
3. know how the word is used (the part of speech; the typical sentence patterns it fits into; what words it is typically used with [collocations]; whether it is formal or informal, polite or rude; who typically uses it; whether or not its use is restricted)

Corpus analysis (see p. 13) can be used to great advantage by teachers and students to determine many of these aspects of vocabulary knowledge. Corpora are particularly useful for identifying word collocations in authentic contexts and studying frequency of use in different types of situations and registers (Read, 2004).

Explicit teaching strategies such as helping students identify key words and discuss their meanings can play an important role for L2 students. However, context appears to be critical especially as a means for consolidating known knowledge in that it provides frequent exposure and allows students to develop the nuances of meaning in particular contexts (Nassaji, 2003).

Teaching Strategies for Developing Vocabulary

Teachers of L2 learners may want to consider the following strategies:

1. Suggest that beginning and low-intermediate students create word banks using index cards on which they write down the words and phrases they do not know the meaning of but that they think may be important (one word or phrase per index card). Have students write the definition of each in either the first or second language and write samples in which they are used in context in the second language on the back of each card. Use the cards for occasional self-drill or drill with a partner to see if the student can remember the definitions without looking at the back of the card. Test students on their words at regular intervals—perhaps once a week (see Richard-Amato, 1993b, 1998; Richard-Amato & Hansen, 1995). Encourage students to "chunk" the words with other words with which they are frequently used (Lewis, 1993). Vocabulary notebooks can serve a similar function and may be a preferred

means for vocabulary building, especially by intermediate to advanced students (Fowle, 2002).

2. In conjunction with item 1 above, stress the importance of using the word or phrase in an appropriate context shortly after the students have been exposed to it and have talked about it with peers or the teacher. Writing the word or phrase down, saying it to themselves, and associating it with known lexicon can be very effective (Sanaoui, 1995).

3. At first, try to focus students on high-frequency words (Lotto & de Groot, 1998; Zimmerman & Schmitt, 2005); later on lexical bundles of words that are used together in academic discourse (Eldridge, 2008). By knowing early on the basic list of 2,000 head words provided by Michael West (1953), Nation and Newton (1997) claimed that students will know 85 percent of the words on a given page for any subject matter (p. 238). Coxhead (2000) compiled a corpus from which she drew 570 word families frequently used in academic texts across subject areas. However, Hyland and Tse (2007) warned that word usage generally varies in different subject areas and that lexical items should be learned in context. Teachers mislead learners when they claim that there is a single word list that can be learned and used across the academic areas.

4. Whenever appropriate, give instruction in the use of *cognates* and partial cognates (words that have similar meaning in the first and second language—Lotto and de Groot (1998); Sunderman and Schwartz (2008). This way, students are more likely to experience some success early on.

5. Teach word families to increase rate of learning; teach commonly used word parts such as prefixes and suffixes (Nation, 2005) and show how they affect the meaning of words.

6. For beginners and low-intermediate students, select materials that include definitions in the margins (preferred) or at the bottoms of the pages on which the more difficult words or phrases are found (Jacobs, Dufon, & Fong, 1994). The inclusion of such help features are very effective and do not interfere with the flow of meaning (Nation, 2001).

7. Advise students to go beyond the word and notice the phrase, clause, sentence, and even the paragraph in which the word is used in order to better guess its meaning and then reconfirm the meaning from multiple clues (Nassaji, 2003).

8. Encourage intermediate and advanced students to use not only the context but a good dictionary to figure out the meaning of unfamiliar lexical items (Knight, 1994).

9. When teaching idiomatic expressions, always choose materials that contain authentic language in order to get a true representation of any given expression. The materials should include information on the expression's frequency of use, distribution, and variations (see D. Liu, 2003, including appendices). The best materials are corpus-based.

10. Begin academic vocabulary development as early as possible as part of mini-content lessons; these can serve as transitions to sheltered and mainstream content later.

11. Encourage lots of reading—extensive reading increases students' vocabulary dramatically (Eskey, 2005; Hu & Nation, 2000).

12. Use intensive reading selections that contain unfamiliar elements that learners can focus on through the preteaching of vocabulary items. Check to see if the materials include self-help features such as glossing, cultural notes, or strategy hints in the margins or at the bottoms of the pages.

13. Make sure vocabulary items are recycled throughout the materials with sufficient frequency. Vocabulary needs to recur often to be remembered (see also Hu & Nation, 2000).

14. Use simplified readers designed to recycle vocabulary for beginners especially (Nation, 2005).

15. Involve both deliberate attention to vocabulary learning and meaning-focused use (Nation, 2005).

16. Give students plenty of opportunity to talk about words and negotiate their meaning with you and/or peers (R. Ellis & He, 1999; Newton, 1995).

17. Provide for peer facilitating/tutoring of students who want additional help with vocabulary.

18. Have dictionaries available in both the target language and the first languages of your students to the extent possible. Training in dictionary use can be beneficial for receptive as well as productive vocabulary knowledge (Nation, 2005).

Reading as an Interactive Process

Many educators and researchers use the term *interactive* to describe the relationship between top-down and bottom-up processing within the individual reader (see especially Carrell, Devine, & Eskey, 1988; Eskey, 2005). One can also think of interactive reading in a different context—as a process during which meaning is created by the reader (see also Zamel, 1992), not only through interaction with the text but also through interaction with others in the class, school, community, and home.

The focus of the interactive model presented in Figure 5.1 is on the L2 reader: the reader's cultural expectations (schema) and values; identity and relationships; prior knowledge and experience; linguistic knowledge and reading proficiency in the first and second language; motivation and attitudes toward L2 learning; dreams and goals; and preconceived notions about the author, if he or she is already familiar to the reader. The L2 reader relates to the L2 text (whatever it might be), to literature of all kinds, to mass media (periodicals, journals, or popular magazines), and to the Internet, or to formal or informal written communication. Out of this relationship comes a preliminary interpretation, or a *created meaning*. This interpretation is accepted or rejected by the L2 reader either in part or as a whole, based on interaction with other readers in the home, at school, in the community, or beyond the immediate environment. If there appears to be a mismatch in interpretation, the L2 reader may return to the text to reread or to reanalyze and *re-create* the meaning. All the while, the student is internalizing skills, testing hypotheses about the meaning, adjusting expectations, and reevaluating preconceived ideas, as well as reaching increasingly higher levels of understanding.

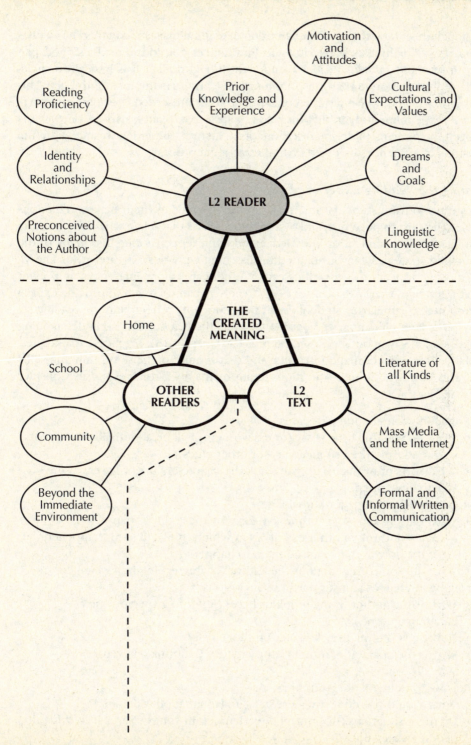

Figure 5.1 Reading as an Interactive Process

Although the interactive conceptualization of reading presented in this chapter has elements of psycholinguistics (psychological influences within the reader's mind, particularly in respect to the L2 Reader component in Figure 5.1), it is basically a sociolinguistic representation in that the community of learners is the main influence. This is also true of the interactive writing conceptualization presented later. Both representations are very rudimentary in that they do not seek to explain how the components work together (perhaps their greatest limitation). Instead, they identify and show the relationships of influences involved in an interactional process.

Facilitating the Reading Experience

Teachers can motivate students of almost any age by having them make predictions about what they are going to read and by asking questions that relate what they are reading to their own lives and prior knowledge and experience (notice that many of the same teaching strategies can be adapted for listening activities). Greater prior knowledge of a topic appears to cause the reader to generate more inferences and fewer incorrect inferences (Barry & Lazarte, 1998). Teachers can do much to provide experiences designed to familiarize students with new concepts reflected in the reading selections. In the later elementary grades and beyond, the teacher can aid understanding by helping students map out ideas (see examples in Chapter 13). Teachers can ask questions that call for reflection and inference and that require higher-level thinking skills and self-reflection, in addition to questions requiring mainly factual responses. Consider the following list:

1. Predicting content and outcomes
   - What do you think the story (or essay, poem) will be about? (Refer students to the title, pictures, subheadings, or other clues.)
   - What sorts of problems do you think the characters might have?
   - What will happen?
2. Relating the text to prior knowledge
   - What reasons does the author give for why these things happened?
     — Can you think of other examples in which things like this happened?
     — What do you think caused them to happen?
   - What are some other actions the author (character) might have taken?
3. Making inferences and supporting conclusions
   - What is the author trying to tell us here? (Refer to a specific line, paragraph, event.)
   - How do you think the character (author) feels?
   - Why is the character (author) happy (angry, doubtful, relieved)?
   - Why do you think so?
4. Relating to self and one's culture
   - What would you do if you were in a similar situation (dilemma)?
   - Do these situations (dilemmas) often happen in your culture? If so, what do people usually do?
   - How does this event (fact, opinion) make you angry (glad, fearful)? Why?

Students can also be asked about organizational strategies and patterns, use of literary devices, and whatever else is appropriate to the situation—or they can be asked to generate questions of their own.

Small-group discussions of readings allow students to share ideas within their own classroom community and test their own hypotheses about what they are reading (see the Other Readers component in Figure 5.1). Because other readers bring to the discussion their own values, prior knowledge, and so on, group discussions can be very potent in an interactive reading process.

See Chapter 13, which offers specific teaching strategies in the three commonly recognized phases of reading: prereading, reading, and postreading. Chapter 13 also includes an in-depth look at ways to promote literacy development at all levels of proficiency development—beginning through advanced.

Other Strategies for Teaching Reading Skills

1. Model the reading process by reading aloud to students and verbalizing the strategies used as you make sense of the text through questioning, clarifying, predicting, and summarizing in a sort of think-aloud protocol (Biancarosa & C. Snow, 2006).
2. Identify and teach key terms and concepts necessary to the comprehension of a specific reading. Include commonly used vocabulary, academic concepts used across subject areas, and items critical to the reading at hand (Richard-Amato & M. A. Snow, 2005b, p. 215; Stevens, Butler, & Castellon-Wellington, 2000).
3. Emphasize the importance of looking for organizational markers that indicate transitions from one idea to the next, clarify relationships among ideas, and assign the relative importance of ideas to the topic. Such markers make readers aware of the overall structure of the presentation, aid comprehension, and help them recall the relevant information (see Jung, 2003).
4. Teach students to take advantage of ancillary learning aids such as prereading questions, graphics, glossing, and cultural notes (Richard-Amato & M. A. Snow, 2005b).
5. Reading rate (in addition to comprehension) is important to reading fluency. Have students practice using a variety of materials with which they are already familiar and which are a little bit below their current reading level (Anderson, 2008). Anderson recommends that the goal for most students be about 200 words per minute with 70 percent comprehension at intermediate and advanced levels. He cautions, however, that not everything students read needs to be read at the same rate. The rate will be influenced by the type of material that is being read and the purpose of the reading task. To prevent needless anxiety, tell students not to worry about comprehension when they are first trying to improve reading rates.
6. Provide for peer facilitating/tutoring of students who want additional help with reading.
7. Whenever possible, have the students self-evaluate. See the sample form on pp. 191–192.

8. Make sure that a wide variety of texts are made available to students. Different genres, diverse topics and purposes, a wide range of levels, various cultural orientations, and so on should be represented. Discuss with students the kinds of rhetorical features used in the different types of texts.

9. Help students to identify the text structure typical of the various genre and the way(s) in which a particular text they are reading may differ (Lenski & Ehlers-Zavala, 2004).

10. Provide plenty of time for sustained silent reading (Cho, 2004) and for extensive reading for pleasure (Lee, 2004).

11. Develop a facility where students have access to technology that allows them to practice their reading skills and learn new ones.

12. Develop a community of readers in the classroom. Give students the opportunity to discuss books in small groups or pairs, share books, recommend books, and so on.

13. Advocate biliteracy whenever possible (Grant & Wong, 2003). Students who can function academically in more than one language and culture have many advantages personally and professionally.

14. Strive to change testing practices that place L2 readers at a disadvantage (Grant & Wong, 2003). Students must achieve a certain level of academic reading proficiency in their new language before they can be fairly evaluated using tests intended for native speakers. According to Cummins (1981a, 1984, 1989), it takes around five to seven years to become academically proficient. (See also Chapter 7.)

Materials for Interactive Reading

Teachers can choose materials (see the text component in Figure 5.1) that are interesting and comprehensible, both semantically and syntactically, and that include some elements slightly beyond the students' present levels. (For more ideas on materials selection, see Chapter 16.) Students can be encouraged to select their own materials for independent reading and for small-group participation.

Writing

Like reading, writing is an interactive process, involving three basic components (see Figure 5.2). The L2 writer (like the reader) can bring to the process his or her own cultural expectations (schema) and values, identity and relationships, prior knowledge and experience, linguistic knowledge and writing proficiency in the first and second language, motivation and attitudes toward L2 learning, and dreams and goals. However, the writer also considers one additional category: the audience. Writers, like speakers, anticipate the possible reactions and so on of those who will read and create meaning out of what is produced.

In addition, the interactive process of writing can include other writers (and readers) at home, in school (mainly the teacher and peers, some of whom will probably be more advanced), and in the community and beyond. Good writers often consult or conference with other writers to ask for their reactions, comments, and suggestions.

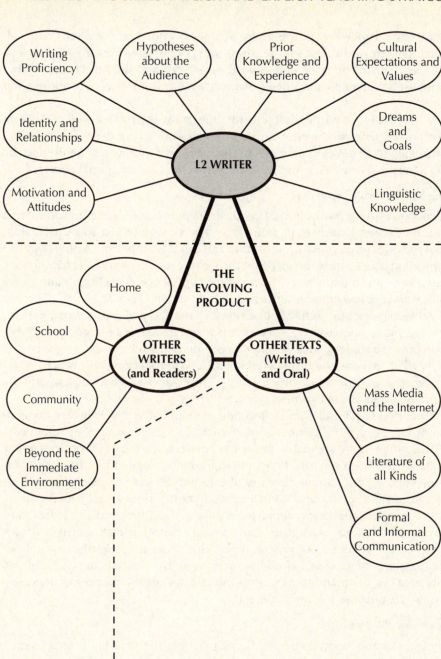

Figure 5.2 Writing as an Interactive Process

The interactive process of writing also includes other texts, written and oral: literature, including stories, drama, essays, novels, and poems; mass media, such as television, newspapers, movies, journals, and popular magazines; and the Internet, as well as formal and informal communication, items that can serve as both sources of information and models.

Because the process of writing is interactive, the evolving product does not belong solely to the person who produced it; rather it belongs in varying degrees to all influences contributing to its development and to the reader who ultimately determines its meaning on a personal level. Thus the product truly reflects a communal effort.

Facilitating the Writing Experience

When students are writing, motivation can come from numerous sources in second and foreign language classes. Experiences with music, poetry, storytelling, role-play, drama, and affective activities often provide motivation and can lead into some highly relevant, exciting topics and issues. Students can begin the writing process with a certain amount of confidence, which can come in part from their experience coauthoring and exposure to other strategies and activities mentioned here and in Chapter 13.

The writing itself can be somewhat personal (letters to pen pals, journal entries, poetry) or more impersonal (lists of various kinds, forms to be filled out, compositions). The kinds of writing a student does depends largely on that student's age, cognitive development, needs, concerns, and proficiency level. However, it is generally best to begin with short pieces of writing before proceeding to longer ones and with description before going on to narrative and expository genres.

L2 writers often require explicit instruction in grammar and vocabulary, depending on the academic writing demands of particular content areas (see especially Chapter 17). Although there are many similarities between learning to write in the first and second language, Frodesen (2001) reminded us that to assume that L2 instruction should be the same as L1 instruction is a mistake. L2 writers have needs that should be specifically addressed. They should be encouraged to notice through reading the structures and discourse features that writers typically use in the different content areas and genres of writing. What kinds of language forms and phrases are used in e-mail messages as opposed to academic reports of various types? How does the language of a journal entry differ from that of an essay? How does a comparative analysis in science differ linguistically from one in literature? L2 writers can also discuss the purpose of a specific piece and how this purpose has been realized.

The Process and the Product

In most writing, students concentrate on the process and the evolving product simultaneously. Murray (1982) explained very early on, "You let the students write.... Writing must be experienced to be learned" (pp. 115–116). The writing process itself involves:

- brainstorming for topics of interest and discussing them with others
- gathering information
- allowing that information to settle into some sort of overall plan (clustering and other graphic organizers might be useful in planning—see Chapters 9 and 13)

- putting the words down on paper
- consulting with others
- revising

Revisions can be particularly important to the writing process. According to Murray (1982), they provide opportunities for the student to "stand back from the work the way any craftsman does to see what has been done. . . . The most important discoveries are made during the process of revision" (pp. 121–122). Because the effective writer frequently pauses, goes back, rereads, rethinks, consults with other writers, rewrites, and writes some more, he or she must be able to concentrate intensely on the composition without interference from the teacher or others who might want to help.

Students may need help before the actual writing begins in order to stimulate thinking and again later, once they have had a chance to hammer out at least part of the piece alone. At that point, students may want to confer with the teacher and/or peers as needed. What points are coming across clearly? What portions are not readily understood? The listener or reader may ask questions or suggest strategies to help. Students then appear to need time to reshape the writing to better communicate what was intended or to move in other directions. Dialoguing with other writers, especially peers, can generate a great deal of enthusiasm for the writing process and can motivate thoughts and feelings that might otherwise remain unexplored. However, having sample products from previous classes for students to look at and analyze can be very helpful for all language learners, even though they want their products to reflect their own individuality.

Focusing mainly on the product also can have benefits, especially for learners who are used to such a focus in their first cultures. Many feel more comfortable with and prefer product-focused and form-oriented learning (see also Canagarajah, 2005). In addition, some students may feel self-conscious about sharing their work with others before they are finished, and, even then, they may want to share it only with the teacher.

Teacher as Model

The teacher can sometimes serve as an effective model for the writing process. Modeling allows students to experience vicariously the frustrations and joys that go into writing and at the same time be exposed to the teacher's own strategies and the forms and conventions of various types of composition. For example, watching the teacher execute a well-developed paragraph on the board or on a transparency can be highly motivating as well as instructive. The teacher can choose a topic or issue to write about (the students may want to make suggestions), brainstorm for ideas, map out a brief preliminary plan, begin a first draft, provide transitions, erase, move materials, modify, consult with the students, rewrite, and use the dictionary. If the teacher does his or her thinking out loud during the process, the students more fully realize that even the teacher has to struggle to communicate. At more advanced levels, the teacher may even want to share previous efforts at writing; analyzing drafts written at different stages of the composition process can be very helpful to developing L2 writers.

Approaching Errors in Written Production

The most effective way to deal with errors may often be an inductive approach—simply underlining or circling the word or phrase in which a problem appears and asking the student to try to identify the error (see also Ferris, 2002). Teachers can guide students to identify errors tied to meaning by asking pertinent questions. In responding to errors in verb tense, for example, the teacher might simply ask, "*When* did this occur?" Often students will recognize the errors themselves, without any lengthy explanation or further probing. Reading pieces aloud in individual conference sessions often makes errors more salient.

At such times, teachers can provide brief explanations to lead students to a better understanding of their errors. At the same time, students can be reminded that errors are perfectly normal during the writing process. Errors can be treated in a matter-of-fact way so that the students do not associate them with the quality of the ideas themselves. In addition, it may be best not to focus on too many errors at once but to point out patterns or prioritize so that students understand the most important problems in their writing. Much depends on what students might be ready for at any given time. For some students, specific activities on recurring errors might help; for others, rewriting and a simple discussion of strategies may be enough to help them improve their writing.

Error correction may sometimes be handled indirectly in writing just as it is with oral production. For example, after students hand in their journals, instead of marking the errors, the teacher may simply react to the entry by repeating the words that the student has used but in the form of a recast in the margin. Thus the teacher's comment serves as a reformulation. For example, if the student writes "On Tuesday my mother sick," the teacher might respond with "I'm sorry your mother was sick." This particular type of correction strategy often comes naturally to a teacher focused on meaning and may work well, especially with reluctant writers who are just beginning literacy development in their new language and need encouragement.

Although most researchers agree that the written modality is highly conducive to a focus on form (e.g., Qi & Lapkin, 2001; Swain, 1998), research on feedback types has produced mixed results. In the study by Qi and Lapkin, the researchers asked two Mandarin speakers learning English to write a description of a picture, compare it with a reformulated draft, and then revise their description; all the while, the learners were expected to reveal their depth of understanding of the mismatches through a think-aloud procedure. Although the completeness and accuracy of think-alouds have been questioned in the literature (see Sachs & Polio, 2007), Qi and Lapkin concluded that the deeper the thinking during the think-alouds, the greater the improvement during the revision process. They argued that reformulation can indeed lead to higher-quality thinking than does the direct error correction condition and therefore may be more helpful to learning. However, Sachs and Polio (2007), in their two studies of English learners, found opposite results. Although reformulations were helpful, error corrections made in purple ink on student's papers (anathema to many teachers' sensibilities) produced the most accurate short-term revisions. Poststudy debriefings, however, caused them to question their findings and conclude that when comparing feedback strategies, long-term outcomes need to be carefully examined. In fact, they warned that their study should not be used as support for claims that the direct error correction condition is most effective in the long term (p. 87). See Chapter 13 for additional strategies and research.

With writers who are at higher proficiency levels, error correction should not just be a matter of conducting what Frodesen and Holten (2003) referred to simply as an "error repair shop." They recommended that teachers combine error correction with lessons on the way in which language and the structure of the discourse intersect. As an example, they pointed to the way in which modal verbs can be used to hedge in argumentative writing. Teachers, too, may want to preteach some structures, not as a response to errors but rather as a model of syntax. Some genres lend themselves to certain structures better than others. Pointing out forms in sample compositions that are typical of certain genres (e.g., a contrastive paper, summary, narration) and having students practice using them could be very beneficial.

Portfolios

Many teachers find it a useful teaching strategy to have students save their work in portfolios so that all concerned can keep abreast of the progress taking place (see pp. 188–189 for more information on portfolios). In periodic evaluative conferences, teachers and students can talk about progress made, strengths observed, and possible future areas of work (see example on pp. 189–190). Students often find such conferences both informative and encouraging.

Additional teaching strategies for writing are presented here. Also refer to Chapter 13 for ways to promote development in writing skills at all levels of proficiency development—beginning through advanced.

Other Teaching Strategies to Facilitate the Writing Process

1. Develop a community of writers in the classroom (see also Collins, 2001). Give students the opportunity to coconstruct products including essays, dramas, stories, poetry, and so on. Computers can be used for coauthoring, commenting on each other's work, dialoguing with the teacher, having written discussions about topics of interest, collaboratively problem solving, and so forth.
2. Provide prompts for beginning learners in their new language (e.g., "On _____ our class visited _____."). Students fill in the blanks. See Gibbons (2005, p. 294).
3. Provide for peer facilitating/tutoring of learners who want additional help with writing. (See Chapter 15.)
4. Give learners opportunities to write about what they are reading (see ideas in Chapter 13).
5. Provide models of quality written work. Such examples can come from former students and can be used anonymously or with permission (Ferris, 2002; Richard-Amato & M. A. Snow, 2005b).
6. Teach the traditional conventions of certain text types, but allow students the freedom to manipulate them according to their own purposes (Gibbons, 2005).
7. Teach students how to use figurative language to clarify meaning and to make their writing more vibrant (Lazar, 2003).

8. Encourage pretask planning for written narratives. Such practice can result in increased fluency (as measured by syllables per minute) and greater syntactic variety (as measured by number of different verb forms used; R. Ellis & Yuan, 2004). Interestingly, in their study R. Ellis and Yuan did not find similar effects for accuracy (see item 11 below for a teaching strategy promoting accuracy).

9. Give students tools for organizing ideas before they write (e.g., graphic organizers or note-taking formats). See Buell and Whittaker (2005).

10. Allow for incubation periods during which students are involved in unrelated activities that do not require deep thought (Krashen, 2001). For example, providing calming background music while students are writing gives them a chance to relax quietly when the situation calls for it and lets ideas incubate for a while before the students are ready to move ahead with them.

11. Avoid putting time pressure on students while they are writing; give them ample time to formulate ideas and to monitor what they are writing, using what R. Ellis referred to as "portable" rules. Such practice can result in greater accuracy (measured by error-free clauses; R. Ellis & Yuan 2004).

12. Although students need due dates, allow them plenty of time to finish written assignments, extending the deadline in some cases (Richard-Amato & M. A. Snow, 2005b).

13. Ask students to rewrite portions of a given selection from a different perspective, or have them rewrite selections from a different point of view (e.g., third-person to first-person or vice versa). Yet another task is to ask more advanced students to rewrite a selection in a different register (Reid, 2001).

14. Give formative teacher feedback. Strategies for improvement while students are working on their papers are generally more effective than giving only summative evaluations on the end product (Black & Wiliam, 1998).

15. Ask students to write marginal annotations to you in their first drafts. In the annotations students can express their composition concerns and questions as they develop their papers (e.g., "Is there a better way to say this?" "Is this clear?" "Is this word appropriate here?" "Should this argument be part of the next paragraph instead?"). Then respond in writing (Creswell, 2000).

16. Allow for peer feedback frequently once students have been given guidelines on how to participate effectively in peer-to-peer sessions (Tsui & Ng, 2000). See p. 328 in Chapter 13 for sample guidelines.

17. Establish staggered deadlines for different stages of product development (e.g., a list of sources, notes based on what was learned from the sources, a graphic organizer containing key ideas and their relationship to each other). See Buell and Whittaker (2005).

18. Whenever possible have students self-evaluate. See sample form on p. 193.

19. If plagiarism appears to be a problem with a particular student or group of students, approach it with sensitivity. Explain that, in the present culture, plagiarism is not acceptable, although it can be very tempting for some students; remind them that in other cultures where community ownership is the norm, it may indeed be acceptable (Flowerdew & Li, 2007). Teach

students alternative ways for incorporating sources (i.e., quoting and/or paraphrasing from sources; see also p. 404).

20. To help facilitate item 1 above, create a workspace where students have access to word-processing programs so they can practice their writing skills and learn new ones (see pp. 402–403). Programs abound that allow students to network among themselves or with others around the world. Corpus data can also be accessed to explore organizational patterns and collocations of words and rhetorical structures that are common to the various genres.

CRITICAL LITERACY

Critical literacy is a way to discover how societies perpetuate and protect the values of their most powerful members. Moreover, it can examine how such power might be shared with those who may have found themselves marginalized. Critical literacy appears to go beyond mere tolerance and a celebration of differences. At its best, it can include multiple literacies and point to ways in which marginalized groups in a given society may gain influence. Students can use the acts of reading and writing to gain a better understanding of their own lives and situations and how they can work to make them better (Freire, 1970b).

Some critical pedagogues argue that rigid forms such as those found in a genre approach to teaching literacy should be avoided. Luke (1996), for example, feels that such forms tend to promote and maintain the injustices inherent in the existing power structures. However, others see a genre approach as a means to penetrate the system, discover what it is all about, and eventually effect change for the better (see Martin, 1993; Richard-Amato, 1996a; Wallace, 1992). Knowing about the various genres and how they are structured makes critical analysis possible. Wells (1999) also stressed the importance of knowing what he called the "genres of power." He urged teachers to give students "every assistance in appropriating them so that they can participate fully in the activities in which they are used" (p. 143).

Hammon and Macken-Horarik (1999) agreed. Based on their research with Australian English as a second language of primary and secondary students, they reported that students should be engaged in a study of textual and cultural practices. They believe that:

> Such engagement includes an awareness of alphabetic codes, comprehension of texts, recognition of the cultural significance of specific genres, the ability to construct well-formed and cohesive texts, and the ability to undertake reflexive and critical analysis of texts.... They [the learners] cannot be expected to run before they can walk. (p. 531)

The authors cautioned, however, that critical literacy should not be treated as an add-on saved only for students operating at advanced levels. Students early on need to make progress toward meeting the goals of the mainstream curriculum so that they can be in a better position to deconstruct on their own terms what they are reading and learning.

Just as teachers in preparation can benefit from having a disciplinary knowledge base to develop a critical perspective on the teaching process (see p. 9), so can their language students benefit from such a base to effect change. In addition, they may be able to develop the metalinguistic strategies necessary to approach literature critically and become successful learners.

Pennycook (1996) perhaps summed it up best by merging the various versions of critical literacy. From his perspective, critical literacy:

> emphasizes the need (a) to view language education as a practice in reading the world; (b) to understand the changing face of that world, especially in terms of shifting media literacies; (c) to link language education to questions of gender, ethnicity, inequality, class, race, and so forth; (d) to consider how the needs to understand, acknowledge, and incorporate student difference and diversity can be taken seriously; and (e) to help develop abilities and awarenesses in our students that enable them to reflect critically on the word and the world. (p. 170)

SUMMARY

An integrated approach to developing skills in a new language can be dynamic and exciting in a natural classroom environment, especially if both explicit and implicit teaching strategies for listening, speaking, reading, and writing and related strategies are used to enhance the learning process.

A balance between implicit and explicit teaching strategies is important to the L2 learner. Deciding which to incorporate at any given time can depend on several factors: immediate needs of the learner; the learner's age and approximate cognitive development; proficiency levels in the second language; interests, goals, and aspirations; communication needs; and academic requirements. Many of the traditional experimental studies accomplished thus far have been for the most part short-term and have, therefore, tended to be biased in favor of explicit teaching and learning. The effects of implicit teaching and learning generally take a longer time to become fully realized and require multiple exposures within a variety of contexts. Unfortunately, sociocultural and affective influences have not been defined and studied yet to any great extent.

Error correction can be direct, indirect, or somewhere in between. In any case, it should go beyond a unit-by-unit, sentence-by-sentence, word-by-word analysis whenever possible. Recasting or reformulations of ungrammatical forms (see pp. 50–51) through the relevant communication is one way to provide indirect correction and can be particularly effective with reluctant language learners—writers as well as speakers. This way, the interaction itself serves as a scaffold on which students can build as they move progressively to more advanced levels of proficiency.

It is important to remember, too, that reading and writing are both interactional processes. Out of the interacting components comes the created meaning (in the case of reading) and the evolving product (in the case of writing).

Critical literacy can be viewed in a more narrow sense (acquiring strategies and skills needed to analyze critically) or in a broader sense (understanding change in the world and how it comes about, associating the teaching of language to issues of personal relevance and concern, increasing awareness, and so forth). Both views can be very important to the emerging individual and collective empowerment of the L2 student within the cultural environment.

QUESTIONS AND PROJECTS FOR REFLECTION AND DISCUSSION

1. What do you think Goodman means by "easy" and "hard" when he refers to language development (pp. 131–132)? To what extent do you agree with his conclusions?

2. How should discrete points of language (e.g., spelling, sounding out consonant clusters, punctuation, rules, and so on) be handled within a natural classroom environment? What does this book recommend? What is your view?

3. Not all the teaching strategies found in this chapter are appropriate for all situations. Choose two or three teaching strategies from this chapter and explain how each might be appropriate for some specific teaching situations but not for others. Give examples.

4. Visit a language classroom in your area on two or more occasions. Describe some of the strategies the teacher uses to help students develop in various skill areas. Observe how the students respond. To what extent do you think the strategies were effective? Make sure you obtain the permission of the school administration and the teacher prior to your observations. Discuss your findings with a small group of peers. What did you learn about teaching and learning from this experience?

5. Create your own diagrams that show how you might conceptualize listening and speaking processes. Discuss them with a small group. Can you improve them in any way based on your group's feedback? Then look at the diagrams for reading and writing in this chapter. Are there any ways you would change them? Discuss with a small group and your class.

6. How important do you think it is for students and teachers to be exposed to text and discourse that presents views that challenge those to which we are typically exposed? How can critical literacy help in this endeavor? How can it be incorporated effectively into classroom activity?

7. ✎ **Journal Entry:** Now that you have read this chapter, create your own list of teaching strategies concerning the teaching of two or more of the following

skills: listening, speaking, pronunciation, reading, vocabulary development, writing. Draw from this chapter, your own experience and prior knowledge, and what you have learned from your instructor and/or your peers. Consider how the teaching strategies might differ for teaching a second language as opposed to teaching a first language and how they might be similar.

SUGGESTED READINGS AND REFERENCE MATERIALS

Bailey, K. (2005). *Practical English language teaching: Speaking*. New York: McGraw-Hill. This easy-to-read book offers teachers, especially those new to the field of English language teaching, a comprehensive view of speaking and what it entails. It contains chapters devoted to the different oral proficiency levels: beginning, intermediate, and advanced. Tasks are presented that are appropriate to each level.

Celce-Murcia, M., Brinton, D., & Goodwin, J. (forthcoming). *Teaching pronunciation: A Course Book and Reference Guide*. New York: Cambridge University Press. This very comprehensive volume presents a description of the sound system of North American English and perspectives on pronunciation pedagogy including theory and practice. Various tools for assessment and exercises to help teachers create communicative activities are also included.

Chen, K. (2005). Preferences, styles, behavior: The composing processes of four ESL students. *The CATESOL, 17*(1), 19–37. This article describes a study that examined the writing-strategy preferences and habits of English learners in a basic writing class at San Francisco State University. The author concludes that due to differences in composing style and process management in individuals, "one-size-fits-all" guidelines may not be in the best interests of the students in an English learners composition setting. Implications for teachers are considered.

Cleghorn, A., & Rollnick, M. (2002). The role of English in individual and societal development: A view from African classrooms. *TESOL Quarterly, 36*(3), 347–372. Although this important article is based on African classrooms, it has much to tell us about code switching, especially in classrooms in which the students and the teacher share the local language and culture. It is the authors' conviction that code switching has been unfairly treated by assimilationists who may consider the home language to be inferior to the target language. The authors argue that code switching can indeed be a useful tool to help students clarify linguistic and cultural misunderstandings and misinterpretations, share beliefs, and raise metalinguistic awareness in meaningful learning environments.

Edelsky, C. (2006). *With literacy and justice for all: Rethinking the social in language and education* (3rd ed.). Mahwah, NJ: Lawrence Erlbaum. In this edition Edelsky offers her most recent philosophy concerning a holistic approach to teaching literacy that takes into consideration important sociocultural, political, historical, and situational factors. Many of her insights have been heavily influenced by practices associated with critical pedagogy and bilingual education.

Ferris, D. (2002). *Treatment of error in second language student writing* (The Michigan Series on Teaching Multilingual Writers). Ann Arbor: University of Michigan Press. This highly readable book presents a guide to making decisions about error treatment and includes many examples from texts. The author discusses issues that teachers often wonder about involving such topics as when and how to correct and the importance of error treatment in the writing process.

Flowerdew, J., & Miller, L. (2004). *Second language listening: Theory and practice.* New York: Cambridge University Press. The authors present state-of-the-art listening theory and practice, including theoretical models, computer applications, and assessment of listening skills. Also included are case studies highlighting classroom practice.

Freeman, D. E., & Freeman, Y. S. (2004). *Essential linguistics: What you need to know to teach reading, English as a second language, spelling, phonics, and grammar.* Portsmouth, NH: Heineman. The aim of this text is to explore how English works and to expose language teachers to the important linguistic concepts necessary to making decisions about what and how to teach skills in language classrooms. The authors present numerous examples and sample activities.

Kroll, B. (2003). *Exploring the dynamics of second language writing*. New York: Cambridge University Press. Presented in this anthology are thirteen chapters by scholars in applied linguistics, all focusing on various aspects of teaching academic writing to L2 learners at colleges and universities. Included are Charlene Polio, Dana Ferris, Jan Frodesen, Christine Holten, Liz Hamp-Lyons, Ann Johns, Ulla Connor, Ilona Leki, and several more. The text is intended for new and continuing teachers and researchers.

Nation, I. S. P. (2001). *Learning vocabulary in another language*. Cambridge, England: Cambridge University Press. This text is a valuable and practical teacher and learner resource on vocabulary development based on an analysis of the research and the author's own teaching experience. The author recommends a systematic approach to vocabulary building, which, he feels, serves learners well.

CHAPTER 6

The Affective Domain

If we were to devise theories of second language acquisition or teaching methods which were based only on cognitive considerations, we would be omitting the most fundamental side of human behavior.

H. D. Brown, 1987

QUESTIONS TO THINK ABOUT

1. Think about your own experiences while studying another language. To what extent did the following help or hinder your success: (a) attitude, (b) motivation, (c) anxiety?

2. What did you and/or your teacher do to lessen your anxiety, increase your motivation, and maintain or improve your attitude? How effective were these strategies?

3. What can you do as a second language teacher to improve the overall affective environment to make your classroom a positive place in which to learn? If you have taught or are currently teaching, which of these strategies have you already tried? What happened?

4. In what ways can stereotypical notions about students from other cultures negatively affect how teachers interact with them? Has a teacher or someone else ever revealed through words or actions a stereotypical notion about you? Tell about the experience. How did it make you feel? Can stereotypical notions about others be avoided? If so, how?

The affective domain includes several variables that can either enhance second language learning or hinder it depending on the context in which they are operating, whether they are positive or negative, the degree to which they are present, and the combinations in which they are found.

Because these variables are difficult to isolate and are often so subtle they can scarcely be detected, studying them objectively as we have tried to do with our current methods seems almost impossible. How does one effectively measure inhibition, for example? or empathy? or attitudes, for that matter? All of these intangible concepts interact with the situational context to form changing patterns that usually operate out of the subconscious. We do know that factors or combinations of factors having to do with *attitudes*, *motivation*, and *level of anxiety* are central to the affective domain. These are strongly influenced by the process of *acculturation*, including the mercurial nature of identity itself, and by certain *personality* variables.

ATTITUDES

The first factor central to the affective domain is attitude. Attitudes develop as a result of experience, both direct and vicarious. They are greatly affected by people in the immediate situational context: parents, teachers, and peers. Attitudes toward self, the target language and the people who speak it (peers in particular), the teacher, and the classroom environment all seem to have an influence on learning. Often the attitudes in one area influence attitudes in other areas. For example, Lucas, Henze, and Donato (1990) found that students' good relationships with and positive attitudes toward their teachers promoted positive attitudes toward school and themselves.

Attitude toward Self

Adelaide Heyde (1979) looked at the effects of three levels of self-esteem—global, specific (situational), and task—on the oral performance of American college students studying French as a foreign language. She found that students with high self-esteem at all levels performed better in the language they were studying. Other early studies have resulted in similar conclusions (Heyde, 1977; Oller, Hudson, & Liu, 1977). In general, successful language learners appear to have higher self-esteem than those who are unsuccessful (Price, 1991).

Most people would probably agree that high self-esteem usually leads to greater self-confidence. But a student may have high global self-esteem and at the same time experience low self-esteem in second language learning environments (Scarcella & Oxford, 1992). Moreover, the degree of self-esteem and/or self-confidence may vary from situation to situation or from task to task. Both may increase as one performs well in a variety of situations. Oller (1981) argued that the relationship between affect and learning is probably bidirectional: We may perform well because our attitude toward self is positive; we may have a positive attitude toward self because we perform well (see also Gardner, Lalonde, & Moorcroft, 1985).

Stevick (1976) emphasized the significance of *self-security*, an important facet of the attitude toward self. "Am I what I would like to be as an intellectual being and also as a social being? Do I have an adequate mind, and am I the kind of person that other people are willing to spend time with?" (p. 229). If the answer to these questions is affirmative, then the individual may be better able to engage in the often humbling process of acquiring a second language.

In emergent participatory classrooms, identity becomes an integral part of the negotiating process but does not always develop smoothly. Based on a multiple case study at a Canadian university, Morita (2004) concluded that

> co-construction of learner agency and positionality is not always a peaceful, collaborative process, but is often a struggle involving a web of power relations and competing agendas. . . . [Learners] use resources and strategies that they have developed in their lives to position themselves favorably. (p. 597)

Morita went on to say that students frequently struggled against identities that were ascribed to them by their instructors and in some cases were further marginalized by them. Yet at times instructors helped students take on more empowered roles in the socialization process.

Morita offered several suggestions for instructors:

1. increase transparency by assisting students to comprehend class discussions
2. explain the purpose of discussion and provide cultural and background information
3. summarize discussion periodically
4. intervene in turn-taking to make sure students get a chance to participate both in small-group and whole-class discussion
5. take advantage of students' perspectives and knowledge by choosing topics that will bring them out both in discussion and during presentations
6. use different types of activities to encourage students with a variety of communicative styles

Thus students are in the best possible position to gain confidence in themselves as intelligent, knowledgeable, and influential persons who have agency within the classroom community.

Attitude toward the Target Language and the People Who Speak It

The attitudes that an individual has toward the target language and the target group (especially peers) seem to have a substantial effect on motivation in particular. Here the stereotyping to which the students have been subjected often plays a large role in determining their own attitudes toward the language they are learning and the people who speak it. Cummins (1997) was convinced that stereotypical labels frequently reflect the power relationships within society as a whole (see also Yep, 2000). Persons from other cultures are often thought of as the deficient and disadvantaged *other* (as opposed to the more normal and enlightened *self*).

Using different terms, Saville-Troike (1976) much earlier reported that the *in-group* (represented by the self) often values characteristics that the *out-group* (represented by the other) is perceived to be lacking—for example, intelligence, cleanliness, human (as opposed to animal) traits, independence, appropriate behaviors concerning time, and the like. A major effect of stereotyping based on race, gender,[1] culture of origin, and so on is to create or perpetuate social distance and social boundaries. Saville-Troike argued that stereotypes build social barriers that are detrimental to one's self-image as a learner.

Similarly, Harklau's (2000) ethnographic study of English-learner identity found that the same students who were once considered exemplary in high school were labeled "difficult" and "underachieving" in their college English as a Second Language (ESL) classes. The change in the students' attitudes due to the different treatment was dramatic. These once determined, hard-working individuals eventually became ill-behaved and combative, and some dropped their ESL program altogether, even though they still felt the need for it.

When negative stereotypes are attributed to second language students in any situation, they may become *internalized* and can undermine attempts at language learning. Not only do negative stereotypes affect the self-esteem of second language students, but they often engender negative reactions and attitudes toward the target language and culture, which generally considers itself to be "the ideal." Students everywhere who are considered linguistically and culturally deficient or disadvantaged because they have a different first language and culture are at serious risk. Their self-esteem is in jeopardy if their teacher and peers fail to show respect for them, their first language, and their culture. If we expect language and cultural minorities to do all the accommodating and fail to reach out to students and meet them where they are, then many of our best minds will be doomed to failure in our school systems and in our society.

Although we may think we have enough evidence to generalize about a society as a whole—even when our conclusions are positive—care should be taken not to label individuals within that society who may or may not fit our stereotypical notions (see Kubota, 1999, 2001, 2004b; Yep, 2000). Persons from all cultures need to be treated as individuals with varying ways of behaving. Kubota (2004b), in particular, challenged the notion that cultural differences are normative or fixed, as those in power might want us to believe. Rather, stereotypical notions are relative and

> shaped by various discourses that serve different political aims. . . . In supporting or rejecting cultural difference or similarity, we need to ask questions such as: Who benefits? Who is oppressed? What concepts are resisted? What ideas are promoted? What are the social, educational, and political outcomes? In interpreting, appropriating, or even critiquing the notion of cultural difference, we need to recognize the political nature of our action as well as the potential consequences. (p. 37)

---

[1] According to Schmenk (2004), gender stereotyping is very prevalent in societies and is sometimes unintentional. She believes that such stereotyping is a discursive construction and that it can affect language learners, especially because language learning is considered by many to be a "feminine domain." See also Eckert and McConnell-Ginet (2003) for a sociocultural perspective on gender issues as they relate to language.

Attitudes toward the Teacher and the Classroom Environment

In classrooms in which mutual respect is lacking, differing values can lead to conflicts between student and teacher and between student and peers. A student who works closely together with another student to complete a project may be perceived as "cheating"; a student who does not guess on the true/false section of a test may be perceived as not caring. In reality, the first student may simply not value competition in completing a task, and the second may not feel comfortable guessing without knowing the answer.

Scarcella (1990) addressed the issue of communication breakdowns and how to help students overcome them. She recommended the following:

- Encourage the development of friendships.
- Emphasize commonalities.
- Create a place in which the experiences, capacities, interests, and goals of every classroom member are simultaneously utilized for the benefit of all.
- Teach all students how their communication styles can be misinterpreted. (p. 104)

Most of us have seen classrooms in which values clashed. In one situation with which I am familiar, the students had been given a group task to identify problems that might be encountered on an American-style "date." Two fairly recent arrivals insisted that the couple must be chaperoned in order to prevent inappropriate behavior, but most students dismissed the idea of a chaperone as silly and argued that such a practice should never be considered in today's world. The discussion turned into a very angry exchange among the students—one that could have been prevented had the majority of students been given a chance to voice differences early on, discuss them, and through discussion gain an appreciation of others and their differing viewpoints.

To ease tensions that might result in this kind of unpleasant exchange, some teachers might feel comfortable using affective activities or *humanistic* techniques. (See Chapter 14, footnote 1, p. 339.) Those advocated particularly by S. Brown and Dubin (1975); Moskowitz (1978, 1999); and Simon, Howe, and Kirschenbaum (1992) seek to create affinity on the part of the students toward the teacher, each other, and the resulting classroom environment.

Moskowitz (1981) set out to gather evidence that the use of such techniques in language classrooms does indeed "enhance attitudes toward a foreign language, rapport with classmates, and the self-image of foreign language students" (p. 149). She conducted two studies using the language students of eleven teachers. The teachers were enrolled at Temple University in courses on humanistic techniques for teaching another language. The subjects were high school students studying a variety of languages: French, Spanish, German, Italian, Hebrew, and English as a second language. Each teacher chose one class (from beginner through advanced) in which to do the study. Often they chose classes that had been apathetic or difficult in some way. They gave three questionnaires prior to the humanistic activities and readministered the questionnaires two months later. Had the students' attitudes changed? In both studies, significant positive increases occurred in students' attitudes toward themselves, the language, and each other.[2] The following four hypotheses were accepted.

Using humanistic techniques to teach a foreign language:

- enhances the attitudes of foreign language students toward learning the target language
- enhances the self-perceptions of foreign language students
- enhances the perceptions of foreign language students toward the members of their language class and how their classmates perceive them
- increases the acceptance of foreign language students for members of the same sex and by members of the opposite sex in their class, thus increasing their cohesiveness (1981, pp. 145–150)

These studies indicated that humanistic activities increase the development of positive student attitudes overall. Moskowitz's later studies (1999), in which she replicated parts of her earlier work, supported similar conclusions.

MOTIVATION

Central also to the affective domain is motivation. Much of the early literature on the subject differentiates between *integrative* motivation and *instrumental* motivation. Gardner and Lambert (1972) defined integrative motivation roughly as a desire to integrate and identify with the target language group and instrumental motivation as a desire to use the language to obtain practical goals such as studying in a technical field or getting a job (see also Dörnyei, 1998; Gardner & MacIntyre, 1991; Hedge, 2000; Noels, Pelletier, Clément, & Valerand, 2000; Shaaban & Ghaith, 2000, for similar definitions). Of course, a student whose motive is to take a language course simply to fulfill a requirement or to please his or her parents, a peer or a small group of other people may have neither integrative nor instrumental motivation. Such a student may do only what it takes to get through the course with a fairly respectable grade and may not go through much of an internalization process. However, some of these students may indeed feel intense social pressure to excel and may do very well even when it comes to internalization.

The very early studies of French classes in Canada done by Gardner and Lambert (1959) and Gardner, Smythe, Clement, and Gliksman (1976) all concluded that integrative motivation is generally stronger than instrumental motivation in predicting French proficiency. However, other evidence in this area frequently appeared contradictory. There were cases in which integration appeared *not* to be a strong motive but in which a certain urgency existed to become proficient in the target language for instrumental reasons. In such cases, instrumental motivation became the main predictor (Lukmani, 1972;

---

[2] In the first study, the students' identities were not revealed, and so the pre–post data were treated as though they came from two independent groups; in the second study, the identity of the students was retained in code so that pre–post data could be matched. Two questionnaires were administered: the Foreign Language Attitude Questionnaire and My Class and Me (see Moskowitz, 1981, p. 150). Sociometric data were collected from each student to see to what extent attitudes changed toward specific peers.

Oller, Baca, & Vigil, 1977). On the other hand, the study of Chinese-speaking graduate students in the United States (Oller, Hudson, & Liu, 1977) indicated that although the students' main reason for wanting to be proficient in English was instrumental, the subjects who characterized Americans positively performed better on a cloze test.[3] Thus the studies appeared to be very inconclusive.[4] In the case of integrative motivation, the target group with which the individual is identifying may not be at all clear. A *global* English identity is possible, too, in the case of English as a world language in which the individual is part of an "imagined community" (Norton, 2001) or a "virtual language community," a term used by Dörnyei (2006).

What appeared earlier to be contradictory findings may simply have been evidence indicating that the various sources of motivation studied are unstable and difficult, if not impossible, to isolate and are certainly not mutually exclusive. In addition, the local culture itself may have an important role to play in both second and foreign language situations.[5] Many questions need to be addressed. What role does culture play in the motivation to learn a foreign language? How about a second language? How do we distinguish the various sources of motivation to begin with? For example, does "integration" mean to become part of the target language group or just to socialize on a casual basis with its members? If it means the latter, then might not instrumental motivation be present as well? Imagine, for example, a person who desires to socialize with the target group in order to integrate but does so in a desire to curry political favor. Or imagine that a person who is part of a marginalized cultural group wants to integrate to show those in power that he or she is indeed capable of learning the language and of academic success. How would one categorize such motives? Even if they could be isolated, how could they be measured? In addition, the person may not want to reveal his or her real feelings—or may not even be aware of them. In the case of an imagined language group, sorting out integrative and instrumental motives would probably never have even been attempted.

Another problem here lies with the distinct possibility that motivation may have been too narrowly defined to begin with. Realizing this, researchers on motivation have begun to turn toward a more situated approach (see especially Dörnyei, 2000, 2006). He calls for a *process-oriented* way of looking at the dynamics of motivation and the manner in which it changes within any given day and over time. To use Dörnyei's (2006) words,

---

[3] A cloze test consists of a passage in which every *n*th word has been deleted; students are to supply the missing words.

[4] Masgoret and Gardner (2003) came to a different conclusion. They found in their meta-analysis of studies conducted by Gardner and associates that what Gardner and Lambert (2003) had referred to earlier as *integrative motivation* actually comprised "integrativeness, attitudes toward the learning situation, and motivation" (p. 174). The researchers concluded that integrative motivation in this sense *is* indeed the major affective factor promoting second language achievement. What others were often looking at was integrative *orientation* rather than integrative *motivation*. They believed that orientations in and of themselves do not of necessity reflect motivation. Because one expresses an integrative orientation does not mean that that individual is motivated to learn the language.

[5] Interestingly, Chen, Warden, and Chang (2005) concluded in their study within a Chinese cultural setting in Taiwan that motivation frameworks need to be reconsidered in cultural settings that are nonwestern. They feel that the way to discover culturally determined motivators lies in a "localized, scientific, research-based approach" (p. 626). See also Dörnyei and Schmidt (2001).

Looking at it from this perspective, motivation is not seen as a static attribute but rather as a dynamic system that displays continuous fluctuation, going through certain ebbs and flows. (p. 51)

Motivation involves not only integrative, instrumental, required, or collective factors but also temporary, situated expectancies; interests of the moment; curiosities; ego enhancement factors; personal satisfaction; and much more (see van Lier, 1996). It also involves the power of *investment* that Pittaway (2004) called a "tool of hope." We need to look at learners' personal investment in reaching goals and in attaining social equity within the new culture. All of these factors appear to interact in complex ways and are far more mercurial in nature than we at first thought. One thing seems clear: Motivation is an extremely important affective factor. Without it, learning any language, first or second, would be difficult at best, if not impossible.

What are some things teachers can do to increase motivation in general? Dörnyei (2001) proposed a taxonomy of motivational categories that includes a variety of dimensions related to teaching practices. In sum:

- motivational conditions (e.g., establishing good rapport between student and teacher, creating a positive classroom environment)
- initial motivation (e.g., gaining student interest, increasing expectancies for success, encouraging positive attitudes)
- sustaining motivation (e.g., using relevant, stimulating tasks)
- encouraging positive, reflective self-evaluation (giving effective feedback)

The complete taxonomy can be found in Guilloteaux and Dörnyei (2008, p. 58).

Teachers' motivational practices that fall within these dimensions and their effects on student motivation should be of interest to us. Guilloteaux and Dörnyei (2008) studied forty English language classrooms in South Korea where they used self-report questionnaires and a classroom observation tool called motivation orientation of language teaching (MOLT). They learned that student motivation is indeed influenced by the teachers' motivational practices.

Guilloteaux and Dörnyei (2008) reported "the results are so robust that they warrant further research in more narrowly defined strategy domains" (p. 72). They concluded also that it would be useful to know which practices are transferable across different learning contexts.

LEVEL OF ANXIETY

The third factor central to the affective domain is level of anxiety. Two types of anxiety have been recognized in the literature on affect:

- *trait* anxiety (a predisposition toward feeling anxious)
- *state* anxiety (anxiety produced in reaction to a specific situation)

In his discussion of the two types, H. D. Brown (1987) early on noted the difference between anxiety that is debilitative and anxiety that is facilitative. Whether the anxiety is an aid or hindrance often depends on the degree to which it is found in the individual.

For example, no anxiety at all might cause the person to be lethargic, whereas a small amount might bring the individual to an optimal state of alertness.

In a study using induced anxiety, MacIntyre and Gardner (1994) found that their control group (the members of which had not been exposed to anxiety-arousal) performed better than the experimental groups during all phases of the learning task set before them. They also concluded that whenever anxiety-reduction strategies are employed, they must be accompanied by reteaching strategies so that students have a second opportunity to learn what was missed during the time when anxiety was high. Based on their research, Gardner and MacIntyre (1993) concluded that if students experience language anxiety too often, the state anxiety may turn into trait anxiety.

Other studies also support the notion that a lowered anxiety level is related to proficiency in the target language (Chastain, 1975; Gardner, Smythe, Clement, & Gliksman, 1976; MacIntyre & Gardner, 1994). In the case of ESL, teachers and peers can promote a lowered level of anxiety by providing a sort of surrogate family to serve as a buffer until the students no longer need it. Sheltered classrooms in the content areas (see Chapters 17 and 18) also provide temporary refuges in which students can receive meaningful input in low-anxiety environments. Although Larsen and Smalley (1972) did not specifically mention the classroom as serving in this capacity, they nevertheless did advocate such a haven. However, students who are sheltered for too long may tend to stabilize prematurely as a result of isolation from target-group peers. A wise teacher involves students with competent speakers, including second language users, as early as possible and helps the students work toward achieving their personal, social, and academic goals. In the case of foreign language teaching, students can receive supplemental instruction, participate in a support group or foreign language club, or learn how to apply relaxation strategies (see especially Campbell & Ortiz, 1991).

Additional potential causes of increased anxiety in both English as a second language and foreign language classes include forcing the students to speak too soon, giving direct corrections while students are speaking, competitiveness among students (see especially K. Bailey, 1995), and incompatible learning styles (see Oxford, Ehrman, & Lavine, 1991). Saito, Horwitz, and Garza (1999) found in their study of university students learning Japanese, French, and Russian that scripts and cultural reading materials with which the students were not familiar caused increased reading anxiety and that students with high levels of reading anxiety received lower grades than those with lower levels of reading anxiety.

Some of the strategies Oxford (1999) recommended to lower anxiety in the language classroom include

- Help students recognize symptoms of anxiety.
- Make students aware that anxiety about language learning can be temporary and generally does not develop into a permanent problem.
- Provide multiple opportunities for success.
- Encourage students to take some moderate risks.
- Help students tolerate ambiguity in a nonthreatening environment.
- Reduce competition.

- Do not expect perfection in performance.
- Use music, laughter, and games to help students relax.
- Be fair and unambiguous in testing.
- Aid students in realistically assessing their own performance.
- Plan activities that address varied learning styles.
- Encourage students to use positive self-talk and reframe negative ideas. (p. 67)

Oxford (1999) also advised teachers to clearly state classroom goals and help students develop strategies to meet them. I would like to modify this recommendation by suggesting that students should be involved as much as possible in setting the goals in the first place. This suggestion is in keeping with the emergent participatory classroom (see Chapter 4).

RELATED FACTORS

Acculturation

Acculturation is very closely related to attitudes, motivation, and level of anxiety. In fact, it was considered an important predictor of target language acquisition by early researchers (Schumann, 1978a; Stauble, 1980). Based on her research of three Spanish-speakers living in the United States, Stauble argued that second language learners succeed "to the degree that they acculturate to the target language group" if no formal instruction is attempted. She stated, "The assumption here is that the more social and psychological distance there is between the second language learner and the target language group, the lower the learner's degree of acculturation will be toward that group" (1980, pp. 43–50).

Schumann's (1978a) earlier research supported the same conclusion. He compared the linguistic development demonstrated by six L2 learners of English—two children, two adolescents, and two adults. The subject who acquired the least was Alberto, a thirty-three-year-old Costa Rican. Of all the subjects, he was the one most socially and psychologically distant from the target language group. He interacted predominantly with Spanish-speaking friends and made no attempt to socialize with English-speaking people. He showed little desire for owning a television set and listened mostly to Spanish music. Although English classes were available, he showed no interest in them. However, as Schumann pointed out, a Piagetian test of adaptive intelligence revealed no gross cognitive defects that might prevent him from learning a second language. The main reason for his low proficiency, according to Schumann, was his lack of desire to acculturate.[6]

The Acculturation Model

To explain the effect of acculturation on the second language acquisition process, Schumann developed the *acculturation model*. According to this model, second language learning is dependent on the amount of social and psychological distance that exists

---

[6] It is interesting to note that, according to Schmidt (1984), the poorest learners in the studies referred to by Schumann and Stauble (1980) were also the oldest. Physical maturation may have been, either directly or indirectly, a contributing factor.

between the learner and the second language culture. When the distances are great, the learner's language tends to prematurely stabilize during the early phases of interlanguage development. The learner may not have received the necessary interaction because of social isolation or may not have given the target language the attention necessary for learning because of psychological distance. Some, too, prefer not to experience the painful process of becoming acculturated and decide to not fully participate in the new culture.

However, Norton (1998) criticized the acculturation model by accusing it of not addressing the powerlessness that immigrants often experience when their values and even their very identity are questioned by the target culture. Thus immigrants having such experiences may be less likely to attempt acculturation. This may have been one reason for Alberto's failure to acquire much English. However, this possibility does not appear to have been explored by Schumann. Pittaway (2004) agreed with Norton but went further to speculate that because Alberto claimed to actually have integrative motivation, a less than accepting community and a lack of the money and time required to take English classes may have prevented him from attempting to close the social gap.

The Nativization Model

Andersen's (1983) *nativization model* also sought to explain why the language of some learners stabilizes prematurely. He cited the effects of what he called *nativization* (not to be confused with the "native-speaker" concept) and *denativization* on the learner. Through nativization, the learner tends to assimilate the target language into an already determined schema of how the second language should be and makes judgments based on knowledge of the first language and culture. Denativization, on the other hand, is an accommodation process in which the learner changes the schema to fit the new language. Andersen was convinced that the learner who tends to denativize is the most likely to become proficient.

Accommodation Theory

Giles's (1979) *accommodation theory* claimed that motivation is the key and that it is closely related to in-group (the first language group) and out-group (the second language group) identification. Giles emphasized how the individual *perceives* social distance rather than the actual social distance as described by Schumann. He argued that feelings of identity are dynamic and dependent on continuing negotiations between and among individuals and groups. Schumann saw these feelings as more constant and slower to change. Premature stabilization, according to Giles's model, occurs during "downward divergence," which takes place when the individual is not strongly motivated in the direction of the out-group.

The Acculturation Process

In his analysis of the literature, H. D. Brown (1987) early on described the four variable stages in the acculturation process.

- *First stage.* The newcomer feels almost euphoric—excited at being in a new (sometimes exotic) place.
- *Second stage.* As the reality of survival sets in, the newcomer moves into *culture shock*, where frustration rises and the individual begins to feel alienated from the target culture. Self-image and security are threatened.
- *Third stage.* This stage marks the beginning of recovery—the newcomer still feels stress but is beginning to gain control over the problems that once seemed insurmountable. This state, which Brown referred to as *anomie* (see Srole, 1956), comprises initial adaptation to the target culture and loss of connection to native culture. The result can be heightened anxiety—a sense of homelessness, or hovering between two cultures. *Anomie* is a critical period in language mastery.
- *Fourth stage.* In this stage of full recovery, the person becomes reconciled to his or her role in the new culture.

Under normal conditions, people becoming acculturated were thought to pass through all these stages at varying rates. They did not necessarily progress smoothly from one stage to the next; regression was thought to be common, depending on circumstances and state of mind.

Ricento (2005) pointed out, however, that many of the earlier approaches to acculturation reflect an assimilationist model (although perhaps unintentionally) in which learners give up their first language and cultural identities in order to take on those of the new culture. The way Ricento and others, including Pavlenko and Lantolf (2000), now look at identity development is quite different. To them identity development is an ever-changing phenomenon that is both complex and variable and may involve membership in multiple cultural groups. Pavlenko and Lantolf, whose view of the acculturation process is based on the self-report of immigrants, described two phases: *the phase of loss* (loss of linguistic identity, loss of frame of reference, loss of inner voice, attrition of first language) and *the phase of recovery and (re)construction* (the appropriation of the voices of others and the emergence of one's new voice and new perspectives). To show the profundity of the loss of the inner voice in particular, the researchers quoted Eva Hoffman (1989):

> I wait for that spontaneous flow of inner language, which used to be my nighttime talk with myself. . . . Nothing comes. Polish, in a short time, has atrophied, shriveled from sheer uselessness. Its words don't apply to my new experiences, they're not coeval with any of the objects, or faces, or the very air I breathe in the daytime. In English, the words have not penetrated to those layers of my psyche from which a private connection could proceed. (Hoffman, 1989, p. 107; also in Pavelenko & Lantolf, 2000, p. 165)

Although Eva Hoffman's loss of inner voice was painful, especially so because her English inner voice had not yet fully emerged, what she was going through was a normal part of the acculturation process. However, the pain of this part of the process may have been eased somewhat had she known that she would be given the opportunity to maintain as much as possible her first language and at least some of her culture. Such an opportunity may have hastened the integration of the old with the new in her last stage of recovery.

First languages and cultures in general should be maintained as much as possible during the acculturation process and beyond for a number of reasons:

- to give the individual access to more than one cultural group
- to keep important aspects of the native culture alive for future generations
- to contribute to a sense of pride in one's self and in one's cultural background

This conclusion is supported by a number of studies. For example, Deyhle (1992), in her study of Navajo students, found that those students whose homes were most traditional, who maintained their own language, and who were involved in the religious and social activities of the community were the most successful in school. Phinney (1993) concluded that teenagers in general are much better adjusted if they have examined their own ethnicity in depth and value its role in their lives. Many have concluded that using students' cultural backgrounds as they begin to learn in another culture is helpful—and may even be necessary to their achieving academic success (Ladson-Billings, 1994; Nieto, 1999).

Personality

Personality, too, is an important factor and is closely related to attitudes, motivation, and level of anxiety. Certain personality characteristics have been known to foster proficiency in the target language. These include:

- a willingness to take risks (Beebe, 1983; H. D. Brown, 1987; Oxford, 1990; Rubin, 1975)
- a relative lack of inhibition (Guiora, Acton, Erard, & Strickland, 1980; Guiora, Beit-Hallami, Brannon, Dull, & Scovel, 1972)
- the ability to tolerate ambiguity (Ehrman, 1999; Oxford, 1999)

Extroversion and assertiveness, although not necessarily beneficial traits (Busch, 1982; Naiman, Fröhlich, & Stern, 1978), can be helpful to the degree that they encourage more output and more interaction in general. Dewaele (2004) discovered that extraverts in formal environments or in situations in which interpersonal stress is high are more fluent than introverts, particularly in those situations. Extraverts also tend to use colloquial words with ease, whereas introverts do not. On the other hand, introverts appear to do better in tasks that call for the memorization of vocabulary and completing written and other tasks that do not only require speaking or learning by doing.

In addition, empathy, under normal conditions, was found to be a positive trait, for it often leads to greater proficiency. Being able to identify with members of the target language group (a trait not always found in extremely extraverted individuals) is important to communication. Guiora, Brannon, and Dull (1972) argued that empathy is essential in order to make our ego boundaries permeable. In other words, we need to be open to the new language and the new people. Schumann (1980) related empathy and ego permeability to a lowering of inhibitions:

> I would submit that empathic capacity or ego flexibility, particularly as operationalized under the concept of "lowering of inhibitions," is best regarded as an essential factor to the ability to acquire a second language. (p. 238)

These characteristics appear outwardly to be most influential when they are in balance. However, the research in this area is inconclusive and may always be so due to the nature of personality and language learning itself. Perhaps if we were to focus on a different kind of research (i.e., descriptive research), we may be able to learn much more about this relationship.

CREATING A POSITIVE SCHOOL AND COMMUNITY ENVIRONMENT

Although the teacher may successfully establish a situated environment conducive to language learning in the classroom, what students face outside of the classroom may have an even greater impact on affect. Unfortunately, English learners are often likely to become the victims of ridicule and sometimes outright hostility. Prejudice can come not only from native-speaking peers but from teachers, administrators, and other school staff members, as well as from the community. However subtle, the form that it takes among teachers and other school personnel can be particularly devastating. Persons of influence can affect the attitudes found in the whole school setting that often extend to the community itself.

I remember an incident that occurred when I was an ESL teacher in a large public high school. One day in the teachers' lounge a fellow teacher asked me, "How's old 'Ho Hum' [a nickname he had given the Asian student we shared] doing today?" I pretended not to know to whom he was referring, although the student's identity was obvious because we had only one Asian student in common. He continued, "You know, what's his name" and then he gave the student's real name. "Oh, he's doing just fine," I replied. As it turned out, old "Ho Hum" went on to maintain close to a 4.0 grade point average throughout school, won the top Junior of the Year Award, and became a star member of the soccer team. Of course, not all English learners can achieve so much, and for those finding their languages and cultural backgrounds devalued, success in school often remains elusive.

Promoting Academic Achievement

Poor academic performance can be due to any number of factors, including, but not limited to

- economic inequality
- ability tracking[7]
- low expectations on the part of teachers
- the pressures of standardized tests
- lack of respect for the individual
- social humiliation
- lack of first language support (see also Nieto, 1999, 2000)

---

[7] Ability tracking (including gifted and talented programs) can be quite devastating to those not making the grade for the upper tracks. Eliminating such tracking, on the other hand, can have very positive effects (see especially Mehan et al., 1992).

Some students do not succeed because negative relationships with persons of the dominant culture have caused them to resist even the appearance of assimilation. Many feel that to succeed means that they must give up too much of their own identity.

The overall school environment and the students' individual relationships with teachers are of utmost importance and often determine whether or not academic success will be achieved. Do the school and the teacher value their languages and cultures? Are the students respected as individuals with knowledge and experience that can be built on and shared?

Of course, we all know of language and cultural minority students who were able to overcome less than ideal conditions. Often these students came from families that took great pride in their traditions and instilled in their children a sense of self-worth. In most cases, these students were encouraged by their parents to do whatever was necessary to succeed academically. An affirmation of self did much to inoculate these students against the insensitivity to which they may have been exposed in school.

Promoting Cultural Understanding

Although we cannot hope to eliminate the prejudice of all insensitive persons with whom our students come into contact, we can, perhaps through awareness training, try to make the overt expression of these prejudices unpopular. Through workshops for teachers and staff, and through the sensitizing of entire student populations and groups within the community, we can achieve a school climate that is supportive for all of our students, not only those in second language classes.

The teacher workshop presented here seemed to be particularly effective in exposing cultural biases. Similar sessions can be held for students and groups within the community. It begins with the following scenario:[8]

> A man and woman dressed in clothes that represent a very "primitive" hypothetical culture walk slowly through the audience. The woman, who is carrying a basket filled with bread, walks a few paces behind the man (her husband). Once they reach the front of the room, they turn to face the audience and kneel down, side by side. The man places his hand on the woman's head while she bows her head down, touching it to the floor three times. She then rises, walks into the audience, and begins to lead people up to the front of the room as though she is preparing for a ceremony. (In this case, it will be a wedding ceremony in which her husband will take a second bride.) First, she quietly leads two men (one at a time) from the audience to the front of the room. The only sounds she utters are pleasing "umms" from time to time. She motions for them to sit in the chairs she has set up previously. She repeats the same procedure, except this time she takes two women from the audience. She motions for them to kneel on the floor. Last, she leads the new bride to a kneeling position beside the husband. She then passes out the bread from her basket. She gives it to the men first, waits a few moments, and then gives some to the women.

---

[8] Although I have not been able to locate the original source of this idea, I saw a version of it presented at the 1980 NAFSA Conference in El Paso.

The moderator asks the audience to describe this society. Usually, the audience guesses that it is a patriarchal society supported by these facts:

- the man walked ahead of the woman when entering
- the women had to sit on the floor while the men got chairs
- the men were fed first
- the husband pushed the woman's head to the floor three times

This audience reaction is expected; they had little choice but to react from their own world view or *weltanschauung*. But in fact, the hypothetical society being portrayed was intended to be matriarchal. Consider the following perspective:

- Men walk ahead of the women to protect them from potential danger.
- Men take more than one wife because there are fewer men than women—and this disparity occurs because men's lives are more dispensable; men are expected to protect women at any cost, and men therefore die younger and in greater numbers.
- Only women can directly receive the spirits who are in the ground. Thus women bow their heads to the ground, whereas the men, who can only receive the spirits indirectly, must place a hand gently on a woman's head. Only during the marriage ceremony can a man receive the spirit directly.
- The bread is served to the men first to ensure the women's safety in case it has been poisoned.

This scenario is almost always followed by a lively discussion about perspectives and how they color views of reality. This kind of activity helps participants look at events from the viewpoints of others and perhaps gain a more global perspective.

Other types of activities that promote cultural understanding are affective activities (Chapter 14), cooperative learning (pp. 382–385), and many other interactive and participatory strategies mentioned throughout this volume. Nieto (2000) pointed out that activities that foster respect and understanding generally reduce the number of racial comments, reduce name-calling, and increase higher academic achievement overall.

The Variable Stages of Ethnicity

Another way to increase awareness of others is to take teachers, students, and community groups through the variable stages of ethnicity (Banks, 1992) by means of role playing in hypothetical situations. Banks's typology applies to situations in which dominant and nondominant groups coexist in a variety of ways. His definitions of these stages are summarized as follows:

Stage 1: *Ethnic Psychological Captivity*
The member of a nondominant group feels rejection and low self-esteem and may avoid contact as much as possible with the dominant group. This individual has internalized the "image" that the dominant society has ascribed to him or her and may even feel shame.

Stage 2: *Ethnic Encapsulation*
The member of a nondominant group reacts to Stage 1 with bitterness and, in some cases, a desire for revenge. As a result, the person may turn inward to his or her ethnic group and reject all other groups, particularly the dominant one. In extreme manifestations of this stage, other groups are regarded as "the enemy" and are seen as racists with genocidal tendencies; members of the nondominant group who try to assimilate into the dominant group are considered traitors.

Stage 3: *Ethnic Identity Clarification*
The individual is able to clarify self in relation to the ethnic group of which he or she is a part, with a resulting self-acceptance and understanding. The person is able to see both positive and negative aspects of his or her own group, as well as the dominant group. To reach this stage, individuals should have gained a certain degree of economic and emotional security and had productive, positive experiences with members of other groups, particularly those in the dominant group.

Stage 4: *Biethnicity*
The individual is able to function successfully in two cultural groups, the primary group and a nonprimary group. Most individuals who belong to a nondominant group are forced to reach this stage if they wish to become mobile socially and economically in the society in general. Interestingly, members of the dominant group do not have to do this and can (and often do) remain monocultural and monolingual all their lives.

Stage 5: *Multiethnicity and Reflective Nationalism*
The individual has learned to function successfully in several ethnic groups. The person still feels loyalty to the primary ethnic group but has developed a commitment to the new culture and to its idealized values as well.

Stage 6: *Globalism and Global Competency*
The individual has developed global identifications and has the skills necessary to relate to all groups. This person has achieved an ideal but delicate balance of primary group, the new culture, and global commitments, identifications, and loyalties.

The road to biethnicity is not easy (see especially Madrid, 1991). Individuals do not necessarily move from one stage to the next in linear fashion. Rather they tend to zigzag back and forth, and some may skip stages altogether. Fortunately, Stage 2 is often bypassed, although some feelings from it may exist temporarily as the person moves from Stage 1 to Stage 3.

I have found that hypothetical role playing allows teachers, students, and community members to "experience" the first three of Banks's stages. First, I ask the participants to decide which groups they want represented (e.g., Latino-American, Korean-American, Vietnamese-American, American Indian, Japanese-American, and so on). Then they decide which group they want to join. Once in the group of their choice, they go through a set of planned activities to help them experience the different stages. In Stage 1, for example, they might bring in pieces of literature, songs, pictures, or anecdotes depicting their people experiencing oppression at the hands of the dominant group. They may want to list negative feelings about the self and the ethnic group created by this experience and discuss how each feeling came about.

A more general activity can also help participants feel the effects of this stage:

- Give each participant a paper hat (a simple headband will do).[9] On each hat write a label such as "dumb," "smart," "good-looking," "unbathed," "conscientious," "lazy," and so on.
- Place the hats on the participants in such a way that no individual can see the label he or she is wearing.
- Help the group members choose a relevant topic for discussion and instruct them to treat each other according to their labels during the discussion.

Most students are amazed at the intensity of the anger or joy they feel based on the treatment to which they are subjected.

At Stage 2, participants may want to discuss the negative feelings they have developed. Once these feelings are fully aired, people are better able to build positive attitudes toward their own ethnic groups, as well as the groups of others. This time, the group may want to share literature and other cultural items that cause them to feel intense pride in their own cultures.

In Stage 3, participants are encouraged to sit back a little and look at the positive attributes and achievements of other groups (e.g., share their literatures, and so forth) and achieve a realistic view of their own ethnic group in relation to others.

Still other culture awareness activities can include group discussions about issues relating to diversity, films, celebrations, and other events that bring school and community together. In emergent participatory classrooms, students are able to determine the issues that most concern them. They can study and research these issues, discuss them, write about them, and perhaps even begin to take actions toward easing the problems (see also problem posing on pp. 99–100). The rewards of such activities can be immeasurable in terms of increased human understanding and personal empowerment.

What Makes a Difference?

I want to stress again that activities and strategies by themselves are not the most important factors in establishing an accepting school and classroom environment. The most important factor by far is *the relationship that has been established between teacher and student and student and student.* If these relationships are not as affirming and positive as they should be, then no activity or strategy, no matter how innovative, will make much difference (see also Cummins, 2000; Nieto, 1999, 2000).

---

[9] This activity was adapted from one Leah Boehne shared with me.

Parental Involvement

Schools should be inviting places where parents and indeed whole families feel welcome. However, schools in the United States, in particular, have not always been so welcoming even with the influx of students from around the world. When parents do not show up for conferences, it may be a mistake to assume they do not care about the education of their children or that they are too busy. According to King and Goodwin (2002), "School norms and structures have historically been, and continue to be, most responsive to parents who are middle-class, able-bodied, U.S. born, and standard-English-speaking individuals" (p. 5). They suggested that the school continually inform parents about educational goals, events, and how their children are doing. They can be invited to join their children on field trips, have breakfast at the school, or view presentations, and they can be given their own room or space within the school where they can meet to plan, hold discussions, or just hang out.

Teachers would be wise to seek parents' ideas for improving the school, both academically and socially; use the home language with the help of interpreters and translators if needed to facilitate communication with parents; encourage bilingual staff members to make home visits and phone calls and in other ways serve as liaisons between school and community; ask questions of parents (perhaps in a survey) about their own schooling, the languages spoken in the home, and their children's expectations and the ways they seem to learn best at home; organize family meetings during which members can share experiences and concerns.

Additionally, special programs can be organized to help meet families' language and cultural needs (see especially the lower Manhattan program described on pp. 514–522). Families need to be encouraged to become partners in the education of their children through such simple acts as reading aloud with them in whatever language feels most comfortable and helping them with homework. If possible, parents should provide books for the home in both languages and encourage their children to read them for enjoyment, analyze and ask questions about them, and/or use them as resources for homework.

Family members can often become important resources in bilingual and second language classes by sharing their own knowledge; this helps other students and the teacher better understand the home and social environment from which each student comes. In all classes, if family members are fluent in the languages being taught, they can be recruited as tutors or teacher aides. Moreover, they often can be effective guest lecturers or facilitators of discussion on topics or issues of relevance.

SUMMARY

Because the concepts related to the affective domain are so intangible and mercurial, they are difficult to define, describe, and measure. Yet despite their ephemeral quality, we cannot give up our attempts to understand what their role might be in second language development. Central to the affective domain are attitudes, motivation, and level of anxiety. They appear to be strongly influenced by acculturation and personality factors.

Attitudes that are largely determined by what our students have experienced and by the people with whom they identify—peers, parents, teachers—influence the way students see the world and their place in it. Motivation also is a strong force in determining how proficient the students will become. In addition, level of anxiety has an effect. If the students are given a chance to try out the language in a nonthreatening environment, they are more likely to go through an acculturation process without it becoming a debilitating experience. If the students' backgrounds and languages are affirmed and accepted, they are in a better position to acculturate while preserving their own cultural identities.

Each student's emotional well-being can be enhanced by a positive school environment. Although prejudices are difficult to eliminate, much can be done to make the environment a better one, not only for language learners, but for all students and their families. Cultural-awareness activities can involve school personnel, students, and community members. They can sensitize people to the needs and feelings of others.

QUESTIONS AND PROJECTS FOR REFLECTION AND DISCUSSION

1. Several language students have mentioned that learning a second language makes them feel "helpless and ineffectual." What demands are typically made on the individual in the following language learning situations that might contribute to this feeling?

   a. a child going to kindergarten in a new culture
   b. a tenth-grader in beginning Spanish as a foreign language
   c. an adult going to work in a new country for the first time
   d. a university English learner attending a class oriented to native speakers

   What affective factors might help or hinder the individual's ability to cope in each situation?

2. Have you ever lived in another culture? To what extent did you experience an acculturation process? Was it more like H. D. Brown's early description (pp. 162–163) or Pavlenko/Lantolf's later description (p. 163)? Or was it a combination of both? Discuss with a small group of peers.

3. Savignon (1983) described an incident involving her son Daniel, a new student in a Paris school. On the first day, he met with more than 100 students at his grade level in the school's courtyard. The school director called out the names of the students. They were to stand and tell what class they were in. When his name was called, he followed the procedure but was immediately chastised for having his hands in his pockets. When he went home that day, he vowed that he would never go back. He had had it with that school. Explain this incident in terms of what you know about attitudes, values, and

the variable stages of acculturation. If you had been Daniel's parent, what would you have said to him to help him put this incident in perspective?

4. What is the difference between sympathy and empathy? Think of examples of each from your own experience. Which one do you think serves the language learner best? Explain.

5. In what ways (other than those mentioned in the chapter) can you aid your own students in developing positive attitudes, strong motivation, and reduced anxiety? Consider kinds of activities, room arrangements, and the general ambiance in the school and classroom environment.

6. Think about your own attitudes toward language minority students. What has been the greatest influence on the formulation of your own attitudes? Have these attitudes changed over time? If so, what has influenced the change? Discuss with a partner or a small group of peers.

7. Plan a culture awareness workshop for school personnel (including the secretaries, custodians, cafeteria help, and so on) in your school. Be very specific about the preworkshop preparation, the workshop itself, and the follow-up. Share your plans with a group of peers to receive their feedback. Make any necessary changes based on what you learn.

8. **Journal Entry:** Write about your own cultural identity and how it has developed and changed. How important has it been to you over the years? Do you have any regrets concerning your cultural heritage? If you have children, what do you want to pass on to them?

SUGGESTED READINGS AND REFERENCE MATERIALS

Arnold, J. (1999). *Affect and language learning.* Cambridge, England: Cambridge University Press. This anthology explores affective factors and how they relate to a holistic approach to the language learning process. The authors represented in this book come from a variety of geographic areas and have varied experiences, backgrounds, and perspectives. They include John Schumann, Earl Stevick, Adrian Underhill, Rebecca Oxford, Gertrude Moskowitz, JoAnn Crandall, Joy Reid, Madeline Ehrman, and many others.

Banks, J. (2007). *An introduction to multicultural education* (4th ed.). Boston: Allyn & Bacon. This book provides a sensitive exploration into the nature of ethnicity and multiethnic education and offers guidelines and strategies for promoting a more pluralistic, global, open society through education. This is a very readable and important book for all teachers.

Dörnyei, Z., & Schmidt R. (Eds.). (2001). *Motivation and second language acquisition* (Tech. Rep. No. 23). Manoa: University of Hawai'i. An examination of theory and research in the area of second and foreign language motivation is presented. Emphasis is placed on the importance of looking at second language motivation in specific environments rather than taking a general approach to the subject. Both quantitative and qualitative research are explored.

Eckert, P., & McConnell-Ginet, S. (2003). *Language and gender*. Cambridge, England: Cambridge University Press. This book offers a very comprehensive look at language and gender from a sociolinguistic perspective, including examples from around the world. It discusses such topics as organizing conversation; the construction, deconstruction, and reconstruction of gender; linguistic and social links; and so forth. The terminology used is clearly defined for novices to this area of exploration.

Igoa, C. (2005). *The phenomenon of uprooting*. In P. Richard-Amato & M. A. Snow (Eds.), *Academic success for English language learners: Strategies for K–12 mainstream teachers* (pp. 115–132). White Plains, NY: Pearson Education/Longman. Drawing from her own journey as a teacher and as an immigrant, Igoa discusses the needs and feelings of immigrant children in our classrooms. She describes ways in which these children can best be accommodated within schools. She includes the stories of two English learners, one from the Philippines and the other from American Samoa.

Richard-Amato, P., & Snow, M.A. (Eds.). (2005). *Academic success for English language learners: Strategies for K–12 mainstream teachers*. White Plains, NY: Pearson Education/Longman. Focusing on the needs of language minority students, this book addresses theoretical foundations for successful teaching in multicultural classrooms. It explores recommended classroom strategies and practices and later relates them to specific content areas such as math, social studies, science, and literature. Chapters by Jim Cummins, Sonia Nieto, Mary McGroarty and Margarita Calderon, Jana Echevarria and Anne Graves, Pauline Gibbons, Deborah Short, Angela Carrasquillo and Vivian Rodrígues, and many more are included.

Schumann, J. (1997). *The neurobiology of affect in language*. Oxford, England: Blackwell. Schumann describes his neurobiological theory and how it relates to cognition. He looks at the kinds of stimuli the learner receives from the environment and how each affects the emotions and behaviors of the learner. He finds a strong connection between stimulus appraisal and motivational theory and, as before, sees affect as critical to the language learning process itself.

Tharp, R., Estrada, P., Dalton, S., & Yamauchi, L. (2000). *Teaching transformed: Achieving excellence, fairness, inclusion, and harmony*. Boulder, CO: Westview Press. This inspiring book presents invaluable information about how social relationships are typically organized in classrooms, how such organization can be changed to promote excellence in learning and teaching, how teacher-student relationships can affect learning in positive ways, the influence of culture on instruction, and the phases of organizing instructional activity. Also included are the authors' five standards for effective teaching: teachers and students producing together, developing language and literacy across the curriculum, making meaning, connecting school to students' lives, instruction in complex thinking, and teaching through conversation.

CHAPTER 7

Language Assessment and Standards

The single most important consideration in both the development of language tests and the interpretation of their results is the purpose or purposes which the particular tests are intended to serve.

L. F. Bachman, 1990

QUESTIONS TO THINK ABOUT

1. Describe your own experiences as a student and/or as a practicing teacher with language testing. Were they mainly positive or negative?

2. For what purposes do you feel second and foreign language students should be assessed in the target language? In each case, what would you want to know?

3. What might a dialogical approach to testing be? How might it differ from other kinds of tests with which you are familiar?

4. Is it possible to design a language assessment program that is both instructive and evaluative? What might it look like? How might you go about justifying your program to your students, their parents, and the school administration?

5. If your classroom is to become as participatory as possible, what implications might this have for testing and assessment?

Although no author can even begin to do justice to the subject of language assessment and standards in a single chapter, I attempt here to present some of the important information and issues that appear to be most relevant to language teachers across the United States and in other places in the world where such information may have relevance.

The chapter begins with a traditional testing framework and looks at test evaluation, selection, and development as we know it today. It then moves to finding a practical way to determine the appropriate placement of second and foreign language students, making testing an integral part of instruction, identifying and assessing learner outcomes, and exploring issues surrounding the use of large-scale standardized tests. The chapter ends with a type of assessment that could have important implications for the future: a dialogical approach to testing.

Misconceptions about testing have been with us a long time—not only as it concerns second language students but all students. For example, many people in the United States and elsewhere have believed that standardized tests are an accurate means for assessing student learning and that such tests are all that we need for such assessment. A single standardized test has often been used to evaluate not only individuals (students, teachers, and administrators) but also programs, schools, and entire school districts. A low score on a standardized test has kept some students from graduating with their classmates. Curriculum has been put on hold in many schools across the United States so that students could be drilled for test taking. State officials in Colorado at one time even considered ranking teacher preparation programs according to how well their graduates' students did on standardized tests. Similar misuse of standardized testing may be occurring today in other places around the world.

Even more troubling is the fact that critical decisions have often been made about second and foreign language students based on their performance on a single language test. Will the student be able to enter a program of choice? Will he or she be able to exit a basic language program and move on to more challenging course work? Important judgments such as these are often based on the very limited data provided by a language test, the scores of which may reflect mainly a knowledge of grammar rules, vocabulary distinctions, and the like. Here I am reminded of the classic story retold by Clark and Clifford (1998) about the scientific investigation of the bumblebee, carried out by an aerodynamic engineer.

> [He] carefully measured the wingspan, body weight, airflow pattern, size and placement of wing muscles, number of wing beats per second, and numerous other of the bee's physiology, and by means of elaborate diagrams, mathematical formulas, and computer-aided calculations, was able to demonstrate conclusively that the bumblebee is incapable of flight. (p. 146)

Similarly, we have often examined students' knowledge of language to come to conclusions about performance capabilities. Does the student of German know the rule governing the subject-AUX inversion following fronted adverbials? Does the student of English know when and how to use the subjunctive? Does the student of French recognize meaning contrasts between the *imparfait* and the *passé composé*? Based on the data obtained from tests of such knowledge, we have often determined that the student is incapable (or capable, as the case may be) of successfully functioning at the level expected—based on the misconception that the ability to use language can be judged by separating it from its context.

Although some of these tests have been improved in recent years by including more authentic testing components (see especially the Test of English as a Foreign Language [TOEFL]), they still should not be used as the only criteria supporting decisions that have had such impact on students' lives. Evaluation of schools and individuals needs to be based on a *variety of assessment procedures*, with formal testing being only one of them.

One aim of this chapter is to explore some other types of assessment, including informal language tests and several formative evaluative tools such as portfolios and performance checklists. We look at a variety of means by which we can determine how our students are doing and whether they have achieved goals and met standards in language development. Performance data are discussed as they relate to decision making and monitoring of student progress in the target language. Even more importantly, alternative ways of testing which look at interaction in instructional environments are examined to see what promise they might hold for finding new ways to test.

The assessment instruments and possibilities for testing described in this chapter may or may not be applicable in different environments around the world, especially in situations where English is taught. Now that many Englishes exist globally, tests need to reflect the appropriate dialects or target languages found in the various cultural settings (see also pp. 6-7 in this volume).

LANGUAGE TESTS: A TRADITIONAL FRAMEWORK

Obviously not everything traditional in language testing can be covered in this section, so I have selected a few concepts that I feel might be most helpful to teachers in classrooms.

According to McNamara (2006), "language tests are procedures for generalizing" (p. 28). The tester generalizes, based on observed performance under test conditions, about what the test taker will be able to do when not operating under test conditions. In language programs, tests are most often given to collect information for making one of the following types of decisions:

- *placement*—placing students appropriately in programs
- *diagnosis*—guiding students' learning activities based on an analysis of the aspects of the target language in which they need to improve
- *achievement assessment*—assigning grades or deciding which students will pass a course based on the extent to which they have attained/achieved course or program objectives

Tests have traditionally been categorized in one of three ways: *norm-referenced* versus *criterion-referenced*, *indirect* versus *direct*, and *discrete point* versus *integrative*.

Norm-Referenced Tests versus Criterion-Referenced Tests

Norm-referenced test scores indicate how well a student does compared to how others do or have done on that same test. When administered on a large scale using accepted statistical procedures, we say that the test is "normed." Results are typically given in terms of a percentile rank. For example, if we say that a student scores in the 96th percentile, that means that the student did better than 96 percent of the test takers on whose test performance the norm was based.

Criterion-referenced test scores, on the other hand, indicate how well the student has performed in terms of specific criteria, objectives, or a level of performance that has been determined independently from how well other students perform on the test. A criterion-referenced test is used mainly for diagnosis and achievement (J. D. Brown & Hudson, 2002). A driver's license test is an example of a criterion-referenced test; one either passes or fails it, based on agreed-on standards. How one compares with others who have taken the test is not relevant. Another example is a teacher certification test. The passing score for this test is based on professional standards of teacher competency. Thus any teacher who demonstrates professional competency on this test will pass.

Indirect Testing versus Direct Testing

Indirect testing does not examine the ability to perform in authentic situations. For example, a test of lexical items relating to history might be used to predict how well a student will be able to function in a history class with competent speakers of the target language. Most would agree that such a test would probably not be a very good predictor in this situation. Indirect tests do not test actual performance; rather they test enabling skills or micro skills that, in theory, "add up" to what might constitute actual performance.

On the other hand, *direct* testing tests abilities actually used in a given context and probably yields a better prediction of performance. For example, tests that assess the ability to gather important ideas from a lecture, write a summary or an essay expressing an opinion, or read and understand academic written discourse, in most cases, tell us more about how a student will perform in the classroom. Performance tasks, performance checklists, and observations in similar settings can also help inform our predictions of student performance.

It is interesting to note here that computer-based assessment has the potential for greater authenticity and can be more interactional (and therefore more direct in some ways) than the paper-and-pencil variety (Bachman, 2000). It is also possible that computer-based assessment can be used for large-scale testing. However, many questions still remain unanswered. What kinds of determinations can be made based on interactions with a computer? Do test takers perform better when tested with the computer, or do they feel intimidated by such testing? How effective is testing by computer? Clearly much more study needs to be done of the possibilities of this means of assessment (see especially Chapelle & Douglas, 2006; Douglas & Hegelheimer, 2007).

Discrete Point Tests versus Integrative Tests

Discrete point tests grew out of a behavioristic/structural approach to language learning and teaching in which contrastive analysis appeared to be the main focus (see p. 23). Discrete point tests examine the knowledge of specific elements in phonology, grammar, and vocabulary in order to determine proficiency in the isolated skill areas of listening, reading, speaking, and writing. Can the student distinguish between "pill" and "bill," for example? Can he or she recognize a past tense form or the present progressive? Does the student know the meaning of "chair" or "hippopotamus"?

Integrative tests, on the other hand, grew out of a developmental/constructivist approach to language learning and teaching. Integrative tests examine a student's ability to use many skills simultaneously to accomplish a task. Can the student answer a question that is typical of conversation? Can he or she determine the meaning of a certain passage? Can he or she tell a story that can be understood, or write an effective letter? Teachers interested in knowing what students can actually *do* in the target language ask these kinds of questions.

Discrete point and integrative tests are not dichotomous in nature but rather represent two ends on a continuum (see Figure 7.1). Most tests generally fall much closer to one end of the continuum than the other. To complicate matters, a test may be integrative in task but discrete point in evaluation. For example, the student may be required to write an essay (integrative in task), but the essay may be evaluated on specific errors in grammar and vocabulary (discrete point in evaluation). Generally speaking, tests that are integrative both in task and evaluation probably tell us more about the proficiency levels of the students, whereas tests that are integrative in task and discrete point in evaluation may be best used for diagnostic purposes.

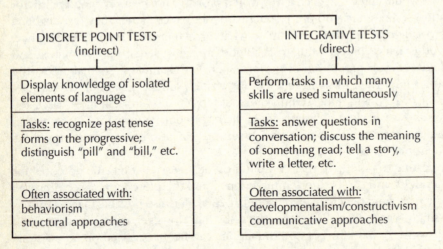

DISCRETE POINT TESTS (indirect)	INTEGRATIVE TESTS (direct)
Display knowledge of isolated elements of language	Perform tasks in which many skills are used simultaneously
Tasks: recognize past tense forms or the progressive; distinguish "pill" and "bill," etc.	Tasks: answer questions in conversation; discuss the meaning of something read; tell a story, write a letter, etc.
Often associated with: behaviorism structural approaches	Often associated with: developmentalism/constructivism communicative approaches

Figure 7.1 Discrete Point/Integrative Continuum

TEST EVALUATION, SELECTION, AND DEVELOPMENT

Language teachers would be wise to learn as much as they can about test evaluation, selection, and development. A knowledge of testing practices helps teachers advocate for their students and strengthens their ability to develop their own tests for classroom use.[1]

---

[1] Please note here that I am only able to provide minimal exposure to some of the important issues involved in test evaluation, selection, and development. For more thorough analyses see Bachman and Palmer (1996) and Stoynoff and Chapelle (2005).

In our postmodern era in which *critical language testing*[2] is stressed, consequences (political and otherwise) take on even greater importance (see also Shohamy, 1998, 2001, 2004). Shohamy (2001) argued that from a critical language testing stance, we need to know several things: who the testers are, their agendas, who the test takers are, the contexts in which the test takers will need to operate in the new language, the persons whom the tests will benefit, the purposes for which the tests will be used, and what is being tested and why (p. 377). Shohamy (2004) pointed to evidence that shows that "language tests are often introduced in undemocratic and unethical ways, mostly for disciplinary purposes and for carrying out the policy agendas of those in power" (p. 73). Such use of tests should give us pause and lead us to expand dramatically our notion of test *validity*. Validity has traditionally been defined as the degree to which a test measures what it is intended to measure. However, any meaningful definition of validity should adequately address the issues that Shohamy has raised.

Bachman and Palmer (1996) identified six qualities of test usefulness that should be part of any expanded analysis of test validity. In the following section, I pose some possible questions concerning each quality for teachers and administrators to consider. (See additional questions that are appropriate for test developers and researchers posed by the authors themselves in their book *Language Testing in Practice*.)

Bachman and Palmer's Six Qualities of Test Usefulness

Reliability (consistency in scores): If the test were to be retaken, how consistent would the results be with those obtained the first time? How consistent are the results from one part of the test to another? How consistent are the results when compared to those obtained on alternative forms of the test? How might inconsistencies in the way the test is given affect consistency in results? If the test is to be evaluated by raters, how consistent are they in their ratings?

Construct Validity (fit between the test scores, the intended interpretations, and decisions to be made): Can we interpret the test scores as indicators of the constructs or areas of language ability we intend to measure? Are the constructs we intend to measure appropriate for and relevant to the decisions to be made? Are the inferences made based on the test results appropriate to the purpose for which the test is given?

Authenticity (the fit between test tasks and the real-life use of language for which the student is being tested): Is the language used in the test natural? Is a context provided for the tasks? How closely does the context correspond to the one in which the students will be expected to operate? What register will they be expected to use? Does the test examine the ability to use the identified register?

Interactiveness (engagement of the test taker's relevant knowledge, strategies, and interest during the test tasks): To what extent are the test taker's knowledge, strategies, and interest relevant to the test tasks?

---

[2] See especially Pennycook (2001) and B. K. Lynch (2001).

Impact (the consequences for the students and other stakeholders—teachers, parents, the community, and so on—and for the education system and society as a whole): Will the use of the test and the decisions made have beneficial consequences for the test takers and other stakeholders? Will the information they receive based on the results be useful to them and to their teacher? What will the impact be on the teacher, the curriculum, and the events of the classroom? What will the impact be on society and education in general?

Practicality (availability of resources needed for the development, administration, and use of the test): Will enough trained persons be available to develop the test, create test tasks, give the test, and score it? What equipment will be needed? Will that equipment be available? What is the cost of the test? Is it affordable? Is there enough time available for giving the test?

Another important consideration when examining the quality of test usefulness has to do with *test bias*, which is basically a fairness issue. Kunnan (2005) stressed that test bias often comes into play when "two groups of test takers with equal ability show a differential probability of a correct response" (p. 786). He mentioned several possible sources of bias. The content of the test may not have represented what students have been taught and, thus, may appear unfamiliar to a specific group of test takers; the language variety may have been different from that with which the student is familiar; directions, scoring, or various procedures may have been ambiguous or unclear; content and language may have reflected stereotypical characterizations based on race, gender, country of origin, and so forth. Kunnan felt that some sort of recourse should be available for test takers subjected to test bias in situations in which they have been unfairly treated as a result of the test.

The Assessment Use Argument

Bachman and Palmer (forthcoming) believe that it is not enough to just make lists of the qualities such as those in the previous section.[3] Instead, specific *claims* concerning such qualities and the *warrants* and *rebuttals* used to back up these claims need to become part of a detailed but flexible framework for developing tests for real-world situations. To provide such a structure, they propose the *assessment use argument* (AUA). The test developer is often called on to not only create a test but to justify its intended uses. The purpose of the AUA is not to prove that the assessment instrument will be a perfect fit for every situation. Indeed that would be impossible. Instead the main purpose of the AUA is to adequately *justify its use to stakeholders* who may include the test developer or a development team, the test user or decision maker, the test takers themselves, parents, school personnel, the community, agencies of various sorts, and so forth. Thus the complexity and details of the AUA are dependent on what it takes to fulfill the purpose of the AUA for specified stakeholders.

---

[3] Also see Bachman (2005).

The *claims* relate to the qualities of the assessment outcomes, or *the degree to which* the outcomes promote

- beneficial consequences for all stakeholders
- equitable decisions based on the outcomes
- sensitivity to important legal requirements and community values
- provision of meaningful information to stakeholders about what is to be assessed
- freedom from bias
- correspondence between the test task and the real-world task that students will be expected to perform
- relevance of the outcomes to the decision maker
- provision of meaningful information to stakeholders about what is to be assessed
- consistency in performance (reliability)

The *warrants* and *rebuttals* have to do with how well and to what degree the qualities of the test hold in a specific situation. Developers of standardized instruments, in particular, must be concerned with providing enough support to convince the stakeholders. According to Bachman and Palmer, not bringing any intended questionable consequence to the fore should be considered unethical.

If the test (or quiz) developer is the teacher, then the stakes are usually fairly low and a more general use of the AUA is in order. In this case, a syllabus, textbook, or curriculum guide may be enough to provide adequate supporting detail. The stakes are somewhat higher if the teacher-developed test will be used to place students according to approximate proficiency level within a language program. In this case, the AUA requires a bit more preparation and justification. On the other hand, if the test developer is creating a standardized measurement to be used in large-scale testing, then the stakes are often extremely high and require a complex AUA that then becomes a public document. In this case, the test developer needs to provide substantial detail and empirical support within all the stages of test development and use: initial planning (including practicality), design (preparing a guide for use), operationalization (developing a set of overarching specifications and creating and ordering specific assessment tasks), and administration (actually giving the assessment and collecting and analyzing the resulting data). Decisions made during each stage need to be revisited and often modified throughout the process.

Because this chapter pertains mainly to teachers in classrooms and not to standardized test developers, only the most rudimentary parts of framework are included. For an in-depth description of the AUA and specific examples of its use, see Bachman and Palmer (forthcoming).

DETERMINING PLACEMENT

Before students can be placed in second language programs in the United States, they must be identified and classified as students needing language support. Generally this has been determined by state law and accomplished at the administrative level of local school districts. According to Durán (2008), "all states use a home-language background questionnaire to identify students whose parents or caretakers report whether a language (in addition to/or) other than English is spoken at home" (p. 294). The answers based on the questionnaire are then used to determine if further screening is necessary to decide the kind of support that is needed and the extent of that support. Because such identification and classification is usually not the job of classroom teachers, it is not covered in this chapter. However, discussions of this topic can be found, particularly in Durán (2008) and several of his sources. Information can also be obtained from the various state governments and local school administrations.

In the United States and many other countries, second and foreign language teachers are often responsible for determining placement according to the approximate proficiency level of each student within each school and sometimes within the language classroom, in cases in which levels are mixed. In such classrooms, students are frequently grouped according to level for specific kinds of work.

The ability to place students with others operating at similar proficiency levels helps in the planning and implementation of workable programs and in facilitating both teaching and learning (see Bachman and Palmer, forthcoming). However, keep in mind that students need to be given many opportunities to interact with those who may be considerably more advanced than they are (see Chapter 3).

Typical Language Behaviors at Various Levels of Proficiency

The typical language behaviors found in Table 7.1 may be useful in assessing a student's performance in contextualized situations. The purpose of such an assessment could be to provide information to help the teacher or assigned tester make informed decisions

TABLE 7.1. TYPICAL LANGUAGE BEHAVIORS OF STUDENTS AT VARIOUS LEVELS OF PROFICIENCY DURING THE PROCESS OF LANGUAGE LEARNING IN THE CLASSROOM

Beginning Student	Typical Behaviors
	Low Depends almost entirely on gestures, facial expressions, objects, pictures, a good phrase dictionary, and often a translator in an attempt to understand and to be understood Occasionally comprehends oral and written words and phrases
	Mid Is beginning to understand spoken language but only when the speaker provides gestural clues, speaks slowly, uses concrete referents, and repeats Speaks very haltingly, if at all; can often respond nonverbally to basic requests Shows increasing recognition of concrete written segments Can create meaning from very simple text but is quite dependent on the teacher for translation and/or simple explanation, pictures, graphic support, and so on May be able to write short utterances independently

(Continued)

TABLE 7.1. (*Continued*)

High

Comprehends more during social conversation but with difficulty; still requires a great deal of repetition

Speaks in an attempt to meet basic needs but remains hesitant; makes frequent errors in grammar, vocabulary, and pronunciation; often falls into silence; is familiar with several common routine expressions and can use some of them in concrete situations; is able to share very basic personal information; is beginning to appropriate more of what others say in familiar situations

Can read fairly simple text, including some academic language

Can write about concrete topics but is restricted in structuring and vocabulary

Intermediate Student

Low

Same as high-beginning

Mid

May experience a dramatic increase in social and academic vocabulary recognition, both oral and written; may understand bits and pieces of academic discourse but depends on visuals and graphic support to grasp more complex meaning

Is able to talk briefly about experiences, needs, simple opinions, and so on and can provide some justification or explanation; can connect ideas but to a limited extent

Has difficulty with idioms generally

Often knows what he or she wants to say but gropes for acceptable utterances, both oral and written

Makes frequent errors in grammar, vocabulary, and pronunciation

Is often asked to repeat and is frequently misunderstood, orally and in writing

Can read short concrete pieces if cultural background information has been provided and if he or she is familiar with the genre itself and key vocabulary

High

Is beginning to comprehend substantial parts of social conversation; often requires repetitions, graphic support, particularly when participating in academic discourse spoken at normal rates

Is beginning to gain confidence in speaking ability; errors are common but less frequent

Can read and write text that contains more complex vocabulary and structures; experiences difficulty with abstract language

Advanced Student

Low

Same as high-intermediate

Mid

Is beginning to comprehend much conversational and academic discourse spoken at normal rates; sometimes requires repetition; idioms still present some difficulty

(*Continued*)

TABLE 7.1. (*Continued*)

Reads and writes with less difficulty; recognizes and is able to use
common organizational patterns, transitions, and cohesive elements;
demonstrates some problems in grasping intended meaning

Speaks more fluently but makes occasional errors; meaning is usually clear; at times, may use vocabulary or structures inappropriately

High

Comprehends normal conversational and academic discourse with
little difficulty; most idioms are understood

Speaks fluently in most situations with few errors; meaning is generally
clear but experiences some regression at times

Reads and writes both concrete and abstract materials; is able to
manipulate the language with relative ease

about student placement in workable (but flexible) groups in second and foreign language classrooms.[4] However, for second language learners in elementary grades and some secondary situations, such placement may not be appropriate, depending on the type of program in which a student is enrolled.[5] Note too that second language learners should also be assessed early on in the academic content areas, preferably in their first language to begin with and in their second language later (see especially Gottlieb, 2006). Depending on the goals and focus of the program, students may need to be assessed on their ability to use language to perform certain tasks.[6]

Table 7.1 contains language behaviors typical of students at various levels of language proficiency.[7] The table is intended to serve as a guide only; developmental and other needs, linguistic or otherwise, must be taken into account. Note that the table focuses on a few easily recognizable behaviors that distinguish each level, although there will be overlap, especially during transitions from one level to the next. Some students may be operating at one level in one or more domains and at another in other domains; for example, a student may be at an intermediate level in reading but at a beginning level in speaking, listening, and writing. The teacher may want to begin the student at the lower level, especially if the domains included at the lower level are speaking and

[4] Table 7.1 may not be applicable in situations in which placement criteria have already been mandated by a governing body such as a school district, state, or nation. However, even in these situations the table may be helpful in cases in which students are informally placed in flexible groups within classrooms of mixed levels.

[5] In many elementary schools today and some secondary schools, the learners are in mainstream programs and second language help is "pushed in" with the assistance of a language specialist or aide. In other mainstream programs, students may be "pulled out" for similar assistance (see Chapter 17).

[6] See especially J.D. Brown, Hudson, Norris, and Bonk (2002).

[7] See also the American Council on the Teaching of Foreign Languages Proficiency Guidelines available on the ACTFL Web site. Although not intended for placement, the following guides to development are other examples that may provide further insight into the proficiency levels of language learners:

1. the Performance Definitions of the Five Levels of English Language Proficiency (TESOL, 2006)
2. the Global Scale of the Common Reference Levels in the Common European Framework (2001)
3. the Canadian Language Benchmarks (see the Centre for Canadian Language Benchmarks Web site)

listening. Students may advance very quickly in these domains and may require a different placement early on. Flexibility is the key in responding to the learners' changing needs. Notice that the list focuses on what the students typically *can* do at each level rather than on what they *cannot* do.

If our goal is to place students by dividing them roughly according to proficiency levels into beginning, intermediate, and advanced classes or groups, then a combination of the following might be all that is needed to make a reasonable determination:[8]

- an oral interview
- a listening comprehension evaluation
- some informal writing
- a reading comprehension task

The *oral interview* process can begin with a picture depicting a universal experience and a group of possible questions arranged on a continuum according to difficulty level (see Figure 7.2 on p. 186).[9] Bachman (personal communication) recommended beginning the oral interview with a question that the tester thinks the student can answer.[10] Following this advice, the tester will probably begin somewhere in the middle of the continuum and then move up or down from there as needed. Thus the student is less likely to feel insulted, threatened, or frustrated by the questions and will probably be more confident about his or her ability to respond adequately. For example, if the picture is of a woman and a man standing next to a laughing female child who is petting a cat, the tester might begin with "What people do you see in this picture?" If the student answers, "a woman, a man, and a child" or "a mother, a father, and their daughter" or something similar, then the tester can move up the continuum to a question that encourages more elaboration ("What is happening in this picture?"). However, if the student is unable to answer the first question, then the tester can move down to a more specific, less difficult question ("What is this?") while pointing to the cat. If there is not a correct response, the tester can move down even further ("Is this a cat?"). Of course the tester should listen for and mentally note errors in grammar, missing articles, and so on in the responses and use such information to inform the placement decision.

Prior to the interview, the tester can have several sets of questions that go with several different pictures. Note that the difficulty of each question asked is determined not only by its degree of specificity but also by its lexical and syntactic complexity and the degree to which the student is familiar with its content. Much depends on the purpose of the test and on the constructs it is supposed to measure.

---

[8] In some situations, the proficiency students have achieved in a specific content area or the degree to which they have mastered specific learning objectives associated with various levels of a course or program may be relevant. In such cases, the test itself should be tied to specific content.

[9] The idea for this continuum is similar to the one supporting the probe questions about industry in Bolivia recommended in Morine-Dershimer, Teneberg, and Shuy (1980, p. 19). Upon request, Roger Shuy was so kind as to locate and send me this citation.

[10] He likened this strategy to the Foreign Service Institute (FSI)/ACTFL notion of a warm-up.

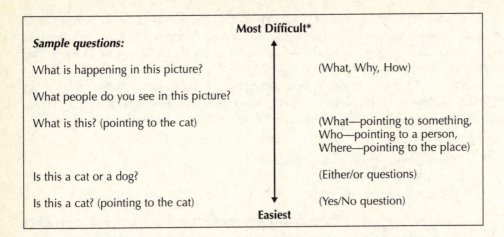

*Note that usually the more general the question, the greater its difficulty. Other factors to consider are its lexical and syntactic complexity and the degree to which the student is familiar with its content.

Figure 7.2 Possible Questions Arranged According to Difficulty

Much of what the tester says depends on what the student says. Student responses should be followed up conversationally as soon as possible. For example, if the tester asks, "What is happening in this picture?" and the student responds, "The little girl is with her mother and her father. She is petting the cat . . . I have a cat, too." The tester might respond to the last part of this response: "Oh, you have a cat? So do I. Do you have any other pets?" and on the conversation goes. The tester needs to flow with the student at this point in an authentic dialogue, rather than continue with the set of questions. Any anxiety felt by the student is likely to become gradually lower as the conversation becomes more and more natural. The tester should be careful to match the difficulty of his or her language to that used by the student throughout. This way, the interaction is largely co-constructed. If the tester is able to accommodate effectively during the co-structuring, then we can be fairly certain that he or she knows intuitively the approximate level at which the student is operating, especially if the student has been given ample chance to speak during the process. Interestingly, Lightbown (1998), in relation to determining students' readiness for particular structures, pointed out that teachers generally are able to make fairly accurate guesses about students' proficiency levels (see Chapter 2). Although the oral evaluation is of necessity highly subjective, the outcome will, in most cases, be reasonably reliable in the case of student placement according to proficiency level.

A *listening comprehension evaluation* can begin with the aforementioned oral interview. To what extent was the student able to understand and respond to the tester's questions? Depending on how the student did during the interview, the tester may or may not move on to other kinds of listening tasks. If the tester decides to move ahead, short clips from television programming or mini-lectures on various topics of general interest followed by the tester's comprehension questions could be used and could reveal much about the approximate level of the student's listening skills.

As with the oral interview, *informal writing* can involve a picture depicting a universal experience. The student may be asked, through the use of oral and/or written questions, to write in the target language about the picture. What does the student see in the picture? What is happening in the picture? Even students who did not perform well during the oral interview should be given the chance to do a writing sample if they are able. Some may prefer to select a topic from several possible choices rather than answer a specific question about a picture. Topics might include family life, friends, the student's country of origin, expectations, and so on. The topics should be appropriate to age and what the tester thinks the student's level might be.

A *reading comprehension task* should contain short passages at different levels of difficulty on a variety of topics such as those mentioned in the previous paragraph. Each passage should be appropriate to the student's approximate age level. Oral and/or written questions should follow each passage to test the student's comprehension. Have the student begin with the excerpt that you and the student think is within his or her approximate level and go up or down from there as needed. It is important to remember that any interpretation given by the student will be heavily influenced by the cultural knowledge necessary to understand a particular passage. Thus having several selections to choose from will probably render a more accurate evaluation.

Once the tester has determined the student's approximate level of operation in one of the four areas (speaking, listening, writing, reading), the testing should be terminated and the next area of testing pursued.

As mentioned earlier, a great deal of overlap exists between one placement level and the next, but that is to be expected. Groups of people are rarely completely homogenous. Our goal should be to assemble groups that, while fairly diverse, are still workable. Within classrooms that are made up of distinguishable mixed-level groups, students should be able to move back and forth between levels depending on the situation, the tasks undertaken, and a multitude of affective factors including motivation, attitude, level of anxiety, and whether they are speaking, listening, reading, or writing (Richard-Amato & M. A. Snow, 2005b, p. 201). Within each level there will still be some variation, which is actually an advantage in that students can benefit by helping each other "stretch" to higher levels of operation, depending on the tasks involved.

Even though these testing procedures may be considered highly authentic by both test takers and their examiners, teachers must take great care in assuring that the evaluation is fair. The kinds of tasks and prompts given to the students during the entire testing process should be reasonably consistent from student to student so that all the performances are elicited under similar conditions. According to Bachman and Palmer's AUA briefly described earlier, teachers need to ask themselves questions about the consistency and meaningfulness of the results and about how the use of a particular testing procedure can be justified. Questions must also be asked about the relationship between the examiner and the test taker. This factor is especially important in oral testing situations. What might be the reaction of the test taker to the examiner's personality or gender, or vice versa? Is the situation likely to be a comfortable one for both the test taker and the examiner? These and many other factors are often culture-bound and can affect the performance itself and the evaluation of that performance.

Teacher-created tests used for the placement can be short, easy to use, and flexible. Furthermore, they can include exactly those items that are appropriate to a specific situation and thus can be quite effective for the initial placement (and later reassessment) of students.

MAKING ASSESSMENT AN INTEGRAL PART OF THE CLASSROOM ENVIRONMENT

Many teachers and language programs are attempting to move away from formal language testing as the sole criteria for placement, diagnosis, and achievement measurement. Teachers are looking for assessment tools that are as authentic and direct as possible and that involve students in tasks typical of an interactive classroom: expressing opinions, telling stories, asking and answering questions, creating meaning while reading and listening, role playing, writing in journals, and so on. Assessment in such situations is ongoing and instructive—in other words, formative as well as summative, process focused in some situations and product focused in others. Such testing provides data not only for the assessment of student progress but also for the continual informal evaluation of teaching practices and entire programs.

Portfolios

One way to manage formative language assessment and make evaluation an integral part of the classroom environment is to use portfolios to gather student work, performance checklists, and other data. Portfolios house collections of representative student work and other performance evaluations compiled over time. Pierce and O'Malley (1992) reminded us that there is no "right" way to design and use portfolios. Rather, the design and use of portfolios should grow out of needs perceived in the specific classrooms for which they are being developed.

Portfolios may contain exemplary pieces of work as well as work in progress, with a separate section for each. Exemplary pieces can be selected by the student independently or by the student and teacher together. To select work for the portfolio, teachers might ask students, "What do you feel should go into this section of your portfolio? Why do you think this particular piece should go in? Why not that one?" In this way, even the selection of writing pieces itself becomes a learning experience, particularly if the classroom is to become as participatory as possible.

Any number of items can be included in a portfolio, such as

- teacher observations and student self-evaluations
- performance checklists in all skill areas (see examples on pp. 191–193)
- preparation notes for writing and discussion (graphic organizers, brainstorming devices, and the like)
- summaries
- illustrations

- conferencing forms (see example relating to peer facilitating in Chapter 15)
- writing samples of various kinds
- reading logs (students keep track of what they read and their reactions to what they read)
- performance logs (students note their reflections and intuitions about what they are doing while they are doing it)
- error analyses (see pp. 45–46)
- oral production samples (transcriptions and/or recordings)
- journal entries
- anecdotal notes based on teacher observation
- student learning journals (see p. 324)
- questionnaires
- videotaped performances

Portfolios may be used in the classroom for the same three purposes of testing already mentioned: placement (or, to be more precise in this case, *re*placement, assuming that the students have already been placed initially); diagnosis; and informally measuring achievement (often used to determine grades). In addition, the data in the portfolios can be used to provide ongoing feedback to students, their parents, and other teachers. The portfolios can even go with the students to the next teacher(s), grade level, or school.

A word of caution here: The teacher and students in the classroom should maintain control over the portfolios, their design and use. Moreover, the assessment itself, for whatever purpose, should be classroom-based in order to maintain the integrity of the portfolio. A portfolio is much more than simply a manila folder used to collect data for summative evaluation; it is an evolving thing that grows as the students grow and develop in the language learning process. It should not be reduced to rating scales and standardized pieces provided only to satisfy the requirements of large-scale testing programs.

As assessment instruments, portfolios can be instructive as well as evaluative within the classroom context. Moreover, they can allow students, teachers, administrators, and parents to see the progress that has been made over time (see also Ekbatani & Pierson, 2000).

Student/Teacher Conferencing

Students themselves are particularly pleased (and sometimes surprised) at the improvement they see in their work. By conferencing individually with the teacher about their portfolios, they often can come to their own conclusions about their progress and see what their strengths are and where they need to improve. Such conferences, if positive and nonthreatening, can be highly encouraging to students at all levels of proficiency.

The following constructed dialogue adapted from Richard-Amato and Hansen (1995—the *Teacher's Resource Book*) shows a teacher and an adolescent student conferencing about the student's progress in reading-related activities. Some of the discussion is focused on a story the students have recently read, "Atalanta," by Betty Miles, in *Worlds Together* (Richard-Amato & Hansen, 1995). The story is about a young girl who decides that she wants to determine her own future rather than have it determined for her by her father.

Sample Dialogue

TEACHER: Well, Alfredo, now that we look back over the last nine weeks, maybe together we can see what has happened here. I can see that you have done a lot of work and, of course, we have talked about much of this before. What do you think is your best piece in all of this?

ALFREDO: I think the letter I wrote to Atalanta's father is the best. I put it on top there [*pointing to his opened portfolio*]. I told her father that she had to make her own decisions about her future.

TEACHER: Why do you like that one so much?

ALFREDO: Well, I think that it is because I will have to do that in my own family. My dad wants me to be a doctor. But, you know, I think I really want to go into my own business. Like a store or something like that. I have talked to my dad about it, but he doesn't really listen.

TEACHER: I think you were wise to try to talk to your dad about this. Maybe if you keep talking, one of these times he will listen.

ALFREDO: Yeah. Maybe I shouldn't give up [*looks back at his paper*].

TEACHER: Are there any other reasons you like this piece? Maybe think about *how* you wrote it.

ALFREDO: Ummm . . . well . . . I don't know. . . .

TEACHER: I see here that you put in a lot of good words to take your reader from one idea to another. See, here you used "not only that" [*points to the paper*] to give Atalanta's father another reason for why she wants to follow her dream. Remember, we talked about using what we called "transitions" to go from one idea to another. Remember . . . we talked about how you needed to use more transitions. And you used that word when you listed your strengths.

ALFREDO: I remember. I really tried to do that . . . you know, what you told me. And I think I did that on other pieces too. See. [*He points to another assignment.*]

TEACHER: Yes, I noticed that too. Well, let's talk about some of the other improvements you've made, and then we'll talk about how you think you can improve in a few other areas. Maybe I can help you here.

Thus the discussion continues as both teacher and student talk about progress and areas for possible improvement. Together they lay out some strategies for the weeks to follow.

Performance Checklists

Performance checklists are very helpful in language assessment and, as mentioned previously, can be made part of the portfolios. However, the criteria looked at should be structured as general performance objectives rather than discrete-skill items. The examples in Figures 7.3.1, 7.3.2, and 7.4 (Richard-Amato & Hansen, 1995) are intended for use in the assessment of reading and writing at intermediate levels. They include instruments for self-assessment in both areas. Self-assessment is particularly helpful in

Name of Student _____ **Date** _____

<u>Part I</u> Check the box that best tells how often you do the things below:

When I read I . . .	usually	sometimes	not very often	comment
understand what the author is trying to say.				
understand most of the details.				
understand the vocabulary.				
read without stopping a lot.				
guess the meaning of a word by looking at the words around it.				
follow the way the author is moving through the text.				
connect what I read to my own life.				
connect what I read to what I already know.				
ask for help when I need it.				
After I read . . .				
I am able to tell someone else about what I read.				
I feel comfortable discussing the reading with others.				
I feel comfortable writing about what I have read.				

<u>**My strengths appear to be:**</u>

<u>**Areas where I can improve:**</u>

Figure 7.3.1 Self-Assessment Reading Checklist, Part I

Part II Put a check in front of the ones that answer the question best.

How many books did you read last month?

❑ a. none
❑ b. one
❑ c. two
❑ d. three
❑ e. more than three

What do you like to read the most? (You can check more than one.)

❑ a. books about science
❑ b. books about math
❑ c. books about history
❑ d. books about animals
❑ e. books about people
❑ f. books about places

❑ g. books about the future
❑ h. books about the past
❑ i. books about the present
❑ j. books about _____
❑ k. books about _____

What kinds of reading do you like most? (You can check more than one.)

❑ a. short stories
❑ b. poetry
❑ c. plays
❑ d. autobiography
❑ e. biography

❑ f. essays that tell the opinions of others
❑ g. novels
❑ h. textbooks
❑ i. _____
❑ j. _____

Where do you do most of your reading?

❑ a. in my classroom
❑ b. at home
❑ c. in the library
❑ d. _____

Which statements best tell how you feel about reading?

❑ a. Reading is one of my favorite activities.
❑ b. I am enjoying reading more and more.
❑ c. Reading is okay, but I like many other activities better.
❑ d. I dislike reading and read only when I have to.
❑ e. I would like reading more if I could read better.

Figure 7.3.2 Self-Assessment Reading Checklist, Part II

Name of Student _____ **Date** _____

Check the box that best tells how often you are able to do the things below:

When I write I . . .	usually	sometimes	not very often	comment
plan beforehand the main things I want to say.				
say what I want to say clearly.				
organize my ideas so others can follow my thinking.				
am able to develop paragraphs.				
use bridges (transitions) to go from one idea to the next.				
use enough details to make myself understood.				
feel comfortable talking about my writing with my teacher.				
feel comfortable talking about my writing with my classmates.				
rewrite to make my ideas easier to understand.				
use words that say exactly what I want to say.				
spell correctly.				
punctuate and capitalize correctly.				

My strengths appear to be:

Areas where I can improve:

Figure 7.4 Self-Assessment Writing Checklist.

emergent participatory classrooms where students are encouraged to become successful learners as quickly as possible. Similar instruments, however, can be developed for teacher assessment of the student, based on observation.

Performance checklists such as those found in these figures can be used to see informally what kinds of profiles emerge for each student and how these profiles change longitudinally. Similar checklists developed by teachers can be used at other proficiency levels and for other skill areas such as listening and speaking.

IDENTIFYING AND ASSESSING LEARNER OUTCOMES[11]

Although in a flexible classroom, lessons themselves must be allowed to go down alternate paths when the situation warrants it, the teacher should have general goals identified through student–teacher dialogue whenever possible. What will the students need to know to be successful in the new language and what will the students need to be able to do? The decided-on goals must be kept clearly in mind when preparing lessons (see Chapter 15). Objectives designed to reach these goals should be specifically laid out by the teacher even though they may change during the course of the lesson itself. Goals such as learning to read better or learning to discuss an issue can lead to specific objectives, which can be verified over a short period of time. For example, being able to identify the protagonist in a story or to recognize a common transition used in discourse is both manageable and testable. Although formal tests or quizzes do not need to be given after every lesson, anything each student accomplishes during a lesson or over a more extended period of time can be noted and made part of the assessment process if that process is pragmatic and ongoing. Even the very informal discussions that take place between student and teacher can serve as checks for comprehension (in the case of reading and listening) or as a means for finding out information about how the student is doing in all areas of language performance. A simple request, such as "Tell me about the story," or questions such as

- "What do you think this essay is all about?"
- "What have you learned about _____?"
- "Do you feel comfortable using this transition here?"
- "Are you having any problems with making this paragraph more clear?"

will tell you a lot about how the student is doing over the short and long terms. Moreover, knowing that the teacher is interested in what the student is working on at the moment or what he or she has accomplished in the past can be extremely motivating.

Observing student behavior during a lesson itself can tell the teacher a great deal about how much the student is learning from both the lesson at hand or a series of

---

[11] Throughout the literature of our field the terms *outcome*, *objective*, and *goal* are used variably (Crabbe, 2003). In the context of this book, the terms *objective* and *outcome* are both used the way Crabbe used them: "to refer to a goal that is specifically defined, usually so that its attainment can be measured in some way" (p. 10).

lessons. In addition, such observation can aid in assessing overall performance and be helpful in providing anecdotal data essential to an informed evaluation of student progress in the various skill areas. Has the student indicated that he or she has knowledge of a selected topic for writing? Is the student generally understood by other students when speaking? Do you usually understand what the student is saying orally and in writing? Do the student's questions about something read reveal logical thinking in the target language? Does the student appear to understand what you and others say? The answers to these and similar questions (although subjective in determination) are extremely beneficial to making decisions during the evaluative process.

Durán (2008) believes we need to reconceptualize our thinking about what classroom achievement is and look to cultural historical activity theory (CHAT) for insight. We learned in Chapter 3 that activity theory acknowledges the learner's sense of identity and agency in addition to his or her basic need to interpret and reinterpret activities according to personal goals and cultural and social orientation. Durán is convinced that it is through classroom interaction that students

> acquire mental and cultural models and scripts for how to act out being competent participants in classroom learning activities, and this includes acquiring competence in using language and language structures to participate in learning activities for communicative purposes. (p. 300)

Such thinking brings us back to Chapter 3 and Vygotsky's *zone of proximal development* in which learners need to operate in order to stretch to higher levels of thinking and performance under guidance. It also brings us back to Bahktin's understanding of *appropriation* and how learners take the language (and knowledge) of others, internalize it, and through a process of refinement use it in creative ways to express their own views and understandings.

Assessment as an ongoing process accomplished daily through classroom interaction can serve as a guide to further instruction based on what students demonstrate they need to learn at any given moment. Erickson (2007) called this kind of assessment *proximal formative assessment*. Through it both learning and assessment are accomplished by means of co-constructed events that take place during the course of learning activities. See similar ideas expressed in the section that ends this chapter: A Dialogical Approach to Assessment.

Any testing that is done in the classroom needs to be carefully contemplated beforehand. Bachman (2007) suggested that teachers ask themselves about

- the beneficial consequences they want to bring about
- the decisions they want to make based on the assessment
- the fairness and values sensitivity of the test
- the information that is needed in order to make the decisions
- how the information may best be obtained: direct observation? informal or formal assessment?

In any case, it is important that the evaluation be meaningful, impartial, generalizable, relevant, and sufficient.

STANDARDS FOR SECOND AND FOREIGN LANGUAGE TEACHING IN THE UNITED STATES

Although this section pertains to standards used in the United States, teachers in similar situations elsewhere may want to consider some of its implications. Standards specify what students should know and what they should be able to do as a result of instruction in the target language. If carefully selected and judiciously implemented, they can help ensure that a program is including relevant skills in personal, sociopolitical, and academic communication, both written and oral.

On first blush, standards, particularly those proposed by forces outside the classroom, appear to fly in the face of participatory language teaching. It is important that standards be considered *guidelines* and that they be universal enough to fit into the agendas of most students and their teachers. Discussing the standards with students who are proficient enough to talk about them meaningfully is essential in working toward an emergent participatory classroom environment. In such an environment, student input is critical to decisions about standards and how they can best be achieved with individual students. Self-assessment is also an important part of the process so that students can eventually become fully functioning learners (see also McNamara & Deane, 1995; Smolen, Newman, Wathen, & Lee, 1995).

English Language Proficiency Standards

An example of standards proposed for English learners can be found in the document titled *PreK-12 English Language Proficiency Standards* published by Teachers of English to Speakers of Other Languages (2006). This document was a revision of the earlier *ESL Standards for PreK-12* (1997).[12] In the 2006 publication, the language proficiency standards were described along with their implications and were coordinated with four academic content areas: language arts, mathematics, science, and social studies. The standards were intended to provide teachers, administrators, states, and school districts with a model for meeting the needs of second language students at all levels, preK through grade 12. See Figures 7.5 and 7.6 (on p. 198) for the anchors and performance definitions.

Next, Figures 7.7 and 7.8 (on pp. 199 and 200, respectively) present sample applications of the language proficiency standards for social, intercultural, and instructional purposes (grade levels 1 to 3) and for mathematics (grade levels 9 to 12). See the entire Teachers of English to Speakers of Other Languages 2006 document to examine applications for other grade levels and various subject areas. The domains covered in each subject area were listening, speaking, reading, and writing; the proficiency levels included levels 1 to 5 that corresponded with the levels indicated in Figure 7.6.

Generally speaking, language assessment of various types can be tied into standards and used to inform teachers, students and their parents, school districts, and other

---

[12] Those undertaking the 2006 project included Margo Gottlieb, Lynore Carnuccio, Gisela Ernst-Slavit, and Anne Katz (with contributions from Marguerite Ann Snow). See also Gottlieb (2006) for further ideas and applications.

Focus of TESOL's English Language Proficiency Standards	Source of Academic Content Standards
1. Communication in English for social, intercultural, and instructional purposes	Teachers of English to Speakers of Other Languages, Inc.
2. Communication of information, ideas, and concepts of language arts	National Council of Teachers of English and International Reading Association
3. Communication of information, ideas, and concepts of mathematics	National Council of Teachers of Mathematics
4. Communication of information, ideas, and concepts of science	National Research Council
5. Communication of information, ideas, and concepts of social studies	National Council for the Social Studies

Figure 7.5 Anchors for PreK–12 English Language Proficiency Standards © 2006 Teachers of English to Speakers of Other Languages

stakeholders about the extent to which students are meeting them. The data needed to test standards within the classroom can be attained in two ways (Katz, 2000):

- traditional testing
- classroom-based assessments that are part of the instructional process

Katz pointed out that students need complex, context-situated testing, encompassing both individual and group performance. She went on to say that the tests should comprise multiple assessments that are authentic, dynamic, and standards-referenced, and that these tests should be used not to rank students (as traditional tests often do) but rather to chart each student's progress. She suggested that the data collected over time include writing samples, group observations, reading inventories, oral proficiency tests, and the like, collected at different times during the year.

Katz also suggested several steps for aligning the standards with the assessments used to determine to what extent they have been achieved. Her steps include making decisions about

1. which standards should be assessed
2. how these standards can be approached through specific activities and in specific contexts
3. whether the assessment tool will be created or selected from ones already developed
4. what the outcome levels will be
5. how it will be determined that the tool used is actually measuring the standard it is supposed to measure.

If the stakes are especially high, Katz pointed out that great care should be taken in choosing the instruments used and gathering corroborating evidence by other means.

Level 1 Starting	Level 2 Emerging	Level 3 Developing	Level 4 Expanding	Level 5 Bridging
English language learners can understand and use . . .				
. . . language to communicate with others around basic concrete needs.	. . . language to draw on simple and routine experiences to communicate with others.	. . . language to communicate with others on familiar matters regularly encountered.	. . . language in both concrete and abstract situations and apply language to new experiences.	. . . a wide range of longer oral and written texts and recognize implicit meaning.
. . . high-frequency words and memorized chunks of language.	. . . high-frequency and some general academic vocabulary and expressions.	. . . general and some specialized academic vocabulary and expressions.	. . . specialized and some technical academic vocabulary and expressions.	. . . technical academic vocabulary and expressions.
. . . words, phrases, or chunks of language.	. . . phrases or short sentences in oral or written communication.	. . . expanded sentences in oral or written communication.	. . . a variety of sentence lengths of varying linguistic complexity in oral and written communication.	. . . a variety of sentence lengths of varying linguistic complexity in extended oral or written discourse.
. . . pictorial, graphic, or nonverbal representation of language.	. . . oral or written language, making errors that often impede the meaning of the communication.	. . . oral or written language, making errors that may impede the communication but retain much of its meaning.	. . . oral or written language, making minimal errors that do not impede the overall meaning of the communication.	. . . oral or written language approaching comparability to that of English-proficient peers.

Figure 7.6 Performance Definitions of the Five Levels of English Language Proficiency ©2006 Teachers of English to Speakers of Other Languages

English learners cannot be expected to meet the same standards or take the same tests as native language students. Standards intended for mainstream students are often measured in large-scale assessments usually given to the majority of students at the program, school district, or state levels. However, according to Gottlieb (2000), such large-scale instruments are generally not valid in the case of English learners.[13] She argued that, because these students are in the process of learning English, they should be held

---

[13] Cummins (1981a) concluded early on that district, state, and nationwide tests are generally not good instruments to use with students learning English. Even students who have been learning English in school for about three years perform about one standard deviation below grade norms in academic English skills.

Standard 1

English language learners **communicate** for SOCIAL, INTERCULTURAL, and INSTRUCTIONAL purposes within the school setting

Domain	Topic	Level 1	Level 2	Level 3	Level 4	Level 5
LISTENING	Directions Instructions	Mimic responses to one-step oral commands supported by gestures, songs, or realia	Follow one- to two-step oral commands supported by gestures, songs, or realia	Follow a series of oral commands supported by gestures, songs, or realia	Follow multistep commands within oral discourse supported by gestures or realia	Follow multistep commands within oral discourse in various contexts
SPEAKING	Feelings Emotions Needs	Respond to everyday oral requests or questions from a partner	Make requests, ask questions, or state reactions to everyday events, situations, or cultural experiences with a partner	Describe or recount reactions to everyday events, situations, or cultural experiences in small groups	Elaborate, using details or examples, reactions to events, situations, or cultural experiences	Present skits reflecting reactions to events, situations, or cultural experiences
READING	Messages Information	Match icons of home, school, or community with individual words with a partner	Associate icons of home, school, or community with short phrases or short sentences expressing their functions (e.g., "Cars stop here.") with a partner	Answer or select questions related to icons, illustrated announcements, invitations, or memos (e.g., "When is the fair?") with a partner	Connect facts or ideas in illustrated announcements, invitations, or memos to new situations with a partner	Infer facts or ideas in illustrated announcements, invitations, or memos
WRITING	Social, cultural, school traditions	Label or match names of peers, teachers, or family members in person or photographs	Create illustrated lists by brainstorming special events or celebrations at school, home, or home country with a partner or in small groups	Describe special events or celebrations at school, home, or home country using drawings or graphic organizers	Explain and give details of special events or celebrations at school, home, or in the home country using drawings or graphic organizers	Produce stories about special events or celebrations and share with peers

Figure 7.7 Standard 1: English Language Learners Communicate for Social, Intercultural, and Instructional Purposes within the School Setting. **Grades 1–3.** © 2006 Teachers of English to Speakers of Other Languages

Standard 3

English language learners **communicate** information, ideas, and concepts necessary for academic success in the area of MATHEMATICS

Domain	Topic	Level 1	Level 2	Level 3	Level 4	Level 5
LISTENING	Quadrilaterals	Identify properties of figures (e.g., opposite sides or angles) in small groups based on visual representations and oral statements	Compare or classify examples of figures with a partner based on visual representations and oral descriptions	Draw or construct figures using materials or computer software with a partner based on oral directions	Respond (through pointing or drawing) to language associated with deductive proofs involving sides and angles of figures with a partner	Follow oral directions to generate transformations of geometric shapes using materials or computer software, and grade-level text
SPEAKING	Problem solving	State or repeat steps in problem solving using manipulatives or visual support	Describe steps in solving problems using tools or technology (e.g., protractors, calculators)	Explain steps used in problem solving assisted by mental math or think-alouds	Present two or more approaches to solving the same math problem as part of a team presentation	Discuss and provide examples of a variety of strategies for solving grade-level math problems
READING	Data displays Data interpretation	Match data in graphic representations from everyday sources (e.g., newspapers, magazines) to text with a partner	Sort and rank, with a partner, information gathered from data on graphs (e.g., stock quotes, sports statistics)	Analyze comparative language to draw conclusions from data in charts, tables, and graphs with a partner	Organize, display, and interpret data from visually or graphically supported material with a partner	Make predictions based on charts and graphs from modified grade-level text
WRITING	Algebra	Copy and label equations, inequalities, or expressions from overheads or models	Describe simple equations, inequalities, or expressions from real-life situations with a partner	Create explanations for equations, inequalities, or expressions with a partner	Provide justifications (e.g., proofs) to solutions of equations, inequalities, or expressions in small groups	Compose word problems that fit equations, inequalities, or expressions

Figure 7.8 Standard 3: English Language Learners Communicate Information, Ideas, and Concepts Necessary for Academic Success in the Area of Mathematics **Grades 9–12.** © 2006 Teachers of English to Speakers of Other Languages.

accountable only for their performance on standards that have been specifically developed for them. Moreover, Gottlieb recommended that the instruments used contain textual information including maps, pictures, diagrams, graphic organizers, and so on and that the tasks and activities reflect the kinds of instruction these students have received in their classes.

Clustering progress indicators by grade level is also problematic. Certain kinds of learning do not necessarily parallel grade level or age. We need to begin where each student is and build from there. To fail to do so ignores the student's individuality and internal process of development.

Possible Washback Effects of Large-Scale Testing

The term *washback effect* is usually used in the literature to refer to the consequence of the test on the curriculum (J. D. Brown & Hudson, 2002). However, there are other effects as well that are associated not only with the test itself but with the use of a test when assessing how well students are meeting standards. Such effects, which can be positive or negative, can have consequences for all the stakeholders including the student, the teacher, parents, the community, and so forth.

The negative effects of the misuse of large-scale testing have greatly troubled teachers over the years. One negative effect that has been particularly troubling is the constant pressure placed on them to improve test scores. Often such pressure has lead to "teaching to the test" (Valdez Pierce, 2003). Although it may be true that teaching to the test can improve students' test scores on a particular test, we need to ask ourselves: at what cost?

One of the costs, according to K. E. Johnson (2006), is that teaching to the test is likely to make teachers feel disempowered:

> it is not surprising that L2 teachers struggle to reject a teach-for-the-test mentality [and] are frustrated by being positioned as managers of curricula rather than as facilitators of the L2 learning process. (p. 248)

Leung and Lewkowicz (2006) concluded that another cost can be a narrowed curriculum. Many schools, due to the early effects of the No Child Left Behind Act of 2001,[14] cut back or even eliminated some of the courses that kept large numbers of students in school. Art, music, physical education, business, tech arts, and even some science programs were seriously affected.

Not only can the misuse of large-scale tests lead eventually to the disempowering of teachers and a narrowed curriculum, but they sometimes result in a dumbing down of

---

[14] The No Child Left Behind Act of 2001 was a revision and reauthorization of the Elementary and Secondary Act of 1965. It required that each state test English learners using a standardized test of English language proficiency and a standardized test of achievement in reading/language arts, mathematics, and science. However, the appropriateness of such testing and its use for English learners has been seriously questioned (see Durán, 2008; Gottlieb, 2006; Menken, 2008). To ease the situation somewhat, accommodated assessments and modified assessments were allowed in individual states (see details in Durán, 2008).

achievement possibilities due to minimal benchmarks (Brindley, 2001). Because the test scores themselves took on such importance, going beyond the benchmarks may not have seemed worth the effort. Teachers often focused on overlearning the basics on which they and their students were to be judged. For the sake of expediency, teachers were tempted to resort to lecture and transmissive teaching strategies at the expense of learner-centered, interactive, and constructivist modes of operation (see Kaufman, 2004).

Falk (2000) warned about many of the same problems. However, she went on to summarize what educational leaders, teachers, parents, and the community can do to make sure standards and assessments are accomplished in the "service of learning." Some of her recommendations included

- helping students instead of using their test scores to punish them through tracking or retention
- developing learning environments based on how students learn best
- educating families, policymakers, and the community at large

Falk suggested that parents and other members of the community learn as much as they can about the curriculum, the assessments being used, and the role these assessments play in the educational system. Most importantly, she encouraged them to make their voices heard.

Bachman (2000) suggested that although the problems concerning the misuse of testing in general were brought to light through concerns often associated with critical social theory, the solutions did not lie with critical social theory itself. He pointed to the importance of adhering to good language testing practice. It is true that many misuses of large-scale assessment in particular can be prevented if those developing the tests and using the tests apply qualities of test usefulness and consider the framework provided by the AUA (pp. 180–181). He also argued that professional ethics play an important role. He pointed to Stansfield (1993) who connected the misuses of language tests to a lack of professional ethics. Bachman urged us to do a better job of education in the area of language testing and to implement a code of professional practice (see also Davies, 1997; Kunnan, 2000; McNamara, 2006; Spolsky, 1981).

Although all of Bachman's suggestions, if heeded, certainly promote good language testing practice, most of the solutions offered to prevent the negative backwash effects described here are often beyond the control of educators themselves and may indeed require political and social solutions. The problem is a very complex one and involves ethics on the part of politicians as well as educators. All players, including the public, can perhaps use a good dose of Bachman's advice concerning what constitutes good testing practice and ethics.

Foreign Language Standards

The standards in Figure 7.9 were first finalized in 1999 following a joint effort of the American Council on the Teaching of Foreign Languages (ACTFL), the American Association of Teachers of Spanish and Portuguese, the American Association of Teachers of French, and the American Association of Teachers of German. A task force earlier had

---

Goal 1: Communication: Communicate in languages other than English

Standard 1.1: Students engage in conversations, provide and obtain information, express feelings and emotions, and exchange opinions.

Standard 1.2: Students understand and interpret written and spoken language on a variety of topics.

Standard 1.3: Students present information, concepts, and ideas to an audience of listeners or readers on a variety of topics.

Goal 2: Cultures: Gain knowledge and understanding of other cultures

Standard 2.1: Students demonstrate an understanding of the relationship between the practices and perspectives of the culture studied.

Standard 2.2: Students demonstrate an understanding of the relationship between the products and perspectives of the culture studied.

Goal 3: Connections: Connect with other disciplines and acquire information

Standard 3.1: Students reinforce and further their knowledge of other disciplines through the foreign language.

Standard 3.2: Students acquire information and recognize the distinctive viewpoints that are available only through the foreign language and its cultures.

Goal 4: Comparisons: Develop insight into the nature of language and culture

Standard 4.1: Students demonstrate understanding of the nature of language through comparisons of the language studied and their own.

Standard 4.2: Students demonstrate understanding of the concept of culture through comparisons of the cultures studied and their own.

Goal 5: Communities: Participate in multilingual communities at home and around the world

Standard 5.1: Students use the language both within and beyond the school setting.

Standard 5.2: Students show evidence of becoming lifelong learners by using the language for personal enjoyment and enrichment.

Figure 7.9 Standards for Foreign Language Learning © 2006 National Standards in Foreign Language Education Project

sent out several drafts to language teaching professionals across the United States to receive their input.

Most of the instruments used in the past to test students on the ability to function in their new language were standardized tests. One such test was the College Board Achievement batteries that rewarded students who had developed impressive vocabularies and had obtained a mastery over the discrete points of language. Tests such as this one ignored the students' abilities to communicate in a target language, participate in other cultural contexts, and gain cultural knowledge and appreciation. However, these tests usually did measure students' abilities to comprehend written text. Sometimes the students' listening skills were assessed through the use of recorded speech (see Valette, 1997).

In 1986, ACTFL developed performance standards in speaking, listening, reading, and writing. The students' abilities to communicate orally were and still are assessed using the Oral Proficiency Interview (criterion referenced) and similar tests in which a tester conducts a very structured interview to determine the student's oral proficiency by comparing the student's speech to strict guidelines. In recent years, task forces have been working on language-specific standards and hope that these standards and the National Standards in Foreign Language Education Project listed previously will lead to greater cultural awareness and the creative use of language in the classroom.

Some of the same washback effects from assessment can also be felt in foreign language testing, especially if the tests are for high-stakes purposes. The testing itself may lead to questionable results, depending on test quality or lack thereof. Teachers may end up teaching to the test. Teachers may also experience disempowerment as a result of a rigid, mandated curriculum no matter from where it comes.

A DIALOGICAL APPROACH TO ASSESSMENT

A dialogical approach to assessment could change dramatically the way we approach the testing of second and foreign language learners (see also Chapter 3). Instead of taking only one measurement, the *actual level of performance*, we would need to find out what the learner can do under guidance, the *potential level of performance*. Newman, Griffin, and Cole (1989) suggested early on that using such testing would require the learner to operate independently during the testing situation until he or she begins to have problems or, in other words, has demonstrated the actual level of performance. At that point, the tester then steps in and the learner's performance is from then on co-constructed with the tester. The more assistance the learner requires to complete the task, the less advanced the learner is considered to be. Thus the testing is rooted in the local context and the results can be highly meaningful. This kind of testing is not that much different from teaching itself when it takes place within the student's zone of proximal development. In the case of teaching itself, a type of incidental assessment is a necessary component for the teacher to mediate within the zone of proximal development. If teachers are not aware that mediation may be called for at opportune moments, then valuable chances for learning can easily be missed.

Lantolf and Thorne (2006), in reference to a forty-year-old paper written by A. R. Luria, clarified the direction that assessment can take and pointed out the difference between diagnostic and prognostic testing in school and laboratory settings:

> A. R. Luria (1961, p. 7) makes a contrast between "statistical" and "dynamic" approaches to assessment. The former, according to Luria, although grounded in sound psychometric principles, assumes inappropriately that a person's solo performance on a test represents a complete picture of what the individual is capable of. The latter, on the other hand, argues that a full picture requires two additional bits of information: the person's performance with assistance from someone else, and the extent to which the person can benefit from this assistance not only in completing the same task or test, but in transferring mediated performance to different tasks or tests. (p. 328)

Thus one more possible component is added to the assessment picture: To what extent can the student transfer what has been learned from the mediated performance to other tasks or tests? Vygotsky himself, according to Lantolf and Thorne (2006), might have wanted to go beyond this question to know to what extent the student is able to transfer what has been learned from the mediated performance beyond tasks to other circumstances. Thus the student's "past is brought into contact with the future" (p. 330). For more information about finding the answers to questions of this type and about a concept that has become known as "dynamic assessment," see Lantolf and Thorne (2006, Chapter 12), Valsiner (2001), and R. Feuerstein, Falik, Rand, and R. S. Feuerstein (2003).

Most current approaches to assessment assume that future performance can be predicted by present performance and do not consider the possibility of the results of mediation and how such mediation might alter future performance. Serious consideration of such possibilities might lead us to new dimensions of language testing and to a new way of looking at the language assessment process itself and what we expect of it.

SUMMARY

Our postmodern era demands a more expanded definition of validity, one that includes the use of tests. Bachman and Palmer, Stoynoff and Chapelle, Shohamy, Kunnan, and others have alerted us to the issues important to acting as advocates for our students in the decision-making process. The rights and needs of test takers and other stakeholders need to be paramount in the evaluation, selection, and development of tests. Bachman and Palmer have presented both the basic qualities of test usefulness and a framework for their application to justify its use to stakeholders. The qualities and the framework are intended not only for large-scale test developers but for teachers as they create their own assessment instruments.

Language assessment does not have to be a mysterious and remote activity accomplished in isolation from what is done in classrooms. The way we test does not need to be that much different from the way we teach; in fact, assessment at its best can become *an integral part of what happens in the classroom*.

Portfolios are a means by which testing can become part of the instructional process. Using portfolios, we can collect performance data to use as a basis for ongoing language assessment. Portfolios can be used to inform decisions made, not only about students and how they are doing in our classrooms but about our own instructional practices. By making language assessment an integral part of our classroom environment, we are making evaluation a formative, authentic, and direct process.

Standards for second and foreign language students can be helpful in guiding curriculum development and assessment within language programs. However, great care should be taken in their application to make sure that they are not used as strait jackets for curriculum planning. Moreover, if we aim to make our classroom as participatory as possible, we should ensure that students are able to have input into decisions about standards and how they are implemented once students are able to do so. If used appropriately, standards can be invaluable in ensuring that programs are giving students the opportunity to develop important skills critical to their success and empowerment.

Dialogical assessment is an area we will want to explore further. It considers what students are able to do as a result of mediation within the zone of proximal development. Such testing could point us to different possibilities for language assessment and how we view it.

QUESTIONS AND PROJECTS FOR REFLECTION AND DISCUSSION

1. What might you include in a test for placing students in a language program? Create a short test that would be useful to you in a specified situation in which you might be likely to teach. Explain how you might use the test to determine levels and how you might justify its use to stakeholders.

2. How would you go about constructing a test for diagnostic purposes in the same specific situation you identified in item 1 above? How might you use it and how might you justify its use to the same stakeholder? You may want to consider the error analysis discussion in Chapter 2, pp. 45–46 and p. 58.

3. If you wanted to use portfolios in a typical classroom in which you might find yourself, what kinds of performance data would you include? Design a plan for the use of portfolios in your classroom. First decide who the students are and what their goals might be for learning the target language. Share your plan with a small group. Ask for their feedback.

4. Interview two or more language teachers in schools in your area. Prepare a list of several questions to ask them about their assessment practices. Before interviewing, compare your list of questions with those of a partner. You may want to modify your list based on what you learn. Make sure you obtain prior permission of the school administration and the teachers you want to interview. After each interview, summarize the responses you received. Share your summaries with a small group of peers. Discuss what you learned about language testing from this experience.

5. How important do you think standards are for teaching language minority students? To what extent would you want them to guide your assessment procedures? How might you go about incorporating them into the way you evaluate students? Do you see any possible dangers in their use? If so, how might these dangers be avoided?

6. The No Child Left Behind Act of 2001 started out on unstable ground. Why do you think this was true? What has happened to it since? To what extent does legislation of this type help English learners? What consequences may result from such legislation? Consider the impact it might have on students, curriculum, school districts, and society as a whole.

7. Now that you have reached the end of Part I, write a paper in which you describe your language teaching philosophy as it now stands. Draw on your own experience, prior knowledge, and what you have learned through current

reading and class discussion. Use your "Exploring Your Current Beliefs about Learning and Teaching Languages" instrument (pp. 20–21) and your journal entries to help you. Include your preferred approach(es) to sociocultural and affective issues, cognitive factors, the role of grammar instruction, error correction methodology and related teaching strategies, and testing/standards. Offer a well-developed rationale for your ideas and examples wherever possible. Keep in mind that the principles you incorporate today may not be the ones you adhere to tomorrow. Much will depend on the knowledge you gain in the future and the teaching and learning experiences you have. You will be asked to revisit your statement of philosophy once you finish Parts II and III of this book.

8. ✎ **Journal Entry:** Portfolios, as evaluative instruments, have been criticized for being "messy," much too subjective, and overly time-consuming. What would you say to educators making such judgments? Are any of these criticisms justified, in your opinion? If you have had experience with portfolios, either as a student or as a teacher, use that experience to inform your thinking.

SUGGESTED READINGS AND REFERENCE MATERIALS

Alvermann, D., & Phelps, S. (2005). Assessment of students. In P. Richard-Amato & M. A. Snow (Eds.), *Academic success for English language learners: Strategies for K–12 mainstream teachers.* White Plains, NY: Longman. The authors characterize what good assessment practices involve and analyze the problems frequently associated with student assessment. They describe several types of bias frequently found in tests: content and conceptual, linguistic, functional, and consequential. Alternative means of assessment that are authentic and performance-based are offered for consideration.

Bachman, L. F., & Palmer, A. S. (1996). *Language testing in practice.* Oxford, England: Oxford University Press. This classic text expands the theoretical concepts presented in Bachman's earlier work, *Fundamental Considerations in Language Testing* (1990). *Language Testing in Practice* discusses in depth the qualities of test usefulness, the development of tests, and various test development projects in which basic principles are applied.

Bachman, L. F., & Palmer, A. S. (forthcoming). *Language assessment practice: Developing language assessments and justifying their use in the real world.* Oxford, England: Oxford University Press. Here the authors discuss guidelines for the development of language assessments. They lay out in substantial detail procedures for the selection, creation, and use of such assessments. Part of the process is the articulation of an assessment use argument (AUA) that justifies the assessment's use to all stakeholders.

Brown, A., & McNamara, T. (2004). "The devil is in the detail": Researching gender issues in language assessment. *TESOL Quarterly, 38*(3), 524–538. The subject of this article is gender bias in language testing. The history of the research on gender bias including discourse-based research is presented and points to the complexity of many relevant issues.

Chapelle, C., & Douglas, D. (2006). *Assessing language through computer technology.* New York: Cambridge University Press. The authors take a careful look at the possibilities of computer-assisted assessment in language classrooms. Their analysis includes the implications—both theoretical and practical—of such assessment and offers guidelines for anyone wanting to implement it.

Council of Europe. (2001). *Common European framework of reference for languages: Learning, teaching, assessment.* Cambridge, England: Cambridge University Press. Included here is a history and clear description of the Common European Framework scales and how they can be used along with a language portfolio framework, a component important to the program. The framework informs instruction and curriculum development, particularly on the European continent. Language learners are encouraged to participate in computer-based self-assessments of their proficiency in the language they are learning.

Durán, R. (2008). Assessing English-language learners' achievement. *Review of Research in Education, 22*(1), 292–327. This seminal article offers alternatives to large-scale testing based on an activity theory perspective to assessment that stresses the complexity of learning. Although he feels that large-scale testing can be useful at some level, Durán is convinced that it has serious limitations: It is isolated from what is happening in the classroom, based on one-dimensional constructs of academic competence, not sensitive to English learners' cultural and social backgrounds, and so on. He mentions ethnography as a possible research tool that could be used to track progression over time, and he stresses the importance of letting assessment take place situationally within the context of the instructional activities themselves.

Gottlieb, M. (2006). *Assessing English language learners: Bridges from language proficiency to academic achievement.* Thousand Oaks. CA: Corwin Press. The author offers many suggestions for the integration of language proficiency and academic content, the assessment of oral language and literacy development, standardized testing and reporting, grading systems, and so on. All the while she emphasizes the importance of fairness and educational equity. Survey formats, rubrics, checklists, charts, and many other useful examples are abundant for use by educators in multiple content areas. The book is particularly helpful as a companion to the *PreK-12 English language proficiency standards* (2006).

Standards for foreign language learning in the 21ˢᵗ century. (2006). Alexandria, VA: National Standards in Foreign Language Education Project. In this volume, the standards are presented along with their implications for learning foreign languages including Arabic, Chinese, classical languages, French, German, Italian, Japanese, Portuguese, Russian, and Spanish. Initial chapters of the book include an overview of foreign language study in the United States, how to go about using the standards, a framework of communicative modes, cultural knowledge and understanding, connecting with other disciplines, and participating in multilingual communities.

PART II

Exploring Methods and Activities

INTERACTIVE METHODS AND ACTIVITIES

Methods are defined generally and in the context of this book as *sets of strategies and techniques accompanied by an articulated underlying theory*. Teachers' desires to know about methods often reflect their need for something concrete that through situated practice can inform their theories. Most do not slavishly adhere to the tenets and practices of established methods but instead use them as interesting sources from which to draw when developing their own methodologies and practices in local contexts. For some they are a starting place. Eventually caring, informed teachers transcend the daily procedures of the classroom in the realization that dialectical relationships are essential to student empowerment. Methods can be considered organic; their selected components can germinate, grow, and change within each individual teacher in each classroom situation.

Activities, on the other hand, are defined in the context of this book as *actions taken for the purpose of reaching certain objectives*. A single activity can serve several objectives, depending on its content and the learning opportunities that it offers. In this sense many of the activities found in this text are prototypes that imaginative teachers can develop in numerous ways to meet the needs of their students.

The activities presented throughout Part II are intended not only for beginners but for intermediate and advanced students as well. (See typical behaviors for each level listed on pp. 182–184.) The activities range from very concrete, requiring minimal levels of interaction and participation, to more abstract, requiring high levels of interaction, negotiation of meaning, and collaboration based on shared knowledge. The greater the possibility for learner agency, the greater the chance that participatory language teaching will become emergent at later levels. However, no matter what the activity involves, it will be perceived quite differently by each student, depending on his or her social and cultural perspective, needs, motives, aspirations, and so on (see *activity theory* described on p. 82).

Many activities and their content will be considered authentic by students and their teachers; others will not. When selecting activities, it is important to remember that authenticity is always seen through the eye of the beholder. Whether considered authentic or not, each activity is designed to challenge students in nonthreatening environments that encourage them to move steadily toward fuller participation in the classroom community and the world outside (see Chapter 4). It is also important to remember that students, as individuals, often prefer different modes of learning (visual, audio, and so on), and sometimes those preferences change for different situations. Thus teachers need to develop a variety of ways to teach and provide students with a variety of ways to demonstrate what they have learned.

The activities in their present state are intended for elementary, secondary, and/or university second or foreign language programs (see Chapter 17 for descriptions of program types and Part IV for "Programs in Action"). However, the content of the activities can be changed to make them appropriate for use in language programs for special purposes, such as preparing students for various fields of study, technical occupations, and the like. Also, although a majority of the activities are recommended for specific age and proficiency levels, most can be adapted to other levels (see the following section on sample adaptations).

Whether used for learning new concepts or for practice with concepts already learned, the activities should be chosen carefully if they are to become part of a workable program (see Chapter 15). Most activities can be successfully integrated with grammar lessons when such lessons are appropriate (see Chapter 2). However, teachers would be wise to keep most programs focused mainly on meaningful communication and to encourage student participation whenever possible. If students do not have input into the decision-making process once they have reached a high enough proficiency level to do so in the target language,[1] and if their languages and cultures are not valued, then what we do in our programs, no matter how creative, will probably fall short of their goal.

The particular features selected for local adaptation from the methods and activities presented here will depend on several factors: the student, the sociocultural situation, and teacher/student preference. Not all of the methods and activities, particularly those requiring physical involvement and some of the other interactive practices, will be appropriate for one or more reasons:

1. The local community and the students themselves may find such activities and practices are not in line with the cultural, historical, or pedagogical practices found in a particular environment and may consider them inappropriate.
2. Teachers may not have adequate preparation in interactive practices.

---

[1] Of course the decision-making process can begin much earlier in any language that the students and teacher already have in common.

3. Teachers may not be fluent enough, especially in foreign language situations, to co-construct knowledge or negotiate meaning.
4. Teachers may be required by school authorities or other entities to use specific teaching practices or to teach from grammar-based books or books focused on other discrete points of language.[2]

It may be a mistake, however, to assume that students, other teachers, and school authorities will not be interested in our experimentation with activities due to cultural constraints. Indeed, others within the cultural environment may support the use of them in the right contexts. Although indoctrination should be avoided in any situation, introducing others to something different may be highly stimulating. The teacher, though, should remain sensitive to the preferences of others and may need to switch gears if others feel uncomfortable or offended by such experimentation.

Parts I and II of this book influence each other bidirectionally: Theory informs practice; practice informs theory. Together the two promote praxis, the marriage of reflection and action (p. 95). See especially the questions and projects suggested at the end of each chapter in Part II.

ADAPTING THE CONTENT OF ACTIVITIES

As mentioned previously, many of the activities recommended in this book can be adapted to several age and proficiency levels. The following is an example of how an affective activity (see Chapter 14) developed for use with adults can be modified for use with children.

Adapting for Age

Describe how you might react when . . .

For adults (mid- to high-intermediate levels)

someone gives you a compliment
you are late for a meeting at which you are the speaker
your boss asks you to work four extra hours and you are very tired
you are left out of a group chosen to represent your school at a forum,
    even though you know you are very highly qualified
you are appointed to lead a peace mission in a country at war

For children (mid- to high-intermediate levels)

your friend says you have a nice smile
your teacher scolds you for coming late to class
your favorite movie is on TV and your mother tells you to go to bed

---

[2] To make the best of such constraints, teachers can often create their own activities based on the required books (e.g., by using pictures in the book for storytelling or for discussion or by modifying the activities when appropriate).

someone offers to treat you to a chocolate sundae
two children in your play group will not let you join their game

The next activity is modified for a different proficiency level. In the activity the students are going on a treasure hunt through the local newspaper. The first group of treasures is for students at beginning levels; the second is for students at intermediate levels. See the descriptions of the levels on pp. 182–184.

Adapting for Proficiency Level

Low- to Mid-Beginning Levels

Directions (should be given orally and demonstrated): You are going on a treasure hunt. You will use the pictures in a newspaper. See how many pictures you can find. Cut out the pictures.

Find something . . .

small
soft
square
made of wood
short
narrow
heavy
made of glass
longer than a pencil

High-Intermediate Levels

Directions (can be given orally and/or in writing): Go on a search in the local newspaper. Discuss the details about what you find with a small group. Ask for their reactions.

Find an article that . . .

describes a rescue
tells a story of oppression
tells about something that can be harmful or even dangerous
describes a social event
tells about a positive action of a political candidate
explains someone's point of view
makes you laugh

Find a picture of something in the newspaper that is used to . . .

beautify something
control something
change something

In the first version of the activity, the items are very concrete and simple; in the second version they are more abstract. Modifications can also be made in the content, depending on various interests, background, goals, and so forth.

CHAPTER 8

Physical Involvement in the Language Learning Process

If the training starts with explicit learning such as audio-lingual that emphasizes error-free production, correct form, and conscious rule learning, the risk is that most children and adults will give up before even reaching the intermediate level.[1]

J. Asher, 1972

QUESTIONS TO THINK ABOUT

1. Recall a time when you studied another language. To what extent were you involved physically in learning that language? Share the practices you considered best. Do you wish you had been involved to a greater or a lesser extent with physical activities?

2. Think of some examples of children's physical involvement while learning their first language. To what extent does learning a first language depend on such involvement?

3. How might it be possible for older children, teenagers, and/or adults to become physically involved with learning another language? What might its effects be?

---

[1] Asher (1972) based his opinion on the early conclusions of Carroll (1960) and Lawson (1971).

THE TOTAL PHYSICAL RESPONSE: TAKING ANOTHER LOOK

In the 1960s, James Asher first offered the total physical response (TPR) as one alternative to the audiolingual approach, which was popular at the time (see description on pp. 23–24). His method, based on techniques advocated much earlier by Harold and Dorothy Palmer (1925), involved giving commands to which students reacted. For example, the teacher might say, "Point to the door," and all the students would point to the door. The imperatives brought the target language alive by making it comprehensible and, at the same time, fun. The students acted with their bodies as well as their minds— in other words, with their total beings. Thus the cognitive process of language learning was synchronized with and partially facilitated by the movements of the body.

Asher looked at the process by which children master the first language to justify his approach: Mother or caretaker directs the child to look at an object, pick it up, or put it in a specific place. Production is naturally delayed until the child's listening comprehension is developed and the child is ready to speak. Thus the child gradually becomes aware of language and what it means in terms of the environment and the situation.

Using TPR strategies, second and foreign language students at all ages could remain silent until ready to speak, usually after about ten hours of instruction. At first they jumped, ran, sang, or did whatever was necessary to show that the request had been comprehended. Advancing gently, at their own rates, the students' aim was to achieve a productive command of the target language. Through this process, they evolved from silent comprehenders of the language to fuller participants in its nuances. After a few weeks of instruction, a typical class might have consisted of approximately 70 percent listening comprehension, 20 percent speaking, and 10 percent reading and writing (Asher, Kusudo, & de la Torre, 1974).

The commands were given to the whole class, small groups, and individuals. Once students acquired basic commands, they responded to double actions such as, "Walk to the window and open it." The teacher or another student demonstrated the appropriate behavior first, making the actions very clear. Then individual students in the class carried out the request. If they did not respond at first, the teacher repeated both the words and the demonstration rather than simply repeating the words. Gradually the requests gained complexity as the students became more proficient. For example, the teacher might have said, "When Lamm opens the window, Maria will run to the door and close it."

The students, when ready, moved into the production phase by volunteering to give the commands while the teacher and other students carried them out. The students were allowed to make mistakes when they first began to speak, thus anxiety was lowered. It was expected that their speech would gradually take on the shape of the teacher's as they gained confidence with their new language.

Although Asher recommended a grammatical sequencing of the materials, the lessons themselves were not focused on grammar; instead they were focused on meaning. The grammar was expected to become internalized inductively. Certain forms seemed more suited than others to the method and were repeated over and over during the natural course of events.

The Research Supporting TPR

Concerning the method itself, Asher admitted that a few teachers remained skeptical of his basic approach for one reason or another. Although some accepted TPR for the teaching of simple action verbs, they questioned its use for teaching the nonphysical elements of language—past and future tenses, abstract words, and function words. To defuse such skepticism, Asher (1972) and Asher, Kusudo, and de la Torre (1974) offered a number of studies, including the following two field tests.

The first field test involved adults who had taken about thirty-two hours of German with an instructor using the TPR. Asher (1972) found that most of the linguistic forms of German could indeed be incorporated into the commands. Tenses were combined by using clauses in sentences such as "While John is closing the door, Annette will turn out the light." Function words were not a major problem because they were ubiquitous and acquired naturally through repetition in a variety of situations. Abstract words such as *honor* and *justice* were manipulated as though they were objects. The words were written on cards. The instructor gave commands in German such as "Andy, pick up 'justice' and give it to Sue."

Although the experimental group had had only 32 hours of training, it did significantly better in listening comprehension than a group of college students who had received 75 to 150 hours of audiolingual/grammar-translation instruction in German. Interestingly, the experimental group, even though it had no systematic instruction in reading, did as well as the control group that had received such training. Asher (1972, 2000) surmised that if students can internalize listening comprehension of a second language, they can make the transition to oral production, reading, and writing with a fair amount of ease.

The second field test reported by Asher, Kusudo, and de la Torre (1974) involved undergraduate college students in beginning Spanish. After about ten hours of concentration in listening comprehension, the students were invited to switch roles with the teacher. As students became ready to do so, they assumed the teacher role and gave the commands for brief periods of time. Reading and writing were also accomplished at the student's individual pace. The teacher wrote on the board any phrases or words that students wished to see in writing. The students eventually were able to create and write skits and problem-solve in the target language.

After 45 hours of instruction, the experimental group was compared with the control groups, whose hours of instruction ranged from 75 to 200. The group exposed to the TPR exceeded all other groups in listening skills for stories. After 90 hours of instruction, the group was given a form of the Pimsleur Spanish Proficiency Test that was intended for students who had completed about 150 hours of college instruction, audiolingual style. Even with almost no direct instruction in reading and writing, the students were beyond the 75th percentile for Level I and beyond the 65th percentile for Level II.

According to Asher, the studies clearly indicated that TPR training produced better results than the audiolingual method. He attributed the success to the fact that TPR utilized implicit learning, whereas the audiolingual approach relied on explicit learning.

However, Asher suggested that an alternative model of teaching might begin the instruction in the implicit mode and end it in the explicit mode. He felt that a student's skills at later levels could be advanced to the point at which teaching rules and correcting errors would be beneficial.

Implementing TPR

Even though Asher (1993, 2000) considered his method the main classroom activity rather than a supplement, he recommended that it be used in combination with other techniques such as skits, role play, and problem solving.

The commands themselves could be arranged around topics of interest: parts of the body, numbers, spatial relationships, colors, shapes, emotions, clothes, giving directions, and so forth. Asher recommended that only a certain number of new concepts be given at one time, depending on the students' levels of understanding.

The following is a list of a few typical commands for use with beginners.[2] These may be modified, expanded, or combined in a variety of ways. Some possibilities for modification are suggested in parentheses.

Stand up.
Sit down.
Touch the floor (desk).
Raise your arm (leg).
Put down your arm (leg).
Pat your cheek (back, arm, stomach, chest).
Wipe your forehead (face, chin, elbow).
Scratch your nose (knee, ankle, heel).
Massage your arm (neck).
Turn your head to the right (left).
Drum your fingers.
Wet your lips.
Pucker your lips.
Blow a kiss.
Cough.
Make a fist.
Shout your name ("help").
Spell your name.
Laugh.
Stretch.
Yawn.
Sing.
Giggle.
Make a face.
Flex your muscles.

---

[2] These commands were adapted from a photocopy (author unknown) distributed by the Jefferson County Schools, Lakewood, Colorado.

Shrug your shoulders.
Wave to me (to _____).
       (name of student)
Tickle your side.
Clap your hands.
Point to the ceiling (door).
Cry.
Mumble.
Talk.
Whisper.
Hum.
Stand up.
Hop on one foot (on the other foot, on both feet).
Step forward (backward, to the side).
Lean backward (toward me, away from me).
Shake your fist (head, hand, foot, hips).
_____, walk to the door (window).
(name of student)
_____, turn on (off) the lights (radio).
(name of student)

Asher intended a lighthearted, relaxed approach to his method, one in which students were encouraged to take on some of the playfulness of childhood, a time when learning language could easily have been made a game and "losing oneself" in it is a natural consequence. Therefore, it is important to give the commands in an easy, nondemanding manner.

A sample lesson for rank beginners might have looked something like this:

The teacher has one or two volunteer students, peer facilitators, or lay assistants (see Chapter 15) come to the front of the room. They are offered chairs through gesture. They sit in them. The teacher also sits in a chair. S/he gives the following commands:

1. Stand up. (The teacher demonstrates by standing.)
2. Sit down. (The teacher demonstrates by sitting.) (Two repetitions of 1 and 2)
3. Stand up. (The teacher motions to the two volunteer students or teacher assistants to stand up. They stand.)
4. Sit down. (The teacher motions to them to sit down. They sit down.) (Two repetitions of 3 and 4)

The teacher turns to the class.

5. Stand up. (Motions to everyone to stand up and they all stand.)
6. Sit down. (Motions to everyone to sit down and they all sit.) (Two repetitions of 5 and 6)

The teacher often compliments with a simple "good" at various points and a lot of smiles. Then he or she continues by giving the commands minus the gestural clues to see if the students are indeed comprehending the words. Gradually other commands such as "step forward" followed by "step backward" are added, following similar procedures.

This continues until the students have a large repertoire of commands that they can comprehend. Often the order of the commands is varied to ensure that students are not simply memorizing a sequence of actions.

Some teachers like to give commands to volunteers or the whole class (as in the previous example) rather than single out individuals. They feel that anxiety is lowered if students are allowed some anonymity, especially at the very beginning levels.[3] In addition, they often prefer to use the method in small doses, perhaps for fifteen minutes or so three or four times a week at beginning levels. Otherwise, the technique might become too tiring for students and the teacher. Also, if the method is used extensively, students may get the impression that the main function of the target language is to give commands. For these reasons, it makes sense to combine this approach with other kinds of activities that reinforce what is being taught, such as cutting and pasting, drawing, painting, chanting, storytelling, singing, and other activities (see later chapters). Another way to reinforce the method is to incorporate key concepts during a common classroom ritual such as grouping students for other activities (see also pp. 294–295, 316, and 342). For instance, the teacher might reinforce colors: "All students wearing the color red come to table 1; all students wearing blue go to table 2." Or, using the same method, the teacher could reinforce months of the year: "All students born in May or June come to table 1." The teacher can continue reshuffling students by giving similar commands until each group has the necessary number of students.

The following are some compatible physical involvement activities that can readily be adapted to almost any age level (provided the students are cognitively ready).[4] Possible alternative words are given in parentheses.

COMPATIBLE PHYSICAL INVOLVEMENT ACTIVITIES

The Pointing Game

With a small group of students, use a collection of pictures such as those found in a magazine or catalog to reinforce concepts already taught. Ask students to point to various specific body parts (a head, an arm), to colors (something green), or to items of clothing (a dress, a sweater).

Identifying Emotions

After the class has acquired simple commands such as "cry" or "laugh," place pictures across the front of the room of people clearly demonstrating such emotional reactions. Students are asked to take the picture of a person displaying a specific reaction (someone crying, someone laughing). Later this same procedure is extended to other descriptions of emotions, perhaps more subtle ones (someone who is sad, someone who is angry).

---

[3] It is interesting to note that even those students who only observed seem to internalize the commands (see Asher, 2000).

[4] I would like to thank Sylvia Cervantes, Carol Gorenberg, and Cyndee Gustke for the basic notions involved in "Dress the Paper Doll," "Working with Shapes," and "Following Recipes."

Dress the Paper Doll

Make a large paper doll of a fully clothed man, woman, or child with an alternate set of clothes and attach it to a bulletin board. Glue Velcro on both to make the alternate paper clothes stick to the figure. Students are asked to place various items of clothing on the doll. Concepts such as *checked, polka-dotted*, and *striped* are taught in the same manner, along with a variety of fabrics and textures (wool, cotton, velvet, or rough, smooth, soft). To teach fabrics and textures, cut different kinds of materials in the shape of the paper clothes and glue them to the paper clothes.

Manipulating Rods

Rods of various colors such as those used in Gattegno's Silent Way (see p. 35) provide realia for teaching numbers, spatial relationships, colors, and the like ("take the *blue* rod," "take *three* red rods," "put the blue rod *beside* a red rod"). Rods are used also in advancing students to more complex structures ("take a red rod and give it to the teacher").

Bouncing the Ball

Concepts such as numbers, days of the week, and months of the year can be acquired or reinforced simply by having the students bounce a ball (Richard-Amato, 1983, p. 35). For instance, each one of twelve students in a circle represents a month of the year. The "March" student is directed to bounce the ball and call out "March, June." The student who is "June" has to catch the ball before it bounces a second time. Conscious attention is centered on the act of catching the ball while the language itself is being internalized at a more or less peripheral level of consciousness.

Working with Shapes

Another idea is to cut squares, rectangles, triangles, and circles out of various colors of construction paper and distribute them to the students. Shapes (hold up the triangle), colors (hold up the green triangle), and numbers (hold up three triangles) can be taught or reinforced. Ordinal numbers can also be introduced by placing several shapes in various positions along the board. A student is asked to place the green triangle in the third position or the eighth position, for example. Each student in the class is then given a small box of crayons or colored pencils and a handout with rows of squares, rectangles, triangles, and circles drawn on it. Commands such as "Find the first row of circles; go to the fifth circle; color it red" are given to reinforce not only the shape but the ordinal number and the color.

As a follow-up, students can cut out of magazines pictures of objects that have shapes similar to those mentioned previously. Another follow-up is to have students cut the various shapes from colored poster board, newsprint, or wallpaper. Have them arrange the shapes into a collage.

Following Recipes

At later levels, making salads, tortilla wraps, or other dishes that do not require the use of an oven or stove top provide a physical experience and also involve students in the cultures of other countries and those within the United States. First display all the ingredients for any given recipe and introduce each item, one by one. Then present each student with a written recipe. An extra-large version to which you and the students can refer can be placed at the front of the room. While you or a student reads the recipe, other students measure, mix the ingredients, and so on. As a follow-up, students bring in favorite recipes to share. These are put together to form a class recipe book to which other recipes can be added.

Information Gaps

Information gaps (Allwright, 1979; K. Johnson, 1979) are created in which one student has information that another does not have but needs. One student gives a set of directions or commands to another student, who carries them out to meet some stated goal. For example, Student A goes to the board and Student B goes to the back of the room and faces the back wall, with a drawing in hand (simple geometric shapes usually work best at first). Student B then gives step-by-step directions to Student A so that Student A can reproduce the drawing. This activity is followed by a debriefing if the directions have not produced a configuration fairly close to the original. If the directions are written down by a teacher assistant as they are given, the specific steps can be analyzed to see how they might be clarified (Richard-Amato, 1983, p. 399).

An alternative is to have Students A and B sit across from one another at a table with a divider made of cardboard between them, high enough so Student B cannot see what Student A is doing. Next give Student A some blocks of various sizes, shapes, and colors. Student B gets a duplicate set of blocks. Student A then is asked to build an original configuration or structure with the blocks. While Student A is accomplishing the task, he or she gives directions to Student B so that he or she can build a similar configuration or structure. Again, a debriefing takes place if there has been a breakdown in communication.

Limitations of TPR

Although the advantages are obvious, there are a few potential drawbacks in using Asher's method. The first concerns the teaching of abstract concepts. Although words such as *honor* and *justice* may be briefly remembered through use of Asher's technique, it is difficult to see how their meanings would become clear unless they are used repeatedly in some sort of meaningful context. Asher attempted to remedy the problem by placing translations of the words into the students' first languages on the back of cards.

Another possible difficulty is the lack of intrinsic sequencing. Although some of the applications described in this chapter do involve a logical sequencing, the method itself does not call for it. No matter how much fun or how fast paced they may be, something is lost if the commands remain isolated from one another and from what we know about human experience. For example, suppose a student is asked to "turn off the light and shout 'help'" (as suggested in the list of commands earlier in this chapter). What motivation does the student have for performing these actions other than to demonstrate that he or she is comprehending? If at some point we could provide a context for such behavior, then perhaps the action would become more meaningful and thus more memorable to the progressing learner. Consider the following situation. A blind person (such as in the classic movie *Wait Until Dark*) has discovered an intruder in her apartment. Cleverly, she turns off the light so that she and the intruder will be equally challenged. In spite of this maneuver, she soon realizes she is definitely in a "no-win" situation. She might shout "help" in order to attract her neighbors. Now the commands have taken on another dimension for a student who might be asked to play the part of the blind person. Strings of seemingly unrelated sentences have taken on meaning and become part of motivated, logical discourse (see Chapter 16). Such thinking has evolved into various versions of what is now known as *total physical response storytelling* (TPRS).

TOTAL PHYSICAL RESPONSE STORYTELLING

Often physical activities can begin with a simple story, read and acted out by the teacher and one or more teacher assistants. Later the teacher can act as a director and the students can perform the parts. Directions can include commands such as "Sit down in the chair" or "Shake hands with Mr. Kim [a character in the story]" or "Tell Hong [another character] to take the book from the shelf." The key words and phrases eventually are written on the board or placed on cue cards. When the students become ready, they take turns being the director while the teacher and other students act out the parts. The students move from predetermined scripts to ones that they create themselves. They may even perform their own creations for other groups.

Skelton (2003) suggested that stories be read as students act them out. Visuals can be used to teach new vocabulary, performances can be practiced and presented, new concepts can be repeated many times in context, and the same vocabulary can be recycled in different contexts. Quick and frequent assessments of understanding of key concepts are recommended and code switching is used as needed (see p. 123, Chapter 5).

Interestingly, Braunstein (2006) found in his research that adult Latino English as a second language students reacted very positively to both TPR and TPRS, even though they held traditional expectations when first coming to class. For more ideas involving storytelling, role play, and drama, see Chapter 11.

THE AUDIO-MOTOR UNIT

Kalivoda, Morain, and Elkins (1971) early on recognized the lack of meaningful sequencing as a weakness in Asher's basic TPR method at later levels and suggested alternative ways of combining commands. Although their ideas may not have been as dramatic as the ones offered in the previous section, they nevertheless added a contextual dimension to the utterances. They called a particular sequence of commands an *audio-motor unit*. A ten-minute recording was played on which a proficient speaker of the language issued a series of commands for twenty actions, all centering on a single topic. The teacher demonstrated the appropriate responses to the commands, using whatever realia were available to make the actions comprehensible. An audio-motor unit might have included such pantomimed or real sequences as "go to the cupboard," "open the cupboard door," "find the largest bowl," "take it out," "set it on the table," and so on. Students were then invited to comply with the commands. Actions could be pantomimed when it was not possible or advisable to use props. For example, climbing a real ladder could be a difficult and even dangerous task, but a pretend ladder was almost as effective, using a little imagination.

Kalivoda et al. liked to consider the audio-motor unit supplemental to a larger program (which, unfortunately, they did not describe). Although one unit generally lasts only about ten minutes, it can be made longer or shorter depending on student needs and the amount of time available.

The authors also liked to include cultural learning in the lessons. Various customs involving eating, preparing food, telephone conversations, and introductions were taught through a series of commands given in the context of real or pretend situations.

To examine the effectiveness of the audio-motor unit, Kalivoda and colleagues (1971) looked at the results of a pilot program in the Southeastern Language Center at the University of Georgia. The students were given intensive six-week courses in Spanish, French, or German. Beginning classes received one ten-minute lesson each day; advanced classes were given only one or two ten-minute lessons a week. The eight participating teachers had received only enough special instruction to make the presentations similar in execution. After the courses were over, the students filled out questionnaires so that their attitudes toward the audio-motor strategy could be studied. Of the 180 students who took part, 90 percent revealed positive attitudes. They thought that the method improved their listening comprehension and increased their vocabularies. Furthermore, they seemed to like the change of pace that it gave to the daily lessons, and they found it stimulating and entertaining. However, a few of the remaining 10 percent found it not difficult enough, boring, or silly. Some students and teachers felt that the written form of the commands should have been given, and a few students thought that they should have been able to participate orally in the lesson.

Six of the eight teachers reacted positively. The benefits they reported are summarized as follows:

1. The vocabulary, structures, and syntax of the language used in their lessons were reinforced by exposure to the audio-motor strategy.
2. Students became strongly interested in the lessons through the physical acting out of cultural aspects.
3. The lessons, even though designed for the development of listening skills, had a real impact on oral production. The teachers noticed increased spontaneity and better pronunciation, although they admitted the latter was difficult to verify.
4. The nonnative teachers of the various languages felt that they improved their own skills with the languages they were teaching.

In spite of these advantages, the audio-motor unit may have suffered somewhat from its dependence on a recording to give the commands. The activities may have become less personalized than and not as flexible as those in Asher's approach, in which teachers used students' names and reacted to their changing needs from moment to moment. This is not to say that it was not a good idea to expose students occasionally to taped voices for which there may be no visual clues to meaning.

I must point out that in both methods the teacher was the controlling force. The interaction was almost completely teacher structured and controlled until the students gained enough proficiency to have more influence. At that time, activities such as "information gaps" mentioned earlier could be implemented, allowing students to have a more significant role in the interactional process.

SUMMARY

Asher's TPR involved giving a series of commands to which the students responded physically. The students themselves remained silent until they were ready for oral production. At that time, they had the option of giving the commands. It was expected that the students would gradually develop their interlanguage and that it would become more and more like the language of their teacher. The main disadvantage, which became most apparent at later levels, was that the commands did not, except in some adaptations, adhere to a logical sequence based on experience. Another disadvantage was that Asher's method was likely to be of limited use in teaching nonphysical elements of language.

TPRS was an outgrowth of Asher's TPR. It appears to have been a recent attempt to add episodic structure and thus greater interest in the language while maintaining the physical involvement. Kusudo, Morain, and Elkins (1971) expanded on Asher's basic method by offering the audio-motor unit which added meaningful sequence. In addition, they considered their method an adjunct to a much larger program rather than the focus. A disadvantage may have been that the recording used to give commands took away some of the personalization and flexibility that was integral to TPR.

In spite of their possible drawbacks, effective adaptations of physical response activities can pay large dividends in terms of student interest, spontaneity, and language development at beginning levels especially. Students' chances for becoming more proficient in their new language can increase when they are allowed to listen first, speak when ready, and be involved in the target language physically.

QUESTIONS AND PROJECTS FOR REFLECTION AND DISCUSSION

1. Why is it important that teachers not consider descriptions of methods and activities "prescriptions" for action? What might happen if they do? How should such descriptions be used?

2. What underlying message might students take from the fact that the teacher usually acts as the authority controlling TPR-type lessons? To what extent do you feel this is necessary at beginning levels? what about at more advanced levels? Is it possible that the teacher might gradually give students greater control and still involve them physically?

3. TPR assumes that students are physically able to carry out the commands. What if they are not? Are there ways TPR can be beneficial to students who may be physically disabled?

4. Prepare your own adaptation of TPR in a five-minute activity and try it out on a small group of fellow students.[5] If the commands are simple

---

[5] At California State University, Los Angeles, I divided the students into small groups for their presentations (often we used empty rooms, offices, etc., to give the groups more space and privacy). I asked students to choose one lesson at some time during the course to present to the whole class following the small-group presentations. Since we only had a limited timeframe, we could accommodate only four or five volunteers each session.

enough, you may demonstrate in a target language with which the group is unfamiliar. In what ways was the activity successful? How can it be improved? Discuss with class members. Begin by briefly sharing your own reactions to the activity.

If you are currently teaching students, use what you have learned to try out a similar activity with them. Make sure the activity you prepare is relevant and appropriate to level. If possible, have the activity videotaped to analyze and discuss with peers. Reflect on its outcome and how you felt about doing it. Pay close attention to student response. Do you see any problems with your lesson? How might it be improved?

5. ✎ **Journal Entry:** Reflect on the activity or activities you carried out in item 4 above. What strategies did you use? How comfortable did you feel with them? Did you think they were effective overall? Why or why not? What were some of the specific problems you encountered? How can they be overcome? Write about what you learned from your peers and instructor during the process. What insights did you gain about learning and teaching from the experience?

SUGGESTED READINGS AND REFERENCE MATERIALS

Asher, J. (2000). *Learning another language through actions* (6th ed.). Los Gatos, CA: Sky Oaks. This is an important source for anyone intending to use total physical response methodology in the classroom. It covers related research and discusses in depth the techniques themselves. The lessons can be readily adapted to teaching languages other than English.

Creative Publications. Worth, IL: Although annual catalogs are not normally found in an annotated reading list such as this, I include this one because it makes available a myriad of hands-on suggestions and manipulatives for teaching concepts in math, geometry, science, social studies, languages, technology, and many other subject areas. The manipulatives include items such as clocks, coins (play money), color tiles, blocks, cubes, cuisenaire rods, dice, dominoes, number boards, pocket wall charts, and so on. Although most of the materials are intended for elementary students, many of them can be used with older students as well.

Larsen-Freeman, D. (2000). The total physical response method. In D. Larsen-Freeman, *Techniques and principles in language teaching*, 2d ed. (pp. 107–119). New York: Oxford University Press. The principles and techniques of the total physical response are discussed and the reader is invited to "experience" it through a description of its implementation in a constructed classroom setting.

Takahashi, N., & Frauman-Prickel, M. (1999). *Action English pictures: Activities for total physical response.* Burlingame, CA: Alta Book Center. Presented here are numerous picture sequences on such topics as school, holidays, home, leisure activities, health and safety, the weather, and so on. The book contains exercise sheets and tear-out pages that can be photocopied to aid the teacher in planning flexible lessons.

CHAPTER 9

Interactive Practices

The essence of language is human activity—activity on the part of one individual to make himself understood, and activity on the part of the other to understand what was in the mind of the first.

O. Jespersen, 1904

QUESTIONS TO THINK ABOUT

1. What kinds of activities do you think might be typical of "interactive" practices?

2. When you learned another language in a classroom, to what extent was your experience interactive? Were you able to discuss issues that were important to you and others in the class? Share a few of the interactive practices that you liked the best.

3. What do you think a "natural" approach might be? Does it sound like something you might feel comfortable drawing from? Why or why not?

4. How can a teacher best modify and enhance academic instruction in the language classroom to make it more easily understood?

Interactive practices in language teaching include activities and strategies of many kinds—some minimally interactive, others highly interactive and requiring substantial negotiation of meaning based on shared knowledge. The requirements of each activity depend mainly on the proficiency level for which it is intended. When selecting activities for adaptation to a particular situation, one needs to consider the context and the sociocultural orientation, age, needs (academic and personal), interests, goals, and aspirations of the participants. Physical approaches (Chapter 8) and most other practices described throughout this book are considered interactive. Many of them can lead to full participation at higher levels of proficiency and eventually to an emergent participatory classroom environment.

The chapter is divided into two sections: "The Natural Approach Revisited" and "Modifying and Enhancing Instruction in the Language Classroom."

THE NATURAL APPROACH REVISITED[1]

The natural approach was first proposed by Tracy Terrell and developed in collaboration with Stephen Krashen. Although it did not embody all that is interactive in language teaching, it did describe an important branch of interactive teaching found in the United States, where historically it marked a turning point in the 1980s and 1990s. Because the natural approach and its extensions are so highly developed and provide such an important resource for teachers, it is discussed in depth in this chapter.

When Krashen and Terrell first developed the natural approach in the early 1980s, they were careful to make no claim that other interactive methods could not match if they relied on real communication as their modus operandi. Like Asher, they reminded us that students acquire the second language in much the same way that people acquire language in natural situations (therefore the term *natural approach*). Some argued that it was not really a method at all but was, in a more general sense, an approach. However, the authors developed the natural approach as a method, and so, for the purposes of discussion, that is the way it is presented here (see Krashen & Terrell, 1983). They based their method on four principles:

1. *Comprehension precedes production.* The students' right to remain silent if they chose to do so was respected. The teacher used the target language predominantly, focused on interactive situations, and provided comprehensible input that was roughly tuned to the students' proficiency levels.
2. *Production emerges in variable stages.* Responses generally began with nonverbal communication, then progressed to single words, two- and three-word combinations, phrases and sentences, and finally complete discourse. Students spoke when ready, and speech errors were usually not corrected directly but rather were recast or reformulated (see pp. 50–51) during the communication. It was thought that the corrections eventually would be incorporated into each student's interlanguage.
3. *The course syllabus focuses on communicative goals.* Grammatical sequencing as a focus was shunned in favor of a topical/situational organization. Discussion

[1] See also Richard-Amato (1995).

centered on items in the classroom, favorite vacation spots, and other topics and issues. Grammar was thought to be acquired mainly through the relevant communication. (Note that current thinking on grammar instruction gives it a much larger role today; see pp. 54–62.)

4. *The activities are designed to lower the "affective filter"* (see description on pp. 73 and 75–76). According to Krashen and Terrell, a student engrossed in interesting ideas was less apt to be anxious than one focused mainly on form. In addition, the atmosphere had to be friendly and accepting if the student was to have the best possible chance for acquiring the target language.

Selected components of the natural approach and its extensions can be combined with aspects of many other compatible methods and activities: total physical response (TPR), total physical response story telling (TPRS), the audio-motor unit, chants, music, games, role play, storytelling, affective activities, and so on (see later chapters). The resulting practices can work together to produce enriched environments in which concepts are taught and reinforced in a variety of ways. Aspects of the natural approach and the methods and activities with which it can be used can be blended to form integrated programs (see Chapter 17). Although recycling was not emphasized in the natural approach literature, it was considered important to many of the teachers who drew from the method. These teachers realized how important it was to recycle concepts in many different ways so that they could be mastered.

Because the focus was on real communication, many demands were made on the time and energy of teachers, who were expected to present a great deal of comprehensible input about concrete, relevant topics, especially at beginning levels. It was not unusual to see language teachers trudging across campus with sacks filled with fruits to talk about and eat, dishes with which to set a table for an imaginary dinner, oversized clothes to put on over other clothes, and additional paraphernalia to demonstrate the notions involved. According to Krashen and Terrell, each teacher's chief responsibility during class hours was to communicate with the students about relevant topics and issues.

The following outline adapted from Krashen and Terrell (1983, pp. 67–70) may be useful in planning units for beginning to low-intermediate students.

PRELIMINARY UNIT: LEARNING TO UNDERSTAND

Topics

1. Names of students	5. Clothing
2. Descriptions of people	6. Colors
3. Family members	7. Objects in the classroom
4. Numbers	8. Parts of the body

Situations

1. Greetings
2. Classroom commands

(Continued)

PRELIMINARY UNIT: LEARNING TO UNDERSTAND (CONTINUED)

I. Students in the Classroom

Topics
1. Personal identification (name, address, telephone number, age, sex, nationality, date of birth, marital status)
2. Description of school environment (identification, description and location of people and objects in the classroom, description and location of buildings)
3. Classes
4. Telling time

Situations
1. Filling out forms
2. Getting around the school

II. Recreation and Leisure Activities

Topics
1. Favorite activities
2. Sports and games
3. Climate and seasons
4. Weather
5. Seasonal activities
6. Holiday activities
7. Parties
8. Abilities
9. Cultural and artistic interests

Situations
1. Playing games, sports
2. Being a spectator
3. Chitchatting

III. Family, Friends, and Daily Activities

Topics
1. Family and relatives
2. Physical states
3. Emotional states
4. Daily activities
5. Holiday and vacation activities
6. Pets

Situations
1. Introductions, meeting people
2. Visiting relatives
3. Conversing on the phone

IV. Plans, Obligations, and Careers

Topics
1. Future plans
2. General future activities
3. Obligations
4. Hopes and desires

5. Careers and professions   7. Work activities
6. Place of work   8. Salary and money

Situations
1. Job interviewing
2. Talking on the job

V. *Residence*

Topics
1. Place of residence   4. Activities at home
2. Rooms of a house   5. Household items
3. Furniture   6. Amenities

Situations
1. Looking for a place to live
2. Moving
3. Shopping for the home

VI. *Narrating Past Experiences*

Topics
1. Immediate past events   4. Holidays and parties
2. Yesterday's activities   5. Trips and vacations
3. Weekend events   6. Other experiences

Situations
1. Friends recounting experiences
2. Making plans

VII. *Health, Illnesses, and Emergencies*

Topics
1. Body parts   4. Health maintenance
2. Physical states   5. Health professions
3. Mental states and moods   6. Medicine and diseases

Situations
1. Visiting the doctor   4. Buying medicine
2. Hospitals   5. Emergencies (accidents)
3. Health interviews

VIII. *Eating*

Topics
1. Foods
2. Beverages

(Continued)

PRELIMINARY UNIT: LEARNING TO UNDERSTAND (CONTINUED)

Situations
1. Ordering a meal in a restaurant
2. Shopping in a supermarket
3. Preparing food from recipes

IX. *Travel and Transportation*

Topics
1. Geography
2. Modes of transportation
3. Vacations
4. Experiences on trips
5. Languages
6. Making reservations

Situations
1. Buying gasoline
2. Exchanging money
3. Clearing customs
4. Obtaining lodging
5. Buying tickets

X. *Shopping and Buying*

Topics
1. Money and prices
2. Fashions
3. Gifts
4. Products

Situations
1. Selling and buying
2. Shopping
3. Bargaining

XI. *Youth*

Topics
1. Childhood experiences
2. Primary school experiences
3. Teen years experiences
4. Adult expectations and activities

Situations
1. Reminiscing with friends
2. Sharing photo albums
3. Looking at school yearbooks

XII. *Giving Directions and Instructions*

Topics
1. Spatial concepts (north, south, east, west; up, down; right, left, center; parallel, perpendicular; and so on)
2. Time relationships (after, before, during)

Situations

1. Giving instructions
2. Following instructions
3. Reading maps
4. Finding locations
5. Following game instructions
6. Giving an invitation
7. Making appointments

XIII. *Values*

Topics

1. Family
2. Friendship
3. Love
4. Marriage
5. Gender roles and stereotypes
6. Goals
7. Religious beliefs
8. Political stands

Situations

1. Making a variety of decisions based on one's values
2. Sharing and comparing values in a nonthreatening environment
3. Clarifying values (see Chapter 14 in this volume)

XIV. *Issues and Current Events*

Topics

1. Environmental problems
2. Economic issues
3. Education
4. Employment and careers
5. Ethical issues
6. Politics
7. Crime
8. Sports
9. Social events
10. Cultural events
11. Minority groups
12. Science and health

Situations

1. Discussing last night's news broadcast
2. Discussing prejudice and racism and what can be done about them.

The students were moved through three overlapping and variable stages in the natural approach: (1) comprehension, (2) early speech production, and (3) speech emergence.

Beyond speech emergence was a fourth stage later recognized by Terrell and others as *intermediate fluency*. The time spent in any one stage differed greatly depending on individual characteristics and preferred strategies, the amount of comprehensible input received, and the degree to which anxiety had been lowered. Some students began speaking after just a couple hours, whereas others needed several weeks. Some children needed several months. The second stage, early speech production, could take anywhere from a few months to one year or longer. The third stage, speech emergence, could take up to three years, but usually the student was considered reasonably fluent in personal communication skills long before that. At this stage, the teacher did most of the talking and students did most of the listening. However, as the students became more proficient, they often assumed the teacher's role in initiating input and the teacher became predominantly an organizer and facilitator.

Stage 1: Comprehension

During this first stage, the students went through a silent period in which they were not forced to speak. They received comprehensible input usually from the teachers and, in some classrooms, peer facilitators and lay assistants (see Chapter 15). Often versions of the TPR were also used. Although the students' main goal was to develop listening skills at this level, many of the activities overlapped into the next higher level, early speech production. Students gave simple responses to the comprehensible input by gesturing, nodding, using the first language, answering "yes" or "no," giving names of people or objects as answers to questions such as "Who has on a yellow dress?" (Kim) or "Do you want an apple or an orange?" (apple). A lot of visuals, explanations, repetitions, and so forth were used. The teacher's speech was a little slower than usual. The intonation was reasonably normal except that key words received a bit of extra emphasis. Students were not called on to respond individually. Instead, questions were directed to the whole group, and one or several could respond. Key terms were written on the board, perhaps the second or third time the students were exposed to them. If students were given written forms of the words too soon, it was thought that they might experience a cognitive overloading that could interfere with learning.

TPR was often used to teach the students some basic vocabulary (see Chapter 8). For example, students might acquire names ("Give the book to Hong"), descriptions ("Take the pencil to a person who has short hair"), numbers ("Pick up three pieces of chalk"), colors ("Find the blue book"), and many other concepts. Notice that TPR was involved to some degree in almost every activity suggested for this level. From my own experience using aspects of the natural approach, I found that it was best if new concepts were introduced gradually and frequent checks for understanding were made before adding other new concepts.

In the sample dialogue that follows, the teacher introduces four colors (red, blue, green, and yellow) and has a strip of construction paper for each color. Notice that the language is very simple. However, the language is expected to become much richer as the teacher begins to build on these concepts.

TEACHER: [*holding up the red strip*] This is red. This is red. [*The teacher then points to a student's red sweater.*] Is this red? [*The teacher begins to nod her head, softly uttering*] Yes.

STUDENTS: [*nodding their heads*] Yes.

TEACHER: [*pointing to a student's red skirt*] Is this red?

STUDENTS: [*nodding their heads*] Yes.

TEACHER: [*pointing to a green sweater*] Is this red? [*She begins to shake her head, softly uttering*] No.

TEACHER:	[*The teacher points to the red strip again.*] Is this red?
STUDENTS:	Yes.
TEACHER:	Yes. This is red. [*again points to the red strip*]
TEACHER:	[*holding the blue strip*] This is blue. This is blue. [*The teacher points to a student's blue scarf.*] Is this blue?
STUDENTS:	Yes.
TEACHER:	[*pointing to a blue door*] Is this blue?
STUDENTS:	Yes.
TEACHER:	Good. Yes, this is blue. [*The teacher points to the red strip.*] Is this blue?
STUDENTS:	No.
TEACHER:	No. [*pointing to the blue strip*] This is blue and this [*pointing to the red strip*] is red.

The teacher continues, adding one color at a time while returning to check for understanding of colors already introduced. After working through the four colors, the teacher gives the strips to various students and asks that they be returned, color by color, for reinforcement. It was thought that the students gradually would begin to comprehend and use the concepts in many different meaningful contexts once more concepts had been learned.

It was important to not introduce too many new concepts at once and to reinforce the ones introduced immediately. For example, the students might use magazines to cut out pictures of objects of each color, paste them on sheets of paper, and label each picture. Or students might draw and color with crayons various objects in different colors according to the teacher's directions. A day or so later the teacher might bring in pieces of clothing of the same colors to see if the student could remember the colors. At that point, the pieces of clothing themselves became the new concepts to which the students were introduced in a similar manner.

Once the students were able to identify simple concepts, the teacher reinforced these and introduced new ones by using a stream of comprehensible input: "Look at Maria's feet. She is wearing shoes. Look at Jorge's feet. He is wearing shoes too. His shoes are brown. Look at his hair. His hair is brown. How many students have brown hair?" (nine) "What is the name of the student with red hair?" (Carolina) "Who is behind the person with the red shirt?" (Yung) "Does Yung have on a shirt or a sweater?" (sweater) "What color is the sweater?" (yellow) The teacher might carry on in this fashion about a wide variety of concrete subjects, stimulated by a picture, an object, a map, and so on.

Other sample activities, which are extensions of the natural approach, are described on the next few pages.[2]

---

[2] Many of these activities can be adapted to several age levels, provided students are cognitively able to deal with their content (see pp. 211–212). They can also be adapted for teaching any language, second or foreign, and for most programs: English for academic purposes (EAP), English for special purposes (ESP), and others.

INTERACTIVE ACTIVITIES

Where Does It Belong?

On the board, sketch and label the rooms of a house (see Figure 9.1). Then briefly talk about the house and its various rooms (e.g., "Look at the house. It is big. It has many rooms. Here is the kitchen. Food is kept in the kitchen. People eat in the kitchen."). Roughly draw a few typical household items in each room, including furniture to help the students correctly identify the room. Cut out pictures of other household items to be placed in the appropriate rooms. On the back of each picture, place pieces of rolled up cellophane tape to make them stick to the board. (Later the tape can be removed, making the pictures reusable.) Give directions such as "Put the stove in the kitchen" or "Put the dresser in the bedroom" to see if the students can correctly place the pictures. An alternative might be to use a magnetic board or a large doll house with miniature furniture.

Items typical of other places can be incorporated in similar activities. Simulated settings such as zoos, farmyards, hospitals, libraries, various work sites, cafeterias, and university campuses can be used.

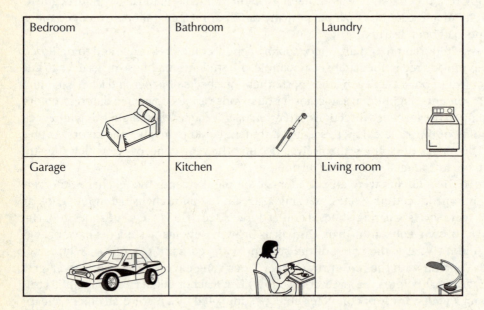

Figure 9.1

Put It On!

Bring in a variety of oversized clothes. Talk about the clothes (e.g., "These are pants. They are blue. Here is the pocket. Point to the pocket"). Have the students put the clothes on (over their own) according to the directions you give. The oversized clothes are taken off using a similar procedure. A camera can be used for recording the highlights of this activity. The photos can be displayed in the classroom and used at a later stage to stimulate discussion.

A follow-up provides the students with clothing catalogs, scissors, glue, and blank sheets of construction paper.[3] Take articles of clothing (which have previously been cut out) as well as a cut-out head, arms, and legs. Show the class how easy it is to create a figure by gluing these items to the construction paper. The figure will probably look very humorous, especially if you have chosen such things as enormous shoes, a little head, and a strange assortment of clothing. Have the students make their own funny figures. Through a cooperative effort, students locate the items each needs to complete a creation. In the process, the same words are repeated over and over, and a great deal of laughter can be generated, lowering anxiety.

Guess What's in the Box[4]

Fill a box with familiar objects. Describe a particular object and have the students guess which object is being described. Once the object has been correctly named, remove it from the box and give it to the student temporarily. Once all the objects have been handed out, ask that the objects be returned: "Who has the rubber band?", and so forth.

Getting Around

For second language learners, make a large map of the campus or school using strips of butcher paper taped together (an alternative might be to block off the various locations with masking tape placed on the floor). The total area should be large enough so the students can stand on it and walk from place to place. Label rooms, buildings, or whatever is appropriate. Make sure it is clear what the various rooms in the buildings are. For example, you might place a picture of medicines in the clinic or pictures of food in the cafeteria. Using TPR, have students move around to various places. Take a tour of the campus or school itself, pointing out these same places. Once the students are familiar with the area, ask them to act as guides to new students of the same first language backgrounds. New students who are not fluent enough to ask directions need to know where things are in order to survive the first few days in a new school.

The People in Our School

Take photos of personnel within your school. Show the photos to your students and talk about the job that each person does. You may want to act out the various roles: custodian, cafeteria helper, secretary, nurse, counselor, teacher, and orchestra director. Have the students point to the picture of the custodian, the principal, and so on. Then ask a volunteer student to act out the roles. See if the others can guess which roles the student is acting out (see Chapter 11 for other role-play activities that would be appropriate to this level and would help reinforce concepts).

Classifying Objects

Have each student make a classification booklet. Any categories can be used, depending on your objectives. For example, one page could be for household items, another for clothing, and a third for sports or camping equipment. Give the students several magazines or catalogs and have them cut out pictures to be categorized. Then ask them to glue the items to the appropriate pages. You can provide comprehensible input about the pictures and do some individual TPR with each

---

[3] Thanks to Teri Sandoval for the follow-up idea.

[4] Thanks to Esther Heise for introducing this idea to me.

student (e.g., "Point to the _____," "Name two objects that are in a kitchen"). Previously acquired concepts can also be reinforced this way.

Following a Process

Students learn to make things (kites, puppets, dolls, pictures, maps, and so on) through a series of simple commands. Demonstrate first before taking the students through the step-by-step processes. Students are not expected to speak; they simply carry out the directions.

Matching

Students match pictures of objects with words placed on heavy paper and cut into puzzle pieces—the word on one puzzle piece, and the picture on the other (Figure 9.2). The kinesthetic matching serves as a clue or as reinforcement.

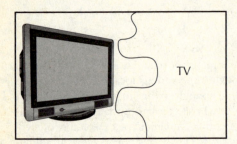 

Figure 9.2

The activities described here represent just a small sampling of many that could be used with students at this stage. Of course, some are more applicable to certain ages than others. However, activities sometimes considered "childish" for older learners are often enjoyed by children and adults alike. A lot depends on how comfortable students feel, no matter their age.

The teacher needs to use lots of manipulative visuals; act out, model, or demonstrate expected responses; use body language to clarify meaning; use high-frequency vocabulary, short sentences, yes/no questions, either/or questions, and other questions that require only one-word answers; and rely heavily on getting the students physically involved with the target language. At the same time, activities need to be varied within any given time period for two reasons: Students' attention spans are often short, and the teacher's stamina is often limited.

Stage 2: Early Speech Production

Getting into Speaking

The transition into the second stage generally began with an extension of many activities used in the comprehension stage. The teacher gradually began to notice changes in the length of the responses. For example, when asked "Who has on a blue dress?" the student might have responded with "Ashwaq has dress" instead of just "Ashwaq." Once the expansions began to appear, they often came naturally and abundantly, especially if the students felt comfortable with the teacher and with the ambiance of the classroom. The speech at first was expected to contain many errors, which were to be dealt with *only* indirectly. Regarding the omission of words in "Ashwaq has dress," the teacher might have responded with "Yes, Ashwaq has on the dress" instead of "No, you should say, 'Ashwaq has on the dress'" (emphasizing *on* and *the*). If allowed to develop their interlanguage naturally, the students were expected to continue expanding their utterances to include a wide variety of structures and eventually complex language.

Some of the activities typical of this stage are described here.

EARLY SPEECH ACTIVITIES

Charts and Other Visuals

Krashen and Terrell (1983) recommended the use of charts and other visuals that make discussion easier and serve as transitions into reading.

Write the following on the board to use as aids to conversation.

Numbers

How many students in the class are wearing jeans?

sneakers?

belts?

glasses?

Follow-up questions:

How many students have on sneakers?

Are any students wearing glasses?

How many?

Clothing

Name of Student	Clothes
Carlos	Jeans
Sung Hee	Dress

Follow-up questions:

Who is wearing jeans?

What is Sung Hee wearing?

The following is an example of a chart used in an English as a second language class to encourage interaction and help the students to get to know one another.

First give each student a copy of the chart below. Then divide the students randomly into pairs. Have them ask each other the questions and fill in the column labeled "Partner 1" on their charts. Then assign each to another partner and ask them to fill in the column for "Partner 2," and so on.[5]

	Partner 1	Partner 2	Partner 3
What's your name?			
Where are you from?			
What language do you speak?			

The teacher can ask follow-up questions and let the students who interviewed the person (whose name the teacher places in the blank) volunteer the answer. The teacher should try to ask at least one or both questions about each student in the class.

What country is _____ from?
                    (name of student)

What languages does _____ speak?
                    (name of student)

The teacher can then ask these questions using the same procedure:

Who is from _____?
                    (name of country)

Who speaks _____?
                    (name of language)

Group Murals

Give each student a space on a huge piece of butcher paper strung across a wall. Give students pencils, rulers, wide felt-tip pens, paints, and brushes to draw pictures in their spaces and place their names at the bottom. Display the butcher paper in the classroom for a week or two, then roll it up and save it. As the students progress in the language, bring out the butcher paper again but for different activities. At first, ask simple questions about each picture: "Look at Juan's picture. What color is the wagon?" "How many apples did Jenny paint?" Later, when the students are in the stage of speech emergence and beyond, they can tell about their own pictures and those of their friends, or they can make up an oral group story incorporating all of the pictures in some way.

Open-Ended Sentences

Extend the streams of comprehensible input to include utterances that the student completes. The open-ended sentences can be placed on the board. Here are some examples:

On Saturdays I _____.
My family likes to _____.
Ho likes to eat _____.

Or have the students bring in family photos to share. Using open-ended sentences placed on the board, have them talk about their relatives pictured in the photos. See the examples below:

My sister likes _____.
My brother is _____.
My cousins are _____.

---

[5] This chart is adapted from one supplied by Linda Sasser of the Alhambra School District in California.

Matrices

Open-ended sentences that are used in certain combinations for specific situations are called matrices. The following are examples.

First Meetings

Hi there, my name is _____.

Nice to meet you. I'm _____.

Are you a new student, too?

Yes, I came from _____.

On the Telephone

Hola.

Hola. Soy _____. ¿Con quién hablo?

Con _____.

At an Office

May I help you?

My name is _____. I have an appointment with _____.

The matrices are not to be drilled using an audiolingual style. Instead, role-playing situations are used in which a variety of responses can be given. Students simply use the matrices as aids and "starters" for as long as they need them (see Chapter 11 for similar ideas). The matrices are placed on cue cards, which can serve as transitions into reading (see Chapters 5 and 13) or be incorporated into chants or lyrics (see Chapter 10).

Asking for the Facts

Show the students simple sale advertisements (Figure 9.3). In a second language class, the ad can come from a local newspaper; in a foreign language class, it can come from a foreign language

CAMERA $250.00
NOW ONLY $189.00

Figure 9.3

newspaper. As an alternative the teacher can show the students pictures of forms that have been filled out: a hospital record, an application for welfare, or a passport (see Figure 9.4). Ask pertinent questions about each.

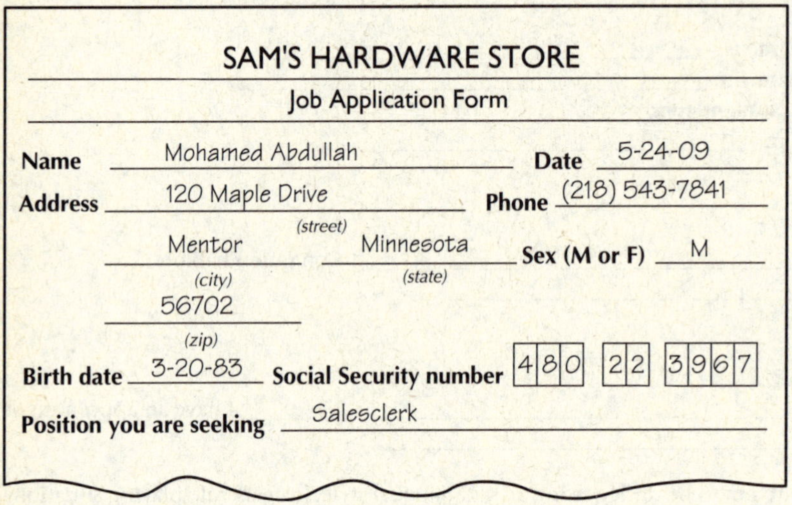

SAM'S HARDWARE STORE
Job Application Form

Name Mohamed Abdullah   **Date** 5-24-09

Address 120 Maple Drive   **Phone** (218) 543-7841
       (street)

   Mentor   Minnesota   **Sex (M or F)** M
    (city)   (state)

   56702
    (zip)

Birth date 3-20-83   **Social Security number** 4 8 0   2 2   3 9 6 7

Position you are seeking Salesclerk

Figure 9.4

Sale Advertisement Questions:
1. What is being sold?
2. How much was it?
3. How much is it now?
4. How much will you save?
5. Is this something you really need?

Job Application Questions:
1. What is the person's last name?
2. What job does the person want?
3. Where does the person live?
4. What is the person's telephone number?
5. When was the person born?

Getting into Reading and Writing

Even though speaking is their major thrust, most of the above activities can be used as transitions into reading and writing (see also Chapter 13). Key words written on the board, TPR commands that students might have listed in their notebooks, cue cards with matrices written on them, words on charts, and other visuals all lead to reading and writing in the target language. Of course, nonliterate learners of all ages, and students whose first language writing system is vastly different from that of the target language, need special attention (see Chapters 5 and 13). However, the teaching is expected to always be done through meaningful interaction rather than by stringing together isolated elements such as phonemes, orthographic symbols, and the like. The natural approach, as first described by Krashen and Terrell, was concerned mainly with oral communication skills. However, the authors agreed for the most part that skills—listening, speaking, reading, and writing—should be integrated rather than taught as separate entities.

Stage 3: Speech Emergence and Beyond

Because students' speech has been emerging all along, to distinguish *speech emergence* as a separate stage seems artificial. Perhaps this is the reason Krashen and Terrell replaced it with the term *extending production* in their book, *The Natural Approach*. During this third stage, the utterances became longer and more complex. Many errors were still made, but if enough comprehensible input was internalized, the errors were thought to gradually decrease as the students moved toward full production. If undue attention was paid to developmental errors, the process of acquiring correct grammatical forms in the new language could have been impeded (see Chapter 3).

At this stage a large number of activities can be used that are somewhat more demanding and challenging but still within reach cognitively: music and poetry (Chapter 10), role playing and drama (Chapter 11), affective activities (Chapter 14), and problem solving or debates at higher levels. Many of the activities already described in this chapter for earlier levels can be extended to provide additional opportunities for development. For example, instead of simply answering questions about an application form, the students might fill one out; instead of just following directions, they might begin to write their own sets of simple directions to see if others can follow them. The following is a sampling of other activities that are typical at this level and beyond.

RELATED INTERACTIVE ACTIVITIES

The People Hunt

Give the students the following list and ask them to find a person who

> has an older sister
> wears glasses
> is laughing
> speaks three or more languages
> is wearing black socks
> hates carrots
> has on a plaid blouse or shirt
> lives north of Maple Street
> has five letters in his or her last name
> lives with a grandparent
> has a six in his or her phone number
> plays a guitar

Then ask them to obtain the signature of a person or several persons in each category. As the students become more advanced, they can find a person who

> has parents who voted in the last election
> has been to Hong Kong within the past five years
> has a family with more than six people in it
> has a sister who likes to ice skate or roller skate
> has lived in more than three countries
> plans to go to college after completing high school

Cartoons

Take several cartoons from the newspaper and cut out the words in the bubbles. Place the cartoons on a blank sheet of paper, providing a place for students to write their own dialogue in the bubbles. Students can exchange cartoons and end up with several versions of the action (see Chapter 11 for more storytelling activities).

Draw this!

Divide the students into groups of four or five. Give one student per group a picture with simple lines and geometric shapes on it. Have these students give directions to their groups so that each group can reproduce the picture without seeing it. The student who comes closest to the original picture in each group gives directions for the next picture. You may want to brief the group on the kinds of directions that will help by giving some key words: horizontal, vertical, diagonal, perpendicular, parallel, a right angle, upper-left corner, lower right, and so on (see Figure 9.5). Pictures should become progressively more difficult as the students become more proficient.

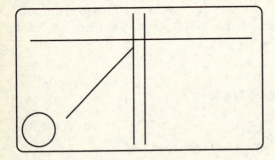

Figure 9.5

Buying Groceries[6]

Set up one corner of the room as a grocery store. Stock the shelves with empty Jell-O boxes, egg cartons, milk cartons, cereal boxes, cleaning supplies, magazines, and so forth. Indicate the prices below the items. Have the students make out a grocery list (see Figure 9.6) and go grocery shopping with fake money that they have made beforehand. Have students take turns

---

[6] Thanks to Cyndee Gustke, who introduced me to a similar idea.

GROCERY LIST

bread
cereal
eggs
milk
flour

Figure 9.6

being shoppers, salespersons, and cashiers. Various situations can be set up to add variety to the shopping expeditions: A shopper may have to ask where a particular item is on the shelves, may need to exchange an item, may have been given wrong change, and so forth. Similar public places can be simulated: a doctor's office, a bank, the post office, a drugstore, a clothing store, a garage. Various lists can be compiled, depending on the task, and the situations can be an extension of matrices (see p. 239).

Whose Name Is It?

Write the name of a student in large letters on a piece of paper. Tape it on the back of a student volunteer. The volunteer asks yes/no questions of the class (they are in on the secret) to determine the name on the paper. "Is the person a female?" (yes) "Is she in the first desk? (no) "Does she like to sing?" (yes) "Is it _____ ?" (no). On it goes until several volunteers have a chance to participate. A variation of this activity is "Guess What's in the Box," described on p. 235 in this chapter. The teacher gives a box with one familiar object in it. The rest of the class asks yes/no questions until the object is named (see Chapter 12 for similar activities).

Following Written Directions

Give students sets of simple directions to follow. The directions should be about topics of interest: how to make a model car, how to make paper flowers, how to decoupage, and so on. See if the students can read the directions and follow them. Have students work in pairs on some projects and in groups on others (see also "Following Recipes" in Chapter 8).

Map Reading

This activity is an extension of "Getting Around," described earlier in this chapter. Write helpful phrases on the board: "turn right (left)"; "go south (north, east, west)"; "go around the corner (straight)"; "on the right (left, north, south, east, west) side of the street"; "in the (middle, far corner) of the block"; "down (up) the street; until you see a mailbox (fire hydrant, bus stop)"; "between the drugstore and the bank"; "across from the hardware store"; and so on. Give the students maps such as the one in Figure 9.7 and have them follow your directions as they trace the route with a pencil. First do a demonstration with the class. Place the map on the overhead projector and trace a route while reading a set of directions aloud. For example, "Start at the bank, go north on Second Street until you get to Central Avenue, turn left, walk straight ahead to the gas station. It's between the grocery store and the bakery." Then divide

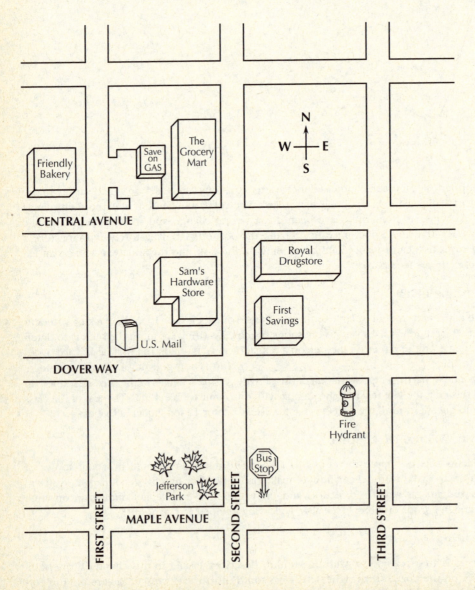

Figure 9.7

the students into pairs and have them give each other directions while they trace the routes on their own maps.

As an alternative, you might combine storytelling with the activities.[7] For example, create a story about a fugitive who moves from place to place in different ways: he walks, runs, darts, crawls, skips, and drives. The students trace the route on their individual maps as you read. Instead of drawing only straight lines, the students can draw broken lines for "walks" (- - - - -), zigzag lines for "runs" (^v^v^v^v^v^v^v^v), sideways carets for "darts" (>>>>>>), wavy lines for "crawls" (~~~~~~~~~), arches for "skips" (mmmm), and a series of plus signs for "drives" (++++++).

Follow-up activities could include having the students draw maps of sections of their own communities and write sets of directions to the various places within them. Have them write mini-stories to go with the directions. Eventually have students participate in similar activities using real street maps of cities or highway maps of whole states or countries.

Sharing Books: The Classroom Library

Place several comfortable chairs in the corner of the classroom along with several bookcases set up at right angles to form a little library where students can read individually, read to each other, and/or discuss books. Books might even be checked out through a system you create.[8] Students may contribute their own books to the collection. The books can be in several different languages for second language students.

Writing Memos

Set up situations in which students write memos. Some suggestions are as follows (see Figure 9.8):

- Your mother is at work. You are leaving for a baseball game. You and some of your friends want to go out after the game for pizza. Write a memo to your mother and tape it to the refrigerator door. Tell her you will be home a little late but not to worry.

Figure 9.8

- You are at home. Someone has called for your brother. He is still at school. Write a note asking him to return the call.
- You have a job as a receptionist. A salesman has come to sell paper products to your boss. Your boss is not in. The salesman asks you to leave a message. It should say that the salesman will be back later.
- You have an appointment with your professor. You need to cancel it because your mother is coming to visit that day. Write a note to give to the professor's secretary. Explain the situation.

Using Local or Foreign Language Newspapers[9]

1. Ask the students to find, cut out, and paste on a large piece of paper a sample of each of the following. Students can work in groups or individually. This kind of activity can begin at much earlier stages if the items are simple enough.

   > the price of a pound of ground meat
   > the low temperature in a major city
   > a number greater than 1,000
   > a face with glasses
   > the picture or name of an animal
   > a sports headline
   > a letter to the editor
   > the price of a used Toyota
   > a city within 50 miles of your own
   > a movie that starts between 1:00 P.M. and 4:00 P.M.
   > an angry word
   > the picture of a happy person
   > a ten-letter word
   > a picture of a bride

2. Have the students look at the commercial ads in a recent paper. Ask them to find three ads for products from other countries. Ask them to find three ads for products made in the state or city in which they now live.
3. Ask older students to look for suitable jobs, apartments, and other items of interest in the want ads. Have them discuss what they have found and tell why these may or may not meet their needs.
4. Ask students to look in the want ads for items to buy. Have them play the roles of potential sellers and buyers. For example, the buyers can make "telephone calls" to the sellers to gather more information about the items. (A fist held to the ear makes a good pretend phone.)
5. Ask students to find an article about an issue that concerns them. Have them discuss the issue with a small group. Ask the group to come up with a plan for action.
6. Finding articles about interesting people in the news can be exciting. Have students plan a "celebrity" party and make a list of those they would like to invite. Have them tell why they would like to meet those they have selected.
7. Ask students to choose a headline and write an alternative story to go with it.

---

[9]These activities have been adapted from the pamphlets "Newspapers in Education," *Albuquerque Journal/Tribune.*

Pen Pals

Mainstream classes or organizations within or outside of the school can write personal letters to second language learners. After several exchanges, the groups might get together to meet for a party or outing.

In foreign language classes, students can write to each other on a regular basis in the target language, write to students studying the same language in another school, or obtain pen pals in the countries where the target language is spoken.

Establish a mailbox center in a quiet area of the classroom. Display directions for writing and information about using the center. Provide a table with three or four chairs, several types of paper, envelopes, and writing tools. To encourage letter writing, you, your assistants, and the advanced students can first write letters so that each student receives one. Schedule a regular time for students to receive, read, and respond to the letters. If students have access to computers, they might correspond through e-mail (see Chapter 16).

Oral History

One way to show respect for the students' backgrounds is to have them develop oral histories of people from their respective countries. Students need to first determine what questions they want to ask members of their families and/or people living in the neighborhood and in the community at large. The questions may need to be translated into each student's native language, and the answers need to be recorded for later transcription and translation into English. The English versions can then be shared with peers from other language groups. Photographs of the people interviewed can accompany the transcriptions. Students may place copies of the oral history transcriptions in the school library so that all students can access them (for similar ideas see Olmedo, 1993).

Stages in the Natural Approach

The three variable stages of the natural approach were expected to flow into one another, and it was difficult to tell where one ended and the next began. If one were to compare these stages with the traditional levels—beginning, intermediate, and advanced—their relationship might have looked like that depicted in Figure 9.9 on p. 248.

At the comprehension stage, students were expected to develop the ability to understand spoken language and respond to simple directions. During this time, students experienced their "silent period" when they were not expected to speak, although they might have responded with a word or two. At the early speech production stage, students were expected to be able to produce a few words and could often recognize their written versions. At the speech-emergence stage, they began to use simple sentences and were able to read and write simple text in the target language. As students became capable of fuller production (sometimes referred to by natural approach advocates as the period of "intermediate fluency"), they were expected to express themselves in a variety of ways and be able to understand much of what was said. (See pp. 182–184 for a more comprehensive list of typical language behaviors found at each level.)

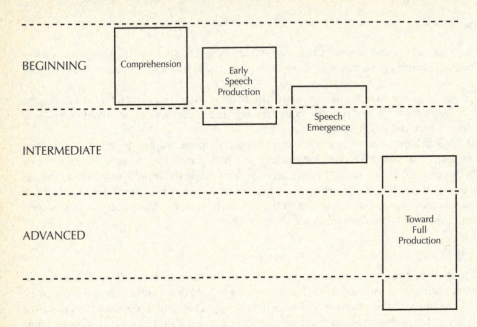

Figure 9.9 Classification of Proficiency Levels

Much overlap existed between one level and the next and one stage and the next. Students may have been beginners at some tasks but advanced learners at others. In addition, an intermediate or advanced student might have been thrown back temporarily into the comprehension stage typical of beginners whenever new concepts were introduced. It has been my observation that students need several "silent periods" as they move from one group of concepts to another.

Limitations of the Natural Approach

Although the natural approach was greatly appreciated as a resource from which to draw, particularly in the United States, it did appear to have limitations. One of these was that the method itself was oriented to oral development with beginning to low-intermediate students. Although this was not a fault in and of itself, teachers needed to be aware that literacy skills required more emphasis than the approach called for and that advanced students needed to be challenged through an increased emphasis on higher thinking skills.[10]

Another limitation was that it did not adequately address the formal teaching of grammar. Originally, Terrell intended that grammar would develop naturally as students

---

[10] Krashen (1995) expands this notion in "What is Intermediate Natural Approach?" in Hashemipour, Maldonado, VanNaerssen (Eds.), *Studies in Language Learning and Spanish Linguistics in Honor of Tracy D. Terrell* (pp. 92–105). New York: McGraw-Hill.

were exposed to sufficient amounts of comprehensible input. Although he acknowledged that formal grammar should have a role, it was not made clear what that role should be until 1991, when Terrell revealed an evolution of his thinking about the formal teaching of grammar, especially in the foreign language classroom.

In an article titled "The Role of Grammar Instruction in a Communicative Approach," Terrell (1991) acknowledged that instruction "is beneficial to learners at a particular point in their acquisition of the target language" (p. 55). He went on to say that instruction gives students structures to use as advance organizers to aid comprehension and help students focus on less noticeable features of language such as word endings. Moreover, such instruction serves as a basis for conscious monitoring and the creation of utterances using structures not yet acquired. However, he did *not* advocate a return to the use of a grammatical syllabus (see also the grammar discussion beginning on p. 54 of this volume).

A third limitation lay in the area of content and tasks. With the natural approach, the content and tasks for beginners were mainly related to everyday survival topics (foods, colors, body parts, interests, and so forth). Although this focus may have been fine for many students, it was inadequate for those who wished to reach academic proficiency sooner in the new language. In their own practices, many teachers began to introduce subject-matter content relating to math, science, social studies, literature, and so forth early on and to involve students in tasks that were more likely to lead to earlier success academically.

In addition, many teachers have related the new concepts taught to meaningful larger contexts to provide a cognitive hierarchical framework for them. Look again at the dialogue about colors on pp. 232–233. Think about how it might differ if it were related to a science unit on flowering plants, for example. Consider the following dialogue, which again is oriented to rank beginners.

TEACHER: Flowers come in many colors. Here is a red flower. [*The teacher holds up a red flower or a piece of one, then holds up another red flower just like the first one.*] Is this a red flower?

STUDENTS: Yes.

TEACHER: [*holding up the same kind of flower, only this time it is yellow*] Is this a red flower?

STUDENTS: [*shaking their heads*] No.

TEACHER: [*pointing again to a red flower*] No. Good. This is a red flower.

Thus the dialogue continues in much the same way as the first one did. The language becomes more enriched (maybe within a day or two) by relating to other qualities that flowers have and by talking about *where* they grow and *how* they grow.

In the first dialogue, the focus is on colors only. In the second dialogue, although the focus is still on colors, the teaching is situated in a larger hierarchical unit: Flowering Plants. Flowering Plants can be part of a still larger unit: Plants. The largest unit including plants and flowering plants might be labeled Living Things (see Figure 9.10 on p. 250).

The other activities mentioned in this chapter can also be situated in larger units and themes, depending on their content. For example, "Guess What's in the Box" can be used for recycling math vocabulary if the box contains items such as a ruler, a compass,

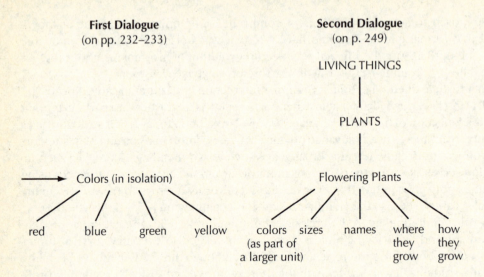

Figure 9.10

a pocket calculator, and the like. "Following a Process" can be situated in an art lesson if it involves a process such as creating hanging mobiles. "Charts and Other Visuals" can be situated in a geography lesson comparing various countries (see Figure 9.11 from Richard-Amato & M. A. Snow, 2005b, p. 207).

Country	Location	Climate
Argentina	South America	Warm Summers Temperate Winters
Canada	North America	Warm Summers Cold Winters
Vietnam	East Asia	Hot Summers Temperate Winters

Figure 9.11 A Chart Used to Clarify a Geography Lesson.
From Richard-Amato and M. A. Snow (1992)

A hodgepodge of activities thrown together does not a curriculum make. If the activities described in this section are used, they should be carefully selected and adapted, and they need to logically fit into a well-planned but flexible hierarchy of units and themes. Within this hierarchy, key concepts need to be reinforced sufficiently to be acquired. Unfortunately, there appeared to be no mechanism inherent in the natural method itself for the recycling of key concepts.

Yet an additional limitation appeared to be the natural approach's penchant for putting the teacher at center stage. Of course, at beginning levels the teacher's input was of utmost importance while the students were beginning to develop proficiency in the language. However, students even at beginning levels needed to begin communicating more with one another and with peers (or others) who were fluent speakers of the language being learned. An emphasis on group/pair work should not have been relegated only to later levels.

MODIFYING AND ENHANCING INSTRUCTION IN THE LANGUAGE CLASSROOM

Teaching language through content starting at beginning and intermediate levels[11] is essential if students are to reach higher levels of academic functioning in their new language and become full participants in the language classroom. See also the teaching strategies intended for content-area teachers (pp. 431–436), the Basic Structure of the Lesson (pp. 366–367), and the Sample Lesson Preparation Format (pp. 367–369). Many of the strategies and basic framework found on these pages are applicable to the second and/or foreign language classroom.

If a language teacher feels inadequate about teaching in specific content areas, then team teaching with a visiting content teacher may be part of the answer. Or the teacher may, with input from the students, choose a theme or topic from a specific content subject with which the teacher already has some familiarity (see discussion of content-based teaching on pp. 374–375). Yet another possibility is to have peer facilitators and/or lay assistants do presentations in the subject areas in which they have expertise (see pp. 377–382). Whoever is doing the teaching needs to use strategies that make it possible for learners to understand what is being taught. We have already considered many implicit and explicit teaching strategies for instruction in specific skill areas in Chapter 5. The following is a list of more general strategies that suggest various ways to modify and enhance instruction regardless of the subject matter or skill being taught.

General Strategies

1. *Enunciate clearly and emphasize key words and phrases through the use of facial expression, gesture, and intonation.* However, avoid making the input unnatural or condescending by speaking too slowly and deliberately.
2. *At first use simple, concrete language and avoid idioms.* New and abstract items can be added gradually as students become ready for them. Cognates and high frequency lexical items are particularly helpful at beginning levels.

---

[11] See typical language behaviors at each level on pp. 182–184.

3. *Reinforce important concepts in many different contexts over time.* Experiencing concepts in a variety of situations helps students internalize the language.

4. *Use visuals to make key concepts as clear as possible.* Pictures, maps, charts, time lines, diagrams, graphic organizers (see Figure 9.12), objects, and props, examples written or drawn on the board or transparencies can help students comprehend what they hear (see especially Richard-Amato & M.A. Snow, 2005b).

5. *Keep lessons short (especially for beginners) and check for understanding frequently.* Having too much to absorb and experience at one time can overwhelm students.

6. *Make lessons part of relevant units/themes.* Isolated segments may seem not worth the time and effort if they are not logically tied to a meaningful whole.

7. *Plan many hands-on activities for beginning students.* Learning in a concrete way can lay the foundation for later work on related but more abstract concepts.

8. *Demonstrate and dramatize when appropriate.* Showing different techniques for creating a picture with oil paints during an art lesson or acting out what it means to "saunter" down the hall when talking about the action of a character in a story can provide important clues to meaning.

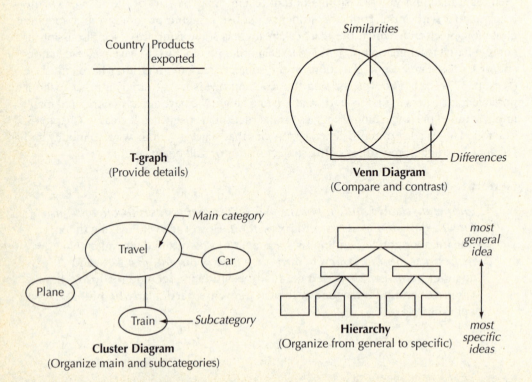

Figure 9.12 Graphic Organizers

9. *Build in redundancy for key vocabulary through direct definition, simplification, and expansion.* The following examples are intended for a lesson in history:

> *Direct definition:* "The country to the north was partitioned. This means that it was divided into parts."
> *Simplification:* "The country to the north was partitioned. It could not be one country anymore."
> *Expansion of ideas:* "The country to the north was partitioned. A single government was not able to hold it together anymore. Each part wanted its own government."

Because students benefit from a rich language environment as they internalize academic concepts and the structural features associated with specific subject areas, expanding the discourse rather than always resorting to simpler forms will probably be the most effective. However, a wise teacher will not overwhelm students with too many new elements at one time. Students can benefit if they have familiar vocabulary and structures on which to build. When students are ready, more complex elements can be added to the discourse.

10. *Be aware of whether or not you are being understood.* For example, if you say that Vincent Van Gogh's paintings were not acclaimed during his lifetime, you might check for understanding by asking, "Were Vincent Van Gogh's paintings liked by very many people when he was alive?" By asking a question to confirm understanding, the teacher can at the same time expose students to different words and still keep the basic meaning.

11. *Give students sufficient wait time before expecting them to volunteer information or answer questions.* Students need time to think and to mentally plan their utterances.

12. *Plan flexible group-work experiences.* Students can benefit greatly from collaborating on projects and learning together (see especially the cooperative learning discussion on pp. 382–385). Group work allows students many opportunities to use the language that is emerging and to share their knowledge with others. It also can give them a chance to take on leadership and facilitator roles.

13. *Allow and even encourage code switching in most situations.* Code switching from one language to another can be very advantageous to language learners as an important means of clearing up linguistic and cultural confusion (Cleghorn & Rollnick, 2002). Not only can it aid communication in this way, but it can facilitate bonding and identity development. In addition, difficult conceptual knowledge can often be better understood when translated into the first language. No matter how good the intentions of the teacher, refusing to allow students to use their first languages is in essence saying that their languages are not good enough. Of course, students may need to be reminded that their first language should not be used to exclude others from discussion.

14. *Interact with individual students as much as possible during noninstructional time or when students are working by themselves.* However, it is important not to hover or be too intrusive or directive when the students are trying to work things out for themselves.

15. *Find out what students already know about a subject or topic to be studied and provide relevant background information as needed.* Language students already have a reservoir of knowledge that can be tapped into at various points during a lesson or before an assignment.

16. *Adapt materials from mainstream textbooks.* Most publishers do not mind your adapting such materials as long as they are used only with your students and you give appropriate credit. However, you may want to check with the publisher to be certain.

    The following is an example of text that has been adapted for low- to mid-beginning learners.

    Original: "Leaving Home," short story by Wendy Hansen (Richard-Amato, 1993b, pp. 39–40).

    > Ella, born of Norwegian immigrants, grew up in a large farm family and was used to daily bread baking and meal preparation for the family and hired hands.

    Adaptation:

    > Ella's mother and father were Norwegian immigrants. They were farmers. The family was large. Ella baked bread every day. She prepared meals every day for the family and the farm workers.

17. *Provide students with tools for learning.* For example, giving high-beginner to intermediate-level students a partial outline on which to enter key ideas or a graphic organizer to fill out can greatly facilitate their learning. Students can eventually use such tools on their own to better comprehend and gain perspective on what they read, and to help them organize what they write. See Figure 9.12 on p. 252 for sample configurations.

18. *Frequently ask students to summarize what they have learned from a given lesson or reading.* Summarization helps learners glean what is important from the lesson or materials and control what they have learned by putting it into some sort of logical perspective. Paraphrasing passages in their own words can be very beneficial as well.

19. *Model and/or present examples of what it is you want the students to do.* Providing scaffolds of knowledge and language use is invaluable in making your expectations known and familiarizing students with typical organizational frameworks and linguistic structures associated with certain subjects and tasks. For intermediate- and advanced-level students, you might display examples of typical organizational patterns along with a list of common connectives (e.g., "however," "on the other hand," "therefore," "first," "second," and so on) and other wording and expressions associated with

specific content areas. Guided practice, too, can be very helpful in getting students off to a good start.

20. *Encourage students to reflect on their learning and the strategies they are using* (see pp. 104–110 for a discussion about learner strategies once students are proficient enough to do so). A reflection on the learning itself and the strategies used may be accomplished by the students orally and/or written down in a journal.

> *Reflections on learning:* "What did I already know before the lesson? What did I learn today? What activities were particularly helpful to me? What do I still want to know or learn about the topic or subject or skill?" Self-evaluation using checklists is also an important means for reflecting on learning (see pp. 191–193 in Chapter 7.
>
> *Reflections on strategies:* "How did I go about completing this activity/task? How should I go about completing activities/tasks of this kind in the future? What strategies did I learn from others? What strategies did I share with others?"

21. *Provide reading materials in the students' first languages and make bilingual dictionaries and other dictionaries available.* Encourage students to initially guess the meaning of an unfamiliar word or phrase from context and then to check their guesses by using the dictionary.

22. *Move students gradually into discussions of issues that are important to their lives* (see Chapter 4).

The development of both interpersonal and academic skills and the language typically associated with each are important to the student's success in the new language and, in the case of second language students, in a new cultural environment. The seeds of academic development can be planted in the language class itself and then nurtured and allowed to grow through further experiences in and out of school. Indeed, we as language teachers have a critical role to play in determining how effective our students will be academically in the language they are learning.

SUMMARY

Interactive practices such as one finds in the discussion of the natural approach can indeed lead to emergent participatory language teaching and can serve as scaffolds upon which participatory practices are gradually built (see Chapter 4).

According to Krashen and Terrell, the foundation of the natural approach rested on four principles: (1) comprehension precedes production; (2) production emerges in variable stages; (3) the course syllabus focuses on communicative goals; and (4) the activities are designed to lower the "affective filter." What one draws from the natural approach can be expanded and improved on by adding activities having to do with literacy skills development, by including academic themes and group/pair work at beginning levels, and by contextualizing learned concepts and incorporating them into broader, hierarchical units.

Selected components of this method like those of other methods and activities described in this book are still relevant and can continue to evolve in different ways in different classrooms and with different teachers.

Modifying and enhancing academic instruction can start from the very beginning of any course in a new language—second or foreign—and can continue during the time that students are with the language teacher and beyond. The purpose of modified and enhanced instruction is twofold: to give the students the basic tools they need for successful academic communication and learning and to move students more quickly along the path to full participation.

QUESTIONS AND PROJECTS FOR REFLECTION AND DISCUSSION

1. Reflect on the process by which you became proficient in a second language. How closely did your progress approximate the variable stages described in the natural approach? To what extent was your progress variable? Did your teachers appear to help or hinder your learning of the language? Explain.

2. Often listening, speaking, reading, and writing are treated as isolated skills by language teachers. How might you integrate them by using interactive strategies? List some specific activities as examples.

3. Incorporate your own adaptations of natural approach practices into an eight-minute lesson for low-beginners (see p. 182). Try out your lesson on a small group of fellow students or peers. Utilize the following Structure for Simulated Lessons and the Sample Lesson Preparation Format on pp. 367–369.

STRUCTURE FOR SIMULATED LESSONS

Note: This structure may need to be adjusted depending on the kind of lesson it is used for and the proficiency level for which it is intended.

1. Perspective (opening)—to your peers (as peers)
   Share with your peers parts of your lesson preparation:
   a. the approximate age and proficiency level of the students for whom this lesson is intended
   b. the concepts that will be introduced in your lesson
   c. the related concepts you are assuming the students already know that you plan to reinforce
   d. the behaviors expected as a result of the lesson
   e. what the follow-up lessons will be (briefly describe one or two)

(Continued)

2. Stimulation and Overview—to your peers (as your students)
    a. gain their interest
    b. explain objectives (items (b) and (d) above modified according to approximate age and proficiency level for whom the lesson is intended)
    c. discover your students' prior knowledge and experience as it relates to the lesson
    d. provide critical background information when needed
    e. when appropriate, explore with the students a few key vocabulary items if necessary to help their understanding of the lesson
3. Instruction/Participation Phase—to your peers (as your students) Implement the lesson itself. Use comprehensible language, clear visuals, demonstrations, and so on
4. Closure with peers (as your students): Ask what they learned, what they liked, and so forth.

The simulated lesson may be in a language unfamiliar to your group if the lesson is easy enough. After presenting your lesson, ask the group as peers in what ways it was effective and how it might be improved. Begin by sharing with them your own reactions to the lesson. You might want to use the following Questions to Guide Evaluative Discussion.

QUESTIONS TO GUIDE EVALUATIVE DISCUSSION

1. What did you find effective about my lesson overall?
2. What appeared to be the overall goal of my lesson?
3. To what extent did I accomplish it?
4. What strategies did I use? How effective were they?
5. Was my lesson appropriate for the age and proficiency level for which it was intended?
6. Was my lesson clearly presented?
7. Were my materials, illustrations, and so on used to advantage?
8. To what extent did I encourage student interaction and participation?
9. How did the students respond to the lesson?
    a. What in the lesson seemed to interest them most?
    b. Did they appear to be challenged by the lesson? In what ways?
10. Did any problems arise? How well did I handle them?
11. How do you think my lesson can be improved overall?
12. What part of the lesson was the most successful? Why?

4. Select applicable strategies from the "Modifying and Enhancing Instruction in the Classroom" section in this chapter. Utilize the Structure for Simulated Lessons on pp. 256–257 and the Sample Lesson Preparation Format on pp. 367–369 to prepare an academic lesson for mid-beginning students. Present your lesson to a group of class members. After presenting your lesson, ask your group in what ways it was effective and how your lesson might be improved. Begin by sharing with them your own reactions to the lesson. You may want to use several of the Questions to Guide Evaluative Discussion on p. 257 as the basis for your analysis.[12]

   If you are currently teaching students, use what you have learned to try out a similar lesson with them. Make sure the lesson is relevant and appropriate to level. Afterwards, reflect on its outcome and how you felt about doing it. Did you see any problems with your lesson? If possible, have your lesson videotaped to analyze and discuss with peers. Reflect on its outcome and how you felt about doing it. Pay close attention to student response. Do you see any problems with your lesson? How might your lesson be improved?

5. Return to the information on adapting content for other age groups or other proficiency levels in the introduction to Part II, pp. 211–212. Use the lesson you prepared for item 4 above and describe how you might adapt it for another age group and/or another proficiency level. Discuss your adapted lesson(s) with a small group to obtain their feedback. What considerations should you take into account in each case?

6. ✎ **Journal Entry:** Reflect on the lessons you carried out in items 3 and 4 above. What strategies did you use in each lesson? How comfortable did you feel with them? Did you think they were effective overall? Why or why not? What were some of the specific problems you encountered? How can they be overcome? Write about what you learned from your peers and your instructor during the process. What insights did you gain about learning and teaching from the experience?

---

[12] Instead you or the course instructor may develop an evaluation format based on instructor/student expectations. The form can then be used for this lesson presentation and for future lesson presentations. You may want to draw from the Questions to Guide Evaluative Discussion and/or Echevarria, Vogt, and Short's (2008) Sheltered Instruction Observation Protocol Model briefly described on pp. 439–440.

SUGGESTED READINGS AND REFERENCE MATERIALS

Baltra, A. (1992). On breaking with tradition: The significance of Terrell's Natural Approach. *The Canadian Modern Language Review*, *48* (3), 265–583. The author of this important article discusses the impact of the natural approach on how we viewed language teaching in both second and foreign language classrooms in the 1980s and 1990s. The article has historical value in that the author made us keenly aware of the method's contribution to the interactive movement in language teaching in the United States in particular.

Banville, S. (2007). E-book: *1,000 ideas and activities for language teachers*. Breaking News English Web site (http://www.breakingnewsenglish.com). This is an excellent resource where teachers can find a large number of workable activities and ideas for consideration. Included are warm-ups, pre- and postreading activities, vocabulary development tasks, role plays, discussion ideas, activities on newspaper use, and more.

Brinton, D., Wesche, M., & Snow, M. A. (2003). *Content-based second language instruction: Michigan Classics Edition*. Ann Arbor: University of Michigan Press. Here the authors explore the developments that have taken place in content-based language teaching since the first version of this book appeared in 1989. They also look at the research supporting content-based language teaching in its many contexts at the university level. Program models are described in-depth and guidelines are given to those in the process of developing content-based language programs.

Echevarria, J., Vogt, M. E., & Short, D. (2008). *Making content comprehensible for English learners: The SIOP model*. Boston: Allyn & Bacon. A model of effective sheltered lessons to use for the observation and evaluation of teachers of English learners is presented here. The model, called the Sheltered Instruction Observation Protocol, or SIOP, can also serve as a valuable tool for the planning lessons in which language and content are learned concurrently.

Kaufman, D., & Crandall, J. (2005). *Content-based instruction in primary and secondary school settings*. Alexandria, VA: Teachers of English to Speakers of Other Languages. This very practical book offers elementary and secondary teachers numerous innovative ideas for improving the learning of both language and content in conjunction with one another.

Krashen, S., & Terrell, T. (1983). *The Natural Approach: Language acquisition in the classroom*. Englewood Cliffs, NJ: Alemany/Prentice Hall. This classic text presents important information for anyone planning to draw from the natural approach. The book clearly describes the method, offers theoretical justification for its use, and presents suggested activities.

CHAPTER 10

Chants, Music, and Poetry

Rhythm and rhyme, assonance and pun are not artificial creations, but vestigial echoes of primitive phases in the development of language, and of the even more primitive pulsations of living matter, hence our particular receptiveness for messages which arrive in rhythmic pattern.

A. Koestler, 1964

QUESTIONS TO THINK ABOUT

1. What do chants, music, and/or poetry have in common? What role might they play in the acquisition of a first language?

2. In your opinion, would older children, teenagers, and adults learning a second language benefit from them also? If so, in what ways?

3. Think about the experiences you have had learning another language. To what extent were you exposed to chants, music, and/or poetry during the process? What effects did they have on your own success?

4. Do you think chants, music, and poetry should be incorporated into a second language program? Explain.

5. How might music and poetry, in particular, be used to make emergent participatory language teaching a more likely possibility (Chapter 4)?

Through word/sound play, many "chunks" of useful language, often found in private speech (see p. 81), can be incorporated into the individual's linguistic repertoire at almost any age or level of proficiency.

The use of prosodic elements, redundancy, and sometimes thoughtless repetition can produce lowered anxiety and greater ego permeability.[1] One might call such play a sort of "palatable audiolingualism." However, unlike audiolingualism, the rhythms and sound repetitions carry the student into sensually appealing activities that go far beyond mere drill. Children and adults alike can receive considerable enjoyment from indulging in such frivolity. The subject matter does not have to be meaningless but can be directly anchored in experience. The messages can be rich and multileveled and can initiate discussions that challenge even the most proficient among the group.

Routines and patterns can provide a stopgap strategy allowing entry into the new culture even before the student is considered "ready." Although the process used to develop routines and patterns is very different from that used for creative speech (Krashen, 1981a; Lamendella, 1979), they can indeed form part of creative speech at a higher level. Myles, Mitchell, and Hooper (1999) found support for this notion in their study of early classroom learners of French as a second language. They concluded that chunks and formulas can actually form the basis for creative construction later on; they can provide "rich linguistic data" which can be reexamined and used to produce creative speech (see also Towell & Hawkins, 1994). Based on corpus research (see p. 13), Schmitt and Carter (2004) claimed that such formulaic speech is commonly used in English. They refer to Erman and Warren's (2000) analysis, which concluded that 52.3 percent of written English and 58.6 percent of spoken English consist of different types of formulaic sequences. It appears that routines and patterns may play a much larger role in the English language than most of us previously thought (see also Watson-Gegeo & Nielsen, 2003).

Meaningful word and/or sound play can provide students with a few tools for communication, especially valuable at beginning levels. Through such play, students can internalize routines and patterns with or without consciously committing them to memory. Students do not even have to understand the meanings of the words within the chunks to use them for social participation (albeit in a limited fashion) and to encourage input from others. One might argue, however, that others may at first assume that students are more fluent than they really are. However, it does not take long to realize the approximate levels of second language students and adjust one's speech accordingly.

CHANTS

The most frequently used chants in language classrooms today are jazz chants developed by Carolyn Graham, an English as a second language teacher and jazz musician. She provided language learners with a rhythmic means for improving speaking and listening skills. Through jazz chants, students can be exposed to natural intonation patterns and

---

[1] Guiora, Brannon, and Dull (1972) discussed the concept of language ego, which refers to the self-identity intricately involved with the risks of taking on a new language. It is responsible for boundaries that can make us extremely inhibited if too strong and impenetrable.

idiomatic expressions in often provocative, sometimes humorous situations. Feelings are expressed in the playing out of the common rituals of everyday life.

Because jazz chants are often in dialogue form, students learn the cultural rules of turn-taking and appropriate ways to communicate specific needs in a variety of situations. The dialogues generally include three kinds of conversational patterns: question/response, command/response, and provocative statement/response.

Graham (1978) suggested that certain steps, summarized here, be taken.

1. The teacher should make sure that students understand the chant's situational context. Vocabulary items and cultural ramifications inherent in the situations require clear explanations.
2. Initially, the teacher, in a normal conversational voice, recites each line of the chant once or twice as needed, and the students repeat in unison. Graham advises the teacher to stop at any point to correct pronunciation or intonation patterns.
3. The teacher establishes a beat by snapping the fingers (usually preferred by students), counting, clapping, or using rhythm sticks. Step 2 is then repeated but this time with a firm beat.
4. The teacher divides the class into two groups (the number of students in each group does not matter). Using the beat already established, the teacher recites the lines. The two groups of students alternately repeat the lines as they are given.
5. The dialogue of the chant is then conducted between the teacher and the class. The teacher takes the first part; the students take the other (without the teacher to model). The teacher can use the recordings that accompany the jazz chants books (see Suggested Readings at the end of this chapter).

In my own experience with jazz chants, I have found it unnecessary to stop and correct students' pronunciation as Graham suggested. Students pick up the modeled pronunciation through repetition. Stopping for correction may place undue emphasis on form rather than meaning.

Chants of any kind can help students internalize matrices (see p. 239) and at the same time reinforce specific vocabulary items. In the following sample chant sound play is embedded through the use of rhyme. The matrix allows for various structures for offering and refusing food. Substitutions can include the names of the foods one wants reinforced. Follow-ups might include physical response activities involving food preparation (see Chapter 8) or other role play taking place in the kitchen (see Chapter 11).

> Would you like a fried egg?
> Would you like a fried egg?
> No thanks. I'm on a diet.
> Please don't fry it.
> Please don't fry it.

Chants can also be used to introduce a unit topic. For example, the following chant introduces a unit on sports events. Typical pictures of sports events can accompany the chant. Follow-ups can include physical response activities (involving basic actions of the sport), sports demonstrations, local news reporting of sports events, or a trip to a sporting event as part of a "language experience" activity (see Chapter 13). The matrix in the following chant offers a means for talking about sports. Word substitutions can easily include a wide variety of events.

> Where do you go? Where do you go?
> Where do you go to see
> a ball go in a basket,
> a ball go in a basket?
>
> Where do I go? Where do I go?
> To a basketball game,
> To a basketball game.
> That's where I go to see
> a ball go in a basket.
>
> All you have to do is ask it.
>
> Where do you go? Where do you go?
> Where do you go to see
> a ball kicked all around,
> a ball kicked all around?
>
> Where do I go? Where do I go?
> To a soc-cer game,
> To a soc-cer game.
> That's where I go to see
> a ball kicked all around.
>
> You keep it on the ground.
>
> Where do you go? Where do you go?
> Where do you go to see
> a girl fly through the air
> a girl fly through the air?
>
> Where do I go? Where do I go?
> To a gym-nas-tics meet,
> To a gym-nas-tics meet.
> That's where I go to see
> a girl fly through the air.
>
> Would you do it on a dare?

There are many ways to orchestrate chants. The class can be divided with males and females chanting different parts, or it can be divided into more unusual sections, such as those wearing green and those not, those born July through December and those born

January through June, and so on. To add variety, parts might be assigned to individual volunteers or to small groups of differing sizes.

Some chants can be partially improvised by students. For example, the students can sit in a circle on the floor.[2] A rhythm is set by the snapping of fingers. The teacher begins the chant with something like "My name is _____. What's your name?" The teacher looks at the student on the right, who responds, "My name is _____. What's your name?" That student looks at the next student on the right, who responds, and so on around the circle. Variations can overlap into affective activities (see Chapter 14). "My name is _____ and I like _____" and "My name is _____ and I prefer _____."

Although these chants are oriented to beginning students, intermediate and advanced students can learn idiomatic expressions through chants as well. Subtle forms of humor, decisions about the appropriateness of utterances, and symbolic content are only a few of the concepts to which students at higher levels can be introduced. Through the cadences, the students' pronunciation and intonation can become more natural without conscious drill. Chants can be combined with songs and even dance (Bell, 1999) and possibly performed for an audience.

MUSIC

Music also can reduce anxiety and inhibition in second language students. Furthermore, it can be a great motivator in that its lyrics are often very meaningful and relevant. Human emotions are frequently expressed in highly charged situations. Through music, language easily finds roots in the experience of students at any age or proficiency level. Often awareness is heightened through its prosodic elements. Kahlil Gibran once said, "The reality of music is in that vibration that remains in the ear after the singer finishes his song and the player no longer plucks the strings." Music can break down barriers among those who share its rhythms and meaning. Its unifying effect can extend across time, nations, races, and individuals.

At beginning levels, music can be used to teach basic vocabulary. Colors, body parts, simple actions, and names of people are only a few of the concepts that can be taught through music. The teacher does not have to be talented in music to make it a memorable experience. A gravely voice can exude as much enthusiasm as a euphonious one. Recordings can provide the accompaniment in some situations. Words can be created and students' names inserted into stanzas coordinated with easy-to-learn melodies. For example, the following are lyrics to sing to the tune of "You Are My Sunshine."

> Your name is Car-los.
> Your name is Car-los.
> You come from Per-u,
> so far away.

---

[2] Thanks to Linda Cobral for sharing this idea with me.

And now you're with us
Until the summer.
And it is here
we want you to stay.

Your name is Sung Lee.
Your name is Sung Lee.
You're from Kor-e-a,
so far away.
And now you're with us
Maybe forever
Even after
your hair turns gray.

Your name is Ni-kom.
Your name is Ni-kom.
You come from La-os,
so far away.
And now you're with us
We are so happy.
We want to sing with you today.

Although Carlos, Sung Lee, and Nikom may not understand all the words the first few times they hear them, they will be highly motivated to find out what is being sung about them. Thus acquisition will be highly likely.

Specific matrices can be reinforced through music. Notice the lyrics of the following song, written to the tune of "Mary Had a Little Lamb."

Danella says, "Come on, let's go.
Come on, let's go. Come on, let's go."
Danella says, "Come on, let's go.
To the zoo on Friday."

Hung an-swers, "That's fine with me.
Fine with me. Fine with me."
Hung an-swers, "That's fine with me.
Let's go to the zoo on Friday."

Friday comes and off they go.
Off they go. Off they go.
Friday comes and off they go.
To see the an-i-mals.

First they see the elephants.
El-e-phants. El-e-phants.
First they see the el-e-phants.
In the mud-dy waters.

Then they walk to the lion's den.
Lion's den. Lion's den.
Then they walk to the lion's den.
To find him pacing back and forth.

The song goes through as many stanzas as the teacher wants to create. Once students become more proficient, they can add their own stanzas. Seeing the words in writing and accompanied by pictures can aid the students' understanding. Physical response activities can also be used, with students pointing to pictures of animals while the song is sung. A trip to the zoo can stimulate additional meaningful experiences or a discussion of zoos and what can happen to the animals when confined to a small area. Note the line about the lion "pacing back and forth."

For those who prefer more "professional" songs, Hap Palmer[3] has provided a series of songbooks, audio recordings, and videos (see the Hap Palmer Web site). Among his more popular songs are "Colors" and "Your Hands up in the Air." In addition, "songs for teaching" Web sites include not only Hap Palmer songs but the words for many other songs in English (e.g., "Counting 1 to 20" and "Months of the Year" by Jack Hartman; "How Much is it?" by Uwe Kind, and so on). Some of the songs on these Web sites are also available in Spanish.

Although these songs are beneficial mainly to beginning students, there are many songs available for intermediate to advanced students. Even the "top ten" can provide one or two. Interestingly, a serious study was done on the appropriateness of music for teaching a second language. Murphey (1992) looked at the characteristics of fifty pop songs and found them to be repetitive, basically simple, conversation-like, and vague enough to allow for very different interpretations. He argued that "these discourse features and the song-stuck-in-my-head phenomenon make them potentially rich learning materials in and out of the classroom" (p. 771). Songs about the relevant issues students might be researching, discussing, and acting on can sometimes be found in the lyrics of previous decades and today. If one uses songs of any kind as text, the lyrics can be duplicated so that students can take their own copies home and share them with families and friends.

When presenting a song in class, you may want to let the students first listen to the recorded song. Then hand out the words and play the song again. The third time the song is played, students will probably want to sing along with you and the recording. Give the students time to ask about unfamiliar words or phrases. A discussion among students relating the song to their own lives and the lives of others can serve as a follow-up.

POETRY

Although poetic elements are contained in chants and music lyrics, poetry should be treated as a separate category. Poems range in length from a few words to a whole book. They are generally concise, sometimes deceptively simple, and often highly charged with emotional content. They can be used at a variety of levels to reinforce ideas, introduce new ones, and explore issues relevant to the students' lives.

---

[3] Thanks to Raquel Mireles for making me aware of these songbooks, audio recordings, and videos.

The following poem by Jack Prelutsky is a favorite, especially among elementary schoolchildren. It reinforces the names of concrete objects in the classroom as it presents a fantasy that we all may have had at one time or another.

The Creature in the Classroom[4]

It appeared inside our classroom
at a quarter after ten,
it gobbled up the blackboard,
three erasers and a pen.
It gobbled teacher's apple
and it bopped her with the core.
"How dare you!" she responded.
"You must leave us . . . there's the door."

The Creature didn't listen
but described an arabesque
as it gobbled all her pencils,
seven notebooks and her desk.
Teacher stated very calmly,
"Sir! you simply cannot stay,
I'll report you to the principal
unless you go away!"

But the thing continued eating,
it ate paper, swallowed ink,
as it gobbled up our homework
I believe I saw it wink.
Teacher finally lost her temper.
"OUT!" she shouted at the creature.
The creature hopped beside her
and GLOPP . . . it swallowed teacher.

Poems may not be understood in their entirety at first. In fact, when students are initially exposed to them, they may understand only a few words. However, after subsequent exposures, they begin to understand more.

The next poem, by Edwin Arlington Robinson, is suitable for students in university or adult programs. It can be used at high-intermediate to advanced levels to reinforce various emotions such as happiness, love, envy, loneliness, and desperation and to teach literary devices such as symbolism and metaphor. The poem leads naturally into a discussion of Richard Cory's life and the seeming irony of his death. What was missing in his life that was essential to his happiness? The cultural ramifications and the social taboos concerning suicide can also be relevant to the discussion. A good follow-up is the classic narrative song of the same title from the Simon and Garfunkel recording *The*

---

[4] © 2002 by Jack Prelutsky. Thanks to Norma Ramirez, who introduced me to this poem.

Sounds of Silence (Eclectic Music Company). In the song, Richard Cory owns a factory, and the narrator, who works for him, envies his lifestyle and is shocked at his death, just as we are. Both poem and song are very powerful and can stimulate not only discussion but compositions as well.

Richard Cory

Whenever Richard Cory went down town,
We people on the pavement looked at him:
He was a gentleman from sole to crown,
Clean favored, and imperially slim.

And he was always quietly arrayed,
And he was always human when he talked;
But still he fluttered pulses when he said,
"Good-morning," and he glittered when he walked.

And he was rich—yes, richer than a king—
And admirably schooled in every grace:
In fine, we thought that he was everything
To make us wish that we were in his place.

So on we worked, and waited for the light,
And went without the meat, and cursed the bread;
And Richard Cory, one calm summer night,
Went home and put a bullet through his head.

In addition to listening to and reading poems written by others, some students, even at beginning levels, may want to write poems of their own. In her book *English Through Poetry*, Christison (1982) recommended concrete poetry, formed from pictures and words. For example, students can draw large butterflies such as the one in Figure 10.1. Once the butterflies have been drawn, words and phrases such as "light," "flying," "beautiful," "in the

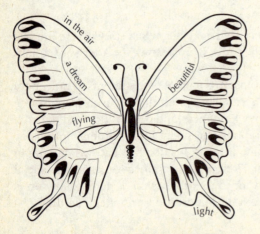

Figure 10.1 Adapted from Christison (1982)

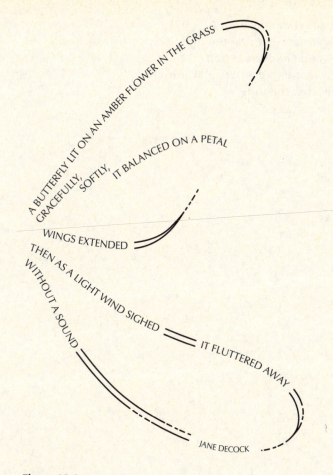

A BUTTERFLY LIT ON AN AMBER FLOWER IN THE GRASS
GRACEFULLY, SOFTLY, IT BALANCED ON A PETAL
WINGS EXTENDED
THEN AS A LIGHT WIND SIGHED
WITHOUT A SOUND
IT FLUTTERED AWAY
JANE DECOCK

Figure 10.2

air," and "a dream" can be written on the wings or the bodies. A butterfly for a student at an intermediate to advanced level might look something like the one in Figure 10.2.[5]

Also recommended for students at intermediate to advanced levels are verse forms such as word cinquain, Japanese tanka, or haiku (see also Moulton & Holmes, 1997). The following are examples, each followed by a summary of the structure that it contains.

Word Cinquain

A cat
Full of mischief
Charges, dances, pounces
Brightens my longest days
A wonder

---

[5] This poem and illustration are by Jane Decock and come from *Harbinger*, published by the Advanced Creative Writing Classes at Jefferson High School in Edgewater, Colorado.

First line: a word or two to name the topic
Second line: two or three words that describe the topic
Third line: three or four words that express action
Fourth line: four or five words that express personal attitude
Fifth line: a word or two to rename the topic

Tanka

Drifting in the sky
Clouds come and go in patterns
I look to the sun
The darkness hovers around
Slowly rain begins to fall

First line: 5 syllables
Second line: 7 syllables
Third line: 5 syllables
Fourth line: 7 syllables
Fifth line: 7 syllables

Haiku

Flowers wave to me
As I pass them in the field. . . .
Gentle, swirling wind

First line: 5 syllables
Second line: 7 syllables
Third line: 5 syllables
(Note: There is generally a break in thought between the second and third lines.)

The verses can be written at first in groups with the help of the teacher or teacher assistants, using pictures to stimulate ideas. Later the students may want to try writing verses on their own.

Whether students are working in groups or individually, they should not be held to exact numbers of words or syllables for structured verse unless they can be shown how a poem might be improved by doing so.

Christison (1982) suggested that events in the students' lives provide the impetus for writing and sharing poetry. For example, students can create greeting cards to give others on special occasions. Birthdays, marriages, graduations, holidays, and other celebrations are ideal times to write and/or illustrate poetry. If the students do not want to write their own poetry, they can search books for appropriate poems to put on their cards, giving credit to their sources.

Christison also recommended having students draw or paint pictures and then find or write poems to go with them. Activities such as these can give students important reasons for reading and writing poetry, thus increasing their exposure to meaningful language.

SUMMARY

Chants, music, and poetry can produce lowered anxiety and greater ego permeability among second language learners. Beginners are often able to internalize chunks of language, allowing them to participate in social situations early on. During initial phases of language development, students often want to communicate but do not have the necessary skills. By having a communicative repertoire (however limited), students can form bonds with competent speakers and thus are positioned to receive more modified language tailored to their needs and more opportunities for interaction.

Intermediate and advanced students also gain benefits from chants, music, and poetry. Idiomatic expressions, subtle forms of humor, decisions concerning appropriateness, and symbolic content can be internalized through these genres. Pronunciation and intonation patterns can become more natural through the use of word/sound play. Students can be exposed to situations in which highly meaningful content can be dealt with on many different levels.

QUESTIONS AND PROJECTS FOR REFLECTION AND DISCUSSION

1. Compare the use of repetition and imitation in the audiolingual method (see Chapter 1) with the use of similar strategies in chants, songs, and poetry. In what ways do you think the latter might render the strategies more "palatable"?

2. What role do you think routines and patterns play in the second language learning process? How might the proficiency level at which students are exposed to routines and patterns make a difference in the role of routines and patterns? Explain.

3. Choose a topic around which to develop a beginning lesson. Find a chant, some lyrics set to a popular song, or a poem to introduce or reinforce some of the key concepts. You may write your own if you wish. Try out your lesson on a small group of fellow students or peers. Utilize the Structure for Simulated Lessons on pp. 256–257 and the Sample Lesson Preparation Format on pp. 367–369.

   After your lesson, discuss its strengths and the ways in which it might be improved. Begin by sharing your own reactions to the lesson. You may want to use the Questions to Guide Evaluative Discussion (p. 257) as the basis for your analysis, or you may use an evaluation format that you or your instructor have developed (see footnote 12 on p. 258).

   If you are currently teaching, use what you have learned to try out a chant, lyrics, or a poem with your students. Make sure the lesson you prepare is relevant to the content they are studying and appropriate to level. If possible, have your lesson videotaped to analyze and discuss with peers. Reflect on its outcome and how you felt about doing it. Pay close attention to student response. Do you see any problems with your lesson? How might it be improved?

4. ✎ **Journal Entry:** Reflect on the lesson(s) you carried out in item 3 above. What strategies did you use? How comfortable did you feel with them? Did you think they were effective overall? Why or why not? What were some of the specific problems you encountered? How can they be overcome? Write about what you learned from your peers and instructor during the process. What insights did you gain about learning and teaching from the experience?

SUGGESTED READINGS AND REFERENCE MATERIALS

Bell, D. (1999). Rise, Sally, rise: Communicating through dance. *TESOL Journal, 8*(1), 27–31. Chants and songs are combined with dance to teach language through the synchronization of voice, rhythm, and bodily movement. The goal is to improve pronunciation and fluency in the new language by placing emphasis on conversational stress patterns and rhythm.

Fisher, M. (2007). *Writing in rhythm: Spoken word poetry in urban classrooms.* New York: Teachers College Press. Although this book is intended mainly for Latino and African-American youth and others in the urban community, it can also provide a highly effective tool for teaching literacy to second language learners in similar environments. Fisher is convinced that spoken poetry often originates in the lived experiences of students and encourages peer-to-peer and larger group interaction for those who want to participate.

Graham, C. (2006). *Creating chants and songs.* New York: Oxford University Press. Suggestions for developing jazz chants and songs for your language learning students in any language are presented with examples and a recording to which students can listen. Other books by Graham of interest are *Jazz Chants: Old and New; Small Talk; Grammar Chants; Jazz Chants for Children; Jazz Chant Fairy Tales; Mother Goose Jazz Chants; Holiday Jazz Chants;* and *Let's Chant, Let's Sing.*

Hanauer, D. (2004). *Poetry and the meaning of life.* Tonawanda, NY: Pippin. The author stresses the importance of using poetry to teach literacy in classes for English learners as well as for other writers and readers. He believes that through poetry students can express themselves more readily and clearly than by other means. Included are vignettes demonstrating ways in which teachers have used poetry in classroom settings.

Moulton, M., & Holmes, V. (1997). Pattern poems: Creative writing for language acquisition. *The Journal of the Imagination in Language Learning, IV,* 84–90. The authors present several types of pattern poems about specific topics such as the five senses, heroes, and other people. Some of the patterns require specific grammatical forms within the poems; others require that each line fulfill a specific purpose such as "name a person," "give three words that describe that person," and so on.

Schmitt, N. (Ed.). (2004). *Formulaic sequences: Acquisition, processing and use.* Philadelphia: John Benjamins. This book presents an analysis of formulaic speech including definitions, hypotheses about the way(s) in which formulaic speech is processed mentally, and related research and important issues.

CHAPTER 11

Storytelling, Role Play, and Drama

Drama is like the naughty child who climbs the high walls and ignores the "No Trespassing" sign. It does not allow us to define our territory so exclusively; it forces us to take as our starting-point life, not language.

A. Maley and A. Duff, 1983

QUESTIONS TO THINK ABOUT

1. How important do you think storytelling is to children acquiring a first language? What about role play or drama?

2. Do you think older children, teenagers, and adults learning a second language might also benefit from storytelling, role play, or drama? If so, in what ways? What is there about these activities that might facilitate the language learning process for them?

3. Recall your own experiences with one or more of these activities in learning another language. What effects do you think they may have had on your own second language development?

4. Think of some ways storytelling, role play, and drama can be incorporated into a second language program.

5. How might stories and drama be used to affirm students' cultural traditions and values?

Storytelling, role play, and drama allow students to explore their inner resources, empathize with others, and use their own experiences as scaffolds on which to build credible action. As a result, students may be able to improve their ability to produce the target language, acquire many of its nonverbal nuances, improve the ability to work cooperatively in group situations, and effectively deal with affective issues.

Before the teacher involves students in storytelling, role play, or drama, a series of warm-ups is recommended to reduce anxiety and to create a welcoming, active environment.

WARM-UPS

The warm-ups included here require almost no verbal language and therefore can be used with true beginners. In addition, they can lower inhibitions and help establish trust and understanding among group members. Begin with a series of simple exercises involving stretching and bending, followed by tightening and relaxing specific muscle groups. The following are two sample warm-up activities.

WARM-UP ACTIVITIES

Circle Mimics

Students form a circle. The first student is asked to make a movement such as hopping on one foot. The second student repeats the movement and adds a new one such as shaking a fist in the air. The third student hops on one foot, shakes a fist in the air, and adds a third movement, and so on around the circle.

Baseball Mime

Throw a make-believe ball across the room to one of your students. After the student "catches" it, motion to the student to join you in a game of catch. Then throw the ball to other students and motion to them to join you also. The game can remain simply a game of catch, or it can develop into a full baseball game if the students are familiar with baseball. Give one student a make-believe bat and station the others around the room at pretend bases. Let the students take over the game.

Once students have worked out tension and lowered inhibitions, they may be ready for storytelling.

STORYTELLING

Stories have traditionally been used to teach, entertain, and explain the unknown. The activities offered here can be coordinated with other practices described in this book. Some of the activities are more appropriate to beginning levels; others to more advanced levels. Most can be adapted to any age level provided they are within the students' range cognitively.

Exposing students to a story before they fully understand the words can be highly motivating for beginners at any age.[1] The same story can be used from time to time in

---

[1] Note that this recommendation appears to fly in the face of the arguments favoring modified language. If the story were simply read aloud with little expression of feeling and there were no physical involvement on the student's part, then it probably would be as meaningless as most other language that is not understood.

different ways until a full understanding is achieved over a period of perhaps several months. Activities such as those presented in this chapter enable the students to participate in the language *before* they are proficient in it. Through the activities described here, curiosity in the target language can be stimulated under the right conditions.

STORYTELLING ACTIVITIES

Story Experience[2]

Level: Beginning

Have the students form a large circle. Choose a story or a narrative poem such as the one that follows. (This particular poem is oriented to children, although adults have enjoyed it too.) Pick out the concrete words that can be easily acted out. Assign to each student a word to act out. Help the students understand what the word means by demonstrating its meaning or showing a picture to illustrate. Then read the story aloud with much feeling. Each student should listen carefully for his or her word. When the word is read, the student crosses the circle, acting it out while moving across. Students on the other side make room as the actors come across.

For the following story excerpt, the teacher should have students act out the following: a fly, a spider, a bird, a cat, a dog, a cow, and a horse.

Excerpt from *There Was an Old Lady Who Swallowed a Fly*[3]

There was an old lady who swallowed a *fly*.
I don't know why she swallowed a *fly*.
Perhaps she'll die.

There was an old lady who swallowed a *spider,*
That wriggled and wriggled and jiggled inside her.

She swallowed the *spider* to catch the *fly.*
I don't know why she swallowed a *fly.*
Perhaps she'll die.

There was an old lady who swallowed a *bird.*
How absurd, to swallow a *bird!*
She swallowed the bird to catch the *spider.*

There was an old lady who swallowed a *cat.*
Well, fancy that, she swallowed a *cat!*
She swallowed the cat to catch the *bird.*

---

[2] This activity has been adapted from one presented by the Barzak Institute of San Francisco at a workshop done for the Jefferson County Public Schools of Colorado in 1979.

[3] This story in its entirety can be found in the version by Ruth Bonne, illustrated by Pam Adams, and published by Child's Play (International). I thank Ernestine Saldivar for introducing me to this version.

There was an old lady who swallowed a *dog*.
What a hog, to swallow a *dog*!
She swallowed the *dog* to catch the *cat*.

There was an old lady who swallowed a *cow*.
I don't know how she swallowed a *cow*!
She swallowed the *cow* to catch the *dog*.
She swallowed the *dog* to catch the *cat*.
She swallowed the *cat* to catch the *bird*.
She swallowed the *bird* to catch the *spider*,
That wriggled and wriggled and jiggled inside her.
She swallowed the *spider* to catch the *fly*.
I don't know why she swallowed a *fly*.
Perhaps she'll die.

There was an old lady who swallowed a horse.
She's dead of course.

Bonne (1973)

The next story-experience activity is oriented toward teenagers and adults. This time, the students in the circle hold cards of various colors: red, yellow, blue, white, and so on. Work with the students to make sure they are able to associate the word with the color to which each student has been assigned. The students are instructed to listen very carefully to the words as the story is read. When the names of their colors are read, they walk across the circle, holding up the colored card.

More than one student may have the same color. The number of students holding each color depends on how many persons are involved at any given time.

A Spring Day

The door opens wide. It is Sasha. Sasha comes to my house every morning at six o'clock. We walk to work together. Today is such a beautiful, warm day. We walk on the long sidewalk. A YELLOW sun peeks through the trees. It is spring. The flowers are opening up—RED flowers, YELLOW flowers, BLUE flowers. We see a man in the street. He is riding a RED bicycle. He is wearing boots and a BLUE hat. He stops riding. He asks, "Have you seen our rabbit? He's WHITE and BLACK, mostly BLACK. He got out of the cage this morning and must have come this way." He points toward the grass behind us. We look in the direction he is pointing. Then at each other.

"No, we haven't," we say at the same time. "Sorry." The man looks very worried. He gets back on his bicycle. He begins to ride away. "Wait," I yell. "I see something here . . . behind the bush. I think . . . I see fur . . . it's WHITE and BLACK—why it is. It's a rabbit and it looks very scared. Look, it's all hunched over." The man turns around and rides back. I pick up the frightened little ball of fur and hand it to him. "Oh, thank you so very much!" exclaims the man. "My little boy will be very happy." He cuddles the rabbit in one arm as he rides away.

Once the students are familiar with the colors and feel comfortable with the activity, they pretend to be the objects as they go across the circle. One can, for example, be the sun; others can be flowers, and so forth. Even the characters and main actions of the story can be acted out or pantomimed once a fuller understanding is achieved.

Using a version of Story Experience, the teacher can pursue one of the following distinct alternatives:

- begin with a core story (the simplest form of the story) that can be gradually expanded by adding more complex syntactic structures and more abstract vocabulary as the students move forward in the language
- begin with the fully developed story and allow the students to "grow into it" over time

Sound Effects

Level: Beginning

Demonstrate the sound effects that accompany the following story.[4] Beginning students only need to listen for the words that cue the appropriate effect (blanks have been inserted where the sound effects should go). Once the students understand the whole story (perhaps at an intermediate level), they can act it out. If they want, they can change the ending or rewrite it completely.

Rosita's Night to Remember

Rosita is alone in the house. Outside she hears the wind blow through the trees _____ (hooing noises). Rain begins to fall _____ (patting of fingertips on the desks). There is a scratching at the door _____ (light touch of fingernails scratching on desks). Maybe it is a lion _____(roaring). Maybe it is a mouse _____ (squeaking). Maybe it is a monster _____ (howling). She is scared. She turns on the radio to drown out the scratching. The radio is playing a song _____ (singing—does not have to be a particular tune). She turns it low _____ (the singing softens), high _____ (it becomes very loud), off _____ (it stops). At the door, the scratching continues _____. She opens the door _____ (creaking). Her dog comes in, jumps up, and gives her a big kiss _____ (kissing sound).

As the students become more proficient, they can write their own scenarios, complete with sound effects. At advanced levels, the mini-dramas can even become part of full-blown radio shows complete with commercials and newsbreaks.

Story Act-Out

Level: Beginning to Intermediate

Read a favorite story aloud while the students listen. Give students a chance to ask questions, then read the story again. Ask for volunteers to take the parts of the characters. Pin a sign with the character's name on each volunteer. Read the story a third time as students act it out, action by action. Then give other volunteers a chance to be the actors.

---

[4] This story is an adaptation of one shared with me by Sylvia Pena.

Bilingual Storytelling

Level: Beginning to Advanced

Bilingual storytelling involves telling a story in some combination of two languages. Often the teacher begins by telling the story in the students' first language and then tells the same story in the second. By offering a story that is well known to the students in their first language, a link can be formed to the students' culture, which is one way of affirming it (Kasser & Silverman, 2001). Familiar stories are much easier to comprehend in the new language once they have been told in the native language. In classrooms where multiple languages are spoken, students can be divided into groups, according to their native language. Advanced students of the second language can be assigned to their own native language groups and can tell the story to the others in both languages.

At intermediate levels and above, the students may read the same story in both languages. Stories can be written by the students in one language and then translated into one or more languages. *Code switching* may be used within the same story. Its parts may be told or written in alternating languages, depending on what is most appropriate for a particular story.

Folktales and legends lend themselves particularly well to bilingual storytelling.

What's the Title?

Level: Intermediate

Read a story to students but leave out the title. Once the students understand the story, let them make up a title for it. Eventually the author's title can be revealed and discussed in relation to the meaning of the story.

Spinning Stories[5]

Level: Intermediate

Tape a stimulating picture with people in it to the wall. After placing students in a circle, ask them what they see in the picture. Write the words on the board as they give them to you so that they will have some starters for a story they will be telling. Have students make up names and short biographical sketches for the people in the picture.

Have the students sit in a circle. Then take a ball of yarn in which you have previously tied knots at varying intervals. Some knots should be close together, others far apart. Give the ball of yarn to one student in the circle. Ask him or her to begin a story about the picture while unraveling the ball of yarn. The student continues to tell the story until he or she reaches the first knot. Then the ball of yarn is passed to the next person, who continues the story until reaching the next knot. The activity continues until every student in the circle has had a chance to contribute.

---

[5] Adapted from an activity shared with me by Esther Heise.

Group Story

Level: Intermediate

Using a language-experience type of activity (see Chapter 13), have the students create a group story. As each student makes his or her contribution, write the utterances on the board, making any necessary corrections indirectly. The stories will probably be very brief at first but will evolve into longer and more complex plots as the students gain proficiency. A series of pictures can be used to stimulate ideas. The teacher can use pictures that codify an issue that is relevant to the students as was used for problem posing (see pp. 99–100).

Silly Stories[6]

Level: Intermediate to Advanced

You and your students can create a story together while a teaching assistant writes it on the board. Begin by offering the first half of a sentence, then ask a volunteer student to finish it. Other sentences can be produced in the same fashion. Pictures can be used to stimulate thought. For example:

TEACHER: The elephant knocked at . . .
STUDENT 1:   . . . the door to my house.
TEACHER: He asked . . .
STUDENT 2:   . . . "Can I borrow a cup of straw?"

Ghost Stories by Candlelight

Level: Intermediate to Advanced

Ask each student to bring a scary story to tell the class in the target language. Have the students sit in a circle on the floor. Light a candle, place it in the center of the circle, and turn off the lights. Students can volunteer by taking the candle from the center and placing it in front of them so it lights up their faces. Then they proceed to tell their stories. The candle is returned to the center as each student finishes his or her story. The teacher should demonstrate the procedure first. Background music, the volume of which can easily be adjusted to fit the situation, can be used to fill the silence between volunteers while adding to the mood. Because this activity may be a little too frightening for young children, you will probably want to limit its use to older children, teens, and adults. A flashlight may be used to substitute for a candle as a safety measure, especially for preadolescents.[7]

Finish the Story

Level: Intermediate to Advanced

Present part of a story and have students finish it orally and/or in writing. At first, most of the story can be given. Later, only a few lines such as those listed here may be necessary to launch students

---

[6] This idea has been adapted from Wright, Betteridge, and Buckby (1984, p. 99).

[7] I want to thank Cesar Montes for suggesting this precaution to me.

into building a climax, followed by the denouement. Students can read their stories aloud to a small group and discuss the meaning of them.

> The boys see a dark shadow fall across the sidewalk. They look up and see . . .
>
> The first day of her trip went well. Then she opened her suitcase. She discovered . . .
>
> Maria heard a loud knock at the front door. A voice shouted, "You must pay your rent or leave now." Maria walked toward the door and . . .

Oral History

Level: Intermediate to Advanced

As part of a study of local history, students tell their own stories and those of their parents, grandparents, friends, and neighbors. Where did they come from? How did they get here (to this town, suburb, city, state, country)? The project can be as broad as the students want to make it. They can include stories about their experiences in the particular locale, how certain buildings came into being, how traditions developed, and so forth. Collections can be made of these stories to share with each other, other classes, and/or visitors to the classroom.

Story Interpretation

Level: Intermediate to Advanced

The following story is one that is sure to interest second language learners in particular because it involves the mixed feelings that often accompany returning to one's homeland.

You can motivate students to read the story by asking them questions about their own longings to return home or about what they think it might be like to return home. Following the story are relevant activities that can heighten its impact.

Excerpt from "Blue Winds Dancing," by Thomas S. Whitecloud

Morning. I spend the day cleaning up and buying some presents for my family with what is left of my money. Nothing much, but a gift is a gift, if a man buys it with his last quarter. I wait until evening, then start up the track toward home.

Christmas Eve comes in on a north wind. Snow clouds hang over the pines, the night comes early. Walking along the railroad bed, I feel the calm peace of snowbound forests on either side of me. I take my time; I am back in a world where time does not mean so much now.

I am alone—alone but not nearly so lonely as I was back on the campus at school. Those are never lonely who love the snow and the pines, never lonely when the pines are wearing white shawls and snow crunches coldly underfoot. . . .

Just as a light snow begins to fall, I cross the reservation boundary. Somehow it seems as though I have stepped into another world. Deep woods in a white-and-black winter night. A faint trail leading to the village.

The railroad on which I stand comes from a city sprawled by a lake—a city with a million people who walk around without seeing one another; a city sucking the life from all the country around; a city with stores and police and intellectuals and criminals and movies and apartment houses; a city with its politics and libraries and zoos.

Laughing, I go into the woods. As I cross a frozen lake, I begin to hear the drums. Soft in the night the drums beat. It is like the pulse of the world. The white line of the lake ends at a black forest, and above the trees the blue winds are dancing.

I come to the outlying houses of the village. Simple box houses, etched black in the night. From one or two windows soft lamplight falls on the snow. Christmas is here, too, but it does not mean much—not much in the way of parties and presents. Joe Sky will get drunk. Alex Bodidash will buy his children red mittens and a new sled. . . . The village is not a sight to instill pride, yet I am not ashamed. One can never be ashamed of his own people when he knows they have dreams as beautiful as white snow on a tall pine.

Father and my brother and sister are seated around the table as I walk in. Father stares at me for a moment. Then I am in his arms, crying on his shoulder. I give them the presents I have brought, and my throat tightens as I watch my sister save carefully bits of red string from the packages. I hide my feelings by wrestling with my brother when he strikes my shoulder in a token of affection. Father looks at me, and I know he has many questions, but he seems to know why I have come. He tells me to go on alone to the lodge, and he will follow.

I follow the trail to the lodge. My feet are light, my heart seems to sing to the music, and I hold my head high. Across white snow fields blue winds are dancing.

Before the lodge door I stop, afraid. I wonder if my people will remember me. I wonder—"Am I Indian, or am I white?" I stand before the door a long time. I hear the ice groan on the lake, and remember the story of the old woman who is under the ice, trying to get out, so she can punish some runaway lovers. . . .

Inside the lodge there are many Indians. Some sit on benches around the walls. Others dance in the center of the floor around a drum. Nobody seems to notice me. It seems as though I were among a people I have never seen before. . . . I look at the old men. Straight, dressed in dark trousers and beaded velvet vests, wearing soft moccasins. Dark, lined faces intent on the music. I wonder if I am at all like them. They dance on, lifting their feet to the rhythm of the drums. . . .

The dance stops. The men walk back to the walls and talk in low tones or with their hands. There is little conversation, yet everyone seems to be sharing some secret . . . they are sharing a mood. Everyone is happy . . . the night is beautiful outside, and the music is beautiful.

I try hard to forget school and white people, and be one of these—my people . . . we are all a part of something universal. I watch eyes and see now that the old people are speaking to me. They nod slightly, imperceptibly, and their eyes laugh into mine. I look around the room. All the eyes are friendly; they all laugh. No one questions my being here. The drums begin to beat again, and I catch the invitation in the eyes of the old men. My feet begin to lift to the rhythm, and I look out beyond the walls into the night and see the lights. I am happy. It is beautiful. I am home.

Possible Follow-up Activities to "Blue Winds Dancing"

1. First, talk about the meaning of the story based on what happens and the reactions of the main character. Ask the students if there are any words or phrases that they do not understand. Ask them to guess at the meanings by using the context.
2. Have volunteers retell the story to a guest who is not already familiar with it (you may want to invite someone in for this purpose).

3. Divide the students into pairs. Have one person take the part of the young man who comes home and the other the part of one of the older men at the lodge. Have them make up a dialogue, write it down, and practice it. Ask volunteers to share their scenes with the class.

4. Divide the students into groups of three. Have them speculate about what it would be like to return to their homelands. Encourage them to share the problems they might have as well as the delights.

Story Writing

Level: Advanced

Students can be given time to write and share their own stories. They may want to make their stories autobiographical, biographical, or fictional. As a culminating activity, put copies of all the stories together in a book with illustrations and a table of contents. The books can be shared with other classes or placed in the school's library to be checked out by anyone who wants to read them.

ROLE PLAY

Role play has high appeal for students because it allows them to be creative and put themselves in another person's place for a while. As Atticus Finch says in Harper Lee's *To Kill a Mockingbird*, "You never really understand a person until you consider things from his view—until you climb into his skin and walk around in it." Role play can be just "play" or it can have serious social implications, such as in sociodrama.

Scarcella (1983) defined sociodrama as student oriented rather than teacher oriented. Students act out solutions to social problems, generally defining their own roles and determining their own courses of action. The enactment is open ended but centers around a clearly stated conflict that is relevant to the students. Only those students who demonstrate a special interest in particular roles are chosen to play them. The steps adapted from F. Shaftel and G. Shaftel (1967) include the following:

1. introduce the topic
2. stimulate student interest
3. present new vocabulary
4. begin to read a story that clearly identifies a problem
5. stop the story at the climax
6. discuss the dilemma
7. select students to play the roles
8. prepare the audience to listen and later to offer advice
9. act out the rest of the story
10. discuss alternative ways of dealing with the problem
11. replay the dramas using new strategies if necessary.

Following are some sample mini-sociodramas (or "role-play situations").

ROLE-PLAY SITUATIONS

For Adults or Teenagers

Sun Kim comes home from school all excited. Jeff, an Anglo-American boy, has asked her for a date. She tells her mother. Her mother is very upset.

"In Korea, you do not do any such thing," her mother reminds her.

"But, Mother, this is not Korea. This is America."

"But we are Korean," her mother insists. "You are Korean. This is not what we do. In time you will be ready. Your father and I will arrange a nice Korean man for you. We will not let you go alone with this man."

"Oh, Mother . . . but . . . I . . ."

For Preadolescents

"Look. I'm as big as you," Anita says to her brother John. She stretches up on her tiptoes. "Why can't I go to the movie with you?"

"Look, Squirt, you stay home this time, okay. The movie is not for you because . . ."

For Young Children

"Mom, come here. Come here. The cat is stuck up in the tree. He won't come down. Come quick."

Mother sticks her head around the door. "Now just a minute, Sally. Don't panic. The first thing we'll do is . . ."

It's important that the students gradually work into the role-play situations. The teacher can ease them into their roles by asking questions such as, "How old are you, Anita? What kinds of movies do your parents want you to see?" When the students seem to feel comfortable in their roles, the teacher can reread the situation and let the actors take it at the point where the story leaves off.

For the more proficient students, another activity that can be adapted to various age groups is acting out roles of characters from literature. Literature can come alive when students play the role of a character with which they are familiar. For example, if they have just read *The Pearl* by John Steinbeck (1947), one student may want to play Juana and another Kino. The characters could be interviewed as they might be on a talk show, or they might be part of a panel discussion on what money and greed can do to one's life. In addition, people from history might be brought back to life for a day or two. For example, one student might play Abraham Lincoln and another Susan B. Anthony. After students read up on their lives and times, these characters can be brought together for a TV show during which they can have discussions about relevant topics. Other characters from history can be pitted against each other in a debate about something current. It would be interesting to see how Henry VIII might feel about divorce or how Joan of Arc might react to feminist issues.

Mid-beginners also can participate in role play. Tools for communication can be taught through role-play situations. Students can be given matrices on index cards to be used as cues. Short scenes can begin with physical response activities in which the teacher plays the role of the director and directs students in their parts ("move to the right, sit down, walk to the table, say, 'Are you ready to order?'"). Matrices such as the following can be tailored to fit different situations. Similar matrices can first be incorporated into chants and lyrics (see Chapter 10).

In a restaurant:

> *[Menus are given to two customers by the waiter who disappears for a few minutes and then returns.]*
>
> Are you ready to order?
> Yes, I will have the _____.
> And you? *[looks at the second person]*
> I will have the _____.

At a farmers' market:

> *[A salesperson is setting out baskets of strawberries. A customer approaches from behind.]*
>
> Excuse me. Can you please tell me where the _____ is/are?
> Oh, yes. It's/they're by the _____.
> Thank you.

Typical greetings, simple compliments, frequently asked questions, and often-used comments can be introduced or reinforced in this manner (see also Bardovi-Harlig, Hartford, Mahan-Taylor, Morgan, & Reynolds, 1996). Public places, in addition to those mentioned previously, can be simulated to serve as settings (a post office, a doctor's office, a library, a hospital). Eventually the students can simply be given an oral description of a situation (no cue cards) to which they respond through role play.

> You are in a restaurant. The waiter comes to take your order. You look at the menu and tell the waiter what you want.
> You are at a booth at a farmers' market. You can't find what you want to buy. You ask the salesperson for help.

The most beneficial kind of role play, however, is that in which the teacher plays a key role. For example, if the teacher is the waiter in the restaurant or the salesperson in a booth at the farmers' market, he or she can provide modified language tailored to each student's approximate level in order to extend the conversation. The teacher can prompt, expand, or offer help as needed. By this means, groups of mixed abilities can be included in the same role-play situation. Starters are offered to some, explanations provided to others, and others are given no help at all if they do not need it. The following is an illustration of how this can work:

In a booth at the farmers' market [*The students have been given play money and have had prior experience counting it.*]
Pedro stands in front of the strawberries.

TEACHER: [*or teaching assistant playing the role of the salesperson*] Strawberries? For you, Pedro? [*She holds up a basket of strawberries.*]

PEDRO: Aaa . . . Straw . . .

TEACHER: Strawberries? Do you want strawberries?

PEDRO: . . . Strawberries . . . [*nods his head*].

TEACHER: [*offering the basket to him*] Do you want to buy the strawberries? Yes? [*points to some play money in the box that serves as a cash register*].

PEDRO: Yes . . . buy.

TEACHER: One dollar. Give me one dollar. [*Pedro takes some play money from his pocket but looks puzzled.*]

TEACHER: One dollar [*points to a dollar bill in his hand*].

PEDRO: One dollar [*gives the teacher the dollar bill*].

TEACHER: Thank you [*takes the money and gives him the basket*].

PEDRO: Thank you.

TEACHER: [*turning to the next customer*] Do you want some strawberries, Nor?

NOR: I want oranges.

TEACHER: Oranges, huh [*moves to the oranges*]. I've got juicy ones for you.

NOR: Juicy?

TEACHER: Yes. Juicy. Lots of sweet juice [*squeezes one to show its softness*].

NOR: Oh yes. Juice.

TEACHER: They cost $1.50 a bag. Do you want a bag?

NOR: Yes. I'll take a bag [*gives the teacher the money and takes the oranges*].

Thus the teacher is able to adjust the input to fit the approximate level of each student. *No cue cards are needed.* With sufficient input, the students can begin to acquire the structures through the interaction.

DRAMA

Even though drama is an integral part of storytelling and role play, it constitutes its own separate category. It includes activities involving roles, plots, and dialogues that are written in play form to be memorized and acted out on the stage or read aloud. In the results of a questionnaire given to University of California, Los Angeles teachers and students, Susan Stern (1983) early on found support for her theory that drama has a positive effect on second language learning. It encourages the operation of certain psychological factors that facilitate oral communication: heightened self-esteem, motivation, and spontaneity; increased capacity for empathy; and lowered sensitivity to rejection (p. 216). Healy (2004) believed that drama involves language learners intimately with its content and encourages them to talk meaningfully about their reflections and opinions. Because they become absorbed in playing out life's experiences, second language students may be able to overcome the self-consciousness generally associated with learning another language. In addition, by losing themselves in the struggles and conflicts of others, they can become better able to make the target language part of their memory store (see the "episode hypothesis" in Chapter 16).

The introductory activities recommended here can be suitable as warm-ups for storytelling and role play as well.

Act It Out

Level: Beginning

At lower proficiency levels, introduce students to simple dramatized emotions. First model the emotions, using exaggerated facial expressions and other movements to illustrate joy, anger, fear, sadness, and doubt. Have students model the emotions as a group (see also "Identifying Emotions" in Chapter 8). Have students refine their abilities to recognize and reproduce emotions by learning to draw them. (See Figure 11.1.)

For further reinforcement, have students find pictures in magazines of people expressing specific feelings. Students can cut out the pictures and paste them in a book of emotions (have them label one page "Joy," another "Fear," another "Anger," and so forth).

At a higher proficiency level, have each student write the name of an emotion on a piece of paper to be put into a grab bag. Each student draws an emotion out of the grab bag and acts it out while the rest of the class guesses which emotion is being portrayed. At another time, the names of specific activities are written on the pieces of paper; the students draw them out and pantomime the activities while the class guesses what activity is being acted out.

Figure 11.1 ©1990 Evans and Moore

TV Show

Level: Beginning

Choose an interesting segment of a TV show such as a soap opera, a serious drama about a relevant issue, or a situation comedy to videotape. Show the video first without sound and let the students decide the emotions that the actors are feeling. Later show the same segment, again without sound, and ask the students to guess what is happening just from facial expressions and actions. Then replay the same segment and listen to the words. How close did the students come to guessing the reality? Discuss. It is not necessary that they understand all the words. Play it again in a few months and have students write and act out additional segments. Eventually, have them write and stage their own shows.

Puppets

Level: Intermediate

Have each student, particularly younger ones, make a puppet out of heavy construction paper and a tongue depressor (see Figure 11.2).[8] For the head, have them cut out two identical shapes from construction paper and staple the edges together, leaving an opening at the neck. Placing a small wad of newspaper inside gives the puppet a three-dimensional effect. Have them place the tongue depressor where the neck should be and staple the paper to it. Yarn can be used for hair. A felt-tip pen can be used to draw eyes, a nose, and a mouth. Have the students give the puppet a name and make it a character in a series of simple dramas or mini-scenarios written and acted out by the students.

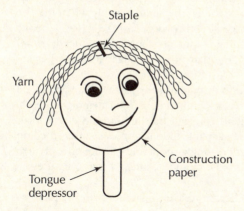

Staple

Yarn

Construction paper

Tongue depressor

Figure 11.2

Prop Box

Level: Intermediate to Advanced

This activity intended for the upper-elementary grades and later is an adaptation of "The Prop Box," created by Judy Winn-Bell Olsen.[9] Have each student bring to class something from home

---

[8] I want to thank Susan Andrews for this idea.

[9] She gives credit to the Creative Environment Center (San Francisco Unified School District) workshop for this suggestion. Prop boxes can be used to teach other lessons, particularly in conjunction with other interactive practices (see especially Chapter 9). For example, one box could include household items, another box could hold camping equipment, and so on.

that he or she does not want anymore. It can be from any room in the house, but it must be something that the teacher can keep. Place all the items in a large box (the prop box). Divide the class into groups of two, three, or four students. Ask each student to reach into the prop box without looking and draw out an item. Have the groups write short dramas or skits that incorporate all the items they have drawn out of the box as props. Students then rehearse the plays with the help of peer facilitators or lay assistants (see Chapter 15) and present them to the whole class.

Readers' Theater

Level: Intermediate to Advanced

Goodman and Tenney (1979) recommended readers' theater as a vehicle for acquiring a second language. The term *readers' theater* comes from the fact that the actors hold their scripts and read from them with expression and feeling. The actors and the narrator generally sit on tall stools arranged in a semicircle in front of the audience. The actors imagine that the wall in back of the audience is a mirror. The actors talk directly to the mirror "images" of the other characters rather than address them directly. In fact, they more or less ignore the presence of the other characters except as they appear in the "mirror." Characters who are supposed to be offstage also sit on stools but keep their backs to the audience, facing the audience only when they enter the stage. The narrator, who addresses the audience directly, plays a large role: He or she sets the scene, introduces the characters, and gives running comments about actions, feelings, and moods. In other words, the narrator provides the glue that holds the dialogue together and makes it comprehensible.

Because readers' theater involves much repetition through rehearsals for presentation, the words eventually become part of the students' repertoires without conscious memorization. The whole class, even the audience, begins to internalize the lines if they are in on the rehearsals. Reading also can be enhanced for the audience if they are able to look at the scripts as the lines are read. Goodman and Tenney were convinced that creating a script and putting on a play can be an excellent culminating activity for units of study. Through it, concepts and structures are acquired and/or reinforced.

Goodman and Tenney suggested that the teacher first have the actors read the dialogue aloud and then ask the audience what was especially effective about the way it was read. The teacher then discusses the drama with the students to create interest in the problems of the characters. The teacher as director should model the roles to encourage the students to put aside some of their own inhibitions. Students then read the parts one more time with added expression and feeling. The audience can be called on for suggestions, including ideas, sound effects, or other elements. The teacher makes sure all the students who want to participate are part of the production in some way. See the following example of a readers' theater script.

An Unusual Birthday Celebration
Narrator: It is mid-afternoon. Two elderly women and a dog are on the sidewalk. They are in front of the ice cream store on Maple Street.
Mabel: Well, Nettie, what will we get today?
Narrator: She smiles at Nettie. Their eyes are dancing.
Nettie: I want something very special today . . . something new.

Narrator: Nettie tugs at her dog's leash.

Nettie: Now you be a good boy and lie down.

Narrator: She points to the sidewalk in front of the glass door. The dog lies down obediently. The two women go into the store.

Mabel: Something new? You're going to try something new? You always want the same old thing. A cone with one scoop of chocolate. You always get that.

Nettie: But today I want something special. Today is my birthday, you know. Seventy-six years old.

Narrator: She looks at all the pictures on the wall. There are ice cream sundaes everywhere. Chocolate and caramel drip from them. They are covered with nuts, whipped cream, and cherries. Her mouth waters. Mabel says . . .

Mabel: Happy birthday!

Nettie: Thank you.

Mabel: Yes. You must get something different to celebrate. Did you hear from your son today? Did he wish you a happy birthday?

Narrator: Mabel's hands flutter in the air. Nettie's smile fades.

Nettie: No. I'm afraid he hasn't . . .

Clerk: What will you have, Ma'am?

Nettie: I think I'll have that . . .

Narrator: She points to a caramel sundae.

Nettie: I'll have . . . that caramel sundae . . . with whipped cream and nuts. No cherry, please. I'm allergic to cherries. They give me hives.

Clerk: Yes, Ma'am. Right away.

Narrator: She turns to look at Mabel. She catches a glimpse of the glass door and the sidewalk outside. Something is wrong. Her eyes open very wide. She screams . . .

Nettie: My dog. Where's my dog?

Narrator: She runs out the door. She looks up and down the street. But she can't find him. She calls and calls . . .

Nettie: He-re Lad-die. He-re Lad-die.

Narrator: . . . in a high voice. A stranger comes out from behind the building.

Stranger: Ma'am, is this the dog you're looking for? He's right here eating ice cream. A little boy dropped his cone . . .

Narrator: Nettie runs around to the side of the building. Sure enough, there in front of her is the dog. He is lapping up the last bit of ice cream from the ground. He makes slurping sounds. Nettie is overcome with joy. She says . . .

Nettie: Oh, my Laddie. Thank goodness he's safe.

Narrator: She rushes over and hugs him. The dog is now licking his chops. Mabel is right behind her.

Nettie: Oh, my sweet Laddie.

Mabel: I guess he wants something special on your birthday too. Just like a dog, you know. They all think they're people. Come on, let's get our ice cream. I don't have all day, you know.

Narrator: The three of them head back to the door of the ice cream store.

Later, students should be encouraged to write and perform their own scripts based on pictures or musical lyrics, poetry, TV shows, issues important to their lives, and so forth. The productions can eventually become whole-class projects from beginning to end.

SUMMARY

Storytelling, role play, and drama through their attention to human experience are likely to have much appeal in the language classroom. When students lose themselves in the characters, plots, and situations, they may experience lower anxiety, increased self-confidence and esteem, and heightened awareness.

Even beginning students enjoy dramatic action right from the start through prelanguage activities or warm-ups, Story Experience, and/or producing sound effects for production. Even being a properties assistant or part of the audience has its rewards.

Not only can students improve their abilities to comprehend and produce the target language, but they quickly learn to work cooperatively in group situations toward mutual goals. Being able to tell their own tales, interpret stories, deal with problems and issues through sociodrama, write, read aloud, and produce mini-dramas gives them early meaningful experiences with the language that they might not otherwise have.

QUESTIONS AND PROJECTS FOR REFLECTION AND DISCUSSION

1. How might dramatic experiences help to make the ego more "permeable" in the sense that Guiora et al. used the term? (See footnote 1 on p. 261.)

2. What role should culture play in choosing a selection around which to build activities? What criteria might you use to guide your choice? Include important constraints that culture might present for individuals and/or groups. What might be the consequences if such constraints are ignored? Give examples.

3. How might storytelling, role play, and drama be used to make emergent participatory language teaching a more likely possibility?

4. Plan a lesson using storytelling, role play, or drama. Be specific about the age levels and proficiency levels of the students for whom it is intended (beginning, intermediate, or advanced). Utilize the Structure for Simulated Lessons on pp. 256–257 and the Sample Lesson Preparation Format on pp. 367–369.

   Present your lesson to a small group of fellow students or peers. Discuss with them the strengths of your presentation and ways in which you might improve it. Begin by sharing your own reactions to your presentation. You may want to use the Questions to Guide Evaluative Discussion (p. 257) as the basis for your analysis, or you may use an evaluation format that you or your instructor have developed (see footnote 12 on p. 258).

If you are currently teaching, use what you have learned to try out a similar lesson. Make sure the lesson is appropriate to cultural sensitivities and level(s). If possible, have your lesson videotaped to analyze and discuss with peers. Reflect on its outcome and how you felt about doing it. Pay close attention to student response. Do you see any problems with your lesson? How might it be improved?

5. ✎ **Journal Entry:** Reflect on the lesson(s) you carried out in item 4 above. What strategies did you use? How comfortable did you feel with them? Did you think they were effective overall? Why or why not? What were some of the specific problems you encountered? How can they be overcome? Write about what you learned from your peers and instructor during the process. What insights did you gain about learning and teaching from the experience?

SUGGESTED READINGS AND REFERENCE MATERIALS

Kasser, C., & Silverman, A. (2001). *Stories we brought with us*. White Plains, NY: Pearson Education. This collection of well-known tales from many countries around the world works well for teachers with multileveled classes in elementary school. Two versions of each story are presented: One is written for a lower proficiency level than the other.

Paran, A. (Ed.). (2006). *Literature in language teaching and learning*. Alexandria, VA: Teachers of English to Speakers of Other Languages. The message of this anthology is that language and literature can be effectively taught together. Language teaching demands a context, and no better context can be found than in the plots, characters, tensions, and issues presented by relevant literature. Included are practical ideas and case studies intended to help English as a second language and English as a foreign language teachers in multiple environments improve their instruction.

Phillips, S. (1999). *Drama with children*. Oxford, England: Oxford University Press. Many ways to get children to participate in drama are included in this book. Ideas are presented concerning managing the classroom and following up with appropriate drama activities. Teachers are encouraged to photocopy selected pages for use in the classroom.

Stern, A. (2001). *Tales from many lands*. New York: McGraw-Hill/Contemporary. This multicultural reader, intended for secondary students and above, presents stories from several different cultures that teachers can read to their students or have students read by themselves. Through the selections and their accompanying activities, teachers are able to help students operating at high-beginning levels to link cultures and build skills at the same time. See also a similar book by Stern entitled *World Folktales* for teachers to use with students at low-intermediate levels.

Wainryb, R. (2003). *Stories: Narrative activities for the language classroom*. New York: Cambridge University Press. This book looks at stories as a way to synthesize experience and the narrative as a type of social discourse. It builds a convincing rationale for using stories to teach language in the classroom. Many activities are suggested that focus on narrative text itself and include travel tales, tall stories, and other kinds of stories.

Wright, A., & Maley, A. (1997). *Creating stories with children*. New York: Oxford University Press. This book includes activity ideas and their alternatives for assisting children in developing their own stories and drama. Scaffolding is one of the main strategies used to move students along in the learning process.

CHAPTER 12

Games

*Game playing, having apparently
originated as a form of instruction,
now appears again to be coming into
its own as an instructional activity.*

T. Rodgers, 1978

QUESTIONS TO THINK ABOUT

1. Do you remember favorite childhood games that helped you to learn your first language? What were some of those games? In what ways did they help you?

2. Are teenagers and adults too old for games that might help them learn another language? Why or why not?

3. What advantages might games have in learning another language?

4. To what extent would you incorporate games into a second language course? How would you use games to teach language?

5. Can you think of a way that games might be used as a link to other cultures? If so, how?

Games are usually associated with fun. Although they can indeed be fun, we should not lose sight of their pedagogical value, particularly in second language teaching. Like most other activities recommended in this book, games can lower anxiety, and thus they can make acquisition more likely. In addition, they can be highly motivating, relevant, interesting, and comprehensible.

Games can develop and reinforce concepts, such as colors, shapes, numbers, and word definitions (see also Lewis & Bedson, 1999); serve as a link to other cultures (Shameem & Tickoo, 1999); add diversion to the regular classroom activities; and even break the ice, particularly in the case of true beginners. Moreover, they can introduce new ideas and provide practice with communication skills (see also computer games discussed on p. 399). Although some games are quiet, contemplative games, others are noisy and require much verbal or physical involvement. Some are meant for small groups, others for large groups. Often classes can be divided into smaller units and several games can be played simultaneously. The teacher, peer facilitators, or lay assistants can help facilitate the individual groups. (See Chapter 15.)

The games recommended here may involve a certain amount of group competition, but competition is generally not the focus (except perhaps in some of the nonverbal games). Games that pit student against student or that may embarrass individuals in front of the class are not included. However, the teacher may want to emphasize a race against the clock or against a previous group accomplishment when appropriate.

The rules of games should be very few and clearly explained. In most cases, students can begin the games and have the rules explained or repeated as the games progress. Demonstrations can also be very helpful.

Most of the games discussed here can be adapted to any age level, provided students are cognitively able to handle their content. In addition, most can be adapted to several proficiency levels (beginning, intermediate, or advanced), according to the difficulty of the tasks involved. None of the games require much money to purchase or create; usually the materials needed can be easily collected or made by the teacher or an assistant.

Even though the categories often overlap, the games are divided into the following types, depending on their emphasis: nonverbal games, board-advancing games, word-focus games, treasure hunts, and guessing games.

NONVERBAL GAMES

Games such as relays or musical chairs help students become acquainted with each other, even before they can speak. Used sparingly, they serve as icebreakers and can be used to bring together students of mixed levels. After hearing the directions for a specific game given in the target language, the more proficient students of various language backgrounds can translate the directions into the first language of other, less proficient students.

Nonverbal games can also be used to form groups for other games and activities. For example, objects such as trees can be made of construction paper and cut into puzzle pieces to be matched (Figure 12.1).

The number of trees depends on how many groups are necessary for the game and the number of students in the class. For example, for Classroom Scrabble (described later in this chapter), if fourteen students need to divide into four teams, you will need to make

Figure 12.1

four trees (two trees cut into three puzzle pieces and two into four puzzle pieces). The students each pick a puzzle piece out of a grab bag and find the students who have the missing pieces to make a complete tree. Thus a group is formed. An alternative is to cut several pictures (one for each group desired) into puzzle pieces, mix them up, and have each student take one piece and find the other people with the pieces that will complete the picture. (For more ideas about forming groups, see pp. 218, 316, and 342.)

BOARD-ADVANCING GAMES

Using game pieces (such as buttons or other small objects) to represent the players, students perform certain tasks written on cards or simply roll the dice to move forward a certain number of spaces. The board itself can be as imaginative and colorful as you want to make it. The spaces need to form some sort of pathway from a starting point to a finishing point (the goal) as in Figure 12.2.

Figure 12.2

Students may take turns drawing cards with specific directions on them ("jump three times," "write your name on the board," "sing a song from your country"). Other students can help interpret and carry out the directions. Once students complete the tasks, they move forward the number of spaces indicated on the cards.

Additional tasks can include giving synonyms or antonyms for specific words, identifying objects on pictures, doing simple math computations, or any kind of task that reinforces concepts or procedures. The "winner" is the one who reaches the goal first.

WORD-FOCUS GAMES

One simple word game involves giving students words to see how many other words they can make from them. For example the following words can be made from the word *teacher: ear, her, teach, reach, cheer, each, hear, here, arch, tea,* and *eat.*

By working with others in a team situation, students learn new words from the other members in the group. Seeing which group can make the most words in a certain time period may add to the excitement and probably will not raise anxiety levels because no individuals are put on the spot.

An alternative is to have teams of students see how many words they can make from a letter grid such as the one shown in Figure 12.3. Students need to move along the connecting lines without skipping any letters. A single letter cannot be used twice in succession but can be returned to if there is an intervening letter. For example, in Figure 12.3, *regret* is acceptable but *greet* is not.

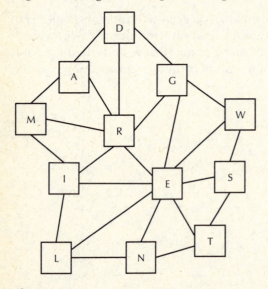

Figure 12.3

A bean-bag toss suggested early on by Evans and Moore (1979) can be adapted to teach antonyms, synonyms, or categories of words. The authors suggested that the teacher make a large playing area on tagboard with a felt-tip pen. The teacher or an assistant then draws circles all over the area and puts one word in each circle (see Figure 12.4).

If the teacher is reinforcing antonyms, each word should have its opposite; for synonyms, each word should have a corresponding word that means the same thing; and for categories, each word should have a corresponding category to which it belongs. A student stands behind a line that has been marked with masking tape and tosses a bean bag. After reading the word on which the bag lands, the student takes a second bean bag and tries to toss it so it will land on the appropriate antonym, synonym, or category member.

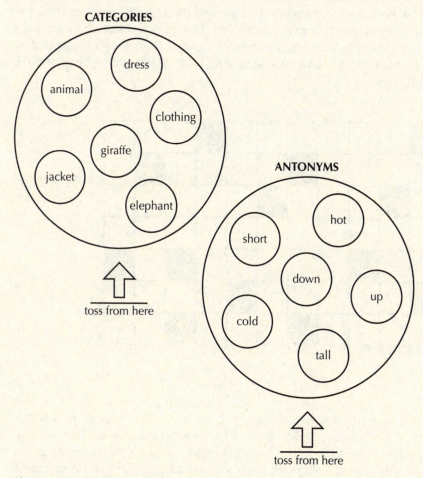

Figure 12.4 ©1979 Evan-Moor

Classroom Scrabble[1] is a particularly effective word-focus game. Divide students into two to four teams with three to four students per team. Draw a Scrabble board on the board (see Figure 12.5 on p. 298). Shade some of the squares; letters placed on these shaded areas receive double their normal count. Give the teams letters cut from

[1] I thank Deborah Floyd for this game idea.

index cards (four consonants and three vowels per team) on which you have written point values (lower point values for frequently used letters, higher point values for the rest).

Write a message in the middle of the board, such as "Peace." The students are to build their words off the letters in the message. Roll up cellophane tape and place it behind each letter to make it stick to the board (later the tape can be removed so the same letters can be used again). The teams take turns, making as many words as they can. All words need to connect to a word already on the board, either horizontally or vertically. Each team's letters are replaced after the turns, a vowel for a vowel and a consonant for a consonant. They are drawn at random by a team member from a reserve guarded by the teacher or an assistant. To keep the game moving, place a limit of about two or three minutes for each turn.

Figure 12.5

One commonly used word-focus game that some teachers choose to avoid is Scrambled Word. The students are given words with the letters scrambled. They are supposed to unscramble them to form the intended word. For example, "cesenic" can be unscrambled to form "science." Although proficient speakers might find this fun, most second language students find such games frustrating. For them, the language may appear to be somewhat "scrambled" to begin with; it seems senseless to cause them additional anxiety.

TREASURE HUNTS

A treasure hunt is a favorite game among second language learners. It allows students to work cooperatively in a group to find the items required to win and at the same time practice communicative skills. Often the items call for a group consensus: The students may have to find something they all agree is beautiful. Condon (1983) suggested the following steps (summarized here) for organizing a treasure hunt. The hunt can take anywhere from ten minutes to an entire day, depending on the number and kinds of items listed. In addition, treasures can differ depending on the age and proficiency levels of the students.

1. Divide the class into groups of from three to six members.
2. Give an identical list of treasures to each group.
3. Read the items aloud for children or less proficient students to make sure they understand the vocabulary.
4. Give a time limit.
5. Say "Go" to indicate when the groups can begin their searches.
6. At the end of the time limit or when one of the groups finishes its search, all the groups get together to check each item, giving points (e.g., 5 points) for each completed item.

Condon mentions a few of the more interesting items that can be included:

1. On a sheet of paper, list five countries the members of your group would like to visit.
2. Find something useless.
3. Make a dinner menu in English.
4. Find a photograph.
5. Collect the autographs of three people not in your group.
6. Find something that smells good.
7. Make a crazy hat for your teacher.
8. Write down six ways of making people laugh.
9. Find a picture of something good to eat.

An alternative activity for intermediate students could be to ask them to search for "treasures" in newspapers or magazines (e.g., a story about a fight against oppression, the report of a successful rescue, and so on). Follow-up activities for newspaper or magazine searches could include group discussion, asking and answering questions about the article in pairs, and so forth.

GUESSING GAMES

Guessing games can be a painless way to reinforce any number of concepts. "Guess What I Am" or "Guess Who I Am," for example, can be used to teach about animals, professions, or people in different age groups (baby, child, teenager, young adult, middle-aged adult, elderly person). Each student pantomimes a particular role, and the class guesses which role is being acted out. The student who guesses the role correctly is "it" and takes the next turn. A time limit can be set so not too much attention is devoted to any one person.

"Guess What I'm Doing" teaches or reinforces concepts associated with activities such as taking a shower, going fishing, doing homework, and so forth. "Guess What I Have" is even more focused on verbalization. The student gives verbal hints as to what object is being described, or the students ask questions about the object (as in "Twenty Questions"). The object may be hidden or in full view. It is important that the class not know beforehand which object is being described.

Alternatives include "Whose Name Is It?" or "What/Who Am I?" In either case, one person is "it," and a sign, which the person cannot see, is placed on his or her back. The name of a classmate or a famous person in world history or a specific occupation has been written on the sign. The person with the sign asks yes/no questions of the class until he or she finds the correct response (e.g., "Do I wear a hat?" "Do I climb ladders?" "Did I live in the nineteenth century?"). The students take turns being "it."

Games come in many different forms and can be gathered from a variety of sources: books on the subject, young people's magazines, department store game sections. However, one important source that should not be overlooked is the second language students themselves. Having students share games from their countries or cultural backgrounds can be a very exciting experience for everyone and can provide many opportunities for practice with the target language.

SUMMARY

Games can be used to develop or reinforce concepts, add diversion to the regular classroom activities, or just break the ice. However, their most important function is to give practice in communication.

It is recommended that competition be downplayed for most games, that the rules be few, and that they be clearly explained and demonstrated where possible.

Although the categories can overlap, the games offered here were divided into the following types depending on their emphasis: nonverbal games, board-advancing games, word-focus games, treasure hunts, and guessing games.

Various sources for game ideas are mentioned, but remember that one of the best sources is the students themselves.

QUESTIONS AND PROJECTS FOR REFLECTION AND DISCUSSION

1. Form a set of criteria to use in the selection of a game for second language classroom use. Give examples of games that you might choose based on the criteria you have developed. Discuss with a small group.

2. How can a game such as a treasure hunt be used to reinforce the teaching of a story? Choose a particular story, describe the story, and tell what "treasures" you might incorporate to reinforce the concepts.

3. Recall one of the favorite games that you played as a child. How might it be adapted for a second language class?

4. Select a topic and the key concepts on which you may have focused in a previous lesson. Find and adapt or create two or three games that you could

use to reinforce the concepts associated with the topic. Try one game out with a group of fellow students or peers. Be specific about its purpose and the age and proficiency levels of the students with whom you might use it (beginning, intermediate, or advanced). Discuss with them the strengths of your presentation and ways in which you might improve it. Begin by sharing your own reactions to the presentation.

If you are currently teaching, use what you have learned to try out one or more games with your students. Make sure the games are appropriate to cultural sensitivities and to levels. If possible, have your presentation videotaped to analyze and discuss with peers. Reflect on the outcomes and how you felt about using the game or games you selected. Pay close attention to student response. Do you see any problems with the game(s) and the strategies you used? How might your overall presentation be improved?

5. ✎ **Journal Entry:** Reflect on the games you used in item 4 above. How comfortable did you feel with this kind of activity? Did you think they were effective overall? Why or why not? What were some of the specific problems you encountered? How can they be overcome? Write about what you learned from your peers and instructor during the process. What insights did you gain about learning and teaching from the experience?

SUGGESTED READINGS AND REFERENCE MATERIALS

Lewis, G., & Bedson, G. (1999). *Games for children*. Oxford, England: Oxford University. The games included in this book are intended for language reinforcement in the classroom. Many of the games included can be used with teenagers as well as children.

Shameem, N., & Tickoo, M. (Eds.). (1999). *New ways in using communicative games in language teaching*. Alexandria, VA: Teachers of English to Speakers of Other Languages. The games presented here, which come from several cultures, are designed to help students become more fluent in the language, learn strategies for socialization, be introduced to content, and develop pragmatic discourse skills. The games involve students in whole-class and small-group activity.

Wright, A., Betteridge, D., & Buckby, M. (2006). *Games for language learning* (3rd ed.). Cambridge, England: Cambridge University Press. A wide variety of games for second language learning are featured in this book, including story games, memory games, psychological games, and so on. They are organized by skill area and language as well as by game type.

CHAPTER 13

Ways to Promote Literacy Development

. . . writing like a reader becomes inextricably bound up with reading like a writer.

V. Zamel, 1992

QUESTIONS TO THINK ABOUT

1. In your opinion, what kinds of activities will best promote reading and writing skills in second language learners? Relate to your own experiences with reading and writing in your first and/or second language. If your opinion is based mainly on your first language experiences with literacy, discuss how the kinds of activities might be different for second language learners.

2. Are there any kinds of activities that you would avoid? Again relate to your own experiences.

3. Do you think reading and writing should be taught simultaneously? Why or why not? To what extent do you feel they should receive separate treatment?

4. To what extent do you think second language teaching should be literature-based? What are some possible advantages and disadvantages of using literature to teach a second language?

5. What do you know about a workshop approach to teach writing? Have you experienced it as a teacher or as a student? If so, reflect on this experience. To what extent were the workshops successful? What problems did you encounter? What problems might second language students encounter with a workshop approach?

The ways to promote development of literacy skills suggested in this chapter are extensions of a natural language framework developed in Chapter 5. They are based on the premise that learning to read and write is a communal process. They assume that the student's major goal in developing literacy skills is to effectively create meaning either as a writer or a reader through collaboration (see also Lee & Smagorinsky, 2000). They also assume that the learner comes to the classroom community with a rich fund of knowledge and experience to share with others within an emergent participatory classroom environment. Sociocultural, cognitive, and linguistic aspects of reading and writing need to come together in the classroom so that progress can occur.

In this chapter, the following topics are discussed:

- The Language Experience Approach
- Literature-Based Curriculum
- Writing Workshops
- Advanced Academic Literacy

THE LANGUAGE EXPERIENCE APPROACH

The *language experience approach* (Van Allen & Allen, 1967) was a precursor to the whole language movement (see Chapter 5). Even though it originally lacked a well-developed theoretical base, its apparent efficacy established it as a viable means for teaching reading to native speakers. Later, several versions were suggested for use with second language students (see especially Dixon & Nessel, 1990; Moustfa, 1989; Nessel & Dixon, 2008). This approach is predicated on the notion that students can learn to write by dictating to the teacher what they already can express verbally. The teacher writes what they say and, as a result, the students' first reading materials come from their own repertoire of language.

Although applications may differ for various age levels and needs, the process begins with the student's experiences (e.g., going on a trip, seeing a movie, looking at a picture, listening to a poem or story). The student first discusses the experience with the teacher and/or fellow students and then dictates a "story" about that experience to the teacher individually. The teacher writes down exactly what the student says, including the errors. The teacher then reads aloud each sentence after it is written, giving the student a chance to make changes. Some may notice their own errors and want to correct them. The teacher may wait until the story is finished before reading it back, making sure the student sees the correspondence between what is being said and what was written. The student is encouraged to read the story either silently or aloud with the teacher, and then copy it into a notebook where it can be revisited again and again as needed.

An interesting alternative, which changes the dynamics considerably, is for the whole class or small groups within the class to dictate a "group" story while the teacher writes it on the board, flip chart, or overhead transparency. What makes this alternative interesting is that the students build on each other's utterances and, through this process, stretch to higher levels of expression.

The stories that the students write in this fashion can be displayed, with their permission, in story collections or on the walls of the classroom for all to read. Students can provide illustrations to accompany their stories, adding another dimension to the printed page. As the students become more proficient reading their stories, they are gradually introduced to textbooks and other materials that are easy and are within their reach cognitively.

Some teachers like to break students' stories down into discrete elements of decreasing size. For example, teachers may cut the story into sentence strips and ask students to put the strips together again to form the whole story. Others may cut the strips into sentence parts or phrases, words, syllables, or even just letters and again ask the students to construct the whole, using increasingly smaller units. Yet other teachers may have students identify letter-sound correspondences by matching them. For example, the teacher might say "find the *b*s in the story." Although this kind of activity may be helpful for some students, for others it can become tedious repetition. The greatest danger is that students may find it frustrating to see their stories turned into scrambled word/sentence/letter puzzles (I always hated those myself) or into seemingly endless phonics lessons. Sometimes teachers use the story as a lesson in semantics (e.g., "Which word means 'to walk slowly'?" "Which word is the opposite of 'dangerous'?"). Although this may benefit some students, most would probably be more motivated by asking and answering questions related to the story's meaning, at least at first. For example, if the students have just written a story about a picture of a man packing his suitcase, comprehension questions could be asked (e.g., "Where is the man going? Point to the sentence that tells that. Why is he going there? How do you know?" and so on).

Applications of the language experience approach can be used at many levels and for many purposes other than composing stories. For example, charts with the information supplied by students can be created, comparisons can be drawn in chart or paragraph form, and idea maps or clustering devices can be generated, just to name a few.

Advantages of the Language Experience Approach

Perhaps the biggest advantage of this approach is that the text is appropriate both cognitively and linguistically because it comes from the students themselves. Moreover, the student's own culture and ideas are encouraged and validated, thereby enhancing self-concepts and fostering the emergence of individual and collective empowerment. Grammar and other discrete point instruction can be used as needed, and small groups of students needing similar instruction can be formed. In the case of a group-created product, students can learn from and build on one another's contributions.

Limitations of the Language Experience Approach and How They Can Be Overcome

One possible limitation of this approach is that students might get the mistaken idea that writing is simply recorded speech. However, through the process of creating text, adjusting, rewriting, and so forth, students eventually learn that the written register is not the same as recorded speech. Certain conventions and abstractions are used in written language that are not usually found in everyday speech. Moreover, students soon realize that the purposes of written language are often very different. They write things down to aid memory, to keep a record, to meet various requirements at school and in the work place, and so on.

A second limitation concerns writing down student errors as part of the dictation procedure. Teachers often express reservations about this practice, thinking that they are reinforcing errors.[1] They are afraid, too, that if students see the teacher writing down their errors, they will think that all is well and that there is no mismatch between their own hypotheses about the language and what proficient users of the language know.

A third limitation involves the teacher acting chiefly as a transcriber, when in fact the teacher could be playing a far more facilitative role. One way to make the experience more participatory is for the teacher and students to become integral parts of a composing process. However, care should be taken that the students have the opportunity to contribute as much as their abilities will allow and that the teacher not overshadow their efforts.

The Teacher in a Facilitative Role

In the following example, the teacher assumes a *more facilitative role* out of which a *collaborative product* is created. Notice that the teacher makes indirect corrections through recasts or reformulations (see pp. 50–51) and uses these corrected forms in the writing. This way, a teacher who feels uncomfortable writing errors does not have to.

TEACHER: [*referring to a story she has just read aloud to the students*] Let's write our thoughts about the story. Did you like the story?

ASSAD: I didn't like the story.

TEACHER: You didn't? Why? Why didn't you like it?

ASSAD: I didn't like when Maria keep the ring. It didn't belong to her.

TEACHER: Do the rest of you feel the same way? Did you not like it when Maria kept the ring? [*Five students raise their hands.*] What do some of the rest of you think?

JORGE: It's okay.

TEACHER: What's okay?

JORGE: To keep the ring. It was her mother's ring.

ASSAD: But her mother gave it to the neighbor.

TEACHER: How many of you agree with Jorge that it was all right to keep the ring? [*Three students raise their hands.*] Okay, what should we write?

JORGE: Write "Some of us want Maria keep the ring. It belonged to her mother."

TEACHER: Some of us wanted Maria to keep the ring? [*She looks at Jorge as she begins to write. Jorge nods. She writes* "Some of us wanted Maria to keep the ring. It belonged to her mother."]

Thus the writing begins as the teacher guides the students, bringing out their ideas and helping them to shape the language. The teacher, in a sense, becomes a coauthor, as well as a facilitator; the teacher asks questions, clarifies meaning, and makes a few contributions of his or her own. Moreover, he or she provides language on which the students can build.

---

[1] Advocates of the more "pure" version of the language experience approach argue that this fear is unjustified and that the benefits of such a practice far outweigh the disadvantages, especially for children and beginners of any age who are in special need of encouragement.

Gradually, students require less guidance from the teacher. They soon may be able to finish, on their own, the compositions begun as collaborations. Later, students may be able to work with partners to create compositions. Eventually, they may be able to write independently but still with ongoing collaboration and help available as needed from the teacher and peers (see Writing Workshops discussed later beginning on p. 325).

LITERATURE-BASED CURRICULUM

Shirley Brice Heath (1996) said, "Literature has no rival in its power to create natural repetition, reflection on language and how it works, and attention to audience response on the part of learners" (p. 776). Many others advocate literature as a powerful resource for the teacher to use as a focus for language teaching (Lazar, 1993; Kay & Gelshenen, 1998; Paran, 2006; Richard-Amato, 1996b).

Even at beginning proficiency levels, teachers can use literature as the pivot around which curriculum can revolve. For example, Story Experience (see pp. 275–277) brings students into literature from the very beginning. Other activities using stories (see Chapter 11) help students as they begin and continue their journey into the language learning process. All the while, writing, speaking, and listening are incorporated as they relate to the literature—both creative (novels, stories, drama, and poetry) and expository (biographical writings, histories, textbooks, essays, and the like). Often listening, speaking, and/or reading events are turned into writing events. In addition, the language experience approach just described can make a major contribution to the development of literacy by providing students with materials they themselves have written or have helped to write.

Why Use Literature as a Pivot?

Literature Is Authentic. It is not usually written solely to teach specific structures or vocabulary (unless we are talking about basal-type readers). Instead its structures and vocabulary grow naturally out of the ideas, plots, dialogues, and situations developed. However, authentic literature does usually have a particular audience in mind. For example, it may be written for persons of a certain age, gender, cultural background, occupation, or level of proficiency in a given language. Also, "authentic" does not mean "unaltered." Literature modified for a specific age or level of proficiency can still focus on meaning (see Bamford & Day, 1996), and its structures and vocabulary can continue to be a product of that meaning. The authenticity of a selection is generally in the eyes of the beholder and is largely determined by the local situation in which that person finds himself or herself.

Literature Can Provide Memorable Contexts for the Language. To support this argument, Oller (1983b) offered the episode hypothesis (see also pp. 392–395), which states "text (i.e., discourse in any form) will be easier to reproduce, understand, and recall to the extent that it is structured episodically" (p. 12). Episodic organization requires both the motivation created by conflict and the logical sequencing that is necessary to good storytelling and consistent with experience. Such organization is found mainly in novels, stories, and drama, although expository literature can contain episodic elements in their examples and illustrations and can ring true to life in other ways.

Schank and Abelson (1977) earlier went even further and related episodic structure to the very way in which memory is organized. According to them, humans not only store information in episodic form but also acquire it that way. Literature using plot lines and characters can engage students emotionally as well as cognitively. As they become involved with the characters, they often become so absorbed that they, at least momentarily, lose the barriers often associated with learning another language.

Literature Illustrates Appropriate Language for Specific Situations. Through literature, students learn what is acceptable and what is not in given situations. They learn the skills involved in turn-taking, what vocabulary and structures to use within specific genres, and how to get certain things accomplished in the new language.

Literature Links Students to Other Cultures and Subcultures. By reading *The Diary of Anne Frank*, for example, students learn about the Jewish culture within Nazi-occupied Europe. From the biography *Isamu Noguchi: The Life of a Sculptor*, they learn what it was like to be a struggling Japanese-American artist during the same time period. From *The Me Nobody Knows*, they learn through poetry about the frustrations of children in the black ghettos of America. Literature can help students appreciate other peoples and their experiences.

When the literature comes from the students' first cultures, it can help bridge a gap between the familiar and the new. Literature can also be a source of pride for students; they can see their own values and traditions reflected in what they read. In addition, literature often presents universal themes, conflicts, and experiences that can bring people together in harmony and mutual respect.

Literature Presents Fodder for Critical Analysis, Discussion, and Writing. It encourages students to draw inferences, interpret, and explore personal, social, and political issues. Students eventually need to be able to explore why certain genres are used and what political purpose is served. The issues might include the racism found in *Huckleberry Finn* and the relevant issues found in other creative pieces and in the expository writing found in editorials, essays, biographies, and so on. All these genre can be very powerful to the extent that, through them, students explore, research, and write about issues important to their lives (see also Collins, 2001). Literature often elicits strong emotional responses that lead to critical analysis and reflection. Moreover, literature often forms a basis for discussion, writing, or further research and provides students with ample opportunities to practice valuable skills such as summarizing and paraphrasing.

Literature Encourages Performance. The performance generated by literature can include reading aloud, acting out, discussion, and debate. Often, rehearsal for performance requires the natural use of repetition (not of the drill-and-skill variety). Choral reading, chants, readers' theater, or memorization of the lines for a drama production all lend themselves to practice with the language.

Components of Literature-Based Lessons

Literature-based lessons comprise three basic phases: prereading, reading, and postreading. In this section, each phase is discussed separately, along with suggested activities and strategies for each. The examples come from *Worlds Together* and its accompanying *Teacher Resource Book* (Richard-Amato & Hansen, 1995) and *Exploring Themes* (Richard-Amato, 1993b), as well as other sources.

Before beginning, a discussion about the learning strategies for reading (see the box) encourages students to think about how they approach reading. After discussing these strategies, ask the students to share what has worked for them. (See also p. 108.)

Before You Read

1. Look the selection over. Think about the title. Are there pictures? If so, look at a few of them. Do they give you any ideas about what the selection will be about? If the selection tells a story, do the pictures give you any clues about what might happen in the story?
2. What do you think you will learn from this selection?
3. Have you already learned some things from personal experience, other selections, or classes that might help you understand this selection?

While You Read

1. Relax and feel the words and sentences flow together.
2. Ask questions of yourself as you read. Does this seem real? Have I experienced this myself? What does this have to do with what the author has just said or what has just happened? What is coming next?
3. Do not stop reading every time you find a word you do not understand. The meaning may come to you as you read further.
4. If a word seems important and the meaning is not coming clear as you read further, then look in the glossary (if there is one) or check a dictionary. You may want to discuss the word's meaning with a classmate or your teacher.
5. If there are parts you do not understand, make a note of them so you can return later.
6. Reread for better understanding. Return to the parts you did not understand. Reread them. Are they more clear to you now? If not, discuss them with a classmate or with your teacher.

After You Read

1. What did you learn from this selection? Has it changed the way you thought before?
2. Did the selection turn out as you expected?
3. Talk about it with others who have read the same selection.

Discussions about strategies should be frequent and can take place at any time during the three phases.

Prereading

Prereading activities have four main purposes:

- to help the student relate the text to prior knowledge and experience
- to heighten motivation for reading the selection
- to gain cultural knowledge helpful to achieving a fuller understanding of what the writer is trying to say
- to learn what knowledge the students already possess about the subject, what they want to know, and, later, what they have learned

Schema theory (see especially Carrell, 1984, 1985; Eskey, 2005) was labeled a "theoretical metaphor" by Grabe (1991), who considered it a useful way to describe the reader's prior knowledge. However, he argued that the notion of *stable* schema structures is a myth and not strongly supported by research.

Despite some skepticism concerning schema theory and the stability of schema, we know that readers bring expectations to a selection that either help or hinder understanding. For students to get the most out of what they read, teachers should help them relate the text to what they already know and have experienced and prepare them for elements of the text that may be puzzling (see also Anderson, 1999).

To facilitate the reading process for all students, consider the following prereading activities.

Asking Specific and Open-Ended Discussion Questions. An example of these kinds of questions comes from *Exploring Themes*, designed for intermediate to advanced young adults. The book begins with a unit titled "To a Distant Shore," which includes autobiographical sketches of four new arrivals. The questions that begin the unit are as follows.

> Think about your own situation. Have you recently arrived on a "distant shore"? Are you planning to make such a move? Even if you cannot answer "yes" to either question, try to imagine what it might be like to leave your home and live far away. What joys are experienced by persons going from one culture to another? What problems do they face? Discuss with your class.

Students can either discuss the questions with the class or in smaller groups (spokespersons can then share the groups' conclusions with the class).

Using Graphic Organizers (Charts, Clusters, and so forth). A learning chart such as the following determines what the students already know and what they think they will learn from the reading (Ogle, 1986). The chart is adapted from *Worlds Together* (intended for adolescents at intermediate levels) and appears before a selection about Martin Luther King, Jr.

A Learning Chart	
What We Know Already About Martin Luther King, Jr.	What We'd Like to Know About Martin Luther King, Jr.

After the students finish the selection, they fill in a third column, "What We Learned About Martin Luther King, Jr."

The next example of a prereading device, in this case a cluster, comes from the same textbook. It begins the unit "What Makes a Hero?"

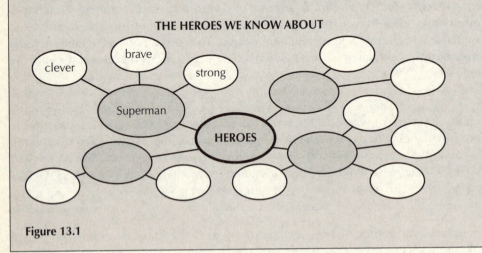

> What do you think it means to be a hero? Perhaps a hero is someone who is unusually brave or has uncommon strength or speed. With your class, name people you think are heroes. They may be famous people (past or present). They may be people you know in your own neighborhood. They may even be make-believe people in movies you have seen or in stories or cartoons you have read. Think about what it is that makes them heroes. With your class make a cluster such as the one in Figure 13.1. Display it in the classroom. You and your classmates may want to add heroes to your cluster after reading this unit.

THE HEROES WE KNOW ABOUT

clever — brave — strong — Superman — HEROES

Figure 13.1

Explicitly Presenting Key Words. Write a few key words from the selection on the board. The students brainstorm or say what comes to mind about these words while the teacher forms a cluster out of the ideas (see Figure 13.2).

The teacher or the students ask questions to clarify and/or extend meaning.

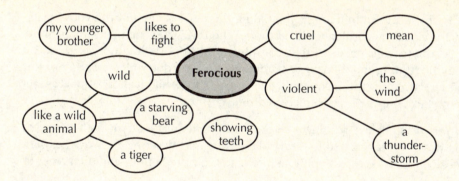

Figure 13.2

Using Prediction Strategies and Anticipation Guides. Students can predict what is going to happen or what they think they might be introduced to in a particular selection. The title, subtitles, and illustrations are helpful in this process. Photos and other artwork or a sample excerpt from the reading can be helpful as well. To add interest, the teacher or a student can write down the predictions as they are given and refer to them later to see which ones come closest to what actually happens or what is learned.

An anticipation guide (Readence, Bean, & Baldwin, 2005) is yet another device to help students build relevant expectations. Such a guide presents the students with statements to which they react. The following precedes the essay "Romantic Deceptions and Reality" in *Exploring Themes*.

Anticipation Guide

It is not unusual for people to have many misconceptions about love and what makes it thrive. Read the following statements. Check the ones you think are true.

a. When you feel that the romance has left your relationship, it is time to move on to a new relationship with another person.
b. It is a bad sign when one partner in a love relationship wants to make changes in the relationship itself.
c. A strong physical attraction for one's partner is necessary in order for a love relationship to blossom.
d. In a lasting relationship, partners have enough in common that they don't need outside activities with other people to lead happy, fulfilling lives.
e. Conflict should be avoided if one wants a love relationship to last.

Now read the following essay. After you read it, you will be asked to look back at your answers to this activity to see if you still feel the same way.

Students are surprised to learn from reading the essay that all of the above statements are false, at least according to the authors. When writing statements for an anticipation guide, the teacher needs to first consider what important concepts are to be learned from the reading and then write statements that will determine whether or not the students already know these concepts. Such an activity is highly motivational as students seek to check out their preconceived notions.

Writing in Journals. Before reading a selection, students write down their thoughts about the issues or topics related to the reading. They may describe their own experiences or those of others, express opinions, or write their predictions and then react to them later.

Previewing the Reading. Teacher-presented previews that include story-specific information such as a vivid description of the characters and the situation and end with a motivator such as "Now read the story and find out how (why) the main character . . ." can be very effective. Chen and Graves (1995) found that listening to a preview of a story was the best prereading alternative offered in their study of high-scoring college freshmen at Tamkang University in Taipei. Four treatments were given, one to each of the four randomly assigned groups: (a) a 200-word preview, (b) a 200-word presentation of background information, (c) a combination of the two, and (d) no prereading assistance at all. Although the posttests given indicated that treatments (a) and (c) were almost equally effective, the authors determined that previewing alone was the most time- and cost-effective.

A word of caution about prereading activities in general: They should not be too long. Sometimes teachers attempt to cover all possible unknowns and expose students to overly lengthy explanations and too many activities. Although students usually appreciate having their curiosity piqued and having a cognitive scaffold on which to build meaning, they do not appreciate putting on hold whatever motivation they may have already gained to read the selection. Sometimes, too, teachers impose their own interpretations on the students beforehand, making it difficult for students to create meaning for themselves.

Reading

Scheduling reading times during class can be very helpful to students. The teacher acts as a facilitator and guide to students needing help, as long as such help is not disruptive to others. The teacher, too, may want to be seen as a reader, reading silently along with the students during these times. Thus the teacher serves as a role model for the students to emulate.

Reading selections may contain clues to meaning in the form of illustrations, subtitles, glossaries, and footnotes. Visuals can establish the mood and/or give added life to characters and situations.

Glossaries (sometimes found at the bottom of pages or in the margins) are particularly important to second language students. The more effective ones offer not only definitions but also common root derivations and clues to help students use the context to determine meaning. Although they may not seem a significant feature, these glossaries are extremely valuable; they provide help *while* the students are reading, when the need to understand is immediate and the motivation is strong.

Once the students have completed the silent reading of a literary piece, they often benefit (especially at beginning to intermediate levels) from hearing the selection read aloud by the teacher or others or by listening to a recording of it. They need to hear the intonation, pauses, rhythm, and pronunciation. If the selection has been recorded, students often want to hear it repeated several times.

One warning concerning reading aloud: Being *forced* to read aloud in front of a group can create needless anxiety and sometimes even fear in many students. Moreover, it is difficult for second language readers to attend to meaning while reading aloud or waiting to be called on. Reading aloud is a specialized skill and should be expected only of volunteers. Reading is generally a quiet activity accomplished in a comfortable environment either at school, in a library, or at home.

Postreading

Postreading activities should enable the student to further create meaning and extend it beyond the context of the selection itself. Here students test their hypotheses about the selection and reread when it is beneficial to do so. They share their interpretations with peers and the teacher in an effort to express themselves and, at the same time, stretch progressively to higher levels of understanding. Consider the strategies presented in the following sections.

Questions for Discussion. Two basic types of questions are discussed here: knowledge-based questions and reflective/inferential questions.

Knowledge-based Questions.   Often these kinds of questions are discussed by the whole class and the teacher. Their main purpose is to ensure that the students have comprehended the main facts or points of the selection. Often they begin with what, who, when, where, and how. They allow students, under the guidance of the teacher, to know what is essential to the creation of meaning. For example, *Life, Language, and Literature* (Fellag, 1993) includes the following knowledge-based questions about Bret Harte's "The Luck of Roaring Camp."

1. What interesting thing happened in Roaring Camp in the beginning of the story?
2. What happened to the baby's mother?
3. What did the citizens of Roaring Camp decide to do with the baby?
4. Who was declared chief caretaker for the infant?
5. How did the baby fare in the camp?
6. How did the town change as a result of the baby?
7. What happened to the baby in the end?

It is important to remember, however, that this kind of information also can be brought out indirectly through reflective and inferential questions.

Reflective and Inferential Questions.   Discussion questions requiring more thought and reflection can perhaps best be handled in small groups in which students have more opportunities for interaction. The teacher circulates among the groups, guiding when necessary. The following examples come from "Making Friends in a New World" in *Worlds Together*. They follow the story about a Vietnamese boy, San Ho, who comes to the United States after the Vietnamese War. Notice that, in this case, cultural expectations are directly referred to.

> - How does San Ho know that he and Stephen [his new stepfather] will be good friends? What does it mean to San Ho to be a good friend? Do you agree with him? What does it mean to be a good friend in the culture you know best? List some words that you think describe a good friendship.
> - San Ho was so filled with fear that he cried in the story. Is it all right to cry? Does the culture you know best encourage or discourage crying? Does age make a difference? Is it different for boys and girls? If so, why do you think it is different?

A spokesperson from each group shares the group's ideas with the class later. The teacher summarizes the ideas as they are shared.

If the questions are personal in nature, pairs of students usually work best. For example, after the story about San Ho, one or more of the following questions are discussed with a partner.

> - Why do you think San Ho felt alone in the crowd of people in the gym? Have you ever felt alone in a crowd? Why do you think this happens sometimes?
> - Our friends are sometimes much older or younger than we are. For example, Stephen, an adult, was San Ho's friend. Have you ever had a friend who was much older or younger than you? Talk about your friend. Why do you think you became friends?

When they are working in small groups, it is important that students select the personal questions they want to discuss. They might prefer to write about these questions privately or not address them at all. These options should always be available.

Discussion questions promoting the expression of opinions and feelings should lead to higher-level thinking skills (application, analysis, synthesis, and so forth). In addition, students should be encouraged to form their own questions—both knowledge-based and reflective/inferential. Having the ability to pose good questions of both types is as important as being able to answer them and is extremely beneficial to cognitive as well as language development.

Short-Term Group Projects and Activities. Short-term group projects and activities often increase student participation (also see the cooperative learning discussion beginning on p. 382). Usually such projects and activities require sharing information. An example is found after reading "Blue Winds Dancing" in *Exploring Themes*. It is the story of a Native American who returns to his reservation with great anxiety as well as anticipation (see the story on pp. 280–282 of this book). Will his people accept him, or has he become too "white"?

Once you have discussed the story, have students research a particular tribe of Native Americans, including the problems they have had. They may want to look at the tribe's history, culture, and contributions to society. Eventually they might share the information they find with a small group.

Other short-term group projects and activities include:

- acting out the story
- adapting the selection for readers' theater (see pp. 288–289)
- forming round-table groups to discuss related problems and possible solutions
- role playing the characters
- forming collections of student writings about or related to the story
- sharing favorite literature about related themes, genre, and so forth

Although suggestions are often made by the teacher or a textbook, short-term projects and activities generated by students themselves are often very effective and can involve students maximally right from the start.

Short-term group projects and activities that are teacher- or textbook-generated work well when they are tied very closely to the selection and critical to creating its meaning. The following chart follows an excerpt from "Sarah, Plain and Tall" in *Worlds Together*.

FINDING DETAILS TO SUPPORT AN IDEA

We know from the story that it has been several years since Mama's death. How do we know that this family still deeply misses her? Give the details from the story that show that each of the following characters misses Mama. With your group, make a chart similar to the one below. Have one member of your group do the writing.

	Details
Caleb	
Anna	
Papa	

Not only do the students have the opportunity to work collaboratively, but they learn how to support a conclusion, a very important skill for academic success.

The last example of a short-term project or activity comes from "To a Distant Shore" in *Exploring Themes*. Here the students use Venn diagrams to draw comparisons. They compare the situations, goals, and other characteristics of four newcomers to the United States. Notice that the things the newcomers have in common are placed in the overlapping area of the circles. Students work with a partner to complete the diagrams (see Figure 13.3).

Forming Discussion and Project Groups. Groups can consist of the whole class and the teacher or of smaller numbers of students. The teacher can move from group to group, serving as a facilitator and guide. The groups can either be formed randomly or carefully planned (see also pp. 218, 294–295, and 342).

Of the two, planned groups have at least two major advantages:

- ethnic and cultural diversity within the groups can be ensured
- students of varying abilities can be assigned to a single group

Thus each group's work is more likely to reflect a variety of perspectives and proficiency levels. The latter is important in that students have a greater chance of being exposed to the language and the thinking of others operating at more advanced levels (see Vygotsky discussion in Chapter 3). However, most teachers recognize that sometimes homogeneous groups are just what's needed in a given situation—e.g., when the task pertains to a particular ethnic or cultural group or when it is intended only for those with specific goals not shared by everyone.

Letting students choose their own groups often works well with adults and mature adolescents. Like the planned groups, they can produce the desired diversity of perspective and ability in some situations. However, this practice sometimes results in hurt feelings and bruised egos. Inevitably there are some who are left out for one reason or another. To allow students more freedom of choice and, at the same time, preserve self-esteem, it may be wise to have students write down the names of those with whom they most enjoy working. Consideration then should be given to those choices when planning workable groups. Although this alternative requires more time and effort, it does pay off in terms of self-esteem and motivation. Most students assume they have been "chosen" by someone and are more inclined to put forth their best effort.

Taking a Closer Look at Literature. Discovering more about literature, including characteristics of various genre types, expository formats, descriptive language, and so forth, can aid in the creation of meaning and enhance the appreciation and enjoyment of literature in general.

The next two examples, Figures 13.4 and 13.5 on pp. 318–319, come from *Worlds Together*. The first one, which follows the story of San Ho, explores the concept of plot or chain of events; the second one, which follows the excerpt from a biography about Martin Luther King, Jr., explores the concept of time line or chronology.

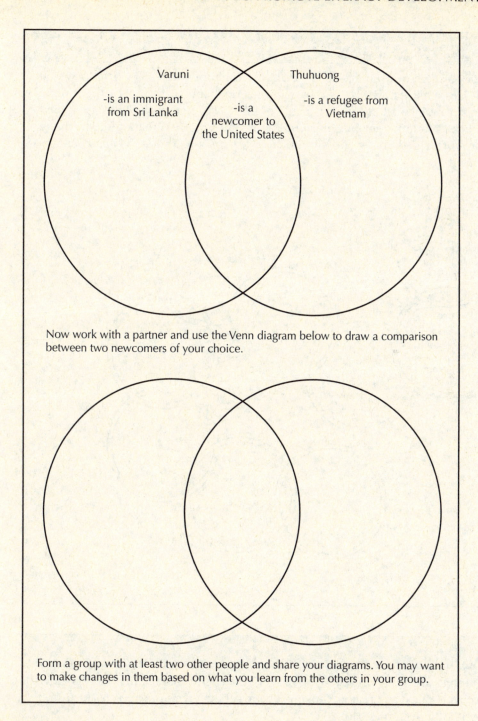

Varuni

-is an immigrant
from Sri Lanka

-is a
newcomer to
the United States

Thuhuong

-is a refugee from
Vietnam

Now work with a partner and use the Venn diagram below to draw a comparison between two newcomers of your choice.

Form a group with at least two other people and share your diagrams. You may want to make changes in them based on what you learn from the others in your group.

Figure 13.3

THE PLOT OR CHAIN OF EVENTS

A plot or chain of events is all the things that happen in a story. It tells which thing happens first, which one happens second, and so forth. See the sample chain below. Like all chains, it is made of links. Notice that the links are joined together. Each link contains an event that is important to creating the meaning of the story. The first four links are filled in for you already. Use as many links as you need.

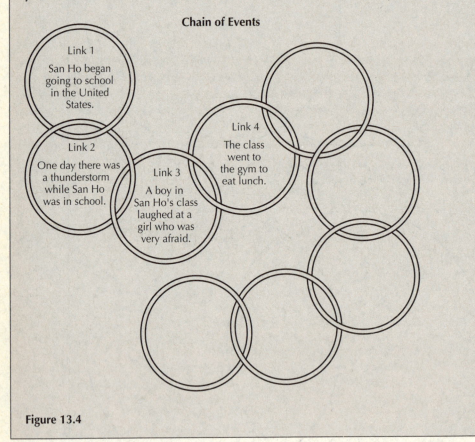

Chain of Events

Link 1

San Ho began going to school in the United States.

Link 2

One day there was a thunderstorm while San Ho was in school.

Link 3

A boy in San Ho's class laughed at a girl who was very afraid.

Link 4

The class went to the gym to eat lunch.

Figure 13.4

A TIME LINE

Biographies are often written in the order of the events that happened. This order of events is called a time line. The time line may begin with the person's birth and end with the person's death.

(Continued)

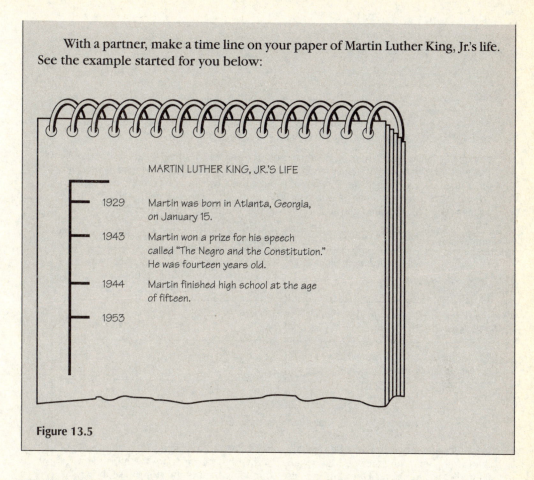

With a partner, make a time line on your paper of Martin Luther King, Jr.'s life. See the example started for you below:

MARTIN LUTHER KING, JR.'S LIFE

1929   Martin was born in Atlanta, Georgia, on January 15.

1943   Martin won a prize for his speech called "The Negro and the Constitution." He was fourteen years old.

1944   Martin finished high school at the age of fifteen.

1953

Figure 13.5

The last examples in this section come from activities developed around John Steinbeck's "The Pearl" in *Exploring Themes*. All four have to do with appreciating descriptive language (see also Lazar, 2003).

Appreciating Descriptive Language

1. Authors often draw their readers into the excitement of a story by appealing to the senses: sight, sound, smell, touch, and taste. For example, John Steinbeck makes the night come alive by appealing to the reader's sense of sound with the words "the little tree frogs that lived near the stream twittered like birds." Find several passages from the story that appeal to the senses listed below and place each in the appropriate category. There may be categories for which you can find no examples.

sight: _____

sound: _____

(Continued)

smell: _____

touch: _____

taste: _____

Discuss your examples with a small group. You may want to add other examples to your list based on what you learn from your classmates.

2. Descriptive language often involves a comparison between two things that are not usually thought to be similar in any way. For example, the statement "Your bicycle leaped forward like a cat" uses such a comparison. Bicycles and cats are not usually compared to one another. Look at the following comparisons from the story in the chart below. Explain each one in the column provided. Then find one additional example of your own to place in the last space.

Comparison	Explanation
Example: "Kino was a terrible machine"	Kino is compared to a machine because he seemed to be fighting without any human feelings or pity for the trackers.
"two of the men were sleeping curled up like dogs"	
"And Kino crept silently as a shadow down the smooth mountain face"	

Discuss each comparison with your class and the teacher.

3. What does Steinbeck mean when he talks about the "music of the pearl," the "Song of the Family," and the "music of the enemy"? Why does he compare the movements of people's lives to music? Does this increase your enjoyment of the story? If so, how?

4. Steinbeck uses many words whose sounds suggest their meanings. The forming of such words is called *onomatopoeia* (pronounced ŏn-ä-mat-ä-pē′-ä). For example, Steinbeck uses onomatopoeia when he says that the baby "gurgled and clucked" against Juana's breast. Find several other examples of onomatopoeia in the story.

Story Grammars. A story grammar describes the structure of a story. It contains elements of storytelling such as theme, setting, characters, conflict, plot, and denouement (resolution). A story grammar is not much different from grammar used to talk about language. It allows students to analyze the parts of a story and see how they relate to one another, just as the grammar of a language shows them the various parts of its structure and how the parts relate to one another. Both grammars are descriptive, and both are useful tools for learning. In Reading in the Content Areas (Richard-Amato, 1990), a text intended for advanced adolescent and adult students of English, Ambrose Bierce's much-loved story "An Occurrence at Owl Creek Bridge" is followed by an analysis of its story grammar (see Figure 13.6).

A story grammar such as the one below allows the reader to see graphically the parts of a story and how they relate to one another. Complete the story grammar, filling in the missing sections. Before you begin, consider a few definitions that may help you with the task. The theme is the main idea of the story. A protagonist is the main character or group of characters who desire something (the main goal). The antagonist, on the other hand, is usually another character or group of characters who, either directly or indirectly, prevent the protagonist from reaching the main goal. The antagonist does not necessarily have to be other characters, however. It can be nature, society, or a flaw within the protagonist. The plot is the series of events or happenings in the story.

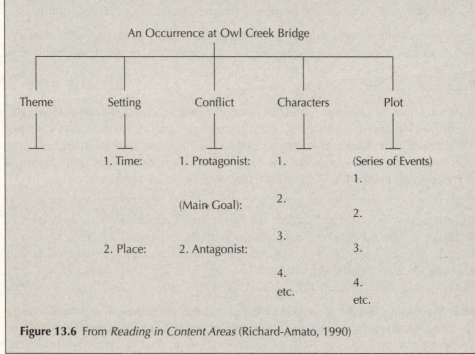

Figure 13.6 From *Reading in Content Areas* (Richard-Amato, 1990)

Individual Activities and Projects. Even though the activities and projects suggested here are individually executed, they, too, are in essence communal. Often students share what they create with the teacher, a partner, or a small group and receive feedback and help when necessary. The examples given here include interviewing, writing in a specific genre, speech writing, journal writing, and independent reading.

Interviewing. One way for students to interact with each other and with people fluent in the target language is through interview. Students not only receive the benefits inherent in the interactional process, but they also develop skills in posing questions, asking questions, recording answers, and sharing what is learned from the experience. Here is an example from "Between Two Cultures," a unit in *Exploring Themes*.

> Are you learning English in a country where it is a commonly used language? If so, write several questions to ask fluent speakers of English. Following are a few sample questions:
>
> —Have you ever been between two cultures? If so, what were the two cultures?
> —What was it like for you to be between two cultures? What were the problems? Were there any advantages?
> —Were there times when you were fearful? Explain.
> —How did you overcome the problems involved in being between two cultures?
>
> Interview several people outside your class. After each interview, write down what you can remember of the answers you received. Share a few of the more interesting answers with your class.

Writing in a Specific Genre.   Students often like to try their hand at writing in a specific genre, be it a poem, short story, or play. It is often helpful to use what they have just read as a model. For example, following the reading of the poem "Desiderata" in *Exploring Themes*, students are highly motivated to express their own feelings and opinions about what is important in life. One of the postreading suggestions is as follows:

> Write your own "Desiderata." Include all of the things that you think are important to leading a full and rich life. Share your paper with a partner. Ask your partner to write a brief response. You may want to react in writing to your partner's response, thus continuing the dialogue.

Speech Writing.   Writing a speech on a topic about which one has strong feelings can be quite exhilarating, especially if it is well received by one's peers. Following the autobiographical piece about Martin Luther King, Jr., in *Worlds Together* (which includes an excerpt from his "I Have a Dream" speech), the students are encouraged to write a speech and share it with a small group.

> Write your own "I Have a Dream" speech. It may be about one dream or about several dreams. You may want to repeat the line "I have a dream . . ." or "I wish . . ." or similar phrases in your speech. Think about what you would like the world to be like. It could be a world without hunger, a world without war, and so forth.

The student is asked to share his or her speech with a small group. He or she can either read it to the group or record it beforehand for the group to listen to. The members of the group are then asked to make a list of the ideas they feel are most important in the speech. These ideas are then discussed, based on such questions as "Do they agree with what has been expressed? Why or why not? What did you like about the speech? Do you have any questions about it?" The student is then asked to rewrite the speech based on what he or she learns from the small group.

Journal Writing.   Journals allow students to express their thoughts in writing and relate what they read to their own lives. They may keep their entries private or share them with others. In a standard journal begun in class, students often describe their ideas and experiences, express their feelings and opinions, and/or talk about hopes and dreams. Sometimes students write about what happens on a given day; other times they choose or are given a specific topic, usually related to what they are reading or studying. There are alternative kinds of journals as well, a few of which are described in this section.

THE REACTION JOURNAL

In a reaction journal, the student reacts to something very specific: a story, a poem, a picture, or a song (Richard-Amato, 1992b). These may have been selected and presented by the teacher or by fellow students. Special days are set aside as "reaction days," when students bring in and present items to which others react in their journals (see the discussion on reaction dialogues on pp. 101–102).

Alternately, the reaction may be to something even more specific such as a line from a story, poem, or essay; a quote from a character in a story or play (see Figure 13.7); a description of an event; or an expressed opinion. It should be something that the student finds interesting or thought-provoking. After dividing the page into two columns in a double-entry journal, students write the item to which they wish to react in the left column and their

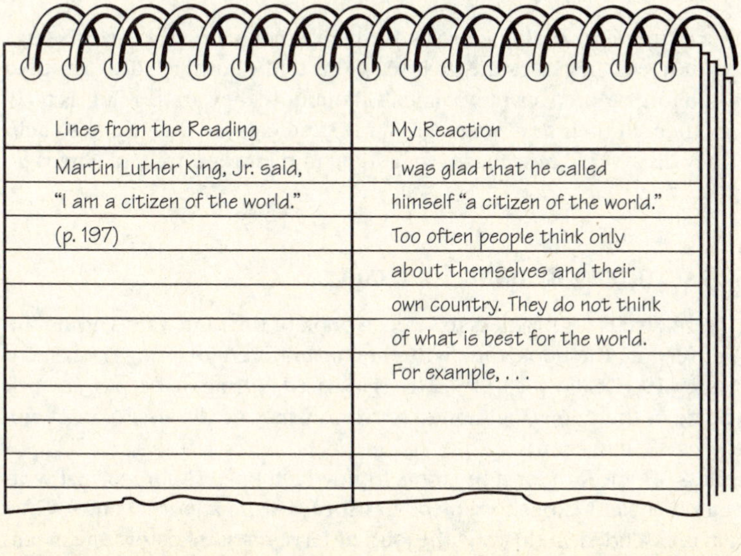

Lines from the Reading	My Reaction
Martin Luther King, Jr. said,	I was glad that he called
"I am a citizen of the world."	himself "a citizen of the world."
(p. 197)	Too often people think only
	about themselves and their
	own country. They do not think
	of what is best for the world.
	For example, . . .

Figure 13.7 The Reaction Journal

reaction in the right column. Students might react by questioning, agreeing or disagreeing, analyzing, and so on.

THE DIALOGUE JOURNAL

Using a standard format or a double-entry format such as the one just described, the students may write about a topic related to what they are reading or studying. The student expresses his or her opinion or feelings in the left column; in the right column, a partner or the teacher responds (see also Henry, 2005). Thus the writing itself becomes a social event and takes on interesting social ramifications through its dialogical nature. Often by the means of dialogue journals, relationships are built and bonds are formed.

Peyton and Staton (1992) pointed out the following additional benefits that can accrue to those participating in dialogue journal writing. They say that such writing:

- makes available discourse adapted to the students' "linguistic, cognitive, and emotional levels"
- facilitates the learning of advanced language functions and structures of reasoned discourse
- presents students with texts that are individualized and progressively more demanding

THE LEARNING JOURNAL

Again the double-entry format is used. However, for this type of journal the student lists in the left column those things that he or she has learned from a given selection. In the right column, the student writes what he or she still wants to learn or how the learned information can be applied.

READING JOURNALS

Somewhat more personal in nature are reading journals. In them, students reveal their feelings about what a character says or does. They can state their reactions to the author's ideas, relate to their own experiences, and so forth. Moreover, they can talk about how they are reading. Is reading becoming any easier for them in their new language? What strategies are they using to help them comprehend? Have they discovered new means for adding to their repertoire of language, both semantically and syntactically?

COAUTHORED READING JOURNALS

A particularly interesting alternative is for partners to select a book of the same title. During the period of time that they are reading the book, they write in a coauthored journal, also called a "buddy book journal" (Bromley, 1995; Gillespie, 1993). This is a shared journal that is passed back and forth between them. Some of the things mentioned previously may be discussed (i.e., emotions, reactions, reading strategies, and so on).

Journal entries, regardless of type, can form the roots from which longer, more formal writings can grow. Many a poem, story, and expository piece has sprung from a journal entry. Thus the usefulness of the journal is extended. In this way, the journal serves as a brainstorming mechanism, a means for generating and clarifying ideas and sorting out information.

Independent Reading.   Through independent reading, students can pursue subjects of interest, perhaps expanding their knowledge and vicarious experiences in areas to which they have been introduced in their lessons.

BOOK REVIEWS

Book reviews can become an integral part of the independent reading process. They can provide a means whereby students share their impressions and make recommendations to others. The following is a sample form.

Book Review	
Title of book:	
Author:	Type of book:
Name of reviewer:	Date:
What was this book about?	
What did you like about this book?	
Was there anything you did not like about this book? Explain.	
Do you think your classmates would like to read this book? Why or why not?	

The reviews can be written or typed on index cards which can then be filed in an accessible place in the classroom, or they can be put into a computer database that is shared by all class members.

WRITING WORKSHOPS

Transforming the classroom into a writing workshop can be an effective way to utilize important resources, including peers, and reinforce the notion that writing is indeed a communal process (see also Chapter 5 on implicit and explicit teaching strategies). The teacher and peers give input when needed. The steps include:

1. coming up with an idea
2. gathering information
3. working out the idea on paper, perhaps graphically at first or in outline form
4. expanding and developing aspects of the idea
5. getting some semblance of order (moving things around, deleting, replacing)
6. providing transitional elements where appropriate

7. rendering the draft more coherent as well as cohesive
8. polishing
9. sharing with an audience, if the student chooses to do so

A word of caution here: Sometimes setting up a workshop results in writing as an isolated activity, removed from other events of the classroom and other language experiences. Care should be taken to ensure that writing remains an integral part of the total curriculum and that its content is related to what the students are reading, listening to, and talking about.

Face-to-Face Conferencing with the Teacher and Peers[2]

Although conferencing is often treated in the literature on second language learning separately, it can be made an integral component in a workshop approach to writing.

Some teachers may be reluctant to utilize peer conferencing, thinking that it is detrimental to the writing process. When looking at responses on questionnaires and interviews of twenty-seven Hong Kong English learners, Tsui and Ng (2000) found that, although peer suggestions had not always led to learning and students had not always trusted the judgment of their peers, it did enable the students to learn from each other, helped them establish a heightened awareness of audience, assisted them in noticing their linguistic problems, and gave them increased feelings of ownership of what they had written.

The conference itself, be it with the teacher or a peer, should occur in an out-of-the-way place, perhaps at a station at the periphery of the classroom (see Figure 15.3 on p. 380) or in a private corner, so that it is not disruptive to others. Not everyone will be ready to conference at the same time, so those who are ready can go to a station when one is available or set up a new one if needed. It should be noted here that some students may be reluctant to join in the conferencing at first. Those not wishing to participate should not be forced to. It has been my experience that eventually almost everyone becomes caught up in the excitement generated by working with others, especially if the environment is positive. Students often receive a better sense of the reader through conferencing. Nevertheless, some students might need a little extra encouragement occasionally from the teacher and peers.

The conferencing groups can be organized in several ways:

- The teacher selects a few students to serve as peer consultants (see also Chapter 15, pp. 377–382). Different people can be chosen for each workshop until all who want to serve, have done so at least once. Each peer consultant is assigned a station. Students can be assigned to specific consultants, select those with whom they feel most comfortable, or go to whomever is available at the time.

---

[2] An alternative would be conferencing through e-mail (see Chapter 16).

- Students can be paired by the teacher to serve as consultants for each other.
- Students can form their own partnerships.

The way in which the conferencing groups are organized may vary from workshop to workshop, depending on the task to be accomplished and on the outcomes desired. At first the writings will probably be rather personal, short, and elementary—a listing of ideas or a cluster, chart, paragraph, or simple poetic form. Later the writings become more academic, longer, and/or more complex—perhaps an essay, report, critique, short story, poem, or one-act play.

The purpose of the conference is different at each phase of the writing process. When ideas are first taking shape, students may want to express these ideas orally and receive feedback. At other points in the process, students may want reactions to what they have written and may ask or be asked specific questions about what they write. At some point, they may want the teacher or a peer with whom they have established rapport to help them find and correct errors. It is important that feedback on errors be given when the student can most benefit from it (see also Chapter 5, pp. 144–145).

It is essential that all the students go through a preparation phase before any conferencing begins. Respect for one another's ideas needs to be stressed and a focus on the positive should be emphasized. Some role play demonstrating effective conferencing should take place during which all students have access to the sample piece of writing being discussed. Such role play can prevent many of the problems often associated with peer conferencing (i.e., overly severe criticism, a focus on "being correct," a failure to offer positive support, and overall lack of preparation; see Ferris, 2002; Hedgcock & Lefkowitz, 1992; Leki, 1990; Yoshihara, 1993).

As part of the preparation for conferencing, the following suggestions can be discussed and/or used in a role play.

WHAT THE WRITER CAN DO DURING THE CONFERENCE

Read the paper aloud to the teacher or peer (you may see some problem areas yourself). You may be asked to read it aloud more than once.
  Ask questions such as the following:

- Which idea or ideas do you find of interest in my paper?
- Is there a main idea that holds it together?
- Are there any ideas that might be best put in a paper on another topic?
- Do you have any questions about what I am saying?
- Is there anything you would say more about if you were me?
- Did you notice any errors that I did not catch?
- How can I correct my errors?

WHAT THE TEACHER OR PEER CAN DO DURING THE CONFERENCE

Listen carefully as the paper is being read. Take a few notes if you want to. If you have trouble understanding the reader, look at the paper with the reader while it is being read. Ask the writer to read it again, if necessary.

Ask questions such as the following:

- What part do you like the best about your paper?
- What idea do you think is the most important?
- Are there any ideas that might be best put in a paper on another topic?
- Why did you choose this topic?
- How do you feel about . . . ?
- Can you tell me more about . . . ?
- When did this happen?
- Should this go first or last?
- What kinds of details might you add here?
- What do you want the reader to learn from this?
- Did you notice any errors that you think need to be corrected?
- How do you want your errors handled? How can I help you with them?
- What do you plan to do now?

The following form can be filled out by the writer as a result of the conference.

Date: _____   Name of Writer: _____

Name of the conference partner: _____

What did you learn from the conference?

What changes do you plan to make on your next rewrite?

The effectiveness of peer conferences has been associated with the quality of the interaction itself. Nelson and Murphy (1993) found in their study of English learners in a writing course at a large urban university that a particular student was more likely to use a peer's suggestions in rewrites when the interaction was cooperative. When the interaction was defensive or a negotiation for meaning was nonexistent, the student was less inclined to use the peer's suggestions. This was also supported by Goldstein and Conrad (1990), who looked at a similar population.

Feedback on Errors

Interestingly, the quality of the revisions may depend on the type of feedback that the student is given. Kepner (1991) found that students studying Spanish in an intermediate class at Wheaton College who had received meaning-focused written feedback rather than error-focused feedback did not "sacrifice accuracy for content." In fact, those receiving surface-error correction feedback wrote subsequent journal entries of far lower ideational quality than those receiving meaning-focused feedback (see Zamel, 1985, who found a similar result in a much earlier study). Kepner concluded, "Correction of discrete errors should occur only at the final stages of editing, when the piece is prepared for 'publishing' or other forms of public display" (p. 306).

Ferris (2002), however, disagreed. She believed that error-focused feedback is more likely to benefit the student if it is given at intermediate stages of the writing process:

> By refusing to provide such feedback until the very last draft, teachers can severely limit these opportunities for needed input. A compromise position is to provide general feedback about errors on preliminary drafts alongside comments about students' ideas and organization: "As you revise this paper, be sure to pay attention to your verb tenses and the placement of commas in your sentences. I've underlined several examples of each type of error on the first page of your essay." On later drafts, the teacher can then shift the emphasis, providing more error feedback. (p. 62)

In addition, Ferris was convinced that students can benefit from feedback both on content and form within the same draft. Throughout her book *Treatment of Error in Second Language Student Writing,* she suggested, among other things, that the teacher:

- discover what the student already knows about error-correction terminology and what he or she prefers concerning error-correction strategies; then design error strategies around each student's preference
- read the student's paper first to find out what the error correction issues might be
- be consistent and clear with error markings and make sure the student understands what the errors are
- do not feel compelled to provide corrections on every writing assignment
- work with students on self-editing strategies, supplementary grammar instruction, and mini-lessons in grammar
- encourage students to take on more responsibility for their own writing over time

Moreover, Ferris concluded (based on a study of English learners) that indirect error correction, which she defined as pointing out errors but not providing the correct form, is more helpful to learners than direct correction. She stated that the greater benefits of indirect error correction are most likely a result of the learners' use of hypothesis testing when discovering their errors, and, because of this, they engage in deeper internal processing.[3]

Earlier Ferris (1997) had examined the comments that an experienced teacher had made on the papers of forty-seven students enrolled in a sheltered English freshman composition class at a California university. She looked at the revised drafts to see how the students had utilized the comments in their modifications and whether the modifications seemed effective. She concluded that, overall, the comments were generally heeded and led to substantial and effective revisions (less than 5 percent were rated negative). The comments that appeared most influential were requests for information, summary comments on grammar, longer comments, and those comments that were text-specific. A strategy that she judged particularly effective was to require students to write a "revise and resubmit" letter reacting to the feedback received, telling how each suggestion would be handled in the revision, and explaining why some would be disregarded. This practice seemed to ensure that it was the student who was in control of the revisions and that, if the reason(s) given for not making a specific revision were strong enough, he or she was justified in not making the recommended change. She noted, too, that teachers need to take great care in structuring any written questions because students are frequently confused by teachers' questions. She cautioned, however, against making broad conclusions based on her study because students operating at proficiency levels lower than those of her subjects and students not already familiar with composition classes taught in the United States might respond very differently. She also suggested that analyzing variations in comments and their effects on revisions across instructors would be helpful.

In a study of article learning in adult intermediate ESL learners, Sheen (2007) compared two kinds of written corrective feedback: direct-only and direct metalinguistic. Direct-only correction was defined as traditional feedback that indicates the location of the error and provides the correct form; direct metalinguistic correction was defined as feedback that indicates the location, provides the correct form, and explains the correction. She found that the direct metalinguistic group outperformed the direct-only group in the delayed posttests and that both groups did better than the control group that received no corrective feedback. She also found that language analytic ability was more positively correlated with the direct metalinguistic than with the direct-only group. Of course, both kinds of written corrective feedback examined in this study were very explicit. One might wonder how these two kinds of corrective feedback would have compared with some of the more implicit kinds of corrective feedback mentioned earlier in this chapter and in Chapter 5.

To date, research on feedback types has obviously produced mixed results. However, in a study described in Chapter 5 by Qi and Lapkin (2001), the researchers found through a think-aloud procedure that their two Mandarin-speaking learners of English thought at a very deep level while looking at a reformulation of their writing as opposed to direct

---

[3] Note that some research shows the opposite. For example, Chandler's (2003) research showed that because the indirect feedback delays confirmation of the students' hypotheses, direct corrections appear to work best. Clearly more research needs to be done in the area of hypothesis testing as it relates to error correction. See also Antón on p. 331.

correction. The subjects had been asked to write a description of a picture, compare it with a reformulated draft, and then revise their description. The researchers came to the conclusion that the deeper the thinking during the think-alouds, the better the improvement during revision. They argued that reformulation can indeed lead to higher-quality thinking than the direct error correction condition and, therefore, may be more helpful to learning.

Interestingly, Antón (1999) had argued earlier that a *dialogic* approach to teaching grammatical forms transcends both explicit and implicit strategies and helps students co-construct hypotheses with their teacher or assistant and then test them. Whereas the *transmission* approach is very explicit and directly corrects students by pointing out their errors, a dialogic approach uses collaboration to reach desired forms. Aljaafreh and Lantolf (1994) advocated a similar approach based on their research of English learners. They concluded that corrections should be approached implicitly at first. As needed, the corrections can become gradually more explicit (see also Chapter 5, pp. 144–145).

Cultural Considerations

Even though there are cultural tendencies within different groups with respect to literacy development, we should not assume that all individuals within these groups have the same tendencies (see also Parry, 1996). All students should be treated as individuals who are capable of bringing a variety of strategies to each situation as it presents itself. Although teachers have become more sensitive to cultural differences and norms concerning writing and approaches to writing, there is a danger when assumptions are made about individual writers, even those from the same culture. For example, some cultures are assumed to use circular organizational patterns when thinking and writing. If the teacher assumes that *all* students from one of these cultures have a hard time with linear organizational patterns, then he or she might very well come to the wrong conclusion and, at the same time, do these students a great disservice (see also Zamel, 1997). Students vary *within and between* cultures, depending on circumstances and experiences and how both are interpreted by the individual. In addition, students are often highly skilled at "hopping borders" and achieving what might be expected in two very different cultural situations without difficulty. Teachers would be wise to explore with each student his or her background and use that background as a transition to help the student develop compositional skills in the new language (see also Nieto, 1999).

Not all students feel comfortable sharing work with others, and they should be given the option of not doing so if they wish. Others enjoy it, and some even like to perform in front of an audience by reading their work aloud. One means for providing an audience for your students from intermediate to advanced levels is to conduct a "writers' theater" (Bobrick, 2007). Students can read aloud from their dialogue journals or other kinds of journals (also known as "talking journals"), read aloud the stories and essays they have written, read scripts dramatically as actors might do (see readers' theater on pp. 288–289), and so forth. Other classes and school personnel, parents, and the community can be invited to these celebrations of student work and achievement.

In this section on a workshop approach to writing, the logistical suggestions I have offered for teacher and peer conferencing is based on what has worked in the classroom situations I have facilitated over the years. It should be noted that there are many other ways in which this type of activity can be carried out, some of which may be more effective than what you see here. For further ideas on a similar subject, see the section on pp. 377–382 detailing peer facilitating. Although the role of the peer is a bit different in peer-facilitating situations, many of the ideas may be appropriate to teacher and peer conferencing and can be easily adapted.

Information about assessment tools, including portfolios (their development and use), can be found in Chapter 7 on language assessment.

ADVANCED ACADEMIC LITERACY

Academic goals need to be pursued right from the beginning in second language classroom settings, especially if students expect to be able to function successfully in academic environments (see also Chapter 17).

Many of the already-mentioned strategies and activities can be adapted for advanced academic applications. For example, the language experience approach can yield a group-generated analysis of an experiment on the effects of one chemical on another; prereading, reading, and postreading strategies and activities can be applied to a seminal article on pre–World War II influences on modern political thought; a writing workshop approach can be used to develop a critical paper on Jungian philosophy; and so forth. The applications are virtually limitless. Most of these applications can utilize a computer to carry out the strategies and activities employed at most levels (see discussion in Chapter 16).

At advanced levels, in particular, students need to be exposed to the kinds of reading and writing (and listening/speaking) tasks that will be expected of them in later coursework: reading abstract materials, taking down the key ideas from lectures, writing critiques and summaries, and so forth. Once students are in a mainstream academic environment, they need a place they can go for assistance and support, perhaps in the form of an adjunct program or a learning center (see examples described in Chapter 18).

Sustained-content language teaching is one important way to prepare students for academic work (see Murphy & Stoller, 2001). These authors maintain that an extended exploration of a single content area (math, social studies, science, geography) or a topic within a content area can enhance students' abilities to learn the language skills associated with advanced literacy development, speaking, listening, academic vocabulary, grammar, and so on. In addition, a sustained approach encourages students to pursue extensive reading in the areas chosen for investigation, use multiple print and nonprint sources, consider various perspectives, and use the critical thinking necessary to successfully form comparisons and evaluate what they read.

Within a second language academic program, students need knowledge and experience (including guided experience) in all areas that are likely to lead to academic success. These areas include but are not limited to the following:

1. *Text-structure schema and conventional text-constructing devices* It is important for students to have knowledge of the text-structure schema and the text-constructing devices commonly used by the academic community within a given society

and a given field of study (see also Hedgcock, 2005). Being familiar with the structures associated with argumentative composition, chronological development, definition, procedural description, and analysis, to name a few examples, is useful to students studying in a variety of fields. The related text-constructing devices such as specific introductory elements, conclusions, headings, transitions, and other organizational signals aid the students in gaining perspective on what they read, seeing relationships, and following lines of thought. In addition, there is evidence that students who have text-structure knowledge comprehend and recall more of what they read than those who do not (see especially Carrell, 1983, 1984, 1985). Not only is such knowledge beneficial to students as readers (and listeners), but it helps students construct their own compositions, so academic audiences can better understand them.

2. *Cognitive and metacognitive strategies for reading and writing in the various academic content areas*   Important strategies for reading as an aid to learning include underlining, highlighting, paraphrasing in the margins, outlining, idea mapping, using the dictionary, identifying key ideas, using context to determine meaning, and many more.

Strategies for writing include brainstorming mechanisms, researching, using quickwrites[4] and graphic representations of ideas (see clustering devices used earlier in this chapter), drafting compositions, combining text structures, and so forth (see especially Kroll, 2003).

Additional tasks such as answering, posing, and anticipating questions; reacting in various ways; summarizing; using specific composition formats and combinations of formats; collecting information for specific writing tasks; preparing for and taking tests; and taking notes involve a wide variety of strategies of their own. Talking about strategies in "What Works for Me" sessions can be extremely beneficial, as can practice with such strategies. However, remember that such practice should not be isolated from the content with which the students are currently involved; on the contrary, the strategies experienced should be an integral part of what the students are learning.

3. *Synthesizing information from a range of materials in a single area of study*   Krashen (1981b) called this kind of reading "narrow reading" (see also Shih, 1992). Such reading is more akin to what students will eventually be doing in their academic coursework (see also Murphy & Stoller, 2001). Shorter, less complex readings can be used first, followed by those that become progressively longer and more complex. These readings can then become the basis for a variety of academic writing (and speaking) experiences. Thus the students can gain the background knowledge necessary for the intelligent, logical treatments of related assignments.

4. *Other areas*   In addition to synthesizing information in a single area of study (item 3 above), Horowitz (1986) early on identified six other categories. Based on an examination of actual writing assignment handouts and essay examinations given to

---

[4] Quickwrites allow students to write down whatever comes to mind without stopping to make corrections or worry about format. It is one way to get preliminary ideas down on paper. Peter Elbow (1993) called the quickwrite an "evaluation-free zone" and strongly encouraged its use in getting students to take risks, follow hunches, and increase their fluency in writing. Students can return later and restructure their quickwrites, making them more palatable to potential readers.

students at Western Illinois University, he found that out of fifty-four examples, the following types of tasks emerged:

Category	Number of Examples
Summary of/reaction to a reading (in psychology, communication arts and sciences, history, home economics, special education, and learning resources)	9
Annotated bibliography (biology)	1
Report on a specified participatory[5] experience (anthropology, psychology, educational foundations, and home economics)	9
Connection of theory and data (communication arts and sciences, psychology, economics, and home economics)	10
Case study (administrative office management, marketing, and psychology)	5
Synthesis of multiple sources (communication arts and sciences, psychology, biology, geology, sociology, accounting, zoology, management, special education, and marketing)	15
Research project (communication arts and sciences, psychology)	5

In studies such as this one, the departments from which the examples come and the number of examples vary from term to term and campus to campus. It is critical that the language instructor know the kinds of tasks that his or her students will be expected to carry out. In addition, knowing the specific nature of the tasks provides valuable information for the instructor who really cares about preparing students for what is to come. Horowitz found that out of the fifty-four tasks, thirty-four of them were highly controlled and accompanied by detailed instructions, calling for specific content organization. Related to these tasks, Horowitz emphasized the importance of the student's being able to select relevant data from sources that are appropriate for the task, reorganize the data in response to questions, and encode data into academic forms of the language.

Rose (1983), in a study similar to Horowitz's, looked at assigned topics for composition and take-home test questions given by faculty members in seventeen departments at the University of California, Los Angeles. The topics and questions generally required knowledge of expository and argumentative modes and the ability to synthesize information and relate it to the theoretical assumptions associated with a given field of study.

Concerning writing for an academic audience, in particular, Reid (1992) stressed the importance the academic community places on traditional formats and accepted

---

[5] The term here probably refers to *participation* rather than *participatory* as it is used throughout this book.

conventions of expression. In her discussion of surface errors in English, she referred to Vann, Meyer, and Lorenz's (1984) survey of academic readers, which found that respondents tended to be least accepting of those errors that were generally associated with the writing of nonnative speakers (e.g., word order and word choice, *it* deletion, tense and relative clause errors). Perhaps the academic audience needs to become more informed about the nature of errors typically made by second language writers so they can see them in light of the normal language development process. Although more instructors are becoming aware of the needs of second language students, the students need to be prepared for the kinds of feedback they may receive from an audience that may or may not respond in a way that is helpful. It is beneficial, too, to give students the opportunity to write for *real* audiences from time to time (see especially Johns, 1993).

Finding out specifically what abilities students will need seems essential to any serious academic preparation program. Also, while students are preparing for future study, instructors should be working closely with content-area teachers or professors, if they are known and available. This collaboration, in all likelihood, will make the transition much easier for students. See Chapter 17 for other ideas about transitioning into academic programs.

SUMMARY

There are many ways we can promote literacy development in a second language. Using versions of the language experience approach, it is possible to begin where each student is. By involving the students in a literature-based curriculum, we can use the power of language to heighten awareness and fully engage their minds. Motivation and guidance can be provided through a workshop approach to writing in which students can take full advantage of the classroom environment. At later levels, the students can take on progressively more advanced reading and writing tasks to prepare for an academic environment, if functioning in such an environment is the goal. All the while, skills can be integrated and allowed to grow naturally out of the content the student is learning.

QUESTIONS AND PROJECTS FOR REFLECTION AND DISCUSSION

1. What is your opinion of the more "pure" application of the language experience approach? To what extent do you think the teacher should take on the role of a facilitator? Might there be a danger in the teacher's contributing too much? Explain.

2. Try out a version of the language experience approach with a small group of peers. Ask them to play the role of students operating at high-beginning to low-intermediate levels (see p. 183 for behaviors typical of those levels). What experience will you give them about which they can write? Decide what your

role will be and how you will handle errors. After your language experience activity, ask your group for feedback. Begin by sharing your own reactions to the activity.

   If you are currently teaching, use what you have learned to try out a similar language experience activity with your students. Make sure the activity is relevant and appropriate to their level. If possible, have the activity videotaped to analyze and discuss with peers. Reflect on the outcome of the activity and how you felt about participating in it. Pay close attention to student response. Do you see any problems with the strategies you employed? How might they be improved?

3. Select a piece of literature that will engage the minds of students and develop several prereading and postreading activities around it. Make sure they are appropriate to your students' ages and proficiency levels. Share your plans with a small group. What is their reaction? Can they suggest any additional activities you might incorporate into your plans?

4. Devise a way to use a writing workshop that relates to and is an extension of a unit you are developing or might develop. How will you set it up? What will you do to prepare your students so that the workshop has the best possible chance for success? Discuss your ideas with a small group.

5. How might you prepare your students for a mainstream academic environment, if that is their goal? Make a list of the tasks you might include. What if their goal were something other than an academic environment? What if their goal were to have the skills necessary to succeed in a specific trade or vocation? What would your list look like in this case? Share your list with a small group and ask for their input.

6. ✎ **Journal Entry:** Reflect on the language experience activity you carried out in item 2 above. What strategies did you use? How comfortable did you feel with them? Did you think they were effective overall? Why or why not? What were some of the specific problems you encountered? How can they be overcome? Write about what you learned from your peers and instructor during the process. What insights did you gain about learning and teaching from the experience?

SUGGESTED READINGS AND REFERENCE MATERIALS

Anderson, N. (2008). *Practical English language teaching: Reading.* New York: McGraw-Hill. Teachers, particularly those new to the field of English language teaching, will find this book valuable. It features background information on the reading process and ideas for teaching reading at the different levels of reading proficiency: beginning, intermediate, and advanced. It also includes the use of textbooks in the classroom, the use of technology, and suggested readings including books, articles, and Web sites.

Collins, P. (2001). *Community writing: Researching social issues through composition*. Mahwah, NJ: Lawrence Erlbaum. Rooted in critical pedagogy, this book contains assignments guiding students in their research of social issues that affect them and the communities in which they live. At the same time, students collaborate as they work on a variety of writing projects that grow out of their investigations. Shorter writing pieces develop into longer compositions as each student progresses in the writing process.

Ferris, D. (2003*). Response to student writing: Implications for second language students.* Mahwah, NJ: Lawrence Erlbaum. The author takes a look at the related research and practices used mainly in ESL classes at the university level. She includes suggestions for dealing both directly and indirectly with errors and for utilizing peer input. She refers to actual samples of student writing and offers guidelines for various kinds of feedback.

Hedgcock, J. (2005). Taking stock of research and pedagogy in L2 writing. In E. Hinkel (Ed.), *Handbook of research in second language teaching and learning* (pp. 597–613). Mahwah, NJ: Lawrence Erlbaum. This reading presents an objective overview of the issues important to the teaching of writing to second language students. It reflects both cognitive and sociocultural approaches to the writing process and supports the importance of genre knowledge, not as a goal in and of itself but as a "vehicle for engaging with core content" (p. 601).

Kucer, S. (2005). *Dimensions of literacy: A conceptual base for teaching reading and writing in school settings* (2nd ed.). Mahwah, NJ: Lawrence Erlbaum. The complex nature of reading and writing processes is emphasized in this book. In response to the era of high-stakes testing, the author gives teachers the tools needed to more fully understand these processes and to become more influential in developing policy. Included are the linguistic, cognitive, and sociocultural aspects of literacy development. It focuses on giving teachers a foundation on which to build their practices, and it provides hands-on activities from which teachers can draw.

Lazar, G. (2003*). Meanings and metaphors: Activities to practice figurative language*. Cambridge, England: Cambridge University Press. Based on the Cambridge International Corpus, this book contains vocabulary activities and lesson designs for teaching intermediate-level students the figurative language associated with many useful English phrases and expressions.

Nessel, D., & Dixon, C. (2008). *Using the language experience approach with English language learners: Strategies for engaging students and developing literacy.* Thousand Oaks, CA: Corwin. This book presents an in-depth look at the language experience approach with practical applications. Examples written by English learners are given along with ways in which these student texts can be used to reinforce and further develop literacy skills.

Paran, A. (Ed.). (2006). *Literature in language teaching and learning.* Alexandria, VA: Teachers of English to Speakers of Other Languages. The message of this anthology is that language and literature can be effectively taught together. Language teaching demands a context, and no better context can be found than in the plots, characters, tensions, and issues presented by relevant literature. Included are practical ideas and case studies intended to help English as a second language and English as a foreign language teachers in multiple environments improve their instruction.

CHAPTER 14

Affective Activities

When given the opportunity to talk about themselves in personally relevant ways, students tend to become much more motivated. The result is that they want to be able to express their feelings and ideas more in the target language. They want to communicate. When this happens, growth becomes a reciprocal process; enhancing personal growth enhances growth in the foreign language.

G. Moskowitz, 1978

QUESTIONS TO THINK ABOUT

1. Think back about what you learned in Chapter 6: The Affective Domain. In your opinion, what were the most important factors discussed there? What do you think "affective activities" might entail? You might want to look ahead in this chapter and scan a few of the activities presented here.

2. Have you ever participated in affective activities and/or used them in the classes you have taught? If so, describe your experience with them. Under what circumstances were they used? What effect did they have on you and/or your students?

3. How do you think affective activities might be used in a second or foreign language class? Do you think they could be of benefit to language learning? If so, in what ways? Do you see possible problems in their use?

WHAT DO LEARNERS VALUE?

Many of the affective activities found in this chapter have grown, either directly or indirectly, from the much earlier interest in *values clarification*. Values clarification and the many strategies associated with it seem quite relevant to today's emphasis on critical pedagogy and its focus on furthering learner identity and agency, although values clarification comes from very different theoretical underpinnings.[1] Raths, Merrill, and Simon (1966) asserted that *valuing* is made up of three categories of subprocesses:

- prizing beliefs and behaviors
- choosing beliefs and behaviors
- acting on beliefs

The approach Raths et al. recommended aimed not at inculcating a specific set of values but rather at helping students work through the process of valuing in order to clarify what it is that gives meaning to their lives. The authors argued that exploring already formed beliefs as well as those that are emerging can be a rewarding experience for students of all ages and can greatly enhance their self-esteem and confidence.

Many teachers now appear convinced that, for second language learners, especially those at intermediate to advanced proficiency levels, affective activities (including values clarification) can add a valuable dimension to the language learning process. If used appropriately by an impartial, accepting teacher, such activities can provide meaningful dialogue in the target language as well as serve as an important means of bonding among students. This can be particularly important in English as a second language (ESL) classes in which many different value systems are brought together (see Chapter 6). An environment that fosters an appreciation of differences can encourage individual growth and decrease hostility. It can also be transformative. Norton and Pavlenko (2004) in their article addressing gender issues in the classroom argued that transformative classroom practices include

> flexible curricula that recognize the diversity of the students' needs, shared decision making in the classroom, teaching and learning that incorporate students' life trajectories, pedagogy that locates student experiences and beliefs within larger social contexts, and practices that encourage students to imagine alternative ways of being in the world. (p. 512)

In spite of their potential benefits, however, affective activities are not for everyone. They are not for the teacher who feels uncomfortable sharing reflections and opinions or the teacher who intends to treat them as therapy sessions, although, as Moskowitz

---

[1] Values clarification finds its roots in humanistic education that assumes that individuals have the freedom to rise above their circumstances. Critical pedagogy, on the other hand, is based on the notion that such freedom may or may not be there and that there are powerful forces determined to hold cultural minorities or persons with diminished influence in a state of oppression (see the Introduction). Some claim that humanism can become a tool to accomplish the goals of colonialism. However, the strategies presented here are not intended to perpetuate such goals. Much depends on the role assumed by the teacher.

(1978, 1991) pointed out, they may be therapeutic. And they are certainly not for the teacher who wants to use them as a way to change the beliefs of others.

If affective activities are to be effective for language teaching, the activities chosen should be compatible with the students' age and proficiency levels and appropriate to the cultural environment in which they are used. Some cultures may consider it offensive to reveal oneself or to probe the thoughts of others. However, Moskowitz (1999) found that affective strategies, if carefully applied with individuals from a variety of cultural backgrounds, can promote harmony and self-acceptance.

For the teacher who decides to implement affective activities, Moskowitz laid down a few ground rules, which can be summarized as follows:

- Students should be given the right to pass, meaning they should not be forced to answer questions or participate.
- They should have the right to be heard.
- They should have the right to see their own opinions respected; no put-downs are allowed.

Moskowitz recommended further that the students have a chance to express afterwards how they felt about specific activities and what they learned from them.

In addition, Moskowitz advised that the activities accentuate the positive in that they be constructive and "low risk" so neither teacher nor student feels threatened by them. Of course, negative emotions cannot be denied when they arise; they should be treated like any other emotions, unless, of course, they involve the expression of perceptions used to diminish someone else. However, not all activities bring about positive reactions, nor should they. For example, we may want to ask students what changes they would like to see in the world or what they think would make their lives better, or similar questions.

WHAT ROLE CAN TEACHERS PLAY DURING AFFECTIVE ACTIVITIES?

Although there appears to be some disagreement in the early literature (Gaylean, 1982; Moskowitz, 1978, 1991; Simon, Howe, & Kirschenbaum, 1992) as to the role of the teacher in affective activities, all seem to agree that the chief duty is that of facilitator. As facilitators, teachers need to encourage honest responses, establish an aura of trust, listen with genuine interest to what students say, and invite sharing—but only what students want to share. Furthermore, teachers should clarify by asking "Is this what you're saying?" or by paraphrasing with statements such as "I think you're saying. . . ."

Most seem to agree that teachers should be free to reveal their own reflections and opinions in the discussions. However, Simon et al. believed that these revelations should occur only at certain times, preferably at the end of the discussion, after students have had a chance to think things through and express their own points of view. Teachers should present themselves as people with values (and sometimes with values confusion). They should be willing to share their own values but not impose them on their students. This way, teachers present themselves as adults who prize, choose, and act according to a valuing process. Teachers should have the same opportunities to share values as any other members of the class, and the particular content of teachers' values should hold no more weight than that of others.

On the basis of my own experience with affective activities, I agree that it is important for the students to realize that teachers, like other people, are engaged in a valuing process. However, it may be naive to think that the teacher's point of view will be perceived as carrying no more weight than anyone else's, particularly when the teacher is acting as a facilitator. The problem then appears to be how teachers can make it known that they are developing and refining their own values without allowing their beliefs to unduly influence their students. Perhaps the answer lies in how we view a facilitator's role as opposed to a participant's role. It is my opinion that the teacher should not attempt to be a facilitator and a participant simultaneously. As a facilitator, the teacher should remain objective throughout the activity. It is the facilitator's job to prepare and lead the students into a particular activity, enforce the ground rules, listen thoughtfully and nonjudgmentally, clarify, accept each student as he or she wants to be accepted, and provide transitions as well as closures at the end of each activity. The participant's role also includes listening thoughtfully and nonjudgmentally, clarifying others' ideas, and accepting others on their own ground, but it does not require that one remain impartial. A participant has the right to state his or her opinions and beliefs about the subject, as long as others' rights to opinions are respected.

For a teacher to express his or her ideas without giving them undue weight, a clear shift of roles should take place, and this shift can be discussed with the students. The teacher can become a participant on occasion, and volunteer students can become facilitators (somewhat akin to the dialectical relationship between student and teacher described in Chapter 3). This role switch not only provides a chance for teachers to model behaviors but also can create a great deal of excitement and motivation for students, who realize that they too can take on the responsibility of facilitating the discussion.

There are other ways in which teachers can express opinions without being overly imposing. For example, the teacher can step down from the role of facilitator without completely reversing roles. However, it may be prudent to do this only when the students ask for the teacher's opinion on a certain issue of interest and only after students have had a chance to express themselves fully, as Simon et al. suggested. The teacher also may want to use himself or herself as an example in a demonstration as part of the preliminary instructions, especially if the issue involved is not a controversial one.

WHEN CAN AFFECTIVE ACTIVITIES BE USED?

Affective activities can be used in the classroom at almost any time, and they can be particularly beneficial in certain situations. On days when students are feeling especially tense or emotionally down, affective activities can have comforting effects. For example, before final exams or other somewhat threatening events, the teacher might attempt an overt enhancement of self-concept by seating the students in a circle and drawing attention to one person at a time. Each student says one thing he or she especially likes about that person. During the session, someone (perhaps an advanced student) can record on separate sheets of paper what is said about each person so that the students can go home at the end of the day with the positive comments in writing (Richard-Amato, 1983).

On lighter occasions, the teacher may want to center on a theme such as "exploring career options" with teenagers and adults or "choosing a pet" with children. Sometimes a particular activity is very compatible with what is being discussed in response to a story, song, or poem. If a character in a story must decide between joining the Peace Corps or taking a high-paying position in her father's law firm, for example, an affective activity on related choices might be in order. Such activities tie content to real life. Flexibility helps the teacher recognize these teachable moments and take advantage of them in ways that maximize the benefits of each activity. Particularly at advanced levels, the teacher may want to use several activities to stimulate thought for writing assignments. Similar activities may also serve as appropriate means for culminating library research.

OTHER IMPORTANT CONSIDERATIONS

Many of the activities presented in this chapter are for small groups (from two to ten students). Groups can be formed in any number of ways:

- Students can be grouped *sociometrically* by having them write down the names of other students with whom they feel most comfortable. After collecting their papers, the teacher can plan what might be some workable groups.
- In an ESL class, the teacher might want to have the various cultures represented in each group or might prefer to group students according to cultures of origin. The act of grouping itself might be an affective activity. Groups can be set up on the basis of favorite pastimes, seasons, restaurants, and the like. For example, the teacher might say, "Today we will have four groups. The group to which you belong will be determined by your favorite season of the year. All people who like fall come to this table; spring to that table," and so on.
- Random units might be formed by having the students simply number off.

The method selected to form groups may depend on the activity chosen, the number of groups needed for the activity, the number of students in the class, and/or whether the groups need to be of equal numbers (see also pp. 218, 294–295, and 316).

Most of the activities suggested in this chapter are intended for intermediate to advanced levels, although a few are oriented to beginners. Most can be modified to accommodate several different proficiency levels and adapted easily to various age groups simply by changing the content (see the section beginning on p. 211). Many of the questions and statements used as examples in the exercises that follow reflect the interests of teenagers and adults but can be changed to reflect those of young children. Topics appropriate to children might include animals, toys, being the youngest or oldest in the family, discipline at home, holidays such as Halloween and Valentine's Day, TV cartoons, what they want to be when they grow up, and so forth. Activities should always be tailored to the needs, interests, and capabilities of the students and should be ones with which the teacher and students feel comfortable.

PREPARING STUDENTS FOR AFFECTIVE ACTIVITIES

Students should be exposed early on to some of the basic vocabulary that is particularly useful for affective activities: *emotions, perceptions, beliefs, reflections, preferences*, and so forth. These can be taught through several of the practices presented in previous chapters. For example, the teacher can introduce low-beginning students to emotions by demonstrating and then asking them to select pictures of persons displaying different emotions (e.g., crying, laughing). Likewise, food preferences can be introduced with food preparation; clothing choices by putting on and taking off selected sweaters, jackets, and other garments; favorite colors by first manipulating objects of various colors. These concepts can be reinforced through discussion or in warm-ups for role play. As students move into the mid-beginning proficiency level (see p. 182), they can begin to express emotions and preferences through activities such as the chants in Chapter 10, where they supply the missing words. Establish a beat by snapping fingers, and then begin and ask students to follow suit: "My name is _____ and I feel _____ [happy, sad, tired]," or "My name is _____ and I like _____ [apples, pizza, movies, dancing, to read]."

Eventually, students move into the high-beginning level, and the vocabulary becomes a little more sophisticated, with words like *beautiful, stubborn, smart, safe*, and *selfish*. As students approach intermediate levels and above (see pp. 183–184), they may pick up such words and phrases as *self-confident, self-conscious, ridiculous, secure, spiteful, stimulated, enthusiastic, open-minded, to know oneself*, and *to lay it on the line*. Many of the words and structures commonly used in expressing emotions, perceptions, beliefs, reflections, preferences, and so forth come naturally through affective activities. There may be times, however, when the teacher wants to provide supplementary vocabulary and perhaps even some open-ended sentences (called "stems" by Moskowitz) to reinforce certain vocabulary and structures by building exercises around them:

> If I were older, I would . . .
> One thing I do well is . . .
> I want my friends to . . .
> I wonder if . . .
> My brother (sister) makes me feel . . .
> People seem to respect me when I . . .
> People can't force me to . . .
> One thing I like about my family is that . . .
> When people tease me, I . . .
> If I could have one wish come true, I would wish for . . .

In addition, students should be encouraged to ask for help when attempting to share something that is temporarily beyond them rather than simply to pass. Students should be invited to consult with more proficient peers or the teacher. Not only does such mentoring benefit the learner, but it can also benefit the student who acts as the "teacher." Thus others can serve in helping roles similar to what the counselors used in conjunction with Curran's counseling learning approach.[2]

If students seem reluctant to use affective activities, starting with activities involving characters in literature may help. For instance, the teacher might have the students read a story with well-developed characters then role play the characters to reveal what they might choose in a particular situation. An easy next step then is to ask, "And what would you have chosen in this situation?" For example, if students are reading about a couple who fight because one wants to buy an expensive home, own a flashy car, and take frequent trips to Europe, whereas the other would rather live modestly, drive a simple, energy-efficient car that runs well, and vacation in the Sierras in a camper, they can role-play the characters in affective activities. Or students might make up a story about the people in a picture and then role-play those characters, using appropriate affective activities. Once comfortable in role-play situations, students may be more at ease doing the same activities without role playing but using their own opinions, emotions, and beliefs.

Another aid for reluctant students (all students may be a little reluctant at first) is to begin with less threatening issues. For example, the teacher might begin with, "Tell us about your favorite movie," rather than something more personal. Several of the ideas presented in the following section may also serve as warm-ups to the other activities.

ACTIVITIES TO FURTHER IDENTITY DEVELOPMENT

IDEAS FOR YOUR CRITICAL CONSIDERATION

Values Survey[3]

Ask students questions and give them three or more choices from which to select. Write the questions and possible answers on a sheet of paper, make copies, and distribute to the class. When giving the instructions, stress that there are no right or wrong answers (see also Schoenberg, 1997).

What kind of gift do you prefer to receive?
_____ something a friend made for me
_____ money so I can buy something I want
_____ a gift that someone special buys for me

How would you most like to spend an afternoon with a friend?
_____ on a picnic in the mountains
_____ at a church activity

---

[2] Curran (1972) described an approach whereby the teacher or others proficient in the target language serve as counselors and linguistic models for students (see Chapter 1). At the beginning, the students are completely dependent on the counselors, who help them translate their utterances from their first language to their second language. As they become more proficient in the new language, they are expected to work toward complete independence.

[3] Adapted from Simon, Howe, and Kirschenbaum (1992).

_____ at the movies
_____ at an arcade in the shopping center
_____ at a political rally

Which is most important in choosing a spouse?
_____ educational level
_____ looks
_____ personality
_____ interests
_____ values

If you had $2,000, what would you do with it?
_____ give most of it to charity
_____ put it in the bank or invest it in the stock market
_____ buy a nice present for myself

Which car would you buy if you could?
_____ a small, hybrid car
_____ a fast sports car
_____ a medium-sized, comfortable car
_____ a pickup truck
_____ a sport utility vehicle (SUV)
_____ an electric car

Which do you like least?
_____ a person who is loud and obnoxious
_____ a person who is dishonest
_____ a person who gossips

What would you most like to do alone?
_____ eat at a restaurant
_____ attend a party
_____ go to a movie
_____ visit the zoo
_____ attend a lecture
_____ go to a local theatrical performance

Where would you like to spend your vacation?
_____ by the ocean where I can surf and swim
_____ in New York City where I can see a Broadway play
_____ at a ski resort where I can ski for ten days
_____ on a camping trip in a remote area

Who would you rather be?
_____ an astronaut preparing for a trip to a far-away planet
_____ a store owner in a successful business
_____ a teacher working with second language students
_____ a mechanic fixing race cars
_____ a social worker working with troubled families
_____ a scientist trying to find a cure for cancer
_____ a carpenter building an energy-efficient home
_____ a politician with hopes of being the president of a large country

Having students complete the same survey several months later to see if their preferences have changed can yield interesting results.

The Search[4]

Write the following on a sheet of paper, make copies, and distribute to the students (see "The People Hunt" in Chapter 8 for a similar activity).

Find someone who . . . (write the name of the person in the blank following each item).

likes to go to libraries _____
has eaten okra _____
has been to a water polo game _____
would like to have a rabbit as a pet _____
saw a funny movie in the last week _____
is trying to break a habit _____
would like to be an actor _____
wants to take a trip to Mars some day _____
plays a guitar _____
has volunteered for a local organization _____
went swimming recently _____
likes to tell jokes _____

Give the students about five minutes and then call time. Ask the whole class questions such as, "Who likes to go to libraries?", "Who has eaten okra?", and so forth.

An alternative might be to have the students take similar search sheets home to use with family members, neighbors, or friends.

Values Voting[5]

One sure way to get all the students involved in affective issues is to use this rapid-fire activity. Begin with the question "How many of you _____?" Students raise their hands if the phrase is true of them. The blank can be filled in with items such as:

have a dog
are afraid of storms
think parents should be stricter with their kids
do not like most movies
plan to go to college
have been in love
wear seat belts in the car
like to eat chocolate
disapprove of smoking cigarettes
want to end all wars
think school is exciting
work part-time
want to get better grades in school
like to sing
are concerned about the environment

[4] Adapted from Moskowitz (1978, pp. 50–52).

[5] Adapted from Simon, Howe, and Kirschenbaum (1992).

The teacher can write these items on the board or on a transparency and follow each with the number of the students who raise their hands. The teacher and students together can then see where the highest and lowest numbers fall.

My Favorite Possession

Have the students decide which objects in their households are most valuable to them. Tell them to imagine that their houses are about to be destroyed by a natural disaster (e.g., earthquake, hurricane). They are each allowed to save only one thing. (All humans and animals are already out of danger.) What one thing would they save and why? Have them talk about their answers in small groups.

A Collage about Me

Give students several magazines out of which they can cut pictures or parts of pictures that reveal something about themselves. Have them make collages—arrange and paste pictures or parts of pictures onto individual poster boards. Items can include favorite activities, colors, foods, clothes, products, sayings, poems, jokes, and so on. After dividing the students into groups of about six, have them talk about their collages and what each item reveals. The collages can then be displayed around the room.

An interesting follow-up might be to have students find the collage made by someone else that comes closest to revealing their own interests and values.

My Own Space

If the room is large enough, give each student (especially younger ones) some bulletin board space. Freestanding bulletin boards work well for this purpose. Each student can use the space for items that are important to him or her but that could be replaced if lost or damaged, such as favorite sayings, reprints of family pictures, art work, compositions, poetry, and pictures from magazines. Students may want to rearrange their spaces from time to time and put up new things.

A Helping Hand[6]

With your assistance, have students make two separate lists (Figure 14.1 on p. 348):

- a list of things they know how to do that they can teach others
- a list of things with which they need help

Collect these lists, choose those tasks that can be worked on in class, and give the students time to help and be helped as appropriate. The activity could be repeated at various times throughout the year and could involve many different tasks.

Students can follow up the activities by answering the following questions:

What is one new thing I learned today?
Who helped me?
What did I help someone do today?
What would I like to learn tomorrow?
Who can help me?

---

[6] Adapted from Farnette, Forte, and Loss (1977, p. 25).

Figure 14.1

Teachers can get into the act if they wish. Teachers can learn things from the students such as how to fold paper birds Japanese-style or how to count in Korean. This can be very challenging and exciting for both student and teacher.

Dear Blabby[7]

Ask the students to play the role of assistant to the famous personal advisor, Blabby. Have them write answers to the following letters (these particular sample letters are oriented toward teenagers).

Dear Blabby,

I can't seem to get this boy at school to talk to me. I try to get his attention by wearing clothes I think he will like and by saying things to attract him. Nothing seems to work. I did catch him staring at me one day, but when I am near him, he ignores me. What can I do? I think I am in love with him.

Lovesick

Dear Blabby,

Last week I did a terrible thing, and I feel very guilty. In fact, I can't do my schoolwork. I just think about what I did all the time. When I was in the hardware store near my house, I was looking at some tools. The next thing I knew, I put a small wrench in my pocket and walked out with it. No one saw me do it, but I feel just awful. My parents always taught me never to steal. How can I make myself feel better?

Guilty in Memphis

---

[7] Adapted from Farnette, Forte, and Loss (1977, p. 59).

Dear Blabby,

I can't seem to make any friends. Everyone around me has friends, and they laugh and talk all the time. But me, I'm alone. I think maybe I'm boring. I just can't think of anything interesting to talk about when I'm with someone. I try to act cool so no one will know what I'm really feeling. I think I'll go crazy if I can't have at least one friend. Help me please.

Only the Lonely

The Most Influential Person

Ask students to think about people who have affected their lives then write about these people, including information such as descriptions (they may have pictures to share), how long they have known them, and what these people did that made such an impact. Divide students into groups to share their writings.

Reaching the Goal

Ask students to decide on a goal (either academic, social, or political) and map their approach to it, trying to anticipate possible obstacles (see Figure 14.2). Work out one to use as an example. When the students have completed the exercise, divide them into small groups for a discussion of their goals and the steps they will take to overcome the obstacles.

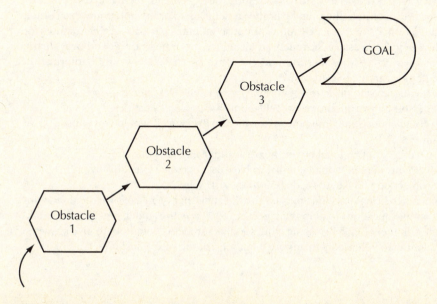

Figure 14.2

A Quote to Live By[8]

Have students choose a favorite quotation such as "To have a friend, you must be a friend" or "If you love something, you must set it free." Provide a few books of quotations from which the students can select their sayings, or give them the option of creating their own or using one from another culture. Divide the class into small groups to discuss the meaning of their sayings. Make available felt-tip pens with which to illustrate the sayings they have chosen. Give each student a poster board or large sheet of paper that can later be displayed in the room. At the high school or university level, the teacher might ask the students to develop effective paragraphs or essays using the quotes as topics.

Journal Keeping

Daily journal entries are a good way to record reactions, emotions, and experiences in the target language (see Chapter 13). Encourage students to make "I" statements, such as "I was angry when I found out that . . ." or "Today I knew that. . . ." From time to time, ask students to hand in their journals for your response, if they feel comfortable doing so. Do not correct mechanical errors; instead write positive and encouraging comments.

Getting to Know You through Interview

Interviews are another good opportunity to practice the target language and to help students clarify values. Keep in mind that students should always have the right to pass.

1. Even though most students may already be acquainted, new students may come in from time to time and need to be introduced. At intermediate or advanced levels, one effective way to do this is to write the questions such as the following on cards (one or two per card), distribute them, and pair the students up to briefly interview each other, using the questions on the cards. Allow about six minutes per pair—three minutes for each interview. Then ask each student to introduce his or her partner and provide the partner's answers to the questions on the card, as well as any other information received. Some sample questions are

    What is your favorite place to spend time by yourself? Describe it.

    What person do you admire most? Tell about that person's qualities.

    If you could choose any time period in which to live, which would you choose? Give your reasons.

    Where would you like to take your next vacation? Explain your choice.

    Which famous person would you like to have as a personal friend? Why?

    What subject do you like to read about the most? Why?

2. Ask students to bring questions to class to ask each other. (You can provide them with a list of sample questions to help them get started.) Have the students sit in a circle, and have one volunteer begin by asking a question. Let students volunteer to give answers. The student who volunteers to answer can then ask the next question.

---

[8] Adapted from Moskowitz (1978, pp. 232–234).

3. Explain that you will interview two students and ask for volunteers. Either or both can answer the questions, which should be nonthreatening in nature.[9] Here are a few possibilities:

  Who is your favorite female athlete? Explain your choice.

  What do you think is the best thing one person can give to another person?

  What kind of person do you usually choose as a friend? What characteristics should he or she have?

  What is the funniest situation you've ever found yourself in?

  Out of all the people in the world, past and present, who is the one you most admire? Why?

  Have you ever made a choice that surprised everyone? What was it?

  Do you have any advice to give us that you think would be good for us to hear?

  Has any news in the paper, on TV, or on the Internet really worried you lately? If so, what was it and why did it disturb you?

  Do you think homosexuals should have the right to marry? Explain.

  What is your biggest problem as a second language student?

  How would you change this school if you could?

  If you could have one question answered about life, what would your question be?

  What would you change about the society in which you live?

  Follow up answers with other appropriate questions before going on to the next question in order to ensure that the intended meaning comes across, or react by simply repeating what the students say. Once you complete the interview, give the class a chance to ask questions too.

  Alternatively, ask the volunteers to select topics about which they would like to be interviewed. You might post a list somewhere in the room to suggest possible categories: sports, movies, vacation, school, dating, socio/political issues, and so on.

4. Invite students, teachers, and administrators (who speak the target language) from outside the class to come in to be interviewed. Students, with your help, can prepare questions beforehand. Other questions will grow out of the interviews themselves.

5. Send the students out into the school or university campus to interview other students. (This is especially appropriate for an ESL class.) Have them form the questions beforehand and then report on the most interesting answers they received.

  Alternatively, have students write up an opinion poll and ask other students outside of class to respond orally while their opinions are recorded on paper. Questions calling for a "yes," "no," or "maybe" answer, such as "Do you think most drugs should be legalized?" are easiest to tabulate. The results can be tallied once the students return to class.

Stand Up and Be Counted![10]

Place five large signs around the room far enough apart so groups have room to form beside them. Label the signs "Strongly Agree," "Agree Somewhat," "Neutral," "Disagree Somewhat," and "Strongly Disagree." Read a statement and ask students to move to the sign that best describes their reaction.

---

[9] Remember that what might seem nonthreatening to one student may not be to another. Sometimes even an innocent question such as "Where does your mother work?" might bring tears to one who has just lost a mother. The teacher simply is advised to use his or her best judgment and encourage the students to do the same in asking questions. As teachers and other facilitators become more experienced and skillful in using affective activities, they may want to take higher risks in some situations in order to maximize the results.

[10] Adapted from Simon, Howe, and Kirschenbaum (1992).

Then have a volunteer from each group tell the whole class why he or she has chosen that particular position. Each group is heard fully before a verbal exchange among groups is allowed. Only one person should talk at a time. Some sample statements to which students can react are:

> Childhood is the happiest time of life.
> Grades in school should be outlawed.
> Pets should be allowed to live in homes for the elderly.
> Most people are dishonest when given the chance.
> Partners should share equally the chores of running a household, regardless of their gender.

In advanced classes, follow up with writing activities or library research if the issues create a lot of interest and, perhaps, controversy.

Concentric Circles[11]

Have students sit on the floor in two concentric circles with equal numbers in each circle. The members of the inner circle should face outward, toward corresponding members of the outer circle, who face inward. Begin with a question such as "What do you find especially difficult about learning a second language?" and ask the students in the outer circle to answer the question first. As soon as a lull in the conversation becomes apparent (after a minute or so),[12] ask the students in the inner circle to answer the same question. Then the inner circle remains stationary while the outer circle rotates clockwise until each student is aligned with the next person to the left. Ask a different question, and this time have the inner circle answer first. After those in the outer circle answer, the inner circle rotates counterclockwise to the next person, and so on. Make sure to give students time to think about the question before you begin the timing.

An alternative, with somewhat different interpersonal dynamics, uses groups of three. One person in each group answers the question while the others listen. When time is called, the second member of each group answers the same question, and then the third member.

Some sample questions are:

> What is one thing you would like to learn to do well.
> Is there anyone in the world with whom you would like to change places? Explain your answer.
> If you could run this school (or university), what would you change about it?
> What do you really like about the person (or people) sitting across from you?
> What is the biggest problem faced by second language students today?
> If you were the president of the United States, what is the first thing you would try to do?
> What was the nicest thing anyone ever did for you?
> What is one thing you wish you had the courage to do?

SUMMARY

One important reason for using affective activities in the classroom is to help students reach an increased understanding of those beliefs and behaviors that give meaning to

---

[11] A version of this activity can be found in Moskowitz (1978, pp. 78–79).

[12] During some affective activities, time is called after each response to indicate that it is now someone else' turn to react. The turn should stay with only one person until the facilitator says that time is up. If that person finishes his or her response early, the remaining time can be used to ask questions to clarify or simply reflect silently until it is the next person's turn.

their lives. At the same time such activities can provide motivating dialogue in the target language about important issues and serve as a way to bring individuals and groups closer together.

Although many benefits can accrue from the use of affective activities, they are not suited to everyone. Teachers who are not comfortable sharing reflections and opinions, who want to turn affective activities into therapy and/or sensitivity training sessions, or who are interested in imposing their own belief systems on others are not good candidates.

The activities themselves should be appropriate to the proficiency and age levels of the students as well as to the cultural environments in which they are used. They should be nonthreatening and constructive in nature. Certain ground rules should be adhered to concerning the right to pass, the right to be heard, and the right to have one's opinion respected. If the classroom atmosphere is warm and accepting and the teacher wise and caring, affective activities can carry the students far in the language learning process.

QUESTIONS AND PROJECTS FOR REFLECTION AND DISCUSSION

1. To what extent do you feel our values are culturally determined? Is there a set of values basic to all cultures? Explain. What role does individual and group experience seem to play in the process of the development of a values system?

2. Green (1983) early on stressed the characteristics of a successful values clarification teacher:

   Use of values clarification in the classroom requires a teacher who (1) is willing to examine his or her own values; (2) can accept opinions different from his or her own; (3) encourages a classroom atmosphere of honesty and respect; and (4) is a good listener. (p. 180)

   What might be the consequences in the classroom for the teacher who tries to use values clarification but who lacks even one of these characteristics?

3. What are several situations in your own teaching for which affective activities could be adapted? Plan in detail a few such activities for at least two situations. You might consider using them as part of a literature or history unit of some kind, as a follow-up to the study of the lyrics of a song, as a unit to commemorate a special holiday, or for any other situation in which such activities might be appropriate.

4. Choose one of the affective activities planned in item 3 above and try it out with members of your class. State clearly the situation, the proficiency and age levels for which it is intended, and the possible follow-ups you would

use. Give the class members a chance to express their reactions to it afterwards. In what ways was it successful? How can it be improved? You may want to begin by sharing your own reaction to your activity.

If you are currently teaching students, use what you have learned to try out a similar activity with them. Make sure the activity is relevant and appropriate to level. If possible, have your lesson videotaped to analyze and discuss with peers. Reflect on its outcome and how you felt about doing it. Pay close attention to student response. Do you see any problems with your activity? How might it be improved?

5. ✎ **Journal Entry:** Reflect on the affective activity you carried out in item 4 above. What strategies did you use? How comfortable did you feel with them? Did you think they were effective overall? Why or why not? What were some of the specific problems you encountered? How can they be over-come? Write about what you learned from your peers and instructor during the process. What insights did you gain about learning and teaching from the experience?

SUGGESTED READINGS AND REFERENCE MATERIALS

Moskowitz, G. (1999). *Enhancing personal development: Humanistic activities at work.* In J. Arnold (Ed.), *Affect and language learning* (pp. 177–193). Cambridge, England: Cambridge University Press. This important chapter presents the logic behind the use of humanistic activi-ties in teaching second languages. Included is the research supporting the positive effects of such activities on the attitudes students have toward themselves, each other, and the language they are learning. Interestingly, teachers, too, noticed improvement in their own self-esteem and in satis-faction with their teaching.

Schoenberg, I. (1997). *Talk about values: Conversation skills for intermediate students.* White Plains, NY: Pearson Education. Topics such as honesty, views toward growing old, gift-giving, and choosing a mate are used to stimulate discussion about values. There are no right or wrong an-swers. The book is intended for use with adults, both young and old. Mature teenagers may find it beneficial as well.

Simon, S., Howe, L., & Kirschenbaum, H. (1992). *Values clarification: A handbook of practical strategies for teachers and students* (2nd ed.). New York: Hart. This book contains a series of activities and explains how to use them for furthering the process of values clarification. It in-cludes decision making, problem solving, and many other means for confirming and developing values. Even though a few of the topics suggested in this book may be a little high risk for most teachers and students, many of the activities lend themselves readily to successful language teaching.

PART III

Putting It All Together: Some Practical Issues

No book can dictate a program or a methodology. What may be good for one group of learners in one particular setting may not be appropriate for those in other situations. The brief descriptions that follow of second and foreign language programs suggest some of their implications for students and for learning. See Chapter 17 for a fuller description of program types in relation to bilingual education and other related programs.

The differences between a second language program and a foreign language program are not always clear, particularly where English is concerned. For example, Kachru (1992, 2005) distinguished English instruction in three groups of countries: the *inner circle* (e.g., the United States, England, Canada, Ireland, Australia, and New Zealand), where English is the language of communication in most situations; the *outer circle* (e.g., the Philippines, India, Singapore, Kenya, Nigeria), where English is used mainly in government, education, and other important domains; and the *expanding circle* (e.g., China, Russia, Japan, Korea, European countries, Arab countries, and South and Central American countries), where English does not have official status and is not routinely used in society but is rapidly becoming a second language in education, business, science, and technology.[1] The various dialects of English in all three circles are called World Englishes (see pp. 6–7 in the Introduction).

Some linguists have divided the programs into more highly refined categories. For example, Nayar (1997) proposed dividing English as a second language programs into two subcategories: ESL, for inner circle situations in which English is the main language of communication, and EAL (English as an associate language), for programs in outer circle countries where there has been a substantial British or U.S. political presence and where English is used in some domains of the society for communication. He defined English as a foreign language (EFL) as English programs in expanding circle situations where there has been no substantial British or U.S. political presence and where English has no

---

[1] See Tollefson (2000) for an enlightening discussion of the three groups identified by Kachru.

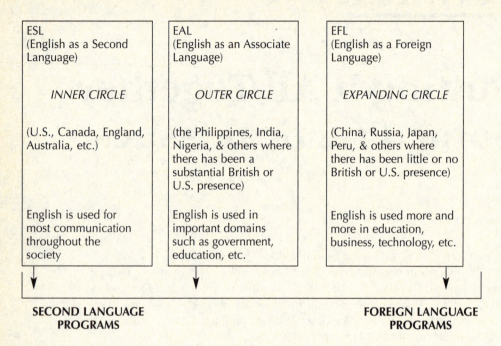

Figure III.1 shows three boxes:

| ESL
(English as a Second Language)

INNER CIRCLE

(U.S., Canada, England, Australia, etc.)

English is used for most communication throughout the society | EAL
(English as an Associate Language)

OUTER CIRCLE

(the Philippines, India, Nigeria, & others where there has been a substantial British or U.S. presence)

English is used in important domains such as government, education, etc. | EFL
(English as a Foreign Language)

EXPANDING CIRCLE

(China, Russia, Japan, Peru, & others where there has been little or no British or U.S. presence)

English is used more and more in education, business, technology, etc. |

SECOND LANGUAGE PROGRAMS   **FOREIGN LANGUAGE PROGRAMS**

Figure III.1 The Second and Foreign Language Continuum

special status as an internal language of communication. See Figure III.1. Interestingly, the numbers of people speaking English outside the inner circle is greater than within, and many varieties of English have developed or are in the process of developing.

Because the following discussion pertains to all languages, not just English, I use only the two basic classifications—second language and foreign language— realizing that there are many distinctions within each and that these distinctions may have quite different implications for teaching. If we think of the two classifications as being on opposite ends of a continuum, with many programs falling somewhere in between, as shown in Figure III.1, we obtain a more realistic picture of the variations.

SECOND LANGUAGE PROGRAMS

Second language programs were referred to in the Introduction (see footnote 10) as programs *in which the target language is the dominant language for communication in the area or domain in which it is being taught.* Generally, students in such programs are interested in learning to survive physically, socially, and academically in their new culture. They are, in most cases, surrounded by the target language in the community, the workplace, and the school or university campus. Sometimes, however, second language students live in communities in which their first language and culture are predominant. This means that, although they have the advantages of first language and cultural maintenance, they may lack the target language input available to those in more integrated situations. For them, having considerable contact with proficient speakers of the target language as part of the curriculum would be especially important to their second language development. For many of these second language learners, cultural identities are multiple, making proficiency in two or more languages or dialects a great advantage.

In outer circle countries, English still falls into the "second language" category to the extent that the student has sustained access to the domain in which it is being used, be it on the job, in dealings with government, or in other settings within the country. However, there are probably as many varieties of English and political ramifications as there are countries and domains in which it is being taught. Often, academic institutions use English as the medium of instruction to some extent, and a substantial use of code switching between English and other languages occurs. In addition, the motivation to acquire the language may not be as strong as it is in other English as a second language programs. Much depends on the extent to which students need the language for their academic, career, and/or social survival.

FOREIGN LANGUAGE PROGRAMS

Foreign language programs were referred to in the Introduction (footnote 10) as programs *in which the target language is not the dominant language in the area or domain in which it is being taught.*

Students have a variety of reasons for participating in foreign language programs. Their goals may be

- *Integrative:* Students may want to communicate with people globally or within their own country who speak the target language, or they may want to survive in another culture where the target language is the main language used.
- *Instrumental:* Students may want to travel, study, or work in another country where the target language is the main language used; they may want to study a particular field or obtain a job within their own local environment that requires that they be bilingual; or they may need the language to fulfill a graduation requirement and/or move on to other levels of study.
- *Personal:* Students may feel that learning another language is cognitively advantageous and enriching in that it can provide new and interesting perspectives.

Students may be in a foreign language program for a combination of these reasons.

There are basically two kinds of foreign language programs: a program in which the foreign language *is not* used as the medium for instruction and a program in which the foreign language *is* used as the medium for instruction.

When the Foreign Language Is Not Used as the Medium for Instruction

This is the most common type of foreign language program. Larsen-Freeman and Freeman (2008) would probably call such a program a *subject-language* program. The language itself is the subject matter for a course offered within the curriculum of a school. They agree with Halliday (2001) that such a program does not focus on any particular subject-area discipline; rather, its focus is often thematic in that it can touch on many disciplines (Halliday used the term *transdisciplinary*). However, Larsen-Freeman and Freeman went beyond Halliday's analysis to include claims of local ownership of the language being learned, especially in the case of English as a subject language.

In a subject-language program, the environment outside the classroom does not usually give students the opportunity to be immersed in the target language. They may require substantial amounts of meaningful interaction because the classroom may be their only source. On the other hand, because they may not receive sufficient opportunities for interaction leading to full participation in the classroom (many foreign or subject-language classes meet only one hour a day), they may find themselves also in need of increased grammar instruction, appropriately timed, taking into consideration age, cognitive development, approximate proficiency level, and learning preferences (see Chapter 2).

A subject-language program has its own implications for curriculum planning as well. For example, instrumental programs that are offered strictly for a single academic purpose (e.g., interpreting research findings in another language) or for other specific purposes (e.g., becoming acquainted with a new medical procedure used in another culture) may not include the development of communication skills at all. In these programs, learning to read and being familiar with a certain technical vocabulary may be all that is needed. Another factor is that students in instrumental programs may be less motivated to interact in the target language because it is not required for their everyday survival.

When the Foreign Language Is Used as the Medium for Instruction

There are at least two types of foreign programs in which the target language is used as the medium for instruction. However, they are not discussed at any length until Chapter 17 and are only mentioned very briefly here.

The first of these are the two-way bilingual programs. These programs are considered "foreign" language programs by the language *majority* students who are enrolled in them (approximately half of the students), but these students are not learning the language as a separate subject; mostly they are learning it through academic disciplinary content. The same is true of the language majority students in the one-way foreign language immersion programs. The students in both these situations are learning a foreign language through academic disciplinary content. See Chapters 17, 19, and 20 for descriptions of these programs.

TEACHERS NEW TO A PARTICULAR CULTURE

Using a framework acceptable to the culture in which they find themselves, teachers from other countries find that they can often be flexible within that framework. Showing respect for the situated environment in which they are teaching, they often discover that a mixture of the familiar and the unfamiliar can be exciting for both teacher and students as they work together to create an environment in which all can thrive. Learners in these cultures often expect foreign teachers to operate in ways different from what they are used to, and they often welcome such differences. Honesty and respect are key on the part of both teacher and students when it comes to cultural differences and ways of acknowledging and accommodating them. We would be wise to remember, too, that even within the same cultural environment, styles of teaching can be quite different and still be within the range of acceptability. We should learn as much about the local situation as we can in order to adjust to it and, at the same time, be ourselves. As in all situations, teachers should be sensitive to individual and cultural preferences. The important thing is for teachers to not impose their own worldviews on other cultural groups.

CHAPTER 15

Devising a Plan[1]

> *Just as there is no one set of ideal teaching materials,*
> *so there is no universal teaching method suited to the*
> *many contexts of language learning . . . . The most*
> *effective programs will be those that involve the whole*
> *learner in the experience of language as a network of*
> *relations between people, things, and events. The balance*
> *of features in a curriculum will and should vary from*
> *one program to the next, depending on the particular*
> *learning context of which it is a part.*
>
> S. Savignon, 1983

QUESTIONS TO THINK ABOUT

1. Think about the kind of program in which you are teaching or might be teaching in the future. Is it a second or a foreign language program, or does it fall somewhere in between? Where might it fall on the continuum in Figure III.1 on p. 356? What do you anticipate some of the implications for teaching will be because of the kind of program it is?

2. Can you think of ways to involve peers who are already proficient in the target language with the students in your classroom? What do you think the advantages might be? What problems might occur?

3. What do you think a syllabus for language teaching should look like? How specific should it be? How might it vary because of the kind of program it is in and the students that it serves?

---

[1] Most of the suggestions in this chapter are intended for second and foreign language teaching situations in which content and/or content themes are the focus. However, many can be adapted to other language teaching situations should the teacher determine that they are appropriate locally.

Van Lier (1996) described a language teaching syllabus as

> a collection of maps with information and options, a guide, but one which leaves the students the freedom to stop where they want to, to travel alone for a while or in groups, to go off on some tangent if it seems interesting, but always coming back to the main road, and keeping the destination in mind. The syllabus—as Triptik—does not tell you where (and how far, how fast) you want to go, it gives you the advice and assistance that you ask for. (p. 20)

A syllabus for language learners can indeed map out either a very rigid and highly specified journey (it's Monday so we must be in Prague) or a journey that begins where the students are and takes them as far as possible in the learning process. The kind of syllabus used often is determined by the local situation in which one is teaching. If emergent participatory teaching is an important goal, then students will have input into planning the trip and into the side tours that interest them or for which they have a need. If they want to stop for more maps, they can. As van Lier (1996) suggested, if students want to pursue something alone occasionally, they can. If they want to travel in groups, they can. What matters is that they stay the course.

In addition, a needs assessment for each student is essential as long as the results are arrived at in a nonjudgmental fashion and agreed to by student and teacher. See the discussion on portfolio use and other types of assessment described in Chapter 7. Such assessment should be negotiated, ongoing, and coordinated with objectives and the instructional phases of classroom work itself.

A single method will not meet the individual or collective needs of students, nor will the concatenation of several methods, strategies, and isolated activities. What is needed is an interweaving of courses of action, each providing what is required at the moment, all working together to form a highly integrated curriculum[2] into which students have had input to the greatest extent possible. In emergent participatory classrooms, the curriculum will reflect students' needs, their goals and aspirations, their ages and competency levels, their learning styles. A workable curriculum will also reflect the teacher's preferences—teachers should feel comfortable with what they are doing.

INTEGRATING METHODS, STRATEGIES, AND ACTIVITIES INTO A FLEXIBLE CURRICULUM

Many possibilities exist for integrating various components into a flexible curriculum. A program that integrates methods, strategies, and activities might be organized at the beginning levels around basic topics and situations similar to those suggested by Krashen and Terrell (see pp. 227–231): body parts, physical actions, clothing, occupations, emotions, recreation, getting things done, and so on. Early on, the program might begin to ease into subject-area concepts, themes, and sociopolitical issues and their

---

[2] *Curriculum*, according to Crabbe (2003), is "an organization of learning opportunities, or means, for achieving certain outcomes, or ends" (p. 10).

related proficiencies. The subject areas might include art, math, business, computer processing, physical education, social and natural sciences, and literature. Whatever the content, it must be relevant to the needs and concerns of the students. It should include areas of knowledge in which the teacher has some expertise, although most areas can be explored by teachers and students together if the program is an emergent participatory one in which dialectical relationships have been established.

Students might first be introduced to key concepts, during low-beginning levels, through physical approaches described in Chapter 8. The same concepts can be reinforced, while new ones are introduced, through activities typical of other interactive approaches described in Chapter 9. As students move toward mid- and high-beginning levels, chants, simple poetry, and/or music lyrics (Chapter 10) can be added either to introduce a set of concepts or to reinforce them. During this period, techniques from storytelling, role play, and drama (Chapter 11) can be highly motivating while providing the many passes through the material necessary for learning to occur. Games (Chapter 12) can be effective if played occasionally to develop or reinforce concepts or to teach the vocabulary and structures of game playing itself. During the high-beginning through advanced levels, if the program is to be participatory, the teacher will need to involve the students to a much greater extent in the planning process. At these levels, the teacher can introduce and reinforce concepts through affective activities (Chapter 14) and through more advanced applications of the previously discussed approaches. All the while, literacy in the target language (Chapter 13) and its related proficiencies can be taught in an integrated fashion rather than as separate sets of skills and subskills.

Various methods, strategies, and activities might also be combined on a much smaller scale, either within a unit (several lessons about the same topic) or a single lesson.

The following are two examples of how several methods, activities, and strategies can be merged *within a unit:* The first example is for children, and the second is for adolescents and adults.

Unit One: An Example for Intermediate-Level Children

Susan Ashby, a teacher in the Alhambra School District of California, illustrates how storytelling, music, affective activities, and poetry can be integrated with aspects of the physical approaches and interactive/emergent participatory teaching. All can work together to produce a unified whole—in this case, a subject-area unit on birds. She suggests that the unit begin with the Mexican folktale, "The Pájaro-cu"—the story of a bird that, at the beginning of the world, appeared before the eagle (the king) stark naked because he had no feathers. The eagle was so offended that he sent the featherless bird into exile. A dove took pity on him and began a campaign to clothe him. Each bird willingly contributed a feather. The result was a bird so colorful and beautiful that he became vain and would have nothing to do with the other birds. He decided to leave the country. The other birds were sent to look for him. In their search, the various birds began to sing out the different calls by which they are now known. Although the lost bird (called the *pájaro-cu*) has never been found, the other birds still sing their characteristic songs but no longer expect an answer.

The meaning of the story can be discussed by asking questions such as the following:

1. Do people, like the Pájaro-cu, ever get sent away—into exile? If so, why?
2. Once the Pájaro-cu became more colorful and beautiful than the other birds, he would have nothing to do with them. Why? Do people ever behave this way? Explain.

To appeal to various modes of learning, the teacher can use any number of different strategies:

- Display a series of colored pictures of birds and talk with the students about the different types of birds and the features that most birds have in common.
- Have students pantomime to the beat of a drum the movements of different kinds of birds: big birds; delicate birds; birds that run, walk, and soar. Using movements to music (see Chapter 10), let students dance, playing the roles of different types of birds.
- Have students sketch and paint the Pájaro-cu, perhaps combining crayons and watercolors to give the hues a jewel-like appearance.
- Help students find sayings such as "Birds of a feather flock together" and "A bird in the hand is worth two in the bush." After discussing the meanings of the sayings, have students choose one or two and draw pictures to illustrate them.
- Stimulate discussion through the use of stories and poetry about birds. Students may want to author or coauthor their own stories and poems and share them with other students.

Other kinds of activities interwoven into a unit on birds may include readings on related topics of interest such as the migratory patterns of birds, their habitats, environmental dangers to bird life, and so forth. Also included might be vocabulary development using key words from the readings, grammatical structures students are ready for, and other more discrete elements of language.

Unit Two: An Example for High-Intermediate to Advanced Young Adults

Sean Banville, whose experience includes teaching in Japan and in the United Arab Emirates, has developed an online unit for teachers accompanied by listening files based on a newspaper article about the death penalty.[3] The unit integrates interactive/participatory practices including pair and larger group work to draw on what students have learned and what they believe about the death penalty. The unit uses a variety of before, during, and after reading, listening, and writing activities.

---

[3] This description is used with the permission of Sean Banville. See similar units on his Breaking News English Web site and in his e-book *1,000 Ideas and Activities for Language Teachers*.

The following is an excerpt from the article on which the unit is based:

The UN Calls for Death Penalty Abolition

A United Nations committee has voted for an immediate worldwide freeze on the use of the death penalty. A total of 99 countries voted in favor of a suspension of capital punishment, while 52 opposed the proposal and the remaining 33 nations did not vote. Those who campaigned against the death penalty said the abolition would "contribute to the enhancement and progressive development of human rights." They said capital punishment has not been a deterrent for crimes and many innocent people are still put to death by mistake.

The unit can begin with warm-up activities for teachers to consider in their planning. One such activity finds students walking around the classroom to ask some of their classmates about the various types of punishment commonly used. They then come back to a partner and share what they have learned. Then in pairs or larger groups they talk about the various methods (e.g., hanging, lethal injection, beheading, firing squad, electrocution, stoning, the gas chamber). Another warm-up can find the students involved in a brief debate with a partner, each taking a side. Among the topics debated are

a. all killing is wrong versus an eye for an eye and a tooth for a tooth
b. the death penalty stops crime versus murders happen with or without it
c. mistakes are made and innocent people die versus no system is perfect
d. the death penalty gives society the message that killing is okay versus "no way"

Before reading/listening activities can involve the students in such activities as deciding whether certain statements such as "The U.N. has banned the use of the death penalty around the world" and "Many countries believe the death penalty does not deter crime" are true or false. Banville considers it important to check their prior knowledge and possible misconceptions.

During reading/listening activities can include cloze exercises called "Gap Fills." For example, the students are to fill in the blanks in the following text example with the words *favor, contribute, immediate, put, against,* and *crimes*.

A United Nations committee has voted for an _____ worldwide freeze on the use of the death penalty. A total of 99 countries voted in _____ of a suspension of capital punishment, while 52 opposed the proposal and the remaining 33 nations did not vote. Those who campaigned _____ the death penalty said the abolition would "_____ to the enhancement and progressive development of human rights." They said capital punishment has not been a deterrent for _____ and many innocent people are still _____ _____ to death by mistake.

After reading/listening activities can include a word search using a corpora data base (see p. 13) for the words *death* and *penalty*. Students are to find collocates, alternate meanings, and synonyms. Afterwards they can be asked to share their findings with a partner, develop questions using the words, and then ask others their questions. A vocabulary activity can have them circling words they do not understand, joining a group and pooling their words with all the group's members, and looking up meanings of the words in various dictionaries. Last they can be asked to write several questions concerning the death penalty with a partner for a survey they will take of their classmates.

In the *after reading/writing activities* teachers can use a pair-work discussion activity containing questions such as "What did you think when you read the headline?" "What is the history of capital punishment in your country?" "Do you think most of the world will oppose the death penalty a decade from now?" Also included is a quickwrite about the death penalty and an Internet search to find information about countries that have/do not have capital punishment.

STRUCTURING LESSONS

Before a lesson structure is devised, some sort of needs/interest assessment should take place, perhaps at the unit level with as much student input as possible. Then general goals and specific concept and behavioral objectives (see especially the Sample Lesson Preparation Format on pp. 367–369) can grow out of the assessment as flexible lessons are developed. After the lesson is completed, lesson evaluation is important. How well has the lesson worked? Does it need to be modified in any way before trying something similar again with the same group? Did it accomplish what it was supposed to accomplish? At this point, student evaluations can be very helpful in determining answers to these questions. Also having a peer observe or record the lesson for future evaluation can be beneficial. See the section on teacher research and professional development in Chapter 17.

Teachers need to remain flexible when structuring the content of their lessons. Some of the best lessons teachers have will be those spontaneous ones that grow out of a special need or interest that presents itself at the moment. In my mind, flexibility is a large part of what good teaching is all about. Wells (1999), too, emphasized that teachers need not be committed to completing a predetermined lesson; instead they might move in directions prompted by student response.

Concerning the structure of lessons for beginners in particular, Wong-Fillmore (1985) concluded early on that teacher lessons that are consistent and well organized and that have a similar framework with clear beginnings and endings appear to be most effective. Familiar routines provide a scaffold for the learning of new materials.[4] Of course, students need to have as much input into the curriculum and lessons as their proficiency allows, and teachers need to flow with students' changing needs and goals.

The following routine outline can, perhaps with some modification, be followed in most lessons *as long as the language used is appropriate for the approximate age and proficiency levels of the students.* This structure is similar to a plan described much earlier by Hunter and Russell (1977) for classroom lessons but with an important difference. Whereas the original Hunter–Russell model appeared to be highly teacher-centered and teacher-controlled, this model allows for greater student input and participation.[5] As the students gain competence, they can gradually take on a larger role in choosing the content and even in the structure of the lessons themselves.

---

[4] Her conclusion is based on a study with colleagues at the University of California at Berkeley. They observed the input given in thirty kindergarten through fifth-grade classrooms over a five-year period. In addition, she observed and recorded teachers in another ten classrooms in which there were English learners.

[5] The same type of plan can be used when appropriate by peer facilitators and lay assistants for their work with small groups and individuals. See the section later in this chapter.

BASIC STRUCTURE OF THE LESSON

1. Perspective (opening)

Ask students questions such as:

> What have you learned to do? (previous activity)
> What concepts have you learned? (previous activity)
> How does it make you feel? proud of yourself? more confident?

Give a preview of the objectives and possibilities for the new lesson.

Help the students to relate the coming activity to their lives and their prior knowledge.

Provide critical background information when needed.

Explore a few key vocabulary items with the students if needed for understanding the lesson.

2. Stimulation

The following are a few options that can be used to gain student interest:

> Pose a question to get students thinking about the coming activity and the major concepts involved.
> Begin with an attention grabber: an anecdote, a short scene acted out by peer facilitators or lay assistants (see pp. 377–382), a picture, or a song.
> Use it as a lead into the activity.

3. Instruction/Participation Phase (teacher/student contributions)

For example:

> Read and discuss the story or poem, sing the song or have it sung, do the chant, present the concepts, search for the issues, agree on expectations, check for understanding, divide into groups, and so on. Encourage student involvement to the largest extent possible, depending on the student's emerging capabilities in the target language.

4. Closure

Address these questions when they are appropriate:

> What did you learn? How does this help you?
> How did you feel about doing the activities?
> How can you use what you have learned in the future?

Give a preview of your plans for future lessons. Get student input.

5. Follow-up

> Use other activities to reinforce the same concepts.
> Give students the opportunity to do independent work in class or as homework.

Note that some elements of the lessons should be downplayed and others emphasized, depending on the situation and the proficiency levels of the students. For instance, a full development of the perspective would probably not be appropriate for low-beginning or young students because not much of it would be understood unless given in the primary language. Simple statements such as "I think you know what watercolors are. It will be fun to see what you do with them" would be sufficient. On the other hand, fully developed, highly comprehensible instructions during the instruction/participation phase would be very appropriate for low-beginning students and young children. Furthermore, the teacher should keep in mind that students will probably, at first, not understand every word in the lesson, nor should they expect to. It takes time and many passes through similar structures and concepts to acquire the target language.

The teacher may want to make a list of or an outline of the important points he or she wants to include during critical parts of the lesson (e.g., directions, rules, introductions, summaries, presentation of key concepts, and so on). In addition, the teacher needs to pace the lesson well so that it moves smoothly and logically from one activity to another. Sometimes lessons can get bogged down in unnecessary repetition and irrelevant detail. That is why careful planning is so critical. In addition, using a variety of strategies and activities throughout the lesson helps to maintain a high level of anticipation and interest on the part of the students.

Van Lier (1996) suggested that lessons be balanced in that they contain both planned and improvised elements. He reminded us that "most students also need points of stability in lessons, and these are achieved by recycling tasks, planning certain sequences of activities in predictable ways, ritual beginnings, endings, and transitions, and so on" (p. 200). The Basic Structure of the Lesson presented earlier provides for the ritual that students often find helpful and safe.

Teachers need to spell out a detailed and focused preparation prior to the lesson—but one that leaves the description of the activity open and flexible. I developed the following lesson preparation format for my students at California State University, Los Angeles. The details of the preparation format used as an example here were adapted from one given to me by Elsa Ortega, a graduate student.

A SAMPLE LESSON PREPARATION FORMAT

Using the Five Senses

Name of student: *Elsa Ortega*
Date: *October 20*
Age level: *teenagers or adults*
Proficiency level: *high-beginning to low-intermediate*

Concepts introduced: Concepts introduced will come from the students themselves as part of the language experience portion of the lesson later on (see p. 303–306). For some, the concepts will be new; for others, they will be recycled. The poetic format demonstrated in the lesson and the punctuation and capitalization often (but not always) found in poems may be new to some students.

(Continued)

Concepts reinforced: A rather extensive range of emotions—happiness, sadness, loneliness, excitement, pride, anger, peacefulness, jealousy, envy, hatred, and so on—and the five senses: sight, sound, taste, smell, and touch.

Behaviors expected as a result of this lesson: Students should be able to demonstrate an understanding of the concepts introduced in the language experience portion of the lesson. They should be able to use with relative ease the poetic format demonstrated, including the way it is usually punctuated, with appropriate elements capitalized.

Materials needed: Several large pictures showing people in situations in which fairly specific emotions are depicted; a board or transparency on which to write; paper (for students), unless they are expected to use their own; thick, medium, and thin felt-tip pens in different colors and/or brushes and paints for artwork.

Description of the activities:

1. Show the students pictures of people in different situations likely to bring about strong emotions (i.e., a teenage girl at the store who cannot get the attention of the salesclerk, a child handing his sick dog to a veterinarian, an old man hugging an old woman). As students mention various emotions, write them in noun form on the board.

2. Ask the students if they remember what the five senses are. Write them on the board.

3. Tell students that they are going to write a poem together about an emotion using the following format:
   Title: Name of the emotion
   Line 1: What color is the emotion?
   Line 2: What does it sound like?
   Line 3: What does it taste like?
   Line 4: What does it smell like?
   Line 5: What does it look like?
   Line 6: How does it make you feel?

4. Choose an emotion that the students are not likely to choose. Using elements of language experience, write a poem with the students, following the above format.

5. Ask each student to choose an emotion and write a poem using the same format (write the format on the board if you have not already done so). Students can work with a partner if they want to.

Here is an example: Happiness

Happiness is a colorful rainbow in the sky.
It sounds like people cheering.
It tastes like soft, sugary cotton candy,
And it smells like jasmine blooming at night.
Happiness looks like people dancing.
It makes you feel good.
                                        Heather Mc Brian

(Continued)

Strategies used to check for understanding: Can the students talk about the various emotions? Do they show a clear understanding of them in their poems? Do they show an understanding of the format and why they are or are not following it exactly? Some may choose to vary it. Do they demonstrate in their own poems that they understand appropriate use of punctuation and capitalization, even though they may deviate from it for a logical reason? Poetry allows for deviation perhaps more than other genres.

Follow-up lesson(s):

1. Ask each student to complete pieces of artwork to accompany their poems. If they prefer, they may cut pictures out of magazines to accompany their poems.
2. Have students share their poems in small groups. Later, ask for volunteers to share their poems with the whole class.

Teachers should do an evaluation of the lesson once it is finished. How did the students respond? What were the strengths of the lesson? What could be improved in the lesson? What insights did the teacher gain about teaching and learning from the lesson?

THEME CYCLES/INVESTIGATIVE INQUIRY

If an emergent participatory classroom is the goal, one way to decide on the content and organization of lessons is to use a *theme cycles* approach (see also Chapter 4) or some similar investigatory process (see also Weinstein, 2001). Lessons associated with theme cycles represent a mutual effort on the part of both the teacher and the students. Of course, students should be proficient enough in the target language to participate as fully as possible.

Theme cycles present not just a general topic as a label around which isolated lessons in math, science, social studies, and their related skills revolve; instead, the topic is a subject for *investigative inquiry.* During the inquiry, students use a knowledge base of math, science, social studies, and so forth from which to draw. The process begins with an investigation that evolves into a negotiated curricular plan. Questions lead to more questions which lead to even more questions and further investigation. Thus the curriculum is constructed in a joint effort between the students and the teacher.

Harste, Short, and Burke (1988) early on outlined procedures for curriculum development using theme cycles. They are summarized as follows:

1. Both teachers and students make a list of topics that interest them and blend the two lists by mutual agreement to form the basic curriculum plan.
2. Through negotiation, one topic is selected as a starting point.
3. Students and teacher create a web or chart, identifying "What We Know" and "What We Want to Know" about the topic (Ogle, 1986). Figure 15.1 illustrates the creation of a chart focused on the topic of space.
4. Students and teachers together develop a list of resources: books, people to interview, places to visit, and so on.
5. Students choose the questions in the "What We Want to Know" column that are the most pressing.

6. With the help of the teacher, students become involved in whole-group, small-group, and individual learning activities to explore the questions selected.
7. New questions are added to the chart as new discoveries are made.
8. At the end of particular segments of study, students present what they have learned to one another.
9. Other charts such as the one in Figure 15.1 are created, and the process continues.

What We Know	What We Want to Know
Mars, Venus, and Jupiter are planets in space. Neil Armstrong and Sally Ride were early astronauts. The sun is a star. The moon revolves around the earth.	What else is there in space? How do you become an astronaut? What is the sun made of? How is it possible to revolve around another object without falling?

Figure 15.1 Topic: Space

Harste et al. stressed the importance of building a supportive classroom environment before trying to negotiate curriculum. Throughout the process, the teacher acts as a facilitator and a participant to ensure the inquiry is being carried out successfully.

INFUSING STANDARDS INTO THE CURRICULUM

Standards are crucial to any successful language program. If they are offered as guidelines, as are the ESL proficiency standards (see p. 196–201) and the foreign language standards (see p. 203), then they can be used flexibly in the classroom without unduly constraining the freedom teachers and students need to progress toward an emergent participatory classroom environment. For example, look at the previous Sample Lesson Preparation Format on using the five senses. The immediate behaviors expected as a result of the lesson include the student's ability to demonstrate the understanding of the specific concepts introduced, to use with relative ease the poetic format that was demonstrated, and to punctuate and capitalize appropriately. These behaviors are closely associated with standards related to being able to grasp content; express oneself in writing, including poetry; and use the conventions involved in punctuation and capitalization for a variety of formats. Standards can also be infused into a theme cycles or investigative inquiry approach and into virtually any lesson preparation format employed in the classroom.

Standards specify what students should know and what they should be able to do as a result of instruction in the target language (see Chapter 7). They can help assure stakeholders (students, teachers, the school, the school district) that relevant skills necessary to reaching personal, sociopolitical, and academic objectives are being included in the language program. If selection and implementation are judiciously carried out, they can help students and teachers clarify what skills are necessary to each student's development as a successful learner and effective citizen in the community, both locally and globally.

One of the dangers of standards of which teachers should be aware has been mentioned already (see Chapter 7). Sometimes teachers and/or the school districts, in their effort to ensure that students meet predetermined standards, use them as strait jackets for the curriculum. Santiago (1997) also talked about this fear. She observed, "Often, teachers are put in a position where they become a hindrance to the learning process by prescribing too closely what children should learn and thereby failing to create the necessary conditions for learning" (p. 74). She went on to say, "We fail our students by saturating them with what we think they should know at a certain age instead of finding out where they are and what they know, and continuing from there" (p. 78). In order to help students stretch to higher levels of understanding, we need to start approximately where they are and build from there. A highly specified curriculum and timetable with little input from teachers and their students leaves almost no possibility for that.

Van Lier (1996) went even further to condemn such preestablished constraints on classrooms. He argued that the curriculum itself must be process-oriented in that it is

> motivated by our understanding of learning rather than by a list of desired competencies, test scores, or other products. The setting of goals and objectives, and the construction and assessment of achievement, are themselves integral parts of the curriculum process, rather than preestablished constraints that are imposed on it from the outside. (p. 3)

Of course, standards by themselves are not inherently evil. It is the way in which they are implemented that can make them seem that way. Many teachers, however, when faced with standards handed down as "edicts from above," have learned to deal with them as best they can (see McKay, 2006). Many try to allow for as much student input and attention to students' immediate needs as possible within even the most rigid systems. Many of these same teachers have fought and continue to fight to have these systems changed so that they are more flexible and in tune with the ever-changing needs of their students.

DECIDING THE FOCUS OF THE INSTRUCTION: PROFICIENCY-BASED, TASK-BASED, OR CONTENT-BASED

There is some disagreement about the proper focus for communicative programs. Some have encouraged a focus on proficiencies/competencies (Omaggio, 2001); others have seriously examined and/or recommended a focus on tasks (e.g., H. D. Brown, 1994; R. Ellis, 2003; Long, 1985; McDonough & Chaikitmongkol, 2007; Nunan, 1989, 1991, 2004; Roebuck, 2000; to name a few); yet others have advocated a focus on content (e.g., Brinton, M. A. Snow, & Wesche, 1989; Crandall, 1993; Crandall & Kaufman, 2002; Kaufman, 2004; M. A. Snow, 2005; M. A. Snow & Brinton, 1997; Stoller, 2004).[6]

Proficiency or Competency-Based Instruction

Proficiency/competency-based programs focus on the "mastery of basic and life skills necessary for the individual to function proficiently in society" (National Center for Educational Statistics, 1982, p. 80).

---

[6] In addition, there are many other alternatives, including theme-based, literature-based, genre-based, and community-based instruction. Most can be directly related or subsumed by the three foci described in this section. For example, product-based instruction relates closely to task-based instruction in cases in which a product is a result of the task at hand. Theme-based, literature-based, and community-based instruction can logically be subsumed under content-based instruction.

Often the syllabus is organized synthetically around learning outcomes that have been divided into sets of skills and subskills (Omaggio, 2001), such as the ability to

- recognize and write common abbreviations
- distinguish certain vowel sounds auditorially
- spell a list of two-syllable words
- verbally produce and write the alphabet
- punctuate a dialogue correctly
- use negatives in obligatory positions
- distinguish between "some" and "any"
- use prepositions of location correctly

Often checklists are used to make sure students have met these proficiencies or competencies before they can move on to the next exercise or the next level.

Task-Based Instruction

Task-based instruction has been defined in various ways over the years, each with a somewhat different orientation. Long (1985) early on defined tasks simply as "the things people will tell you they do if you ask them and they are not applied linguists" (p. 89). These "things" might include filling out a form, typing a letter, checking a book out of the library, writing an essay, and so on. A task-based syllabus is generally context specific and is grounded in a highly specified needs identification. Once the needs have been identified, they are classified into task types (e.g., tasks related to a specific content area; tasks related to working in a bank or driving a car). Task difficulty is assessed within each task type; a syllabus is prepared, and teaching procedures and materials are selected and/or developed. Meaning is negotiated as the learners try to accomplish goals related to each task. Language ability is developed through this interactive process (R. Ellis, 2003).

Nunan (1991) related task-based instruction to experiential learning. He gave an example using steps to develop a pedagogic task:

1. Identify the target task (e.g., giving personal information in a job interview).
2. Provide a model (e.g., students listen to and extract key information from an authentic or simulated interview).
3. Identify the enabling skill (manipulation drill to practice *Wh-* questions with *do-* insertion).
4. Devise a pedagogic task (interview simulation using role cards). (p. 282)

Nunan claimed that this procedure provides students with the opportunity to accomplish the following:

- develop language skills meeting their needs
- be exposed to native-speaker [I would change this to "proficient-speaker"] or user language
- receive explicit instruction and guided practice
- mobilize emerging skills by rehearsing

H. D. Brown (1994) added to our knowledge of tasks by asserting that some tasks may be synonymous with teaching techniques (e.g., a role-play task/technique or a problem-solving task/technique). According to him, "[task-based instruction] views the learning process as a set of communicative tasks that are directly linked to the curricular goals they serve, and the purpose of which extend beyond the practice of language for its own sake" (p. 83). Brown presented important questions for teachers such as: Do the tasks specifically contribute to communicative goals? Are their elements carefully designed and not simply haphazardly or idiosyncratically thrown together?

In more recent years the meaning of *task* has been elaborated on and has become more nuanced in definition. For example, Bygate, Skehan, and Swain (2001) referred to a task as "an activity, susceptible to brief or extended pedagogic intervention, which requires learners to use language, with emphasis on meaning, to attain an objective" (p. 11).

Many, including Nunan (2004), considered task-based learning a type of communicative language teaching (see also Savignon, 1991). Kumaravadivelu (2006), however, disagreed and attempted to place task-based language teaching into yet a different framework by arguing that it is not a methodological construct and that different methods can be used to achieve its goals. He pointed to the three foci of tasks: *language* centered (explicit focus on form), *learner* centered (focus on functional properties), and *learning* centered (focus on negotiation of meaning and problem solving with no explicit focus on form).

Crabbe (2003, 2007) viewed tasks as part of a hierarchy in which a task is considered "a unit of communicative activity designed to facilitate learning" (2007, p. 119). Under each task in his proposed framework were *learning opportunities*, which he called units of "cognitive or metacognitive activity associated with learning." Learning opportunities included the following ingredients: input, output, interaction, feedback, rehearsal, language understanding, and learning understanding. In Crabbe's perspective, learning opportunities do not favor one approach or method over another and are greatly influenced by the local situation.

Interestingly, the behaviors that tasks produce are ever-changing and dependent on the individual's motives, personal and social history, negotiations with other participants, and so forth (see Coughlan & Duff, 1998). Task-based research that treats subjects as controllable objects has been questioned. Roebuck (2000) explained it this way:

> Part of the perceived controllability of tasks, however, stems from the belief that subjects, although so named, can be manipulated by the intentions of the researcher and, in particular, by task instructions. Thus, subjects are treated as objects and are denied the agency attributed to true subjects. (p. 79)

McDonough and Chaikitmongkol (2007) used a case-study approach to look at teachers' and learners' reactions to a task-based EFL course in Thailand. The results indicated that the learners had been encouraged to become more independent and that the course had acknowledged their academic needs. The authors called for empirical research to explore questions concerning the effectiveness of task-based courses in promoting second language learning, the implementation of task syllabi, teacher preparation, and so on in order to assist teachers in designing and implementing their own task-based courses.

The tasks themselves need to be examined within the social milieu of which they are a part and not looked at in isolation only from a teacher's or researcher's perspective. The perspective that is crucial here is that of the learner and the behaviors that the task has produced within that individual.

Content-Based Instruction

Using content-based instruction, the teacher leads the students through the process of learning language and content concurrently. The language skills needed to function in a new language environment are integrated with the particular content being taught.

Content-based instruction originated in 1986 with Bernard Mohan who claimed in his book *Language and Content* that both should not (and could not) be isolated from one another. He argued that content provides the best context for language teaching in that it is both natural and very rich in meaning (Brinton & M. A. Snow, 2008).

Three prototype models of content-based instruction were identified early on by Briton, M. A. Snow, and Wesche (1989). They are, briefly:

- *theme based:* Within the language classroom, the teacher integrates language teaching with various themes or topics often related to content-area subjects.[7] The language used and the assignments given are tailored to the students' proficiency levels and the themes or topics chosen are generally of high interest and relevancy. See the description of the Alhambra School District program for grades K–3 beginning on p. 469.
- *sheltered:* Within a content-area classroom specially designed for language learners, the teacher of the subject being taught (e.g., math, science, social studies) helps language learners gain access to it through language. The language used to teach the content is highly contextualized. The teacher usually has had at least some preparation in strategies for integrating language and content instruction for second language learners. See the examples in the Artesia High School program description beginning on p. 463.
- *adjunct:* A language instructor teaches a course for second language learners in conjunction with a subject they are taking. The language instructor works closely with the content-area teacher to provide the assistance needed to comprehend lectures, take notes effectively, write papers of various kinds, make sense of the text, and so on. See an example of this in the Saint Michael's College program description beginning on p. 447. An alternative is the *simulated adjunct model.* Using this model, subject-related units are designed for language learners, encouraging them to augment what they are learning in their subject-area class through additional reading and other assignments (Brinton & M. A. Snow, 2008).

---

[7]Survival topics taught at beginning levels of second language development such as getting a job, going to the doctor, and so forth are not generally considered content based but, rather, task based (see the previously mentioned Bygate et al., 2001, definition).

In each of these models, the content itself serves as the organizing principle underlying decisions made about language teaching and the sequencing of the language instruction (Brinton & M. A. Snow, 2008).

One problem with attempting to teach academic course content in second language classes themselves is that language teachers often lack confidence in their ability to teach certain content (Kaufman, 2004). One possible solution is for the language teacher to collaborate with content-area teachers and perhaps even link courses or team-teach.

Another alternative is to select the first prototype discussed earlier: a theme-based program. Using this model, language teachers can teach themes or topics about which they do have some expertise. For example, Brinton et al. (1989) early on advocated (among other things) that topics such as ocean fish (science), travel destinations (geography), the effects of illegal drugs on society (health), and so on be used and that language skills be integrated around them. Any of the themes or topics chosen, depending on the students' needs and interests, could last for a short time period or be extended over a long time period (see *sustained-content language teaching;* Murphy & Stoller, 2001). Themes and topics extended over a long time period would probably be most appropriate for students operating at high-beginning to advanced levels, although preparation for them could begin much earlier. Using this model, the themes or topics are generally selected by the teacher (hopefully with student input), and the modified language is specially tailored to students' needs.

Regardless of the way in which students are prepared to function academically, Snow, Met, and Genesee (1989) and M. A. Snow (2005) stressed the importance of students' learning both *content-obligatory language* (structures, lexical items, and functions typically used in a given content-area) and *content-compatible language* (structures and lexical items that pair naturally with the given content area). Some researchers have studied classroom discourse to identify functions. For example, A. Bailey, Butler, LaFramenta, and Ong (2001) looked at science classrooms in an elementary school and found that comparison, definition, description, evaluation, and justification were among the functions used. Corpus searches (see p. 13 in this volume) might be a way to locate both obligatory and content-compatible language used to perform certain functions within the various fields of study.

It is expected that students, once they have a basic knowledge of the content obligatory and content-compatible language associated with specific content areas, will be placed in the appropriate sheltered, adjunct, or mainstream courses (see Chapter 17 for further description of each type of course).

Which Focus Appears Most Promising?

The answer to this question depends mainly on which makes the most sense cognitively for the situation in which it is to be used. Because task-based instruction is oriented to carrying out a task or procedure, it would be most appropriate for language learners studying in highly specific technical fields or contexts in which the goals are often narrowly focused. An example might be an English for special purposes program in which students are studying specific medical techniques or computer technology.

It might also be appropriate for those operating at true beginning levels who need to be able to carry out certain basic tasks just to survive in a second language environment. Overall, however, content-based instruction appears to make the most sense cognitively as a focus for situations in which successful communication and/or academic competency are the goals. In such situations, tasks generally need something to belong to in the way of highly developed content. Although it is true that some task-based lessons may be attached to a very general theme or topic, a course that jumps from task to task lacks both cohesion and a reason for being.

It should be mentioned here that both task-based and content-based teaching have their critics. Hinkel (2006) argued that neither has been sufficiently tested to determine its effectiveness and that both may not be appropriate or workable in global contexts. However, Hinkel also pointed to the increased opportunities each provides language learners for communication that has a purpose and for furthering both language and skill goals in an integrated fashion.

A major problem with proficiency/competency-based instruction is that it tends to lead to a syllabus that concentrates on isolated elements of language for study. It is not much different in this respect from the grammar-based approaches of the past. Here I am reminded of Newmark's (1983) seminal article, "How Not to Interfere with Language Learning." He said that we learn language in natural chunks, exponentially, rather than additively. The "interference" occurs when we artificially isolate parts from wholes. This is exactly what a proficiency/competency-based curriculum seems to do. This is not to say that proficiencies and competencies are not important. On the contrary, they should be part of the curriculum but not the focus of the curriculum.

All three foci can become part of a workable hierarchy and integrated into an effective program for students who need to survive and thrive both socially and academically (see Figure 15.2). For example, if the *content* were ocean fish and involved the types of fish, where they live, how they live, the effects of global warming on their habitat, and the dangers of overfishing, then the *tasks* might involve finding out as much as possible about ocean fish and sharing that information with a small group, helping the class and the teacher set up an aquarium in the classroom to study, describing the animals in the aquarium, and so on. Proficiencies and competencies might involve

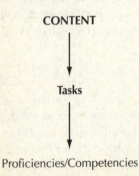

Figure 15.2 Focus Hierarchy

being able to spell the names of various ocean fish, correctly punctuate a paragraph about the habitat of various ocean fish, and so forth.

USING PEER FACILITATORS AND LAY ASSISTANTS

In an ideal second language teaching situation, every student would receive the following:

- plenty of opportunity for interaction leading to full participation and eventually emergent participatory experiences
- a sufficient number of opportunities to enhance self-image and develop positive attitudes
- opportunities to become part of outside speech communities and enter into extended dialogue in the new language (Curran & Stelluto, 2005)
- opportunities to establish social relationships in and out of the school environment
- regular encouragement, motivation, and challenges
- frequent feedback including recasts (see Chapter 2)
- appropriate linguistic models (competent users of the target language are usually best)[8]
- formal grammar instruction when beneficial to the language learning process (see pp. 54–62)

The quantity or amount of each necessary to learn the target language depends on the individual student and each situation. However, to ensure that student needs are met, peer facilitators and/or lay assistants may prove to be necessary additions to the program. Like the teacher, they can facilitate communication through negotiating for meaning, offering modified language tailored to each student's needs, and giving encouragement and feedback. They can provide a social bridge to the rest of the students in the school and to the community. In addition, they can serve as linguistic models to help prevent premature stabilization and share language information prepared by the teacher when needed. It is important that peer facilitators not appear as linguistic "experts" when working with language learners. See Hall, Hendricks, and Orr (2004) for an illuminating discussion of nonnative speaker and native speaker collaboration in the classroom. Peer facilitators (like native speakers) need to be cooperative partners working together with the language learners. Peer facilitators, as their name suggests, need to "facilitate" learning, not dominate it.

Potential peer facilitators who are fluent in the target language are usually available within the schools themselves. For example, foreign language classes can draw from the advanced students in the language, adult programs from the community at large, ESL classes at junior and senior high schools and universities from the student body at large,

---

[8] It is important to stress here that peer facilitators are a lot more than just "linguistic models"; their more important role is that of cooperative partners working together with language learners to facilitate their learning.

and elementary school classes from the upper grades. If tasks are not cognitively demanding, peer facilitators can be much younger. However, younger peer facilitators generally require more supervision from the teacher than older ones. Lay assistants who are fluent in the target language can be invaluable at all levels and are often an overlooked community resource.

In their investigation of bilingual students working with less proficient peers in content-area classes, Klingner and Vaughn (2000) found that scores on the English vocabulary tests improved significantly on the posttests, both for those needing help and those doing the helping. The finding that both the students and their peer facilitators/tutors benefited supports the conclusions of much earlier research on peer facilitating/tutoring (see Richard-Amato, 1992a, for a summary of that research).

Peer facilitators and lay assistants should meet certain qualifications: They should have the necessary skills, enjoy helping others, have a lot of patience, be supportive, and be willing to work hard. In addition, they need preparation workshops (especially effective at secondary and adult levels) to aid them in the following areas:

- development of cultural sensitivity (see also Chapter 6)
- knowledge of the instructional procedures the teacher chooses to use
- familiarity with the materials available
- pertinent background information on the students with whom they will be working—cultural information, individual background information, and so on
- strategies for creating friendly, supportive relationships

See the following chart for strategies that might be discussed at a preparation workshop for peer facilitators and lay assistants.

STRATEGIES FOR HELPING OTHERS

- Learn the student's name and use it frequently.
- Be friendly. Get to know the student.
- Be a good listener. Encourage the student to talk. Ask questions to find out more or to clarify what the student is saying.
- Work cooperatively with the student as a partner rather than as an "expert."
- Recognize and show enthusiasm for the student's accomplishments. Praise genuinely, and make praise as specific as possible. Try to build intrinsic motivation by getting the student to reflect on what he or she has done. Phrases like "You should be very happy that you were able to _____" encourage the student to be self-motivating.
- Find out more about the student's culture, learning preferences, background, goals, and aspirations.

(Continued)

- Be accepting of the student's right to his or her own opinions and beliefs. Avoid put-downs.
- When asking questions, give the student enough time to respond. Be patient.
- Give the student sufficient time to work at his or her own pace without feeling hurried.
- If the student does not understand a concept after several attempts, go to something that you know the student can do successfully. Later when you return to the more difficult task, it may come more easily.
- If the student is obviously troubled or upset, give him or her a chance to talk to you about it. The task at hand can wait.
- Use language that the student can understand. Repeat and/or rephrase frequently if the student is a beginner. Use pictures and/or act out concepts whenever necessary.
- Keep directions short and simple.
- Be honest. If you do not know the answer to a question, admit it. Often you and the student can find answers together.
- If the student is proficient enough in a language you have in common, ask the student to reflect on and give you input about his or her perceived needs and feedback on what is being learned and how it is being learned.
- Remember that the teacher is there to help you when you need it. Do not hesitate to ask for assistance.

In addition to preparation workshops, peer facilitators and lay assistants need to meet with the teacher regularly to develop flexible lessons and talk about possible problems and various approaches. Student input is essential whenever possible. On p. 380 is an evaluation checklist to ensure frequent communication between the teacher and peer facilitator or lay assistant concerning student progress. Students should be conferred with regularly to discuss progress and future directions and plans (see sample conference on p. 189–190).

Room Arrangements[9]

Two room plans have worked well for me in incorporating peer facilitators and lay assistants (see Figures 15.3 and 15.4 on pp. 380–381). Consider their possibilities for your own classroom.

In Figure 15.3, each peer facilitator or lay assistant has a *private work station* where the students to whom he or she has been assigned go for assistance. These students remain at the tables in the center of the room while working on their own. This particular configuration can be very effective when the tasks are mainly one-to-one, requiring a certain degree of privacy.

Figure 15.4, on the other hand, illustrates the *flexible cluster work station* where the students assigned to a particular peer facilitator or lay assistant sit together with the

[9] From Richard-Amato (1992a, pp. 282–283).

EVALUATION CHECKLIST

Name of peer facilitator or lay assistant _____

Date _____

Name of student _____

1. What did the student accomplish today?
2. Were there any problems?
3. How does the student feel about what he or she is learning? What can you do to better meet the student's needs?
4. What activities will you work on tomorrow?
5. Can the teacher help you in any way?

Comments:

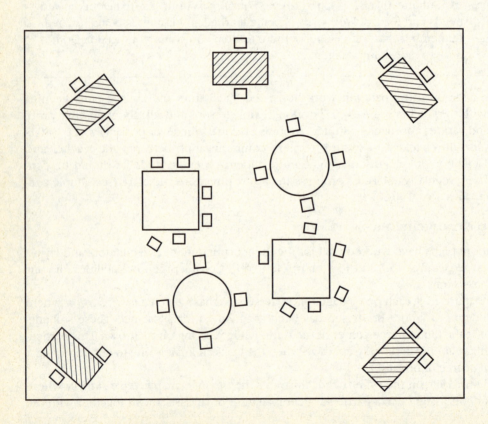

Figure 15.3 Private Work Stations

facilitator/assistant at the apex. This arrangement is ideal for group instruction or a group project. However, the cluster is flexible enough so that by rearranging the desks, the peer facilitator and lay assistants can still work somewhat privately with one or more members of the group.

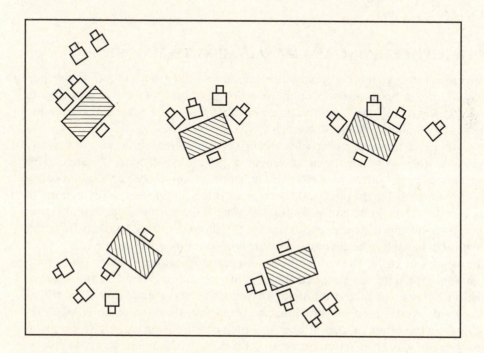

Figure 15.4 Flexible Cluster Work Stations

Comfortable chairs are found at each table. The tables with diagonal lines running through them are work stations for the peer facilitators and lay assistants. The teacher, too, might have a work station. Note that for whole-class activities, all the students can be at the tables in the middle.

Movable desks cluster around the tables that serve as work stations for peer facilitators and lay assistants. A similar station may be set up for the teacher. Note that for whole-class activities, the tables can be moved to the periphery of the room and the movable desks can be moved to the center to form a circle or any other configuration needed.

The task of organizing a program using peer facilitators and lay assistants may at first appear overwhelming. However, once the aides are familiar with procedures and are assigned to workable groups (perhaps three or four students of similar proficiency levels), the program seems to take on a momentum of its own. At that point, the time and talents of the teacher can be put to optimal use. The teacher is able to concentrate on students needing special help, peer facilitators and lay assistants wanting additional guidance, whole-class activities, and overall structural concerns.

In spite of the potential overall effectiveness of peer facilitators and lay assistants, I have been careful not to overuse them. The class was divided according to one of the work station configurations described previously two to three times a week, depending on what was being studied. On the other days the whole class met for other lessons that I facilitated; groupings depended on what needed to be accomplished at any given time.

COOPERATIVE LEARNING AS A MANAGEMENT TECHNIQUE[10]

In cooperative learning, students help other students within groups of four to five persons in an effort to reach goals. Cooperative learning approaches can be effective in both second and foreign language teaching situations and at many age levels from the late elementary grades through adult levels.

In cooperative learning, an *interdependence* is established among the students in each group as they strive for the achievement of group or individual objectives. This approach draws from both behaviorism and humanism; more recent applications draw from postmodernism. On the one hand, it frequently offers group rewards (in the form of points or grades) as its prime motivation; on the other, it urges students to develop more fully their own individual identities while respecting those of others. Students, however, need to be able to handle the cognitive challenges cooperative learning presents.

The results of early studies done on cooperative learning (Slavin, 1983) indicated great potential for some aspects of the approach to produce academic success, especially in classes of mixed ethnicity. In almost all the studies (89%) in which group rewards were based on individual achievement, there were noted achievement gains. On the other hand, in studies in which only individual grades were given or a group grade was given based on a group product, achievement was roughly the same as that found in the control classes. Moreover, several studies indicated that medium to low achievers seem to benefit most and that their accomplishments were not made to the detriment of high achievers (Armstrong, D.W. Johnson, & Balow, 1981; Martino & D.W. Johnson, 1979).

One possible drawback of cooperative learning (if it is used extensively at beginning to intermediate levels with second or foreign language students) is the possibility of premature stabilization (see Chapter 2). Wong-Fillmore (1985) reported that students who are not proficient in the target language do not provide adequate models for each other. This appeared to be true also to a certain extent in the immersion programs (see Chapter 17). However, Crandall (1999) felt that this argument was overblown. She stated:

> Possibilities of uncorrected or miscorrected student contributions are less important in the overall development of second language competence than opportunities for negotiation of meaning and interaction. (p. 242)

---

[10] I wish to thank Carole Cromwell, Linda Sasser, and Leslie Jo Adams for sharing their ideas about cooperative learning with me. Note that it is improbable that each will agree with every one of my conclusions.

Cooperative learning groups can provide comfortable environments in which the students can practice giving output and negotiating for meaning (see Long & Porter, 1984; Pica & Doughty, 1985; Porter, 1986). The danger seems to come when not-yet-competent peers are the *major* source of input during the language learning process.

Versions of cooperative learning can be incorporated very successfully in most subject areas, especially in intermediate to advanced language classes and mainstream content-area classes. It is particularly effective in the latter, where language learners can be grouped with more competent speakers of the target language, even though they may not be more knowledgeable, content-wise. Cooperative learning, too, provides for changing leadership depending on the content and skills being learned and on who can best teach what to whom. Wells (1999) described similar flexible collaboration this way:

> most activities involve a variety of component tasks such that students who are expert in one task, and therefore able to offer assistance to their peers, may themselves need assistance on another task. But it can also happen that in tackling a difficult task as a group, although no member has expertise beyond his or her peers, the group as a whole, by working at the problem together, is able to construct a solution that one could not have achieved alone. In other words, each is "forced to rise above himself," and, by building on the contributions of its individual members, the group collectively constructs an outcome that no single member envisaged at the outset of the collaboration. (pp. 323–324)

Wells went on to say that there is nothing wrong with collaboratively trying to solve problems for which no one person has the answer in a sort of "pooling of ignorance." It is at these times when the greatest advances in learning are often made.

Kagan (1986) described five distinct types of cooperative learning, which are briefly summarized in the following. (The examples for possible use are mine.) Types 2 to 5 seem to work best with groups of mixed ethnicity (in the case of ESL) and mixed ability levels. In addition, many other versions of these basic types have evolved over the past few years.

1. *Peer tutoring:* Teammates teach each other simple concepts. This type is often used for math or language arts and is particularly applicable in a mainstream content-area class that includes second language learners.
2. *Jigsaw:* Each member of the group is given the chief responsibility for a specific portion of the learning unit. These members work with the members of other groups who have been given the same assignment. They form "expert groups." However, eventually each member should learn the whole unit by sharing information with the others in the group. This type of cooperative learning is often used in the mastery of text material in social sciences. For example, a unit on the contributions of women in a specified country might be studied by each group. One group member might be responsible for women's contributions to science, another for their contributions to literature, a third for their contributions to politics, and so forth. Each student is graded individually on his or her understanding of the whole unit.

3. *Cooperative projects:* The members of the group work together to complete a group project such as a presentation, a composition, or an art project. Members receive individual grades based on the evaluation of the group product.

4. *Cooperative/individualized projects:* Students work alone on a particular assignment or project but their progress contributes to a group grade. They may help each other so that each group can achieve the best possible results.

5. *Cooperative interaction:* Students work as a unit to learn. However, there is no group grade. Each member of the group is graded individually even though completion of the unit (e.g., a lab experiment, panel discussion, dramatic presentation) requires a cooperative effort.

Although these suggestions are mainly for long-term projects, some very simple applications of cooperative learning can be incorporated in short-term activities at any level for which the specific content is appropriate. Some examples are:

1. In a version of the activity commonly known as *numbered heads together*, the class is divided into several groups of four or five, and each student is given a number within the group. Each student (depending on the number assigned) does one small portion of the group's work. For example, if a class in adult basic education is studying cultures, the teacher might give the groups several short passages, each describing an important custom in the United States. The person who is assigned the number 4 in each group could be responsible for reading the passage about how late one can be to a dinner party without being considered rude. The same person is then responsible for sharing this information with the others. The person assigned number 3 could do the same for a passage describing who is expected to pay when one is asked to go to a movie, and so forth. Any number of topics can be handled in this manner.

2. *Think/pair/share* requires students to think about a question or issue, share their thoughts in pairs, and then share them with the class or a larger group (Kagan, 1994). For example, if the students are presented with a question about saving the environment for future generations, they might first want to jot down the aspects of the environment that need protection and what might be done in each case; get together with a partner and share these ideas for the purpose of getting feedback; and last, tell the whole class or a large group about their ideas, which by now have probably been modified more than once to reflect what they have learned in the process. At each stage, they are given the opportunity to more fully develop their ideas before presenting them to the whole class or a large group (see also Crandall, 1999).

3. The members of each group can study together for a test or work together to complete an assignment.

4. The group can complete a short-term group project such as a brief skit, a description of a scene, a collage, or a small-group discussion. Each member receives a group grade.

In his book *Cooperative Learning: Resources for Teachers*, Kagan (1985) described a highly structured cooperative learning system consisting of team building, management techniques, and rewards based on a fairly complex system of points. However, some teachers might prefer to downplay behavioristic goals (points and other extrinsic motivational devices) and concentrate on humanistic goals (personal development and respect for others) and postmodern goals (identity and agency, empowerment, and action on issues of importance). In spite of the early claims made for cooperative learning in its unadulterated forms, my experience suggests that similar results can be achieved by focusing on the development of intrinsic motivation and encouraging students to focus on what they have accomplished.

One research study on cooperative/collaborative group work brought mixed results for English learners. Leki (2001) found in her research at a large state university in the United States that English-speaking bilingual students often felt intimidated and found their efforts thwarted while working with native-English speakers. When they did find their work yielding positive results, it was usually because the teacher had intervened to make sure they received equal opportunities to participate.

Several researchers were among those who found evidence for one or more of the following conclusions (Cowie, Smith, Boulton, & Laver, 1994; Felder & Brent, 1996; Jacob, Rottenberg, Patrick, & Wheeler, 1996; D.M. Johnson, 1994; Leki, 2001; Tinto, 1997).

Group learning overall appears most successful in situations in which it:

- is well organized
- is structured to give equal roles to language minority students when they are mixed with native speakers
- is carefully monitored and frequently assessed by a teacher who intervenes when necessary
- requires participants to have prior instruction in working in groups effectively
- presents tasks that engage the group's interest and for which the outcomes are not predetermined
- offers language learners multiple opportunities for receiving the interaction necessary for acquisition

See McGroarty and Calderón (2005) for further information on cooperative learning models and the research supporting cooperative learning.

WORKING WITH LARGE AND MIXED-LEVEL CLASSES

Teachers of second language students are often overwhelmed with large class sizes. Classrooms filled with fifty or more students are not uncommon, especially in cities where significant numbers of immigrants live. More often than not, teachers find in these classrooms a microcosm of needs, languages, cultural backgrounds, goals, and proficiency levels. These levels can range anywhere from low-beginning to high-intermediate levels and above. Some students may have not had much experience with formal schooling in their own countries; many may be struggling with the rejection and frustration of not being able to get their most basic needs met in a culture that seems indifferent to them. Trying to meet all of the challenges may lead to teacher burn-out unless appropriate strategies are used to make the job more manageable. (See especially Chapters 4, 5, 6, and 13 of this book.) The following are suggestions that may help teachers manage overly large classes and mixed levels.

1. *Multiactivity approach with one teacher:* The teacher can instruct one group of students while a second group is working independently. A third group can be conferring in pairs, and a fourth group can be sharing their work in small clusters of four or five students. The teacher can call time after about twenty minutes or so, depending on the requirements of the tasks and the attention spans of the students. Once time is called, the students move to another group. Possible alternatives include:

   a. What each group is doing can be coordinated in some way with what the other groups are doing, if the students are of similar proficiency levels. For example, the first group may participate in a strategy discussion with the teacher about a writing assignment that has been given, the second group may be actually doing the writing assignment (having already discussed it with the teacher), the third group may be conferring about what they have just written with a partner (having already completed the work of groups 1 and 2), and the fourth group may be sharing what they have written with the cluster of four or five students (having already completed the work of groups 1, 2, and 3). Prior to the four tasks, all the students may have been reading or doing a different assignment independently and will continue to work independently until the teacher calls them to join the first group, starting the process.

   b. The work done by the groups may not be coordinated at all with each other, but instead each group may represent a different approximate proficiency level. Each group works on something appropriate to that level, but only one group has the teacher during any one twenty-minute segment. The teacher is the one who rotates. Very careful preparation is necessary to ensure that all the groups are working on something challenging, perhaps to reinforce what they have just learned or confer with a peer(s) about what they have just done.

   c. Give a short writing assignment for all students to work on at their desks. Paragraphs of different types—descriptive, informative, comparative, or argumentative—may work well here. Place your most proficient students (after some preparation), each at a different work station. See Figure 15.3 on p. 380. Students, when they are ready, go to an available station to discuss what they have written. They then go back to their desks to do a revision based on the discussion. When finished with the second draft, they show their work to the same peer for more discussion. They can either revise a second time or, if they are satisfied and think they have the best draft they can do, they turn it into the teacher.

   d. Use some version of cooperative learning. For many of the activities, the proficiency levels will be mixed, but this should not be cause for concern.

Students of mixed levels learn much from each other as they work to accomplish group goals.

2. *Multiactivity approach with one teacher and peer facilitators and/or lay assistants:* See the previous discussion in this chapter on pp. 377–382. Possible ways to utilize facilitators/assistants include the following:

a. Peer facilitators and lay assistants can each be assigned to a group operating at an approximate proficiency level; however, no one person should have more than four or five students in his or her group. The teacher can take a group as well, or the teacher can rotate, teaching coordinated mini-lessons, answering questions, and helping to facilitate discussions. Facilitators/assistants work with their assigned students, individually or as a group, with their assigned students in specific problem areas (grammar, usage, basic organization) as determined by past work. They meet frequently with the teacher to make plans and address concerns.

b. Set up several stations around the room with a different (but coordinated) activity at each station. The teacher and the facilitators/assistants are each assigned to a station. The students rotate from station to station when time is called.

c. Have most of the students work independently while small groups of students are called out to a station for related instruction based on a perceived need or interest (e.g., a grammar/usage problem, special instruction on some aspect of academic content or skill area). Facilitators/assistants are each assigned to a station for which they have been prepared beforehand. Try to have a variety of purposes for station call-outs so that all students are called out at some time or another.

d. After you give instruction followed by an activity, ask facilitators/assistants to walk around the room with you to give assistance to individual students as needed.

These are just a few ideas for working with large and/or mixed-level classes. Many of the activities presented throughout Part II of this book can be adapted for use with such classes. Grouping suggestions on pp. 218, 294–295, 316, and 342 can be utilized to great advantage in many cases along with the writing workshop description found on pp. 325–332.

SUMMARY

Developing a methodology for both second and foreign language classrooms involves the synthesis of emerging theory and practice into a program that works. Developing such a program often means drawing from several methods, strategies, and activities in order to create an integrated curriculum that will meet the needs of the students and the situation. Motivational goals, the particular concepts being taught, learning and teaching preferences, cultural factors, and age and competency levels of the students are all important considerations.

For beginners and low-intermediate students in particular, lessons need to be structured in such a way that students will receive optimal exposure to important concepts. The lessons should be well organized and contain familiar routines in order to serve adequately as vehicles for new information. Content needs to be modified to be appropriate for various age and proficiency levels. For intermediate and advanced students, theme cycles or other investigative procedures that require greater proficiency in the target language may offer the most challenges for both students and their teachers in emergent participatory classrooms.

Focusing the instruction on content appears to be cognitively sound for most programs, particularly when relevant tasks and proficiencies are allowed to grow out of the content chosen. The resulting proficiencies can be tied into important standards that may have been infused into the program.

Peer facilitators and other assistants can be prepared to help the teacher provide sufficient opportunities for interaction and participation, social interaction in and out of school, self-image enhancement, encouragement, and motivation. At the same time, they can serve as linguistic models to help prevent premature stabilization. In addition, the peer facilitators and other assistants can help make it possible for students to move from undemanding to more cognitively demanding tasks and to integrate the four skill areas as they flow with the students' needs and interests.

Versions of cooperative learning also can serve as effective classroom management tools, particularly in intermediate to advanced second language classes or mainstream content-area classes in which second language students are included. When the conditions are favorable, students can make substantial strides in communicative and academic competence through cooperative efforts.

QUESTIONS AND PROJECTS FOR REFLECTION AND DISCUSSION

1. Plan a workshop for a small group of peer facilitators and other assistants. What important preparation will you want them to have?

2. Can you think of a few units for which you might want to incorporate some version of cooperative learning? Briefly describe how these units might be organized.

3. Teachers have described themselves as "challengers or agents of change," "nurturers," "cooperative leaders," "innovators," "providers of tools," and "artists," among other things (see de Guerrero & Villamil, 2000). How do you see your own role(s) as a teacher? In what ways and under what circumstances do you think your role(s) might change?

4. Develop a flexible theme-based unit (a series of several lessons centered around a theme) for a language classroom situation at a beginning or

intermediate level.[11] After considering what you think your students' objectives might be and what standards they will try to reach, decide some of the major concepts you will teach and reinforce throughout and the skills you will help them develop. Describe the unit in writing. Include a brief description of the lessons and what activity or activities will be included in each. Develop fully one of the lessons. Utilize the Structure for Simulated Lessons on pp. 256–257 and the Sample Lesson Preparation Format on pp. 367–369.

Present your lesson to a group of fellow students or peers. Make sure you first describe your unit briefly and state clearly how this lesson fits into the other lessons within your unit. After your presentation, discuss with your class the strengths of your presentation and ways in which you might improve it. Begin by sharing your own reactions to your presentation. You may want to use the Questions to Guide Evaluative Discussion (p. 257) as the basis for your analysis, or you may use an evaluation format that you or your instructor have developed (see footnote 12 on p. 258).

If you are currently teaching, use what you have learned to try out a similar lesson with your students. Make sure the activity is relevant and appropriate to their level. If possible, have your lesson videotaped to analyze and discuss with peers. Reflect on its outcome and how you felt about doing it. Pay close attention to student response. Do you see any problems with your lesson? How might it be improved?

5. ✎ **Journal Entry:** Reflect on the lesson(s) you carried out in item 4 above. What strategies did you use? How comfortable did you feel with them? Did you think they were effective overall? Why or why not? What were some of the specific problems you encountered? How can they be overcome? Write about what you learned from your peers and instructor during the process. What insights did you gain about learning and teaching from the experience?

SUGGESTED READINGS AND REFERENCE MATERIALS

Brinton, D., Wesche, M., & Snow, M. A. (2003). *Content-based second language instruction: Michigan Classics Edition.* Ann Arbor: University of Michigan Press. Here the authors explore the developments that have taken place in content-based language teaching since the first version of this book appeared in 1989. They also look at the research supporting content-based language teaching in its many contexts at the university level. Program models are described in depth and guidelines are given to those planning to develop content-based language programs.

---

[11]Situations might be one of the following: an elementary, secondary, or university second or foreign language program; an adult basic education program; or a language program for special purposes such as preparing students for specific technical occupations.

Crandall, J. (1999). Cooperative language learning and affective factors. In J. Arnold (Ed.), *Affect and language learning* (pp. 226–245). Cambridge, England: Cambridge University Press. Crandall presents a very clear analysis of cooperative language learning and how it relates to affect. She describes many of its applications (along with potential problems) and gives a convincing rationale for its use.

Ellis, R. (2003). *Task-based language learning and teaching.* Oxford, England: Oxford University Press. In this highly readable book, Ellis includes research and practice in the area of tasks as they relate to listening comprehension, interaction, production, assessment, evaluation, and other issues in second language acquisition. His analysis is as objective as it is comprehensive.

Gebhard, J., & Oprandy, R. (1999). *Language teaching awareness: A guide to exploring beliefs and practices*. Cambridge, England: Cambridge University Press. This book offers assistance to teachers wanting to better their teaching through the process of discovery. It includes very practical guidelines to use while observing, keeping a journal, collecting other kinds of data, working with supervisors, and so forth.

Kaufman, D., & Crandall, J. (2005). *Content-based instruction in primary and secondary school settings*. Alexandria, VA: Teachers of English to Speakers of Other Languages. This very practical book offers elementary and secondary teachers numerous innovative ideas for improving the learning of both language and content simultaneously.

McGroarty, M., & Calderón, M. (2005). Cooperative learning for second language learners: Models, applications, and challenges. In P. Richard-Amato & M. A. Snow (Eds.), *Academic success for English language learners: Strategies for K–12 mainstream teachers* (pp. 174–194). White Plains, NY: Longman/Pearson Education. Here the authors discuss the conditions for the use of cooperative learning in second language learning settings. They talk about the various models and their foci on the psychosocial and affective aspects of the classroom and on cognition. Included also are the findings of current research on the benefits of cooperative learning in elementary and middle school contexts in the United States and abroad.

McKay, P. (Ed.). (2006). *Planning and teaching creatively within a required curriculum for school-age learners.* Alexandria, VA: Teachers of English to Speakers of Other Languages. Teaching within the constraints of a required curriculum does not necessarily mean that teachers need to sacrifice their creativity. Through collaboration with students and with others in the school environment, they can still provide enriching experiences for young learners and delve into issues that challenge them.

Underhill, A. (1999). Facilitation in language teaching. In J. Arnold (Ed.), *Affect and language learning* (pp. 125–141). Cambridge, England: Cambridge University Press. Here Adrian Underhill defines three different kinds of teacher: the Lecturer (one who has knowledge of the topic but pays little attention to teaching techniques and methodology); the Teacher (one who has both knowledge of the topic and is skilled in a range of methods and procedures for teaching it); and the Facilitator (one who has both knowledge and skills but also has insight into the students and seeks to enable them to be responsible for their own learning). He provides insight into each of the three roles teachers most often assume in the classroom.

CHAPTER 16

Tools for Teaching Languages: Textbooks, Computer Programs, and Videos

...part of the task of selection, then, becomes the selection of segments of real world knowledge and experience.

R. Crymes, 1979

QUESTIONS TO THINK ABOUT

1. Think about textbooks you used when you were trying to learn another language. On what did they appear to focus (grammar, functions, meaning)? To what extent were they effective in furthering your own language development?

2. To what extent have you used computers in a classroom either as a student or as a teacher? Describe the situation. How well did they work? What kinds of programs would you want to have available for your language students? Why?

3. Do you think videos might have a place in the second or foreign language classroom? If so, what kinds of videos would you use? How would you use them?

Many of the materials suggested up to this point—television programs on video, newspapers and periodicals, stories and other pieces of literature, catalogs, magazines, games, reference books, lyrics to popular songs, maps, pictures, photographs, and others—are not specifically intended for use in language teaching. However, commercial products especially designed for second language, foreign language, or bilingual teaching can be invaluable if they are chosen carefully. Such materials can provide challenging content, aid organization, give guidance when needed, complement and/or constitute lessons, and introduce and reinforce concepts. Moreover, they can serve as important resources in emergent participatory classrooms and allow for self-access learning.

The purpose of this chapter is not so much to advocate specific student textbooks, computer programs, or videos but rather to provide guidelines for evaluating and selecting these important teaching tools.

TEXTBOOKS

Some teachers and many publishers long for the days when one set of materials (complete with student texts, workbooks, teacher manuals, and audio/visual components) was considered the answer to language teaching needs. Today most of us realize that much more is needed to build a program. Perhaps with the shift in emphasis to interactive/participatory practices and academic content, publishers feel even greater pressure to provide materials that are communicative and logically motivated and that lead students to further inquiry. This is as true of large programs with multiple levels as it is of supplemental programs or materials that teachers themselves have developed. Moreover, many educators are already insisting that materials require teachers and students to be more active and creative and that they focus on relevant, meaningful content. Some teachers are even turning entrepreneur and publishing their own materials in an attempt to fill the gap.

A problem with many texts is that they are often written as though the readers already speak the target language and know the culture (see Cleghorn & Rollnick, 2002). In addition, the proficiency level for which the materials are written are often uneven and inconsistent. For example, directions may be written for high proficiency levels whereas the lesson content itself may be at a much lower level—the level for which the book was intended. In addition, the text materials are often bland and basically formS-focused (see Chapter 2), although communicative activities may be added for practice (Tomlinson, 2001).

We need to ask ourselves: What kind of textbook content most effectively promotes language learning? In answer to this question, Oller (1983a) offered the episode hypothesis.

The Episode Hypothesis

This hypothesis states that "*text (i.e., discourse in any form) will be easier to reproduce, understand, and recall, to the extent that it is motivated and structured episodically*" (1983a, p. 12, italics added). Episodic organization requires both motivation created by conflict and the kind of logical sequencing necessary to good storytelling. It needs to be consistent with experience.

As mentioned in Chapter 13, Schank and Abelson (1977) related episodic structure to memory itself. They argued that humans both acquire and store information in episodic form. Oller (1979) agreed and went one step further by applying this theory to the classroom:

> Language programs that employ fully contextualized and maximally meaningful language necessarily optimize the learner's ability to use previously acquired expectancies to help discover the pragmatic mappings of utterances in the new language into extralinguistic contexts. Hence they would seem to be superior to programs that expect learners to acquire the ability to use a language on the basis of disconnected lists of sentences. (pp. 31–32)

Many traditional second and foreign language texts written over the years contain disconnected lists of sentences or, at best, sentences that are related but not part of any motivated or logical discourse.

Consider the following example, consisting of a group of items related only in that each illustrates the same grammatical form.

EXAMPLE 1

1. *We're having* a grammar test today.
2. Bob *is having* a party tomorrow.
3. The Smiths *are having* a good time in Paris.
4. My sister *is having* a baby in June.

(Pollock, 1982, p. 7)

Now read the next typical passage, in which the dialogue is temporally structured but lacks sufficient motivation or conflict as well as logical sequencing.

EXAMPLE 2

Tomás is visiting Ralph and Lucy.

Ralph: How long can you stay, Tomás?

Tomás: I'm going to leave tomorrow afternoon. I'm taking the bus.

Lucy: I like taking the bus, but Ralph doesn't.

Ralph: What do you want to do tomorrow, Tomás? Do you want to sleep late?

Tomás: No, I like to get up early. Let's go to the park. Do you like playing tennis?

Ralph: I don't like to play, but Lucy likes tennis. She plays every day.

Lucy: Ralph likes jogging. Let's go to the park early tomorrow morning. Tomás and I can play tennis, and you can go jogging, Ralph.

(Sutherland, 1981, p. 11)

To reinforce the importance of episodically meaningful text, look at the following questions keyed to these two examples.

QUESTIONS FOR EXAMPLE 1

1. Who is having a good time in Paris?
2. Who is having a party tomorrow?

Can you answer these questions without referring back to the text? Why not? Probably because Bob and the Smiths are not important to us; they do not connect meaningfully to our experience, nor do they connect in any meaningful way to each other.

QUESTIONS FOR EXAMPLE 2

1. Who is visiting?
2. What does the visitor plan to do?
3. Who likes to ride on buses?
4. What does Lucy like to do?
5. Who likes jogging?

Although the sentences to which they refer are temporally related and perhaps slightly motivated, these questions are almost as difficult to answer as those for Example 1. Why? They are not logical according to our experience. Their only reason for existence seems to be to expose the student to the present progressive tense and gerunds and to teach the comparative structure: "I like taking the bus, but Ralph doesn't," or "I don't like to play, but Lucy likes tennis." People in normal conversation do not speak like this because in natural discourse we are not concerned with exposing others to specific grammatical forms.

In addition, the conversation in Example 2 does not flow logically. When Tomás says, "I'm going to leave tomorrow afternoon. I'm taking the bus," we might expect Lucy or Ralph to respond with, "Oh, you're leaving so soon!" or something similar. Instead, Lucy says, "I like taking the bus, but Ralph doesn't." Our sense of expectancy is violated. Grice (1975) related this sense of expectancy to the maxim of relation that is essential in normal discourse.

Compare the first two examples with Example 3.

EXAMPLE 3

Darlene: I think I'll call Bettina's mother. It's almost five and Chrissy isn't home yet.
  Meg: I thought Bettina had the chicken pox.
Darlene: Oh, that's right. I forgot. Chrissy didn't go to Bettina's today. Where is she?
  Meg: She's probably with Gary. He has Little League practice until five.
Darlene: I hear the front door. Maybe that's Gary and Chrissy.
  Gary: Hi.
Darlene: Where's Chrissy? Isn't she with you?
  Gary: With me? Why with me? I saw her at two after school, but then I went to Little League practice. I think she left with her friend.

Darlene: Which one?

   Gary: The one next door . . . the one she walks to school with every day.

Darlene: Oh, you mean Timmy. She's probably with him.

   Gary: Yeah, she probably is.

Darlene: I'm going next door to check.

(Brinton & Neuman, 1982, p. 33)

Without looking back at Example 3, see if you answer the questions.

QUESTIONS FOR EXAMPLE 3

1. Who has disappeared?
2. When was she last seen?
3. Where are they going to look for her?
4. How do the characters feel about her disappearance?

Did you feel the need to check back for the answer to each question? Probably not. Why? Because the structure of the discourse is consistent with our own experience, and the dialogue is motivated and logical. As a result, we automatically become involved with the language at a subconscious as well as conscious level; we experience a heightened awareness. We are concerned about the little girl's disappearance, just as the people in the story are.

In spite of what we have learned about language learning and teaching over the past thirty years or more, many of today's textbooks still contain the same kinds of content one finds in examples 1 and 2. It is difficult to understand why so many publishers—and some teachers—still cling to the notion that content such as this promotes language learning in classrooms.

Although the episode hypothesis is universal in that it is based on the logic of experience, that experience reflects the culture of which it is a part. The frames of experience in a particular text may be unfamiliar; certain dialogues simply may not occur in some cultures. For example, a discourse in which someone decides on a nursing home for an elderly parent may confuse or offend students from cultures in which extended families are the norm. Prereading activities can be very useful in preparing students for the cultural schemata to which they will be exposed (see also Chapters 5 and 13). However, when English is being taught as a foreign language, choosing a text that relies on the source culture (the culture where English is being taught) is important because it reinforces a culture that is both acceptable and familiar to the learner. An alternative might be to select a text that reflects many cultures in this context.

Selection Guidelines

Of course, the episode hypothesis may not appear to be directly applicable to textbooks that are expository in nature and focus on academic content, nor will it seem applicable to supplemental textbooks that emphasize grammar, vocabulary development, listening, reading, and writing. However, the more the textbooks involve aspects of storymaking itself such as conflict, dialogue, characters, and so on in their examples and supporting materials, the easier it will be for the students to internalize their content, according to the episode hypothesis.

When you select textbooks, supplemental or otherwise, you may want to ask yourself several important questions using the following list as a guide. Not all of these questions will be appropriate in every situation; you will need to choose those questions that you find most relevant.

Purpose and Motivation

- What underlying assumptions about language and language learning are reflected in the materials? Do you agree with these assumptions?
- Are the topics and themes covered in the materials inviting? Do you think they will interest your students?
- Do the materials encourage students to reflect on their own learning strategies and to develop new ones?
- Do the materials encourage students to inquire further about the issues covered? Do they encourage student participation in learning? Do they encourage students to become active thinkers and independent learners?
- Do the activities encourage use of creative language and negotiated meaning in a variety of situations? Do they seem to have a good chance of actually resulting in improved language use?
- If there are characters and they are second or foreign language learners, are they presented positively? Are their values respected? Are they given positive roles within the material? Do the materials promote positive attitudes toward all cultures, including the target language culture? Will the activities enhance self-concepts among your students and boost confidence?

Appropriateness

- Are the materials appropriate to the language needs, goals, interests, and expectations of your students? Look not only at content but at the illustrations, range and format of activities, language level, and so on.
- Does the level of the material rise appropriately over the course of the text? Does the content become gradually more complex and academically challenging?
- If the material is part of a series, does the book dovetail nicely with those that precede and follow? Is there a clearly defined approach and "voice" that runs through all the books?
- Do activities above the beginning level call for critical thinking, or do they probe mainly for factual information and detail?

Format

- Are the materials attractive and inviting? Is there ample white space for students to write (if they are to own the books)? Are the illustrations pedagogically effective or simply decorative?

- Are skill areas largely integrated, or are they approached as disconnected separate entities? (See Chapter 5.)
- Do the activities represent a wide range of varied tasks?
- Are concepts recycled several times, from unit to unit, or are they introduced and then forgotten?
- Are directions clearly written, at a level your students will understand? Often directions are written at a much higher level than the content of the activity itself.
- Do prereading activities adequately prepare and motivate students, calling on prior knowledge, without being too long or tedious?

Authenticity

- Are students encouraged to relate the content of the material to their own lives? Are they encouraged to draw on prior knowledge?
- Do the conversations and activities seem motivated and logical according to real experience? Is the grammar natural, or has it obviously been selected to illustrate a grammar point?
- Do you think your students will consider the reading selections authentic? If the materials have been adapted from the original source, is the adaptation effective and real?

Teacher Resources

- Are the teacher resource materials clearly written and pedagogically useful? Do they contain helpful teaching suggestions? Are a range of teaching options provided?
- Do the teacher materials include ways to evaluate student progress? Are these tied coherently to the student materials? Are self-evaluation tools available for the students in the student materials?

Keep in mind also that textbook titles are sometimes misleading. Titles that imply a cast of characters, and contain the words *interactive* or *communicative*, do not always identify truly interactive/communicative materials. Often these books are grammar-, competency-, or function-based texts disguised to look communicative. It pays to check the content carefully before ordering them for student use.

COMPUTER PROGRAMS

Computers have brought about great changes in the way people communicate and learn, not only in western cultures but in many countries around the world (see Hanson-Smith & Riling, 2006). In addition to assisting and facilitating the language learning process and exposing students to intercultural communication, they have created a language of their own. This language includes mixtures of languages, symbols in the form of icons and graphic displays, and sounds (speech, music, and so on).

One important question is: To what extent is computer use beneficial to language learners? Zhao (2003) argued that few conclusions can be reached in answering this question. So much depends on how the technology is used in addition to the fact that there are many other variables related to who the learners are and the environment in which the technology is used (see also Chapelle, 2001). Each use of the computer needs to be evaluated on its own merits and possibilities in relation to each student.

Traditionally software used in computer-assisted language learning (CALL) programs has been of the "drill-and-test" type—the computer plays "teacher" and imparts information; the students apply the information and then are tested. Those who give wrong answers on the test are cycled back for further instruction and practice. Some programs allow teachers to use an authoring system to set up similar lessons by using already established content, or by selecting items from a series of possible choices, or by creating new content for the program. Authoring programs are available that do not require the teacher to know advanced techniques or complex computer language. In addition, some Web sites (e.g., Blackboard) allow teachers to display notes, exercises, and tests that students can access (Lismore, 2007).

Drill-and-test discrete point materials are still plentiful and can be appropriate in the right situations. Hoffman (1995/1996) reminded us early on that such programs can be beneficial to the curriculum, if used appropriately. She argued that computers can effectively reinforce structural knowledge of a language and recommended that students be given an index of such programs, arranged from easy to difficult. Students can then choose programs in the areas in which each needs work, eliminating those in areas already mastered. Self-study activity can probably best be accomplished in a laboratory where students can work at their own pace.

Although it may be used effectively for individual study, discrete-point software can often lead to boring repetition and reduced motivation. It is important generally to use classroom computer programs that have a highly integrative rather than a discrete-point focus (McLoughlin & Oliver, 2005). Using computers as communicative tools not only teaches computer language and skills but also helps students reach other language, academic, and sociocultural objectives.

Many excellent communicative programs are available today that are constructivist in nature. These include

- simulation programs in which students can take fantasy trips and choose from among many options: where to go, what to eat, and so forth
- interfacing programs in which students can hear prerecorded messages and interact with the computer by pressing particular keys or touching certain areas of the screen
- expository writing programs in which students are asked questions to clarify their thinking about compositions that are in the planning stages
- creative writing programs in which students can create and illustrate stories with graphics or create poems, sometimes with line-by-line assistance for special patterns (rhymes, limericks, haiku, and so on)

- problem-solving programs in which students are immersed in a wide variety of problem-solving strategies, some of which even have features that allow the student to "teach the computer" to complete a task

Computer Games

Although not usually meant for language teaching per se, computer games can provide language learners with challenges in the target language. They can present simulations that call for students to make decisions, and they can require interaction with others involved in the game. Computer games are currently available in many content areas. For example, one such program introduces children to concepts involved with graph plotting; students are asked to plot their own designs. Another program takes younger learners on a simulated safari journey through a grid-like environment where they decipher clues in order to find the hiding place of a "mystery" animal. In the process, they get practice in making inferences, creating tactics, and collecting and organizing clues.

Other computer games can be useful in language learning (primarily for older learners). These include chess, word games, memory games, teasers with missing numbers, and many more.

When choosing a software program, Bishop (2001) suggested that we consider the following:

- educational soundness
- ease of use by students and teachers
- age appropriateness
- cultural sensitivity
- visual appeal
- cost effectiveness

Teachers may find a checklist like the one in Figure 16.1 on pp. 400–401 helpful in evaluating software programs.

Canale and Barker (1986) suggested that computers could make available integrative programs that serve many of the same purposes for which language itself is used (see also Levy & Stockwell, 2006; McLoughlin & Oliver, 2005). Such programs could be used as tools for thought (self-directed language), tools for social interaction (other-directed language), and tools for play and artistic endeavors in which the emphasis is on self-expression. Canale and Barker were convinced that the activities should be intrinsically motivating, provide for independence on the part of the language student, and involve problem solving in many different situations. Testing by computer, programs for analyzing pronunciation, and more interactive uses of the computer such as video conferencing and telecollaborative projects are among the many possibilities for computer use. Many of these uses involve multimedia.

Today we have sophisticated multimedia programs utilizing computers, printers, CDs, DVDs, players, monitors, scanners, digital cameras, and other electronic devices, some of which have recording capabilities. Amanti (2001) suggested, among other

---

SOFTWARE PROGRAM EVALUATION

Title of the program: _____

Publisher: _____

Name of reviewer: _____

Date reviewed: _____

Languages in which the program is available: _____
_____

1. **Use**

    How easy is the program to install? ❏ Very easy ❏ Easy ❏ Confusing or complicated ❏ Very difficult

    How easy is the program to operate and navigate? ❏ Very easy ❏ Easy ❏ Confusing or complicated ❏ Very difficult

    Comments:

2. **Appropriateness**

    For what audience is this program intended? ❏ ESL ❏ EFL ❏ Bilingual ❏ Sheltered ❏ Other, specify _____

    For what ages or grade levels is the program designed? ❏ Primary ❏ Secondary ❏ Adult

    Is the program appropriate for that age group or grade level? ❏ Very appropriate ❏ Acceptable ❏ Inappropriate

    Comments:

    For what approximate proficiency level is the program designed? ❏ Beginner ❏ Intermediate ❏ Advanced

    Is the program appropriate for that proficiency level? ❏ Yes ❏ No

    Comments:

    What kind of use is the program most appropriate for? ❏ Classroom use ❏ Self-study at home or in a lab ❏ Other, specify _____

    Comments:

3. **Cultural sensitivity**

    If the program includes characters, was the author careful not to stereotype them by ethnicity, race, country, or origin? ❏ Yes ❏ No

    Are any characters second language speakers? If so, are they given mainly positive traits? ❏ Yes ❏ No

    Is the language employed in the program sensitive to diverse ethnicities, races, and countries of origin? ❏ Yes ❏ No

    Comments:

(Continued)

Figure 16.1 Software Program Evaluation

---

4. **Visual appeal**

   The design of this program is: ❏ Very appealing ❏ Somewhat appealing ❏ Unattractive ❏ Very unattractive

   Comments:

5. **Cost-effectiveness**

   Price of program: _____

   How often might I use this program in my classroom? ❏ Daily ❏ Weekly ❏ Once or twice during the course ❏ Other, specify _____

   Comments:

6. **Educational soundness**

   What instructional options does the program provide? ❏ Individual work ❏ Group work ❏ Pair work ❏ Other, specify _____

   Description of the program:

   What are the program's stated objectives?

   Does the program, in your opinion, fulfill its objectives? ❏ Yes ❏ No

   Comments:

7. **Recommendation**

   Overall evaluative comments:

   What do you recommend? ❏ Purchase ❏ Don't purchase ❏ Other, specify _____

Figure 16.1 Software Program Evaluation (*Continued*)

things, that students use multimedia tools to author original programs. She offered one idea in which students of various proficiency levels collaborate to make a multimedia presentation of a field trip, including photos that can be scanned into a computer file and for which captions can be written, retelling the event. Students can then narrate a slide show presentation by reading the text on each slide, using a computer microphone. Amanti suggested that activities such as these give even shy students a chance to produce the language in a nonthreatening environment. Text and graphics (e.g., tables, charts, graphs, animation) can be used with sound to create programs of many kinds. However, Amanti emphasized the need for setting up guidelines, evaluation criteria, and organizational plans before students embark on projects of this nature.

Involving students in special media projects can be effective, but Kessler and Plankans (2001) recommended going a step further by having students actually *create* instructional materials. They argued that learners understand what is helpful to them in the learning process and what is not. Because the learners are stakeholders, individuals with different learning styles, often computer-literate already, and affected by the environment in which they will be using computers, they should be part of the program development process whenever possible.

Whether or not teachers and their students actually create instructional programs, one should be mindful of the kinds of programs on the market that can serve as practical tools for student learning. Some of the best programs available today involve word processors and the Internet.

Word Processors

Using a word-processing program can be frustrating, exhilarating, and almost always challenging to the language learner. The language used is fully contextualized and can be very creative. Perhaps the best time for students to begin is at late beginner/early intermediate levels after they have acquired a repertoire (however limited) of language structures and vocabulary. Children, too, provided they can handle the experience cognitively, are able to work in word-processing programs, especially if the programs are designed with them in mind. Some programs use extra-large characters on the screen, and the menu choices are pictorial for ease of understanding.

Students seem to learn best when they are eased into word processing gradually, with the help of the teacher, peer facilitators, other assistants, or other learners. For a student who has never been introduced to a computer before, one way to begin is to type something about the student that he or she can comprehend with the keyboard, perhaps using the student's name. The student can then respond verbally while the teacher or aide types the words as they are said. The student can eventually proceed from the comprehending and writing of very short messages to understanding and producing fully developed text. Commands can be learned gradually, as they are needed. A good example is provided by Schneider (1997). In her class for intermediate-level English learning adults at San Francisco City College, she first has her students copy a paragraph or two into the computer. Then she has them change the tense from present to past. In a computer lab, her students learned to cut, copy, paste, rewrite passages, and make requested changes. Later, they learned to select and use the find and replace commands. For example, students may have changed the name "Sylvia" to the name "Nasim" or another male name. Of course, this change necessitated other changes, which the students were able to recognize if they had already worked on agreement of forms. Being able to delete material, move whole passages to other parts of a document, select and change formats, write and send messages, and perform numerous other functions does much to facilitate the writing process. Interestingly, Li and Cumming (2001) were among the researchers who found that second language writers tend to revise more when using a word processor than when writing with pen and paper. The researchers found, in addition, that second language writers also tend to plan their composition as they write using the word processor rather than plan it beforehand.

Some programs are specifically designed to guide the writer through the preliminary phases of writing. For example, a few programs ask a series of questions to aid users in targeting the purpose for a specific composition. Be careful, though, of programs that give general reactions such as "How interesting!" or "Nice job!" regardless of what the student has actually written. Also be wary of programs that accuse students of such offenses as being "wordy" if the sentences are too long. Some of these programs may focus students on mechanics at the expense of meaning, or may make students overly concerned with sentence length as opposed to clarity.

In most programs, students can store ideas and draw on them as they write, often from a "window" opened on the screen where they are creating new text.

The Internet

For many students, the World Wide Web can be an exciting resource for research and information gathering and a helpful source of valuable information that may not be available on the shelves of their libraries. To other students, it can be a confusing maze of information so unreliable that it cannot be trusted. In reality, the Web can be both of these things, but when good research strategies are applied, the Web can be very helpful, especially when used in conjunction with other resources.

Software programs known as browsers provide access to search engines that, in turn, help identify appropriate sites on the Web and aid users in navigating a complex network of hypertext[1] documents or sites. The user types a topic, keyword, or phrase into a search box and the search engine hunts for related sites—often generating thousands of sites, some of which have little to do with the subject. The more specific the keywords, the more focused the results. Sometimes a broad search (like a stroll through library stacks) can produce unexpected treasures. It may be best to begin with a fairly broad search to see what is available and then narrow it down to something manageable. Stress to your students the importance of evaluating what they find on the Web. Who wrote the information? How credible is the author? How current is the information? Is it fact or opinion? Is it relevant to the topic being researched? Does the information include full citations that can be verified? Are the author's sources reliable? Does the source give you the information you need to link to other relevant sites? Government sources (.gov) and education sources (.edu) can generally be trusted to provide reliable information; commercial sites (.com), may require closer scrutiny. Cultural factors come into play here as well. Whose cultural view is the most influential on specific Web sites? How biased is the information provided there? What language is used? The answers to these questions will often determine whether the viewers comprehend the information included on the Web site and the extent to which it will be considered credible.

Materials found on the Web should be given proper credit if referred to, paraphrased, or quoted in the user's own work. As with using information from any other source, quotes should be placed around exact words taken and page numbers should be included in the citations where possible. Long passages and graphics require

---

[1] *Hyper-* means "beyond" or "above." Hypertext allows users to create text that is beyond traditional text in that it can provide nonlinear links to other texts and visual and sound media. It combines a set of links and can subordinate one link to another.

permission unless the user is an educator and is using the materials for instructional purposes only. Should that be the case, then properly crediting the source may be all that is necessary under fair use guidelines. Egbert (2005) suggested that educators consider using materials clearly labeled "copyright-free" to be absolutely safe, or secure written permission from the copyright owner.

Plagiarism occurs when a person tries to pass off someone's else's work as his or her own or paraphrases the words too closely without using quotes or setting the words off as a quote, even though indirect credit may be given. According to Flowerdew and Li (2007), plagiarism operates at different levels:

> On one level there are the so-called paper mills, online services that provide academic term papers for a fee. On another level there is . . . textual plagiarism, or the copying of sections of one text in the composition of another. To combat these practices, at both levels, an increasing number of plagiarism detection software applications are being developed and put into use. Ironically, however, in some cases, the same companies are both operating paper mills and offering antiplagiarism services. (p. 161)

Plagiarism is frowned upon and, in some countries and cases, considered unlawful. Cultural misunderstandings about it often occur which should be handled as tactfully as possible, particularly when second language learners are involved.

Using the Internet for Class Work and Personal Communication

Even if the classroom has only one computer, that computer can be utilized to great advantage. Of course, it helps to also have a computer lab,[2] even if it has to be shared with the rest of the school. Taking turns and flexible grouping can give all students some time at the computer and encourage them to interact, learn from one another, and coordinate projects. The Internet can give students immediate access to encyclopedias, e-books, e-journals, data bases for research, and many other useful resources. Web-based iCALL (intelligent CALL) programs can also be accessed and are now capable of at least a limited amount of interaction and feedback. In addition, parser-based CALL programs that are designed to evaluate natural language including syntactic and even semantic student input are now available (Blake, 2007). Of course, such programs still have their imperfections and produce a number of false responses at present, according to Blake.

The Internet can provide highly motivating activities to aid class work and collaboration and further communication skills through *computer-mediated communication* (CMC). CMC encourages students to use language for authentic communicative

---

[2] Ware (2005) has several ideas for interaction in the computer lab. They involve side-by-side social interaction during which the students communicate with each other in writing (often less threatening than oral interaction) and the students collaborate on group projects and teach each other informally, often appropriating instructional language they have heard their teacher or peers use. Thus, the students are able to learn from each other and expand their repertoire of computer-related language.

purposes. Some examples include creating a classroom Web site and using e-mail and word processing to provide practice and increase confidence in the ability to communicate. Setting up a classroom Web site is a relatively simple task, and many software programs are available to help with this process. Such a Web site can provide learning resources for students, links to other sources, and opportunities for students to get to know one another. Content might include writing guidelines and tips, sample compositions representing various genres, a dictionary designed for students in bilingual or other language programs, topic ideas for compositions, and anything else the students might find useful. A classroom Web site might also include more personal information—biographies that students create or information in students' first languages about their home cultures.

Leslie Jo Adams has used e-mail projects with her high-intermediate English learners to improve their writing skills. Each student acquires an e-mail address from an Internet service provider. The students and the teacher exchange initial personal information, and then students are assigned writing topics such as "All About Me," "My School," "My Favorite Holiday," and "My Goals for the Future"—topics that will help them feel more confident writing about themselves. Once they are ready, she connects them with students from other classes and often with English learners from other states or countries.[3]

E-mail exchanges can allow students within the same class to extend discussions beyond the classroom. Classroom assignments involving problem-solving activities, writing assignments, information gathering, and so on can be done in collaboration with partners through e-mail. Students tend to feel very comfortable connecting with peers through e-mail, and such discussions are often lengthy and cover longer periods of time than those that occur in the classroom. Kamhi-Stein (2000c), while teaching a Teachers of English to Speakers of Other Languages (TESOL) methods course at California State University, Los Angeles, used a World Wide Web bulletin board on which her native and nonnative students could interact with each other about what they were learning and the possible applications of what they had learned.

Students can join national and international networking groups. One such group is called a listserv, which allows people to send out e-mails to everyone who has joined. Generally, a listserv includes people who have interests in common and gives its members access to all sorts of information. Through it, members can exchange ideas and air disagreements about relevant issues.

Perhaps one of the more imaginative types of CMC to date is a *MOO*[4] or a MOO-like system that can place the user in a kind of "global village" (Pennington, 2003). Pennington described it this way:

> MOO interactions have the special characteristic that users can assume one or more imaginary identities and keep their real identity hidden, thus encouraging playfulness

---

[3] She accesses a Web site that provides partner teachers from a variety of places here and abroad.

[4] MOO means multiuser domain—object oriented.

and experimentation. MOO interactions may therefore have some value in stimulating student writers to develop ideas and "freeing" them to experiment with different authorial voices and writing styles. (p. 298)

Many young second language writers and readers are attracted to what are called online fan communities (Thorne & Black, 2007). Fans of certain books, television shows, movies, comics, and video games borrow characters, plots, settings, and so on from these sources and mix them all together to create "cross-over" fanfiction. They mix languages and other cultural items and even blend social registers. According to Thorne and Black, fanfiction allows learners to bond with each other as they assert their identities on line.

The Internet enables students to develop skills so they can operate in a variety of language communities such as chat rooms and sites featuring politics, local concerns, sports, and so on. *Wikis*, such as the online encyclopedia Wikipedia, are also available. They allow students to edit the content of the site itself.

Other Internet possibilities that encourage interaction, imagination, and organizational skills include

- podcasting[5] or setting up audio files or videos on the Internet which others can download to their own computers (Kessler, 2006)
- becoming a blogger[6] and developing a sense of authorship (Bloch & Crosby, 2006)
- developing Web sites on line that provide audio guides that take users on trips to various places such as the Metropolitan Museum of Art or the Museum of Modern Art (Ferris, 2006)

In addition, specially created WebTexts can be beneficial particularly to second language readers. They offer scaffolds for reading (McCloskey and Thrush, 2005), providing students with vocabulary items, knowledge about other cultures and about literature itself. WebTexts encourage students to seek supplementary information independently at the click of a mouse. Students can see pictures of well-known people or the various objects being written about. They can access the precise information they need in order to fully comprehend the text.

Concordancing

An extremely valuable classroom use of the Internet involves teachers and their students in *concordancing*. Together they can examine collections of authentic discourse data or *corpora* to discover how language is used in specific contexts (see p. 13). These electronic databases can be used to research collocational patterns (lexical items and the words that typically are used together) and formats that include turn-taking

---

[5] *Podcasting* allows students to listen to music or other kinds of programming using their computers or a mobile device. Programming can include news podcasts such as those produced by CNN, teacher-created podcasts intended for students or colleagues, or student-created podcasts (see especially Costa, 2006).

[6] The term *blog* comes from *Web* + log.

and other features of social and academic discourse. Hypotheses can grow out of the data and can aid the language learning process once the teachers and students are able to test these hypotheses by exploring additional data. Such research can be challenging and fun for the students who eventually might be able to collect and test the data on their own once they are ready for such ventures. Starting out with a very small corpus and then moving to one that is a bit larger can help facilitate the process without overwhelming learners. By using corpus analysis, students can become familiar with a variety of registers and learn the vocabulary and structures typical of many fields of study.

Internet Sites for Teachers

Egbert (2005, pp. 155–156) found that by using a search engine to find several specific topics on the Web, the teacher may be led to many useful sites. Among the terms to search are: "lesson plan" + English as a second language (ESL); "software reviews" + ESL; language listserv; and "free ESL materials" + teachers. She also suggests three guidelines for using technology (2005, pp. 173–174), summarized as follows:

1. Do not use technology only because it is available. Make sure it is appropriate.
2. Technology is not an end in itself. Focus instead on whether or not the technology you are considering can help students reach language and content goals.
3. Learn from your students. Many of them are computer-savvy already.

Technology Standards

Teachers of English to Speakers of Other Languages (TESOL) published the *TESOL Technology Standards Framework* in 2008. The framework was intended for use in both ESL and EFL settings.[7] TESOL was very careful to point out that the goals and standards were intended to serve as a guide *only* and that their focus was not on technology itself, but rather on language teaching and learning. In addition to the goals and standards laid out, the framework included performance indicators and selected vignettes to illustrate the various uses of technology in context (see details in the publication). Although the framework included goals and standards for language learners as well as for the preparation of their teachers, only the goals and standards for language learners will be presented in Figure 16.2 on p. 408.

VIDEOS

Videos are another potentially valuable tool for language learning. Gersten and Tlustý (1998) explored whether video exchanges between peers (grades 8–12) learning EFL in different countries would have a positive effect on their students' performance and participation. Their study looked at a cultural video exchange project between volunteer students from Prague and their counterparts in Regensburg, Germany. Members of the two groups communicated through letters written in English and then met to

---

[7] The Technology Standards Project Team included Deborah Healey, Volker Hegelheimer, Phil Hubbard, Sophie Ioannou-Georgiou, Greg Kessler, and Paige Ware.

Technology Standards For Language Learners

Goal 1: Language learners demonstrate foundational knowledge and skills in technology for a multilingual world.

Standard 1: Language learners demonstrate basic operational skills in using various technology tools and internet browsers.

Standard 2: Language learners are able to use available input and output devices (e.g., keyboard, mouse, printer, headset, microphone, media player, electronic whiteboard).

Standard 3: Language learners exercise appropriate caution when using online sources and when engaging in electronic communication.

Standard 4: Language learners demonstrate basic competence as users of technology.

Goal 2: Language learners use technology in socially and culturally appropriate, legal, and ethical ways.

Standard 1: Language learners understand that communication conventions differ across cultures, communities, and contexts.

Standard 2: Language learners demonstrate respect for others in their use of private and public information.

Goal 3: Language learners effectively use and critically evaluate technology-based tools as aids in the development of their language learning competence as part of formal instruction and for further learning.

Standard 1: Language learners effectively use and evaluate available technology-based productivity tools.

Standard 2: Language learners appropriately use and evaluate available technology-based language skill-building tools.

Standard 3: Language learners appropriately use and evaluate available technology-based tools for communication and collaboration.

Standard 4: Language learners use and evaluate available technology-based research tools appropriately.

Standard 5: Language learners recognize the value of technology to support autonomy, life-long learning, creativity, metacognition, collaboration, personal pursuits, and productivity.

Figure 16.2 From *TESOL Technology Standards Framework* © 2008 by Teachers of English to Speakers of Other Languages, Inc. Used by permission.

exchange the videos each had made. The students did the research, wrote the scripts, made revisions, rehearsed and acted out various scenes, interviewed people, and produced and evaluated their videos. The Czech students focused their video on the city of Prague. They included information about the history of the city; its historical monuments; famous artists, politicians, musicians, and writers; architecture; and food. Shooting locations included a school, Saint Vitus Cathedral, the National Theatre, Prague Castle, and local restaurants. The video also featured excerpts from a well-known Czech play and interviews with a range of people including English-speaking tourists and the director of the National Theatre. Finally, the students performed historical reenactments and told stories.

Interviews with students afterwards revealed that they found the experience helpful in developing English proficiency and in using English to communicate in an international setting. The authors noted that the success they discovered seemed to be due to the students' motivation to communicate in English for authentic purposes, the pride they took in sharing aspects of their culture with a real audience, and their treatment of video as an effective tool for communication and self-evaluation. Such videos can be transferred to a computer with a video capture card and then clipped to a Web page to become part of a Web site by using a hypertext transfer protocol (HTTP).

Commercially produced videos can also be used in a variety of ways as the focus of classroom lessons. Lessons can be built around all kinds of available videos, including music videos, documentaries, sports highlights, television talk shows, commercials, soap operas, and situation comedies. In addition, they can allow students to experience various countries from around the world and explore global issues. Kip Cates (2007) stated, "Video provides an exciting way to have students travel the world, learn about its cultures, engage in global issues and practice language skills—all while seated in the classroom." Simple question-and-answer sessions, discussions, or writing assignments based on what students have seen can comprise the follow-up. Tracy Cramer (2008) developed a year-long, learner-centered unit for young adults learning English at Kansai Gaidai University in Osaka, Japan, based on the documentary series "Families of the World."[8] The child narrators in the thirty-minute videos take viewers on a journey through a typical day in the lives of two families (one urban and the other rural) in several countries around the world including Brazil, Canada, China, Egypt, France, India, Thailand, Ghana, and many more. The narrators talk about home, school, and community life; religious traditions; agriculture; and so forth. Students are asked to research the countries and share what they learn. They may research such topics as the form of government, politics, economics, history, language policy, the environment, and many other issues of global interest such as loss and preservation of traditions, roles of men and women, and so on. The teacher presents brief lectures on various topics and uses handouts, pictures, maps, music, and other realia to help the students understand and appreciate the various cultures. Students are involved in group discussions as well as activities to further their development of basic skills and vocabulary. Tracy calls the materials "a work in progress" and modifies them frequently using student feedback.

Interactive video, which combines the benefits of both video and computer, can also serve as an excellent tool for developing communicative skills in a language. Requirements for using interactive video include a DVD player and a computer with monitor and keyboard. The benefits of interactive video can be great. Chief among these is the ability to show real people in compelling scenarios that allow students to contribute input. For example, a video may show a mom and dad arguing about whether their teenage daughter should be allowed to take a weekend trip with several friends, including her boyfriend.

---

[8] For more information, go to the "Families of the World" Web site, from which study guides can be downloaded.

After we hear the parents' opinions, the characters turn to the camera and ask for help in resolving their dispute. Several pieces of advice flash on the monitor, and students are asked to read these and then press buttons representing their choices. After one character comments on the advice that has been given, the scenario continues. In some interactive videos, the continuation is based on student input. Finally, the video characters seek help from an "expert" who is part of the computer program. Similar current programs can be found by using a search engine to look for topics such as "interactive video for language teaching" or similar terms.

Interactive video can also be used to teach the listening skills necessary for academic success. For example, while watching a lecture on some topic of interest, students may be asked to press keys whenever they hear a main idea. At the end of the lecture, all the main ideas may appear on the monitor, and students are asked to type questions referring to these ideas. After each question is formed, the speaker on the video answers it. An inherent problem with this kind of program is, of course, that students may ask questions for which the speaker has no answers.

Interactive video dictionaries are also available. A student types a word; the computer provides a definition and checks for spelling. If it finds an error, it presents the student with the correct spelling. A speaker on the screen then pronounces the word and demonstrates its use in context. The word may also appear on the screen in a sample sentence.

Many publishers produce videos to accompany their classroom materials. These range from videos keyed directly to multilevel programs to videos licensed from network television. As with software, video materials should be evaluated before classroom use. Do they serve a useful pedagogical purpose for the intended audience?

Hollywood-type films recorded on DVDs can also be used in the classroom. Carefully selected films can form the center of lessons for language learners, providing experience with authentic listening and practice in speaking and writing.

Films based on classic literature can provide connections between the printed word and the screen. For example, Herman Melville's *Billy Budd*, Jane Austen's *Sense and Sensibility*, Pearl Buck's *The Good Earth*, William Golding's *Lord of the Flies*, Charles Dickens' *A Christmas Carol*, and E. M. Forster's *Room with a View* are a few from British and American literature that are available. Instructors teaching in other cultures may be able to find other films reflecting the culture of the learners. Sometimes the book may be available in a language translation and the film may be dubbed in that language.

Hess and Jasper (1995) described a particularly interesting approach of using scenes from *Great Expectations* to complement reading assignments from the novel. The process included these steps:

- Students viewed the film segments with the sound off.
- In small groups, they wrote what they thought was being said.
- Students were assigned a character and asked to write down that character's words as they watched the same scenes again, this time with

the sound on. The scenes were played repeatedly, so students could check for accuracy.
- Students regrouped and recreated the dialogue, using their transcriptions.
- Students approximated the dialogue without their transcriptions.
- Finally, students watched the scenes once more and then moved on to the next reading assignment.

Interspersed with reading, viewing, and recreating dialogue were discussions about cultural and personal issues, including the students' reactions to the film segments and how they might relate to their own lives. A culminating activity was to compare the book and the film after viewing the film in its entirety.

SUMMARY

The episode hypothesis argues that text that is motivated and structured episodically is more easily incorporated into the learner's linguistic repertoire than other kinds of text. Many language textbooks, however, are written mainly to teach specific grammar points, competencies, or structures and give little thought to what constitutes meaningful prose. This is not to say that grammar- or competency-based books should never be used. There is a place for such books, particularly as supplements. However, textbooks that consider emotions as well as intellect are perhaps more likely to help students acquire language than those that do not.

The selection and use of textbooks, computer programs, and videos are not tasks that should be treated lightly. In order for these tools to be maximally useful, their substance and the activities they promote should reflect the basic philosophy of the teacher and the goals of the students. If the students' main goals are to communicate effectively and learn subject matter in the target language, then tools should be chosen that are consistent with those objectives. This means that the materials should allow for active participation on the part of the learner, thus augmenting their agency.

QUESTIONS AND PROJECTS FOR REFLECTION AND DISCUSSION

1. Discuss how the following considerations might affect the teacher's choice of textbooks and other materials.
   a. culture in which the materials are to be used
   b. size of the class
   c. experience of the teacher in teaching the target language
   d. proficiency level of the teacher in the target language

   What other considerations should be taken into account?

2. How might you incorporate the types of materials/equipment listed below into the language curriculum? Several suggestions for using most of them have been mentioned throughout this book. You can probably think of many additional means for incorporation. Give specific examples.

   a. teacher-made materials
   b. student-made materials
   c. magazines and newspapers
   d. catalogs
   e. pictures and photographs
   f. television shows on video
   g. a computer laboratory shared with other classes, a single computer in the classroom, or a computer for every student in the classroom

3. With a small group of peers, set up important criteria for evaluating textbooks in terms of their episodic organization where applicable and other aspects you feel are important in making your decisions. You may want to draw criteria from the sample form and adapt suggestions presented earlier for software program evaluation.

Example:

	(Check one)		
	Yes or	**No**	**Comment**
Episodic Organization			
Are the characters believable?	_____	_____	
Is the dialogue logical?	_____	_____	
Is foreshadowing present?	_____	_____	
	_____	_____	
Other Important Aspects			
Are the materials appropriate to age level?	_____	_____	
Are the materials appropriate to proficiency level?	_____	_____	
Are key concepts recycled?	_____	_____	
	_____	_____	

You might want to refine the evaluation by using such categories as "usually," "sometimes," "never," and so on and/or giving numerical values to each.

Once you have completed your evaluation instrument, locate at least three to five language textbooks and/or supplementary materials. Analyze them using appropriate items from criteria you and your peers create. Which of these materials would you select for use in a hypothetical or real teaching situation (see footnote 11 on p. 389)? Justify your choices.

4. If you have access to computer software, select four programs for preview (they need not be specifically for language teaching). Which of the four would you select to use with your students? Justify your choices and explain how each might fit into your program, hypothetical or real.

5. ✎ **Journal Entry:** How might a knowledge of the episode hypothesis help you in selecting materials other than textbooks and in planning lessons that may involve computer or video use? Write about the possibilities.

SUGGESTED READINGS AND REFERENCE MATERIALS

Chapelle, C. (2005). Computer-assisted language learning. In E. Hinkel (Ed.), *Handbook of research in second language teaching and learning* (pp. 743–755). Mahwah, NJ: Lawrence Erlbaum. This article presents a comprehensive look at where CALL is today and the associated research. The author discusses some of the important issues involved as they relate to second language learning.

Chapelle, C., & Jamieson, J. (2008). *Tips for teaching with CALL: Practical approaches to computer-assisted language learning.* White Plains, NY: Pearson Education. Teachers who want a basic introduction to CALL will find this text very helpful. It includes ways to use the computer to teach literacy skills, grammar, vocabulary, and so on. The book comes with a CD-ROM that demonstrates various applications.

Egbert, J., & Hanson-Smith, E. (2007). *CALL environments: Research, practice, and critical issues* (2nd ed.). Alexandria, VA: Teachers of English Speakers of Other Languages. This book offers very practical advice and suggestions to language teachers and discusses the relevant issues and research associated with using CALL in diverse environments and with a wide variety of language learners. Each chapter ends with project ideas and questions concerning the issues.

Hanson-Smith, E., & Riling, S. (Eds.). (2006). *Learning languages through technology.* Alexandria, VA: Teachers of English Speakers of Other Languages. Authors from different parts of the world share different uses of technology and the important issues with which they are associated. Included are chapters by Vance Stevens (United Arab Emirates) on teacher communities of practice, Reppen and Vásquez (United States) on using academic writing modules, Marti Sevier (Canada) on issues involving vocabulary acquisition, In-Seok Kim (South Korea) on developing a

Web-based listening course, and many more. Recommended Web sites, tools, and software programs can be found in the appendices.

Levy, M., & Stockwell, G. (2006). *CALL dimensions: Options and issues in computer assisted language learning*. Mahwah, NJ: Lawrence Erlbaum. Offered here is a detailed analysis using description and examples of CALL and how it is used today in many contexts and with several languages. Among the dimensions considered are design, evaluation, computer-mediated communication, theory, research, practice, and technology.

Pennington, M. (2003). The impact of the computer in second language writing. In B. Kroll (Ed.), *Exploring the dynamics of second language writing* (pp. 287–309). Cambridge, England: Cambridge University Press. Emphasizing the importance of the use of computers in current pedagogy, the author discusses implications of computer use for the writing process itself, interacting within a network environment, choosing computer tools for differing interactive purposes, and encouraging agency.

CHAPTER **17**

Teaching Language through the Content Areas and Professional Development

Educators must understand the complex variables influencing the second language process and provide a sociocultural context that is supportive while academically and cognitively challenging.

V. Collier, 1999

QUESTIONS TO THINK ABOUT

1. What does it mean to "teach language through the content areas"? How important do you think it is to do so? Consider differences between second and foreign language teaching situations.

2. If you were teaching history, science, or some other content subject, how might you teach language through it?

3. What problems do you think language minority students might have in mainstream classes such as history, science, or some other content subject? If you were their second language teacher, how would you help to a prepare them for the transition to a mainstream course?

4. How can all teachers of language minority students best improve their teaching practices across the content areas?

Students in academic settings need to have command of the new language for abstract thinking and problem solving. Whether the skills related to functioning at abstract levels are taught in self-contained classrooms in which a variety of subject areas are covered or in classrooms set up for the purpose of teaching specific subject matter, the lessons need to become increasingly more challenging academically, and the environment needs to be accepting.

Although there is considerable overlap, two types of language proficiency are critical to the success of second language (L2) students in a school environment: academic and interpersonal. Academic language proficiency typically takes approximately five years or more to develop fully (see Collier, 1987; Collier & Thomas, 1997; Cummins, 1981a, 1984, 1989; Klesmer, 1994; Ramirez, Yuen, & Ramey, 1991). Interpersonal language, generally, is learned within two years (Cummins 1981a, 1984). However, it is important to remember that there is a great deal of overlap between academic and interpersonal language use.

This chapter focuses on programs in the United States, although teachers elsewhere might have similar programs and might benefit from reflecting on and discussing what is presented here. Teachers of English as a second language (ESL), bilingual education, and foreign languages can teach the target language through basic academic content or academic themes, drawing from many of the methods and activities described in previous chapters. For example, physical approaches might be used to teach math skills ("Draw an octagon. Divide it in half with a vertical line.") or physical education directives ("Line up. Count off by fours."); interactive activities can be used to demonstrate how to blend colors for an art project; and chants can help students remember important information about history or science. No matter what kinds of activities are adapted or created, they need to make increasingly greater cognitive demands on the students.

Once students are ready for higher levels within the content areas, they can be introduced to more difficult concepts through concrete approaches at first and more abstract ones later. For example, beginning students might watch a teacher demonstrate and explain a science experiment and then be asked to do the experiment themselves, following specific oral directions. Intermediate students might perform experiments using only written directions, whereas more advanced students might be required to conceptualize an experiment and write about the expected results under various conditions. At first the teacher can scaffold instruction extensively while students are trying out the skills they are learning. Then that support can gradually be lessened as students become increasingly more independent (Biancarosa & C. Snow, 2006).

In this section, we explore the various approaches that can be used to teach language through content learning and the political implications of each. Most foreign language courses in the United States are subject courses taught independent of other content areas. ESL, on the other hand, is often taught in conjunction with one or more content-area programs: a submersion program, an immersion program consisting of sheltered content-area classes, and/or a bilingual program.

SUBMERSION

Students whose first language is different from that of the school and community are often "submerged" in content-area classes in which they are a minority among proficient speakers. Often they suffer socially and feel isolated. If they had been in an ESL or bilingual program right from the beginning, they would no doubt have been able to form friendships with others going through similar experiences. Not only that, but students in submersion classrooms frequently find themselves at a disadvantage academically. What they hear can be incomprehensible to them, and they are sometimes treated as intellectual inferiors. The teachers generally do not understand their languages and know very little about their cultures. A first language may be regarded as a hindrance (subtractive)[1] to a mastery of the second. The students may or may not have the opportunity to be tutored individually. Sometimes the students are placed in what are known as "pull-out" programs that frequently put them at an even greater disadvantage, because they may miss concepts introduced in the general classroom while they are receiving pull-out instruction.[2] On the other hand, if the pull-out instruction is carefully coordinated with what is happening in the classroom, then it may be of benefit, depending on the situation. Another factor to consider is that, in some cases, these students have to deal with the social stigma sometimes associated with being pulled out in front of their peers. Much depends on how sensitively the program is handled.

In many schools, particularly elementary schools, a "push-in" program is used whereby a language specialist or aide comes into the mainstream classroom and works with one or more second language students. In such cases, the work is typically coordinated with what the language proficient students (often native speakers) are learning. Any stigma that may be associated with receiving extra help can be lessened or perhaps even avoided if the push-in work is coordinated with other group work participated in by the rest of the class during the same time frame. One possible problem is that language learners may not get the help they need if there are not enough qualified persons to do the assisting.

Some schools (K–12) in the United States have submersion programs referred to in the literature as *inclusion* programs in which English learners, along with other students with special needs, are placed fully in mainstream classes early on, usually without the benefit of any special outside help. The content-area teachers into whose classes English learners are placed are expected to meet most of the students' needs and provide appropriate instruction and an adapted curriculum. Therefore the effectiveness of such programs depends mainly on how well the content-area teachers have been prepared. Even if they are prepared, class size may not allow for sufficient time to

---

[1] Lambert (1974) identified two treatments of primary languages within a second language environment: subtractive and additive. A language is said to be *subtractive* when it is considered detrimental to the learning of the second language and *additive* when it is thought to be beneficial.

[2] A pull-out program is one in which the students are taken out of their regular classes for certain portions of the day in order to receive special help with the target language.

devote to their second language students who often require several hours of individual attention.

Examples of inclusion programs for English learners can be found, particularly in the state of Florida where it appears to have been the preferred placement "even though many of these classrooms provided insufficient opportunities for second language (L2) development" (Harper, Platt, Naranjo, & Boynton, 2007, p. 644). In Florida, inclusion for English learners appears to have been favored to avoid the inequities and any discrimination that might result from separation into ESL, sheltered, and bilingual classes. Although such reasoning may appear to some to be commendable, in reality inclusion often results in an equity imbalance when English learners are not given the support or specialized services they need to achieve mainstream goals. Indeed, this was a concern of several district-level Florida ESL administrators who were interviewed in a study done earlier by Platt, Harper, and Mendoza (2003). The researchers concluded based on these interviews that the consequences of inclusion can be profound if "specialized language support is considered peripheral rather than essential to the success of English language learners" (p. 128). However, if class sizes are small and if all teachers have sufficient expertise in second language teaching, inclusion can become a viable option for many second language students.

Mainstreaming

A chief goal of ESL and sheltered classes is to prepare students to function effectively in mainstream content-area classes. In ideal situations, the students are gradually transitioned into these classes once they are considered socially and academically ready. Before students are mainstreamed, they are generally evaluated by both the language specialist and the content-area teacher to make sure they know the basic concepts involved and have the necessary skills for academic work. These skills may include note-taking and study skills; basic research skills, including summarizing and paraphrasing; and test-taking skills, including writing answers in paragraph form. Students may be placed first in mainstream classes such as physical education, art, music, and math and later in the more language-dependent natural and social sciences. The subject matter for beginners during initial transitioning is generally cognitively undemanding, the materials are context-embedded, the content-area teacher is aware of the students' need for modified language tailored to their needs, and the atmosphere is one of acceptance rather than rejection.

Sometimes a mainstream class is paired with an *adjunct* course for English learners (see especially Saint Michael's College International Center described on pp. 447–453). In an adjunct course, students receive assistance with language and content learning from a language teacher who works in conjunction with the mainstream course instructor. Adjunct courses have been attempted mainly at the college/university levels, probably because schedules are generally more flexible there than they are in secondary schools.

Unfortunately, second language students are often submerged in mainstream classes too soon simply because other programs have not been made available to them. Sometimes parents have insisted that they be put in "regular" classes (see the previous discussion on inclusion). Duff (2005) made clear to us what can happen when students are submerged or mainstreamed too early:

> ELLs [English language learners] and their parents often seek expedited mainstreaming and thus removal from physically and socially isolated groups of ESL students—and then experience frustration and disappointment with lower-than-expected grades and/or with social alienation once they are mainstreamed. Social, linguistic, and academic support is typically inadequate after students enter the mainstream. (p. 57)

Students in some states are required by law to remain in ESL for one year only and, as a result, may be mainstreamed long before they are ready.

IMMERSION

All immersion programs have at least one thing in common: The students are *at similar levels of proficiency* in their new language, meaning that they generally receive input specifically tailored to their needs. There are three kinds of immersion programs: foreign language, second language, and heritage language.

Foreign Language Immersion

In foreign language immersion programs, most (if not all) of the students are from the language majority population and are part of the dominant cultural group. They are placed in content-area classes in which a foreign language is the medium for communication and instruction. Usually the first language is added gradually later on for some of the subject-area content. The Thunder Bay French immersion program described on pp. 490–494, in which all the students are from English-speaking homes, is a typical example. In foreign language immersion programs, the new language is additive and generally has the support of the parents and the community. Usually the parents have requested the program for their children and are often instrumental in setting up the program. The teacher is, in most cases, familiar with the students' first language and knows (and is often part of) their culture.

    All of these factors contribute to the high student self-esteem often found in such programs. These factors also clearly differentiate foreign language immersion programs from submersion programs, in which children are typically at a disadvantage as the content becomes more demanding. Affective advantages, coupled with the cognitive benefit of modified input, probably account for the significant difference in the results of both programs. Children appear to thrive in foreign language immersion programs; in submersion programs they often do not (see especially Cummins, 1981b).

Second Language Immersion

Second language immersion is found in classes that separate English learners from the mainstream so that they may participate in an environment that is established with their special needs in mind. They include ESL, sheltered content, and adjunct classes. In these classes, the input is still adjusted to the students' needs, but their first languages and cultures are often very different (unlike foreign language immersion). In these classes (often referred to as *structured immersion* classes), unmodified input is gradually added as the students become ready for it. The students are considered part of the non-dominant groups in the community, even though their numbers may be greater than those of the dominant group. Their teacher may or may not be familiar with their first language and culture. However, the teacher usually has a background in current language and content teaching practices and often has some knowledge of the various language and cultural backgrounds of the students.

Heritage Language Immersion

Heritage immersion programs are mainly intended for those learners who have never become proficient in their native languages but are concerned with keeping their native languages and cultures intact, alive, and healthy. *Heritage language learners* are interested in establishing and preserving bonds with each other and the traditions of their cultures that are often centuries old (see the Acoma program described on pp. 523–526). By learning and maintaining their languages, they are able to pass them on to their children and stimulate their children's interest in doing the same, generation after generation. By this means they can hang on to the values and traditions that have brought them joy and pride in the past. Heritage immersion programs can empower learners, enabling them to meet the future as bilingual and bicultural persons who can function effectively in more than one world (Baker, 2006). The native language also allows them to communicate with and understand their elders and learn from them and others in the community.

However, in today's world, indigenous groups in the United States in particular still struggle with the injustices of the past. Many have seen their languages and cultures almost totally wiped out by ignorance and attempts at forced assimilation. Now some of them (such as the Acoma and other indigenous groups) are trying to revive their languages and cultures by becoming heritage learners in immersion programs.

Another example of a heritage program was developed by the Ojibwe tribe near Mille Lacs, Minnesota, where the elders became concerned when they realized that younger members of the community were unable to participate in traditional ceremonies because they did not know the language. A learning center was established in Rutledge, Minnesota, to revitalize the dying language and culture. Larry Smallwood, a founder of the center, lamented, "Our parents and grandparents went to boarding school, and the language was beaten out of them. Those that didn't lose it didn't teach it to their children because they didn't want their children to face the same thing they did" (*Minneapolis Star Tribune*, July 19, 2000, p. B1). Thus the descendants of the Ojibwe today learn their language in the same way one might learn a "foreign" tongue—a sad commentary on the state of minority languages in our country!

Heritage learners of a different kind are sometimes found in foreign language immersion programs (see especially the Concordia Language Villages program description on pp. 484–490). These learners do not come from homogeneous communities as do tribal heritage learners. They are often third- or fourth-generation immigrant students whose parents may not know the language of their ancestors and who missed out on learning the language themselves. They take great pride in their cultural backgrounds and are usually supported by their parents in the endeavor to revive both language and some of the culture in the home. Heritage learners in this situation often see learning the language of their heritage as a chance to open up career opportunities and broaden their horizons culturally by being bilingual.

BILINGUAL EDUCATION IN THE UNITED STATES

Bilingual education involves teaching students in some combination of their first and second languages. It has been in existence around the country for the past two centuries in one form or another. The Bilingual Education Act of 1968 and the *Lau v. Nichols* Supreme Court decision of 1974 gave impetus to bilingual education in recent decades. Today there are basically three types of bilingual education programs:

- *transitional programs.* language minority students learn most of the subject matter in the first language until they are ready to be gradually transitioned to all-English classes, usually after considerable time spent in the ESL component of the program
- *maintenance programs.* students continue throughout much of their schooling to learn a portion of the subject matter in their first language in order to continue improving their skills while they are developing their academic proficiency in English
- *enrichment programs.*[3] a portion of the subject matter is taught in the second language primarily to broaden cultural horizons or in anticipation of some future move or visit to another culture, rather than for the purpose of immediate survival. A single program may be enrichment for some and maintenance for others (see two-way bilingual education beginning on p. 423)

Bilingual programs for language minority students can generally be characterized as either *one-way* or *two-way*. In one-way programs, students are all from the same first language (L1) background (e.g., Spanish speakers learning English in the United States or English speakers learning French in Canada). The first case involves *language minority students;* the second case involves *language majority students*. On the other hand, in two-way programs, students are from two L1 backgrounds and are learning each other's first languages (e.g., Mandarin speakers learning English and English speakers learning Mandarin, all in the same program). In both the one-way and two-way programs, students receive mainstream curriculum through some combination of their first and second languages. The type of program and the people running it usually determine how the two languages are combined and how much time is devoted to each language.

---

[3] Collier and Thomas (1999) used the term *enrichment program* to mean something entirely different: They referred to programs which teach cognitively challenging and complex content as opposed to remedial programs which teach watered-down content. Bilingual programs (especially maintenance ones) are enrichment programs, according to their definition, because they are able to teach grade-level content in the first language, keeping students from falling behind while they are learning the second language.

One-Way Bilingual Education

Language minority students in one-way programs begin their education in a new culture by learning at least some of the core academic content in their first language. They can generally avoid missing out on important concept formation while they are trying to master their new language, and what they learn in their first language is often easily transferred to their second language (Collier, 1995).[4] Some of these programs are maintenance or *late-exit* programs in which students continue learning at least a portion of the content in their first language, allowing them to develop their skills in the primary language. Unfortunately, most one-way bilingual programs for language minority students in the United States today are transitional or *early-exit* programs. In other words, once students have acquired a sufficient amount of the target language to survive (often in social situations), the bilingual component of their schooling is dropped. This is troublesome for two reasons: (a) Students are often not ready for academic mainstreaming, because their academic skills are not yet highly developed in the second language; and (b) students are not able to function with maximal effectiveness in our multicultural society, a society that *needs* people who are highly literate in more than one language.

If all of these programs were maintenance (as opposed to transitional), we as a nation would have a tremendous language resource on which to draw. Ironically, we spend much time and energy improving and expanding our foreign language programs to benefit our citizens, and yet we almost daily discourage the natural resource that many of our students already possess but need to develop—their first languages.

According to Cummins (1981b), an important goal of any second language program should be to develop proficient bilinguals (see the threshold hypothesis[5]). He reported:

> studies were carried out with language minority children whose L1 was gradually being replaced by a more dominant and prestigious L2. Under these conditions, these children developed relatively low levels of academic proficiency in both languages. In contrast, the majority of studies that have reported cognitive advantages associated with bilingualism have involved students whose L1 proficiency has continued to develop while L2 is being acquired. Consequently, these students have been characterized by relatively high levels of proficiency in both languages. (p. 38)

Cummins further stated that a major success of bilingual programs in elementary schools in particular is that they encourage students to take pride in their native

---

[4] This is true mainly for *sequential* bilingual learners who are acquiring their second language *after* the first one has been learned. The person who is a *compound* or *simultaneous* bilingual learner, on the other hand, has acquired both languages together from early childhood and probably does not need bilingual education. However, bilingual education in some form may still be of benefit so that the learner continues to develop both languages throughout his or her schooling.

[5] The threshold hypothesis argues that being proficient in one language facilitates proficiency in another. There are two thresholds involved: (a) a higher threshold dividing the *proficient bilingual* (one who has obtained high levels of proficiency in both languages) from the *partial bilingual* (one who is proficient in one of the languages), and (b) the lower threshold dividing the partial bilingual from the *limited bilingual* (one who has only low-level skills in both languages).

languages and cultures, a necessity if the students are to have positive attitudes not only toward themselves but toward the target language and the people who speak it.

One of the problems facing bilingual education associated with ESL programs is that only one or two students may speak any given language within a particular school. Most school districts require a minimum number of students in order to make the hiring of a bilingual teacher feasible. A second problem is that sometimes it is difficult to find qualified teachers, especially in languages for which there are fewer speakers. Often first language speakers can be hired as classroom tutors, but unfortunately these people often cannot do much more than aid in mainstream situations. In any case, it is important for teachers to encourage students to maintain their first languages and emphasize the advantages and increased opportunities for those who become proficient bilinguals.

Language majority students in one-way immersion bilingual programs usually have the desire to be immersed in a foreign language within their own communities. See the previous discussion of foreign language immersion in this chapter.

Two-Way Bilingual Programs

Two-way programs have gained popularity in the United States in recent years among students, their parents, and whole communities. In most cases, these programs are voluntary and require parental permission. The students who enroll include

- language minority students who are learning English
- language majority students who already speak English but who want to learn the language of the newcomers

The two groups serve as linguistic models for each other in their respective languages. The students are generally together for the entire school day, except when they are working on specific language instruction in their new languages. Exceptions to this integration are "developmental" programs, in which basic core content is first taught in the primary language for both groups. In such programs, students do not become fully integrated with each other for core curriculum until later. However, they are integrated for art, music, physical education, and other subjects in which the work is less cognitively demanding (see especially the Valley Center program mentioned later and described on pp. 507–514).

Goals of two-way bilingual programs include learning the content-area subject matter and becoming proficient in both languages. These programs usually last at least through elementary school and sometimes follow students into the middle school and beyond. The Valley Center program, for example, is contemplating expanding its presence into the high school as it moves with its students into the upper grades.

A very early two-way immersion bilingual education program comprising Spanish and English began in the San Diego City Schools. Students included Spanish-speaking children who began their schooling in Spanish and who eventually learned English and English-speaking children who also began their schooling in Spanish (similar to a foreign language immersion program) and who eventually developed their English skills.

Subject-matter content was taught only in Spanish in grades 1 through 3; in grades 4 through 6, half of the content was taught in Spanish and the other half in English. (English reading was begun in the second grade, however.)

Spanish-speaking children were in the majority in the San Diego program, and test results focused mainly on them. Herbert (1987), for example, compared students who had been in the two-way bilingual program with students who had received ESL without bilingual education. Controlling for ethnicity, gender, socioeconomic status, grade level, and the differences in pretest scores, he found that students in the two-way bilingual program did significantly better at all levels tested, grades 4 through 6, on the Comprehensive Tests of Basic Skills (CTBS) math and reading tests. Moreover, they were reclassified one year earlier on the average than those students who only had ESL. Positive results were also found in a much broader analysis done later by Collier and Thomas (1999; see pp. 425–427 in this chapter).

Another important factor concerning two-way immersion programs is that not only do the language minority children begin with the language with which they are most comfortable (their first language), but they serve as "models" in their first language for the English-speaking students, thereby raising their self-esteem. Self-esteem is a critical factor and should not be overlooked when we examine program effectiveness (see Chapter 6).

A similar affective advantage can be found in the Spanish/English two-way language in Valley Center, California, and the Cantonese/English two-way language program in lower Manhattan. (See their descriptions in Chapter 20.) The Valley Center program is considered *developmental* in that the students are introduced to their new language (either Spanish or English) as they become ready for it. The Manhattan program, in contrast, is considered *immersion* in that all the children learn in Cantonese starting on the first day, whether they are English-speakers or Cantonese-speakers.

Collier and Thomas (1999) also stressed the development of self-esteem and other sociocultural and affective processes such as the establishment of positive relationships and anxiety reduction. According to the researchers, an affirming sociocultural environment, which is most likely to occur in two-way programs, is necessary to three important interdependent processes:

- language development
- academic development
- cognitive development

If any one of these processes is arrested for any reason, the other two will be arrested as well. For example, if cognitive development is interrupted (which is what generally happens in monolingual programs), language development and academic development will be simultaneously—and negatively—affected.

In two-way immersion bilingual education, the language majority students experience many of the same frustrations as the language minority students in the program. They are thrown into a language in which they cannot communicate, their linguistic models come from unfamiliar backgrounds, and they are not sure how to deal with the resulting problems. Because of their uncertainty and strong desire to learn, they begin to understand and accommodate their new friends and the new language.

Accommodation is no longer a one-way street, with the language minority students doing all the adjusting (see also Nieto, 1999, 2000). As a result, bonds form between the two groups, and the language majority students begin to affirm and respect their language learning counterparts.

Bilingual Education: What Does the Research Indicate?

Perhaps the most extensive research to date on bilingual education programs in the United States was done by Virginia Collier and Wayne Thomas (1997, 1999; Collier, 1987, 1995; Thomas & Collier, 1996, 1998, 2002), researchers at George Mason University. Their analysis included more than 1 million language minority student records collected from twenty-three school districts in fifteen states beginning in 1982. They followed these students for as long as the students remained in these school districts, looking at their academic achievement over time as measured by school district tests given at each grade level in math, science, social studies, reading, and writing. Collier and Thomas (1999) reported that when comparing various programs intended for language minority students, including ESL and bilingual education, that two-way bilingual education was most effective. The average scores of English learners at the end of two-way programs were above the 50th national percentile. The next most effective programs for language minority students were one-way, late-exit programs, in which average scores for students at the end of their schooling was at the 50th national percentile. Students in both one-way and two-way programs took a minimum of five to six years to reach the 50th percentile, thus closing the achievement gap in their second language. In other words, they made fifteen months' worth of progress in every ten months of school.

Less effective were transitional one-way programs using current instructional approaches (average final scores for these were at the 32nd national percentile); transitional one-way programs using traditional instructional approaches (24th national percentile); ESL content-based programs (22nd national percentile); and finally ESL pull-out programs (11th national percentile). Interestingly, a prior analysis of 42,000 student samples (Thomas & Collier, 1996) found little difference between programs in the very early grades. It was not until the content became more demanding in the later grades that differences among programs became significant. In addition, students overall appeared to do best in programs that did *not* focus on discrete points of language taught in a highly structured, sequenced curriculum in which the learner passively received knowledge. Rather, they did best in programs in which they were active learners.

The conclusions reached by Collier and Thomas, particularly concerning the two-way programs, has not gone without its critics. According to Zehr (2005), Krashen had argued earlier that the first-grade students in the two-way programs had high scores in English to begin with, suggesting that they may have already known English prior to coming to school. He also thought that the two-way programs may have come out best because students who score high in English have a tendency to remain in these programs longer than they would have in other kinds of bilingual programs. However,

Zehr reported that Collier countered the first argument by saying that the scores were high for first-graders in only one school and that they were high because the test given in that school was easy and the children had been in school since prekindergarten, unlike the children in most of the other schools in the study. Zehr went on to quote Donna Christian from the Center for Applied Linguistics who had suggested that *self-selection* might have affected the results. "If students in two-way immersion are found to do better than their peers in other programs, it is difficult to know if this is because of the effects of the two-way immersion program itself, or due at least in part to inherent differences among the student populations and their families" (Zehr, 2005, p. 7). It is clear that more research needs to be done on the various kinds of bilingual programs to see which produce the best results. However, as with any program, the results may be influenced greatly by who is teaching in the programs and who the students are.

In earlier analyses, Thomas and Collier's (1996, 1998) data and observations supported the following conclusions.

Language minority students in bilingual programs appear to do best overall when:

- The teaching staff is of high-quality.
- Challenging academic instruction is given in the first language for as long a time period as possible (at least six years), while the students are also receiving progressively more of the same kind of instruction in the second language. (Collier and Thomas call this kind of instruction in both languages *enriched,* as opposed to remedial, meaning it builds on what the students already know and speeds up not only academic development but cognitive and linguistic development as well.)
- Current interactive approaches are used in which students are actively involved in a discovery process and in cognitively complex learning (e.g., whole language, learning through the academic content areas, cooperative learning, and problem solving).
- The two languages are separated for instruction by subject area or theme, regular time slots, and/or teacher (that is, one teacher represents one language; a different teacher represents the other).
- The non-English language is used for at least 50 percent of the time spent on instruction and as much as 90 percent in the early grades.
- Students are integrated with English speakers in the two-way programs in a balanced ratio of 50:50 or 60:40 but not below 70:30.
- The school environment is supportive and affirming.
- Administrators within the school wholeheartedly back the program.
- The two languages are given equal status, thus creating self-confidence among all students.
- Close collaboration is established between parents and the school.
- The program is considered a gifted and talented program for all students.

In the United States, students who first enter at the secondary levels generally go into ESL and sheltered programs, because bilingual education is typically not an option for them. Although they would also benefit from participating in a bilingual program, lack of access to one may not be quite as harmful to them as it is to younger learners because those entering as secondary students often have highly developed academic skills in their first languages to begin with. According to Collier and Thomas, adolescents seem to do best (a) when English is taught through academic content, (b) when thinking and problem-solving strategies are focused on, (c) when attention is paid to the students' prior knowledge, (d) when the first language and culture are respected, and (e) when multiple measures are used in ongoing assessment.

Collier (1995) and Collier and Thomas (1999) went further to conclude that the evidence overwhelmingly indicates that *proficient bilinguals develop cognitive advantages over, and generally outperform, monolinguals on school tests* (see also Bialystok, 2001).[6] This may be one reason that two-way bilingual programs and one-way immersion programs are sought by many language majority parents today for their children. Research indicates that language majority students participating in these programs benefit from becoming proficient in two languages and are not at a disadvantage academically by learning content through another language (see also Genesee, 1987; Genesee, Lindholm-Leary, Saunders, & Christian, 2006; Harley, Allen, Cummins, & Swain, 1990). Lambert and Cazabon (1994) found high levels of self-esteem and academic/personal satisfaction in both language majority and language minority students in the two-way programs (see also Christian, 1996). Of course, we need a lot more research, especially on the impact of two-way programs on language minority students. Individual programs differ a great deal depending on who is running them, and some two-way programs may be better than others for those in the minority.

Politics and Bilingual Education in the United States

In spite of all its advantages, bilingual education overall in the United States has been a political football in recent decades. Its challengers' voices reached a crescendo in the mid-1990s with a group called U.S. English who made it their mission to establish English as the "official" language of the United States government, arguing that the citizens' common bond as a people would be preserved. Fortunately, they did not succeed. What they failed to realize was that by attempting to make English official, they risked bringing about the opposite effect—increased divisiveness rather than unity. Quebec provides an example of what can happen when the speakers of any language group try to dominate the speakers of another. Another example is Slovakia (see King, 1997), where more than 10 percent of the population is ethnic Hungarian, but the country nevertheless made Slovak its official language, requiring that it be spoken in state hospitals to patients who did not understand it and by teachers in staff meetings at Hungarian language schools. Needless to say, this action drove a further wedge between two peoples who were finally beginning to heal the wounds of the

---

[6] It is interesting to note that bilingualism also has advantages in the area of cognitive control for bilingual children who are able to maintain this advantage as they become adults and that being bilingual serves as a defense against cognitive decline due to the normal aging process (Bialystok, Craik, Klein, & Viswanathan, 2004).

past. King pointed to more fortunate countries in which two or more languages have coexisted in relative harmony: Finland (with its Swedish minority), Switzerland (where German, French, Italian, and Romansh are all considered "national" languages), India (which officially recognizes nineteen languages, English among them), among other examples. Most countries around the world consider other languages additive rather than subtractive; such countries more often than not encourage bilingual education and treasure its results.

In the United States, however, the status of minority languages has been another story. Some have worried that immigrants will be less motivated to learn English if we "coddle" them too much with education in their own languages, multilingual drivers' tests, or other measures that might aid them before they can fully understand the main language of the country. This fear seems to me to have been unwarranted. In my own experience with immigrants over the years, I have yet to meet one immigrant who has not wanted to learn English. In Los Angeles alone, thousands of immigrants are turned away from English classes each year because there simply are not enough classes to go around. Most immigrants realize the importance of learning English and are desperately trying to do just that.

Perhaps the worst threat to bilingual education (as well as to ESL) began with the English-only movement and the Unz initiative known as California Proposition 227, approved by the voters of that state in 1998. Proposition 227 required that bilingual education be done away with altogether and that "structured English immersion" (i.e., a crash course in ESL) be limited to one year. Such a limitation meant that students were often thrown into mainstream classes where their teachers did not have the time or the expertise to give them appropriate English language instruction or the support they still needed. The initiative was intended to allow for few exceptions, regardless of parental preferences or students' individual needs or aspirations. Unfortunately, attempts to consider similar (but even more strident) measures have spread to other states, where their advocates have achieved or are attempting to achieve more successes. Colorado is one state that has managed to vote down a similar initiative to do away with bilingual education and require English immersion after only one year of ESL. Colorado's parents of children in its one- and two-way programs, along with many other advocacy groups, fought and succeeded in defeating this potentially harmful piece of legislation.

If we legally inhibit bilingual education, we are in essence infringing on the rights of parents, states, and local communities to choose what they think is best for their children. Much of the rationale of the English-only movement has been based on an *assimilationist* viewpoint (as opposed to a *pluralistic* viewpoint). For example, in her book titled *Forked Tongue,* R. Porter (1990) argued that it is not appropriate for public schools to use resources to promote bilingualism because it is an unrealistic goal. Instead, she thought that our goal should be to make all children part of the mainstream society. Although it is true that children need to be able to function successfully in the mainstream society, there is no research to suggest that they need to do it at the expense of their own languages and cultures. Being proficient in two or more languages is now and always will be a tremendous advantage to successful members of our society and responsible citizens of our world. Bilingualism *is* an appropriate goal not only for our schools, but for our country as a whole. In fact, this goal becomes more and more critical as our nation becomes increasingly more diverse.

PROGRAM POSSIBILITIES FOR ENGLISH LEARNERS[7]

Alternative paths indicated in Figure 17.1 find English learners beginning their schooling in the new culture in a native language program—transitional (early-exit) or maintenance (late-exit)—and/or in an ESL program. In some elementary schools, English learners are placed in a mainstream class with a push-in or pull-out ESL component (described earlier in this chapter). In the most effective native language programs and ESL programs or programs with ESL components, students' social, linguistic, and academic needs are the focus. If the initial program is a late-exit maintenance bilingual program, then students may go from there directly into *academic mainstream classes* (follow the path of the arrows in Figure 17.1).

If the only option is ESL and/or an early-exit transitional bilingual program, the students, once they are considered ready, may transition to *sheltered classes* if they are available and then into the *academic mainstream classes* where there are no ESL components. Instead *adjunct classes* coordinated with mainstream courses may be an option for them, especially at the college/university level.

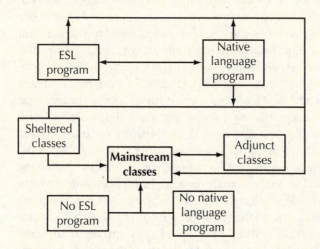

Figure 17.1 Program Options for English Learners. Also in Richard-Amato and M. A. Snow (2005b, p. 201)

---

[7]Although the main focus in this section is on English learners, many of the concepts presented are applicable in other second language situations in which students are struggling to gain access to both language and culture. Several of the strategies listed beginning on pp. 431–436 may also be applicable to foreign language and bilingual education situations as well.

Unfortunately, in many schools across the United States today, students have neither an ESL nor a native-language program; instead many find themselves in a sink-or-swim situation with little or no help from second language specialists.

Krashen (1984) early on presented a gradual transitional design (see an adapted version in Figure 17.2). As we can see, the main goal is to eventually teach *all academic subject matter in English*. However, the first language is maintained somewhat through enrichment.[8]

Level	Mainstream	Sheltered	First Language
Beginning	Art, music, physical education	ESL	All core subjects
Intermediate	Art, music, physical education	ESL, math	Social and natural sciences
Advanced	Art, music, physical education, math	ESL, social and natural sciences	Enrichment
Mainstream	All subjects	—	Enrichment

Figure 17.2 Program for English Learners. Adapted from Krashen (1984)

English learners at beginning levels are mainstreamed only into subject areas in which the concepts are generally concrete and less demanding cognitively. For some students (especially those in high school), home economics and industrial arts might be added as additional mainstream electives. Students study all core subjects in their first language. During intermediate levels, the same students might add typing to their mainstream course selections and sheltered mathematics, but the remainder of the core subjects are still taught in the first language. At advanced levels, students are mainstreamed in most subjects except the social and natural sciences, which are taught in sheltered environments. The first language is used mainly for enrichment, as Krashen originally suggested. The amount of time spent in ESL at each level depends on the particular needs of each student. If teaching core subjects in the first language is not possible through the intermediate levels, then these subjects are taught in the second language within sheltered classes beginning at intermediate levels. However, Krashen, who himself is a strong proponent of bilingual education, would probably agree that the program could be improved substantially if students were able to continue using the first language for at least half of their core subjects throughout their academic program as they are able to do in the maintenance programs.

---

[8] The term *enrichment* here may in reality result in a sort of token treatment of the first language. The importance given to it depends on those operating the program. Hopefully the first language is used for academic as well as social communication in situations that really matter. Program directors might want to consider using the first language for a portion of the subject-matter teaching, provided that adequate teaching staff and materials are available.

What Can a Content-Area Teacher Do?

Teachers of mainstream, sheltered, and adjunct classes in the various content areas can do much to lower the cognitive and affective burdens of the students, particularly if maintenance bilingual education is not in place or fully developed. They can modify their teaching to meet three basic objectives:

- integrate the student (in the case of mainstream classes)
- communicate effectively with the student
- teach language and the subject matter in a manner conducive to learning

The following are some suggestions to help content-area teachers meet these goals (see also the section "Modifying and Enhancing Instruction in the Language Classroom" on pp. 251–255). Although the majority of ideas can be adapted to almost any situation, a few may not be relevant for your particular classroom. Their relevance will usually depend on the age levels, proficiency levels, and cognitive development of the students with whom they are to be used. The Sheltered Instruction Observation Protocol (SIOP) described later in this chapter can also provide a valuable framework for planning lessons, not only for English learners but all students.

For Mainstream Teachers

1. *Provide a warm environment in which help is readily available to the student:* One way to do this is to set up a "buddy" system in which proficient speakers of English are paired with English learners. Other useful management tools include peer facilitating and cooperative learning (see Chapter 15). Individual instruction and group work can increase the chances that the student will receive the necessary help.
2. *If possible, use a "satisfactory/unsatisfactory" grade option until the English learner is able to compete successfully with proficient speakers:* Students may be ready sooner than expected, as many of them adapt very rapidly. Often the students, particularly those who are older, will already have a high level of academic understanding in the first language and may even surpass many monolingual English speakers once they have learned the new language.
3. *Record your lectures or talks:* Students need to be able to listen to these as many times as necessary for understanding.
4. *Ask some of your proficient English-speaking students to simplify the textbook by rewriting the chapters:* The job can be made as easy as possible by giving each proficient speaker just a few pages to simplify. The simplified materials not only aid English learners but other students who may find the regular text too difficult. The students who do the rewriting benefit also in that the task may serve as a review for them. The teacher can edit these simplifications as needed.
5. *Choose proficient English-speaking students who take effective, comprehensible notes to make copies of their notes for English learners:* By this means, the latter can be provided with study aids.

For Mainstream, Sheltered-Class, and Adjunct Teachers[9]

1. *Plan lessons that are related to the students' lives, utilize a number of visuals, and provide for "hands-on" kinds of involvement:* For example, drawing, coloring, and labeling maps in geography and pinpointing where the students came from is far more valuable to them than simply listening to a talk about maps.

2. *Communicate individually with the English learners as much as time permits:* Avoid using complicated words or complex sentences at first. Speak slowly but keep the volume and intonation as normal as possible. Use few idioms. Incorporate body language. Those whose main goal is to communicate use these strategies subconsciously, for the most part.

3. *Avoid forcing students to speak:* Allow them to speak when they are ready—in other words, when they volunteer. Students' right to a "silent period" (see Chapter 3) needs to be respected, especially when they are being introduced to new concepts.

4. *Reassure the students that their own languages are acceptable and important:* If other students from the same language group are present, do not insist that they use only English in class. *Code switching* from one language to another can be very beneficial to language learners and can be an important means of communicating, bonding, and establishing identity. In addition, difficult concepts can often be better understood when translated into the first language. No matter how good the intentions of the teacher, refusing to allow students to speak in their first languages is in essence saying that their languages are not good enough. Of course, students may need to be reminded that first languages should not be used to exclude others from discussion.

5. *Make most corrections indirectly by repeating what the students have said in correct form:* For example, suppose the student says, "My book home"; the teacher can repeat, "I see. Your book is at home." Remember that ungrammatical forms are to be regarded as normal while the student is progressing toward proficiency in the language. When the student is ready to move to another level, the indirect correction will have a good chance of being picked up and internalized after it is heard several times in a variety of situations. You might keep track of the errors students are making and work on these errors in small groups. Overcorrection of grammar and pronunciation errors can raise anxiety levels and may prevent normal language development from occurring.

   In written production, a few suggestions can be made for improvement as long as they are balanced with positive comments. Keep suggestions simple and offer only what you think each student can handle at his or her proficiency level. It is important to focus first on making the student's ideas as clear as possible. Written comments and suggestions made by the teacher can contain new structures and vocabulary on which the students can build as they begin to stretch cognitively to higher levels of meaning and expression.

---

[9] Note that many of the strategies included here are also presented, some in greater detail, in Richard-Amato and M. A. Snow (2005b).

6. *Accents should not be corrected:* Language learners cannot be expected to sound like native speakers, although some of them may over time.

7. *Try to answer all questions that the students ask but avoid overly detailed explanation:* Simple answers that get right to the point are understood best. If possible, point to objects and pictures or demonstrate actions to help get the meaning across.

8. *If you are in a situation in which lectures are appropriate, try to make them as comprehensible as possible, but avoid "talking down" to the students:* Speak slowly (but not too slowly). Emphasize (but do not overemphasize) key words and phrases through intonation, gesture, facial expressions, and redundancy. Write key concepts on the board or on an overhead transparency as you are talking.

   Give concrete examples. Use pictures and charts, the mapping out or expansion of ideas, acting out, simplifications, or whatever is necessary to ensure understanding. Definitions, comparisons, and the like can be incorporated in the lectures to clarify new words and concepts. For example, in a history lesson you might say, "The government's funds were depleted. It was almost out of money." Thus the phrase "funds were depleted" is made more comprehensible.

   Try to provide a rich language environment by providing new elements in the discourse rather than always replacing complex items with simpler forms. However, problems can occur when too many new elements are introduced at once. Using cognates and high-frequency vocabulary gives students something familiar on which to build. More difficult items can be added gradually over time as the student becomes more proficient in the language.

9. *Check to see that what you are saying is understood:* Frequently ask questions such as, "Do you understand?" or "Do you have any questions?" and be very aware of the feedback you receive. Students may even nod their heads but still not understand. Blank stares or puzzled looks are sure signs that you are not being understood. Often it is better to ask more specific questions directly related to the preceding utterance. For example, after saying, "In Arizona, rainfall is minimal during most of the year," you might check for understanding by asking, "Does it rain much in Arizona?" Asking a question such as this to confirm interpretation is yet another means by which you can expose students to new words and concepts without losing the meaning of the message.

10. *Use confirmation checks if you are not sure you are understanding what the student is saying:* Questions such as "Is this what you're saying?" can help to confirm that you have understood correctly.

11. *Give students sufficient wait time before expecting answers:* Students need time to formulate their ideas. Often teachers try to avoid silence and move too quickly to another student for an answer. If, after a sufficient time, you still do not receive a response, you might want to rephrase the questions and/or answer it yourself. The question–answer process that takes place in a nonstressful, supportive environment helps students to acquire the appropriate language associated with turn-taking.

12. *Establish consistent patterns and routines in the classroom:* Procedures for taking roll, moving to work stations, organizing lessons, and so on make it possible for students to be comfortable in familiar contexts and to focus more directly on the new concepts they are learning and the unfamiliar tasks to which they are introduced.

13. *Encourage students to use their bilingual dictionaries when necessary or to ask questions when they do not understand important concepts:* Help them to guess at meanings first by using the context. Assure them that they do not have to understand every word to comprehend the main idea.

14. *Reinforce key concepts continually in a variety of situations and activities:* Hearing about the concepts once or twice is not enough. Students need to be exposed to them several times through a wide range of experiences in order to best facilitate internalization.

15. *Summarize and review frequently:* If routinely accomplished, summaries and reviews provide reinforcement, help students focus on what is important, and put what they have learned into perspective. They can also provide a framework for the learning that is to come.

16. *Whenever possible, utilize tutors who speak the native language of the students:* Such help is especially important to students operating at beginning to intermediate levels.

17. *Avoid ability tracking:* Students should not be placed in certain classes due to general ability as determined by a test or someone's observation. Such tracking can be very demoralizing to students. *Fluid grouping* within classes, on the other hand, allows students to be placed temporarily in a group due to a specific need (e.g., problem with pronoun use) or interest (wants to learn more about global warming). If they are grouped by a particular interest, they can self-select the books they will read on the topic with the help of the teacher. If the book turns out to be too difficult, another can be selected. The student can then share what he or she has learned with the group.

    ESL and sheltered content classes are formed on the basis of proficiency level in the language, which is much different from being placed because of general ability. Once the student becomes more advanced in the language, he or she moves to a higher level. The students realize that they are assigned to a class or group but only temporarily. Once they become more proficient in the language, they should be moved to a different level.

18. *Request that appropriate content-area books be ordered for the library in the students' native languages:* These can be particularly useful to students in comprehending the concepts while the second language is being mastered. They also provide the students with a means for maintaining and developing skills in the native language.

19. *Become informed as much as possible on the various cultures represented by your students:* Knowing how particular students might react to classroom events and being able to interpret nonverbal symbols could help prevent misunderstanding and confusion. Be careful, however, not to stereotype the

student with cultural labels. Individuals within a given culture are often very different from one another.

20. *Acknowledge and incorporate the students' cultures whenever possible:* For instance, differing number systems can be introduced in math, customs and traditions in social science, various medicines in natural science, native dances and games in physical education, songs in music, ethnic calendars in art, haiku in literature, and so on. In addition, holidays can be celebrated, languages can be demonstrated for appreciation, and literature with translations can be shared. It is important also to include discussions of issues related to ethnicity and race so that recognition of other cultures and a respect for diversity is not limited to celebrations and the like. In addition, students usually prefer to be treated as individuals and not simply as products of a specific cultural environment.

21. *Prepare the students for your lessons and reading assignments:* You might ask them what they already know about the subject. Encourage them to look for main ideas by giving them at least a partial framework or outline beforehand to get them started. Ask them to predict outcomes and then to verify their predictions.

22. *Demonstrate and/or provide models of work that make clear your expectations and stimulate creativity:* How might they go about completing a particular assignment? Approximately how long should the final product be? What sorts of things might it include? What linguistic conventions should be followed concerning mechanics, spacing, and so on? What might be some good strategies to use? Well-written papers from former students (used anonymously or with permission) can be helpful to learners.

23. *Give students sufficient time to complete assignments:* For shorter assignments, even a few extra minutes can be important. Longer assignments may require an extra day or two or maybe even an extra week.

24. *Discuss some of the new vocabulary, cultural items, and structures they might find in reading selections:* If possible, provide a glossary of new vocabulary and cultural items that they can keep beside them as they read.

25. *Frequently have students self-evaluate and reflect on their learning:* Using checklists or asking students how they think they are doing helps them to determine what they have accomplished and where they want to go.

26. *Increase possibilities for success:* Alternating difficult activities with easier ones allows the English learners to experience early successes. Of course, the tasks as a whole should gradually become more academically challenging as the students become more proficient.

27. *Familiarize yourself with the language required of your content area:* What key vocabulary items are necessary? What kinds of language structures, transitions, ways of organizing are particular to your content area? What types of analyses are common? English learners will need to be made aware of the typical genres and language used in your field in order to better understand the oral and written discourse and comprehend textbooks, lectures, and other presentations. By using activities focused on both language requirements and

the content to be learned, students are in a better position to learn both simultaneously.

28. *Provide learning guides and examples for English learners to use:* Study guides, steps to take to complete a process, partial outlines on which students fill in the missing items, sample lecture notes (mentioned previously), sample text with the important points highlighted or underlined, sample marginal notes, and so on will all help.

29. *Explain to students how to synthesize information from many sources: periodicals, books, data collected by students, personal observation and reflection, and so forth:* Show them how such information can be integrated into a paper or an oral presentation.

30. *Demonstrate learning strategies you think will be helpful to students as they go about their work:* Ask them to reflect on the strategies they are already using to take tests, remember important information to which they are exposed, understand what they read, develop their vocabulary, approach a composition, work through a math problem, read a map, and so on.

31. *Be aware of linguistic and other problems that could hinder the student's progress:* Resource persons who may be in a position to offer assistance are the ESL teacher or other language specialist, a guidance counselor, the school nurse, community resources, the student's parents, and so forth.

PROGRAM POSSIBILITIES FOR FOREIGN LANGUAGE STUDENTS

One-way and two-way bilingual education are both appropriate designs for foreign language (language majority) students. Both can ensure that students develop skills in their first language, even though it is also being fostered at home and in the community. Through both programs, students of approximately the same proficiency and age levels are given appropriately adjusted input and interactional opportunities in the various subject areas (see especially the descriptions of the Thunder Bay early immersion program in Chapter 19 and the two-way programs in Chapter 20). The *language village concept* is also a possibility to consider. (See the description of the Concordia Language Villages in Chapter 19.) Students may want to combine traditional foreign language study in their local schools with a portion of a summer spent in a village where they are immersed in the foreign language of their choice.

Unfortunately, traditional foreign language programs (which Larsen-Freeman and Freeman, 2008, refer to as subject-language programs) in the United States involve students in the target language for only a small portion of each day. Because the classroom is probably the only source of input for the student, unless he or she also participates in a village concept program, it is vitally important that the class time be spent mainly on meaningful communication through interaction. However, because students may not receive a sufficient amount of input, even though the focus is on interaction, they will probably need additional grammar instruction (see Chapter 2), in order to facilitate the learning process—especially those students who are cognitively able to use rule application.

PROFESSIONAL DEVELOPMENT: TEACHER RESEARCH, OBSERVATION, AND EVALUATION

Professional development needs to occur throughout teachers' careers if they are to continue to grow and attain ultimate satisfaction in their chosen fields. Nowhere is this more true than in teaching language minority students. The challenges are great as teachers strive to help these students achieve both academic and personal goals. Taking classes, participating in workshops, collaborating with other teachers, participating in peer reviews, keeping journals, and so forth are among the ways teachers can develop professionally.

Teachers can take at least two actions to add to their knowledge about what is happening in their schools and how they are doing in their classrooms. Both can incorporate several of the previously mentioned suggestions as well as other means leading to professional development. One involves *teacher research;* the other involves *teacher observation and evaluation,* which can become part of a research data base.

Teacher Research

No matter what type of program teachers find themselves in, teacher research is critical in helping better their practices. Many do participate in teacher research but usually on a very informal basis. In fact, these teachers may not even realize that they are doing any research at all. Many informally assess the strategies *while* and/or *after* using them. Do they and their students feel comfortable with these strategies? Were the outcomes what they anticipated? How might they change their strategies for a better result? What new strategies do they want to try?

Bassano and Christison (1995), both very experienced teachers and authors, asked their students in ESL classes questions about what their teachers were doing right, what had helped them most in acquiring the language, which activities they preferred, and whether the curriculum was meeting their needs. They used the collected data for self-evaluation. The authors reported, "Like many teachers involved in classroom observation and data collection at the time, we did not view our activities as research, nor did we believe that our work was particularly significant for the language teaching profession" (p. 89). Good teachers, just by progressing through a normal day, are involved in informal research. They determine from students' reactions, test results, and analyses of their students' work how well they have taught and in what ways they may need to improve. Their data may also include feedback, not only from students, but from parents, administrators, and other teachers. If they want to create emergent participatory classroom environments, they find out what issues most concern and/or interest their students and use these as foci of the curriculum. This strategy is particularly effective at intermediate to advanced levels in the case of second language classrooms or any level in bilingual classrooms. It is important to know that teaching itself can constitute informal research and can become a rich and transformative experience.

Kumaravadivelu (2003) advocated for a more systematic and strategic look at classroom events, problem identification, and possible solutions. He argued that teachers need to acquire skills and knowledge that allow them to analyze and evaluate their own teaching. Like Bassano and Christison, he believed that teachers need to ponder what is working and what is not. All this becomes part of the *culture of teaching*. Asking colleagues to observe your teaching and then sitting down with them to discuss your strengths and how you might improve adds yet another dimension to your analysis. A video recording can be very helpful during the discussion.

There are also many resources for those teachers wishing to participate in more formal types of teacher research, the results of which they eventually plan to make public. One such resource is Donald Freeman's book *Doing Teacher Research: From Inquiry to Understanding* (1998). Freeman argued that to investigate the classroom in a rigorous way, research must be redefined so that it becomes part of the teaching process itself. The research begins with thinking out one's assumptions about teaching and learning and then uses these assumptions to develop the questions from which the inquiry flows. It means being open to changing predetermined thinking by challenging it at every step of the way so that the results will be transformative. According to Freeman, questions for research should be open-ended and have the potential to produce understandings and principles rather than specific solutions or courses of action. Usually, such "research-able questions" (to use his term) lead to other questions for similar research. An example of one of Freeman's research-able questions is: What is the impact of praise on group dynamics? This question requires the teacher to look at the main question and the subquestions that grow out of it from the student's point of view. The teacher's data may include, among other things, an examination of journals and diaries; observations and documentation of student behaviors; a videotaped record of classroom events; a transcription of what the students say, indicating gestures and pauses; and, perhaps, recorded interviews with the students.

The following questions are among those Freeman (1998) said can be made part of the framework included in any teacher research plan (p. 122):

What is the inquiry?
What are the research-able questions/puzzles here?
What are the supporting questions/puzzles?
What is the background or rationale of the research?
Where will the research be done?
Who will be the participants in your study?
What data are relevant to the research questions?
How do you/the researcher plan to collect them?
How will you/the researcher analyze them?
What is the provisional time line or schedule?
Why will the research matter?

Michael Wallace (1998), in his book *Action Research for Language Teachers*, took a more personal approach to teacher research. He saw it as problem focused with intended outcomes that are very pragmatic. The problems researched may relate to classroom management, using appropriate materials, teaching in areas such as reading and speaking, student behavior, and so forth. Data might include field notes and logs, diaries, journals, personal accounts, verbal reports (such as think-aloud) transcribed into protocols, interviews, questionnaires, case studies, and the like (see also J. Gebhard & Oprandy, 1999). An analysis of the data then becomes the basis for evaluation and decision making. Wallace asserted that action research can be used by teachers in conjunction with results of academic research of various kinds to inform decisions. However, unlike experimental research, it does not attempt to make general statements or make extensive use of statistical analysis. Its main goal is to encourage and facilitate reflective thinking and professional development.

Teachers collectively may use their own research to help them form evaluations and make decisions as part of an effort to reform their school. For example, they may want to take a look at groups of students who drop out of school to discover some of their reasons for doing so. They may want to know to what extent the academic and career needs of language minority students are being met. They may want to know what the attitudes of teachers are toward students who come from different cultural and language backgrounds.

The types of research teachers are able to do depends mainly on the questions they want to answer and the constraints within the school and classroom. Often lack of time and resources, large class sizes, and scheduling problems make more formal investigations very difficult. However, for teachers who are able to pursue teacher research, the dividends can be great in terms of their own professionalism and increased understanding about the learning process and the factors affecting it in their schools and classrooms. However, teacher research should never become just another burdensome endeavor in which teachers feel compelled to participate. Even at its most informal levels, teacher research can produce valuable information to inform practice and improve teaching overall.

Teacher Observation and Evaluation

The Sheltered Instruction Observation Protocol (SIOP) described by Echevarria, Vogt, and Short (2008) may be a useful tool to help teachers improve their teaching strategies and effectively plan lessons. Based on the premise that language and content can be learned through sheltered academic instruction, SIOP provides a model for sheltered instruction. Linda Stratton (personal correspondence), who has used the SIOP model extensively in teacher training at Colorado College and in District 11 in Colorado Springs, reported that this observation protocol is emphasized in the teacher preparation programs with which she is familiar, mainly as a model for sheltered instruction, a tool for self-evaluation, and a guide to lesson preparation.

However, these are not its only important uses. As its name implies, it was originally intended for teacher observation and involved scoring teachers in the categories summarized as follows:

- *preparation.* definition of content objectives and language objectives for students; use of appropriate content concepts, incorporation of supplementary materials; adaptation of content; meaningful, integrative activities
- *building background.* explicit linking of concepts to students' backgrounds; linking between prior learning and new concepts; explaining key vocabulary
- *comprehensible input.* use of language appropriate to proficiency level; explanation of academic tasks; use of variety of techniques

- *strategies.* opportunities for student use of strategies; use of scaffolding; variety of question types or tasks to encourage higher-order thinking
- *interaction.* opportunities for interaction and discussion; effective use of grouping configurations; sufficient wait time for responses; use of the first language for clarification
- *practice/application.* providing hands-on materials/manipulatives; applications of knowledge through activities; integration of language skills
- *lesson delivery.* supporting content and language objectives; encouraging student engagement; appropriate pacing
- *review/assessment.* reviewing key vocabulary and content concepts; providing feedback on student output; assessment of comprehension and learning

The teacher being observed is scored in each category and subcategory on a scale of zero to 4 (4 is the best score). Echevarria et al. suggest that the scores be used for collaborative discussion of a specific lesson between a teacher and a supervisor or between teacher and peers. The specific indicators and their descriptions within each category, the scoring forms, and other critical information can be found in their book *Making Content Comprehensible for English Learners: The SIOP Model* (third edition). The authors recommend videotaping a lesson because they feel that such an audiovisual tool can be particularly helpful to the teacher and can include student reactions as the lesson progresses.

The authors caution that care must be taken in the use of the scores, considering all the variables that may affect them such as time of day, student dynamics, and so on. The authors recommend that conclusions not be based only on a single lesson or observation. Observations over time yield a more reliable assessment.

Margie Brown (personal correspondence), who has used SIOP successfully for several years in District 11 of Colorado Springs, also has a few recommendations. She suggests that evaluators meet with the teachers prior to the observations to learn which categories (and the indicators within them) the teachers want to focus on. Some categories appear to fit certain lesson purposes better than others, and teachers often have intuitions about where they might need improvement. She also likes to use the narrative descriptions for the indicators rather than the rating numbers and have the teachers themselves begin the post-observation discussions by sharing their reflections on how they think the lesson went and what they think they need to work on.

SUMMARY

To succeed in producing individuals who can function with maximum effectiveness in a pluralistic society, we need to be concerned with the development not only of interpersonal skills but also of academic language skills in both first and second languages. Lessons should be made progressively more challenging academically regardless of the program used to teach language and content simultaneously.

Several programs and combinations of programs have much to offer our language minority students. They include ESL through locally developed content programs, sheltered classes, mainstream courses, adjunct classes, and maintenance bilingual programs. Extensive research indicates that maintenance bilingual education is particularly effective in preparing students for the mainstream and for society as a whole. Language majority students in the two-way bilingual education programs, wherever they are found, seem to benefit as well.

Teachers of language minority students need to capitalize on what their students already have—their first languages and cultures. Beginning where these students are and building from there is indeed the responsibility of our schools—and one we cannot minimize except to our detriment as a nation.

Professional development is extremely important to teachers and the myriad programs in which they are teaching. Teacher research and observation and evaluation are among the tools that teachers can use to improve their strategies and overall effectiveness in the classroom.

QUESTIONS AND PROJECTS FOR REFLECTION AND DISCUSSION

1. Do any of the schools in your area have a bilingual program? If so, plan a visit on two or more occasions. Describe the program. What are its goals? How are the two languages handled within the program? How is academic subject matter interwoven into the curriculum? Does the program seem to be well received by the students in the program? by the other students and staff members in the school? by the community surrounding the school? Do you think it is effective? Why or why not? Make sure you obtain the permission of the school administration and the teacher prior to your observations. Discuss your findings with a small group of peers. What did you learn about teaching and learning from this experience?

2. Plan a program in which you would incorporate one-way or two-way bilingual education. Consider these questions: For what age levels or grade levels is your program intended? How would you set it up? Describe its components (e.g., instruction in the primary language, instruction in the second language, sheltered content, mainstream content, formal language instruction, assessment)? How might the various components relate to one another? You might want to include a diagram to graphically illustrate how the students would move within your program. Share your program with a small group to get their input. You may want to make changes based on what you learn.

3. Choose strategies from the suggestions for mainstream, sheltered-class, and adjunct teachers in this chapter and apply them to a specific lesson you prepare for a small group of high-intermediate English learners who are about to enter a sheltered class. Make sure you state clearly the situation and what you have done previously to prepare the students for the transition. Utilize the

Structure for Simulated Lessons on pp. 256–257 and the Sample Lesson Preparation Format on pp. 367–369.

Present your lesson to a small group of fellow students or peers. Discuss with them the strengths of your presentation and ways in which you might improve it. Begin by sharing your own reactions to your presentation. You may want to use the Questions to Guide Evaluative Discussion (p. 257) as the basis for your analysis, or you may use an evaluation format that you or your instructor have developed (see footnote 12 on p. 258).

If you are currently teaching, use what you have learned to try out a similar lesson with your students. Make sure the lesson is relevant and appropriate to level. Afterwards, reflect on its outcome and how you felt about doing it. Did you see any problems with your lesson?

4. Revisit your "Exploring Your Current Beliefs about Learning and Teaching Languages" response on pp. 20–21 and your statement of philosophy (see item 7 on pp. 206–207) to see what you might want to modify or change. Write a short paper about how your beliefs and philosophy may have evolved since then based on what you learned from Parts II and III of this book, other sources, and the teaching experiences you have had, both simulated and/or real. Has your identity as a teacher or a prospective teacher changed in any way as a result?

5. ✎ **Journal Entry:** Reflect on the lesson(s) you carried out in item 3 above. What strategies did you use? How comfortable did you feel with them? Did you think they were effective overall? Why or why not? What were some of the specific problems you encountered? How can they be overcome? Write about what you learned from your peers and instructor during the process. What insights did you gain about learning and teaching from the experience?

SUGGESTED READINGS AND REFERENCE MATERIALS

Baker, C. (2006). *Foundations of bilingual education and bilingualism* (4th ed.). Clevedon, England: Multilingual Matters. This important book presents an introduction to bilingual education and bilingualism and the important related issues. Topics covered are bilingualism and cognition, revitalizing endangered languages, bilingualism and the deaf, identity and empowerment through bilingual education, and many more.

Clarke, M. (2007). *Common ground, contested territory: Examining the roles of English language teachers in troubled times*. Ann Arbor: University of Michigan Press. The author examines the many issues in today's schools that teachers find problematic. The book is based on the premise that teachers themselves need to be the ones in charge of practices affecting students such as planning lessons, selecting activities and materials, and deciding on assessment and evaluation practices. A companion to this book which may interest the reader is titled *A Place to Stand* by the same author.

Crawford, J., & Krashen, S. (2007). *English learners in American classrooms: 101 questions, 101 answers*. New York: Scholastic. This book is a starting place for those wanting a brief introduction to some of the issues and misconceptions commonly associated with teaching English learners. Those desiring more in-depth coverage can turn to the list of supporting sources at the back of the book.

Díaz-Rico, L., & Weed, K. (2005). *The crosscultural, language, and academic development handbook* (3rd ed.). Boston: Allyn & Bacon. This is a valuable resource for ESL and bilingual teachers and administrators across the United States. The book brings together current research, history, theories, important concepts, and illustrative examples, all in an effort to enlighten those working with diverse populations.

Echevarria, J., Vogt, M. E., & Short, D. (2008). *Making content comprehensible for English learners: The SIOP Model.* White Plains, NY: Pearson Education. Presented here is a model of effective sheltered lessons to use for the observation and evaluation of teachers of English learners. The SIOP model can also serve as a valuable tool for planning lessons in which language and content are learned simultaneously.

García, O. (2009). *Bilingual education in the 21st century: A global perspective*. Malden, M. A.: Wiley-Blackwell. This comprehensive text examines the theories and strategies associated with bilingual education as it is practiced around the world. The author builds a case for the benefits of bilingual education for all children and offers a viable framework for its implementation.

Genesee, F., Lindholm-Leary, K., Saunders, W., & Christian, D. (Eds.). (2006). *Educating English language learners: A synthesis of research evidence.* New York: Cambridge University Press. Presented here is an overall review of the research conducted over the past two decades on oral language acquisition, literacy development, and the academic achievement of English learners in schools across the United States, K–12. Bilingual education is examined to determine what role its different forms might play in the process of becoming academically proficient. Most of the chapters end with a useful chart displaying details from the relevant studies.

Palmer, A., & Christison, M. (2007). *Seeking the heart of teaching*. Ann Arbor: University of Michigan Press. The authors take the reader on a journey into the teaching profession and examine how teachers can grow and evolve within it. They encourage teachers to reflect on both their personal and professional development and how this development can increase their sense of fulfillment as teachers.

Richard-Amato, P., & Snow, M. A. (Eds.). (2005a). *Academic success for English language learners: Strategies for K–12 mainstream teachers.* White Plains, NY: Pearson Education/Longman. Focusing on the needs of language minority students, this book addresses theoretical foundations for successful teaching in multicultural classrooms. It explores recommended classroom strategies and practices and later relates them to specific content areas such as math, social studies, science, and literature. Chapters by Jim Cummins, Sonia Nieto, Mary McGroarty and Margarita Calderon, Jana Echevarria and Ann Graves, Pauline Gibbons, Deborah Short, Angela Carrasquillo and Vivian Rodrígues, and many more are included.

PART **IV**

Programs in Action

To be maximally effective, all programs for language-minority students need to be developed locally; they need to grow out of perceived needs and desires of the particular students served. Even so, we can learn much from programs such as those presented in this section. Reading about how other teachers, past and present, have implemented and developed methods, activities, and methodologies (including situated decisions about content, how and when to correct, how to incorporate a silent period, and so forth) can give teachers a wealth of information from which to draw. Exploring the ways in which vital questions have been answered by others can give real insights into what might work in certain situations, with specific groups of learners.

The programs described here have been divided into English as a second language (ESL) programs (Chapter 18), foreign language programs (Chapter 19), and two-way bilingual and heritage language programs (Chapter 20). Several different levels are represented—elementary through university, including adult basic education. Some are district-wide programs; others take place in a single school or college/university setting. An immersion foreign language village, a sheltered English program, a life-skills program using community resources, a college English language program, a university support program, two two-way bilingual education programs, and a heritage language program are only a few of the many presented here.

CHAPTER 18

ESL Programs

As I stated in Chapter 17, a program possibility to consider for K–12 English learners might be one that combines ESL with locally developed versions of mainstreaming, sheltered classes, and maintenance bilingual education. Adjunct courses might be created, particularly at the college and university levels. Although none of the programs described in this chapter has claimed to be a model as such, all have features worthy of careful examination. The programs include a college English language program (Saint Michael's College in Colchester, Vermont), a university support program (California State University, Los Angeles), a life-skills adult basic education program (the North Hollywood Adult Learning Center in Hollywood, California), a secondary sheltered English program (Artesia High School in Artesia, California), an elementary district-wide program (Alhambra School District in Alhambra, California), and a kindergarten ESL program within a Spanish bilingual school (Loma Vista Elementary in Maywood, California).

Some of the descriptions focus on the overall design of the programs, others on specific elements within them. Although the programs were developed originally for specific age groups and purposes, the basic designs and activities need not be used exclusively in these situations. An imaginative teacher can probably see many ways in which some of their features might be adapted for local educational settings.

A COLLEGE ENGLISH LANGUAGE PROGRAM[1]

The School of International Studies (SIS), established in 1954 at Saint Michael's College in Colchester, Vermont, is one of the oldest centers of its kind in the United States, and it is one of the first (if not the first) to incorporate sheltered and adjunct courses into its curriculum. Over the years, four major programs have evolved: the Intensive English Program (IEP), the Academic English Program (AEP), the Special English Program,[2] and the Master of Arts in Teaching English as a Second Language (MATESL) Program. In this chapter, only two of these programs are described: the IEP and the AEP.

The Intensive English Program

The IEP, which serves approximately forty to sixty students each semester, is not restricted to students having academic interests only; thus it is varied in its approach and offerings. The program is available to students year-round with openings every four weeks. The students generally remain in the program for anywhere from twelve to sixteen weeks, depending on their needs and interests.

Because the program serves a wide spectrum of students, its goals are both general and academic. It offers five levels of instruction, from low-beginning to advanced. Once students have completed a series of tests, they are placed at the appropriate level. Students operating at the lowest levels focus on oral activities in all classes; reading and writing activities are introduced to support oral language development.

Students at higher levels have a somewhat different schedule. In the morning, they take what is known as "the Core" which consists of integrated instruction in reading, writing, and grammar. Following the Core, students attend either a reading lab (i.e., a reading skills development class) or a grammar lab where they receive additional individualized help with grammar. In the afternoon, an oral skills class is offered along with a listening lab Monday, Wednesday, and Friday (MWF) and a special topics class Tuesday and Thursday (TTH). The lab classes may take place in the classroom or in the Language Learning Resource Center, which offers audio, video, and computer-assisted instruction for individualized or group work. See Figure 18.1 on p. 448 for a sample schedule.

The Reading Lab

The reading lab provides additional work in reading skills. Typical activities include reading-rate exercises; practice with previewing, skimming, and scanning texts; text organization activities; and vocabulary development exercises. Students are also introduced to extensive reading materials, and they read about specific topics, such as the history of Vermont or issues concerning business. For novice readers, the selections are on cassettes so that students can hear them read aloud. The work is individualized and

---

[1] I am very grateful to Sally Cummings and Carolyn Duffy at Saint Michael's College for allowing me to include this description.

[2] The program is specially designed for groups from other countries who want a short-term language and cultural program tailored to their needs (e.g., a group of Colombian high school students wanting to improve their academic English skills while learning about culture in the United States).

9:00–11:00	Core	Reading Writing Grammar
11:15–12:00	Reading Lab Grammar Lab	
1:00–3:05 (MWF)	Oral Communications Skills Class Listening Lab	
1:00–3:30 (TTH)	Special Topics Class (elective)	

Figure 18.1 A Typical IEP Schedule

learner centered in that students plan what they will work on with their instructor as a guide. Students also select books for independent reading from the program's library (again under the guidance of the instructor). They respond to what they are reading either by writing in their journals or by giving oral and/or written reports.

The Core

The core curriculum uses an integrated-skills approach. Each unit has a theme around which reading, writing, and grammar revolve. The required texts are supplemented with films, guest speakers, field trips, and authentic related readings. For example, in the reading component, a unit on education and learning styles is supplemented by an article about student test scores from *The New York Times*. A component of the Core is devoted to specific grammar instruction, drawing from the unit's theme-based materials.

During the writing component, students write letters requesting information about alternative schools in the area. In the afternoon oral skills component, students conduct phone interviews and take a field trip to an alternative school. Viewing the classic movie *Stand and Deliver* provides a culmination of the work accomplished up to this point. The in-depth discussion and writing activities that follow allow the students to synthesize what they have learned.

The Listening Lab

The listening lab has a dual function: (a) it extends and enriches what students are learning in the oral skills class, and (b) it provides an opportunity to practice aural skills through materials that students themselves have chosen. Students can focus on activities to improve general comprehension; specific items such as numbers, prepositions, or reduced forms; or academic skills such as note-taking.

The Oral Communication Skills Class

This class, which is usually coordinated with the listening lab, includes work with both academic and conversational oral and aural skills. Themes and topics introduced in the morning Core are continued in the oral communication skills class. Activities typical of this class include listening to academic lectures, conducting interviews, listening and responding to guest speakers, participating in role plays, creating videos, and participating in debates. A component of this class is devoted to pronunciation work and introduces students to individualized pronunciation programs such as *Pronunciation Power* for individual practice.

The Special Topics Class

Examples of special topics classes from which students can choose are as follows:

1. Current Events: High-intermediate and advanced students read and discuss human interest articles from *The New York Times*.
2. Games and Puzzles: Students at all levels select games consonant with their proficiency levels. Popular choices are Jeopardy and Clue. Word games of various sorts and number puzzles are among the many options available.
3. English through TV: Students view news items, commercials, and clips from television programs. This way, they can acquire new vocabulary and improve their listening skills. In addition, the lively discussions generated by shows enable students to practice communication skills.
4. Business English: High-intermediate and advanced students study aspects of business and take field trips to area businesses.

The Academic English Program

The AEP serves as a bridge to academic coursework and involves intensive English study that prepares students for the academic courses typically found at American colleges and universities. It evolved out of a need to provide a transition to the campus mainstream. Before the program was established in 1972, students often found themselves floundering for up to a year or more in courses for which they were not adequately prepared, culturally or linguistically. Drawing on Cummins's distinction between the context-rich learning environments (as represented by the ESL classes) and the context-reduced learning environments (as represented by undergraduate mainstream classes), a rationale was developed for the establishment of the AEP.

The program's courses are credit bearing, and students who successfully complete them can transfer the credits to their undergraduate degree programs either at Saint Michael's College or at other institutions. The courses integrate both content-based and language-based teaching procedures and are taken over a two-semester time period. Students may enter the program either directly from the IEP or by applying to the program. Acceptance is based on scores from the Test of English as a Foreign Language (TOEFL) and/or the English Language Proficiency Test. In addition, students take a test in academic skills prepared by the SIS. This test includes an authentic academic lecture and reading followed by a multiple-choice/essay task. Teacher recommendations and prior academic performance are part of the data used to determine appropriate placement within the program. All students entering the AEP from the IEP are first required to take a course that focuses on academic readings, lectures, and note-taking.

Within the AEP itself there are two levels: Level 1 and Level 2. Level 1, offered the first semester, is oriented to intermediate students. These students take a cooperative course, a sheltered course in college reading and writing, and a course in advanced grammar. The cooperative course has evolved over the years to include an adjunct program. It features mainstream academic content, taught by regular undergraduate faculty, and a language component, taught by a language teacher from the SIS. Level 2 is offered in the second semester and is oriented toward advanced students who take sheltered courses in literature, advanced college writing, and two mainstream undergraduate courses. A special undergraduate elective, Oral Presentation Skills, has been added for international students and can be taken by Level 2 students. See Figure 18.2.

Level 1		Level 2	
Cooperative Course (adjunct)	(3–4 credits)	Introduction to Literature (sheltered)	(3 credits)
Academic English for the Cooperative Course (sheltered)	(1 credit)	Advanced College Writing (sheltered)	(3 credits)
College Reading and Writing (sheltered)	(3 credits)	Oral Presentation Skills (sheltered; elective)	(3 credits)
Advanced Grammar (sheltered)	(1 credit)	Two undergraduate courses (mainstream)	(6 credits)

Figure 18.2 AEP Courses and Credits

The Cooperative Course (Adjunct)

The first cooperative course offered at the AEP was a sheltered course in chemistry, taught by a mainstream undergraduate professor and a language instructor from the SIS. The course was sheltered in that the students taking it were all international students and the language was modified for their comprehension. Soon it became apparent that it might be better to include proficient English speakers so the international students could gain the skills needed to function in mainstream situations; thus changes were made. The course soon lost the characteristics inherent in a sheltered program and began to resemble instead an adjunct program. Now the language instructor from the SIS attends all lecture and discussion sessions, takes notes, and, when appropriate, records all classroom events on cassettes. The language instructor then conducts an adjunct language class in the AEP for the international students in which the concepts and academic language requirements of the cooperative course are integrated. Following are the goals of the adjunct class:

> The development and integration of:
> academic language proficiency
> a solid knowledge of the content
> discussion/interaction skills
> academic grammatical competence
> library research skills
> study skills

The cooperative course became so successful that it was offered in numerous content areas: biology, human genetics, nutrition, business, economics, political science, mass communication, religious studies, and philosophy. Sally Cummings and Carolyn Duffy, both instructors at the SIS, report significant benefits of the course based on their discussions with undergraduate faculty, the international students themselves, and the proficient English speakers in the cooperative courses.

1. Benefits to members of the undergraduate faculty:
   a. The cooperative teaching approach caused many of them to reexamine their own teaching styles.
   b. They gained a better understanding of the tasks that face international students in an academic course.
   c. Their courses improved due to the new and necessary viewpoints contributed by the international students.
2. Benefits to the international students:
   a. Their opportunities for interaction with proficient English speakers increased substantially even after the course ended.
   b. They were more confident and more active class participants in all their classes once they had taken the cooperative course.
3. Benefits to proficient English speakers:
   a. They gained a new awareness of international students through the sharing of cultural values and experiences.
   b. They learned about other points of view.

College Writing (Sheltered)

The second course in Level 1 is the sheltered course in college reading and writing. This course integrates academic reading, writing, listening, and other academic skills. However, its central focus is on writing for academic purposes.

Advanced Grammar (Sheltered)

This course focuses on problem areas of grammar and allows for even more language work and additional reinforcement. When possible, coordination with the college reading and writing course allows instructors to address in greater depth student errors that surface in writing.

Introduction to Literature (Sheltered)

Students in Level 2 take a sheltered course called Introduction to Literature, which includes selections from both American and international literature. They read, discuss, and write about the novels, short stories, poetry, and plays they read. One special feature of this course is that sometimes the plays they read are the same plays that the theater department is producing. The students are often invited to attend rehearsals.

Advanced College Writing (Sheltered)

The second course in Level 2 is a course in sheltered advanced college writing. Here students further develop their writing competence by exploring rhetorical modes of academic discourse. In this course they become aware of their own developing writing styles. In addition to reading and writing essays in various rhetorical modes, they complete a library research paper. Importance is placed on peer and student–teacher conferences throughout the revision process.

Oral Presentation Skills (Sheltered)

This course was developed at the request of undergraduate faculty once they realized that the international students needed more work in oral presentation skills. The course includes extemporaneous speaking; a focus on pronunciation problems, if needed; and a PowerPoint project, among other topics.

Mainstream Undergraduate Courses

In addition to the courses mentioned, Level 2 students take two mainstream courses of their choice at the undergraduate level. Before making their selections, the students are advised by the director of International Student Affairs. Once in the mainstream, they are invited to return to their teachers in the SIS, particularly their composition teachers. They are also encouraged to use the college writing center, whose tutors are trained to assist international students. At times, they seek tutorial help from MATESL practicum students.

Support Services

Student assistants organize and execute the international student orientation program and serve as hosts for international students during their first week on campus. The student assistants meet the international students at the airport, take them to a local bank, serve as English language conversation partners, and in many other ways assist them and serve as their support group.

The director of International Student Affairs conducts campus and community orientation sessions and provides ongoing support for all international students. In addition, this person serves as a liaison between the SIS and student affairs offices such as housing and health services. The Program Activities Coordinator plans evening and weekend trips off campus and publishes a weekly bulletin highlighting upcoming events of interest, cultural information, and language-related quizzes and puzzles.

The SIS itself attempts to maximize the interaction and integration of the international students with their English-speaking peers. The Program Activities Coordinator also organizes additional activities and involves the international students in volunteer work such as serving dinner at the local soup kitchen for the homeless, planting and harvesting a garden for the Food Shelf, or assisting at Special Olympics events.

The SIS also sponsors weekly afternoon coffee hours during which the international students are integrated with mainstream students who are studying foreign languages. The coffee hours offer at least two benefits for all students who attend. First, they increase the opportunities for students to interact in the languages they are trying to learn. Second, students have a chance to increase their knowledge of the various cultures represented and make new friends.

Yet another service provided by the SIS is the individual study components of the English Language Program, which utilize a computer-assisted instructional component for grammar, a self-study reading lab, and a writing center. The latter is staffed by students in the Master of Arts in Teaching English as a Second Language program who set up individual conferences with the international students to discuss their writing. Participation in the writing center also benefits the M.A. students themselves by giving them the opportunity to work with international students and obtain the advantages that such authentic experiences provide.

Future Directions

One might wonder how the SIS could better provide for the needs of international students. A major strength of the SIS is its flexibility; it can change in response to the needs of its students and in the light of current theory and research in the field of second language learning and teaching. Because of increased student interest in theme-based content in upper levels of the IEP, the SIS is extending this method of organization to the lower levels as well. The SIS has found that highly motivating themes such as tourism and global issues (e.g., environment and peace education) are an excellent way to integrate language development and content. Moreover, such themes encourage analysis, synthesis, and the critical evaluation of information.

The success of its cooperative courses has spurred the AEP staff to make plans to develop additional courses for students at Levels 1 and 2. Experience has shown that the most successful cooperative courses are academic courses that (a) utilize the background knowledge of the international students and (b) incorporate writing as a major learning tool. These factors will be included as criteria for the development of new cooperative courses. In addition, the AEP will coordinate more closely with the cooperative course and the sheltered reading and writing course in order to maximize language and content integration.

A UNIVERSITY SUPPORT PROGRAM: PROJECT LEAP[3]

Overview of the Project

Project LEAP (Learning English for Academic Purposes), a six-year project at California State University, Los Angeles, was funded by the U.S. Department of Education Fund for the Improvement of Postsecondary Education. Its main goal was to make the undergraduate general education curriculum more accessible to the university's language minority student population by enhancing the support system developed by the Educational Opportunity Program (EOP).

The students included in Project LEAP were the same students in the already existing EOP, whose program was aimed at bilingual, low-income, first-generation college students, both immigrant and native English-speaking. Thirty-three percent of the students in EOP had been admitted to the university on special admission status because their SAT scores and high school grade point averages did not qualify them for regular admission.

The EOP Study Group Program

The students in the EOP Study Group Program were advised by counselors to select certain sections among the general education courses required of all incoming freshmen.

---

[3] I want to thank Ann Snow and Janet Tricamo, codirectors of Project LEAP, for making their materials and program available to me.

These sections were paired with one-credit study group courses[4] taught by trained peer leaders. Each study group met for three hours a week with its peer leader, who had attended the same lectures and completed the same course readings as the students. The students received assistance from the peer leader in comprehending course content, preparing for exams, developing individual study skills, and practicing group study techniques. Each peer leader was considered a facilitator of the many activities planned for the group.

The peer leaders (generally recommended by faculty members) were either upper-division or graduate students. They had themselves received at least a B in the courses with which their study groups were paired. They were required to complete an initial eighteen-hour training program and were closely observed and evaluated weekly during their first quarter of employment as peer leaders. In addition, they attended biweekly staff training meetings.

Project LEAP

The four major goals of Project LEAP were

1. to improve and expand the existing EOP study group courses.
2. to provide faculty development training for the professors teaching regular general education courses.
3. to effect curriculum modification to institutionalize language-sensitive instruction.
4. to gain project continuity and dissemination by training future instructors and peer leaders of the study group courses.

To meet these goals, Project LEAP prepared peer leaders to address more effectively the academic language (as well as content) needs of their assigned students; instructed content-area faculty teaching the general education courses in strategies for teaching academic literacy; developed a language- and content-based curriculum that could be used in all group study courses on campus, even after the project was completed; and created and/or adapted materials for the targeted general education courses.

During the project's first year, three general education courses were targeted: biology, history, and introductory psychology. Attached to each of these courses was a LEAP study group course, led by a peer and a professional language specialist. The course aimed to integrate content instruction and related academic language skills. The time frame for the study group course was extended from three to four hours per week, and two credits were earned instead of one. During the second year of the project, political science, sociology, and speech were targeted, and during the third year, anthropology, health science, and a laboratory biology course. In the second three-year grant, faculty who taught upper-division courses were trained, and courses in departments which did not previously participate, such as business and engineering, were targeted.

---

[4] The study group courses in the already existing program and in Project LEAP were similar in concept to the adjunct courses described in Chapter 17 and those at the Center at Saint Michael's College in Colchester, Vermont (see previous program).

Academic Content/Language Teaching Strategies

LEAP Group Study Courses

In addition to working with academic content and language, the LEAP study group courses taught students self-sufficiency and interpersonal communication skills so they might participate more actively in their assigned groups. A question–answer format was used by group leaders who initially prepared the pertinent questions (both knowledge based and inferential) from the lectures and readings. Once students gained experience in answering questions, they brought in more of their own questions as they took greater responsibility for the group's effectiveness. Study skills presentations were made at least three times each quarter by the peer leader or a study skills specialist from the university's Learning Resource Center. Actual course material was used in the presentations. Practice quizzes were given often by the peer leaders to emphasize the content of the readings or to help the students prepare for exams.

The following questions are from the peer leader self-evaluation form.

Discussion Leading

1. Did everyone participate in the discussion?
2. Did you give the students enough time to respond and wait until they were through?
3. Did you give reinforcement for correct and partially correct answers?
4. Did you make sure all the words used in the discussion were clear to the students?
5. Did you redirect the students' questions back to the group?
6. Did you test the students even though they said they understood the material?
7. Did the students do more talking than you did?
8. Was the level of difficulty of questions or materials appropriate?

Study Skills

1. Did you explain the study skill clearly?
2. Did you give the students ample opportunity to implement the skill?
3. Did you explain how they can benefit by using this skill?
4. Did you relate it to your subject area?
5. Did you explain how it can be applied to other areas?
6. Will you remember to refer to this skill again throughout the quarter?

Quizzes and Tests

1. Was it short enough for the students to complete in the allotted time period?
2. Was the level of difficulty appropriate?
3. Did you review the quiz immediately after the students completed it?
4. Did you ask the students to explain how they got their answers?
5. Do the students who missed a question know why they missed it and where to go to find the correct answer?
6. Did you make notes of the questions that were frequently missed, so that you can test the students again later?

The General Education Courses

The strategies presented here were designed by the LEAP study group leaders, language specialists, and course instructors for use in the general education courses. All the strategies were aimed to help the students learn the content and improve their academic language regardless of their language background. They included the following:

1. Students submitted assignments in stages (especially longer papers) instead of the previous "one-shot" term paper assignment.
2. The course syllabus made all expectations explicit.
3. A variety of instructional techniques accommodated diverse learning styles in the classroom. These included increased wait time, avoiding "spotlighting" students, and group work.
4. Guidelines made explicit the critical thinking or analytical requirements of assignments.
5. More interaction between faculty and students was encouraged. For example, one visit to the professor during office hours was made a course requirement.
6. Students were made more accountable for keeping up with reading assignments through pop quizzes, chapter study guide assignments, and so on.
7. Lectures were improved by reviewing key concepts from the previous lecture; writing an agenda on the board for each class session; explicitly defining general academic vocabulary; referring less frequently to cultural, generational, or class-based references that might not be part of the students' background experiences.

The following are samples from some of the activities used in the general education courses. Although each sample is intended for a specific course, with some modification it could be adapted for other courses.

LIST-MAKING EXERCISE: RECONSTRUCTION[5]

To answer a complicated question, you first need to compile all of the relevant information. Eventually, you will be able to answer the question: Was the Civil War and Reconstruction Era a watershed in the South? Why or why not?

1. List all of the evidence that shows change. List all of the evidence that shows continuity.

Change	Continuity
a.	
b.	
c.	

---

[5] Contributed by Carole Srole.

Sample Textbook Survey[6]

Understanding how your textbook is organized will help you with your studies. If you familiarize yourself with the basic content and organization of the text, reading it for academic purposes will be easier because you will understand the basic purpose of each section and chapter.

I. **Instructions:** Working in small groups, fill in the blanks below.
Name of course: _____
Title of textbook: _____
Author(s): _____
Author(s') qualifications (e.g., university degree, professional affiliation, etc.): _____
Copyright date: _____
Has the book been revised? _____

II. **Instructions:** Working in groups, survey your textbook and decide which of the following features it contains. Place a check in the appropriate column. Then, by analyzing each of the sections, determine the purpose that each serves. Be ready to share your ideas with the entire class.

	Yes	**No**
Table of contents		
Bibliography		
Name index		
Subject index		
Preface		
Glossary		

III. **Instructions:** Using your textbook and working in small groups, answer the following questions or locate the requested information. Be prepared to explain how you found the information to the rest of the class.

1. What were the author's goals in writing the book? Where did you find the information?
   _____
   _____

2. Look at the table of contents. Is the organization of topics easy to follow?
   _____
   _____

3. On what page(s) will you find a discussion of stereotyping?
   _____
   _____

4. How did you find the page number?
   _____
   _____

5. How does the author explain stereotyping?
   _____
   _____

---

[6] Contributed by Gloria Romero, Carolina Espinoza, and Lía Kamhi-Stein.

6. If you wanted to read the entire article quoted on page _____, where could you find the complete reference?

_____

_____

Grammar Exercise: Error Analysis[7]

I. Instructions: The following sentences were taken from student papers. Working in pairs or small groups, analyze the structural or grammatical problems and discuss ways to rewrite the sentences.

1. The incentive was to have people buy American products instead of foreign trade.
2. Industrialization led to a transformation from an agrarian to an industrial economy, which caused much more social problems and a social class system.
3. Also government supported the business by passing vagrancy laws. These laws made business profitable. By using blacks to work in there company.
4. In 1914 congress passed the Clayton act prohibited unfair trading practices.
5. An example of this was the Sugar treaty. The sugar treaty was good for the business because they saved money in two way's and they were that they paid low wages, and did not have to pay tariff's to the Hawaiian government.

Identifying Cause and Effect[8]

I. **Instructions:** Identifying the cause and effect of events and movements is a critical part of any study of history. Sometimes students don't make a clear differentiation between the cause and its results or may even mistake one for the other. Identify the causes and effects in the following statements.

Example:

The owl and the pussycat went to sea in a beautiful pea green boat. They felt the need to get away.

Cause: They felt the need to get away.
Effect: The owl and the pussycat went to sea in a beautiful pea green boat.

1. The Emancipation Proclamation and the freeing of the slaves did not produce a society with complete equality for African Americans, and their condition remained desperate.

   Cause:
   Effect:

2. Because of the development of birth control, women could delay having children or avoid having them altogether; consequently, women had the opportunity to acquire an education or pursue a career.

   Cause:
   Effect:

---

[7] Contributed by Nick Zonen.

[8] Contributed by Nick Zonen.

Research on Project LEAP

The results of program evaluation conducted at the conclusion of the first three years revealed that, overall, the performance of students in the Project LEAP study group courses approximated or exceeded that of the students in the language-enhanced general education courses. Specifically, students enrolled in the study group courses earned a higher percentage of As and Bs than those who did not participate in the study groups. Furthermore, the course grade point averages of the study group students were equal to or higher than those of comparison students in six of the nine courses. Analysis of open-ended questionnaires indicated that the Project LEAP students were very positive in their evaluation of both the study groups and the enhanced general education courses. The students reported that the project had assisted them in developing their reading, writing, and note-taking skills in particular, but many noted that they needed to improve their reading skills further.

From the faculty perspective, follow-up evaluation after six years revealed that participants were more aware of their students' language needs and had incorporated academic literacy instruction on a regular basis into their courses. They reported positive results both in content learning and in the written performance of their students. In addition, other benefits accrued. Several faculty participants published articles describing their academic literacy enhancements in such discipline-specific journals as *The History Teacher* and *Advances in Physiology Education*. Others applied Project LEAP principles to newly identified need areas such as training graduate laboratory instructors or developing strategies for teaching very large classes. Several departments changed faculty hiring practices, requiring experience and interest in teaching linguistically and culturally diverse students. Finally, more than sixty faculty members across the campus adopted the multistep writing assignment and library research activity developed in Project LEAP.

Resources

More detailed descriptions of Project LEAP can be found in the following:

Snow, M. A., & Kamhi-Stein, L. D. (2002). Teaching and learning academic literacy through Project LEAP. In J. Crandall & D. Kaufman (Eds.), *Case studies in TESOL practice: Content-based instruction* (pp. 169–181). Alexandria, VA: Teachers of English to Speakers of Other Languages.

Snow, M. A. (1997). Teaching academic literacy skills: Discipline faculty take responsibility. In M. A. Snow & D. M. Brinton (Eds.), *The content-based classroom: Perspectives on integrating language and content* (pp. 290–304). White Plains, NY: Longman.

A LIFE-SKILLS ADULT BASIC EDUCATION PROGRAM[9]

In an attempt to meet the needs of adults who were struggling not only with learning a new language but also with providing a living for themselves and their

[9] I would like to thank the program's original coordinator Sandra Brown, who provided the information on which this summary was based. Thanks also goes to Harriet Fisher, Rheta Goldman, Roberto Martinez, Ethel Schwartz, Katie Treibach, and the many others I talked with during my observation.

families, the North Hollywood Adult Learning Center made the community part of its classroom.

The 500 students who were enrolled in the program represented many different cultural groups from around the world: Hispanic (70%), Asian (12%), Middle Eastern (9%), and European (4%). The remaining 5 percent were native English speakers who were taking courses outside of the basic ESL program. The curriculum itself consisted of six levels of ESL, from beginning to advanced; a reading lab for students with special problems in reading; a language skills lab which emphasized writing, spelling, and grammar; and a high school lab for those desiring a GED certificate or a high school diploma. In the latter three, the ESL and proficient English-speaking students were mixed.

Incorporating Community Resources

Every month, the activities were built around specific life-skills units such as the following:

Community Resources

- the community and its members
- autobiographical data
- cultural–social integration
- the world around us
- police–fire–paramedic services
- the telephone
- the post office
- leisure-time activities
- athletic activities
- entertainment activities
- recreational activities
- educational services
- schools
- libraries

Government and the Law

- vehicles and the law
- law and legal services
- taxes
- current issues

Consumer Economics

- individual/family economy
- physical concerns
- financial services

- consumer rights
- insurance
- consumerism
- general shopping skills
- food shopping
- meals
- clothing shopping
- housing

Mental and Physical Health

- medical care
- nutrition
- personal hygiene
- dental care
- safety and home

Occupational Knowledge

- vocational training/counseling
- job searches
- the interview
- on-the-job skills

These topics and the information related to them served as an important part of the content through which the structures, vocabulary, and pronunciation of English were taught. Integral to these units were trips that the students at all levels took to city government offices, occupational centers, markets, commercial businesses, factories, music/arts centers, libraries, museums, parks, hospitals, and many other places in and around the city.

On one such trip to the farmers' market, Rheta Goldman, a teacher of intermediate ESL, asked her students to find the answers to the following questions:

> What animals are in the window of the pet shop?
> Find the post office. What shops are next to the post office?
> What's the name of a store where you can get shoes repaired?
> Go to the farmers' market newspaper stand. Can you buy a newspaper in your
> native language?
> How much does it cost?
> What kind of food can you buy at the shop next to Gill's Ice Cream Shop?
> Find the glassblower. Write the names of four glass animals you can buy there.
> How much does a fresh-baked pie cost from Du-Bar's Bakery?
> What kinds of pies do they have today? Name three.

In addition to the trips and related activities, the students were exposed to films and real-life materials. Also, a variety of representatives from the community visited the classrooms: an immigration attorney to give advice on becoming citizens; a speaker from the Red Cross to help the students be better prepared in the event of a major earthquake; a representative from the Department of Consumer Affairs to inform them of their rights as consumers; and police officers to make them aware of strategies to use in protecting themselves from crime, to name a few. In connection with the units, the students also participated in classroom activities such as role play, dialogues, conversations, discussions, and writing activities commensurate with their proficiency levels.

To aid other teachers in setting up similar programs, the coordinator and teachers at North Hollywood compiled extensive lists of ideas in several areas: community services, consumer education, cultural awareness, employment, family life, government/citizenship/law, health, and recreation. The following is an example.

Community Services

Real-life materials/transparencies.

1. *Post office* forms
2. *Bank* forms, statements, checks, travelers' checks
3. *Telephone* directory pages of zip code maps; emergency telephone numbers; telephone bills
4. *Driver's license* application form, test, change of address form
5. *Traffic signs* parking/traffic citation forms; bus, train, airline schedules; bus maps from local bus company; road maps from the local chamber of commerce

6. *School* (elementary, secondary, adult) enrollment forms; school report card; announcement of school activity

7. *Library* card applications

Brochures. Police department (home protection, self-defense, drugs, and so on); fire department (fire prevention); automobile club and National Safety Council (traffic safety); Department of Motor Vehicles (driver manual); library; building and safety department (earthquake safety); adult school (schedule of classes); city council member, state assembly member (booklets on local agencies and services).

Audiovisuals. Television programs, movies, recordings of telephone conversations (students were told prior to hearing the recordings that they were only simulations) with police and fire departments, telephone directory assistance operators; bus, train, taxi, and airline personnel; conversations in the community—at the post office, bank, with child's teacher, and so on; telephone reports of weather, and current road conditions; Teletrainers—actual telephone conversations with a control unit, and so forth.

Speakers. Police officer (home protection or self-defense, with film and demonstration); firefighter (with film on fire safety and exit procedures); paramedics (with demonstration of life-saving equipment and techniques); AAA and National Safety Council representatives (with films on traffic safety); library aide; elementary, secondary and/or adult school principal; city council member on community services; United Way representative.

Trips. Fire station; police department; post office; bank (before it opens); library; telephone company; local elementary school; airport.

Subjects for Discussion, Dialogue, Role Playing, and Other Activities. *At the post office*. Sending, insuring, picking up packages; buying stamps, airletters, correctly addressing letters; and so on.

At the bank. Savings/checking; deposit/withdrawal; safe deposit boxes, and so on.

Emergency services. The role of police in home and self-protection; fire prevention; reporting a fire, a prowler, a break-in, an auto accident, calling the paramedics; what to do in case of a fire, earthquake, break-in, rape attempt; experiences with and attitudes toward police.

Telephone. Emergency calls; long-distance calls; taking messages; using the telephone directory; social and business calls; a report of a disconnected phone.

Transportation. Car, taxi, bus, train, airline schedules; map-reading activities; locating local services; geography of local areas; traffic safety; dangers of hitchhiking; obtaining a driver's license; what to do at the gas station or garage; asking directions.

Education. Registering child/self in school; conference with child's teacher, counselor, principal, nurse; participation in child's school activities; report cards; education in the United States compared with education in other countries; levels and types of education; special education; private schools; new approaches to education; admission requirements to colleges and universities.

Library. Card application; overdue books; reserving books; foreign-language books; using children's books.

Philanthropic organizations. Becoming involved in volunteer activities; charities; charity drives; animal protection agencies.

Community Volunteers

One of the most interesting aspects of the program was its utilization of volunteers from the community. Eighteen community workers arrived every week to assist the teachers in classrooms, tutor students, or help out wherever they were needed. They came primarily from the ranks of homemakers and retirees. Although they received no monetary rewards for their time, they did receive numerous rewards of a different kind. Their individual birthdays were celebrated, articles in school papers were written to honor their accomplishments, and special days were set aside to recognize the work they did. Ranging in age from twenty-six to eighty-two, they formed a dependable resource. Some were there only one or two hours a week; others worked fifteen to twenty hours. The volunteers determined, in advance, their own schedules and signed contracts confirming the agreement (see the sample contract, Figure 18.3 on p. 464).

Once officially accepted as staff members, the volunteers were given mailboxes and their names were added to the check-in sheets. After an orientation, they went to their assigned classrooms where they were trained by the teacher with whom they would be working. In addition to the orientation and training, the volunteers were given suggestions in writing concerning general strategies to use when working with students. (See Chapter 15 in this volume for a similar list intended for peer facilitator and lay assistant training.) They also received self-evaluation checklists containing items about cooperation with others, following the teacher's directions, being friendly and encouraging, and so forth.

A SECONDARY SHELTERED ENGLISH PROGRAM[10]

We learned in Chapter 17 that a sheltered class is a kind of immersion situation in that the students are at similar levels of proficiency in the target language. We also learned that the teacher may be familiar with their first languages and usually has a knowledge of their cultures. A sheltered class can provide the modified language necessary for the

---

[10] Thanks to Pam Branch, Lilia Stapleton, Marie Takagaki, Ted Marquez, and many others with the ABC Unified School District who made it possible for me to observe their sheltered class program and include it in this chapter.

**North Hollywood Adult Learning Center
Volunteer Job Description and Agreement**

POSITION TITLE: Adults Basic Education Tutor

PLACE: _____ Reading Lab   _____ High School Lab

_____ Language Skills Lab   _____ English as a Second Language

PROGRAM OBJECTIVES: To assist students who want to learn to improve their basic
skills in English as a second language or to earn a GED
certificate or a high school diploma.

TIME COMMITMENT: Days _____   Hours _____
_____   _____

RESPONSIBILITIES:
- To work under the guidance and supervision of the teacher to whom you have been assigned
- To work with either individuals or groups according to the needs of the teacher and students
- To follow the teacher's plans for each session
- To assist the teacher in any way the teacher feels will be of benefit to the students
- To be reliable and on time on regularly scheduled days
- To sign in and out on the sign-in sheet
- To inform the office or teacher if you must be absent (The volunteer does not: diagnose student needs, prescribe instruction, select materials, evaluate student progress, or counsel students.)

QUALIFICATION:
- A positive attitude, interest and enthusiasm in working with adult basic education students
- Ability to work cooperatively with school personnel and other volunteers
- Adequate communication skills
- Dedication to fulfill all of the obligations of the position

TRAINING: BY THE TEACHER TO WHOM YOU ARE ASSIGNED

I have read and understand the above and agree to conscientiously carry out the responsibilities as described.

x_____

Figure 18.3 Volunteer Job Description and Agreement

student to acquire the target language through content-based instruction. At the same time, it can serve as a surrogate family of sorts or a temporary buffer between the student and the mainstream.

Artesia High School in Artesia, California, was one of the schools in the ABC Unified School District that created a highly developed network of sheltered classes. The school offered thirty-six sections of ESL and sheltered classes to approximately 350 English learners who represented twenty-one different languages. All the students in what was called the Diverse Language Program (ESL only) were eligible to take the special courses. Pam Branch, the school's program coordinator, reported:

> What immersion has taught us is that comprehensible subject matter teaching *is* language teaching; students can profit a great deal from subject-matter classes in which the conscious focus is on the topic and not on language. Classes are taught in English, but native speakers are excluded in order to make the teacher's input more understandable for limited-English students.

Students in this program began with two periods of ESL and three sheltered classes in specific subject-matter areas (see Figure 18.4 on p. 466). Later, they were able to add other sheltered classes (see Figure 18.5 on p. 467). Gradually, they became fully mainstreamed, first in those areas that required less command of English and later in all subjects. Bilingual aides provided primary language support for the students.

Identification and Evaluation

A home language survey and supplementary questionnaire was used to identify English learners in the school district. Once the student was identified, he or she took one or more selected standardized tests of basic skills and completed an informal writing sample. Each student was then rated on an oral language observation matrix that was similar to the American Council on the Teaching of Foreign Languages proficiency levels 1 through 5. On the basis of these measures, students were placed in either Level I, II, or III.

Description of Each Level

Level I (akin to the beginning levels described on p. 182–183) included two periods of ESL: *Skills I* and *Conversation I*. At this level, the students could also choose from among several sheltered courses (see Figure 18.4).

Skills I focused on survival skills such as telling time, using the telephone, filling out application forms, and so forth. *Conversation I* emphasized various topics of interest such as those recommended by Krashen and Terrell (1983; see Chapter 9). In both classes, physical approaches and interactive teaching appeared to minimize anxiety and provide sufficient modified language. The sheltered classes at this level required tasks that were cognitively undemanding and heavily context embedded. For example, in *Art,* students were given a wide variety of art experiences in which they could express themselves freely while studying composition and color as these were used in drawing, painting, and making three-dimensional objects. *Geography* also relied on concrete concepts for which pictures, maps, and globes were used. Drawing or making papier-mâché maps in relief provided a great deal of hands-on activity. *Horticulture* found students planting and caring for a garden after diagramming and labeling the plants in a basic plan. The course not only helped students acquire the language through concrete tasks but may have even opened up some possible jobs for

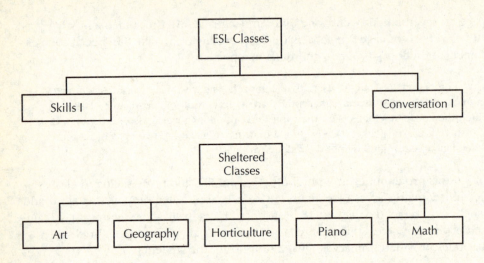

Figure 18.4 Level I

the future. *Piano* offered individualized instruction on the use of electric keyboards with headsets. Students could elect to continue *Piano* into the next level. Students were placed in *Math* (in Levels I and II) according to their math ability rather than their level of proficiency in English. Problems were worked out on the board, and vocabulary banks were used to help students remember words already learned and add new words for future work. Because word problems were a continuing difficulty, the teacher helped students break down the problems into various steps, making the tasks more manageable.

Level II (akin to the intermediate levels described on p. 183) included two periods of ESL: *Skills II* and *Conversation II*. At this level, the students had more choices from among sheltered classes (see Figure 18.5).

Skills II and *Conversation II*, like their counterparts at Level I, extended survival skills through a topical organization, adding vocabulary appropriate to students' needs. At this level, the tasks were more cognitively demanding but were still highly context embedded. *Careers* looked at various vocational possibilities and helped the students discover their strengths and areas where they might need improvement. The course aimed to help students discover the kinds of jobs for which they were best suited. The students received practice in interview technique by role playing (see Chapter 11). *Cultures/Geography* helped students gain an appreciation of many different cultures in relation to their geographical advantages and constraints. *Civics* took a historical approach to the American governmental system, its organization, and the ramifications of its tenets. *Health* covered the human body and emphasized prevention and control of common diseases. *Musical Theater* presented American culture as depicted through Hollywood's version of Broadway musicals. *State Requirements* included a variety of units mandated by the state of California: mental health,

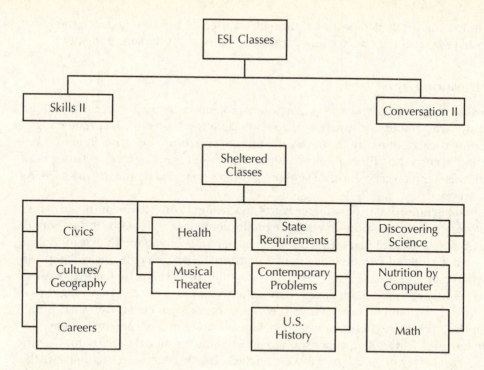

Figure 18.5 Level II

first aid (students received a certificate after completion of the unit), and fire and accident prevention. *Contemporary Problems* was a sort of catchall course highlighting issues on consumerism and interpersonal relations. Topics covered in this course included money management, credit, insurance, self-awareness, alternative lifestyles, sexuality, and parenting. *U.S. History* was taught through frequent dramatizations of events, bringing the past alive and making it meaningful to the students. *Discovering Science* included experiments and much realia to explain physical phenomena. *Nutrition by Computer* exposed students to the benefits of a balanced diet and at the same time introduced them to computers, a rather unusual but effective combination. Students charted daily food intake, categorized foods into groups, and planned well-balanced meals.

Mainstream classes were gradually added beginning at Level II. Students were required to take mainstream physical education and could elect to take other mainstream courses such as typing or home economics.

Level III (akin to the advanced levels described on pp. 183–184) was tailored for advanced students who were into a full schedule of mainstream courses except for English. Literature was at the core of the program, and the basic skills (listening, speaking, reading, writing) were integrated into the activities. Students were reclassified from

Level III ESL once they demonstrated through a variety of means (similar to the initial battery of tests) that they were ready to move on to more challenging activities.

Staff Development

One reason for the apparent success of Artesia's program in helping students to acquire English was the emphasis the school placed on staff development. All seventeen ESL/content-area teachers received special training in presenting effective modified language and in correcting through recasting and expansion (see Chapter 2). This special training was part of a series of after-school inservices provided by the district's ESL resource teachers.

Alfredo Schifini and other language arts and reading consultants in the Los Angeles area conducted workshops in writing/reading activities for the ABC Unified School District. Schifini stressed that introducing the main points of a lesson increases the use of contextual clues for comprehension of the material. Recapping the major points on the board or an overhead also increases the possibility of learning. He felt that lectures ladened with jargon are inappropriate in a sheltered class. Instead he thought that oral interaction should be used extensively. Students could be engaged in small-group tasks such as science experiments, map-making, creating murals, preparing skits, and similar activities. It was the teacher's job to demonstrate or model the task for the students to then carry out. He advised teachers, when choosing textbooks, to consider the readability, print size, paragraph length, and types of illustrations used. He recommended mapping or other kinds of graphic organization as useful techniques for helping students obtain meaning from the materials. About sheltered classes, he reminded the teachers,

> Sheltered English classrooms do not involve any magical approach to teaching. Certainly there is no "quick fix." . . . The potential exists with the sheltered model to provide truly meaningful instruction for a wide range of LEP [limited English proficient] students. It is important to restate that sheltered English should not be viewed as a substitute for bilingual education, but rather as a component in a carefully planned out developmental program designed to facilitate academic success.[11]

In addition to the inservicing provided by the ABC Unified School District, several of the staff members at Artesia graduated from the master's degree program in teaching second languages offered through a joint effort between the district and California State University, Los Angeles. All the courses in the program were taught locally to make them even more attractive to the teachers.

Staff members working in the program came to the conclusion that a sheltered program is an effective means for teaching the target language to diverse primary-language groups for whom bilingual education was not considered a possibility.

---

[11] Here it should be noted that the school discontinued its bilingual program in Spanish, some think to its detriment (see Chapter 17), when it began the sheltered program.

AN ELEMENTARY DISTRICT-WIDE PROGRAM[12]

To meet the needs of its English learners, kindergarten through grade 3 (K–3), the Alhambra School District in Alhambra, California, developed a multifaceted program and thematic curriculum. The program itself integrated features of several of the methods and activities discussed in Part II of this book: physical approaches, interactive language teaching including chants, storytelling, drama, and others.

Demographics

The district, which served thirteen elementary schools, had a total of 3,583 English learners, representing about thirty languages. Based on the information gained from the home language surveys required of each student, the most common languages were Spanish, Vietnamese, Cantonese, Mandarin, and Cambodian. However, languages less common to ESL classrooms were also found in this diverse student population, including Punjabi (India), Urdu (Pakistan), Illocano (northwestern Luzon, part of the Republic of the Philippines), and Tongan (Tonga, an island group in the South Pacific).

Although many of the language minority children from other countries came from large urban population centers, there were many who came from the isolated rural regions of China and Latin America as well. In spite of the fact that most of the parents stated that the goal for their children was a postsecondary degree, only a few of these parents had themselves obtained such a degree; however, many of them did have some formal education beyond the secondary level.

Assessment and Placement

If a language other than English was spoken in the home, the student was tested at the district's Elementary Orientation and Assessment Center. All elementary students were assessed in the primary language and in English.

The district developed and was using on a trial basis Chinese and Vietnamese tests, drawing from the English and Spanish LAS format. When appropriate (for children in grades 3 and above), the district also assessed performance in mathematics and English reading and obtained an English writing sample.

The students who were classified by the district as English learners generally were operating from low-beginning to intermediate proficiency levels (see pp. 182–183). Usually they were placed in one of three types of classrooms: bilingual, language development, or language development cluster. In all three types of classrooms, a bilingual paraprofessional was present whenever possible to assist in the instruction.

---

[12] I wish to thank Linda Sasser formerly from the Alhambra School District in Alhambra, California, for making available the information on which this summary is based. Thanks also to the other people in the Alhambra School District who contributed, either directly or indirectly, to the development of the thematic curriculum: Lilia Sarmiento, Mary Ellen De Santos, Lourdes Brito, Marie Ibsen, Linda Naccarato, Sharon Oliver, Gina Tesner, Virginia Torres-Lopez, Cathy Tyson, and Florence Wong.

A Bilingual Classroom

Bilingual classes were offered in kindergarten through sixth grade in Spanish, Cantonese, and Vietnamese; each class had a teacher who spoke the first language. The teacher was required to have bilingual authorization granted by the state of California.[13] In addition, the number of students had to be great enough to warrant the creation of a bilingual class.

A Language Development Classroom

This classroom was an intensive English environment for students operating from low-beginning to low-intermediate proficiency levels. It was taught by a state authorized bilingual or language development teacher.

A Language Development Cluster Classroom

This was a transitional classroom that included English learners operating at intermediate to advanced levels, native English speakers, and language minority students who were designated as English-fluent. The English learners were usually placed in this classroom after they had been in the language development classroom long enough to obtain the necessary skills. The teacher had to be a certified bilingual or language development teacher.

Staff Development

In an attempt to better meet the needs of language minority students, all of the K-3 teachers in the district participated in staff development sessions. Grouped by grade level, the teachers were given information about the language learning process, conditions conducive to learning, and the recommended methodology. Teachers had a chance to try out various activities and strategies on each other and receive peer feedback. From time to time, they were asked to reflect on what they had learned and on their own growth as developing teachers. Linda Sasser, an ESL program specialist for the school district, reported that the teachers' comments on the staff development sessions were generally very positive and that she and the district were encouraged by the enthusiasm.

The Thematic Curriculum

The thematic curriculum developed for K-3 was incorporated into all four classroom plans as described on pp. 472-475. It was based on the premise that learning is most likely to occur when ideas and activities are integrated and interrelated in the classroom as they are in life. The thematic units link several disciplines (literature, social science,

---

[13] Due to the passage of Proposition 227 (see footnote 3 on p. 507), waivers had to be obtained for students to enroll in these classes.

art, and so forth) around a central idea or theme. The district felt that such an organization would encourage the following:

- an emphasis on processes for constructing meaning, solving problems, and discovering relationships
- greater teacher–student involvement in planning and implementing the curriculum
- increased individual work appropriate to each student's developmental level and interests
- more effective and productive use of instructional time
- greater student involvement in dynamic, experiential learning through the myriad of resources provided

The following are graphic representations of the themes developed by the district (with teacher input) and used for K–3 (see Figures 18.6, 18.7, 18.8, 18.9). Literature, appropriate to the proficiency and age levels of the students, was selected by the teachers to accompany each theme.

Activities

The activities mentioned here are only a few of those recommended to teachers using the thematic organization. The activities, most of which were both flexible and adaptable, could be used at virtually any elementary grade level and in any thematic unit. They included clustering and other graphic devices such as Venn diagrams (see Chapter 13), concrete poetry (see Chapter 10), the language experience approach (see pp. 303–306) alternative types of journals (see pp. 323–324), and many more. In addition, the following were included in the recommendations:

ACTIVITY RECOMMENDATIONS

Dramatic Corner

Level: Low- to high-intermediate

Set aside a place in the classroom where the children can go and role-play real-life situations related to the theme being studied (buying a coat, taking a pet to the veterinarian, selling shoes). The scenery can be designed by the children and all the necessary props can be provided by the children or made available by the teacher. This activity can enable children to experiment with language in relatively risk-free environments.

Circle Story

Level: Mid- to high-beginning

On a large sheet of paper, the children are asked to draw a circle, divided like a pie (see Figure 18.10 on p. 476). In each section of the pie, they make a drawing to represent an event in the story.

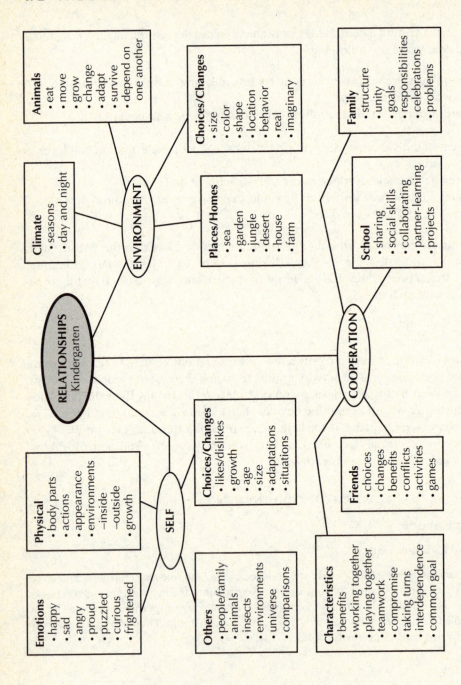

Figure 18.6 Theme: Relationships, Alhambra School District

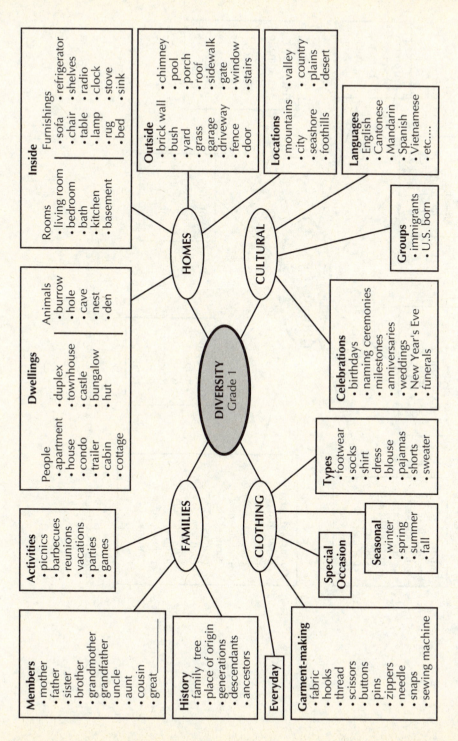

Figure 18.7 Theme: Diversity, Alhambra School District

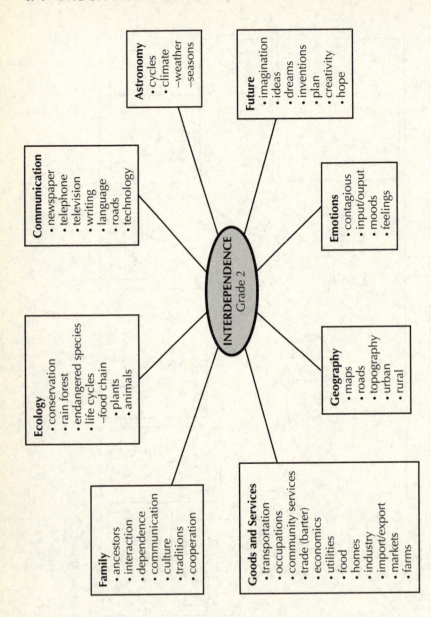

Figure 18.8 Theme: Interdependence, Alhambra School District

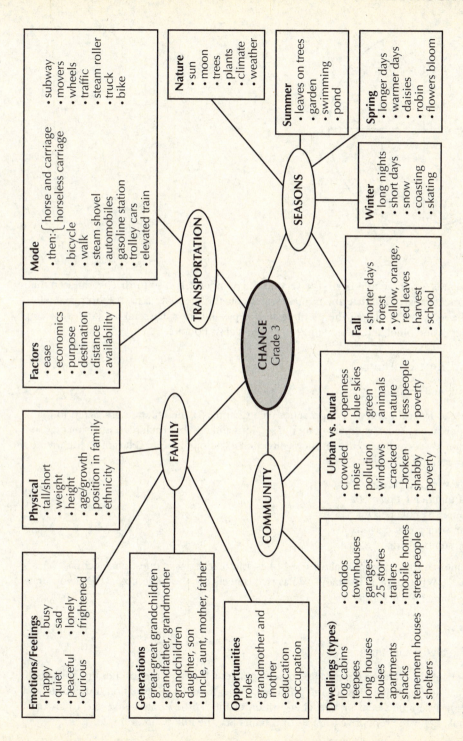

Mode
- then: horse and carriage
  horseless carriage
- bicycle
- walk
- steam shovel
- automobiles
- gasoline station
- trolley cars
- elevated train
- subway
- movers
- wheels
- traffic
- steam roller
- truck
- bike

Nature
- sun
- moon
- trees
- plants
- climate
- weather

Summer
- leaves on trees
- garden
- swimming
- pond

Spring
- longer days
- warmer days
- daisies
- robin
- flowers bloom

Winter
- long nights
- short days
- snow
- coasting
- skating

Factors
- ease
- economics
- purpose
- destination
- distance
- availability

Fall
- shorter days
- forest
- yellow, orange,
  red leaves
- harvest
- school

TRANSPORTATION

SEASONS

CHANGE
Grade 3

Physical
- tall/short
- weight
- height
- age/growth
- position in family
- ethnicity

FAMILY

COMMUNITY

Urban vs. Rural

Urban	Rural
• crowded	• openness
• noise	• blue skies
• pollution	• green
• windows	• animals
–cracked	• nature
–broken	• less people
• shabby	• poverty
• poverty	

Emotions/Feelings
- happy
- quiet
- peaceful
- curious
- busy
- sad
- lonely
- frightened

Generations
- great-great grandchildren
- grandfather, grandmother
- grandchildren
- daughter, son
- uncle, aunt, mother, father

Opportunities
- roles
- grandmother and
  mother
- education
- occupation

Dwellings (types)
- log cabins
- teepees
- long houses
- houses
- apartments
- shacks
- tenement houses
- shelters
- condos
- townhouses
- garages
- 25 stories
- trailers
- mobile homes
- street people

Figure 18.9 Theme: Change, Alhambra School District

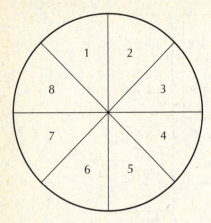

Figure 18.10 Circle Story

The first event is given the number 1, the second the number 2, and so forth. The children then cut the segments apart, eliminate the numbers, and give the pieces to a partner to reassemble. They tell the story by looking at the pictures and/or pasting their reassembled circles on construction paper and binding them together to create a class booklet.

Draw and Remember

Level: Low- to mid-beginning

Using strategies from the physical approaches (see Chapter 8), the children are asked to fold a sheet of paper into a predetermined number of sections and number each section. Using crayons, the children draw according to the teacher's directions. The pictures are relevant to the theme's content. For example:

> Pick up your red crayon.
> In box number 1, draw a ball.
> Put your red crayon down.
> Pick up your green crayon.
> In box number 4, draw a chair.

After the children have drawn in all of the boxes, the teacher asks questions such as "What's in number 2?" "What color is the ball?" "What two objects are the same color?" "Did you draw something orange? What was it?"

Echo Chants

Level: Mid- to high-beginning

In an echo chant, the children repeat a line or a portion of a line after the teacher or another student has read it aloud first. The chant provides a "soft focus" on intonation, inflection, and pronunciation. A simple poem or a teacher-written chant can be easily converted to an echo chant by looking for the repetitive phrases or refrains. See the following example.[14]

---

[14] The source of this poem is unknown.

Poem	**Echo Chant**
Snow on the cars.	**Teacher:** Snow on the cars.
Snow on the bus.	**Students:** On the cars.
Snow on the vans.	**Teacher:** Snow on the bus.
Snow on us!	**Students:** On the bus.
Snow in the puddles.	**Teacher:** Snow on the vans.
Snow in the street.	**Students:** On the vans.
Snow in the gutters.	**Teacher:** Snow on us!
Snow on my feet!	**Students:** Snow on us!
	Teacher: Snow in the puddles.
	Students: In the puddles.
	Teacher: Snow in the street.
	Students: In the street.
	Teacher: Snow in the gutters.
	Students: In the gutters.
	Teacher: Snow on my feet!
	Students: Snow on my feet!

Within the theme curriculum, teachers were encouraged to use whole-group activities (chanting, role playing, creating graphic representations, discussing, and so on) and small-group instruction (using the Magnetic Way[15] to learn concepts related to the theme, reviewing with a partner, sharing homework). In addition, the centers were set up where students could go during various times of the day. The following list describes centers and examples of activities taking place in each center.

Book Corner: Share a big book with a friend; choose a book to read
Art Corner: Explore color by mixing any two colors; draw pictures for a collaborative story
Manipulative Area: Sequence four pictures; cut pictures of kitchen items out of magazines
Discovery Corner: Investigate water evaporation; experiment with the effects of the sun on a planted seed
Listening Area: Follow directions on a cassette tape; listen to a story on a cassette tape

Homework related to the theme was expected of each student. Students were asked to share stories, rhymes, or chants with someone at home and come back with the responses; count the number of chairs or lamps in their house; interview adults to discover their opinions; and so forth.

Teachers were encouraged by the district to adhere to the following practices that were considered consonant with the philosophies supporting physical and interactive

---

[15] The Magnetic Way, made available by Creative Edge, Inc. (Steck-Vaughn), consists of a large magnetic board with pieces representing people, houses, buildings of various sorts, furniture, and so on that stick to the board. Overlay pieces (e.g., clothing, interchangeable store fronts) can be placed on top.

approaches (see Chapters 8 and 9): maintain a low-stress environment, allow for a silent period, generally focus on content rather than form, adjust input to accommodate the student, use an appropriate rate, check for understanding, and give timely feedback on student performance.

A KINDERGARTEN ESL PROGRAM WITHIN A SPANISH BILINGUAL SCHOOL

At Loma Vista Elementary School in the heart of Maywood, California, a Spanish-speaking community, every class had two components: ESL and Spanish bilingual education.[16] The kindergarten was no exception.

Beverly McNeilly, a teacher of the ESL component of the kindergarten program, took a holistic approach to teaching English to her thirty-one students. In her class, English, was the vehicle by which the students were exposed to stories, films, songs, games, and other items of interest. Structured ESL lessons represented only a small portion of the program; they were the first to go if any spontaneous opportunity presented itself. For example, one day the class watched tree trimmers as they sawed off the limbs of an old tree outside the window. The teacher abandoned her planned lesson and talked to the children about what they observed.

The Subject Matter, Activities, and Classroom Management

The subject matter itself was integrated into a variety of skill areas. Target vocabulary words were generally presented in an introductory lesson and then used again throughout the day, whether in math, science, art, physical education, or music. The words were reinforced naturally in the course of events. For example, as part of an art project in a unit on ocean life, the children created starfish and coral for a mural. In math, they chose which of several drawings are "true octopi" (the ones with eight legs). Music found the children dancing to aquatic sounds on a recording as they imagined how a shark, crab, whale, or dolphin might move. The reading lesson for the day consisted of a game in which the children used magnets to "catch" fish on which letters of the alphabet had been written. A science display featured shells and sand for the children to explore. The entire room environment reflected the topic in other ways with pictures, bulletin boards created by the children, and books on the theme (see Figure 18.11).

The teacher and her assistants, including one or two peer teachers from the fifth grade, managed a variety of activities for small-group participation. Group size varied from six to nine members depending on the task at hand and the number of assistants available. Instead of rigidly defined groups and timetables, fluid grouping was used. Several centers were set up each day that focused on related concepts. For example, one day during the study of mathematics, the children were divided into groups to participate in some of the activities from the still popular *Mathematics Their Way* by Lorton (1994). One group found how many designs they could make with only three Tinkertoys.

---

[16] Loma Vista Elementary School is in the Los Angeles Unified School District.

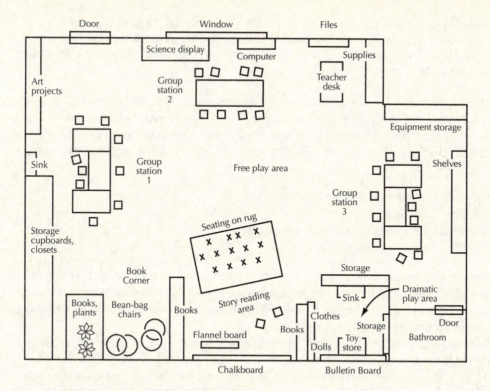

Figure 18.11 A Floor Plan of the ESL Kindergarten

Another group explored the different ways of separating six cubes into two piles. Other groups made geometric shapes with rubber bands and sequential patterns with rocks and shells. The amount of time needed to complete a task depended on each group. Ongoing informal evaluation and periodic pretesting and posttesting of key objectives provided evidence that children were mastering the concepts.

For these lessons, groups were formed based on a placement test that accompanies the Lorton book. However, usually the small-group activities were not sequentially organized and the children were allowed to select their own groups. Because they were allowed the freedom of choice, interest and curiosity remain at high levels. There were times when the group into which a student wanted to go was full (all the chairs were taken). In that case, the student had two choices. He or she either could move to another activity or participate in free or dramatic play in the areas designated for those purposes. It was in these areas that the child could reinforce concepts just learned or pursue other goals of immediate interest.

The teacher claimed that she was often heartened to see the themes with which they had been working reflected in their choices of play activity. She reported,

When we discussed transportation, block play produced trains and rocket ships. When we were concentrating on body parts, the table in the dramatic play area was an operating table, as amateur doctors came out with appropriate original language. To me, having a child produce "I'm a doctor. What's the problem? Let me see your leg"— a combination of words that had never been taught her—is so much more rewarding than having little parrots.

A physical approach (Chapter 8) was combined with drama (Chapter 11) and songs and poetry (Chapter 10) to reinforce concepts. Props and pictures were used to aid understanding. For example, a skit about a firefighter's day included the following song, which was sung to the tune of "Frère Jacques." The children acted out the words as they sang the song.

> Are you sleeping? Are you sleeping?
> Firefighters, firefighters.
> Alarm bells are ringing, alarm bells are ringing.
> Ring, ring, ring . . . ring, ring, ring.

Because the lyrics were accompanied by action, even true beginners could respond to the cues after observing their more advanced classmates. Children who were operating at the low-beginning level began to sing along with the words. Thus children at all levels were accommodated in this activity.

The teacher frequently read aloud stories related to the units. Some of the children "read" the stories to each other later in the book corner, prompted only by the pictures. One of McNeilly's favorite stories to read to the children was Esphyr Slobodkina's *Caps for Sale* during a unit on clothing. She generally simplified the story to ensure understanding. She reported that because she often repeats the same story several times in a row, she was not surprised to hear expressions from it used by the children in other situations. For instance, "Hats for sale! Does anybody want to buy a hat?" the next day became "Pencils for sale!" when one of the students was handing out the pencils.

Nursery rhymes were also used. One day she exposed the children to "Baa, Baa, Black Sheep," and the next day she asked if they could remember it. In unison they said, "Baa, baa, black sheep, you have any wool?" This made more sense to them than the original syntax, indicating that they were focused more on meaning than on form. Other nursery rhymes such as "Pat-a-Cake" and "Pease Porridge Hot" were introduced as they related to the topics at hand. The rhymes were memorized by the children and seemed to serve a function similar to chants (Chapter 10), appealing to the senses through their rhythmic and other poetic qualities.

McNeilly's attitude toward error correction was that "only global errors that impede communication" should be corrected. She accepted most surface form errors and primary language responses, which she considered to be perfectly healthy and normal at first. She felt that if the children are not overly corrected, they will be able to develop the self-confidence they need to acquire the language naturally.

To build self-esteem, she gave the children responsibilities in the classroom. Even the rituals that begin the class each day were handled almost entirely by children, including the flag salute and attendance procedures. Children were given center stage whenever possible. On some occasions, they held the book from which the teacher read aloud; on other days, they steadied the flannel graph so it would not fall over when others stuck figures to it, illustrating a story that was being read. In addition, the children's own drawings were copied and made into booklets for the book corner.

The following was one of the integrated units the teacher liked to use.

Topic: Food

Whole Class Activities

Introduce vocabulary with real objects.
Use a grab bag of fruits and vegetables.
Have a fruit-tasting party.
Play the song "Alice's Restaurant."[17]
Ask children to hold pictures of food and respond to the verbal cues.
Make vegetable soup from items brought from home.

Small Group Follow-Up Activities

Make macaroni collages.
Use cookie cutters in dough made of clay.
Put illustrated cookbooks in the book corner.
Make collages, gluing pictures of food onto paper plates.
Fingerpaint in chocolate pudding.
Practice writing in thin layers of Jell-O crystals placed in trays.
String popcorn.
Bake cookies.
Set up a supermarket in the play area with food boxes, cans, and so forth; have the children "go shopping."

A Typical Day

11:00–11:45 A.M.

Greeting. The teacher greeted the students and they greeted her back.
Calendar coloring took place. Today's numeral on a large calendar at the front of the room was colored in by a child volunteer. The teacher and students sang the song "What is the day to be happy?" which cued the answer to the question "What day is it today?"
Attendance. Children were learning to respond to visual cues. The teacher held up flash cards and asked, "Is the person with this last name here today?"
Quick review of this week's concepts through the use of a picture dictionary.
Large-group ESL lesson. With use of posters and other realia, the Chinese New Year, which was coming soon, was discussed. Comparisons between the Chinese New Year and holidays that the children celebrate with their families were drawn.

---

[17] Hap Palmer Educational Children's Songs, http://www.happalmer.com/.

11:45–12:25 *P.M.*

Small-group activities. Children chose one or more of the following:
  Make paper firecrackers for the Chinese New Year.
  Play a game involving guessing how many pennies are in "red packets" (made previously in preparation for the Chinese New Year).
  Listen to *The Story about Ping* by Marjorie Flack as it was being read in the book corner.
  Decorate paper plates with water colors; plates would later be assembled into a giant dragon for the Chinese New Year parade.
  Dramatic free play.

12:25–12:45 *P.M.*

Cleanup and nursery rhymes. All the children participated in the cleanup.
Then the children retired to the rug. The "teacher of the day" (a child volunteer) led in a chanting of some of the nursery rhymes the children had learned.

12:45–12:55 *P.M.*

Recess. Outdoor free play with sand toys, balance beams, and a climbing apparatus for psychomotor and large-muscle development. At this time the children were transitioned to the Spanish component of the program.
The Spanish bilingual teacher was also on the playground with her group of children. When recess was over, the teachers returned to their respective rooms, each with a different group.

CHAPTER 19

Foreign Language Programs

Many foreign language students have found that they can indeed acquire a second language in the classroom, particularly if interactional and participatory strategies are employed. The five programs selected for illustration here were chosen because they contain features that may be of special interest to foreign language teachers, but none is intended as a model for replication.

The first program is the Concordia Language Villages, a unique concept in foreign language teaching, utilizing immersion in creative ways to develop and maintain French, German, Russian, Chinese, Korean, Spanish, Norwegian, Finnish, Swedish, and several other languages. Next is an early immersion program in four elementary schools in Thunder Bay, Ontario, Canada, where children learned French through exposure to the various subject-matter areas. Third is the Instituto Cultural Argentino Norteamericano (ICANA) in Buenos Aires, Argentina. Its approach to English as a foreign language made it one of the fastest-growing binational centers in South America. Next we discuss a middle school Spanish language program at Millikan Junior High School in Los Angeles, California. Students at this school began with an exploratory course in the seventh grade that prepared and motivated them for the two years of Spanish that followed. Last is the Spanish program at Artesia High School in Artesia, California. There students studied the target language mainly through classroom interaction but in the traditional one-period-a-day mode.

In this chapter, as in the previous one, the descriptions focus on the more salient characteristics of each program, sometimes on the overall organization and other times on specific activities and strategies. Although the programs were designed for particular age groups and specific purposes, most of the ideas can be readily adapted to other age levels and programs.

A VILLAGE IMMERSION PROGRAM FOR GLOBAL UNDERSTANDING, LANGUAGE DEVELOPMENT, AND MAINTENANCE[1]

Tucked into the forests and amid the low-lying lakes of northeastern and central Minnesota is Concordia Language Villages. Its roots go back to the summer of 1961 when Concordia College[2] brought together seventy-two children (ages nine to twelve) to learn German by immersing them in the language and culture provided by the German "village."

Today there are twelve villages, each representing a different language and culture. Thousands of children, teenagers, and young adults now participate each year. Denise Phillippe, Associate Director for Curriculum and Staff Development, reported that in 2000 alone there were 9,084 villagers in addition to the 1,223 staff members hired that year. The staff members included deans, the counseling/teaching staff, facilitators for the various types of programs, nurses and their assistants, managers of stores and banks, maintenance people, lifeguards, and a cadre of the best cooks and bakers available. The participants and staff arrived from all fifty states and the District of Columbia, as well as from forty-eight countries around the world.

The Villages

The villages form miniature cultural enclaves, each with its own ethnic arts and crafts area, a dining hall where ethnic foods are served, sleeping quarters, showers, a library, an onsite clinic, large and small group meeting areas, an athletic field, a store, a bank, and even its own authentic currency. Most have a beach as well. Participants can learn French, Chinese, Danish, Finnish, German, Japanese, Korean, Norwegian, Russian, Spanish, or Swedish in eleven of the villages. The twelfth village is home to English as a second language (ESL) learners and uses the nearby city of Moorhead as an extension of its English-speaking community. Of these villages, five are permanent and are located on the 830 acres owned by Concordia College on Turtle River Lake near Bemidji, Minnesota.

Local and international civic groups, governments, and individuals have supported Concordia's efforts (financially and otherwise) to create permanent environments

---

[1] Thanks to the many people at Concordia Language Villages for opening up their programs to me for the better part of a week. During my visitation, I had the opportunity to observe teacher/counselor/staff/participant orientations, village life (including classes), and a teacher education class. I ate many fine meals in the dining halls of various villages, witnessed several cultural presentations, and interviewed numerous students. Special thanks go to administrators and staff who supplied the details on which this summary is based and who made my trip so enjoyable: Christine Schulze, Denise Phillippe, Sarah Happel, Donna (Daniele) Clementi, Heidi Hamilton, Laurie (Larisa) Iudin-Nelson, Jennifer (Zhenya) Ryan Tishler, Garrette (Ludo) Heysel, Tove Dahl, Karla (Yukari) Pratt, Paul (Di Baoluo) DelMain, Kerisa (Kike) Baedke, and Ruben Ayala-Brener. Thanks also to the following students for their reflective input: Annika (Gabi) Brink, Eric (Olivier) Reeves, Alex (Antone) Reeves, Mark (Marco) Sheskin, Tiffany (Iliana) Hughes, Julie (Julia) Thompsen, Katherine (Satomi) Lonsdorf, Mike (Ryu) Van Deusen, and Rachel (Reiko) Kerry. I owe a special debt of gratitude to Denise Phillippe, who served as a most gracious guide as well as a main source of information.

[2] Concordia College is a liberal arts Lutheran college in Moorhead, Minnesota. However, the purpose of the language villages is not to teach or promote any specific religion, and all participants are welcome, regardless of religious background.

surprisingly similar to the countries they represent. For example, those entering the village of Salolampi soon discover that the dining hall, Jyringin Talo, is fashioned after a nineteenth-century train station in Finland, and several log cabins and a rustic sauna have been imported directly from that country. In Skogfjorden, villagers can eat at Gimle, a large dining hall whose brick walls are the backdrops for Norwegian artifacts and whose ceiling is covered with intricate rosemaling. At Waldsee, participants are intrigued by the Gasthof and other buildings that are modeled after typical structures in Germany, using the traditional architectural style known as Fachwerk or half-beam. Lac du Bois and El Lago del Bosque feature buildings that are typical of those found in France and Spain, respectively.

These villages are not just for show. In the summer of 2000, 47 percent of the villagers who had attended the previous year returned, a strong indication that something very important is happening. In addition to helping students develop a second language and learn aspects of another culture, the villages serve as a means of extending the languages and cultures of generations of immigrants living throughout Minnesota. This use is supported by Heritage Learners, whose goal is to develop and maintain the language of their ancestors. These learners can be found in varying numbers among the villagers, across most language groups. It should be noted here that the German government has recently established a grant for Waldsee; one-half of this grant will be for curricular projects and the other half for two-week scholarships. In addition, the Sons of Norway offers about $40,000 each year in scholarships to students who want to develop and/or maintain their skills in Norwegian.

Christine Schulze, the executive director, reminds us that while preserving one's heritage is important, the primary goal of the villages is to ensure that "young people are prepared to be responsible citizens in our global community." Christine was a villager herself at El Lago del Bosque in 1970 and later joined the staff, where she has remained for twenty-six years. She knows firsthand about Concordia Language Villages' deep commitment to global concerns. These are evident in the topics for study and discussion, as well as the simulations presented in the villages. The topics for study and discussion are wide-ranging but relate either directly or indirectly to environmental and ecological concerns, international issues, diversity, and tolerance.

Moreover, Concordia Language Villages believes that forming relationships in the villages with people from around the world and immersing oneself in another language and culture brings a greater openness to different world views and ways of doing things. Although the village cultures are still "American" in many ways, the participants feel that they are experiencing something "culturally different." Usually, they go away with attitudes toward other peoples of the world that are positive and lasting.

Village Philosophy and the Practices of Village Teaching

Concordia Language Villages seeks to educate students for responsible global citizenship by establishing *communities of learners* in which each villager is a valued member. Through the immersion experience, villagers are encouraged to become lifelong learners as well as proficient speakers of the language of their village.

Their teachers are vital to this experience. During orientation week, new teachers are introduced to the practices common to village teaching, summarized in the following:

1. The target language is used by the staff and villagers except when English is needed to meet safety and/or emotional needs of the participants. This practice is based on the principle that villagers need to hear and use the target language in a variety of contexts. These contexts can include completing routine tasks, meeting personal needs, actively participating in cultural activities and events, formal and informal discussions, and academic classroom experiences.

2. Early in the language learning process, participants are taught village-centered phrases and words—whatever is needed to participate in the daily life of the village. All signs and labels are written in the target language. The village itself is used as a classroom. Nature hikes, canoe trips, and the like provide much of the language content. It is believed that as the villagers gain the competence necessary to meet their basic needs, their speech will begin to include more abstract language in more complex contexts as interaction spreads beyond the concerns of the immediate village.

3. Error correction is handled through the modeling of correct forms and meanings rather than by the use of direct correction. However, that does not mean that forms and nuances in meaning are never the focus. On the contrary, villagers often receive direct instruction in structure and semantics within their academic work.

4. Culture is reflected throughout all the programs and is lived every day. The villagers, especially for the evening programs, organize for and participate in special cultural experiences and presentations.

Types of Programs Available[3]

One-week, two-week, and four-week language programs are offered in the villages during the summer. The first two programs earn no credit and are often taken by participants seeking an introduction to a specific language and culture. The one-week sessions offer initial exposure and camp survival tips for children ages seven to eleven and older children and teenagers ages eleven to fifteen. These sessions focus on very basic language instruction, arts and crafts, sports, and other hands-on experiences, depending on the interests of the age group. Sometimes a student who has already gained proficiency in one foreign language will sign up for a one-week session in another language just to see what it's like.

The two-week sessions are for participants ages eight to eighteen who have been divided into beginning, intermediate, and advanced levels. These sessions are similar in content to the one-week sessions except that they offer a more in-depth immersion experience complete with cultural simulations, cooking experiences, singing and dancing, and many other activities. Participants often take a two-week session to "brush up" on a language they have already studied in school during the academic year.

---

[3] It should be noted that while costs to participants are not exorbitant, scholarships are available for those needing financial assistance for any of the sessions with the exception of the language abroad programs. Contributors to the scholarship funds include individuals, state agencies, foundations and corporations (both domestic and foreign), the Passport Fund program, and Concordia Language Village store sales.

One-month programs are accredited by the North Central Association for Colleges and Schools and give villagers (grades 9–12) high school credit for language study that is equivalent to 180 hours of instruction. These sessions generally are taught by highly qualified, certified teachers and include speaking, reading, composition, vocabulary development strategies, and grammar. They are quite rigorous and require a frequent performance-based evaluation of each villager. Once final grades are given, written evaluations are sent to each participant's parents and school.

Other programs are available as well. One of the more popular sessions is the French Voyageurs program for eleven- to eighteen-year-olds. One-week, two-week, or four-week sessions are available. The participants not only learn French, but they learn how to survive physical challenges. The young voyageurs live in tents at a permanent campsite on Turtle River Lake. Their days are often spent canoeing on the many lakes and rivers in the area just as the French Canadian fur traders did in the nineteenth century. In a similar vein, the German Grüne Welle (Green Wave) for students ages fourteen to eighteen exposes participants to German language and culture through experiences in a wilderness setting. The focus for this course is the environment and/or important historical events.

Many students follow up a village experience with one-month credit programs abroad. Not too long ago, eighty-six students visited France, Germany, Japan, or Spain. They interacted daily with proficient speakers of the target language and were able to participate in many rich cultural events, as well as explore historical sites and museums. A one-week homestay with a family was also part of the agenda. Although much of the time was spent experiencing the language and culture, some time was set aside for a more formal study of both. To be eligible for a language abroad program, students must have at least intermediate proficiency and a minimum of two years (or its equivalent) of high school credit in the target language. Candidates are assessed through a telephone interview to ensure that they are fluent enough to fully benefit from the experience abroad.

Teachers seeking graduate credit in education or direct involvement as villagers can enroll in programs especially designed for them. A graduate course offered through Concordia College offers immersion teaching techniques. This course is taught in English by Donna Clementi, the dean of Teacher Seminars. In it, she presents the Concordia Language Villages educational philosophy of teaching, shares various methods of curriculum implementation, and helps teachers develop thematic units. During these seminars, teachers are given the opportunity to visit the villages while they are in session. In addition, teachers can become language learners themselves in week-long immersion workshops in French, Spanish, and German. Many take these courses to brush up on their own language skills or to find out what immersion is all about by experiencing it themselves.

Other programs in the village include

1. *The village weekend programs,* which run from October through May, in French, German, Spanish, Chinese, and Japanese. They are recommended to students in elementary, middle, junior, and senior high schools who are studying those languages in their schools and who want to "live" the language for a weekend. Typically, a whole class or combined classes will participate in a weekend program.

2. *Adult programs,* which run September through May, in Finnish, Norwegian, Swedish, Spanish, Japanese, French, and German. For persons eighteen years old and over, these range from three-day to week-long sessions. According to Sarah Happel, Assistant Director for Public Relations, most adults enroll in these programs to sharpen their language skills. The courses include a workshop in rosemaling (a Norwegian art form); Norwegian Vinterfest, featuring cross-country skiing and folk dancing; a trip abroad to Norway; and immersion courses in each language.

3. *College credit programs,* are for advanced learners of French, German, and Spanish. Students must be in high school to enroll in these courses, and they must have had three years of high school language study or its equivalent. An interview determines whether a prospective student has sufficient fluency to handle the work. Three one-month courses such as: (a) Race, Gender, and Power in the Francophone World, (b) Germany after the Wall: Modern German Culture and Civilizations, and (c) Latin American Culture and Civilizations are offered during the summer at their respective villages. They generally are taught by international and American scholars as well as educators who are both fluent in the target language and experienced in immersion techniques.

4. *Elderhostel programs,* which are held in April, May, and October, are taught in German, Finnish, and Swedish. Again, the courses focus on language and cultural experiences in a village environment. Only persons age fifty-five and over are eligible.

The Teaching Staff

The teaching staff is required to attend a multivillage orientation to gain more understanding of the mission and philosophy of the Concordia Language Villages and become acquainted with each other. Actual preparation for village life and teaching is accomplished by the dean of each village, a variety of specialists, and returning staff members. Village counselors and teachers must be proficient speakers of the target language and have some formal educational background in the language and culture.

The dean of each village hires staff members, makes policy and salary decisions, plans the overall curriculum and schedule, and has final say in the overall management of the village. Two facilitators—for the credit program and the noncredit program—work closely with the dean on scheduling and other matters. They also serve as resource persons for the teachers in their respective programs. Certified teachers (or their equivalents) teach the one-month credit courses and assess the progress of each villager. Counselors usually conduct the noncredit sessions; sometimes assist credit teachers with their duties; serve as program leaders for cultural activities, including global awareness; and plan or assist in the organization of the evening programs and other cultural events. Both teachers and counselors are expected to be active participants in the daily life of the villages, take on cabin counseling responsibilities, and encourage the villagers as they move forward in the language learning process. The remaining staff, in addition to carrying out the duties relevant to their positions, also participate in village activities when appropriate. Knowledge of the target language is preferred but not required of support staff members, including health care providers and kitchen personnel. All hired persons are expected to play a role in creating the best cultural immersion environment possible, regardless of position.

Initial Placement

Concordia Language Villages is moving toward self-placement procedures, especially in the credit courses. They have found that fewer changes are necessary if students are allowed to place themselves under the supervision of a facilitator. First the villagers complete the written portion of the self-placement procedures. With the aid of a facilitator, they then group themselves into beginning, intermediate, and advanced levels by comparing their own writing to that of other villagers and/or to writing samples typical of various levels. Once with a group, the villagers move into the oral phase of the assessment process by discussing in the target language the answers to the questions they have just written. Again with the help of a facilitator, they regroup (if necessary) based on what they learn about their own abilities to communicate orally. Then they group themselves yet again after reading posters that have been placed on the walls. In English, each poster describes language behaviors most typical of the levels. Together, the posters form a continuum, stretching around the room. For example, the first poster might feature such items as "Can I say my name in _____?" "Can I count to 100?" A poster at a more advanced level might ask, "Do I feel comfortable talking about abstract topics such as the environment or politics?" "Can I read an abstract chapter from a textbook and understand most of it?" By this time, the students and the facilitator have a pretty realistic view of where each participant falls in relation to the rest of the group, making placement reasonably accurate.

The Curriculum

The immersion experience in the villages is rich and varied. Villagers are expected to interact daily with teachers, counselors, facilitators, and other villagers, many of whom are operating at higher levels. Thus the villagers are likely to receive a great deal of language directed at them (some of it comprehensible and some not) and are encouraged to participate in negotiated communication, albeit limited at first. They eat meals and share cabins with seven or eight other villagers and a teacher/counselor, often in "family" groupings. Some of the villagers have been known to experience a bit of language and cultural shock as they attempt to get their needs met in the new environment.

Although what is taught differs from village to village, teacher to teacher, and year to year, the curriculum across the villages includes similar elements: the village itself as content, global concerns, cultural traditions, music, dancing, ethnic arts and crafts, cooking, sports, history, literature, and current events. Some villages use a flexible syllabus in which the villagers have input. Textbooks are used, but they do not determine the agenda.

For example, the French Village dean, Garrette Heysel, reports that in his program lessons are planned around a theme adopted by the whole village for a specified period of time. Themes have included the 1960s, the Ivory Coast, the color blue (ending with an evening program on artists, including Van Gogh), a day in a French student's life, and many more. Teachers are reminded that no matter what the theme, they are to incorporate listening, speaking, reading, and writing activities into units appropriate to the level they are teaching.

In other villages, the curriculum is a bit more dependent on written texts or a predetermined syllabus. For example, the Russian Village dean, Laurie Iudin-Nelson, has developed textbooks and a collection of Russian songs that form the curriculum for village teachers who wish to use them. The textbooks include basic greetings and phrases, topics of interest, grammar, and activities to ensure reinforcement and the recycling of key concepts. Laurie, who is herself a musician, has made folk, Romany, and contemporary Russian songs an integral part of the language learning process as well. A balalaika ensemble, folk dancing, a Russian choir singing folk and liturgical music, and informal campfire singing are among the musical experiences that form the basis for many language lessons.

In all the villages, the use of authentic materials to support the curriculum is considered essential. Literary pieces and songs, guest lectures, recorded television and radio programming, films, newspapers, and magazines often become the focus of units and lessons. Because there are generally ten or fewer students per class, teachers are often able to individualize the curriculum itself to better meet the needs of each student.

Preparation for "International Days" is also part of the curriculum. The villagers and staff members come together two days during the summer to celebrate world languages and cultures with parents and members of the community. An international buffet is prepared and served, colorful presentations are given, and village experiences are shared.

A FRENCH IMMERSION PROGRAM FOR ELEMENTARY STUDENTS[4]

Background

In the mid-1980s, a group of Thunder Bay, Ontario, parents (of mainly Finnish or Italian origin) approached the Lakehead Board of Education to request a French immersion program for their children. They wanted their children to learn French so they would have more career flexibility. Why did they choose an immersion program over a more traditional program? They believed, as do many parents in Canada, that foreign language immersion does, in fact, produce bilinguals. Their views were compatible with those of the Ontario Ministry of Education, which concluded that immersion is an optimal means for achieving a high level of competency in French. Immersion programs (see Chapter 17) involve a far more extensive and meaningful experience

[4]I wish to thank the following who shared information about their programs with me and allowed me to observe French immersion classes in their respective schools: Ken Cressman, George Rendall, Lise Bagdon, Colette Aubry, John Brusset, Carol Nabarra, Glenn Coriveau, and Roy Fossum. My thanks also to Nicole Gaudet, one of the district's education officers, and to Wendy Hansen for providing transportation and lodging.

with a language than can be provided by the more traditional core programs, in which students study the language for one period a day, or the more recently developed extended programs in which at least one content-area class is taught in the second language, in addition to the core.

Also, research has shown that learning about subjects in a second language does not adversely affect their skills in their first language. Lapkin and Swain reported as early as 1984 that any fears concerning this issue have no basis in reality. In the Thunder Bay example, this was at least partially due to the fact that the children belonged to the majority culture and that English dominated their lives outside of the school environment. (Only 3% of Thunder Bay households claim French as their home language.) Lapkin and Swain reported:

> The English achievement results for students in the early total-immersion programs indicate that, although initially behind students in unilingual English programs in literacy skills, within a year of the introduction of an English Language Arts component into the curriculum, the immersion students perform equivalently on standardized tests of English achievement to students in the English-only program. (1984, p. 50)

They claimed that this was true even for students who were not introduced to English until grades 3 or 4. They pointed out, too, that after grade 4, French immersion students sometimes outperformed their English-only peers in some aspects of English language skills. The immersion students' achievement in the subject areas (math, science, social studies, and so forth) compared favorably to that of their English-only peers.

In general, most students could expect to be competent in French intake skills (listening and reading) by the time they finished elementary school. However, in the output skills (speaking and writing), they were often less competent until they had considerable contact with proficient French speakers. The only children that the organization of Canadian Parents of French found to be less than adequate candidates for immersion were those who exhibited a lack of ability in auditory discrimination or memory. Problems in these areas were usually detected in the first year of kindergarten, and affected students could be steered early on into English-only programs.

Program Description

In the first two years of the Thunder Bay program in the four elementary schools participating, the language for instruction was 100 percent French (except in emergency situations). In addition, all communication within the classroom was in French. In the second, third, fourth, and fifth grades, English was added but was limited to 75 minutes per day of English language arts. French was the language for instruction 75 percent of the time, English 25 percent of the time. During grades 6, 7, and 8, 50 percent of the instruction was in French and 50 percent in English. By the end of the eighth grade, the students had studied history, geography, math, science, and other subjects in both languages. The subjects covered a wide range of content areas at each level (see Figure 19.1 on p. 492).

Grade	K	1	2	3	4	5	6	7	8
French	X	X	X	X	X	X	X	X	X
Math	X	X	X	X	X	X	*	*X	
Environmental Studies	X	X	X	X	X	X	X		
Science								*	X
Music	X	X	X	X	X	X	*X	*X	*X
Physical Education	X	X	X	X	X	X	*X	*X	*X
Art	X	X	X	X	X	X	*X	*X	*X
History								X	*
Geography								*	X
English			*	*	*	*	*	*	*

Figure 19.1 French Immersion Curriculum
* Subjects taught in English
X subjects taught in French
Adapted from Programme d'Immersion Précoce, Lakehead Board of Education.

The concepts to which the students were exposed in the French immersion program were comparable to those in the regular English-only classroom.[5] In listening, the goals included helping children to listen with interest and selectivity at appropriate levels in a variety of experiences. They were taught to judge validity, make comparisons, make inferences, draw conclusions, generalize, and understand intent. During speaking, children learned to articulate their ideas and feelings confidently in a supportive environment, extend and synthesize various speaking skills (drama, role play, discussion, and others), and develop opinions through interaction with the teacher and peers. They learned to tell stories, interpret pictures, name and describe objects, explain events, evaluate, and question using verbal as well as nonverbal clues. Students were exposed to a variety of reading materials, such as legends, folktales, poems, plays, cartoons, novels, magazine articles, recipes, and newspapers. They learned to respond to print within the environment (e.g., names, labels, signs), comprehend and respond to ideas, relate pictures to print, recognize plot, understand relationships, follow directions, distinguish fact from opinion, check for bias, predict outcomes, and so forth. Writing involved being able to label components on maps and diagrams; record personal experiences in their own words; adapt style to intended purpose; write from dictation; and create stories, poetry, diaries, letters, sets of directions, expositions, and reports. Even by the end of kindergarten, children appeared to have acquired a fairly extensive vocabulary in French; they were able to follow instructions and comprehend simple stories. They could answer questions appropriately, participate effectively in drama, and sing a number of songs.

---

[5] The concepts listed here are paraphrased from the *Core Language Guide* made available by the Lakehead Board of Education. No attempt has been made to list all of the goals set down by the board. A few of the more typical ones have been selected for inclusion.

Because the immersion classes focused on subject matter rather than the target language itself, it was important that the teachers have an adequate knowledge of the subject areas they were teaching in and that they be proficient speakers of French. It was also important for the students to associate specific teachers with French and others with English. For this reason, the school district always assigned teachers to classes taught in the same language. This was especially important when there was a possibility that the same students would be present in more than one class taught by the same teacher.

Enrollment and Transportation

Enrollment was on a first-come, first-served basis, and transfers from other immersion programs were accepted, provided there was room. Transportation was generally available for those accepted into the program, making it possible for a larger number of students to be involved. Students within the urban area were bused from designated neighborhood pick-up points to the schools, and for those in the rural areas, transportation arrangements could made at a reasonable cost.

Support Services

The schools with French immersion programs maintained an ever-expanding collection of books and reference materials in French. The teachers looked for materials to purchase that were oriented to the particular needs of immersion students. However, audiovisual resources appeared to be in ample supply, and new ones were ordered yearly.

Assistance was available for enrichment or remediation from a bilingual resource teacher or a qualified special education resource teacher. Parents of children with severe problems were counseled, and recommendations were given depending on the type of problem and the resources available at each school.

The home itself was considered a "support service." Nicole Gaudet, an education officer for the district, reports, "Because the parents have made a decision about the education of their children to be in French immersion programs, they are more involved in their children's education." Parents seemed more than happy to read stories in English to their children at home, work with teachers to provide experiences with proficient French speakers whenever possible, take their children to French cultural events, and volunteer to aid in classroom ventures.

Strengths and Weaknesses of the Program

Ken Cressman, the principal of Redwood Public School, was convinced that the French immersion program in his school had benefited the entire student body. When French cultural events were arranged, they were planned not only for the French immersion students but for everyone. It was his feeling that any cultural activity—be it singing, mime, or drama, even in another language—could be enriching for all students. In addition, he observed that the French immersion students had improved the ambiance of the school in general because they tended to be more tolerant of other cultures and differences among people. When asked if one segment of the school had benefited most from the immersion program, he targeted the core French program as having perhaps received the most advantages. Although the students in this program took French for only one period a day, they profited from exposure to French immersion students with whom they could sometimes converse in a limited fashion and from whom they could often receive help with their homework.

Nicole Gaudet was also convinced that French immersion had been a real boon to the environment of all the participating schools. Because of the increased support and interest of the parents of the children, the schools' parent associations tended to thrive, and the atmosphere of the schools became more positive.

However, both Cressman and Gaudet agreed that improvements could have been made. Lack of materials appropriate to French immersion was a problem. Most of the materials came from Francophone programs and were intended for native French speakers. However, teachers were busy creating their own materials and translating the ones intended for the English-only programs. Another problem was in recruiting enough teachers with expertise and fluency to meet the growing needs. In addition, Cressman and Gaudet stressed the need for developing a long-range plan for inservicing to help teachers keep current once they had been hired.

Because these weaknesses were not inherent in the immersion programs themselves, both administrators believed they could be overcome with additional funds and further effort on the part of everyone involved with the programs.

A BICULTURAL INSTITUTE FOR CHILDREN, ADOLESCENTS, AND ADULTS[6]

The Instituto Cultural Argentina Norteamericano (ICANA), a private, nonprofit organization, was founded in 1927 in Buenos Aires. Its primary goal was to link the education and cultural communities of Argentina and the United States. Blanca Arazi, the school's former director, believed that the Institute's popularity over the years was due mainly to the communicative methodologies that had emerged in its courses. She credited interactive language teaching (see Chapter 9) for serving as the main impetus for this radical departure from a reliance on grammatical approaches as the basis for language development. She was convinced that these approaches served as "the central most important means for gaining linguistic skills."

Students

The student population at the Institute was quite heterogeneous and included students of all ages and proficiency levels. The students represented diverse cultural and economic backgrounds. In spite of all their differences, however, they had one thing in common: their desire to communicate in English, both in oral and written forms. Their goals at each level were mainly instrumental. At the adult level, goals included preparing for travel to English-speaking countries, being promoted in jobs for which fluency in English was an important asset, and bettering themselves personally as well as professionally. At the

---

[6] Thanks to Blanca Arazi, the former director of ICANA, for sharing this information with me.

adolescent level, goals included preparing for the job market, attending school or traveling in English-speaking countries, understanding English lyrics, communicating through the use of computers, and enriching their personal lives. For children, the goals included understanding English songs, working with computers, playing American games, and understanding English-language cartoons.

Teachers

The Institute had 210 teachers, most of whom had college degrees from local universities. Those who did not have college degrees came from the ranks of public translators; others were preparing to graduate from teacher education programs. Regardless of their background, all instructors were required to attend the ongoing inservice programs offered by the Institute. The emphasis was on keeping instructors informed about current happenings in the field and giving them the opportunity to share ideas and discuss problems. At inservice sessions, the teachers were taught strategies on how to provide modified language that could be understood and how to facilitate the language learning process without interfering with it, imposing their own ideas and values on those expressing opinions, or spoon-feeding the language to their students. In addition, teachers were asked to reflect on their own experiences in learning a foreign language. What seemed to facilitate the process for them? What problems did they face? Each inservice program had a specific focus and stated goals. Teachers from all over Argentina as well as neighboring countries participated in the program, making it a very rich and stimulating experience.

Classes

At ICANA, classes were divided according to age level. Some classes were for children, others for adolescents, and yet others for adults. All classes were appropriate for one of three proficiency levels: beginning, intermediate, and advanced (see pp. 182–184). Students could select from among the four-month courses offered. Some of them met twice a week; others met three or four times a week. Some met for two-hour sessions; others met for two and one-half hours. Classes for adults at advanced levels were generally longer in duration than those for adults at lower levels, adolescents, and children. Intensive courses met during the summer for three hours per session.

Students at all levels generally paid tuition; however, there were free conversation sessions with proficient speakers of English, interactive labs in which students practiced their listening skills, and video sessions during which students watched five-minute video segments and participated in prepared activities relating to the segments.

The classes revolved around topics of general interest such as the environment, health care and nutrition, exercise, sports, science, education, travel, and sociology. All topics were connected to everyday life as much as possible, and all activities, including oral and written activities, grew out of the main topics. Grammar and pronunciation were dealt with in a nontraditional way within the lessons themselves and only when needed.

Within the classes, students worked in pairs and other small groups in which they actively participated in activities designed to help them move quickly in the interlanguage development process. They frequently were involved in "mixers," activities involving interaction with the whole class and the facilitator/teacher. By participating in such activities and correcting their own mistakes—sometimes with peer help—students were able to internalize new language skills. Typical activities are described in the following paragraphs.

Small-Group Work

Working in pairs and other small groups was particularly stimulating for the students and seemed to maximize their effectiveness in the new language. If the issue being discussed was somewhat controversial, then a spokesperson from each group tried to convince the other groups that his or her group was right. If the other groups were not easily convinced, then a vote settled the matter and the groups accepted its results. However, that did not mean that minds had been changed. The students knew that it was acceptable to disagree with one another. In small groups, the facilitator/teacher circulated among the groups and did not interfere but rather encouraged students to talk and become actively involved.

Mixers

Occasionally, all students were asked to interact with one another within a time limit set by the facilitator/teacher. Generally, a question or problem was posed, and students had to actively answer the question or see if they could solve the problem. The teacher and the students often alternated roles as they became facilitators and guides, resource people, managers, and so forth.

Other Kinds of Activities

Affective/humanistic activities were called "field study" activities at the Institute. Through them, the teachers and students got to know each others' interests, likes, dislikes, weekend activities, favorite foods, and so on. Field study activities seemed to lower barriers among students and create a highly supportive environment.

Games focusing on discussion, action, group competition, problem solving, or guessing provided a strong motivation to learn English. At the same time, they served as a review of structure and vocabulary from previous lessons.

Preparatory activities such as prelistening and prereading activities were used to give contextualization to the course content. Such activities tended to increase the relevance of whatever happened during the ensuing classroom events and gave students a chance to think about and plan a course of action.

Other activities included the use of maps, charts, graphs of comparison, radio or newspaper stories, directions, open dialogues, debates, discussions, role plays, and improvisations. Whatever the activity, it had to be appropriate to students' age and proficiency levels, and it must appeal to their interests. The facilitator/teacher was asked to provide an example of what the students were supposed to do for each activity. Students needed to know what was expected of them so that they would not become frustrated.

Language Assessment

In order to place students in the appropriate courses, the Institute administered a battery of tests in all four skill areas. Created by the Institute, these tests included an oral interview and a written multiple-choice test. Children completed only the oral interview portion unless they already had developed some literacy in their first language and English.

Once students were placed at the appropriate proficiency level, they were evaluated twice by means of specially designed oral and written tests and by selected standardized tests.

Texts

In addition to some of the standard textbooks on the market in English as a foreign language, the programs relied heavily on what they called "real-life" materials. Such materials included articles and advertisements from newspapers and magazines, songs, television shows (including soap operas), and the work that the students themselves had done. At the levels intended for children, books about the *Sesame Street* characters, such as Big Bird and Cookie Monster, were used daily. At all levels, importance was placed on involvement and the lowered anxiety and inhibitions that can result from high participation.

A MIDDLE SCHOOL SPANISH PROGRAM[7]

Background

Millikan Junior High School in the Los Angeles Unified School District served a very large language minority population in the 1990s: Latin (30%), Asian (30%), Anglo (30%), and black (5%). The remaining 5 percent of the students represented various ethnic backgrounds.

At that time the Foreign Language Department opened its courses in Spanish and French to all who wanted to take them, including students in its special education programs. The department's faculty was firmly committed to the idea that the foreign language experience is for all who seek a liberal education and that, through this experience, increased understanding and personal growth results, regardless of ethnic background or other circumstances.

The students' motivation for studying a foreign language was generally instrumental— to fulfill academic requirements. However, many of the students were interested in developing basic interpersonal communication skills.

The Goals of the Foreign Language Department

The department adopted the goals set by the California Foreign Language Framework. These consist of developing individuals who could

- communicate accurately and appropriately with representatives of other languages and cultures.
- understand themselves as individuals shaped by a given culture.

---

[7] Thanks to Brandon Zaslow, who served as the chair of the Foreign Language Department at Millikan Junior High School, for providing me with the information on which this summary was based.

- function appropriately in at least one other culture.
- exhibit sensitivity to cultural differences in general.

Members of the department were convinced that these goals could be achieved if the program stressed mainly communication rather than grammar rules and memorizing vocabulary items. The governing principle of the department's programs was "to learn content and culture through language and to learn language through content and culture."

More specifically, the department expected that students would be able to function in informal environments, understand simple face-to-face conversation, and deal with relevant academic and survival topics. In addition, students were expected to be able to determine overall meaning from written discourse, create meaning through writing, and transfer learned material to new situations.

Description of the Spanish as a Foreign Language Program

The department offered two programs in Spanish: Spanish as a Foreign Language and Spanish for Spanish Speakers. For the purpose of this chapter, only the Spanish as a Foreign Language Program—Level 1 will be described in depth. Its two-year program (Levels 1 and 2) served approximately 200 students each year and sought to bring eighth- and ninth-graders to intermediate levels in Spanish by the end of the second year. A ten-week exploratory Spanish module was offered to seventh-graders to introduce them to basic concepts and give them an overview of what to expect. Often, these students became group leaders in the Level 1 classes and sometimes served as resources for the other students.

The following practices were a few of those developed by the department and adhered to by the teachers (one full-time and two part-time) in the Spanish as a Foreign Language Program.

Instruction was to be appropriate to the learners' levels of proficiency in each of the skill areas.

Students were to perform in a wide range of culturally valid situations.

Lessons needed to challenge students to interact with increasingly demanding academic content.

Students were to perform a wide range of communicative tasks (emphasis on higher-level thinking skills).

Teachers needed to use paralinguistic clues (visuals, objects, and so on) and modify their speech to make what they said comprehensible (simplification, expansion, restatement, slower speed, use of cognates).

Teachers frequently needed to confirm and clarify responses and check for comprehension.

Guided practice was considered both meaningful and personalized.

Teachers were to provide opportunities for paired and small-group interactions and use strategies that provided for various learning styles.

The following is an overview of the Level 1 program and a description of sample activities.

An Overview

Unit 1: First Encounters

Introducing oneself; saying where you are from
Understanding and spelling names and places
Greeting and leave-taking; saying how you feel; being polite
Understanding prices; giving and receiving phone numbers
Asking and telling times and dates
Discussing the weather/seasons/temperature
Role playing in the target culture and U.S. contexts

Unit 2: Active Lives

Describing daily activities in and out of school
Asking questions about activities
Expressing what one desires/hopes/needs to do
Expressing what one likes/dislikes doing
Role playing in the target culture and U.S. contexts

Unit 3: Friends and Family

Identifying others (friends and family)
Describing self and others
Talking about feelings
Talking about activities related to friends and family
Talking about sports
Talking about pets
Talking about living space at home
Talking about routine care of the home
Role playing in the target culture and U.S. contexts

Unit 4: Daily Life

Talking about daily routines (discussing similarities and differences)
Focus on weekdays and weekends
Talking about clothes (colors/combinations)
Learning about healthful living/the body/medical care
Talking about food (marketing/restaurants/invitations for meals)
Talking about school/physical layout/activities in more detail
Role playing in the target culture and U.S. contexts

Unit 5: Community Life

Identifying places in various communities (maps/directions)
Talking about community/cultural activities
Talking about community resources
Talking about travel
Role playing in the target culture and U.S. contexts

Unit 6: The Working World

Identifying abilities
Discussing career preferences
Identifying professional opportunities
Making plans for the future

SAMPLE ACTIVITIES

The Low-Beginning Level

The first samples come from the unit *El Cuerpo* (The Body) that had been developed for Spanish as a Foreign Language Program students who were operating at the low-beginning level (see p. 182). Its major goal was to help students develop listening comprehension and a large receptive vocabulary. Speech was encouraged but not expected at this point.

The unit's activities described below draw from communicative and physical approaches (Chapters 8 and 9) and Story Experience (Chapter 11).

1. Using aspects of physical approaches, students are asked to touch specific body parts: head, chest, stomach, back, arms, hands, fingers, legs, knees, and feet. However, not all items are introduced at once. First, two items are introduced, followed by a check for understanding. Then a third item is added, followed by a check for understanding, and so on.

2. Students are divided into groups. Each group is given a life-size doll made of construction paper. Aspects of the Story Experience (see pp. 275–277) are then used to tell the story of a terrible accident involving the doll, which represents a real person (see the following). The students are each given a number and are instructed by the teacher to place the bandages (sticking putty) on the various injured body parts. The students often understand only the words for the body parts, the word *bandage*, the command *put*, and some of the words that were made clear through visual aids.

    The teacher says in Spanish, "Carlos has had a terrible accident [points to the picture of a person with mild injuries]. He was hit by a car. Doctors, doctors, what should we do?" The teacher holds up a card with a huge question mark on it and shrugs his or her shoulders as if puzzled. "Put a bandage on his head, Doctor 1." Doctor 1 in each group puts the bandage on the doll's head. The teacher repeats the question and asks the students to put bandages on other parts, until all the targeted body parts have been recycled. Then the teacher says, "Carlos is well now" [shows a picture of the same person obviously recovered]. "Take the bandage off his/her head, Doctor 2," and so forth until all the bandages have been removed.

3. For further reinforcement, students cut out pictures of the various body parts from magazines and glue them onto a blank sheet of paper to form bodies of their own creation. Then they are asked to label the parts.

The High-Beginning Level

Next are sample activities from a unit titled *Bienvenidos* (Welcome). This unit had been developed for students who were operating at the high-beginning level (see p. 183). The unit focused on encouraging positive attitudes toward Mexico and on specific communicative demands such as being able to greet others, talk about time, make appointments, plan schedules, order food in a restaurant, buy necessary items for survival, and so on. It centered around a story line in which the students pretended to be participating in a year-abroad program in Mexico. They arrived at their respective Spanish-speaking homes where they needed to be able to get things done with language. The following are a few of the activities from the unit, which was designed to last about six weeks. Note that the new concepts and structures the students encounter are recycled many times in a variety of circumstances.

1. Students make simulated telephone calls to their hosting peers. They give their names and spell them, and they ask many questions such as what to pack for their stay and so on.
2. Students write down the addresses of their hosts. Then they each write to their host, indicating their feelings about visiting the host's country.
3. Once in the host's village or city, students change their watches to reflect the time in the time zone they have entered, if it is different from their own.
4. Students take the roles of hosts or guests as they introduce themselves and tell where they are from. Consideration is given to appropriate forms: first-name using *tú* or title plus last name using *usted*. Versions of this activity are repeated as needed.
5. Each student chooses favorite activities from a list provided by the host. The lists include events such as soccer games, concerts, dining out, and shopping. They then talk about the dates and starting times of the activities in which they will be participating.
6. Students are given calendars on which they write down the events in which they will participate. What is the event? Where is it? When does it start? Will someone pick them up? If so, at what time? Must they meet a person somewhere? If so, where and at what time? Students can also enter other events such as birthdays of the host family members, holidays, and so on.

Strengths and Weaknesses of the Program

One of the strengths of the program was its exploratory module for seventh-graders, which gave them insight into what it might be like to learn another language. However, according to Brandon Zaslow, chair of the Foreign Language Department, its main strength was its focus on relevant content and culture—but this was also where its chief weakness seemed to lie. The high schools into which the program fed often adhered to traditional, structure-based programs, making transitions difficult and sometimes painful for the students who matriculated with high expectations for continued relevant study. In spite of this problem, most of the students were able to adjust and do very well in their new settings as long as they had at least some opportunity to express themselves creatively in Spanish.

A HIGH SCHOOL SPANISH PROGRAM[8]

Working against problems common to many high school foreign language programs, Christina Rivera used communicative methods as much as possible in her Levels I and II (first and second year) Spanish classes at Artesia High School in Artesia, California. One of the constraints under which she worked was that she must cover a certain amount of formal grammar so that the students were ready for study at subsequent

---

[8] I am grateful to Christina Rivera for making her program available to me.

levels. A second constraint was that she met with her students only one period a day, five days a week. Yet a third constraint was that, as in other California schools, the students were not always in foreign languages classes by choice. Often they were there to satisfy graduation or college entrance requirements. Thus many of Rivera's students brought to her classes less than positive attitudes.

Nevertheless, it was her hope that, by the end of the program, the students would be able to communicate effectively and appropriately in the target language. She also hoped that students would become more sensitive to cultural differences. Activities in her classes, for the most part, centered around the students' world: their objectives, their personal attempts to deal with uncertainties, and their efforts to comprehend and speak another language.

Level I

Before beginning the instruction in Spanish, Rivera took time to educate the students in the theories on which her methods were predicated. She felt that as a result of this, students would be less apt to find her methods "strange" and would be more apt to try.

Using an outline similar to what Krashen and Terrell (1983) suggested (see pp. 227–231), she worked on receptive skills first with Level I students. Body language, gestures, facial expressions, and tone of voice were all important in the initial phases. Through physical approaches (see Chapter 8), students learned colors by manipulating pieces of colored paper. They learned about the objects in their immediate environment, food, clothing, and many other relevant concepts by manipulation of various items. They used pictures and props to act out scenes, and the teacher used visuals as she told familiar stories. Also, students played Bingo, because it did not require them to respond orally. Simple treasure hunts (see Chapter 12) were designed that required students to find objects of certain colors or that had other specific characteristics.

Grammar was introduced at early levels. However, the concepts were generally easily learned and applied. Many of the grammar activities were assigned as homework.

The following activities combining interactive practices, including physical approaches, were typical.

1. Describe a picture from a current magazine and follow up by making statements or requests.
   Example: "This is a picture of some skirts. Notice the colors. This one [points to a skirt] is green. Jane [a student in class] is wearing a skirt. Her skirt is green. This one [points to another skirt] is pink. Point to the pink skirt."
   Follow-up: Thumbs up means "yes"; thumbs down means "no." "This skirt [points to a pink skirt] is green [thumbs should be pointed down]. This skirt [points again to the pink skirt] is pink [thumbs should be pointed up]."
2. Ask students to draw or cut out pictures of items in a category (food, clothing, kitchen utensils, and so on). Then ask them to hold up pictures of specific items. Have them take specific pictures to various places around the room.
3. Using pictures, facial expressions, and gestures, introduce the students to some of the more common emotions: happy, sad, angry, bored, fearful, and so on.

Hold up cue cards on which the names of the different emotions have been written. Have the students point to the picture that clearly expresses the specific emotion indicated.
4. Using numbered pictures, ask the students to say the number of the picture described by the teacher.
5. Have the students make "self collages" with items that they feel best express themselves. Later in the year they can discuss these with class members in the target language.

As the students progressed to higher-beginning levels, the teacher used mass media because of their relevance and contextuality. Rivera found commercials particularly effective. Students acted out the commercials with props as the teacher gave directions. Much later, students wrote and acted out their own commercials. Other activities Rivera felt were appropriate to this level are as follows.

1. Using a real suitcase, real clothing, and other items for travel, students prepare for an imaginary trip. The teacher asks the students to place the items in the suitcase that they would take to Acapulco, Aspen, or some other specific destination.
2. The students are shown a picture from a magazine. They are asked to name what they see. A list of the items mentioned is written on the board.
3. Students make a chart consisting of several of their names, the clothes they are wearing, and the color of each item (see a similar activity in Chapter 9).
4. Matrices such as the following are used as starters for scenarios:
   ¿Cuánto cuesta el _____?
   Está de venta. ¿Le cuesta _____?
   ¡Qué bueno! (¡Qué malo!)
   Necesito un _____.
   ¿Por qué no vas a _____?
   ¿Cuánto cuesta?
   Cuesta _____ mas o menos.
5. Students write in a journal each day using the target language. The teacher guides them at first. They begin by writing down their favorite colors and favorite items of clothing. At later levels, the writing becomes freer as students write about their feelings and thoughts.

A study of culture was also included as the students progressed. Discussions were conducted entirely in the target language, aided by props, maps, and other visuals. Cultural information was frequently woven into other activities such as listening to music and playing games.

Level II

Level II students (those in their second year of language study) were usually somewhere in the high-beginning to low-intermediate levels. Rivera was convinced that many of them regressed over the summer because they had almost no exposure to the target language during that time. However, after spending a few weeks completing activities similar to those described previously, the students soon moved into the intermediate levels, if they were not there already. Students at this level were expected to listen to Spanish language broadcasts during a part of each day for several days in a row.[9] They may have heard traffic reports, time/temperature/weather reports, commercials, horoscope readings, song dedications, listener call-ins, interviews, sports reports, the news, or lyrics to music. They were encouraged to tape the broadcasts for repeated listening experiences. They were asked to write down what items they understood from each report. As they listened to the same reports repeatedly, they were pleased to find that they understood more of the broadcasts. Through this process, students were exposed to proficient Spanish speakers using contemporary, idiomatic speech. They learned to take advantage of cognates, intonation, and other clues to meaning.

Affective activities (see Chapter 14) were favorites among Rivera's students at this level. Keep in mind that the students had spent some time preparing for humanistic activities all along. For example, at previous levels, emotions were identified through communicative practices and physical approaches, and journals allowed students to express their likes, dislikes, and their attitudes in general. In addition, the collages contributed to their willingness to reveal themselves in low-risk situations.

A few of the activities used are as follows.

1. To reinforce the terminology describing human emotions, the teacher reads a soap opera melodramatically. Cue cards with the names of various emotions are held up by the teacher or an assistant as the story is read. The students as a group act out the emotion that is being displayed.
2. Students are asked in the target language to draw a happy baby, a mad father, and so forth. Then they are instructed to draw the following:
   a. a father who has just heard that his teenager has smashed the family car
   b. a mother seeing an *A* on her child's report card
   c. a girl seeing her boyfriend with her best friend
   d. a cheerleader after falling off the human "pyramid"
3. Students hold up small cue cards with the names of emotions written on them. Each card is held up in response to statements in the target language made by the teacher. The following are some examples.
   a. When someone is mean to me, I feel . . .
   b. At a party, I feel . . .
   c. Before a test, I feel . . .
   d. With my family, I feel . . .
   e. At the doctor's office, I feel . . .
4. Students are asked to name songs that make them feel happy, sad, like dancing, and so on.
5. Students draw and label pictures about their favorite activities. They then interview each other about the activities depicted.

---

[9] Credit for this idea is given to Lynne La Fleur.

Eventually, the students were able to discuss problems, goals, and everyday matters in the target language. Although they may not be able to converse in perfect Spanish by the end of the second year, they seemed to communicate with a minimum of anxiety.

Rivera insisted that her main goal throughout the levels was to create as natural a learning environment as possible. She felt that she still had a long way to go in creating an optimal classroom. However, she modestly admitted that she was coming closer to her vision with each passing year.

CHAPTER 20

Two-Way Bilingual and Heritage Tribal Language Programs

Two-way bilingual programs have been gaining popularity across the United States despite the political climate of the past decade or so. Parents, students, and teachers have been opting for these programs, developing and supporting them in the communities where they have been thought to be highly beneficial. Based on their extensive research, Collier and Thomas (1999) reported that although one-way bilingual programs have produced excellent results, two-way bilingual programs appear to be most effective overall (see Chapter 17).

The first two programs described in this chapter are the developmental Spanish/English program in the Valley Center Union School District in California and the immersion Cantonese/English program in Public School No. 1 on the lower east side of Manhattan in New York City. Both programs are highly respected in their communities—and for good reason. The third description is of a heritage tribal language program on the Acoma Pueblo reservation in New Mexico.

Heritage tribal language programs are becoming increasingly important to many indigenous groups in the United States. They teach the language of one's culture in an attempt to preserve and/or revive it for future generations (see the discussion in Chapter 17). Unfortunately, many of our tribal languages have been lost in the United States or are in danger of being lost due to unwise practices of government and educational systems. By learning their heritage languages, students are able to connect or in some cases reconnect with family and/or community members and with traditions that may be centuries old, as in the case of the Acoma culture.

You will notice that the voice or point of view of the third description differs from that of the other programs described in Part IV. Out of respect for the Acoma culture and its values, the story is told by Christine Sims, who is a tribal member herself and lives in the Acoma Pueblo. Her voice resonates with the love she has not only for the Keres language and the community and culture of which it is a part but for all indigenous languages and cultures that may be in danger of being lost.

A DEVELOPMENTAL SPANISH/ENGLISH PROGRAM[1]

One of the more exciting two-way language programs in bilingual education in the last decade is the voluntary Two-Way Developmental Bilingual Program (kindergarten through eighth grade) located at the Valley Center Union School District in California, a semirural community north of San Diego. Valley Center is home to many children of migrant farm workers as well as to children from middle-class and upper-middle-class families. The school district's population of 3,000 students is approximately 52 percent European-American, 26 percent Mexican-American, and 11 percent Native American. Norma Badawi, director of Special Projects, reported that in 2000, about 700 children (26% of the total school population) were in the two-way developmental bilingual program with the consent and encouragement of their parents. These students were served by twenty-three bilingual teachers and several bilingual aides throughout the school day.[2]

The program is "two-way" in that Spanish-speaking children learn English and English-speaking children learn Spanish. The program, which began in 1983, has met the challenges of time and has developed accordingly to better meet the needs of its students and remain in compliance with California's Proposition 227.[3] Students and their parents are motivated by the benefits often associated with being bilingual: greater economic opportunity, increased self-esteem (particularly for minority children who become "Spanish experts" to those children learning Spanish), more career opportunities, a better understanding of other cultures, greater cognitive flexibility, and a stronger bond between the school and the community.

This program first arose out of a need to help students learn a second language while simultaneously developing skills in their first language. Dr. Sarah Clayton, assistant superintendent and architect of the program, began in the early 1980s by soliciting the support of the school board, administration, teaching staff, and community. She presented her initial ideas to every group that would listen. When asked what recommendation she might give to others trying to begin similar programs, Dr. Clayton answered, "Persist but never insist. Don't look for satisfaction in the short term. Start small and add

---

[1] I want to thank Lydia Vogt, Lucy Haines, Norma Badawi, and Dr. Sarah Clayton for sharing their program with me. Thanks also go to the bilingual teachers whose classes I had the pleasure to observe—Natalie Weston, Mary Susan Stone, and Geri Geis—and to Debbie Mixon (math and science teacher) and Susan Benz (an aide and parent of a student in the program) for providing me with insights into their particular roles and the program in general. I am especially grateful to Lydia Vogt, who organized my visit and served as a most gracious and knowledgeable guide, and to Kathryn Z. Weed, who made me aware of the program in the first place.

[2] It is interesting to note that in kindergarten through third grade, no more than twenty students were allowed in a class (mandated by state law); in grades 4 through 8, twenty-six or twenty-seven was the average.

[3] As mentioned in Chapter 17, Proposition 227, the English Language Education for the Children in the Public Schools Initiative, required that language minority children be taught only in English with a few exceptions. One of the exceptions was a student with special educational needs who had obtained a parental waiver to be placed in an alternative program such as bilingual education. In the early grades, a parental waiver could be granted only after the child had been placed for thirty days in a structured English immersion class at the beginning of each year.

on every year rather than trying to do it all at once. Have long-term goals, and be patient enough to achieve them."

In her case, patience paid off. The program has received accolades from various sources. In 1988, the California School Boards Association recognized the Valley Center Union School District for its exemplary bilingual program. In 1994, The British Broadcasting Communications Corporation presented the program live, via satellite, to their British radio audience. That same year, the California Association for Bilingual Education awarded the district the Outstanding Elementary Program Award for substantial contributions to bilingual education. However, Dr. Clayton stated that her greatest satisfaction came when several students from the first class graduated from college.

The District's Philosophy

Lydia Vogt, principal at the elementary school and a strong supporter of bilingual education, shared with me the program's basic philosophy. The following are excerpts from her handout that help provide a foundation for the program's existence and the district's work in the community.

> The Valley Center Union School District bilingual program is based upon the premise that biliteracy is desirable and attainable. Biliteracy enhances the student's potential for functional and creative thinking while providing the means for expanded communication.
>
> Future benefits in higher education and in the economic segment of society are extensive for bilingually educated students entering the work force and seeking their place in society.
>
> Because the education of children is most effective when it is a cooperative effort between the home and the school, close communication is established and maintained between the two environments.

Valley Center's close proximity to Mexico as well as to San Diego and Los Angeles, two ethnically diverse business centers, underscores the need for a global approach to learning and maintaining languages. Foreign trade among the Pacific Rim countries requires communication in multiple languages. The increasing need for bilingual graduates, fortunately, has not gone unnoticed by the district's school board, administration, and teaching staff and the surrounding community.

Program Description

In this program, both Spanish and English learners develop and maintain grade-level skills in two languages. The program is "developmental"[4] in that the students begin their study of the core subjects (language arts, math, science, social studies) in their first language while developing fluency in their second language. In the fourth grade, students formally make the transition to study core subjects in their second language. By the fifth grade, students continue to use the district's grade-level curriculum but are able to do

---

[4] In this context, *developmental* programs are in direct contrast to *immersion* programs in which students are taught the core subjects in their second language from the beginning, whereas the first language remains on hold and is gradually added later.

so in both English and Spanish. The ratio of first language (L1) instruction to second language (L2) instruction throughout the grades is as follows. (See Figure 20.1 on pp. 510–511 for the specifics of this progression.)

	First Language Instruction (%)	Second Language Instruction (%)
Kindergarten and first grade	90	10
Second grade	80	20
Third grade	70	30
Fourth grade (beginning of year)	60	40
Fourth grade (end of year)	50	50
Fifth through eighth grade	50	50

High academic standards are maintained throughout the program in both languages. Although most children enter the program in kindergarten, exceptions can be made up to the fourth grade but only after a careful screening to ensure that all students admitted to the program can handle the work. The school district attempts to maintain a balance between English speakers and Spanish speakers in any given classroom so each group has equal access to the other's language. To participate in the program, all students must have their parents' written permission or signed waivers (in the case of language minority students), and all teachers must have bilingual certification or be close to receiving it. In addition, language minority students in the lower grades can participate in the program only after being in a structured English immersion class for thirty days each school year in order to comply with the requirements of Proposition 227.

Approach to Teaching

Within the program itself, students receive instruction from a team of teachers and their assistants who are prepared to teach language through content. The teachers believe that learning basic skills in the first language under the right circumstances does not interfere with or delay the learning of the second (see also Chapter 17).

As mentioned earlier in reference to the Valley Center program, Spanish-speaking children are referred to as "Spanish experts." Note that English-speaking children are also known as experts—they are the "English experts." On days when Spanish is the focus for subjects such as music and art, the Spanish experts act as leaders and are responsible for helping the English learners; on days when English is the focus, the reverse is true. However, according to first-grade teacher Natalie Weston, the children are reminded early on that their goal is to eventually become "bilingual experts." Not only do they become experts in each other's languages, but they become very familiar with each other's cultures through music, games, ethnic food preparation, celebrations, and literature, as well as formal and informal discussions.

Grade Level	Student	Instruction in Spanish	Instruction in English	Alternating Languages
K	ELL	Language arts, math, science, social studies, health	ESL vocabulary development, physical education	Openings/closings, music, poetry, art, classroom management discourse
	SLL	SSL vocabulary development	Language arts, math, social studies, science, health, physical education	
1	ELL	Language arts, math, science, social studies, health	ESL vocabulary development, guided reading, physical education	Literature (stories), math application, music, poetry, art, opening calendar, classroom management discourse
	SLL	SSL vocabulary development, guided reading	Language arts, math, science, social studies, health, physical education	
2	ELL	Language arts (including concept development for content areas), math, science, social studies, health	ESL vocabulary development, guided reading, spelling, writing, physical education	Literature (stories), music, poetry, art, classroom management discourse
	SLL	SSL vocabulary development, guided reading, spelling, writing	Language Arts (including concept development for content areas), math, science, social studies, health, physical education	
3	ELL	Language arts, math, science, social studies (first two trimesters), classroom management discourse, opening calendar	ESL vocabulary development, guided reading, spelling, writing, health, physical education, social studies (third trimester)	Handwriting, music, art
	SLL	SSL vocabulary development, guided reading, spelling, writing, social studies (first two trimesters), classroom management discourse, opening calendar	Language arts, math, science, social studies (third trimester), health, physical education	

4	ELL	Language arts (first semester), maintenance (second semester)	ESL vocabulary development, guided reading, spelling, writing, physical education, chorus, geography lab, computers	Math, social studies, science, art, music, drama, dance, language arts (second semester), classroom management discourse (languages alternate by unit)
	SLL	SSL vocabulary development, guided reading, spelling, writing	Language arts (first semester), maintenance (second semester), physical education, chorus, geography lab, computers	
5	ELL		ESL (Monday–Thursday, 40 min. each day), physical education, chorus, geography lab, computers	Language arts, math, social studies, science, health, art, music, drama, dance, classroom management discourse (languages alternate by unit)
	SLL	SSL (Monday–Thursday, 40 min. each day)	Physical education, chorus, geography lab, computers	
6	ELL	Social studies, science	ESL (first semester), language arts, math, physical education, band, exploratory (second semester)	None
	SLL	SSL (first semester) social studies, science	Language arts, math, physical education, band, exploratory (second semester)	
7 & 8	ELL	Future Teachers Program*	Future Teachers Program*	Social studies, language arts, science, math
	SLL			

Notes: ELL = English language learner; SLL = Spanish language learner; SSL = Spanish as a second language; ESL = English as a second language. Both groups are together for all course work except for SSL and ESL. Kindergarten through third grade are on the trimester system; grades 4 through 8 are on the semester system.
* Students tutor children in the primary grades.

Figure 20.1 Progression to Proficiency in English and Spanish

During the early phases of the program's L2 instructional phase (Figure 20.1 on pp. 510–511), vocabulary development in the core subjects is the focus. The teachers and aides use modified input, pictures, acting out, and gestures to make the content clear in the language they are teaching. As students become increasingly more proficient, they become less dependent on the teacher. At this point, pair work and small-group work are used so students can practice L2 communication with peers, learn the benefits of cooperation, and complete group work in the content-area subjects.

Student-made books help the children develop literacy, first in their primary language and then in their second language. Family histories (replete with pictures and drawings), community reports (students go out into the community to collect data), descriptions of places and events, and fictional stories are among the more common student-made projects. Moreover, parents are encouraged to become actively involved in their children's education. Students interview parents, read their stories to them, ask for reactions, and write them down to share with the class or small group, if they wish. Meanwhile students are gradually introduced to the literature of both languages.

Teachers are encouraged to develop much of their own curriculum in both languages based on relevancy and what they feel is essential to meeting the academic, psychological, and social needs of their students. Susy Stone, a teacher in the middle school, reports "What I like best about this program is the fact that we can serve such diverse needs and populations and have the flexibility to adapt our program to students' needs as these needs change."

Language Assessment

To determine the English language proficiency level of students whose home language is not English, various forms of the Language Assessment Scales (LAS) were used. The results of the assessment, along with principal/teacher recommendations and a description of available programs, are sent to the parents in a language they can understand. Generally speaking, parents placing their children in the two-way bilingual program know that they can request a reassignment at any time to a classroom where English is the only language of instruction. Parents are also informed that a child placed in bilingual education will be carefully monitored throughout the program. If the student is not doing as well as expected, he or she receives intervention and support programs available to all students in the primary grades. For example, if the student is having difficulty with reading in his or her first language, he or she may be placed temporarily in the Reading Recovery program where one-to-one assistance is given. If a student is having problems with math, he or she may be placed in a math lab for whatever time is necessary. Other possible assistance can be found in the Title I reading intervention.[5] One program employs trained literacy aides who work under the supervision of Title I teachers. In addition, there are after-school tutoring programs at all levels.

---

[5] Title I funds were intended for educational programs to help students in poverty.

School-to-Home Program

During the summer months, bilingual personnel from the school district are invited into many of the students' homes to work on literacy training with students, their siblings, and their parents. They help family members prepare various projects (called Continuing Learning Projects) that they later present or "showcase" at a potluck meal at the end of the summer. The projects—often elaborate—represent a wide range of study; projects in language arts, science, social studies, and math are the most common.

Funding

Funding for the two-way bilingual program comes primarily from the district's general funds and other categorical moneys the district might receive. Supplementary funds from the Economic Impact Aid-Limited English Proficient account have helped to pay for bilingual aides, staff development for teachers and/or aides for instructing those learning English as a second language (ESL), bilingual materials, and parental involvement projects. Title VII funds[6] have been applied over the years to help pay the coordinator's salary and to supplement the hiring of bilingual aides.

Parental Advisory Committees

The English Learner Advisory Committee meets six times a year. Parents of students learning English must constitute a majority of the committee, and at least two-thirds of the members must be migrant parents elected by their peers. Among their duties are (a) advising on the development of the district Master Plan for English Learners and the goals and objectives for such learners, including migrant education goals; (b) assisting in carrying out a district-wide needs assessment for English learners at each school; (c) reviewing and evaluating programs; and so on. Meetings follow a predetermined agenda and are conducted in language(s) best understood by the members.

In addition, there is an advisory group for the parents of native English-speaking children who are learning Spanish. Although the requirements and duties of this group are not as clearly defined, they operate in a fashion similar to that of the English Learner Advisory Committee. They advise the two-way developmental bilingual program and focus on the special needs of the Spanish learners in that program.

Conclusion

School districts planning to develop two-way developmental bilingual programs of their own might heed the words of Lucy Haines, principal of the elementary school and former Special Projects Director. Lucy recommends that school districts have systems in place for problem solving as each program moves forward. "What you start may not be what you have or want tomorrow," she said, reflecting on her own role in the process

---

[6] Title VII, an amendment to the Elementary and Secondary Education Act of 1965, provided funds earmarked for programs supporting language minority students.

of change. She saw her own school district's program evolve over the years into a program of which she and her colleagues are very proud.

In 2001, the school was unified with two other districts to encompass kindergarten through grade 12. That meant eighth-graders were given the opportunity to continue their bilingual education into grade 9. Everyone involved in the program has been enthusiastic about the possibilities for the program as the school district extends it into the higher grades.

AN IMMERSION CANTONESE/ENGLISH LANGUAGE PROGRAM[7]

In the middle of Chinatown,[8] on the lower east side of Manhattan in New York City, is Public School No. 1, also known as the Alfred E. Smith School.[9] From outward appearances, the school seems not that much different from many other inner-city elementary schools: Its brick and stone structure is very old; there is no grass, only sidewalk, between the school and the street and it sits in the shadow of the taller buildings nearby. Upon entering this school, however, one realizes that there is something quite different happening here. Although the steps going up to all four floors are steep and worn, the walls and even the doors are alive with exemplary student projects, student-created pictures and collaborative murals depicting not only symbols of the students' cultures but the daily lives that reflect those cultures. Evidence that a *community of learners* exists here is found everywhere—from the workroom reserved for parents to the nooks and crannies where "power lunches" take place, during which business professionals read and learn with children, one-to-one. Collaboration is also found in the school's classrooms, where students are working to accomplish goals through group participation and inquiry-based learning (similar to "theme cycles" found on p. 369–370). Moreover, students' individual endeavors are considered "works in progress" until they are finished and evaluated. The students learn by apprenticeship, but at the same time, they are held responsible for their own learning. Moreover, they are instilled with the belief that it is each student's right and obligation to critically analyze and question what they read and hear.

---

[7] Appreciation goes especially to Good Jean Lau, Resource Specialist for the Cantonese/English language program, who made my visit possible and who so graciously made time in her very busy schedule to welcome me to the school, set up a schedule for my observations, and serve as a guide and resource person. I also want to thank Principal Marguerite Straus, who met with me and answered all of my many questions about the school and the program itself, and the teachers in the program who so willingly allowed me to observe in their classes and shared with me materials and ideas: Ellen Wong (prekindergarten), Lillian Joe (kindergarten), and Susie Tsang (grade 2). Appreciation also goes to Delores Tucker (school coordinator) and Angela Loguercio (program coordinator) for talking with me at length about their innovative program, Everybody Wins.

[8] Chinatown has more than 150,000 residents, making it one of the largest Chinese communities outside of Asia. However, the inhabitants within this multicultural enclave come not only from China but also from Malaysia, Thailand, Korea, Burma, Vietnam, and many other countries.

[9] Alfred E. Smith was governor of New York (1919–1920) and the Democratic candidate for president in 1928.

Public School No. 1, as its name suggests, was the first public school in New York City. It was organized in 1806 by a group of philanthropists who wanted the city's poor children to have a free education. At first, its forty-two students met in the basement of a tenement. Since then, the school has moved several times with each population increase, finally arriving in 1897 at its present location at 8 Henry Street, where it became known to New Yorkers as the "school of immigrant children."

Based on statistics collected in 2000, the school has 680 students (78.2% Asian, including Pacific Islanders, Alaskan Natives, and Native Americans; 12.5% Hispanic; 8% black; and 1.3% white). Of these students, 11 percent are recent immigrants. Cantonese is the first language of the majority of its students (364), followed by English (117). The remainder speak a variety of first languages, including Mandarin, Fukinese, and Spanish. Ninety percent of the children qualify for the free school lunch program.

The School's Mission

Public School No. 1's mission includes the following goals:

1. to help children develop the skills needed to benefit from the multicultural community and the world at large
2. to expand children's awareness of their environment and help them to become lifelong learners within that environment
3. to help children develop critical thinking skills as well as oral and written communication skills
4. to create a rigorous learning environment within which children are encouraged to reach high standards[10]

To accomplish its mission, the school requires that all teachers make the standards clear to the children and help them stretch to levels beyond their current capabilities. Students are expected to gain a disciplinary knowledge which can then be used to solve problems and serves as a basis from which they can continue to grow and learn. Teachers are required to establish environments that make such learning possible. Within their classes, the students are taught to self-evaluate and are given the opportunity to develop the tools necessary to meet the state and school district standards for which they will be held accountable.

The school's principal, Marguerite Straus, states:

> Public School 1 provides a language-rich environment in which children become readers, problem solvers, and responsible participants in the community. . . . We are committed to high rigorous standards [referring to the state and district standards] with the belief and expectation that all children can learn. Cooperative learning, peer tutoring, and inquiry-based learning challenge children to think critically and communicate successfully.

---

[10] The word *standards* throughout this section refers to the "New Standards" established by the New York City Public Schools. They differ from the "old" standards in that they include tougher performance objectives that are measurable by means other than multiple-choice tests. The older standards were based on "minimum competency" tests, and, as a result, some students were judged competent and others were not. The Board of Education felt that these tests did not provide enough information about how well the students were performing.

Report cards that are aligned with the state and school district standards are sent to each student's home on a regular basis. A variety of assessment tools (including exams in English language arts and mathematics) provide input into determining whether or not students are meeting the standards. In addition, assessing behaviors based on performance descriptors and evaluating student portfolios are an integral part of the process. In 2000, 56.4 percent of the students at Public School 1 had met the standards, in contrast to similar school populations in the district where only 37 percent had done so.

The standards themselves are well delineated at each grade level. For example, Reading Standard 1 intended for grade 1 is as follows.

First-Grade Reading Standard 1: Reading Habits

- *Independent and Assisted Reading*
  We expect first-grade students to
    read four or more books every day independently or with assistance
    discuss at least one of these books with another student or a group
    read some favorite books many times, gaining deeper comprehension
    read their own writing and sometimes the writing of their classmates
    read functional messages they encounter in the classroom (for example, labels, signs, instructions)
- *Being Read to*
  We expect first-grade students to
    hear two to four books or other texts (e.g., poems, letters, instructions, newspaper or magazine articles, dramatic scripts, songs, brochures) read aloud every day
    listen to and discuss every day at least one book or chapter that is longer and more difficult than what they can read independently or with assistance
- *Discussing Books*
  We expect students finishing first grade to be able to
    demonstrate the skills we look for in the comprehension component of Reading Standard 2: Getting the Meaning
    compare two books by the same author
    talk about several books on the same theme
    refer explicitly to parts of the text when presenting or defending a claim
    politely disagree when appropriate
    ask others questions that seek elaboration and justification
    attempt to explain why their interpretation of a book is valid
- *Vocabulary*
  We expect first-grade students to
    make sense of new words from how the words are used, refining their sense of the words as they encounter them again

notice and show interest in understanding unfamiliar words in texts that are read to them

talk about the meaning of some new words encountered in independent and assisted reading

know how to talk about what words mean in terms of functions (e.g., "A shoe is a thing you wear on your foot") and features (e.g., "Shoes have laces")

learn new words every day from talk and books read aloud

Reading Standards 2 and 3 involve getting the meaning and learning the print-sound code, respectively. The following books are among those recommended to support the Grade 1 standards in reading.

Read-Aloud Books

Bourgeois, Paulette, *Franklin in the Dark*

Dorros, Arthur, *Abuela*

Lindgren, Astrid, *Pippi Long Stocking*

Martin, Bill, *Knots on a Counting Rope*

Palacco, Patricia, *The Keeping Quilt*

Sendak, Maurice, *Chicken Soup with Rice*

Viorst, Judith, *The Good-Bye Book*

Warner, Gertrude Chandler, *The Boxcar Children* (series)

Yee, Paul, *Roses Sing on New Snow: A Delicious Tale*

Level 1 Texts

D.C. Heath & Co., Little Readers, Bloksberg, *The Hole in Harry's Pocket*

Houghton Mifflin, Little Readers, deWinters, *Worms for Breakfast*

Rigby, Literacy 2000, *Jack & the Bean Stalk*

Simon & Schuster, Alladin Paperbacks, Rockwell, *Apples & Pumpkins*

William Morrow & Co., Mulberry Books, Hutchins, *Tidy Titch*

Wright Group, Sunshine Science Series, Cutting, *Ants*

Wright Group, Sunshine, Set 1, Cowley, *Quack, Quack, Quack*

The texts in the second group are considered richer in meaning, more challenging, and more complex in story structure than those in the first group. To learn about the remaining reading standards and standards in other areas such as writing, mathematics, and so on and for other grade levels, see the New York City Public Schools Web site.

Across the school district, the standards are benchmarked for grades 4, 8, and 10. At grade 4, the portfolios of the district's students are examined by district representatives, who meet four times a year to look at student work and evaluate teaching practices used to reach the goals developed for the portfolio system. District-wide staff development meetings are conducted once a month for teachers, administrators, staff developers, and district representatives. Attendees read and discuss professional books and articles as they relate to district standards and talk about how the standards themselves are being implemented and assessed.

The International Academy Dual [Two-Way] Language Program

More than 21 percent of the students (144 students) are currently enrolled in the Academy (prekindergarten through fifth grade). Within the program, ninety-one Cantonese speakers are learning English, thirty-two English speakers are learning Cantonese, and twenty-one speakers of a mixture of languages are learning English and Cantonese. Both English and Cantonese are respected equally—English as the language of the broader world outside the community and Cantonese as the language of the community. The students in this program are expected to meet the same state and district standards intended for all students in the school. Of the school's forty-four teachers, seven teach in the two-way language program and are proficient in both languages. Unfortunately, in 2001 the school was unable to hire aides because the Title VII grant funding had run out. However, they have attempted to overcome this problem by relying on student teachers and interns from the local high schools for assistance until more funding comes their way.

The Academy, which began in 1995, has four goals: (a) to provide a complete elementary school education conducted in two languages, Cantonese and English; (b) to develop bilingual proficiency and multicultural understanding and respect; (c) to enable children to achieve high standards in all academic areas; and (d) to utilize the Academy as a comprehensive example of two-way language instruction in order to reform, restructure, and upgrade education for all students in the school.

The program is designed to promote literacy in both Cantonese and English from prekindergarten through grade 5. It includes an extended day program on Thursday afternoons from 3:30 to 5:30 to provide additional instruction in the Chinese culture and the Cantonese language. The extended day program also offers daycare centers, music/dance classes, a buddy reading program, recreational activities, and other academic programs. During the regular school day, the ratio of Cantonese to English used varies depending on the teacher, the content or theme, and the students in the program. Often instructions are given in both languages. The Academy is considered "immersion" because the students are exposed to their second language right from the start, and, in the case of Cantonese learners, it is used almost exclusively in the extended day program.

Students learn to read and write in both languages through a literature-based program utilizing themes as its basic method of organization. The instruction in mathematics and science involves hands-on activities and strategy development that encourage students to think through problems and find solutions. The children serve as expert linguistic models for each other in their respective first languages, and the teachers, because they are fluent in both languages, serve as models as well. Students are often involved in self-directed research and spend considerable amounts of time choosing the best of their own work to put in the portfolios that they then share with parents and other interested parties.

Typical instructional activities involve reading books in both languages,[11] learning to follow directions, exploring the neighborhood and community (libraries, stores, the police station, the hospital), using numbers, recognizing written symbols in both languages, and

---

[11] See especially *Asia for Kids*, a catalog published by Master Communications, Inc., in Cincinnati, Ohio. It offers many bilingual books in English and several Asian languages including Cantonese. It also includes music and lyrics, games, and manipulatives.

so forth. Other activities involve storytelling using historical literature from both cultures, field trips into the community, celebrations to commemorate Chinese and American holidays, music, art, calligraphy, games, dance, crafts, and meal preparation.

Traditional tutoring by adults, peer tutoring, and cross-grade tutoring are provided after school for those children who need and desire it. Reading Recovery, a one-to-one intervention program, is available to the children in grade 1. Small Group Instruction (a push-in program) is available at any grade level.

An important part of the evaluation of the students in the Academy is completed by the teacher using a fairly comprehensive checklist. The areas evaluated in both Cantonese and English include the use of receptive language, the use of expressive language and articulation, cognitive development and language skills, and a knowledge of Chinese culture. (See Figure 20.2.)

Child's Name _____	Rating: 0 = Not Yet
	1 = Rarely
Grade Level _____	2 = Sometimes/
	Occasionally
Date _____	3 = Frequently
	4 = All the Time
Teacher _____	N/A = Not Applicable

	(Cantonese)	(English)
1. Receptive Language		
Follows simple directions	( )	( )

	(English)
2. Expressive Language and Articulation	
Speaks clearly	( )
Expresses thoughts understandably	( )
Uses short phrases	( )
Uses complete sentences	( )
Engages in conversation with adults and/or peers	( )
Retells story in sequence	( )
Relates an experience, event, or story in own words	( )
Subtotal: Expressive Language and Articulation	**(English) = _____**

	(English)
3. Cognitive Development and Language Skills	
Associates letters of the alphabet with their sounds	( )
Recognizes initial sounds and letters in words	( )
Recognizes final sounds and letters in words	( )
Uses inventive spelling	( )
Recognizes letters of the alphabet (uppercase)	( )
Recognizes letters of the alphabet (lowercase)	( )
Writes upper-case letters	( )
Writes lower-case letters	( )
Uses conventional spelling	( )
Finds own topics for writing	( )
Writes simple stories with assistance from adults	( )
Reads on level	( )
Creates independent research projects	( )
Writes independently	( )
Applies the mechanics of writing correctly	( )
Subtotal: Cognitive Development and Language Skills	**(English) = _____**

Figure 20.2 Evaluation Form *(Continued)*

---

4. Expressive Language and Articulations   **(Cantonese)**
   Speaks clearly   ( )
   Is able to use basic daily colloquial language   ( )
   Is able to recite simple songs and poems   ( )
   Engages in conversation with adults and/or peers   ( )
   Retells simple story in sequence   ( )
   Relates an experience, event, or story in own words   ( )
Subtotal: Expressive Language and Articulations   **(Cantonese) = _____**

5. Cognitive Development and Language Skills   **(Cantonese)**
   Copies characters   ( )
   Recognizes numerals   ( )
   Writes numeral (   )   ( )
   Recognizes basic sight vocabulary   ( )
   Comprehends simple characters   ( )
   Writes simple characters   ( )
   Recognizes complex characters   ( )
   Writes complex characters   ( )
   Writes phrases   ( )
   Writes sentences   ( )
   Writes simple stories with minimal assistance from adults   ( )
Subtotal: Cognitive Development and Language Skills   **(Cantonese) = _____**

Chinese Culture: Has the teacher provided the following?	**Yes**	**No**
* Introduction of holidays, writing, calligraphy	( )	( )
* Children's literature, poems, and songs	( )	( )
* Arts and humanities (includes fine arts, performing arts)	( )	( )
* Other _____	( )	( )

Figure 20.2 Evaluation Form (*Continued*)

Staff Support and Development

The team of staff members in the Academy consists of a resource specialist, a community coordinator, and one classroom teacher at each grade level. The team meets regularly to coordinate the program and plan across the grades.

Untenured teachers keep a professional portfolio for at least one year. In it they keep data for any teacher research in which they are involved and responses to various topics of their choice. The portfolios are given to the administrators at the end of the academic year for review and are then placed in the main office where all staff members have access to them. These teachers meet once a month to share their problems and concerns, reflect on their teaching, and plan for the future.

Breakfast talks held every Friday morning are open to all teachers and staff in the school. At these forums, teachers discuss their teaching strategies and their students' work. They share successes and failures, often challenge one another's ideas about best practices, and help each other become more reflective practitioners. In addition, a group of teachers meets every Tuesday morning to report to their colleagues the highlights of their discussions. They talk about new research and analyze alternative methods of assessment to determine whether students are meeting state and local district standards.

At the end of each school year, a celebration is held called "The Images of Excellence." Here the contribution of every teacher and student in the school is recognized, and student work from throughout the year is displayed for all to see and admire.

Parent and Community Involvement

Public School No. 1 prides itself on its close association with parents and the community. Parents are invited to play an integral role in their children's education. To promote good teacher–parent communication, letters, announcements, calendars, and questionnaires are sent to the home in three languages: Cantonese, English, and Spanish. Translators are provided for meetings and consultation sessions. Assistance is available for new immigrant families, and services such as the New York University Dental Program, health screenings, and annual eye and ear testing are provided. When appropriate, referrals are made to community agencies, health clinics, and family counseling services. In addition, workshops are conducted for parents throughout the academic year based on a needs assessment. These workshops include ESL (for parents and other family members) and sessions involving how their children learn to read and write, computer use, standards assessment, parenting skills, family health, and social issues. Families may visit a variety of educational and cultural institutions in the community on specially organized trips. Parents actively participate in family literacy activities, open houses, parent–teacher conferences, school assemblies, and cultural celebrations. Moreover, they often help out in the classroom and are involved in making important decisions. For example, parents played a large role in developing drafts of the Parent Handbook, which is available to all parents, and they had input into the criteria to be included in the report cards. Perhaps most important, they were given their own workroom in the school where they hold workshops and meetings, work on crafts, disseminate information to other parents and the community, and aid in assessing the needs of newcomers to the school.

To assist their children with reading, parents are encouraged to read to them as often as possible, and have their children read to them; let the children help select the books they will read together; teach their children nursery rhymes and songs; tell and encourage the telling of stories; talk about everyday print (signs, announcements, recipes, and so on); and accept without criticism their children's attempts at reading.

Principal Marguerite Straus asks all parents/guardians to read and sign a School-Parent Compact (see Figure 20.3).

Community groups, local high schools, and New York University offer several programs to help Public School No. 1 students academically and in other ways as well. For example, America Reads provides tutors from New York University to assist with reading; Brooklyn Manhattan International High School and Cascade High School supply interns to help teachers individualize the curriculum in any area in which students need assistance. Everybody Wins, which sponsors the power lunches mentioned previously, is a privately funded, nonprofit organization founded by Arthur Tannenbaum in 1991.[12]

---

[12] This organization provides reading partners for 2,200 children in New York, New Jersey, and Connecticut and for 5,000 children across the nation.

School–Parent Compact
Public School No. 1

The school and parents working cooperatively to provide for the successful education of the children agree:

The School Agrees

1. To offer flexibility in scheduling parent meetings so that working parents, single parents, homeless/shelter parents have equal opportunity to meet with teachers.
2. To provide timely information regarding all programs in school and in District No. 2.
3. To provide translations that are accurate and clear for all parents in all necessary languages.
4. To provide an excellent education in a supportive, caring atmosphere.
5. To provide activities for parents to learn parenting strategies, as well as educational workshops and information about related services in the community.

The Parent/Guardian Agrees

1. To play an active role in supporting their child's education and to attend as many PTA meetings as possible, parent conferences, and parent orientations.
2. To check with their child daily for school communications; review and respond when appropriate.
3. To be sure children are in school each day on time.
4. To review child's homework and provide opportunity for sharing classroom experiences.
5. To be an active participant in school-parent involvement policy.

| Principal: _____ | Parent: _____ |
| | for Title 1 and all children |

Figure 20.3 School-Parent Compact

Once a week for one and a half hours, business professionals who have formed partnerships with students come to school to share lunch, books, and conversation with their "partners." Funding for this activity is generally provided by the companies involved, and buses pick up the professionals from their places of work and return them after lunch.

Conclusion

Once the students leave the International Academy Dual [Two-Way] Language Program, they are able to choose the middle school they wish to attend. Unfortunately, none of New York City's middle schools offer two-way language programs at the time of this writing. However, such programs were under consideration for the future. Because the students live in such a rich linguistic and cultural environment, it is hoped that, in the meantime, they will not forget their Cantonese and the knowledge they have gained about the Chinese culture. It is likely that their abilities to self-motivate, self-evaluate, and actively seek the information they need will remain with them as they continue through their schooling at all levels.

MAINTAINING AMERICAN INDIAN LANGUAGES: A PUEBLO INDIAN LANGUAGE IMMERSION PROGRAM

by Christine Sims, Acoma Pueblo[13]

Today, many American Indian tribes across the United States are faced with the challenge of maintaining their ancestral tribal languages in the midst of an English-speaking dominant society. Although recent influences have accelerated the pace of language shift toward English in many tribal communities, these developments were first set in motion as a result of U.S. federal government policies of the late nineteenth and early twentieth centuries. Government education policies at the time specifically targeted American Indian children, with the intent of assimilating them and coercing them to abandon native languages, cultures, and tribal practices (Adams, 1998).

For many tribes, these policies took their eventual toll on many indigenous languages (Hinton, 2001). Today, it is estimated that perhaps only 20 out of approximately 175 extant American Indian languages are being learned as first languages by American Indian children (Krauss, 1992, 1996). The remaining languages are at various stages of vitality, thus raising a critical concern about their survival among many tribes.

Although Pueblo Indian tribes of the southwest have been able to retain their languages far longer than other American Indian tribes, they too are beginning to experience the threat of a language shift toward English, especially among school-age and young adult populations. In response, some tribes, such as the Pueblo of Acoma in northwestern New Mexico, have initiated community-based language programs for young tribal members. The Keres language, spoken by the Acoma community, is one of seven distinct dialects of this language family. There are six other languages represented among the twenty-two different tribes of New Mexico.

The Beginning of a Language Retention Initiative

The Pueblo of Acoma, a tribe of approximately 3,000 members, established its own community-based Acoma Language Retention Program in 1997. Since that time, a number of language initiatives have been started in the community, including summer immersion camps for youth, adult culture and language classes, and, more recently, Keres language instruction in a public elementary school and a local high school.

While the Acoma Keres classes at Laguna-Acoma High School are fairly recent (since 2002), the approach to teaching language is based on the same methodologies used in the tribe's summer immersion camps and other community-based language initiatives. These classes are unique in their primary emphases on oral language development rather than native literacy to teach language. This is in accordance with the wishes of the tribal leadership and elders who have emphasized the need for

---

[13]Christine Sims is an assistant professor in the Department of Language, Literacy, and Sociocultural Studies in the College of Education at the University of New Mexico. She received her doctorate from the University of California at Berkeley, focusing on Native American language maintenance and revitalization issues. She is an enrolled member of the Pueblo of Acoma and resides on the Acoma Pueblo reservation in northwest New Mexico.

younger generations to learn to speak the language because of the critical role it plays in the daily sociocultural and religious life of the Acoma people.

This focus on maintaining an oral-based tradition is a feature that has not always been appreciated by school administrators unfamiliar with Pueblo Indian perspectives regarding their languages. Pueblo Indian communities have generally shied away from public dissemination about their cultures and languages, including their inclusion in formal school settings. Therefore, most tribal communities, such as the Acoma Pueblo, have had to consider in what manner they want to see their languages introduced into schools, what is taught, and who teaches their languages. By 2002, the Acoma tribe had secured an agreement with the local public school district regarding these particular issues. Today, the tribe, through its Acoma Language Retention Program, plays a major role in selecting tribal members from the Acoma community to teach Keres classes to kindergarten through sixth grade students and to students at the middle school-, and secondary-levels who are enrolled in two public schools. The Keres high school classes are briefly described in the following sections.

Goals of Acoma Language Retention

The goals of the Acoma Language Retention Program are to (a) restrengthen and maintain the Acoma language as an oral spoken language, (b) restrengthen and maintain intergenerational processes of language teaching and learning, and (c) create language learning experiences that develop a lifelong interest in learning and using the Acoma language.

Because Acoma elders and leaders maintain that the spoken language is critical for the continuance of the community's cultural life, much of the content of what is taught in the high school immersion classes is based on the tribe's cultural calendar of events, the daily life experiences of family and community that students share, and the traditional teachings that are part of the community's sociocultural life.

The General Structure of the Keres Classes

Both middle school and high school Acoma students receive instruction in the Keres language for fifty-five minutes daily, four days a week. The classes are offered as electives, and students have the opportunity to take a Keres class for two semesters. A third and fourth semester of instruction is being considered for future development to allow for students' continued language development; however, this will depend on what instructional resources are available in the future. At the local high school, a Keres language classroom is available for students and instructors to use throughout the day. It allows for space in which to conduct class instruction as well as an area for materials development for the instructors. There are ample display areas for student work and instructional materials that help make the Acoma Keres classroom an inviting place to learn.

The small number of students who attend these classes make for an ideal teaching environment. Students are able to receive individual attention and help from their instructors. Classes can have as few as three or as many as thirteen students. A team of Keres speakers who have been selected by the Acoma Language Retention Program and who have undergone training in using language immersion methodologies and strategies conducts the classes. The Program has always tried to utilize a team of speakers to teach the

Keres classes. At least two speakers, therefore, are always available. This allows students to hear models of Keres spoken by fluent speakers in the daily discourse of conversation and interaction. It also allows students to observe speakers utilizing the various social rules of language that are part of the Pueblo's social traditions and practices.

A typical class day in the high school Keres class involves the use of the language as soon as students enter the classroom. The instructors use the Keres language exclusively with students throughout the time they spend together. Students are not necessarily grouped according to their level of speaking ability. Instead, the instructors work with students at whatever level they are when they come to class. The Keres instructors have found that the students who have some comprehension of the language are actually able to help their peers. This is a practice that is encouraged by the teachers. Students are told that in this class, "there is no such thing as cheating when learning your language." The instructors have been trained to be supporters of their language learners, which is obvious from the constant positive feedback that students receive whenever they make any attempts to use the language.

Learning the Social "Rules" of Keres

One of the first social rules that students learn is the proper way in which to enter their Keres classroom. A number of different greetings are appropriate for the time of day. Students soon learn that languages such as Keres are complex in their morphology and that they must pay attention to such details as how many people they are greeting. Is it one, two, or three or more? Students learn by listening and watching their instructors adjust their greetings according to these aspects. The same is true at the end of class: Students must pay close attention to whether they bid farewell as an individual or whether they leave with another classmate or a group of students. Such features of the language are not taught as strict grammatical lessons but rather through instructor modeling, student observation, and actual practice.

In addition to such social protocols, students are introduced to a variety of lessons throughout the year that coincide with cultural events occurring on a cyclical basis. These lessons may be ones that the instructors prepare in anticipation of language that students will be apt to hear and use in family or community settings. The lessons are centered around themes that may include such topics as traditional dances, songs and stories; community preparations for feast days; preparing dance regalia, or other community-centered events. Students also learn how they are related to one another through kinship based on a matrilineal clan system. English names take a backseat to the individual Acoma names students have been given at birth by their families. Over time, students learn to identify each other exclusively by their given native names as well as their clan affiliations.

In addition, students learn through basic conversational practice how to use "everyday talk" with each other and their instructors and, when the occasion arises, to use the language of respect with elders, parents, relatives, and tribal leaders. Male and female forms of speech are also quickly learned as the fluent speakers model these terms and phrases in their everyday conversation. The overall focus throughout these lessons is to make language learning practical and immediately useful for students.

Linking Language Learning to the Community

A unique feature of how students learn language in these classes is the link that instructors strive to emphasize through experiential learning involving the community. The underlying philosophy of the program is that younger members must learn to recognize that the value in learning language is its practical and immediate application to situations beyond the classroom setting. In this manner, instructors try to plan for trips during which they accompany students off campus to visit elders in the village, assist the tribe's traditional leaders with community work activities, or assist at public community gatherings. Such opportunities are vivid reminders to students that oral Keres continues to be a crucial aspect of life in the community. They learn that they too are linked to a language community through their social relationships with other speakers.

The Community's Involvement

The Acoma Language Retention Program has been instrumental in making sure that the Keres language classes in the public schools remain consistent with the community's perspectives regarding the teaching of their language. In contrast to programmatic planning that is typically the prerogative of school administrators, this initiative is closely tied to the community's long-term plan for language maintenance. Moreover, the involvement of community members who teach Keres fills a vacuum that the district itself cannot provide at this time. In 2002, the New Mexico state legislature passed a new law requiring alternative certification of individuals who teach Native culture and language in New Mexico public schools. The intent behind this law is to provide the opportunity for tribes to designate their own community resources for teaching Native students their tribal heritage languages in school settings. The Pueblo of Acoma has begun to utilize this law to place its most strategic human resources in local public schools where the Acoma Tribal Council has sanctioned Keres language instruction.

Periodically, the instructors at the high school call on various members of the community to visit the classes, talk to students, and mentor them in short-term projects. This has included, for example, individuals who are expert craftspeople in various traditional arts, elders who have traditional cultural knowledge, and other community members who have specialized skills.

Although the Keres teaching team is always busy with weekly lesson planning and materials development, they are also involved, from time to time, in mentoring new community members who have recently joined the language retention program. As part of the training that new "interns" receive, they are sometimes paired with "veteran" language instructors, so that they can observe first-hand how to work effectively with beginning language learners as well as incipient speakers. In this way, the connection to community is again utilized as a means for teaching and learning. This has been an important aspect of preparing Native speakers to teach tribal heritage languages. It is also the means by which all members of the community come to realize the important role they play in the survival of their own tribal heritage language.

PART V

Case Studies: Teacher Narrations to Stimulate Professional Dialogue[1]

Five case studies are offered in this section to stimulate reflection and a discussion of multiple perspectives and to develop an awareness that there is no simple solution to problems that teachers face on a day-to-day basis. Each case involves a different age group, kindergarten through the college/university level.

There are many different ways to use these case studies. When I used them in my own teacher education classes, I divided the participants into groups of four or five, depending on the age levels at which they were teaching or planning to teach. Each group received only the case that pertained to their particular level (often I would end up with more than one group at any given level). I asked the participants to read the case study description first, then discuss the issues involved and what they might have done in that particular situation. One member of the group jotted down the group's ideas.

Then I asked them to read the second part of each case describing what the teacher did in each situation. Another group discussion took place as the participants reacted to what the teacher had actually done and they sometimes modified their initial ideas, depending on what they learned. Next a spokesperson from each group shared the case and the ideas of the group with the class. This procedure seemed to work. The discussions of the relevant issues were

---

[1] Case Study 1 was written by Cathrene Connery, assistant professor at Ithaca College, and was based on data collected for her doctoral dissertation at the University of New Mexico, Albuquerque (2006), *The Sociocultural-Semiotic Texts of Five- and Six-Year-Old Emergent Biliterates in Nonacademic Settings.* Case Studies 2 and 3 are from *Diversity in the Classroom: A Casebook for Teachers and Teacher Educators* (1993), edited by Judith Shulman and Amalia Mesa-Bains. They are used by permission of Lawrence Erlbaum Associates, Mahwah, New Jersey. Case Study 4 came from the author's own experiences at Alameda High School in Lakewood, Colorado, and Case Study 5 was constructed by the author for this edition. Other sources of case studies for reflection and discussion can be found in Hafernik, Messerschmitt, and Vandrick (2002) and in Tinker, Sachs, and Ho (2007).

quite lively. However, most groups came to the conclusion that there were no easy answers, once the issues had been fully aired. Later, participants wrote their own case studies, based on their own experiences as learners and teachers, to share with their groups. They were asked to include the critical facts and choose an incident that was likely to lead to a multifaceted discussion.

CASE STUDY 1: MOTIVATING BETO (Kindergarten)

Mariposa Elementary School had experienced a surge in enrollment after the first forty days of school. Due to a teacher shortage, very few qualified candidates were left to fill a half-time kindergarten vacancy. Even fewer individuals wanted to teach in what had been described as one of the city's "pocket of poverty" schools. A month after a second social studies teacher was hired, Mariposa's principal began to search for another teacher because the current kindergarten teacher was not treating the children with the sensitivity and respect they deserved.

When I took over the small class in mid-December, I was either the third or fourth teacher the children had been introduced to in four and a half months. Driving down the street toward the school one day in March, I reflected on how such a trauma may have impacted Umberto, a child in my class from a working-class, immigrant, Spanish-speaking home. Beto (we called him by this nickname) seemed to exhibit most of the characteristics associated with the low-beginner proficiency level in English. However, I was worried. After two and a half months, Beto had not spoken to me in English or Spanish unless directly requested to do so in a one-to-one testing situation.

After visiting his home, I encouraged him to draw as best he could his sisters, relatives in Mexico, and what he thought the new baby arriving soon would look like. Instead, despite my efforts, he appeared content just to watch his peers cut out shapes, scribble "sentences," and respond to the colorful big books we all shared. He would address me mainly through his friend Francisco.

I was quite confident that Beto and I had made an emotional connection during our first introduction. Recognizing the child's traditional values, shy nature, and adjustment challenges, I continued to treat him with caring and respect and to make attempts to engage him in both languages. Unfortunately, his previous teacher had given him an English name that barely resembled his own, adding to his further alienation. As soon as I took over the class, I referred to him by his first name or *apodo* (family nickname). I also called him "*mijo*" or "dear one." I interacted with him by asking questions, making comments, offering compliments, and providing instructions as though we were equal conversationalists. His bright eyes reflected intelligence and curiosity, and his actions indicated that he comprehended many of my messages. One day his small hand voluntarily melted into mine as we walked together to other parts of the school. But it disturbed me that in two and a half months he still had not addressed me in his first or second language. He still relied mainly on Francisco to make known his needs or requests and he still preferred to watch his peers engage in their activities. What could I do to get him to communicate directly with me and to participate more in the activities of the classroom, without pressuring him?

WHAT DID THE TEACHER DO?

One day I decided to include myself in one of Beto and Francisco's play sessions. After watching the two boys play cars during self-selected activity time, I asked about their friendship in Spanish. Beto grinned when I suggested we write something about the two friends. Graciously suspending their game, the two boys dictated to me while I transcribed the following short description through translations, gestures, and nods: *Umberto es reyno. Francisco es su amigo. Los niños juegan Nintiendo. Los niños veen televisión. Los niños comen galletas. El fin.*

I then proposed we also include an English translation of their description. The boys heartily agreed, supplying me with the words they knew sentence by sentence. Their English version read as follows: *Umberto is king. Francisco is his friend. The boys play Nintendo. The boys watch television. The boys eat cookies. The End.* The children concluded the writing session by agreeing to title the work, "*Los dos amigos,*" or, "The Two Friends."

The next day, I presented each boy with a typed copy in both languages of what they had dictated. Beto and Francisco agreed to illustrate the text for their evening homework. Francisco joined me in reading and re-reading aloud each sentence over and over again and we discussed what the boys might draw. After I left to attend to other students, I noticed from across the room that Francisco was reading the description to Beto, who then began to mouth the words to himself without looking at the text.

Two days later, Beto submitted his illustrated version of the description. He and Francisco presented it to the class. With Francisco sitting by his side, Beto pointed to words in the text from our author's chair as they read the description aloud in Spanish and then in English. Beto's silence in English and Spanish appeared to have ended.

One day in late spring, Beto approached me and asked me how to draw a turtle. Out of the handful of signs we had explored together, this symbol proved to be the most significant. The turtle motif appeared on most of his work thereafter. He began to seek out others to dictate sentences and stories about turtles. Pictures of turtles and hearts appeared mysteriously on my desk. He even requested books and magazines about turtles from the library. His turtle creations extended from the end of school into the summer and proved to be a source of motivation, bringing him further into the world of biliteracy, as he began to share his work with friends and family.

CASE STUDY 2: MY "GOOD YEAR" EXPLODES: BRINGING IN THE PARENTS (Elementary School)

I thought it had been a good year. My second-grade class of thirty-two bilingual students was a joy to teach. Like me, a third of my students were Japanese immigrants. Another third were Japanese Americans who were born in the United States, and the rest were from a mix of ethnic backgrounds. The entire class had progressed in math, according to their scores on a standardized test of basic skills. With three weeks left of the school year, I was confident that I had covered all the math requirements in the state framework. Moreover, because of strong parent involvement and participation, we had enjoyed a variety of enrichment activities such as art, music, dance, and other performing arts.

Early one spring morning as I prepared for class, Grace—the PTA president—walked in. Grace was a Caucasian parent and a regular volunteer in my classroom. With just five minutes to class time, she handed me a letter and said, "Don't read this now because it will make you unhappy. Wait until after school."

My puzzled look prompted her to say more. "Some parents felt you could have done a better job teaching our children. Do you think you really did a good job this year?"

I couldn't believe what I was hearing. The bell rang, but I ignored it and opened the letter. As I read, tears filled my eyes. I was too shaken to begin class. Instead, I went straight to my principal, Mr. Bryant.

Grace followed me in. Mr. Bryant seemed to be expecting me; he had been given a copy of the letter. "You may leave," he said to Grace, who was by now in tears herself. "We didn't mean to hurt you," she said to me. "We wanted you to know how we felt."

When Grace was gone, Mr. Bryant gave me a hug, offered me tea, and sent another teacher to cover my class. As I regained my composure, we discussed the letter. I learned that copies signed by parents had been sent to the principal, the district office, and the school board. Apparently, the letter had been triggered by the news that I would be teaching a combination class next year. When parents realized that I might be teaching their children again, they decided to express their concern that I had inappropriately taught the basic concepts, particularly in math.

The children had been allowed to explore and learn with manipulatives. Parents felt that they hadn't brought home enough paper-and-pencil homework and math worksheets. They also thought that if their children were in my class next year, they would not progress at the rate of other students. They apparently wanted their children to spend their math time on rote memorization, drill and practice, and traditional tasks.

My mind raced back to a visit I'd had with one of the mothers early in the year. She had come to me holding a stack of worksheets that her daughter had completed in first grade. "Look how much more she was learning last year," the mother had said.

I had explained to her my firm belief that my hands-on approach and problem-solving strategies were far more effective for all my students than traditional "drill and skill" methods. I told her that I used the requirements in the state framework and that I had attended numerous workshops and training programs to learn how to incorporate these techniques into my teaching. The children, I pointed out, felt challenged and were highly motivated to learn math as a result. The mother had listened intently, and I thought she heard my message.

On back-to-school night, I had carefully explained my strategies to all the parents. Throughout the school year I also kept a running communication about all curriculum, special projects, and student progress and concerns through letters, telephone calls, and weekly student checklists. Parents had numerous opportunities to contact me, but no one ever did.

WHAT DID THE TEACHER DO?

Our school has always encouraged active parent participation. My classroom was no exception. The parents who seemed unhappy with my math curriculum helped regularly in my classroom. They saw me teach hands-on, integrated math lessons, and they watched their children engage in critical thinking and problem-solving activities. To reinforce skills with limited-English-proficient students, I often used concrete materials, visuals, sheltered English techniques, or—when I could—the child's primary language. Never did I feel that my teaching abilities were in doubt.

In the days that followed my talk with Mr. Bryant, I conferred with other teachers, the principal, other administrators, and even professors. I wanted to know what they thought, but most of all I needed emotional support. My pride and dignity had been wounded when my professionalism and integrity were questioned. Worse, I had been accused of doing a disservice to the children. I was haunted by thoughts that I had brought this on myself, and I was full of guilt.

The network of colleagues supported me. They felt that the parents' actions reflected not a failure of mine with the children but a lack of parent acceptance of new teaching strategies. They bolstered me with reminders that I had been selected as a mentor teacher and my work was regarded as outstanding.

But I am still puzzled. Why did parents think that their children would have different experiences in other teachers' classrooms? Each school year we address the various curriculum areas in many parent education workshops taught by mentor teachers, administrators, and specialists in the curriculum development areas. My teaching approaches are not different from those of the majority of teachers at my school. We share philosophies and use similar techniques.

Was it a personality conflict between the parents—such as Grace—and me? Was it a cultural problem, rooted in differing communication styles, learning expectations, or traditions? Why couldn't parents come directly to me when concerns first arose? Did they feel they should have had more control over what happened in the classroom? What was the true catalyst for their action?

Since this incident, our staff has had many collegial meetings to brainstorm ways of averting such problems in the future. A schoolwide grievance committee has been established, composed of the administrator, paraprofessionals, teachers, and parents. We have also established a procedure for communications. Parents must meet with the teacher first. If issues remain unresolved, all parties meet with the administrator. The final recourse is the executive parent body.

But I often still ask myself how I missed seeing warning signs. I have always put much effort into my work. It was terribly disturbing to face this quandary at the end of school. I was ready to quit the very profession I loved and to which I have dedicated years of service. Did I cause these parents to react the way they did? What did I do wrong? What should I do in the future if parents and I disagree about how best to teach their children?

CASE STUDY 3: PLEASE, NOT ANOTHER ESL STUDENT (Middle School)

Sam Garcia, the Spanish bilingual counselor, stood outside my classroom door, grinning sheepishly as he pointed me out to the new student. I knew why they were at my door, and without really intending it, I stopped talking in mid-sentence and blurted out, "Oh, no, not another ESL student!" Glaring at Sam I shook my head in despair and moaned, "You can't do this to my program."

He looked beyond me; his eyes refused to meet mine.

"See the boss."

"But I have!"

"You'd better go see him again. Rumor has it we're the only school that'll take in these kids the rest of the year."

"Damn," I muttered. I felt so powerless. The middle school I had chosen to teach in because of its diverse student population, its location near the heartbeat of the city, its array of special programs—Spanish bilingual, Chinese bilingual, reading demonstration, band, and home economics—was now testing my strength, my endurance, my creativity.

Sam disappeared, and the dark eyes of my new student caught mine. The class watched us closely. "*Bienvenido, Fernando, bienvenido a los estados unidos, a San Francisco, a nuestra clase.*"

Later, during my prep period, the last of the day, I was as usual too tired to do any "prepping." I looked down the list of names and dates in my roll book. It was May 1 and twenty new students, including Fernando, all zero-level English, had entered my classroom since February. My "program" had been sorely affected—not enough books, paper, chairs, tables, dictionaries. Even worse, there was not enough teacher time for students thrust so abruptly into a new language and culture. From my experience teaching in Central America, I knew that these students were arriving in this country after completing their school year in December and then traveling during summer vacation to this new country, expecting to enter school in March or April to begin a new year. Unfamiliar with our September–June school year, they had no idea that school would soon be ending. Nevertheless, here they were, assigned to my combined sixth-, seventh-, and eighth-grade Spanish bilingual classroom. And so far, the best I had been able to do was give each a hasty welcome, then move silently closer to hysteria over how I could make the transition work for everyone.

I knew I had to think of something quickly. The week before, eleven-year-old Araceli didn't make it to the girl's bathroom in time; she hadn't been able to remember where it was and had been too shy to ask another student. The long corridors circle the building, and sometimes, on certain floors (who knows why), the bathrooms are locked. Araceli, embarrassed and frightened, went home. I, her new teacher, felt guilty, frustrated, and angry. We both needed help.

WHAT DID THE TEACHER DO?

It was too late in the year for extra help in the classroom, but I thought of my colleague Carolyn, teaching in the basement, publishing poems and stories, putting on plays, and enjoying the fruits of her year-long emphasis on writing and creative learning. She taught the sixth-grade honors class during the same two-hour block my Spanish bilingual students were with me for English as a second language and science instruction. I wondered . . . how about pairing up each ESL student in my class with a native speaker from her class?

We met, talked, and agreed! Yes! And the planning began. How should we pair the students? We went over our class lists, noting problem students. I pointed out that many of the newly arrived Spanish-speaking girls would be most comfortable with a female partner because they come from Latino school systems that traditionally separate the girls from the boys. Carolyn mentioned that she had a number of Asian girls who also were accustomed to working with each other. We made as many pairs of girls as we could. After that, our pairing was based on an attitude of "let's try these two and see if it works out; if not, we'll change it."

In planning the substance of the partnership program, I thought of my original goals in initiating the contact with Carolyn: I wanted someone besides myself to befriend my bilingual students, and I wanted my students to feel important and wanted in their new country. My aim was to provide culturally relevant material in English and Spanish that would help them learn another language and make friends too.

I put together a packet of basic information that students expect to learn when they are studying a new language. The packet contained days of the week, months of the year, numbers, simple dialogues, the alphabet (for spelling purposes), weather words, and a map of San Francisco with questions about addresses and phone numbers. I had spent a number of years teaching in Central and South America and knew that certain games such as Bingo (*loteria*), Simon Says (*Simón dice*), and Twenty Questions (*veinte preguntas*) crossed cultural boundaries; therefore, I included them in the packet and also introduced simple crossword puzzles based on the new vocabulary students would acquire in each language.

The packet was prepared in both English and Spanish with a blank page for writing between each section, because we knew the students would want to practice writing their new vocabulary. Even though the material was available in both languages, I pointed out to Carolyn that it was important to keep instruction in each language as separate as possible so that students did not rely on back-to-back translation as a method of learning a new language. Therefore, we agreed that our Monday session would focus on the material in English and the Friday session would be held in Spanish. Back in our own classrooms, we would have our students record their experiences and feelings about the partnership program in their journals in the language of their choice.

Carolyn and I will never forget the first partnership session. The initial meeting of partner with partner was heavy with apprehension. Some paired students couldn't even bear to look at each other out of nervousness, shyness, and fear. We passed out a curriculum packet to each student, had the students write their names on the packet cover, and gave initial instructions. Silence. I thought I had made a big mistake. And then, as minutes passed, there began tentative talk. Within ten minutes, Carolyn and I were able to grin at each other. As we looked around the room, we saw body language, sign language, and drawing for communication. We heard laughter, words being repeated, introductions, and yells for help too! We saw and felt an intensity of learning that had an energy of its own. Kids were interacting with kids and their attention to each other was 100 percent!

Looking back, we felt more could have been done. We found that once the students began using the simple learning packet, they had many questions that could have been answered if they each had their own bilingual dictionary. We had only two globes, yet students' natural curiosity led them to want a map of the world to find out where a partner's native country was located. Even the students born in the United States had often moved from state to state or city to city, so we needed maps of the United States to allow them to show and talk about their many homes. Once the English-speaking students had mastered the pronunciation of the Spanish alphabet, they were eager to try reading in Spanish, but we had too few books.

Beyond supplies for the program, we wondered about the curriculum itself for next year. How could we challenge the students? What about science? Could students work on experiments together? What about having the students work on major interdisciplinary projects that incorporate English language arts and science?

As a trained bilingual teacher, I knew the value of native language instruction. I knew that my most successful bilingual students were those who had received the most instruction in their native language. I agreed that whatever we decided to work on in our Monday and Friday sessions would have to be presented to the students in my own classroom in prior lessons in their native language. In that way we would be building on what students already knew and understood. In addition, this approach would help the students understand the material presented to them in a new language.

We wondered about ways to pair and group the students. Given the short amount of time we initially had to put the program together, we certainly had paid too little attention to the pairings. There had been some problems. Also, absences had caused problems. These situations led us to the following questions: Do the students always have to be in pairs? Maybe they could form cooperative groups of four. Do they have to stay with the same partner all year? Wouldn't it help stretch their experiences by matching them in a variety of ways throughout the year? As teachers, we might also observe the partners and learn from their behavior. Which kids were helpful? Why? Was it behavior that we could model so that those less helpful could improve? We were excited. We were onto something. We agreed to meet at the end of the summer to lay out next year's plan.

In June, a few days after school was over, I found Alonzo Jones' journal in Carolyn's classroom and read this entry:

> This is the first time I've heard that we will meet with the ESL class about teaching them English. For our field trip together I don't know what it will be like. But I believe that it will be fun. Somehow I will do what I can to communicate and help my partner.

It's comforting for me to know that I need not be alone with my ESL students, that I have Alonzo and many others like him to help me out. I had based my Spanish bilingual program on the premise that I, as the classroom teacher, was the only one who could work with Spanish-speaking newcomers to our school. I now realize my mistake. Learning about a new language and culture can come not only from a teacher but from one's English-speaking peers.

CASE STUDY 4: CONFLICT RESOLUTION ON CAMPUS (High School)

Teaching ESL high school students was a job I had always wanted. I had taught immigrants from Mexico several years before and had learned a lot from the experience. When I was asked to direct an ESL center in a large suburban high school, I jumped at the chance.

The next thing I knew, I was teaching forty-one students from eight different countries around the world, including several from Laos and Vietnam. I had been warned by our district coordinator to watch out for possible conflicts between the Laotians and the Vietnamese in the center due to a history of animosities between the cultures from which they had come. To head off any conflicts, I had decided to expose all of my students to affective and conflict-resolution activities from time to time so that they might see each other as individuals with similar concerns and needs, rather than as enemies. The activities appeared, for the most part, to be working. In fact, it was noted by the district office that, at our school, we had established an atmosphere of mutual respect. When we were asked to help quell an unpleasant situation at another school in the district by visiting and talking with the groups involved, we were confident that we might be able to do some good.

Among the students who went with me to help was one of our Laotians named Samavong, a young man of eighteen whom the others knew to be a fighter from his youth in Laos. He had scars to prove it, and he wore them as badges of honor. He was studious and bright and was learning English very quickly. Not only that, but he seemed to have overcome the hatred that he had at first felt for the Vietnamese in the class and had even become good friends with one of them. The two were among the emissaries who came along, and, particularly because they had become friends, they seemed to make an impression on the students at the other school. Little did I know at the time that it was our *own* school we had to worry about and that the trouble that was brewing was coming from *outside* our classroom.

One day as I was passing the office belonging to one of our vice principals, he motioned me in. With a somewhat quizzical expression on his face, he asked, "Did you hear about the big fight in the parking lot during lunch?"

My heart sank. "No," I replied. "I didn't. What happened?"

"Well it seems as though some of *your* (emphasizing "your") Laotian students beat up some of *our* Cowboys out there." Now the Cowboys were a type of gang in the school who were known by the pick-up trucks they drove and the baseball caps they wore. They also chewed tobacco. He continued, "The one who started the whole thing was that little one of yours with the scars on his face."

"Oh, you mean Samavong." He went on to tell me that I really ought to control my students better. I asked him if anyone had been hurt and he said that, luckily, no one had been this time, but that it could happen again and maybe with tragic results.

I left feeling very sad and disappointed. Why hadn't my students told me about it? Although I had had most of the Laotians that morning, some of the others in my afternoon class could have mentioned it. They must have known. And why hadn't they been able to handle the conflict in the first place? They had done so well with conflict resolution in the classroom. I knew, too, that the vice principal had always seemed to resent my students and me and would, no doubt, make a "federal case" out of this incident. I knew also that I had to do something to try to change the whole situation, including his attitude, but I wasn't sure where to start or what to do first.

WHAT DID THE TEACHER DO?

To begin with, I rather frantically enlisted the help of the multicultural education director who had been working at our school for several months. Although he had been aware of some of the animosity between the two groups, he (like me) had not realized the tension had begun to build. He suggested that we sit down right away with the two groups and encourage them to air their grievances. I thought it was a good idea. The Cowboys complained that the Laotians were purposely "getting in their faces" as they walked down the hallways. The Laotians said that they didn't like being called names or being made fun of. We talked about how disappointed we both were in their behavior and how it could affect the whole school if things didn't change. By the end of the session, most of the students had agreed (maybe it was just to appease us) that they were going to try and get along better in the future.

Then I decided to do an inservice for the entire staff. I had already done one inservice in the early fall which I thought had been fairly successful. I had never been trained to do inservicing and was filled with fear at the thought of it. But somehow I found it easy to talk about the students and their efforts to learn English and become part of American society. I stressed the importance of their being accepted along with their cultures and languages. I also talked about strategies content-area teachers might use to make the content of their classes more accessible. I had spent a lot of time thinking about strategies beforehand and managed to come up with some ideas to start with. Then I divided the participants into content-area groups to come up with their own ideas and share them with the rest of us. I was glad I did that, because we all learned from each other. The only problem was that the vice principal to whom I referred earlier was not there. I wanted to ensure that his presence would be more likely next time so I asked him to facilitate a group during the inservice. He almost seemed pleased at the request and accepted, much to my relief.

Sometime later, I recruited two of the Cowboys who were good students to serve as peer facilitators for the ESL students. Although one of them dropped out (perhaps due to peer pressure), the other got to know several of the ESL students quite well. He even agreed to serve as a "buddy" to one of the Laotians in a course in mainstream science. Over time, we noticed a gradual softening of attitudes among students in both groups, and eventually we even included some of the Cowboys in our occasional parties. But the day I knew for sure that the bitterness was beginning to evaporate was when two Laotian boys came to school with baseball caps on their heads. (I was glad to see, however, that there was no evidence of chewing tobacco.) In spite of everything, Samavong remained aloof and told me privately one day that, although he could act friendly toward the Cowboys, he would never really trust one.

CASE STUDY 5: A MULTICULTURAL CHALLENGE (College/University)

This is my first year teaching freshman English at a medium-sized community college in Los Angeles. I am not very experienced at teaching, nor am I very experienced at working with language minority students, but I really want to help them succeed in college. I am a Caucasian woman, thirty-three years old, divorced with two children. I drive my car to work each day from Santa Monica where I live in a mostly white neighborhood. I attended a multiracial high school, but I graduated from a mainly white university. I have always gotten along well with people of other races, and I enjoy the cultural diversity found in the Los Angeles area.

My most recent challenge is a student named Miguel from Argentina. Miguel really tries, but, like many of my other students, he can't seem to follow directions for assignments, and he did not do well on the midterm exam. I thought I had given very complete, clear lectures about authors, items of historical/cultural significance to the literature we were reading, and explanations of literary terminology such as symbolism, irony, and so on. But he says he can't understand me very well, nor can he understand the other students in the class when they participate in class discussion (which is not very often). Miguel is very quiet, so I didn't realize he was having trouble until now. Up to this point, he has only turned in one written assignment for which he received a B. The other day, I did a little checking and found out that he has never been in our college ESL program. He says that he scored very high on the TOEFL (Test of English as a Foreign Language), including the TWE (Test of Written English), so the administration put him in a regular schedule of courses. He is definitely failing my course, and I suspect he is failing others as well. Now it is too late for him to drop it. Another problem Miguel is having is that he does not seem to be getting along very well with the African-American students in my class. He told me that one of them (Aaron) started an argument with him and shoved him while he was in the library. I don't know what the conflict is all about, but I do know it is having a negative effect on the attitude of my whole class. I want to do well in this environment. Teaching is something I don't want to give up. What should I do? How can I best teach these students?

I should also tell you that I am now on a committee to make suggestions about curriculum, requirements, and so on for our language minority students. What can our college do to better serve students such as Miguel? What should the ESL program at our college be doing to better prepare these students for the mainstream? As far as I know, they are not doing much to help in the transition.

WHAT DID THE TEACHER DO?

First I tried to help Miguel solve the problem he was having with Aaron and the other African-American students. I asked him and Aaron to see me after class. I tried as best I could to lead them into a discussion of what had happened—not to pin the blame on anyone but to talk about how each one felt about the incident in the library. Although no one apologized, I think they came to a better understanding of each other's point of view. Later, on the advice of another instructor at the college, I did some group activities during which we talked about how we could get along better with one another. It did seem to help overall. I began to notice that the atmosphere of the classroom became a bit more positive and that the students were showing a little more tolerance toward one another.

As far as Miguel's skills go, I really didn't make much difference there. He managed to eke out a D for the semester. However, I think I might try some different strategies in my teaching in general. I just read a book about teaching second language students and I got some ideas that I think might work. I plan to do a lot more group work, ask students to share feelings and opinions more, and do a lot with peer consultation on compositions. Also I need to use more visuals including charts, maps, and other realia to make clear what I mean. I don't want to give up lecturing completely. I just want to make my lectures better for all students, not just language minority students.

The committee I served on was very helpful to me. I'm not sure how much I contributed, but I certainly learned a lot! Two of the members talked about establishing an adjunct program in which mainstream courses are paired with language courses conducted by language specialists. The language specialists would help the students understand the vocabulary and key concepts taught in the mainstream course, assist students with their compositions, help them with the comprehension of the lectures (which would be taped) and assigned readings, and refer them to materials on similar topics in their first languages. They also talked about setting up tutoring sessions (led by proficient English speakers) in the library. These recommendations will be made to the administration next week.

REFERENCES

Abrahamsson, N., & Hyltenstam, K. (2008). The robustness of aptitude effects in near-native second language acquisition. *Studies in Second Language Acquisition, 30*(4), 481–509.

Ackerman, P. (2003). Aptitude complexes and trait complexes. *Educational Psychologist, 38*(2), 85–93.

Adams, D. W. (1998). Fundamental considerations: The deep meaning of Native American schooling, 1880–1900. *Harvard Educational Review, 58*(1), 1–28.

Aljaafreh A., & Lantolf, J. (1994). Negative feedback as regulation and second language learning in the zone of proximal development. *The Modern Language Journal, 78*, 465–483.

Allen, J., & VanBuren, P. (1971). *Chomsky: Selected readings*. Oxford, England: Oxford University Press.

Allwright, R. (1979). Language learning through communication practice. In C. J. Brumfit & K. Johnson (Eds.), *The communicative approach to language teaching* (pp. 167–182). Oxford, England: Oxford University Press.

Altwerger, B., & Resta, V. (1986, May). *Comparing standardized tests scores and miscues*. Paper presented at the annual convention of the International Reading Association, Philadelphia, PA.

Alvermann, D., & Phelps, S. (2005). Assessment of students. In P. Richard-Amato & M. A. Snow (Eds.), *Academic success for English language learners: Strategies for K–12 mainstream teachers* (pp. 311–341). White Plains, NY: Pearson Longman.

Amanti, C. (2001). Technology for English language learners. *NABE News, 25*(1), 7–9.

Ammar, A., & Spada, N. (2006). Recasts, prompts, and L2 learning. *Studies in Second Language Acquisition, 28*(4), 543–574.

Andersen, R. (Ed.). (1981). *New dimensions in second language acquisition research*. Rowley, MA: Newbury House.

Andersen, R. (Ed.). (1983). *Pidginization and creolization as language acquisition*. Rowley, MA: Newbury House.

Anderson, N. (1991). Individual differences in strategy use in second language reading and testing. *Modern Language Journal, 75*, 460–472.

Anderson, N. (1999). *Exploring second language reading: Issues and strategies*. Boston: Heinle.

Anderson, N. (2005). L2 learning strategies. In E. Hinkel (Ed.), *Handbook of research in second language teaching and learning* (pp. 757–771). Mahwah, NJ: Lawrence Erlbaum.

Anderson, N. (2008). *Practical English language teaching: Reading*. New York: McGraw-Hill.

Antòn, M. (1999). The discourse of a learner-centered classroom: Sociocultural perspectives on teacher–learner interaction in the second-language classroom. *The Modern Language Journal, 83*(3), 303–318.

Armstrong, B., Johnson, D. W., & Balow, B. (1981). Effects of cooperative versus individualistic learning experiences on interpersonal attraction between learning-disabled and normal-progress elementary school students. *Contemporary Educational Psychology, 6*, 102–109.

Arnold, J. (Ed.). (1999). *Affect and language learning*. Cambridge, England: Cambridge University Press.

Asher, J. (1972). Children's first language as a model for second-language learning. *Modern Language Journal, 56*, 133–139.

Asher, J. (1993, January). *The total physical response*. Paper presented at the California Education Association meeting, San Francisco, CA.

Asher, J. (2000). *Learning another language through actions* (6th ed.). Los Gatos, CA: Sky Oaks.

Asher, J., Kusudo, J., & de la Torre, R. (1974). Learning a second language through commands: The second field test. *Modern Language Journal, 58*, 24–32.

Atkinson, D. (2002). Toward a sociocognitive approach to second language acquisition. *The Modern Language Journal, 86*(4), 525–545.

Auerbach, E. (2000). Creating participatory learning communities: Paradoxes and possibilities. In J. K. Hall & W. Eggington (Eds.), *The sociopolitics of English language teaching* (pp. 143–164). Clevedon, England: Multilingual Matters.

Bachman, L. F. (1990). *Fundamental considerations in language testing*. Oxford, England: Oxford University Press.

Bachman, L. F. (2000). Modern language testing at the turn of the century: Assuring that what we count counts. *Language Testing, 17*(1), 1–42.

Bachman, L. F. (2005). Building and supporting a case for test use. *Language Assessment Quarterly, 2*(1), 1–34.

Bachman, L. F. (2007, November). *Five things to think about before using a language assessment.* Paper presented at the Oxford University Press Teachers' Day, Ewha Women's University, Seoul, South Korea.

Bachman, L. F., & Palmer, A. (1996). *Language testing in practice*. Oxford, England: Oxford University Press.

Bachman, L. F., & Palmer, A. (forthcoming). *Language assessment practice: Developing language assessments and justifying their use in the real world.* Oxford, England: Oxford University Press.

Bailey, A., Butler, F., LaFramenta, C., & Ong, C. (2001). *Towards the characterization of academic language* (Final deliverable to OERI/OBEMLA, Contract No. R305b60002). University of California, Los Angeles: National Center for Research on Evaluation, Standards, and Student Testing.

Bailey, K. (1995). Competitiveness and anxiety in adult second language learning: Looking at and through the diary studies. In H. D. Brown & S. Gonzo (Eds.), *Readings on second language acquisition* (163–205). Englewood Cliffs, NJ: Prentice Hall Regents.

Bailey, K. (2005). *Practical English language teaching: Speaking*. New York: McGraw-Hill.

Bailey, N., Madden, C., & Krashen, S. (1974). Is there a "natural sequence" in adult second-language learning? *Language Learning, 21*(2), 235–243.

Baker, C. (2006). *Foundations of bilingual education and bilingualism*. Clevedon, England: Multilingual Matters.

Bakhtin, M. (1981). *The dialogic imagination*. Austin: University of Texas Press.

Bakhtin, M. (1986). *Speech genres and other late essays.* Austin: University of Texas Press.

Baltra, A. (1992). On breaking with tradition: The significance of Terrell's natural approach. *The Canadian Modern Language Review, 48*(3), 564–593.

Bamford, J., & Day, R. (1996). Comments on Jeong-Won Lee and Diane Lemonnier Schallert's "The relative contribution of L2 language proficiency and L1 reading ability to L2 reading performance: A test of the threshold hypothesis in an EFL context": Two readers react. *TESOL Quarterly, 32*(4), 747–751.

Banks, J. (1992). The stages of ethnicity. In P. Richard-Amato & M. A. Snow (Eds.), *The multicultural classroom: Readings for content-area teachers* (pp. 93–101). White Plains, NY: Longman / Pearson Education.

Banks, J. (2007). *An introduction to multicultural education* (4th ed.). Boston: Allyn & Bacon.

Banville, S. (2007). *1,000 ideas and activities for language teachers* [E-book]. Breaking News English Web site. Available from www.breakingnewsenglish.com.

Bardovi-Harlig, K. (1992). The use of adverbials and natural order in the development of temporal expression. *International Review of Applied Linguistics in Language Teaching, 30,* 199–220.

Bardovi-Harlig, K. (1995). The interaction of pedagogy and natural sequences in the acquisition of tense and aspect. In F. R. Eckman, D. Highland, P. W. Lee, J. L. Mileham, & R. R. Weber (Eds.), *Second language acquisition theory and pedagogy* (pp. 157–181). Mahwah, NJ: Lawrence Erlbaum.

Bardovi-Harlig, K. (2000). *Tense and aspect in second language acquisition: Form, meaning, and use.* Boston: Blackwell.

Bardovi-Harlig, K., Hartford, B., Mahan-Taylor, R., Morgan, M. J., & Reynolds, D. W. (1996). Developing pragmatic awareness: Closing the conversation. In T. Hedge & N. Whitney (Eds.), *Power, pedagogy and practice* (pp. 324–337). Oxford, England: Oxford University Press.

Barry, S., & Lazarte, A. (1998). Evidence for mental models: How do prior knowledge, syntactic complexity, and reading topic affect inference generation in a recall task for nonnative readers of Spanish? *Modern Language Journal, 82*(2), 176–193.

Bartolomé, L. (2003). Beyond the methods fetish: Toward a humanizing pedagogy. In A. Darder, M. Baltodano, & R. Torres (Eds.), *The critical pedagogy reader* (pp. 408–429). New York: RoutledgeFalmer.

Bassano, S., & Christison, M. A. (1995). Action research: Techniques for collecting data through surveys and interviews. *CATESOL Journal, 8*(1), 89–104.

Beebe, L. (1983). Risk-taking and the language learner. In H. Seliger & M. Long (Eds.), *Classroom-oriented research in second language acquisition* (pp. 39–66). Rowley, MA: Newbury House.

Bell, D. (1999). Rise, Sally, rise: Communicating through dance. *TESOL Journal, 8*(1), 27–31.

Bellack, A., Kliebard, H., Hyman, R., & Smith, F. Jr. (1966). *The language of the classroom*. New York: Teachers College, Columbia University.

Bialystok, E. (1994). Representation and ways of knowing: Three issues in second language acquisition. In N. Ellis (Ed.), *Implicit and explicit learning of languages* (pp. 549–569). London: Academic Press.

Bialystok, E. (2001). *Bilingualism in development: Language, literacy, and cognition*. New York: Cambridge University Press.

Bialystok, E., Craik, F., Klein, R., & Viswanathan, M. (2004). Bilingualism, aging, and cognitive control: Evidence from the Simon task. *Psychology and Aging, 19*(2), 290–303.

Bialystok, E., & Fröhlich, M. (1977). Aspects of second-language learning in classroom settings. *Working Papers on Bilingualism, 13*, 2–26.

Bialystok, E., & Haykuta, K. (1999). Confounded age: Linguistic and cognitive factors in age differences for second language acquisition. In D. Birdsong (Ed.), *Second language acquisition and the critical period hypothesis* (pp. 161–181). Mahwah, NJ: Lawrence Erlbaum.

Biancarosa, G., & Snow, C. (2006). *Reading next: A vision for action research in middle and high school literacy: A report to Carnegie Corporation of New York* (2nd ed.). Washington, DC: Alliance for Excellent Education.

Birdsong, D. (1992). Ultimate attainment in second language acquisition. *Language, 68*, 706–755.

Birdsong, D. (Ed.). (1999). *Second language acquisition and the critical period hypothesis*. Mahwah, NJ: Lawrence Erlbaum.

Bishop, A. (2001). An expert's guide to products for the multilingual classroom. *NABE News, 25*(1), 12–13.

Black, P., & Wiliam, D. (1998). *Inside the black box*. London: King's College School of Education.

Blake, R. (2007). New trends in using technology in the language curriculum. *Annual Review of Applied Linguistics, 27*, 76–97.

Bloch, J., & Crosby, C. (2006). Creating a space for virtual democracy. *Essential Teacher, 3*(3), 38–41.

Block, D. (1996). Not so fast: Some thoughts on theory culling, relativism, accepted findings and the heart and soul of SLA. *Applied Linguistics, 17*, 63–83.

Block, D. (2003). *The social turn in second language acquisition*. Edinburgh, England: Edinburgh University Press.

Bobrick, M. (2007). From talking journals to writers' theater. *Essential Teacher, 4*(3), 36–38.

Bradlow, A., Pisoni, D., Akahane-Yamada, R., & Tohkura, Y. (1997). Training Japanese listeners to identify English /r/ and /l/: IV. Some effects of perceptual learning on speech production. *Journal of the Acoustical Society of America, 101*, 2299–2310.

Braidi, S. (2002). Reexamining the role of recasts in native-speaker–nonnative-speaker interactions. *Language Learning, 52*, 1–42.

Branigan, H. (2007). Syntactic priming. *Language and Linguistics Compass, 1*(1–2), 1–16.

Braunstein, L. (2006). Adult ESL learners' attitudes toward movement (TPR) and drama (TPR story-telling) in the classroom. *CATESOL Journal, 18*(1), 7–20.

Breen, M., & Candlin, C. (1979). Essentials of a communicative curriculum. *Applied Linguistics, 1*(2), 90–112.

Brindley, G. (2001). Outcomes-based assessment in practice: Some examples and emerging insights. *Language Testing, 18*, 393–407.

Brinton, D. (2005). Wahchadooin? Teaching reduced speech! *CATESOL News, 37*(3), 4–6.

Brinton, D., & Neuman, R. (1982). *Getting along* (Book 2). Englewood Cliffs, NJ: Prentice Hall.

Brinton, D., & Snow, M. A. (2008, May). *The evolving architecture of content-based instruction.* Paper presented at Teachers of English to Speakers of Other Languages Virtual Seminar, http://tesol.org.

Brinton, D., Snow, M. A., & Wesche, M. (1989). *Content-based language instruction.* New York: Newbury House.

Brinton, D., Wesche, M., & Snow, M. A. (2003). *Content-based second language instruction: Michigan Classics Edition.* Ann Arbor: University of Michigan Press.

Bromley, K. (1995). Buddy journals for ESL and native-English-speaking students. In I. A. Heath & C. J. Serrano (Eds.), *Teaching English as a second language* (2nd ed., pp. 71–75). Guilford, CT: Dushkin/McGraw-Hill.

Brown, A., & McNamara, T. (2004). "The devil is in the detail": Researching gender issues in language assessment. *TESOL Quarterly, 38*(3), 524–538.

Brown, H. D. (1987). *Principles of language learning and teaching.* Englewood Cliffs, NJ: Prentice Hall.

Brown, H. D. (1994). *Teaching by principles: An interactive approach to language pedagogy.* Englewood Cliffs, NJ: Prentice Hall.

Brown, H. D. (2006). *Principles of language learning and teaching* (5th ed.). White Plains, NY: Pearson Education.

Brown, H. D. (2007). *Teaching by principles: An interactive approach to language pedagogy* (3rd ed.). White Plains, NY: Pearson Education.

Brown, J. D., & Hudson, T. (2002). *Criterion-referenced language testing.* Cambridge, England: Cambridge University Press.

Brown, J. D., Hudson, T., Norris, J., & Bonk, W. J. (2002). *An investigation of second language task-based performance assessments.* Honolulu: University of Hawai'i Press.

Brown, R. (1973). *A first language: The early stages.* Cambridge, MA: Harvard University Press.

Brown, R., Cazden, C., & Bellugi, U. (1973). The child's grammar from I to III. In C. Ferguson & D. Slobin (Eds.), *Studies of child language development* (pp. 295–333). New York: Holt, Rinehart & Winston.

Brown, S., & Dubin, F. (1975). Adapting human relations training techniques for ESL classes. In M. Burt & H. Dulay (Eds.), *New directions in second language learning, teaching, and bilingual education* (pp. 204–209). Washington, DC: Teachers of English to Speakers of Other Languages.

Brumfit, C. J., & Johnson, K. (Eds.). (1979). *The communicative approach to language teaching.* Oxford, England: Oxford University Press.

Bruner, J. (1978). The role of dialogue in language acquisition. In A. Sinclair, R. Javella, & W. Levelt (Eds.), *The child's conception of language* (pp. 241–256). New York: Springer-Verlag.

Brutt-Griffler, J., & Samimy, K. (1999). Revisiting the colonial in the postcolonial: Critical praxis for nonnative-English-speaking teachers in a TESOL program. *TESOL Quarterly, 33*(3), 413–432.

Buell, C., & Whittaker, A. (2005). Enhancing content literacy in physical education. In P. Richard-Amato & M. A. Snow (Eds.), *Academic success for English language learners: Strategies for K–12 mainstream teachers* (pp. 455–465). White Plains, NY: Pearson Longman.

Busch, D. (1982). Introversion–extraversion and the EFL proficiency of Japanese students. *Language Learning, 32*(1), 109–132.

Butterworth, G., & Hatch, E. (1978). A Spanish-speaking adolescent's acquisition of English syntax. In E. Hatch (Ed.), *Second language acquisition: A book of readings* (pp. 231–245). Rowley, MA: Newbury House.

Bygate, M., Skehan, P., & Swain, M. (2001). Introduction. In M. Bygate, P. Skehan, & M. Swain (Eds.), *Researching pedagogic tasks, second language learning, teaching and testing* (pp. 1–20). Harlow, England: Longman.

Byram, M. (1998). Cultural identities in multilingual classrooms. In J. Cenoz & F. Genesee (Eds.), *Beyond bilingualism* (pp. 96–116). Clevedon, England: Multilingual Matters.

Campbell, C., & Ortiz, J. (1991). Helping students overcome foreign language anxiety. In E. Horwitz & D. Young (Eds.), *Language anxiety: From theory and research to classroom implication* (pp. 153–168). Englewood Cliffs, NJ: Prentice Hall.

Canagarajah, A. S. (1999). *Resisting linguistic imperialism in English teaching*. Oxford, England: Oxford University Press.

Canagarajah, A. S. (2005). Critical pedagogy in L2 learning and teaching. In E. Hinkel (Ed.), *Handbook of research in second language teaching and learning* (pp. 931–949). Mahwah, NJ: Lawrence Erlbaum.

Canagarajah, A. S. (2006). TESOL at forty: What are the issues? *TESOL Quarterly 40*(1), 9–34.

Canale, M. (1983). From communicative competence to communicative language pedagogy. In J. Richards & R. Schmidt (Eds.), *Language and communication* (pp. 2–27). London: Longman.

Canale, M., & Barker, G. (1986). How creative language teachers are using microcomputers. *TESOL Newsletter 20*(1), Suppl. 3, 1–3.

Canale, M., & Swain, M. (1980). Theoretical bases of communicative approaches to second language teaching and testing. *Applied Linguistics, 1*(1), 1–47.

Carbaugh, D. (1996). *Situating selves: The communication of social identities in American scenes*. Albany: State University of New York Press.

Carrasquillo, A., & Rodríguez, V. (2005). Integrating language and science learning. In P. Richard-Amato & M. A. Snow (Eds.), *Academic success for English language learners: Strategies for K–12 mainstream teachers* (pp. 436–454). White Plains, NY: Pearson Longman.

Carrell, P. (1983). Some issues in studying the role of schemata, or background knowledge, in second-language comprehension. *Reading in a Foreign Language, 1*(2), 81–92.

Carrell, P. (1984). Evidence of a formal schema in second-language comprehension. *Language Learning, 34*(2), 87–112.

Carrell, P. (1985). Facilitating ESL reading by teaching text structure. *TESOL Quarterly, 19*(4), 727–752.

Carrell, P., Devine, J., & Eskey, D. (1988). *Interactive approaches to second language reading*. New York: Cambridge University Press.

Carroll, J. (1960). Wanted: A research basis for educational policy on foreign language teaching. *Harvard Educational Review, 30*, 128–140.

Carroll, S. (2001). *Input and evidence: The raw material of second language acquisition*. Amsterdam, the Netherlands: Benjamins.

Carroll, S., & Swain, M. (1993). Explicit and implicit negative feedback: An empirical study of the learning of linguistic generalizations. *Studies in Second Language Acquisition, 15*(3), 357–386.

Carter, R., (2001). Vocabulary. In R. Carter & D. Nunan (Eds.), *The Cambridge guide to teaching English to speakers of other languages* (pp. 42–47). Cambridge, England: Cambridge University Press.

Cates, K. (2007, March). *Teaching global awareness through video*. Preconvention Institute presentation at the 41st Annual Convention of Teachers of English to Speakers of Other Languages, Seattle, WA.

Cazden, C. (1972). *Child language and education*. New York: Holt, Rinehart & Winston.

Celce-Murcia, M. (1985). Making informed decisions about the role of grammar in language teaching. *TESOL Newsletter*, *29*(1), 9–12.

Celce-Murcia, M. (1993). Grammar pedagogy in second and foreign language teaching. In S. Silberstein (Ed.), *State of the art TESOL essays* (pp. 288–309). Alexandria, VA: Teachers of English to Speakers of Other Languages.

Celce-Murcia, M. (2002). Why it makes sense to teach grammar through context and through discourse. In E. Hinkel & S. Fotos (Eds.), *New perspectives on grammar teaching in second language classrooms* (pp. 119–134). Mahwah, NJ: Lawrence Erlbaum.

Celce-Murcia, M., Brinton, D., & Goodwin, J. (forthcoming). *Teaching pronunciation: A course book and reference guide.* New York: Cambridge University Press.

Chamot, A. (1990). Cognitive instruction second language classroom: The role of learning strategies. In J. Alatis (Ed.), *Georgetown University Round Table on Languages and Linguistics 1990: Linguistics, language teaching and language acquisition: The importance of theory, practice and research* (pp. 497–513). Washington, DC: Georgetown University.

Chamot, A. (2005a). Learning strategies instruction. *Annual Review of Applied Linguistics*, *25*, 112–130.

Chamot, A. (2005b). The cognitive academic language learning approach (CALLA): An update. In P. Richard-Amato & M. A. Snow, M. A. (Eds.), *Academic success for English language learners: Strategies for K-12 mainstream teachers* (pp. 87–102). White Plains, NY: Pearson Longman.

Chandler, J. (2003). The efficacy of various kinds of error feedback for improvement in the accuracy and fluency of L2 student writing. *Journal of Second Language Writing, 12*, 267–296.

Chang, A. C., & Read, J. (2006). The effects of listening support on the listening performance of EFL learners. *TESOL Quarterly*, *40*(2), 375–397.

Chapelle, C. (2001). *Computer applications in second language acquisition.* New York: Cambridge University Press.

Chapelle, C., & Douglas, D. (2006). *Assessing language through computer technology*. New York: Cambridge University Press.

Chapelle, C., & Jamieson, J. (2008). *Tips for teaching with CALL: Practical approaches to computer-assisted language learning.* White Plains, NY: Pearson Longman.

Chastain, K. (1975). Affective and ability factors in second language learning. *Language Learning*, *25*(1), 153–161.

Chaudron, C. (1985). A method for examining the input/intake distinction. In S. Gass & C. Madden (Eds.), *Input in second language acquisition* (pp. 285–302). Rowley, MA: Newbury House.

Chaudron, C. (1991). What counts as formal language instruction? Problems in observation and analysis of classroom teaching. In J. Alatis (Ed.), *Georgetown University Round Table on Languages and Linguistics 1991. Linguistics and language pedagogy: The state of the art* (pp. 56–64). Washington, DC: Georgetown University.

Chen, H., & Graves, M. (1995). Effects of previewing and providing background knowledge on Taiwanese college students' comprehension of American short stories. *TESOL Quarterly*, *29*(4), 663–686.

Chen, J., Warden, C., & Chang, H. (2005). Motivators that do not motivate: The case of Chinese EFL learners and the influence of culture on motivation. *TESOL Quarterly*, *39*(4), 609–633.

Chen, K. (2005). Preferences, styles, behavior: The composing processes of four ESL students. *CATESOL Journal, 17*(1), 19–37.

Cho, K. S. (2004). Teachers' voices in EFL teacher training: Reactions to a sustained silent reading experience. *The International Journal of Foreign Language Teaching, 1*(1), 17–20.

Chomsky, N. (1959). Review of B. F. Skinner, "Verbal Behavior." *Language*, *35*, 26–58.

Chomsky, N. (1980). *Rules and representations*. New York: Columbia University.

Chomsky, N. (1995). *The minimalist program*. Cambridge, MA: MIT Press.

Christian, D. (1996). Two-way immersion education: Students learning through two languages. *The Modern Language Journal*, *80*(1), 66–76.

Christian, D., & Genesee, F. (2001). *Bilingual education*. Alexandria, VA: Teachers of English to Speakers of Other Languages.

Christison, M. A. (1982). *English through poetry*. Hayward, CA: Prentice Hall.

Clark, J., & Clifford, R. (1988). The FSI/ILR/ACTFL proficiency scales and testing techniques: Development, current status, and needed research. *Studies in Second Language Acquisition*, *10*(2), 129–148.

Clarke, M. (1980). The short-circuit hypothesis of ESL reading: When language competence interferes with reading performance. *The Modern Language Journal*, *64*, 114–124.

Clarke, M. (1994). The dysfunctions of the theory/practice discourse. *TESOL Quarterly*, *28*, 9–26.

Clarke, M. (2003). *A place to stand: Essays for educators in troubled times*. Ann Arbor: University of Michigan Press.

Clarke, M. (2007). *Common ground, contested territory: Examining the roles of English language teachers in troubled times*. Ann Arbor: University of Michigan Press.

Cleghorn, A., & Rollnick, M. (2002). The role of English in individual and societal development: A view from African classrooms. *TESOL Quarterly*, *36*(3), 347–372.

Collier, V. (1987). Age and rate of acquisition of second language for academic purposes. *TESOL Quarterly*, *21*, 617–641.

Collier, V. (1995). *Promoting academic success for ESL students: Understanding second language acquisition for school*. Elizabeth, NJ: Teachers of English to Speakers of Other Languages—Bilingual Educators.

Collier, V. (1999). Acquiring a second language for school. In I. A. Heath & C. J. Serrano (Eds.), *Teaching English as a second language* (pp. 16–21). Guilford, CT: Dushkin/McGraw-Hill.

Collier, V., & Thomas, W. (1989). How quickly can immigrants become proficient in school English? *Journal of Educational Issues of Language Minority Students*, *16*, 187–212.

Collier, V., & Thomas, W. (1997). *School effectiveness for language minority students*. Washington, DC: National Clearinghouse for Bilingual Education.

Collier, V., & Thomas, W. (1999). Making schools effective for English language learners, Parts 1–3, *TESOL Matters*, *9*, 4–6.

Collins, P. (2001). *Community writing: Researching social issues through composition*. Mahwah, NJ: Lawrence Erlbaum.

Condon, C. (1983). Treasure hunts for English practice. In J. Oller Jr. & P. Richard-Amato (Eds.), *Methods that work* (pp. 309–312). Rowley, MA: Newbury House.

Connery, C. (2006). *The sociocultural-semiotic texts of five- and six-year-old emergent biliterates in non-academic settings*. Unpublished doctoral dissertation, University of New Mexico, Albuquerque.

Conrad, S. (2005). Corpus linguistics and L2 teaching. In E. Hinkel (Ed.), *Handbook of research in second language teaching and learning* (pp. 393–409). Mahwah, NJ: Lawrence Erlbaum.

Cook, V. (1999). Going beyond the native speaker in language teaching. *TESOL Quarterly*, *33*(2), 185–209.

Corder, S. P. (1967). The significance of learners' errors. *International Review of Applied Linguistics in Language Teaching*, *4*, 161–169.

Costa, C. (2006). My adventure in podland. *Essential Teacher*, *3*(4), 38–41.

Coughlan, P., & Duff, P. (1998). Same task, different activities: Analysis of a SLA task from an activity theory perspective. In J. Lantolf & G. Appel (Eds.), *Vygotskian approaches to second language research* (pp. 173–193). Norwood, NJ: Ablex.

Council of Europe. (2001). *Common European framework of reference for languages: Learning, teaching, assessment*. Cambridge, England: Cambridge University Press.

Cowie, H., Smith, P. K., Boulton, M., & Laver, R. (1994). *Cooperation in the multi-ethnic classroom*. London: David Fulton.

Cox, M. I. P., & Assis-Peterson, A. A. (1999). Critical pedagogy in ELT: Images of Brazilian teachers of English. *TESOL Quarterly, 33*(3), 433–452.

Coxhead, A. (2000). A new academic word list. *TESOL Quarterly, 34*(2), 213–238.

Crabbe, D. (2003). The quality of language learning opportunities. *TESOL Quarterly, 37*(1), 9–34.

Crabbe, D. (2007). Learning opportunities: Adding learning value to tasks. *ELT Journal, 61*(2), 117–125.

Cramer, T. (2008). Using "Families of the World" videos to develop language skills and awareness of global issues. *Global Issues in Language Education Newsletter, 67*, 12–14.

Crandall, J. (1993). Content-centered learning in the United States. *Annual Review of Applied Linguistics, 13*, 111–126.

Crandall, J. (1999). Cooperative language learning and affective factors. In J. Arnold (Ed.), *Affect and language learning* (pp. 226–245). Cambridge, England: Cambridge University Press.

Crandall, J., & Kaufman, D. (2002). *Case studies in content-based instruction in higher education*. Alexandria, VA: Teachers of English to Speakers of Other Languages.

Crawford, J., & Krashen, S. (2007). *English learners in American classrooms: 101 questions, 101 answers*. New York: Scholastic.

Creswell, A. (2000). Self-monitoring in student writing: Developing learner responsibility. *ELT Journal, 54*(3), 235–244.

Crymes, R. (1979, October). *Current trends in ESL instruction*. Paper presented at the Indiana Teachers of English to Speakers of Other Languages Convention. Washington, DC.

Cummins, J. (1981a). Age on arrival and immigrant second language learning in Canada: A reassessment. *Applied Linguistics, 1*, 132–149.

Cummins, J. (1981b). The role of primary language development in promoting educational success for language minority students. In California State Department of Education, *Schooling and language minority students: A theoretical framework* (pp. 3–50). Los Angeles: California State University, Evaluation, Dissemination and Assessment Center.

Cummins, J. (1984). *Bilingualism and special education: Issues in assessment and pedagogy*. San Diego, CA: College-Hill Press.

Cummins, J. (1989). *Empowering minority students*. Sacramento: California Association for Bilingual Education.

Cummins, J. (1997). Minority status and schooling in Canada. *Anthropology and Education Quarterly, 28*, 411–430.

Cummins, J. (2000). Negotiating intercultural identities in the multilingual classroom. *CATESOL Journal 12*(1), 163–178.

Curran, C. (1972). *Counseling-learning: A whole-person model for education*. New York: Grune and Stratton.

Curran, C. (1976). *Counseling-learning in second languages*. Dubuque, IL: Counseling-Learning.

Curran, M., & Stelluto, D. (2005). Opportunities for adult ESOL learning to revision and envision their social identities. *TESOL Quarterly 39*(4), 781–785.

d'Anglejan, A. (1978). Language learning in and out of classrooms. In J. C. Richards (Ed.), *Understanding second and foreign language learning* (pp. 218–278). Rowley, MA: Newbury House.

Davies, A. (1997). Demands of being professional in language testing. *Language Testing, 14*, 328–339.

Davies, M. (2006). Paralinguistic focus on form. *TESOL Quarterly, 40*(4), 841–855.

Day, R. (1984). Student participation in the ESL classroom or some imperfections in practice. *Language Learning, 34*(3), 69–102.

Deacon, T. (1997). *The symbolic species: The co-evolution of language and the brain*. New York: Norton.

de Guerrero, M., & Villamil, O. (2000). Exploring ESL teachers' roles through metaphor analysis. *TESOL Quarterly, 34*(2), 341–351.

De Jong, N. (2005). Can second language grammar be learned through listening? An experimental study. *Studies in Second Language Acquisition, 27*(2), 205–234.

DeKeyser, R. (1995). Learning second language grammar rules: An experiment with a miniature linguistic system. *Studies in Second Language Acquisition, 17*(3), 379–410.

DeKeyser, R. (1998). Beyond focus on form: Cognitive perspectives on learning and practicing second language grammar. In C. Doughty & J. Williams (Eds.), *Focus on form in second language acquisition* (pp. 42–63). Cambridge, England: Cambridge University Press.

DeKeyser, R. (2000). The robustness of critical period effects in second language acquisition. *Studies in Second Language Acquisition, 22*(4), 493–533.

DeKeyser, R. (2003). Implicit and explicit learning. In C. Doughty & M. Long (Eds.), *Handbook of second language acquisition* (pp. 313–348). Malden, MA: Blackwell.

de la Fuente, M. J. (2002). Negotiation and oral acquisition of L2 vocabulary: The roles of input and output in the receptive and productive acquisition of words. *Studies in Second Language Acquisition, 24*(1), 81–112.

Derwing, T., & Munro, M. (2005). Second language accent and pronunciation teaching: A research-based approach. *TESOL Quarterly, 39*(3), 379–397.

DeVilliers, P., & DeVilliers, J. (1973). A cross-sectional study of the acquisition of grammatical morphemes in child speech. *Journal of Psycholinguistic Research, 2*, 267–278.

Dewaele, J. (2004). Individual differences in the use of colloquial vocabulary: The effects of sociobiological and psychological factors. In P. Bogaards & B. Laufer (Eds.), *Vocabulary in a second language: Selection, acquisition, and testing* (pp. 127–153). Amsterdam, the Netherlands: John Benjamins.

Deyhle, D. (1992). Constructing failure and maintaining cultural identity: Navajo and Ute school leavers. *Journal of American Indian Education, 31*, 24–47.

Díaz-Rico, L., & Weed, K. (2005). *The crosscultural, language, and academic development handbook* (3rd ed.). Boston: Allyn & Bacon.

Dixon, C., & Nessel, D. (1990). *Language experience approach to reading (and writing)*. Englewood Cliffs, NJ: Prentice Hall.

Donato, R. (1994). Collective scaffolding in second language learning. In J. Lantolf & G. Appel (Eds.), *Vygotskian approaches to second language research* (pp. 33–56). Stamford, CT: Ablex.

Dörnyei, Z. (1995). On the teachability of communication strategies. *TESOL Quarterly, 29*(1), 55–85.

Dörnyei, Z. (1998). Motivation in second and foreign language. *Language Teaching, 31*, 117–135.

Dörnyei, Z. (2000). Motivation in action: Towards a process-oriented conceptualisation of student motivation. *British Journal of Educational Psychology 70*, 519–538.

Dörnyei, Z. (2001). *Motivational strategies in the foreign language classroom.* Cambridge, England: Cambridge University Press.

Dörnyei, Z. (2006). Individual differences in second language acquisition. *AILA Review, 19*, 42–68.

Dörnyei, Z., & Schmidt, R. (Eds.). (2001). *Motivation and second language acquisition* (Tech. Rep. No. 23). Manoa: University of Hawai'i.

Dörnyei, Z., & Skehan, P. (2003). Individual differences in second language learning. In C. Doughty & M. Long (Eds.), *The handbook of second language acquisition* (pp. 589–630). Malden, MA: Blackwell.

Doughty, C. (1991). Second language instruction does make a difference: Evidence from an empirical study of second language relativization. *Studies in Second Language Acquisition, 13*(4), 431–470.

Doughty, C. (2001). Cognitive underpinnings of focus on form. In P. Robinson (Ed.), *Cognition and SLA* (pp. 206–257). New York: Cambridge University Press.

Doughty, C., & Long, M. (Eds.). (2003). *The handbook of second language acquisition*. Malden, MA: Blackwell.

Doughty, C., & Williams, J. (1998). Pedagogical choices in focus on form. In C. Doughty & J. Williams (Eds.), *Focus on form in classroom second language acquisition* (pp. 1–11). Cambridge, England: Cambridge University Press.

Douglas, D., & Hegelheimer, V. (2007). Assessing language using computer technology. *Annual Review of Applied Linguistics, 27*, 115–132.

Dressler, C., & Kamil, M. (2006). First- and second-language literacy. In A. August & T. Shanahan (Eds.), *Developing literacy in second-language learners: Report of the National Literacy Panel on language-minority children and youth* (pp. 197–238). Mahwah. NJ: Lawrence Erlbaum.

Duff, P. (2005). ESL in secondary schools; Programs, problematics, and possibilities. In E. Hinkel (Ed.), *Handbook of research in second language teaching and learning* (pp. 45–63). Mahwah, NJ: Lawrence Erlbaum.

Dulay, H., & Burt, M. (1974). Natural sequences in child second-language acquisition. *Language Learning, 25*(1), 37–53.

Dunn, B. (1994). *Mi semestre de español: A case study of the cultural dimension of second language acquisition*. Unpublished manuscript, University of Massachusetts, Amherst.

Dupuy, B. (1999). Narrow listening: An alternative way to develop and enhance listening comprehension in students of French as a foreign language. *System, 27*, 351–361.

Durán, R. (2008). Assessing English-language learners' achievement. *Review of Research in Education, 32*(1), 292–327.

Dvorak, T. (1977). *Grammatical practice, communicative practice, and the development of linguistic competence.* Unpublished doctoral dissertation, University of Texas at Austin.

Echevarria, J., Vogt, M. E., & Short, D. (2008). *Making content comprehensible for English learners; The SIOP Model.* White Plains, NY: Pearson Education.

Eckert, P., & McConnell-Ginet, S. (2003). *Language and gender.* Cambridge, England: Cambridge University Press.

Edelsky, C. (2006). *With literacy and justice for all: Rethinking the social in language and education* (3rd ed.). Mahwah, NJ: Lawrence Erlbaum.

Edelsky, C., Altwerger, B., & Flores, B. (1991). *Whole language: What's the difference?* Portsmouth, NH: Heinemann.

Edelsky, C., & Johnson, K. (2004). Critical whole language practice in time and place. *Critical Inquiry in Language Studies: An International Journal, 1*(3), 121–141.

Egbert, J. (2005). *CALL essentials: Principles and practice in CALL classrooms.* Alexandria, VA: Teachers of English to Speakers of Other Languages.

Egbert, J., & Hanson-Smith, E. (2007). *CALL environments: Research, practice, and critical issues* (2nd ed.). Alexandria, VA: Teachers of English to Speakers of Other Languages.

Egi, T. (2007). Interpreting recasts as linguistic evidence: The roles of linguistic target, length, and degree of change. *Studies in Second Language Acquisition, 29*(4), 511–537.

Ehrman, M. (1999). Ego boundaries and tolerance of ambiguity in second language learning. In J. Arnold (Ed.), *Affect and language learning* (pp. 68–86). Cambridge, England: Cambridge University Press.

Ekbatani, G., & Pierson, H. (Eds.). (2000). *Learner-directed assessment in ESL.* Mahwah, NJ: Lawrence Erlbaum.

Elbow, P. (1993). Ranking, evaluating, and liking: Sorting out three forms of judgment. *College English, 55*(7), 187–206.

Eldridge, J. (2008). A reader responds to K. Hyland and P. Tse's "Is there an 'academic vocabulary'?" *TESOL Quarterly 42*(1), 109–112.

Ellis, N. (Ed.). (1994). Introduction: Implicit and explicit language learning—An overview. In N. Ellis (Ed.), *Implicit and explicit learning of languages* (pp. 1–31). San Diego, CA: Academic Press.

Ellis, N. (1996). Sequencing in SLA: Phonological memory, chunking, and points of order. *Studies in Second Language Acquisition, 18*, 91–126.

Ellis, N. (1998). Emergentism, connectionism, and language learning. *Language Learning, 48*(4), 631–664.

Ellis, N. (2002). Frequency effects in language processing: A review with implications for theories of implicit and explicit language acquisition. *Studies in Second Language Acquisition, 24*(2), 143–189.

Ellis, N. (2003). Constructions, chunking, and connectionism: The emergence of second language structure. In C. Doughty & M. Long (Eds.), *Handbook of second language acquisition* (pp. 63–103). Malden, MA: Blackwell.

Ellis, N. (2005). At the interface: Dynamic interactions of explicit and implicit language knowledge. *Studies in Second Language Acquisition, 27*(2), 305–352.

Ellis, N. (2006). Cognitive perspectives on SLA: The associative–cognitive CREED. *AILA Review, 19*, 100–121.

Ellis, R. (1984). *Classroom second language development*. Oxford, England: Pergamon.

Ellis, R. (1985). Teacher–pupil interaction in second-language development. In S. Gass & C. Madden (Eds.), *Input in second language acquisition* (pp. 69–85). Rowley, MA: Newbury House.

Ellis, R. (1986). *Understanding second language acquisition*. Oxford, England: Oxford University Press.

Ellis, R. (1987). Interlanguage variability in narrative discourse: Style in the use of the past tense. *Studies in Second Language Acquisition, 9*(1), 12–20.

Ellis, R. (1990). *Instructed second language acquisition*. Malden, MA: Blackwell.

Ellis, R. (1993). Interpretation-based grammar teaching. *System, 21*(1), 69–78.

Ellis, R. (1994). A theory of instructed second language acquisition. In N. C. Ellis (Ed.), *Implicit and explicit learning of language* (pp. 79–114). San Diego, CA: Academic Press.

Ellis, R. (1997). *Second language acquisition*. Oxford, England: Oxford University Press.

Ellis, R. (2001). Introduction: Investigating form-focused instruction. *Language Learning, 51*(Suppl. 1), 1–46.

Ellis, R. (2003). *Task-based language learning and teaching*. Oxford, England: Oxford University Press.

Ellis, R. (2004). The definition and measurement of L2 explicit knowledge. *Language Learning, 54*(2), 227–275.

Ellis, R. (2006). Current issues in the teaching of grammar: An SLA perspective. *TESOL Quarterly, 40*(1), 83–107.

Ellis, R., & He, X. (1999). The roles of modified input and output in the incidental acquisition of word meanings. *Studies in Second Language Acquisition, 21*(2), 285–301.

Ellis, R., & Loewen, S. (2007). Confirming the operational definitions of explicit and implicit knowledge in Ellis (2005): Responding to Isemonger, *Studies in Second Language Acquisition, 29*(1), 119–126.

Ellis, R., Loewen, S., & Erlam, R. (2006). Implicit and explicit corrective feedback and the acquisition of L2 grammar. *Studies in Second Language Acquisition, 28*(2), 339–368.

Ellis, R., & Sheen, Y. (2006). Recasts in second language acquisition. *Studies in Second Language Acquisition, 28*(4), 575–598.

Ellis, R., Tanaka, Y., & Yamazaki, A. (1994). Classroom interaction, comprehension, and the acquisition of L2 word meanings. *Language Learning, 44*(4), 449–491.

Ellis, R., & Yuan, F. (2004). The effects of planning on fluency, complexity, and accuracy in second language narrative writing. *Studies in Second Language Acquisition, 26*(1), 59–84.

Elman, J., Bates, E., Johnson, M. H., Karmiloff-Smith, A., Parisi, D., & Plunkett, K. (1996). *Rethinking innateness: A connectionist perspective on development*. Cambridge, MA: MIT Press.

Engeström, Y. (2001). Expansive learning at work: Toward an activity theoretical reconceptualization. *Journal of Education and Work, 14,* 133–156.

Erickson, F. (2007). Some thoughts on "proximal" formative assessment of student learning. In P. Moss (Ed.), *Evidence in decision making: Yearbook of the National Society for the Study of Education 106* (pp. 186–216). Malden, MA: Blackwell.

Erman, B., & Warren, B. (2000). The idiom principle and the open choice principle. *Text, 20,* 29–62.

Ervin-Tripp, S. (1974). Is second language learning like the first? *TESOL Quarterly, 8,* 111–127.

Eskey, D. (2005). Reading in a second language. In E. Hinkel (Ed.), *Handbook of research in second language teaching and learning* (pp. 563–580). Mahwah, NJ: Lawrence Erlbaum.

Evans, J., & Moore, J. (1979). *Art moves the basics along: Animal units.* Carmel, CA: Evan-Moor.

Evans, J., & Moore, J. (1990). *Art moves the basics along: Units about children,* (2nd ed.). Carmel, CA: Evan-Moor.

Falk, B. (2000). *The heart of the matter: Using standards and assessment to learn.* Portsmouth, NH: Heinemann.

Fanselow, J. (1977). The treatment of error in oral work. *Foreign Language Annals, 10,* 583–593.

Fanselow, J. (1992). *Contrasting conversations: Activities for exploring our beliefs and teaching practices.* White Plains, NY: Longman.

Farnette, C., Forte, I., & Loss, B. (1977). *I've got me and I'm glad* (ABC Unified School District, Cerritos, CA). Nashville, TN: Incentive Publications.

Felder, R., & Brent, R. (1996). Navigating the bumpy road to student-centered instruction. *College Teaching, 44,* 43–47.

Felix, S. (1988). UG-generated knowledge in adult second language acquisition. In S. Flynn & W. O'Neil (Eds.), *Linguistic theory in second language acquisition* (pp. 277–294). Dordrecht, the Netherlands: Kluwer Academic.

Fellag, L. R. (1993). *Life, language, and literature.* Boston: Heinle.

Ferguson, C. (1975). Toward a characterization of English foreigner talk. *Anthropological Linguistics, 17*(1), 1–14.

Ferris, D. (1997). The influence of teacher commentary on student revision. *TESOL Quarterly, 31*(2), 315–339.

Ferris, D. (2002). *Treatment of error in second language writing classes.* Ann Arbor: University of Michigan Press.

Ferris, D. (2003). *Response to student writing: Implications for second language students.* Mahwah, NJ: Lawrence Erlbaum.

Ferris, D. (2006). Using art institution web sites for English teaching. *Essential Teacher, 3*(3), 42–45.

Feuerstein, R., Falik, L., Rand, Y., & Feuerstein, R. S. (2003). *Dynamic assessment of cognitive modifiability.* Jerusalem: ICELP Press.

Fisher, M. (2007). *Writing in rhythm: Spoken word poetry in urban classrooms.* New York: Teachers College Press.

Flege, J. E., & Liu, S. (2001). The effect of experience on adults' acquisition of a second language. *Studies in Second Language Acquisition, 23,* 527–552.

Flowerdew, J. (1994). *Academic listening: Research perspectives.* Cambridge, England: Cambridge University Press.

Flowerdew, J., & Li, Y. (2007). Plagiarism and second language writing in an electronic age. *Annual Review of Applied Linguistics, 27,* 161–183.

Flowerdew, J., & Miller, L. (2004). *Second language listening: Theory and practice.* New York: Cambridge University Press.

Flynn, S. (1987). Contrast and construction in a parameter setting model of L2 acquisition. *Language Learning, 37*(1), 19–62.

Flynn, S. (1990). Theory, practice, and research: Strange or bliss bedfellows? In J. Alatis (Ed.), *Georgetown University Round Table on Languages and Linguistics 1990: Linguistics, language teaching and* *language acquisition: The importance of theory, practice and research* (pp. 112–122). Washington, DC: Georgetown University.

Foster, P. (1998). A classroom perspective on the negotiation of meaning. *Applied Linguistics, 19*, 1–23.

Fotos, S. (2005). Traditional and grammar translation methods. In E. Hinkel (Ed.), *Handbook of research in second language teaching and learning* (pp. 653–670). Mahwah, NJ: Lawrence Erlbaum.

Fotos, S., & Ellis, R. (1991). Communication about grammar: A task-based approach. *TESOL Quarterly, 25*(4), 605–628.

Foucault, M. (1980). Power/knowledge: Selected interviews and other writings, 1972–1977. New York: Pantheon Books.

Fowle, C. (2002). Vocabulary notebooks: Implementation and outcomes. *ELT Journal, 56*, 380–388.

Freed, B. (1978). *Foreigner talk: A study of speech adjustments made by native speakers of English in conversation with non-native speakers.* Unpublished doctoral dissertation, University of Pennsylvania, Philadelphia.

Freeman, D. (1991). "Mistaken constructs": Reexamining the nature and assumptions of language teacher education. In J. Alatis (Ed.), *Georgetown University Round Table on Languages and Linguistics 1991. Linguistics and language pedagogy: The state of the art* (pp. 25–39). Washington, DC: Georgetown University.

Freeman, D. (1992). Language teacher education emerging discourse and change in classroom practice. In J. Flowerdew, M. Brock, & S. Hsia (Eds.), *Perspectives in second language teacher education* (pp. 1–21). Hong Kong: City Polytechnic of Hong Kong.

Freeman, D. (1998). *Doing teacher research: From inquiry to understanding.* Boston: Heinle.

Freeman, D. E., & Freeman, Y. S. (2004). *Essential linguistics: What you need to know to teach reading, ESL, spelling, phonics, and grammar.* Portsmouth, NH: Heinemann.

Freire, P. (1970a). *Cultural action for freedom.* Cambridge, MA: Harvard Educational Review.

Freire, P. (1970b). *Pedagogy of the oppressed.* New York: Seabury.

Freire, P. (1985). *The politics of education: Culture, power, and liberation.* New York: Bergin & Garvey.

Fries, C. (1945). *Teaching and learning English as a foreign language.* Ann Arbor: University of Michigan Press.

Frodesen, J. (2001). Grammar in writing. In M. Celce-Murcia (Ed.), *Teaching English as a second or foreign language* (3rd ed., pp. 233–248). Boston: Heinle.

Frodesen, J., & Holten, C. (2003). Grammar and the ESL writing class. In B. Kroll (Ed.), *Exploring the dynamics of second language writing* (pp. 141–161). Cambridge, England: Cambridge University Press.

Fuller, J., & Gundel, J. (1987). Topic prominence in interlanguage. *Language Learning, 37*(1), 1–18.

Gaies, S. (1977). The nature of linguistic input in formal second language learning: Linguistic and communicative strategies in ESL teachers' classroom language. In H. D. Brown, C. Yorio, & R. Crymes (Eds.), *On TESOL '77* (pp. 204–212). Washington, DC: Teachers of English to Speakers of Other Languages.

García, O. (2009). *Bilingual education in the 21st century: A global perspective.* Malden, MA: Wiley-Blackwell.

Gardner, R., Lalonde, R., & Moorcroft, R. (1985). The role of attitudes and motivation in second language learning: Correlational and experimental considerations. *Language Learning, 35*(2), 207–227.

Gardner, R., & Lambert, W. (1959). Motivational variables in second-language acquisition. *Canadian Journal of Psychology, 13*, 266–272.

Gardner, R., & Lambert, W. (1972). *Attitudes and motivation in second-language learning.* Rowley, MA: Newbury House.

Gardner, R., & MacIntyre, P. (1991). An instrumental motivation in language study: Who says it isn't effective? *Studies in Second Language Acquisition, 13*(1), 57–72.

Gardner, R., & MacIntyre, P. (1993). On the measurement of affective variables in second language learning. *Language Learning, 43*(1), 157–194.

Gardner, R., Smythe, P., Clement, R., & Gliksman, L. (1976). Second-language learning: A social-psychological perspective. *Canadian Modern Language Review, 32,* 198–213.

Gary, J. (1975). Delayed oral practice in initial stages of second-language learning. In M. Burt & H. Dulay (Eds.), *New directions in second language learning, teaching, and bilingual education* (pp. 89–95). Washington, DC: Teachers of English to Speakers of Other Languages.

Gass, S. (1982). From theory to practice. In M. Hines & W. Rutherford (Eds.), *On TESOL '81* (pp. 129–139). Washington, DC: Teachers of English to Speakers of Other Languages.

Gass, S. (1997). *Input, interaction, and the second language learner.* Mahwah, NJ: Lawrence Erlbaum.

Gass, S. (2003). Input and interaction. In C. Doughty & M. Long (Eds.), *Handbook of second language acquisition* (pp. 224–255). Malden, MA: Blackwell.

Gass, S. & Mackey, A. (2002). Frequency effects and second language acquisition: A complex picture? *Studies in Second Language Acquisition, 24*(2), 249–260.

Gass, S., & Mackey, A. (2006). Input, interaction and output. *AILA Review, 19,* 3–17.

Gass, S., & Selinker, L. (2001). *Second language acquisition: An introductory course.* London: Lawrence Erlbaum.

Gass, S., & Veronis, E. (1994). Input, interaction, and second language production. *Studies in Second Language Acquisition, 16,* 283–302.

Gattegno, C. (1972). *Teaching foreign languages in schools: The silent way* (2nd ed.). New York: Educational Solutions.

Gaylean, B. (1982). A confluent design for language teaching. In R. Blair (Ed.), *Innovative approaches to language teaching* (pp. 176–188). Rowley, MA: Newbury House.

Gebhard, J., & Oprandy, R. (1999). *Language teaching awareness: A guide to exploring beliefs and practices.* Cambridge, England: Cambridge University Press.

Gebhard, M. (1999). Debates in SLA studies: Redefining classroom SLA as an institutional phenomenon. *TESOL Quarterly, 33*(3), 544–554.

Gee, J. P. (1990). *Social linguistics and literacies: Ideology in discourses.* London: Falmer Press.

Gee, J. P. (1992). *The social mind.* London: Bergin & Garvey.

Gee, J. P. (1994). Orality and literacy: From the savage mind to ways with words. In J. Maybin (Ed.), *Language and literacy in social practice.* Clevedon, England: Multilingual Matters.

Genesee, F. (1987). *Learning through two languages: Studies of immersion and bilingual education.* Cambridge, MA: Newbury House.

Genesee, F., Lindholm-Leary, K., Saunders, W., & Christian, D. (2006). *Educating English language learners: A synthesis of research evidence.* New York: Cambridge University Press.

Genishi, C. (1999). Poststructural approaches to L2 research. *TESOL Quarterly, 33*(2), 287–291.

Gersten, B. F., & Tlusty, N. (1998). Creating international contexts for cultural communication: Video exchange projects in the EFL/ESL classroom. *TESOL Journal, 7*(2), 11–16.

Ghim-Lian Chew, P. (1999). Linguistic imperialism, globalism, and the English language. In D. Graddol & U. H. Meinhof (Eds.), *English in a changing world* (pp. 37–47). Erfurt, Germany: Association for Internationale de Linguistique Appliquée.

Gibbons, P. (2003). Mediating language learning. *TESOL Quarterly, 37*(2), 247–273.

Gibbons, P. (2005). Writing in a second language across the curriculum. In P. Richard-Amato & M. A. Snow (Eds.), *Academic success for English language learners: Strategies for K–12 mainstream teachers* (pp. 275–310). White Plains, NY: Pearson Longman.

Giles, H. (1979). Ethnicity markers in speech. In K. Scherer & H. Giles (Eds.), *Social markers in speech* (pp. 251–289). Cambridge, England: Cambridge University Press.

Gillespie, J. (1993). Buddy book journals: Responding to literature. *English Journal, 82*, 64-68.

Gliedman, J. (1983). Interview (with Noam Chomsky). *Omni, 6*(2), 113-118.

Goldstein, L., & Conrad, S. (1990). Student input and negotiation of meaning in ESL writing conferences. *TESOL Quarterly, 24*(3), 443-461.

Goodman, J., & Tenney, C. (1979). Teaching the total language with readers theater. *CATESOL Occasional Papers*, No. 5, 84-89.

Goodman, K. (1986). *What's whole in whole language*. Portsmouth, NH: Heinemann.

Gore, J. M. (1992). What we can do for you! What can "we" do for "you"? Struggling over empowerment in critical and feminist pedagogy. In C. Luke & J. M. Gore (Eds.), *Feminisms and critical pedagogy* (pp. 54-73). New York: Routledge.

Gottlieb, M. (2000). Standards-based, large-scale assessment of ESOL students. In M. A. Snow (Ed.), *Implementing the ESL standards for pre-K-12 students through teacher education* (pp. 167-186). Alexandra, VA: Teachers of English to Speakers of Other Languages.

Gottlieb, M. (2006). *Assessing English language learners: Bridges from language proficiency to academic achievement*. Thousand Oaks. CA: Corwin Press.

Grabe, W. (1991). Current developments in second language reading research. *TESOL Quarterly, 25*(3), 375-406.

Graham, C. (1978). *Jazz chants*. New York: Oxford University Press.

Graham, C. (2006). *Creating chants and songs.* New York: Oxford University Press.

Granger, C. (2004). *Silence in second language acquisition*. Tonowanda, NY: Multilingual Matters.

Grant, E., & Wong, S. (2003). Barriers to literacy for language-minority learners: An argument for change in the literacy education profession. *Journal of Adolescent and Adult Literacy, 46*(5), 388-394.

Green, K. (1983). Values clarification theory in ESL and bilingual education. In J. Oller Jr. & P. Richard-Amato (Eds.), *Methods that work* (pp. 179-189). Rowley, MA: Newbury House.

Gregg, K. (1984). Krashen's monitor and Occam's razor. *Applied Linguistics, 5*(2), 79-100.

Grice, H. P. (1975). Logic and conversation. In P. Cole & J. L. Morgan (Eds.), *Syntax and semantics: Speech acts 3* (pp. 365-372). New York: Seminar Press.

Gries, S. (2005). Syntactic priming: A corpus-based approach. *Journal of Psycholinguistic Research, 34*, 365-399.

Guilloteaux, M., & Dörnyei, Z. (2008). Motivating language learners: A classroom-oriented investigation of the effects of motivational strategies on student motivation. *TESOL Quarterly, 42*(1), 55-77.

Guiora, A., Acton, W., Erard, R., & Strickland, F. (1980). The effects of benzodiazepine (Valium) on permeability of ego boundaries. *Language Learning, 30*(3), 351-363.

Guiora, A., Beit-Hallami, B., Brannon, R., Dull, C., & Scovel, T. (1972). The effects of experimentally induced changes in ego states on pronunciation ability in second language: An exploratory study. *Comprehensive Psychiatry, 13*, 421-428.

Guiora, A., Brannon, R., & Dull, C. (1972). Empathy and second language learning. *Language Learning, 22*(2), 111-130.

Hafernik, J., Messerschmitt, D., & Vandrick, S. (2002). *Ethical issues for ESL faculty: Social justice in practice*. Mahwah, NJ: Lawrence Erlbaum.

Hahn, L. (2004). Primary stress and intelligibility: Research to motivate the teaching of suprasegmentals. *TESOL Quarterly, 38*(2), 201-223.

Hall, J. K., Hendricks, S., & Orr, J. (2004). Dialogues in the "global village": NNS/NS collaboration in classroom interaction. *Critical Inquiry in Language Studies: An International Journal, 1*(2), 63-88.

Hall, J. K., Vitanova, G., & Marchenkova, L. (Eds.). (2005). *Dialogue with Bakhtin on second and foreign language learning: New perspectives.* Mahwah, NJ: Lawrence Erlbaum.

Hall, J. K., & Walsh, M. (2002). Teacher-student interaction and language learning. *Annual Review of Applied Linguistics, 22*, 186-203.

Halliday, M. A. K. (1979). Towards a sociological semantics. In C. J. Brumfit & K. Johnson (Eds.), *The communicative approach to language teaching* (pp. 27-46). Oxford, England: Oxford University Press.

Halliday, M. A. K. (2001). New ways of meaning: The challenges to applied linguistics. In A. Fill & P. Mühlhäusler (Eds.), *The ecolinguistics reader: Language ecology and environment* (pp. 175-202). New York: Continuum.

Halliday, M. A. K., & Hasan, R. (1976). *Cohesion in English*. Cambridge, England: Cambridge University Press.

Hammond, J., & Macken-Horarik, M. (1999). Critical literacy: Challenges and questions for ESL classrooms. *TESOL Quarterly, 33*(3), 528-544.

Hammond, R. (1988). Accuracy versus communicative competency: The acquisition of grammar in the second-language classroom. *Hispania, 71*, 408-417.

Han, Z. (2002). A study of the impact of recasts on tense consistency in L2 output. *TESOL Quarterly, 36*(4), 543-572.

Han, Z. (2004). *Fossilization in adult second language acquisition*. Clevedon, England: Multilingual Matters.

Han, Z. (2007). Pedagogical implications: Genuine or pretentious? *TESOL Quarterly, 41*(2), 387-393.

Han, Z., & Selinker, L. (2005). Fossilization in L2 learners. In E. Hinkel (Ed.), *Handbook of research in second language teaching and learning* (pp. 455-470). Mahwah, NJ: Lawrence Erlbaum.

Hanauer, D. (2004). *Poetry and the meaning of life*. Tonawanda, NY: Pippin.

Hanson-Smith, E. (2000). *Technology-enhanced learning environments*. Alexandria, VA: Teachers of English to Speakers of Other Languages.

Hanson-Smith, E., & Riling, S. (2006). *Learning languages through technology*. Alexandria, VA: Teachers of English to Speakers of Other Languages.

Harklau, L. (2000). From the "good kids" to the "worst": Representations of English language learners across educational settings. *TESOL Quarterly, 34*(1), 35-67.

Harley, B. (1998). The role of focus-on-form tasks in promoting child L2 acquisition. In C. Doughty & J. Williams (Eds.), *Focus on form in classroom second language acquisition* (pp. 156-174). Cambridge, England: Cambridge University Press.

Harley, B., Allen, P., Cummins, J., & Swain, M. (Eds.). (1990). *The development of second language proficiency*. Cambridge, England: Cambridge University Press.

Harper, C., Platt, E., Naranjo, C., & Boynton, S. (2007). Marching in unison: Florida ESL teachers and No Child Left Behind. *TESOL Quarterly, 41*(3), 642-651.

Harste, J., Short, K., & Burke, C. (1988). *Creating for authors*. Portsmouth, NH: Heinemann.

Harste, J., Woodward, V., & Burke, C. (1984). *Language stories and literacy lessons*. Portsmouth, NH: Heinemann.

Hartsuiker, R., Pickering, M., & Veltkamp, E. (2004). Is syntax separate or shared between languages? Cross-linguistic syntactic priming in Spanish/English bilinguals. *Psychological Science, 15*, 409-414.

Hatch, E. (1978). Acquisition of syntax in a second language. In J. C. Richards (Ed.), *Understanding second and foreign language learning* (pp. 34-69). Rowley, MA: Newbury House.

Hatch, E. (1983). *Psycholinguistics: A second language perspective*. Rowley, MA: Newbury House.

Hatch, E., Shapira, R., & Gough, J. (1978). "Foreigner-talk" discourse. *ITL Review of Applied Linguistics, 39/40*, 39-60.

Hayes-Harb, R. (2006). Native speakers of Arabic and ESL texts: Evidence for the transfer of written word identification processes. *TESOL Quarterly, 40*(2), 321-339.

Healy, C. (2004). Drama in education for language learning. *Humanising Language Teaching, 6*(3), 1-12.

Heath, S. B. (1996). Re-creating literature in the ESL classroom. *TESOL Quarterly, 30*(4), 776-779.

Hedegaard, M. (1990). How instruction influences children's concepts of evolution. *Mind, Culture, and Activity, 3*, 11-24.

Hedgcock, J. (2005). Taking stock of research and pedagogy in L2 writing. In E. Hinkel (Ed.), *Handbook of research in second language teaching and learning* (pp. 597-613). Mahwah, NJ: Lawrence Erlbaum.

Hedgcock, J., & Lefkowitz, N. (1992). Collaborative oral/aural revision in foreign language writing instruction. *Journal of Second Language Writing, 1*(3), 255-276.

Hedge, T. (2000). *Teaching and learning in the language classroom*. Oxford, England: Oxford University Press.

Hendrickson, J. (1976). *The effects of error correction treatments upon adequate and accurate communication in written compositions of adult learners of English as a second language.* Unpublished doctoral dissertation, The Ohio State University, Columbus.

Henry, A. (2005). Writing in the margins of classroom life: A teacher/researcher partnership using dialogue journals. In L. Pease-Alvarez & S. Schecter (Eds.), *Learning, teaching, and community: Contributions of situated and participatory approaches to educational innovation* (pp. 69-87). Mahwah, NJ: Lawrence Erlbaum.

Henzl, V. (1973). Linguistic register of foreigner language instruction. *Language Learning, 2*, 203-222.

Herbert, C. (1987). *San Diego Title VII two-way bilingual program*. (San Diego Unified School District). San Diego, CA.

Hess, N., & Jasper S. P. (1995). A blending of media for extensive reading. *TESOL Journal, 4*(4), 7-11.

Heyde, A. (1977). The relationship between self-esteem and the oral production of a second language. In H. D. Brown, C. Yorio, & R. Crymes (Eds.), *On TESOL '77* (pp. 226-240). Washington, DC: Teachers of English to Speakers of Other Languages.

Heyde, A. (1979). *The relationship between self-esteem and the oral production of a second language.* Unpublished doctoral dissertation, University of Michigan Press, Ann Arbor.

Higa, M. (1963). Interference effects of intralist word relationships in verbal learning. *Journal of Verbal Learning and Verbal Behavior, 2*, 170-175.

Higgs, T., & Clifford, R. (1982). The push toward communication. In T. Higgs (Ed.), *Curriculum, competence, and the foreign language teacher* (pp. 57-79). Skokie, IL: National Textbook.

Hilliard, A. (1989). Teachers and cultural style in a pluralistic society. *NEA Today, 7*(6), 65-69.

Hinkel, E. (Ed.). (2005). *Handbook of research in second language teaching and learning*. Mahwah, NJ: Lawrence Erlbaum.

Hinkel, E. (2006). Current perspectives on teaching the four skills. *TESOL Quarterly, 40*(1), 109-131.

Hinton, L. (2001). Federal language policy and indigenous languages in the United States. In L. Hinton & K. Hale (Eds.), *The green book of language revitalization in practice* (pp. 39-48). San Diego: Academic Press.

Hoffman, E. (1989). *Lost in translation. A life in a new language*. New York: Dutton.

Hoffman, S. (1995/1996). Computers and instructional design in foreign language/ESL instruction. *TESOL Journal, 5*(2), 24-29.

Holquist, M. (2002). *Dialogism: Bakhtin and his world*. London. Routledge.

Horowitz, D. (1986). What professors actually require: Academic tasks for the ESL classroom. *TESOL Quarterly, 20*(3), 445-462.

Hu, M., & Nation, P. (2000). Unknown vocabulary density and reading comprehension. *Reading in a Foreign Language, 13*, 403-430.

Hulk, A. (1991). Parameter setting and the acquisition of word order in L2 French. *Second Language Research, 7*(1), 1-34.

Hulstijn, J. (2002). Towards a unified account of the representation, processing and acquisition of second language knowledge. *Second Language Research, 18*, 193-223.

Hulstijn, J. (2003). Incidental and intentional learning. In C. Doughty & M. Long (Eds.), *The handbook of second language acquisition* (pp. 349-381). Malden, MA: Blackwell.

Hunter, M., & Russell, D. (1977). How can I plan more effective lessons? *Instructor, 87*, 74-75.

Hyland, K., & Tse, P. (2007). Is there an "academic vocabulary"? *TESOL Quarterly, 41*(2), 235-253.

Hyltenstam, K., & Abrahamsson, N. (2003). Maturational constraints in SLA. In C. Doughty & M. Long (Eds.), *The handbook of second language acquisition* (pp. 539–588). Malden, MA: Blackwell.

Hymes, D. (1970). On communicative competence. In J. Gumperz & D. Hymes (Eds.), *Directions in sociolinguistics* (pp. 35–71). New York: Holt, Rinehart & Winston.

Hymes, D. (1972). On communicative competence. In J. Pride & J. Holems (Eds.), *Sociolinguistics* (pp. 269–293). Harmondsworth, England: Penguin.

Ikeda, M., & Takeuchi, O. (2003). Can strategy instruction help EFL learners to improve their reading ability? An empirical study. *JACET Bulletin, 37*, 49–60.

Ioup, G. (2005). Age and second language development. In E. Hinkel (Ed.), *Handbook of research in second language teaching and learning.* Mahwah, NJ: Lawrence Erlbaum.

Ioup, G., Boustagui, E., El Tigi, M., & Moselle, M. (1994). Reexamining the critical period hypothesis: A case study of successful adult SLA in a naturalistic environment. *Studies in Second Language Acquisition, 16*, 73–98.

Isemonger, I. (2007). Operational definitions of explicit and implicit knowledge: Response to R. Ellis (2005) and some recommendations for future research in this area. *Studies in Second Language Acquisition, 29*(1), 101–118.

Ishida, M. (2004). Effects of recasts on the acquisition of the aspectual form -te i-(ru) by learners of Japanese as a foreign language. *Language Learning, 54*(2), 311–394.

Iwashita, N. (2001). The effect of learner proficiency on interactional moves and modified output in nonnative–nonnative interaction in Japanese as a foreign language. *System, 29*, 267–287.

Iwashita, N. (2003). Positive and negative input in task-based interaction: Differential effects on L2 development. *Studies in Second Language Acquisition, 25*(1), 1–36.

Izumi, S. (2002). Output, input enhancement, and the noticing hypothesis: An experimental study on ESL relativization. *Studies in Second Language Acquisition, 24*(4), 541–577.

Izumi, S., & Bigelow, M. (2000). Does output promote noticing and second language acquisition? *TESOL Quarterly, 34*(2), 239–278.

Jacob, E., Rottenberg, L., Patrick, S., & Wheeler, E. (1996). Cooperative learning: Context and opportunities for acquiring academic English. *TESOL Quarterly, 30*(2), 253–280.

Jacobs, G., Dufon, P., & Fong, C. (1994). L1 and L2 vocabulary glosses in L2 reading passages: Their effectiveness for increasing comprehension and vocabulary knowledge. *Journal of Research in Reading, 17*(1), 19–28.

Jain, M. (1969). *Error analysis of an Indian English corpus.* Unpublished manuscript, University of Edinburgh.

Jenkins, J. (2000). *The phonology of English as an international language.* Oxford, England: Oxford University Press.

Jenkins, J. (2006). Current perspectives on teaching world Englishes and English as a lingua franca. *TESOL Quarterly, 40*(1), 157–181.

Jespersen, O. (1904). *How to teach a foreign language.* London: Allen & Unwin.

Johns, A. (1993). Written argumentation for real audiences: Suggestions for teacher research and classroom practice. *TESOL Quarterly, 27*(1), 75–90.

Johns, A. (2003). Genre and ESL. EFL composition instruction. In B. Kroll (Ed.), *Exploring the dynamics of second language writing* (pp. 195–217). Cambridge, England: Cambridge University Press.

Johnson, D. M. (1994). Grouping strategies for second language learners. In F. Genesee (Ed.), *Educating second language children: The whole child, the whole curriculum, the whole community* (pp. 183–211). Cambridge, England: Cambridge University Press.

Johnson, J. (1992). Critical period effects in second language acquisition: The effect of written versus auditory materials on the assessment of grammatical competence. *Language Learning, 42*(2), 217–248.

Johnson, K. (1979). Communicative approaches and communicative processes. In C. J. Brumfit & K. Johnson (Eds.), *The communicative approach to language teaching* (pp. 192–205). Oxford, England: Oxford University Press.

Johnson, K. E. (2006). The sociocultural turn and its challenges for second language teacher education. *TESOL Quarterly, 40*(1), 235–257.

Johnson, M. (2004). *A philosophy of second language acquisition*. New Haven, CT: Yale University Press.

Johnston, B. (1999). Putting critical pedagogy in its place: A personal account. *TESOL Quarterly, 33*(3), 557–565.

John-Steiner, V. (1985). The road to competence in an alien land: A Vygotskian perspective on bilingualism. In J. Wertsch (Ed.), *Culture, communication, and cognition: Vygotsky in perspective* (pp. 348–372). Cambridge, England: Cambridge University Press.

John-Steiner, V., & Mahn, H. (1996). Sociocultural approaches to learning and development: A Vygotskian framework. *Educational Psychologist, 31*(3/4), 191–206.

John-Steiner, V., & Souberman, E. (1978). Afterword. In L. Vygotsky, *Mind in society* (pp. 121–140). Cambridge, MA: Harvard University.

Jones, L., & von Baeyer, C. (1983). *Functions of American English: Communication activities for the classrooms*. New York: Cambridge University Press.

Jung, E. H. (2003). The effects of organization markers on ESL learners' text understanding. *TESOL Quarterly, 37*(4), 749–759.

Kachru, B. B. (1992). *The other tongue: English across cultures* (2nd ed.). Urbana: University of Illinois Press.

Kachru, Y. (1994). Sources of bias in SLA research: Monolingual bias in SLA research. *TESOL Quarterly, 28*(4), 795–799.

Kachru, Y. (2005). Teaching and learning of world Englishes. In E. Hinkel (Ed.), *Handbook of research in second language teaching and learning* (pp. 155–173). Mahwah, NJ: Lawrence Erlbaum.

Kagan, S. (1985). *Cooperative learning: Resources for teachers*. Riverside: Spencer Kagan, University of California.

Kagan, S. (1986). Cooperative learning and sociocultural factors in schooling. In *Beyond language: Social and cultural factors in schooling language minority students* (pp. 231–298). Los Angeles: California State University, Evaluation, Dissemination and Assessment Center.

Kagan, S. (1994). *Cooperative learning*. San Juan Capistrano, CA: Kagan Cooperative Learning.

Kalivoda, T., Morain, G., & Elkins, R. (1971). The audio-motor unit: A listening comprehension strategy that works. *Foreign Language Annals, 4*, 392–400.

Kamhi-Stein, L. (2000a). Adapting U.S.-based TESOL education to meet the needs of nonnative English speakers. *TESOL Journal, 9*(3), 10–14.

Kamhi-Stein, L. (2000b). Integrating computer-mediated communication tools into the practicum. In K. E. Johnson (Ed.), *Teacher education* (pp. 119–135). Alexandria, VA: Teachers of English to Speakers of Other Languages.

Kamhi-Stein, L. (2000c). Looking to the future of TESOL teacher education: Web-based bulletin board discussions in a methods course. *TESOL Quarterly, 34*(3), 423–455.

Kasper, G. (1984). Pragmatic comprehension in learner–native speaker discourse. *Language Learning, 34*(1), 1–20.

Kasser, C., & Silverman, A. (2001). *Stories we brought with us*. White Plains, NY: Pearson Education.

Katz, A. (2000). Changing paradigms for assessment. In M. A. Snow (Ed.), *Implementing the ESL standards for pre-K-12 students through teacher education* (pp. 137–166). Alexandra, VA: Teachers of English to Speakers of Other Languages.

Kaufman, D. (2004). Constructivist issues in language learning and teaching. *Annual Review of Applied Linguistics, 24*, 303–319.

Kaufman, D., & Crandall, J. (2005). *Content-based instruction in primary and secondary school settings*. Alexandria, VA: Teachers of English to Speakers of Other Languages.

Kaufman, D., & Brooks, J. G. (1996). Interdisciplinary collaboration in teacher education: A constructivist approach. *TESOL Quarterly, 30*(2), 231–251.

Kay, J., & Gelshenen, G. (1998). *America writes: Learning English through American short stories*. New York: Cambridge University Press.

Kepner, C. (1991). An experiment in the relationship of types of written feedback to the development of second-language writing skills. *Modern Language Journal, 75*(3), 305–313.

Kessler, G. (2006). A multimedia lab on your desktop. *Essential Teacher, 3*(3), 34–37.

Kessler, G., & Plakans, L. (2001). Incorporating ESOL learners' feedback and usability testing in instructor-developed CALL materials. *TESOL Journal, 10*(1), 15–20.

King, R. (1997). Should English be the law? *Atlantic Monthly, 279*(4), 55–64.

King, S., & Goodwin, A. L. (2002). *Culturally responsive parental involvement: Concrete understandings and basic strategies.* New York: American Association of Colleges for Teacher Education.

Kleifgen, J. (1985). Skilled variation in a kindergarten teacher's use of foreigner talk. In S. Gass & C. Madden (Eds.), *Input in second language acquisition* (pp. 59–68). Rowley, MA: Newbury House.

Klein, W. (1995). Language acquisition at different ages. In D. Magnusson (Ed.), *The life-span development of individuals: Behavioral, neurobiological, and psychosocial perspectives*: A synthesis (pp. 244–264). New York: Cambridge University Press.

Kleinmann, H. (1977). Avoidance behavior in adult second-language acquisition. *Language Learning, 27*(1), 93–105.

Klesmer, H. (1994). Assessment and teacher perceptions of ESL student achievement. *English Quarterly, 26*(3), 8–11.

Klingner, J. K., & Vaughn, S. (2000). The helping behaviors of fifth graders while using collaborative strategic reading during ESL content classes. *TESOL Quarterly, 34*(1), 69–98.

Knight, S. (1994). Dictionary use while reading: The effects on comprehension and vocabulary acquisition for students of different verbal abilities. *Modern Language Journal, 78*(3), 285–289.

Koestler, A. (1964). *The act of creation*. New York: Macmillan.

Kramsch, C. (2000). Social discursive constructions of self in L2 learning. In J. Lantolf (Ed.), *Sociocultural theory and second language learning* (pp. 133–153). Oxford, England: Oxford University Press.

Kramsch, C. (Ed.). (2002). *Language acquisition and language socialization*: Ecological perspectives. New York: Continuum.

Krashen, S. (1973). Lateralization, language learning, and the critical period: Some new evidence. In *Language learning: Second language acquisition and second language learning* (pp. 63–74). Oxford, England: Pergamon.

Krashen, S. (1981a). *Second language acquisition and second language learning*. Oxford, England: Pergamon.

Krashen, S. (1981b). The case for narrow reading. *TESOL Newsletter*, December, p. 23.

Krashen, S. (1982). *Principles and practice in second language acquisition.* Oxford, England: Pergamon.

Krashen, S. (1984). Immersion: Why it works and what it has taught us. *Language and Society, 12*, 61–64.

Krashen, S. (1985). *The input hypothesis: Issues and implications*. London: Longman.

Krashen, S. (1995). What is intermediate natural approach? In P. Hashemipour, R. Maldonado, & M. van Naerssen (Eds.), *Studies in language learning and Spanish linguistics in honor of Tracy D. Terrell* (pp. 92–105). New York: McGraw–Hill.

Krashen, S. (1996). The case for narrow listening. *System, 24*, 97–100.

Krashen, S. (2001). Incubation: A neglected aspect of the composing process? *ESL Journal 4*(2), 10–11.

Krashen, S., & Terrell, T. (1983). *The natural approach: Language acquisition in the classroom*. Englewood Cliffs, NJ: Alemany/Prentice Hall.

Krauss, M. (1992). The world's languages in crises. *Language 68*, 4-10.

Krauss, M. (1996). Status of Native American language endangerment. In G. Cantoni (Ed.), *Stabilizing indigenous languages* (pp. 16-21). Flagstaff: Northern Arizona University Center for Excellence in Education.

Kroll, B. (Ed.). (2003). *Exploring the dynamics of second language writing.* New York: Cambridge University Press.

Kubota, R. (1999). Japanese culture constructed by discourses: Implications for applied linguistics research and ELT. *TESOL Quarterly, 33*(1), 9-35.

Kubota, R. (2001). Discursive construction of the images of U.S. classrooms. *TESOL Quarterly, 35*(1), 9-38.

Kubota, R. (2004a). Critical multiculturalism and second language education. In B. Norton & D. Toohey (Eds.), *Critical pedagogies and language learning* (pp. 30-52). Cambridge, England: Cambridge University Press.

Kubota, R. (2004b). The politics of cultural difference in second language education. *Critical Inquiry in Language Studies: An International Journal, 1*(1), 21-39.

Kucer, S. (2005). *Dimensions of literacy: A conceptual base for teaching reading and writing in school settings* (2nd ed.). Mahwah, NJ: Lawrence Erlbaum.

Kumaravadivelu, B. (1994). The postmethod condition: (E)merging strategies for second/foreign language teaching. *TESOL Quarterly, 28*(1), 27-48.

Kumaravadivelu, B. (1999). Critical classroom discourse analysis. *TESOL Quarterly, 33*(3), 453-484.

Kumaravadivelu, B. (2001). Toward a postmethod pedagogy. *TESOL Quarterly, 35*(4), 537-560.

Kumaravadivelu, B. (2003). *Beyond methods: Macrostrategies for language teaching.* New Haven, CT: Yale University Press.

Kumaravadivelu, B. (2006). TESOL methods: Changing tracks, challenging trends, *TESOL Quarterly, 40*(1), 59-82.

Kunnan, A. J. (2000). Fairness and justice for all. In A. J. Kunnan (Ed.). *Fairness and validation in language assessment* (pp. 1-14). Cambridge, England: Cambridge University Press.

Kunnan, A. J. (2005). Language assessment from a wider context. In E. Hinkel (Ed.), *Handbook of research in second language teaching and learning* (pp. 779-794). Mahwah, NJ: Lawrence Erlbaum.

Lado, R. (1977). *Lado English series.* New York: Regents.

Ladson-Billings, G. (1994). *The dreamkeepers: Successful teachers of African American children.* San Francisco: Jossey-Bass.

Lam, W., & Wong, J. (2000). The effects of strategy training on developing discussion skills in an ESL classroom. *ELT Journal, 54*, 245-255.

Lambert, W. (1974, March). *Culture and language as factors in learning and education.* Paper presented at the Annual TESOL Convention, Denver, CO.

Lambert, W., & Cazabon, M. (1994). *Students' views of the Amigos program* (Research Report No. 11). Santa Cruz, CA, and Washington, DC: National Center for Research on Cultural Diversity and Second Language Learning.

Lamendella, J. (1979). The neurofunctional basis of pattern practice. *TESOL Quarterly, 13*, 5-20.

Lantolf, J. (Ed.). (2000). *Sociocultural theory and second language learning.* Oxford, England: Oxford University Press.

Lantolf, J. (2005). Sociocultural and second language learning research: An exegesis. In E. Hinkel, (Ed.), *Handbook of research in second language teaching and learning* (pp. 335-353). Mahwah, NJ: Lawrence Erlbaum.

Lantolf, J., & Thorne, S. (Eds.). (2006). *Sociocultural theory and the genesis of second language development.* Oxford, England: Oxford University Press.

Lapkin, S., & Swain, M. (1984). Research update. *Language and Society, 12*, 48-54.

Larsen, D., & Smalley, W. (1972). *Becoming bilingual: A guide to language learning*. New Canaan, CT: Practical Anthropology.

Larsen-Freeman, D. (1978). An explanation for the morpheme accuracy order of learners of English as a second language. In E. Hatch (Ed.), *Second language acquisition: A book of readings* (pp. 371–382). Rowley, MA: Newbury House.

Larsen-Freeman, D. (1991). Second language acquisition research: Staking out the territory. *TESOL Quarterly, 25*(2), 315–350.

Larsen-Freeman, D. (1996). Impressions of AILA 1996. *AILA Review*, No. 12, 87–92.

Larsen-Freeman, D. (2000). The total physical response method. In D. Larsen-Freeman, *Techniques and principles in language teaching* (2nd ed., pp. 107–119). New York: Oxford University Press.

Larsen-Freeman, D. (2001). Teaching grammar. In M. Celce-Murcie (Ed.), *Teaching English as a second or foreign language* (3rd ed., pp. 251–266). Boston: Heinle.

Larsen-Freeman, D. (2002). Making sense of frequency. *Studies in Second Language Acquisition, 24*(2), 275–285.

Larsen-Freeman, D. (2003). *Teaching language: From grammar to grammaring*. Boston: Thomson-Heinle.

Larsen-Freeman, D., & Freeman, D. (2008). Language moves: The place of "foreign" languages in classroom teaching and learning. *Review of Research in Education, 32*(1), 147–186.

Larsen-Freeman, D., & Long M. (1991). *An introduction to second language acquisition*. London: Longman.

Lave, J., & Wenger, E. (1991). *Situated learning: Legitimate peripheral participation*. New York: Cambridge University Press.

Lawson, J. (1971). Should foreign language be eliminated from the curriculum? *Foreign Language Annals, 4*, 427.

Lazar, G. (1993). *Literature and language teaching: A guide for teachers and trainers*. Cambridge, England: Cambridge University Press.

Lazar, G. (2003). *Meanings and metaphors: Activities to practice figurative language*. Cambridge, England: Cambridge University Press.

Lazaraton, A. (2001). Teaching oral skills. In M. Celce-Murcie (Ed.), *Teaching English as a second or foreign language* (3rd ed., pp. 103–115). Boston, MA: Heinle.

Lee, C., & Smagorinsky, P. (Eds.). (2000). *Vygotskian perspectives on literacy research: Constructing meaning through collaborative inquiry*. New York: Cambridge University Press.

Lee, S. (2004). The robustness of extensive reading: Evidence from two studies. *The International Journal of Foreign Language Teaching, 1*(3), 13–19.

Leeman, J. (2003). Recasts and second language development: Beyond negative evidence. *Studies in Second Language Acquisition, 25*(1), 37–63.

Leki, I. (1990). Potential problems with peer responding in ESL writing classes. *CATESOL Journal, 3*, 5–19.

Leki, I. (2001). "A narrow thinking system": Nonnative-English-speaking students in group projects across the curriculum. *TESOL Quarterly, 35*(1), 39–67.

Lenneberg, E. (1967). *Biological foundations of language*. New York: Wiley.

Lenski, S. D., & Ehlers-Zavala, F. (2004). *Reading strategies for Spanish speakers*. Dubuque, IA: Kendall/Hunt.

Leont'ev, A. (1981). The problem of activity in psychology. In J. Wertsch (Ed.). *The concept of activity in Soviet psychology*. Armonk, NY: Sharpe.

Leung, C., & Lewkowicz, J. (2006). Expanding horizons and unresolved conundrums: Language testing and assessment. *TESOL Quarterly, 40*(1), 211–234.

Levelt, W. (1989). *Speaking: From intention to articulation*. Cambridge, MA: MIT.

Levis, J. (2007). Computer technology in teaching and researching pronunciation. *Annual Review of Applied Linguistics, 27*, 184–202.

Levy, M., & Stockwell, G. (2006). *CALL dimensions: Options and issues in computer assisted language learning*. Mahwah, NJ: Lawrence Erlbaum.

Lewis, G., & Bedson, G. (1999). *Games for children*. Oxford, England: Oxford University Press.

Lewis, M. (1993). *The lexical approach: The state of ELT and a way forward*. Hove, England: Language Teaching Publications.

Li, J., & Cumming, A. (2001). Word processing and second language writing: A longitudinal case study. *International Journal of English Studies, 1*(2), 127–152.

Lightbown, P. (1983). Exploring relationships between developmental and instructional sequences. In H. Seliger & M. Long (Eds.), *Classroom-oriented research in second language acquisition* (pp. 217–243). Rowley, MA: Newbury House.

Lightbown, P. (1998). The importance of timing in focus on form. In C. Doughty & J. Williams (Eds.), *Focus on form in classroom second language acquisition* (pp. 177–196). Cambridge, England: Cambridge University Press.

Lightbown, P., & Spada, N. (2006). *How languages are learned* (3rd ed.). Oxford, England: Oxford University Press.

Linell, P. (1995). Troubles with mutualities: towards a dialogical theory of misunderstanding and miscommunication. In I. Marková, C. Graumann, & K. Foppa (Eds.), *Mutualilties in dialogue* (pp. 176–213). Cambridge, England: Cambridge University Press.

Lismore, P. (2007). Teaching with technology. *Essential Teacher, 4*. Alexandria, VA: Teachers of English to Speakers of Other Languages. Retrieved July 7, 2007, from http://tesol.org.

Liu, D. (2003). The most frequently used spoken American English idioms: A corpus analysis and its implications. *TESOL Quarterly, 37*(4), 671–700.

Liu, J. (1999). Nonnative-English-speaking professionals in TESOL. *TESOL Quarterly, 33*(1), 85–102.

LoCastro, V. (1994). Learning strategies and learning environments. *TESOL Quarterly 28*(2), 409–414.

Loewen, S. (2005). Incidental focus on form and second language learning. *Studies in Second Language Acquisition, 27*(3), 361–386.

Loewen, S., & Philp, J. (2006). Recasts in the adult L2 classroom: Characteristics, explicitness and effectiveness. *Modern Language Journal, 90*, 536–556.

Long, M. (1981). Input, interaction, and second language acquisition. In H. Winitz (Ed.), *Native language and foreign language acquisition: Annals of the New York Academy of Sciences, 379*, 259–278.

Long, M. (1983a). Linguistic and conversational adjustments to non-native speakers. *Studies in Second Language Acquisition, 5*(2), 177–193.

Long, M. (1983b). Native speaker/nonnative speaker conversation in the second-language classroom. In M. Clarke & J. Handscombe (Eds.), *On TESOL '82: Pacific perspectives on language learning and teaching*. Washington, DC: Teachers of English to Students of Other Languages.

Long, M. (1985). A role for instruction in second language acquisition. In K. Hyltenstam & M. Pienemann (Eds.), *Modelling and assessing second language acquisition* (pp. 77–99). Clevedon, England: Multilingual Matters.

Long, M. (1991). Focus on form: A design feature in language teaching methodology. In K. de Bot, R. Ginsberg, & C. Kramsch (Eds.), *Foreign language research in cross-cultural perspective* (pp. 39–52). Amsterdam, the Netherlands: John Benjamins.

Long, M. (1996). The role of the linguistic environment in second language acquisition. In W. C. Ritchie & T. K. Bhatia (Eds.), *Handbook of second language acquisition* (pp. 413–468). San Diego: CA: Academic Press.

Long, M. (2003). Stabilization and fossilization in interlanguage development. In C. Doughty and M. Long (Eds.), *The handbook of second language acquisition* (pp. 487–536). Malden, MA: Blackwell.

Long, M. (2007). *Problems in SLA*. Mahwah, NJ: Lawrence Erlbaum.

Long, M., Adams, L., McLean, M., & Castanos, F. (1976). Doing things with words—verbal interaction in lockstep and small group classroom situations. In J. Fanselow & R. Crymes (Eds.), *On TESOL '76* (pp. 137-153). Washington, DC: Teachers of English to Students of Other Languages.

Long, M., & Doughty, C. (2003). SLA and cognitive science. In C. Doughty & M. Long (Eds.), *The handbook of second language acquisition* (pp. 866-870). Malden, MA: Blackwell.

Long, M., Inagaki, S., & Ortega, L. (1998). The role of implicit negative feedback in SLA: Models and recasts in Japanese and Spanish. *Modern Language Journal, 82*, 357-371.

Long, M., & Porter, P. (1984). *Group work, interlanguage talk and classroom second language acquisition.* Paper presented at TESOL 1984, Houston, TX.

Long, M., & Robinson, P. (1998). Focus on form: Theory, research, and practice. In C. Doughty & J. Williams (Eds.), *Focus on form in classroom second language acquisition* (pp. 15-41). Cambridge, England: Cambridge University Press.

Lorton, M. B. (1994). *Mathematics their way.* White Plains, NY: Pearson Education.

Lotto, L., & de Groot, M. (1998). Effects of learning method and word type on acquiring vocabulary in an unfamiliar language. *Language Learning, 48*(1), 31-69.

Lozanov, G. (1978). *Suggestology and outlines of suggestopedy.* New York: Gordon and Breach.

Lucas, T., Henze, R., & Donato, R. (1990). Promoting the success of Latino language minority students: An exploratory study of six high schools. *Harvard Educational Review, 60*(3), 315-340.

Luke, A. (1996). Genres of power? Literacy education and the production of capital. In R. Hasan & G. Williams (Eds.), *Literacy in society* (pp. 308-338). New York: Longman.

Lukmani, Y. (1972). Motivation to learn and language proficiency. *Language Learning, 22*(2), 261-273.

Luria, A. R. (1961). Study of the abnormal child. *American Journal of Orthopsychiatry. A Journal of Human Behavior, 31*, 1-16.

Lynch, B. K. (2001). Rethinking assessment from a critical perspective. *Language Testing, 18*(4), 351-372.

Lynch, T. (1997). Nudge, nudge: Teacher interventions in task-based learner talk. *ELT Journal, 51*(4), 317-325.

Lyster, R. (1998). Recasts, repetition, and ambiguity in L2 classroom discourse. *Studies in Second Language Acquisition, 20*, 51-81.

Lyster, R., & Mori, H. (2006). Interactional feedback and instructional counterbalance. *Studies in Second Language Acquisition, 28*(2), 269-300.

Lyster, R., & Ranta, L. (1997). Corrective feedback and learner uptake: Negotiation of form in communicative classrooms. *Studies in Second Language Acquisition, 19*, 37-66.

Macaro, E. (2003). *Teaching and learning a second language: A guide to recent research and its applications.* London: Continuum.

MacIntyre, P. D., & Charos, C. (1996). Personality, attitudes and affect as predictors of second language communication. *Journal of Language and Social Psychology, 15*, 3-26.

MacIntyre, P. D., & Gardner, R. (1994). The effects of induced anxiety on three stages of cognitive processing in computerized vocabulary learning. *Studies in Second Language Acquisition, 16*(1), 1-17.

Mackey, A. (1999). Input, interaction, and second language development: An empirical study of question formation in ESL. *Studies in Second Language Acquisition, 21*, 557-587.

Mackey, A., Gass, S., & McDonough, K. (2000). How do learners perceive interactional feedback. *Studies in Second Language Acquisition, 22*, 471-497.

Mackey, A., & Philp, J. (1998). Conversational interaction and second language development: Recasts, responses, and red herrings? *Modern Language Journal, 82*, 338-356.

Madrid, A. (1991). Diversity and its discontents. In L. Samovar & R. Porter (Eds.), *Intercultural communication: A reader* (6th ed., pp. 115-119). Belmont, CA: Wadsworth.

Mahn, H., & John-Steiner, V. (2002). The gift of confidence: A Vygotskian view of emotions. In G. Wells & G. Claxton (Eds.), *Learning for life in the 21st century: Sociocultural perspectives on the future of education* (pp. 46-58). Malden, MA: Blackwell.

Makoni, S. (2005). Toward a more inclusive applied linguistics and English language teaching: A symposium. *TESOL Quarterly, 39*(4), 716-719.

Maley, A., & Duff, A. (1983). *Drama techniques in language learning: A resource book of communication activities for language teachers*. Cambridge, England: Cambridge University Press.

Marinova-Todd, S., Marshall, D. B., & Snow, C. (2000). Three misconceptions about age and L2 learning. *TESOL Quarterly, 34*(1), 9-34.

Martin, J. (1993). Genre and literacy—modelling context in educational linguistics. *Annual Review of Applied Linguistics, 13*, 141-172.

Martino, L., & Johnson, D. W. (1979). Cooperative and individualistic experiences among disabled and normal children. *Journal of Social Psychology, 107*, 177-183.

Masgoret, A., & Gardner, R. (2003). Attitudes, motivation, and second language learning: A meta-analysis of studies conducted by Gardner and Associates. *Language Learning, 53*, 167-210.

Master, P. (1994). The effect of systematic instruction on learning the English article system. In T. Odlin (Ed.), *Perspectives on pedagogical grammar* (pp. 229-252). Cambridge, England: Cambridge University Press.

Master, P. (1995). Consciousness raising and article pedagogy. In D. Belcher & G. Braine (Eds.), *Academic writing in a second language* (pp. 183-204). Norwood, NJ: Ablex.

Matusov, E. (1998). When solo activity is not privileged: Participation and internalization models of development. *Human Development 41*, 326-349.

McDonough, K., & Chaikitmongkol, W. (2007). Teachers' and learners' reactions to a task-based EFL course in Thailand. *TESOL Quarterly, 41*(1), 107-132.

McCarthy, D. (1930). *The language development of the pre-school child*. Minneapolis: University of Minnesota.

McCloskey, M. L., & Thrush, E. (2005). Building a reading scaffold with webtexts. *Essential Teacher, 2*(4), 48-51.

McDonough, K., & Mackey, A. (2008). Syntactic priming and ESL question development. *Studies in Second Language Acquisition, 30*(1), 31-48.

McGroarty, M., & Calderón, M. (2005). Cooperative learning for second language learners: Models, applications, and challenges. In P. Richard-Amato & M.A. Snow (Eds.), *Academic success for English language learners: Strategies for K-12 mainstream teachers* (pp. 174-194). White Plains, NY: Pearson Longman.

McKay, P. (Ed.). (2006). *Planning and teaching creatively within a required curriculum for school-age learners*. Alexandria, VA: Teachers of English to Speakers of Other Languages.

McKay, S. (2000). Teaching English as an international language: Implications for cultural materials in the classroom. *TESOL Journal, 9*(4), 7-11.

McLaughlin, B. (1978). The monitor model: Some methodological considerations. *Language Learning, 28*(2), 309-332.

McLaughlin, B., Rossman, T., & McLeod, B. (1984). Second language learning: An information-processing perspective. *Language Learning, 33*(2), 135-158.

McLoughlin, C., & Oliver, R. (2005). Maximising the language and learning link in computer learning environments. In P. Richard-Amato & M.A. Snow (Eds.), *Academic success for English language learners: Strategies for K-12 mainstream teachers* (pp. 363-374). White Plains, NY: Pearson Longman.

McNamara, M. J., & Deane, D. (1995). Self-assessment activities: toward autonomy in language learning. *TESOL Journal, 5*(1), 17-21.

McNamara, T. (2006). Validity and values: Inferences and generalizability in language testing. In M. Chalhoub-Deville, C. Chapelle, & P. Duff (Eds.). *Inference and generalizability in applied linguistics: Multiple research perspectives* (pp. 27–45). Amsterdam, the Netherlands: John Benjamins.

Mehan, H. (1979). *Learning lessons.* Cambridge, MA: Harvard University.

Mehan, H., Datnow, A., Bratton, E., Tellez, C., Friedlaender, D., & Ngo, T. (1992). *Untracking and college enrollment* (Research Report No. 4). Santa Cruz: University of California. National Center for Research on Cultural Diversity and Second Language Learning.

Mendes Figueiredo, M. (1991). Acquisition of second language pronunciation: The critical period. *CTJ Journal, 24,* 41–47.

Menezes de Souza, L. M. (2005). A change of skin: The grammar of indigenous communities in Brazil. *TESOL Quarterly, 39*(4), 724–728.

Menken, K. (2008). English learners left behind: Standardized testing as language policy. Clevedon, England: Multilingual Matters.

Mohan, B. (1986). *Language and content.* Reading, MA: Addison-Wesley.

Morine-Dershimer, G., Tenenberg, M., & Shuy, R. (1980). *Participant perspectives of classroom discourse. Part II: Why do you ask? Final report.* Washington, DC: National Institute of Education.

Morita, N. (2004). Negotiating participation in SLA communities. *TESOL Quarterly, 38*(4), 573–603.

Morley, J. (1991). The pronunciation component in teaching English to speakers of other languages. *TESOL Quarterly, 25*(3), 481–520.

Morley, J. (2001). Aural comprehension instruction: Principles and practices. In M. Celce-Murcie (Ed.), *Teaching English as a second or foreign language,* (3rd ed., pp. 69–100). Boston: Heinle.

Morley, J., Robinett, B. W., Selinker, L., & Woods, D. (1984). ESL theory and the Fries legacy. *JALT Journal, 6*(2), 171–207.

Morrison, D. M., & Low, G. (1983). Monitoring and the second language learner. In J. C. Richards & R. Schmidt (Eds.), *Language and communication* (pp. 228–250). London: Longmann.

Moskowitz, G. (1978). *Caring and sharing in the foreign language class: A source book on humanistic techniques.* Rowley, MA: Newbury House.

Moskowitz, G. (1981). Effects of humanistic techniques on attitude, cohesiveness, and self-concept on foreign language students. *Modern Language Journal, 65,* 149–157.

Moskowitz, G. (1991). *Caring and sharing in the foreign language class.* Scarborough, Ontario: HarperCollins.

Moskowitz, G. (1999). Enhancing personal development: Humanistic activities at work. In J. Arnold (Ed.), *Affect in language learning.* (pp. 177–193). Cambridge, England: Cambridge University Press.

Moulton, M., & Holmes, V. (1997). Pattern poems: Creative writing for language acquisition. *The Journal of the Imagination in Language Learning, IV,* 84–90.

Moustfa, M. (1989). CI plus the LEA: A long term perspective. *The Reading Teacher, 41*(3), 276–287.

Moyer, A. (1999). Ultimate attainment in L2 phonology. *Studies in Second Language Acquisition, 21*(1), 81–108.

Moyer, A. (2004). *Age, accent and experience in second language acquisition.* Clevedon, England: Multilingual Matters.

Murphey, T. (1992). The discourse of pop songs. *TESOL Quarterly, 26*(4), 770–774.

Murphy, J. M., & Stoller, F. (2001). Sustained-content language teaching: An emerging definition. *TESOL Journal, 10*(2/3), 3–5.

Murray, D. (1982). *Learning by teaching: Selected articles on writing and teaching.* Upper Montclair, NJ: Boynton Cook.

Myles, F., Mitchell, R., & Hooper, J. (1999). Interrogative chunks in French L2: A basis for creative construction? *Studies in Second Language Acquisition, 21,* 49–80.

Naiman, N., Frohlich, M., & Stern, H. H. (1978). *The good language learner.* Toronto: Ontario Institute for Studies in Education.

Nakahama, Y., Tyler, A., & van Lier, L. (2001). Negotiation of meaning in conversational and information gap activities; A comparative discourse analysis. *TESOL Quarterly, 35*(3), 377–406.

Nassaji, H. (2003). L2 vocabulary learning from context: Strategies, knowledge sources, and their relationship with success in L2 lexical inferencing. *TESOL Quarterly, 37*(4), 645–670.

Nation, P. (2000). Learning vocabulary in lexical sets: Dangers and guidelines. *TESOL Journal, 9*(2), 6–10.

Nation, P. (2001). P. (2001). *Teaching and learning vocabulary*. Rowley, MA: Newbury House.

Nation, P. (2005). Teaching and learning vocabulary. In E. Hinkel (Ed.), *Handbook of research in second language teaching and learning* (pp. 581–596). Mahwah, NJ: Lawrence Erlbaum.

Nation, P., & Newton, J. (1997). Teaching vocabulary. In J. Coady & T. Huckin (Eds.), *Second language vocabulary acquisition* (pp. 238–254). Cambridge, England: Cambridge University Press.

Nayar, P. B. (1997). ESL/EFL dichotomy today: Language politics or pragmatics? *TESOL Quarterly, 31*(1), 9–38.

Nelson, G., & Murphy, J. (1993). Peer response groups: Do L2 writers use peer comments in revising their drafts? *TESOL Quarterly, 27*(1), 135–141.

Nelson, P. (2005). Making it happen: From interactive to participatory language teaching (3rd ed.). *Korea TESOL Journal, 6*(1), 133–136.

Nemtchinova, E. (2005). Host teachers' evaluations of nonnative English-speaking teacher trainees—a perspective from the classroom. *TESOL Quarterly, 39*(2), 235–261.

Nessel, D., & Dixon, C. (2008). *Using the language experience approach with English language learners: Strategies for engaging students and developing literacy.* Thousand Oaks, CA: Corwin.

Newman, D., Griffin, P., & Cole, M. (1989). *The construction zone: Working for cognitive change in school.* Cambridge, England: Cambridge University Press.

Newmark, L. (1983). How not to interfere with language learning. In J. Oller Jr. & P. Richard-Amato (Eds.), *Methods that work* (pp. 49–58). Rowley, MA: Newbury House.

Newton, J. (1995). Task-based interaction and incidental vocabulary learning: A case study. *Second Language Research, 11*, 159–177.

Nicholas, H., Lightbown, P., & Spada, N. (2001). Recasts as feedback to language learners. *Language Learning, 51*(4), 719–758.

Nieto, S. (1999). *The light in their eyes: Creating multicultural learning communities*. New York: Teachers College, Columbia University.

Nieto, S. (2000). *Affirming diversity: The sociopolitical context of multicultural education* (3rd ed.). White Plains, NY: Longman.

Nobuyoshi, J., & Ellis, R. (1996). Focused communication tasks and second language acquisition. In T. Hedge & N. Whitney (Eds.), *Power, pedagogy and practice* (pp. 261–270). Oxford, England: Oxford University Press.

Noels, K., Pelletier, L., Clément, R., & Vallerand, R. (2000). Why are you learning a second language? Motivational orientation and self-determination theory. *Language Learning, 50*(1), 57–85.

Norris, J., & Ortega, L. (2000). Effectiveness of L2 instruction: A research synthesis and quantitative meta-analysis. *Language Learning, 50*(4), 417–528.

Norton, B. (1997). Language, identity, and the ownership of English. *TESOL Quarterly, 31*(3), 409–429.

Norton, B. (1998). Rethinking acculturation in second language acquisition. *Prospect: A Journal of Australian TESOL, 13*, 4–19.

Norton, B. (2000). *Identity and language learning: Gender, ethnicity and educational change.* Essex, England: Pearson Education.

Norton, B. (2001). Non-participation, imagined communities and the language classroom. In M. Breen (Ed.), *Learner contributions to language learning: New directions in research* (pp. 159–171). Harlow, England: Longman.

Norton, B., & Pavlenko, A. (2004). Addressing gender in the ESL/EFL classroom. *TESOL Quarterly*, *38*(3), 504–514.

Norton, B., & Toohey, K. (Eds.). (2004). *Critical pedagogies and language learning*. Cambridge, England: Cambridge University Press.

Nunan, D. (1989). *Designing tasks for the communicative classroom*. Cambridge, England: Cambridge University Press.

Nunan, D. (1991). Communicative tasks and the language curriculum. *TESOL Quarterly*, *25*(2), 279–295.

Nunan, D. (2004). *Task-based language teaching*. Cambridge, England: Cambridge University Press.

O'Brien, I., Segalowitz, N., Freed, B., & Collentine, J. (2007). Phonological memory predicts second language oral fluency gains in adults. *Studies in Second Language Acquisition*, *29*(4), 557–582.

Ochs, E., & Schieffelin, B. (1984). Language acquisition and socialization: Three developmental stories and their implications. In R. Shweder & R. Levine (Eds.), *Culture theory: Essays on mind, self and emotion* (pp. 276–320). New York: Cambridge University Press.

Ogle, D. (1986). K–W–L: A teaching model that develops active reading of expository text. *The Reading Teacher*, *39*(4), 564–570.

O'Grady, W. (1999). *Toward a new nativism. Studies in second language acquisition*, *21*(4), 621–633.

Oh, S.-Y. (2001). Two types of input modification and EFL reading comprehension: Simplification versus elaboration. *TESOL Quarterly*, *35*(1), 69–96.

Ohta, A. (2000a). Rethinking interaction in SLA. In J. Lantolf (Ed.), *Sociocultural theory and second language learning* (pp. 51–78). Oxford, England: Oxford University Press.

Ohta, A. (2000b). Rethinking recasts: A learner-centered examination of corrective feedback in the Japanese language classroom. In J. Hall & S. Verplaeste (Eds.), *The construction of second and foreign language learning through classroom instruction* (pp. 47–71). Mahwah, NJ: Lawrence Erlbaum.

O'Keeffe, A., McCarthy, M., & Carter, R. (2007). *From corpus to classroom: Language use and language teaching*. Cambridge, England: Cambridge University Press.

Oller, J. Jr. (1979). *Language tests at school*. London: Longman.

Oller, J. Jr. (1981). Research on the measurements of affective variable: Some remaining questions. In R. Andersen (Ed.), *New dimensions in second language acquisition research* (pp. 14–27). Rowley, MA: Newbury House.

Oller, J. Jr. (1983a). Some working ideas for language teaching. In J. Oller Jr. & P. Richard-Amato (Eds.), *Methods that work* (pp. 3–19). Rowley, MA: Newbury House.

Oller, J. Jr. (1983b). Story writing principles and ESL teaching. *TESOL Quarterly*, *17*(1), 39–53.

Oller, J. Jr., Baca, L., & Vigil, A. (1977). Attitudes and attained proficiency in ESL: A sociolinguistic study of Mexican-Americans in the southwest. *TESOL Quarterly*, *11*(2), 173–183.

Oller, J. Jr., Hudson, A., & Liu, P. (1977). Attitudes and attained proficiency in ESL: A sociolinguistic study of native speakers of Chinese in the United States. *Language Learning*, *27*(1), 1–27.

Oller, J. Jr., & Obrecht, D. (1969). The psycholinguistic principle of informational sequence: An experiment in second-language learning. *International Review of Applied Linguistics in Language Teaching*, *7*(2), 117–123.

Oller, J. Jr., & Richard-Amato, P. (Eds.). (1983). *Methods that work*. Rowley, MA: Newbury House.

Olmedo, I. (1993). Junior historians: Doing oral history with ESL and bilingual students. *TESOL Journal*, *2*(4), 7–10.

Omaggio, A. (2001). *Teaching language in context: Proficiency-oriented instruction* (3rd ed.). Boston: Heinle.

O'Malley, J., & Chamot, A. (1990). *Learning strategies in second language acquisition*. Cambridge, England: Cambridge University Press.

Ortega, L. (1999). Planning and focus on form in L2 oral performance. *Studies in Second Language Acquisition, 21*(1), 108–148.

Ortega, L., & Byrnes, H. (Eds.). (2008). *The longitudinal study of advanced L2 capacities.* New York: Taylor & Francis/Psychology Press.

Ortega, L., & Iberri-Shea, G. (2005). Longitudinal research in second language acquisition: Recent trends and future directions. *Annual Review of Applied Linguistics, 25,* 26–45.

Oxford, R. (1990). *Language learning strategies: What every teacher should know.* New York: Newbury House.

Oxford, R. (1999). Anxiety and the language learner: New insights. In J. Arnold (Ed.), *Affect and language learning* (pp. 58–67). Cambridge, England: Cambridge University Press.

Oxford, R., & Cohen, A. (1992). Language learning strategies: Crucial issues of concept and classification. *Allied Language Learning, 3*(1), 1–35.

Oxford, R., Ehrman, M., & Lavine, R. (1991). Style wars: Teacher–student style conflicts in the language classroom. In S. Magnan (Ed.), *Challenges in the 1990s for college foreign language programs* (pp. 1–25). Boston: Heinle.

Pakir, A. (2005). Applied linguistics proper? Relocation, reorientation, and realignment. *TESOL Quarterly, 39*(4), 720–724.

Pallotti, G. (2007). An operational definition of the emergence criterion. *Applied Linguistics, 28*(3), 361–382.

Palmer, A., & Christison, M. (2007). *Seeking the heart of teaching.* Ann Arbor: University of Michigan Press.

Palmer, H., & Palmer, D. (1925). *English through actions.* London: Longman Green.

Panova, I., & Lyster, R. (2002). Patterns of corrective feedback and uptake in an adult ESL classroom. *TESOL Quarterly, 36*(4), 573–596.

Paran, A. (Ed.). (2006). *Literature in language teaching and learning.* Alexandria, VA: Teachers of English to Speakers of Other Languages.

Parry, K. (1996). Culture, literacy, and L2 reading. *TESOL Quarterly, 30*(4), 665–692.

Pavesi, M. (1984). The acquisition of relative clauses in a formal and in an informal setting: Further evidence in support of the markedness hypothesis. In D. Singleton & D. Little (Eds.), *Language learning in formal and informal contexts* (pp. 151–163). Dublin: Irish Association for Applied Linguistics.

Pavlenko, A., & Lantolf, J. (2000). Second language learning as participation and the (re)construction of selves. In J. Lantolf (Ed.), *Sociocultural theory and second language learning* (pp. 155–177). Oxford, England: Oxford University Press.

Pennington, M. (2003). The impact of the computer in second language writing. In B. Kroll (Ed.), *Exploring the dynamics of second language writing* (pp. 287–309). Cambridge, England: Cambridge University Press.

Pennington, M., & Ellis, N. (2000). Cantonese speakers' memory for English sentences with prosodic clues. *The Modern Language Journal, 84,* 372–389.

Pennycook, A. (1989). The concept of method, interested knowledge, and the politics of language teaching. *TESOL Quarterly, 23*(4), 589–618.

Pennycook, A. (1996). TESOL and critical literacies: Modern, post, or neo? *TESOL Quarterly, 30*(1), 163–171.

Pennycook, A. (1999). Introduction: Critical approaches to TESOL. *TESOL Quarterly, 33*(3), 329–348.

Pennycook, A. (2001). *Critical applied linguistics: A critical introduction.* Mahwah, NJ: Lawrence Erlbaum.

Peyton, J. K., & Staton, J. (1992). *Dialogue journal writing with non-native English speakers: An instructional packet for teachers and workshop leaders.* Alexandria, VA: Teachers of English to Speakers of Other Languages.

Phillips, S. (1999). *Drama with children*. Oxford, England: Oxford University Press.

Phillipson, R. (1992). *Linguistic imperialism*. Oxford, England: Oxford University Press.

Philp, J. (2003). Constraints on "noticing the gap": Nonnative speakers' noticing of recasts in NS–NNS interaction. *Studies in Second Language Acquisition, 25*(1), 99–126.

Phinney, J. S. (1993). A three-stage model of ethnic identity development in adolescence. In M. E. Bernal & G. P. Knight (Eds.), *Ethnic identity: Formation and transmission among Hispanics and other minorities* (pp. 61–79). Albany: State University of New York Press.

Piaget, J. (1979). *The development of thought*. New York: Viking.

Pica, T. (1994). Research on negotiation: What does it reveal about second-language learning conditions, processes, and outcomes? *Language Learning, 44*(4), 493–527.

Pica, T., & Doughty, C. (1985). Input and interaction in the communicative language classroom: A comparison of teacher-fronted and group activities. In S. Gass & C. Madden (Eds.), *Input in second language acquisition* (pp. 115–132). Rowley, MA: Newbury House.

Pienemann, M. (1984). Psychological constraints on the teachability of languages. *Studies in Second Language Acquisition, 6*(2), 186–214.

Pienemann, M. (1988). Determining the influence of instruction on L2 speech processing. *AILA Review, 5*, 40–72.

Pierce, L. V., & O'Malley, J. M. (1992). *Performance and portfolio assessment for language minority students*. Washington, DC: National Clearinghouse for Bilingual Education.

Pinker, S. (1994). *The language instinct: How the mind creates language*. New York: William Morrow.

Pittaway, D. (2004). Investment and second language acquisition. *Critical Inquiry in Language Studies: An International Journal, 1*(4), 203–218.

Platt, E., Harper, C., & Mendoza, M. (2003). Dueling philosophies: Inclusion or separation for Florida's English language learners? *TESOL Quarterly, 37*(1), 105–133.

Polio, C., & Gass, S. (1998). The role of interaction in native speaker comprehension of non-native speaker speech. *Modern Language Journal, 82*, 308–319.

Pollock, C. (1982). *Communicate what you mean*. Englewood Cliffs, NJ: Prentice Hall.

Poole, D. (1992). Language socialization in the second-language classroom. *Language Learning 42*(4), 593–616.

Porter, P. (1986). How learners talk to each other: Input and interaction in task-centered discussions. In R. Day (Ed.), *Talking to learn: Conversation in second language acquisition* (pp. 200–222). Rowley, MA: Newbury House.

Porter, R. (1990). *Forked tongue: The politics of bilingual education* (2nd ed.). Scranton, PA: Basic Books.

Postovsky, V. (1977). Why not start speaking later? In M. Burt, H. Dulay, & M. Finocchiaro (Eds.), *Viewpoints on ESL* (pp. 17–26). New York: Regents.

Prabhu, N. S. (1990). There is no best method—Why? *TESOL Quarterly, 24*(2), 161–176.

PreK–12 English language proficiency standards. (2006). Alexandria, VA: Teachers of English to Speakers of Other Languages.

Price, M. (1991). The subjective experience of foreign language anxiety interviews with high-anxious students. In E. Horwitz & D. Young (Eds.), *Language anxiety: From theory and research to classroom implications* (pp. 101–108). Englewood Cliffs, NJ: Prentice Hall.

Qi, D., & Lapkin, S. (2001). Exploring the role of noticing in a three-stage second language writing task. *Journal of Second Language Writing, 10*, 277–303.

Ramírez, J., Yuen, S., & Ramey, D. (1991). *Longitudinal study of structured English immersion strategy, early-exit, and late-exit transitional bilingual education programs for language minority children. Executive summary: Final report*. San Mateo, CA: Aguirre International.

Raths, L., Merrill, H., & Simon, S. (1966). *Values and teaching*. Columbus, OH: Merrill.

Ravem, R. (1978). Two Norwegian children's acquisition of English syntax. In E. Hatch (Ed.), *Second language acquisition: A book of readings* (pp. 148–154). Rowley, MA: Newbury House.

Read, J. (2004). Research in teaching vocabulary. *Annual Review of Applied Linguistics, 24,* 146–161.

Readence, J., Bean, T., & Baldwin, R. (2005). Language, culture, diversity, and the reading/writing process. In P. Richard-Amato & M.A. Snow (Eds.), *Academic success for English language learners: Strategies for K–12 mainstream teachers* (pp. 150–173). White Plains, NY: Pearson Longman.

Reber, A., Walkenfeld, F., & Hernstadt, R. (1991). Implicit and explicit learning: Individual differences and IQ. *Journal of Experimental Psychology: Learning, Memory, and Cognition, 17,* 888–896.

Reid, J. (1992). Helping students write for an academic audience. In P. Richard-Amato & M.A. Snow (Eds.), *The multicultural classroom: Readings for content-area teachers* (pp. 210–221). White Plains, NY: Longman.

Reid, J. (2001). Writing. In R. Carter & D. Nunan (Eds.), *The Cambridge guide to teaching English to speakers of other languages* (pp. 28–33). Cambridge, England: Cambridge University Press.

Reigel, D. (2008). Positive feedback in pairwork and its association with ESL course level promotion. *TESOL Quarterly, 42*(1), 79–98.

Ricento, T. (2005). Considerations of identity in L2 learning. In E. Hinkel (Ed.), *Handbook of research in second language teaching and learning* (pp. 895–910). Mahwah, NJ: Lawrence Erlbaum.

Richard-Amato, P. (1983). ESL in Colorado's Jefferson County Schools. In J. Oller Jr. & P. Richard-Amato (Eds.), *Methods that work* (pp. 393–397). Rowley, MA: Newbury House.

Richard-Amato, P. (1984). *Teacher talk in the classroom: Native and foreigner.* Unpublished doctoral dissertation, University of New Mexico, Albuquerque.

Richard-Amato, P. (1988). *Making it happen: Interaction in the second language classroom.* White Plains, NY: Longman.

Richard-Amato, P. (1990). *Reading in the content areas: An interactive approach for international students.* White Plains, NY: Longman.

Richard-Amato, P. (1992a). Peer teachers: The neglected resource. In P. Richard-Amato & M. A. Snow (Eds.), *The multicultural classroom: Readings for content-area teachers* (pp. 271–284). White Plains, NY: Longman.

Richard-Amato, P. (1992b, July). Using reaction dialogues to develop second-language writing skills. Keynote speech at the TESOL Summer Institute, Comenius University, Bratislava, Slovakia.

Richard-Amato, P. (1993a, April). *An interactive approach to reading in a second language.* Paper presented at the 27th Annual Convention of TESOL, Atlanta, GA.

Richard-Amato, P. (1993b). *Exploring themes.* Reading, MA: Addison-Wesley.

Richard-Amato, P. (1995). The natural approach: How it is evolving. In P. Hashemipour, R. Maldonado, & M. VanNaerssen (Eds.), *Studies in language learning and Spanish linguistics in honor of Tracy D. Terrell* (pp. 70–91). New York: McGraw-Hill.

Richard-Amato, P. (1996a). *Making it happen: Interaction in the second language classroom,* (2nd ed.). White Plains, NY: Longman.

Richard-Amato, P. (1996b, November). *Until I saw the sea: Creating heightened awareness in language learners.* Plenary presented at the Puerto Rico TESOL 23rd Annual Convention and Fourth Central American and Caribbean Regional TESOL Conference, Ponce, Puerto Rico.

Richard-Amato, P. (1997). Affect and related factors in second and foreign language acquisition. In *TESOL's voices of experience series.* Alexandria, VA: Teachers of English to Speakers of Other Languages.

Richard-Amato, P. (1998). *World views: Multicultural literature for critical writers, readers, and thinkers.* Boston: Heinle.

Richard-Amato, P. (2001, April). *Sharing power: Rethinking the teacher's role*. Plenary presented at the 32nd Annual CATESOL Conference, Ontario, CA.

Richard-Amato, P. (2002). Sharing power in the ESL classroom. *ESL Magazine*, January/February, 16–18.

Richard-Amato, P. (2003). *Making it happen: From interactive to participatory language teaching* (3rd ed.). White Plains, NY: Pearson Longman.

Richard-Amato, P., & Hansen, W. A. (1995). *Worlds together: A journey into multi-cultural literature*, Reading, MA: Addison-Wesley.

Richard-Amato, P., & Hansen, W. A. (1995). *Worlds together: A journey into multi-cultural literature: Teacher's resource book*, Reading, MA: Addison-Wesley.

Richard-Amato, P., & Lucero, R. (1980). *Foreigner talk strategies in the ESL classroom.*, University of New Mexico, TESOL Institute.

Richard-Amato, P., & Snow, M. A. (Eds.). (1992). *The multicultural classroom: Readings for content-area teachers*. White Plains, NY: Longman.

Richard-Amato, P., & Snow, M. A. (Eds.). (2005a). *Academic success for English language learners: Strategies for K–12 mainstream teachers*. White Plains, NY: Pearson Longman.

Richard-Amato, P., & Snow, M. A. (2005b). Instructional strategies for K–12 mainstream teachers. In P. Richard-Amato & M. A. Snow (Eds.), *Academic success for English language learners: Strategies for K–12 mainstream teachers* (pp. 197–223). White Plains, NY: Pearson Longman.

Richards, J. C. (1991). Content knowledge and instructional practice in second-language teacher education. In J. Alatis (Ed.), *Georgetown University Round Table on Languages and Linguistics 1991. Linguistics and language pedagogy: The state of the art* (pp. 76–99). Washington, DC: Georgetown University.

Richards, J. C. (1998). *Beyond training*: Perspectives on Language Teacher Education. New York: Cambridge University Press.

Richards, J. C., & Lockhart, C. (1996). *Reflective teaching in second language classrooms*. New York: Cambridge University Press.

Richards, J. C., & Rodgers, T. (2001). *Approaches and methods in language teaching: A description and analysis* (2nd ed.). New York: Cambridge University Press.

Riggenbach, H. (1993). *Discourse analysis and spoken language instruction*. Paper presented at the TESOL Institute, San Bernardino, CA.

Rivers, W. (Ed.). (1987). *Interactive language teaching*. New York: Cambridge University Press.

Roberts, M. (1995). Awareness and the efficacy of error correction. In R. Schmidt (Ed.), *Attention and awareness in foreign language learning* (pp. 163–182). Honolulu: University of Hawaiʻi Press.

Robinson, P. (2001). Individual differences, cognitive abilities, aptitude complexes and learning conditions in second language acquisition. *Second Language Research, 17*(4), 368–392.

Robinson, P. (2005). Cognitive abilities for implicit, explicit, and incidental L2 learning. *Studies in Second Language Acquisition, 27*(2), 235–268.

Rodgers, T. (1978). Strategies for individualized language learning and teaching. In J. C. Richards (Ed.), *Understanding second and foreign language learning* (pp. 251–273). Rowley, MA: Newbury House.

Roebuck, R. (2000). Subjects speak out: How learners position themselves in a psycholinguistic task. In J. Lantolf (Ed.), *Sociocultural theory and second language learning* (pp. 79–95). Oxford, England: Oxford University Press.

Rogoff, B. (1990). *Apprenticeship in thinking: Cognitive development in social context*. New York: Oxford University Press.

Rosa, E., & O'Neill, M. (1999). Explicitness, intake, and the issue of awareness. *Studies in Second Language Acquisition, 21*, 511–556.

Rose, M. (1983). Remedial writing courses: A critique and a proposal. *College English, 45*, 109–128.

Rosenblatt, L. (1985). Viewpoints: Transaction versus interaction, a terminal rescue operation. *Research in the Teaching of English*, *19*(1), 96–107.

Rost, M. (2005). L2 listening. In E. Hinkel (Ed.), *Handbook of research in second language teaching and learning* (pp. 503–528). Mahwah, NJ: Lawrence Erlbaum.

Rubin, J. (1975). What the "good language learner" can teach us. *TESOL Quarterly*, *9*(1), 41–51.

Rutherford, W., & Sharwood-Smith, M. (1988). *Grammar and second language teaching*. New York: Newbury House.

Sachs, R., & Polio, C. (2007). Learners' uses of two types of written feedback on a L2 writing revision task. *Studies in Second Language Acquisition*, *29*(1), 67–100.

Saito, Y., Horwitz, E., & Garza, T. (1999). Foreign language reading anxiety. *Modern Language Journal*, *83*(2), 202–218.

Sanaoui, R. (1995). Adult learners' approaches to learning vocabulary in second languages. *Modern Language Journal*, *79*(1), 15–28.

Santiago, R. (1997). Imagination in the teaching of reading: A descriptive analysis. *The Journal of the Imagination in Language Teaching*, *IV*, 74–78.

Saussure, F. (1959). *Cours de linguistique générale*. New York: McGraw-Hill.

Savignon, S. (1983). *Communicative competence: Theory and classroom practice: Texts and contexts in second language learning*. Reading, MA: Addison-Wesley.

Savignon, S. (1991). Communicative language teaching: State of the art. *TESOL Quarterly*, *25*(2), 261–277.

Savignon, S. (1997). *Communicative competence: Theory and classroom practice*, (2nd ed.). New York: McGraw-Hill.

Savignon, S. (2005). Communicative language teaching: Strategies and goals. In E. Hinkel (Ed.), *Handbook of research in second language teaching and learning* (pp. 635–651). Mahwah, NJ: Lawrence Erlbaum.

Saville-Troike, M. (1976). *Foundations for teaching ESL*. Englewood Cliffs, NJ: Prentice Hall.

Scarcella, R. (1983). Sociodrama for social interaction. In J. Oller Jr. & P. Richard-Amato (Eds.), *Methods that work* (pp. 239–245). Rowley, MA: Newbury House.

Scarcella, R. (1990). *Teaching language minority students in the multicultural classroom*. Englewood Cliffs, NJ: Prentice Hall.

Scarcella, R., & Oxford, R. (1992). *The tapestry of language learning: The individual in the communicative classroom*. Boston: Heinle.

Schachter, J. (1974). An error in error analysis. *Language Learning*, *24*(2), 205–214.

Schachter, J. (1990). On the issue of completeness in second language acquisition. *Second Language Research*, *6*(2), 93–124.

Schank, R., & Abelson, R. (1977). *Scripts, plans, goals, and understanding*. Mahwah, NJ: Lawrence Erlbaum.

Schmenk, B. (2004). Language learning: A feminine domain? The role of stereotyping in constructing gendered learner identities. *TESOL Quarterly*, *38*(3), 514–524.

Schmidt, R. (1990). The role of consciousness raising in second language learning. *Applied Linguistics*, *11*(2), 129–158.

Schmidt, R. (1993). Awareness and second language acquisition. *Annual Review of Applied Linguistics*, *13*, 206–226.

Schmidt, R. (1994). Implicit learning and the cognitive unconscious: Of artificial grammars and SLA. In N. C. Ellis (Ed.), *Implicit and explicit learning of language* (pp. 165–210). San Diego, CA: Academic Press.

Schmidt, R. (2001). Attention. In P. Robinson (Ed.), *Cognition and second language instruction* (pp. 3–32). New York: Cambridge University Press.

Schmitt, N. (2000). *Vocabulary in language teaching*. Cambridge, England: Cambridge University Press.

Schmitt, N. (Ed.). (2004). *Formulaic sequences in action: Acquisition, processing and use*. Philadelphia: John Benjamins.

Schmitt, N., & Carter, R. (2004). Formulaic sequences in action: An introduction. In N. Schmitt (Ed.), *Formulaic sequences: Acquisition, processing and use* (pp. 1–22). Philadelphia: John Benjamins.

Schneider, L. (1997). How to turn your ESL lesson into a computer assisted language learning (CALL) lesson. *CATESOL News*, December, 12.

Schoenberg, I. (1997). *Talk about values: Conversation skills for intermediate students*. White Plains, NY: Longman.

Schumann, J. (1978a). The acculturation model for second-language acquisition. In R. Gingras (Ed.), *Second language acquisition and foreign language teaching* (pp. 27–50). Arlington, VA: Center for Applied Linguistics.

Schumann, J. (1978b). *The pidginization process: A model for second language learning*. Rowley, MA: Newbury House.

Schumann, J. (1979). Lecture presented at the First TESOL Institute, University of California, Los Angeles.

Schumann, J. (1980). Affective factors and the problem of age in second language acquisition. In K. Croft (Ed.), *Readings in ESL* (pp. 222–247). Cambridge, MA: Winthrop.

Schumann, J. (1997). *The neurobiology of affect in language*. Malden, MA: Blackwell.

Scovel, T. (1988). *A time to speak. A psycholinguist inquiry into the critical period for human speech*. Rowley, MA: Newbury House.

Segalowitz, N. (2003). Automaticity and second languages. In C. Doughty & M. Long (Eds.), *The handbook of second language acquisition* (pp. 382–408). Malden, MA: Blackwell.

Siedlhofer, B. (2005). Pronunciation. In R. Carter & D. Nunan, D. (Eds.), *The Cambridge guide to teaching English to speakers of other languages* (pp. 56–65). Cambridge, England: Cambridge University Press.

Seliger, H. (1977). Does practice make perfect? A study of interaction patterns and L2 competence. *Language Learning, 27*(2), 263–278.

Selinker, L. (1972). Interlanguage. *International Review of Applied Linguistics, 10*, 209–230.

Semke, H. (1984). The effects of the red pen. *Foreign Language Annals, 17*, 195–202.

Shaaban, K., & Ghaith, G. (2000). Student motivation to learn English as a foreign language. *Foreign Language Annals, 33*, 632–642.

Shaftel, F., & Shaftel, G. (1967). *Role-playing for social values*. Englewood Cliffs, NJ: Prentice Hall.

Shameem, N., & Tickoo, M. (Eds.). (1999). *New ways in using communicative games in language teaching*. Alexandria, VA: Teachers of English to Speakers of Other Languages.

Sharwood-Smith, M. (1981). Consciousness-raising and the second language learner. *Applied Linguistics, 2*, 159–169.

Sharwood-Smith, M., & Truscott, J. (2005). Stages or continua in second language acquisition: A MOGUL solution. *Applied Linguistics, 26*, 219–240.

Sheen, Y. (2006). Exploring the relationship between characteristics of recasts and learner uptake. *Language Teaching Research, 10*, 361–392.

Sheen, Y. (2007). The effect of focused written corrective feedback and language aptitude on ESL learners' acquisition of articles. *TESOL Quarterly, 41*(2), 255–283.

Shih, M. (1992). Beyond comprehension exercises in the ESL academic reading class. *TESOL Quarterly, 26*(2), 289–318.

Shin, S. (2005). *Developing in two languages: Korean American children in America*. Clevedon, England: Multilingual Matters.

Shohamy, E. (1998). Critical language testing and beyond. *Studies in Educational Evaluation, 24*(4), 331–345.

Shohamy, E. (2001). *The power of tests: The critical perspective on the uses of language tests*. Harlow, England: Pearson Education.

Shohamy, E. (2004). Assessment in multicultural societies: Applying democratic principles and practices to language testing. In B. Norton & K. Toohey (Eds.), *Critical pedagogies and language learning* (pp. 72–92). Cambridge, England: Cambridge University Press.

Shulman, J., & Mesa-Bains (Eds.). (1993). *Diversity in the classroom: A casebook for teachers and teacher educators*. Hillsdale, NJ: Lawrence Erlbaum.

Simon, S., Howe, L., & Kirschenbaum, H. (1992). *Values clarification* (2nd ed.). New York: Hart.

Sinclair, J., & Coulthard, M. (1975). *Toward an analysis of discourse: The English used by teachers and pupils*. London: Oxford University Press.

Skelton, E. (2003, June). *Total physical response storytelling for English language learners and content area lessons.* Paper presented at the Secondary ESL Leadership and Advocacy Institute, University of Colorado, Denver.

Skinner, B. F. (1957). *Verbal behavior*. New York: Appleton-Century-Crofts.

Slavin, R. (1983). When does cooperative learning increase student achievement? *Psychological Bulletin, 94*(3), 429–445.

Slobin, D. (1971). *Psycholinguistics*. Glenview, IL: Scott Foresman.

Slobin, D. (1973). Cognitive prerequisites for the development of grammar. In C. Ferguson & D. Slobin (Eds.), *Studies of child language development* (pp. 175–208). New York: Holt, Rinehart & Winston.

Smoke, T. (1998). *Adult ESL: Politics, pedagogy, and participation in classroom and community*. Mahwah, NJ: Lawrence Erlbaum.

Smolen, L., Newman, C., Wathen, T., & Lee, D. (1995). Developing student self- assessment strategies. *TESOL Journal, 5*(1), 22–27.

Snow, M. A. (1997). Teaching academic literacy skills: Discipline faculty take responsibility. In M. A. Snow & Brinton, D. M. (Eds.), *The content-based classroom: Perspectives on integrating language and content* (pp. 290–304). White Plains, NY: Longman.

Snow, M. A. (2005). Integrated language and content instruction. In E. Hinkel (Ed.), *Handbook of research in second language teaching and learning* (pp. 693–712). Mahwah, NJ: Lawrence Erlbaum.

Snow, M. A., & Brinton, D. (Eds.). (1997). *The content-based classroom: Perspectives on integrating language and content*. White Plains, NY: Pearson Education.

Snow, M. A., & Kamhi-Stein, L. D. (2002). Teaching and learning academic literacy through Project LEAP. In J. Crandall & D. Kaufman (Eds.), *Case studies in TESOL practice: Content-based instruction* (pp. 169–181). Alexandria, VA: Teachers of English to Speakers of Other Languages.

Snow, M. A., Met, M., & Genesee, F. (1989). A conceptual framework for the integration of language and content in second/foreign language instruction. *TESOL Quarterly, 23*(2), 201–217.

Sorace, A. (2003). Near-nativeness. In C. Doughty & M. Long (Eds.), *Handbook of second language acquisition* (pp. 130–151). Malden, MA: Blackwell.

Sorenson, A. (1967). Multilingualism in the northwest Amazon. *American Anthropologist, 69*, 670–684.

Spada, N., & Lightbown, P. (2008). Form-focused instruction: Isolated or Integrated? *TESOL Quarterly, 42*(2), 181–207.

Spolsky, B. (1981). Some ethical questions about language testing. In C. Klein-Braley & D. K. Stevenson (Eds.), *Practice and problems in language testing* (pp. 5–21). Frankfurt, Germany: Peter D. Lang.

Sridhar, S. N. (1994). A reality check for SLA theories. *TESOL Quarterly, 28*(4), 800–803.

Srole, L. (1956). Social integration and certain corollaries: An exploration study. *American Sociological Review, 21*, 709–716.

Standards for foreign language learning in the 21st century. (2006). Alexandria, VA: National Standards in Foreign Language Education Project.

Stansfield, C. (1993). Ethics, standards, and professionalism in language testing. *Issues in Applied Linguistics, 4*(2), 15–30.

Stauble, A. (1980). Acculturation and second language acquisition. In R. Scarcella & S. Krashen. (Eds.), *Research in second language acquisition* (pp. 43–50). Rowley, MA: Newbury House.

Steinbeck, J. (1947). *The pearl.* New York: Viking.

Stern, A. (2001). *Tales from many lands.* New York: McGraw-Hill/Contemporary.

Stern, S. (1983). Why drama works: A psycholinguistic perspective. In J. Oller Jr. & P. Richard-Amato (Eds.), *Methods that work* (pp. 207–225). Rowley, MA: Newbury House.

Stevens, R. A., Butler, F. A., & Castellon-Wellington, M. (2000). *Academic language and content assessment: Measuring the progress of ELLs.* Los Angeles: University of California, National Center for Research on Evaluation, Standards, and Student Testing.

Stevick, E. (1976). Teachers of English as an alien language. In J. Fanselow & R. Crymes (Eds.), *On TESOL '76* (pp. 225–228). Washington, DC: Teachers of English to Students of Other Languages.

Stevick, E. (1980). *Teaching languages: A way and ways.* Rowley, MA: Newbury House.

Strauss, C., & Quinn, N. (1997). *A cognitive theory of cultural meaning.* Cambridge, England: Cambridge University Press.

Stoller, F. (2004). Content-based instruction: Perspectives on curriculum planning. *Annual Review of Applied Linguistics, 24*, 261–283.

Stoynoff, S., & Chapelle, C. (2005). *ESOL tests and testing.* Alexandria, VA: Teachers of English to Speakers of Other Languages.

Sunderman, G., & Schwartz, A. (2008). Using cognates to investigate cross-language competition in second language processing. *TESOL Quarterly, 42*(3), 527–536.

Sutherland, K. (1979). Accuracy vs. fluency in the second language classroom. *CATESOL Occasional Papers,* No. 5, 25–29.

Sutherland, K. (1981). *English alfa* (Teacher's ed.). Boston: Houghton Mifflin.

Swain, M. (1975). Writing skills of grade 3 French immersion pupils. *Working Papers on Bilingualism, 7*, 1–38.

Swain, M. (1985). Communicative competence: Some roles of comprehensible input and comprehensible output in its development. In S. Gass & C. Madden (Eds.). (1985), *Input in second language acquisition* (pp. 235–253). Rowley, MA: Newbury House.

Swain, M. (1993). The output hypothesis: Just speaking and writing aren't enough. *The Canadian Modern Language Review, 50*, 158–164.

Swain, M. (1995). Three functions of output in second language learning. In G. Cook & B. Seidlhofer (Eds.), *Principles and practice in applied linguistics: Studies in honour of H. G. Widdowson* (pp. 125–144). Oxford, England: Oxford University Press.

Swain, M. (1998). Focus on form through conscious reflection. In C. Doughty & J. Williams (Eds.), *Focus on form in classroom second language acquisition* (pp. 64–81). Cambridge, England: Cambridge University Press.

Swain, M. (2000). The output hypothesis and beyond: Mediating acquisition through collaborative dialogue. In J. Lantolf (Ed.), *Sociocultural theory and second language learning* (97–114). Oxford, England: Oxford University Press.

Swain, M. (2005). The output hypothesis: Theory and research. In E. Hinkel (Ed.), *Handbook of research in second language teaching and learning* (pp. 471–483). Mahwah, NJ: Lawrence Erlbaum.

Swain, M., Brooks, L., & Tocalli-Beller, A. (2002). Peer–peer dialogue as a means of second language learning. *Annual Review of Applied Linguistics, 22*, 171–185.

Swain, M., Lapkin, S., & Barik, H. (1976). The cloze test as a measure of second language proficiency for young children. *Working Papers on Bilingualism, 11*, 32–43.

Szmrecsanyi, B. (2005). Creatures of habit: A corpus linguistic analysis of persistence in spoken English. *Corpus Linguistics and Linguistic Theory, 1*, 113–149.

Takahashi, N., & Frauman-Prickel, M. (1999). *Action English pictures: Activities for total physical response.* Burlingame, CA: Alta Book Center.

Tarone, E. (2002). Frequency effects, noticing, and creativity: Factors in a variationist interlanguage framework. *Studies in Second Language Acquisition, 24*(2), 287–296.

Taylor, B. (1980). Adult language learning strategies and their pedagogical implications. In K. Croft (Ed.), *Readings in English as a second language* (pp. 144–152). Cambridge, MA: Winthrop.

Taylor, B. (1983). Teaching ESL: Incorporating a communicative, student-centered component. *TESOL Quarterly, 17*(1), 69–87.

Technology standards framework. (2008). Alexandria, VA: Teachers of English to Speakers of Other Languages.

Terrell, T. (1983). The natural approach to language teaching: An update. In J. Oller Jr. & P. Richard-Amato (Eds.), *Methods that work* (pp. 267–283). Rowley, MA: Newbury House.

Terrell, T. (1991). The role of grammar instruction in a communicative approach. *Modern Language Journal, 75,* 52–63.

Tharp, R., Estrada, P., Dalton, S., & Yamauchi, L. (2000). *Teaching transformed: Achieving excellence, fairness, inclusion, and harmony.* Boulder, CO: Westview Press.

Tharp, R., & Gallimore, R. (1988). *Rousing minds to life: Teaching, learning, and schooling in social context.* Cambridge, England: Cambridge University Press.

The Random House book of poetry for children. (1983). New York: Random House.

Thomas, M. (1998). Programmatic ahistoricity in second language acquisition theory. *Studies in Second Language Acquisition, 20*(3), 387–405.

Thomas, W., & Collier, V. (1996). Language-minority student achievement program effectiveness. *NABE News, 19*(6), 33–35.

Thomas, W., & Collier, V. (1998). Two languages are better than one. *Educational Leadership, 55*(4), 23–26.

Thomas, W., & Collier, V. (2002). *A national study of school effectiveness for language minority students' long-term academic achievement.* Santa Cruz, CA: Center for Research on Education, Diversity and Excellence.

Thonis, E. (1984). Reading instruction for language minority students. In California State Department of Education, *Schooling and language minority students: A theoretical framework* (pp. 147–181). Los Angeles: California State University, Evaluation, Dissemination and Assessment Center.

Thorne, S. (2000). Second language acquisition theory and the truth(s) about relativity. In J. Lantolf (Ed.), *Sociocultural theory and second language learning* (pp. 219–243). Oxford, England: Oxford University Press.

Thorne, S., & Black, R. (2007). Language and literacy development in computer-mediated contexts and communities. *Annual Review of Applied Linguistics, 27,* 133–160.

Tinker Sachs, G., & Ho, B. (2007). *ESL/EFL cases: Contexts for teacher professional discussions.* Hong Kong: City University of Hong Kong Press.

Tinkham, T. (1997). The effects of semantic and thematic clustering on the learning of second language vocabulary. *Second Language Research, 13*(2), 138–163.

Tinto, V. (1997). Enhancing learning via community. *Thought and Action, 13,* 53–58.

Tollefson, J. W. (2000). Policy and ideology in the spread of English. In J. K. Hall & W. Eggington (Eds.), *The sociopolitics of English language teaching* (pp. 7–21). Clevedon, England: Multilingual Matters.

Tomaselli, A., & Schwartz, B. (1990). Analyzing the acquisition stages of negation in L2 German: Support for UG in adult SLA. *Second Language Research, 6*(1), 1–38.

Tomlinson, B. (2001). Materials development. In R. Carter & D. Nunan (Eds.). *The Cambridge guide to teaching English to speakers of other languages* (pp. 66–71). Cambridge, England: Cambridge University Press.

Toohey, K. (2000). *Learning English at school: Identity, social relations and classroom practice.* Clevedon, England: Multilingual Matters.

Toth, A. (2005). What not to teach when teaching pronunciation. *CATESOL Journal, 17*(1), 125–131.

Towell, R., & Hawkins, R. (1994). *Approaches to second language acquisition.* Clevedon, England: Multilingual Matters.

Tsui, A., & Ng, M. (2000). Do secondary L2 writers benefit from peer comments? *Journal of Second Language Writing, 9*(2), 147–170.

Underhill, A. (1999). Facilitation in language teaching. In J. Arnold (Ed.), *Affect and language learning* (pp. 125–141). Cambridge, England: Cambridge University Press.

Ur, P. (1984). *Teaching listening comprehension.* Cambridge, England: Cambridge University Press.

Valdez Pierce, L. (2003). Teaching to the test: Best practice? *TESOL Matters, 13*(3), 1, 6.

Valette, R. (1997). National standards and the role of imagination in foreign language learning. *The Journal of the Imagination in Language Learning, IV,* 18–25.

Valsiner, J. (2001). Process structure of semiotic mediation in human development. *Human Development, 44,* 84–97.

Van Allen, R., & Allen, C. (1967). *Language experience activities.* Boston: Houghton Mifflin.

van Lier, L. (1996). *Interaction in the language curriculum: Awareness, autonomy, and authenticity.* London: Longman.

van Lier, L. (2000). From input to affordance: Social-interactive learning from an ecological perspective. In J. Lantolf (Ed.), *Sociocultural theory and second language learning* (pp. 245–259). Oxford, England: Oxford University Press.

Vann, R., Meyer, D., & Lorenz, F. (1984). Error gravity: A study of faculty opinions of ESL errors. *TESOL Quarterly, 18*(4), 427–440.

VanPatten, B. (1986). Second language acquisition research and the learning/teaching of Spanish: Some research findings and their implications. *Hispania, 69,* 202–216.

VanPatten, B. (1996). *Input processing and grammar instruction: Theory and research.* Norwood, NJ: Ablex.

Vygotsky, L. (1962). *Thought and language.* Cambridge, MA: MIT Press.

Vygotsky, L. (1978). *Mind in society.* Cambridge, MA: Harvard University Press.

Wagner-Gough, J., & Hatch, E. (1975). The importance of input data in second-language acquisition studies. *Language Learning, 25*(2), 297–308.

Wainryb, R. (2003). *Stories: Narrative activities for the language classroom.* New York: Cambridge University Press.

Walker, L. (2001). Negotiation syllabi in the adult ESL Classroom. *CATESOL News, 32*(4), 5–7.

Walker, R. (2005). Using student-produced recordings with monolingual groups to provide effective, individualized pronunciation practice. *TESOL Quarterly, 39*(3), 550–558.

Wallace, C. (1992). Critical literacy awareness in the EFL classroom. In N. Fairclough (Ed.), *Critical language awareness* (pp. 59–92). London: Longman.

Wallace, M. (1998). *Action research for language teachers.* Cambridge, England: Cambridge University Press.

Wallerstein, N. (1983). *Language and culture in conflict: Problem posing in the ESL classroom.* Reading, MA: Addison-Wesley.

Walsh, S. (2002). Construction and obstruction: Talk and learner involvement in the EFL classroom. *Language Teaching Research, 6*(1), 3–24.

Ware, P. (2005). Maximizing face-to-face and online interaction in the computer lab. *Essential Teacher, 2*(4), 38–41.

Waring, R. (1997). The negative effects of learning words in semantic sets: A replication. *System, 25,* 261–274.

Watanabe, T. (1992*). Making it happen: Interaction in the second language classroom* (Japanese translation). Chiyoda-Ku, Japan: Kenkyu-sha Publishers.

Watson-Gegeo, K. A., & Nielsen, S. (2003). Language socialization in SLA. In C. Doughty & M. Long (Eds.), *Handbook of second language acquisition* (pp. 155–177). Malden, MA: Blackwell.

Weedon, C. (1987). *Feminist practice and poststructuralist theory*. London: Blackwell.

Weinstein, G. (2001). Developing adult literacies. In M. Celce-Murcia (Ed.), *Teaching English as a second or foreign language* (3rd ed., pp. 171–186). Boston: Heinle.

Wells, G. (1981). *Learning through interaction: The study of language development*. Cambridge, England: Cambridge University Press.

Wells, G. (1999). *Dialogic inquiry: Toward a sociocultural practice and theory of education*. Cambridge, England: Cambridge University Press.

Wertch, J. (1979). From social interaction to higher psychological processes: A clarification and application of Vygotsky's theory. *Human Development, 22*, 1–22.

Wesche, M., & Ready, D. (1985). Foreigner talk in the university classroom. In S. Gass & C. Madden (Eds.), *Input in second language acquisition* (pp. 89–114). Rowley, MA: Newbury House.

Weslander, D., & Stephany, G. (1983). Evaluation of an English as a second language program for Southeast Asian students. *TESOL Quarterly, 17*(3), 473–480.

West, M. (1953). *A general service list of English words*. London: Longman, Green.

White, L. (1989). *Universal grammar and second language acquisition*. Philadelphia: John Benjamins.

White, L. (1990). Second language acquisition and universal grammar. *Studies in Second Language Acquisition, 12*, 127–128.

White, L., Spada, N., Lightbown, P., & Ranta, L. (1991). Input enhancement and L2 question formation. *Applied Linguistics, 12*, 416–432.

Widdowson, H. G. (1978). *Teaching language as communication*. Oxford, England: Oxford University Press.

Widdowson, H. G. (1979). *Explorations in applied linguistics*. Oxford, England: Oxford University Press.

Widdowson, H. G. (1996). Proper words in proper places. In T. Hedge & N. Whitney (Eds.), *Power, pedagogy and practice* (pp. 62–78). Oxford, England: Oxford University Press.

Wigglesworth, G. (2005). Researching L2 learning processes. *Annual Review of Applied Linguistics, 25*, 98–111.

Wilkins, D. A. (1979). Notional syllabuses and the concept of a minimum adequate grammar. In C. J. Brumfit & K. Johnson (Eds.), *The communicative approach to language teaching* (pp. 91–98). Oxford, England: Oxford University Press.

Williams, J. (2005). Form-focused instruction. In E. Hinkel (Ed.), *Handbook of research in second language teaching and learning* (pp. 671–691). Mahwah, NJ: Lawrence Erlbaum.

Winitz, H. (1996). Grammaticality judgment as a function of explicit and implicit instruction in Spanish. *The Modern Language Journal, 80*(1), 32–46.

Winn-Bell Olsen, J. (1977). *Communication starters and other activities for the ESL classroom*. Englewood Cliffs, NJ: Prentice Hall.

Winne, P. (2001). Self-regulated learning viewed from models of information processing. In B. Zimmerman & D. Schunk (Eds.), *Self-regulated learning and academic achievement: Theoretical perspectives* (pp. 153–189). Mahwah, NJ: Lawrence Erlbaum.

Wong, S. (2006). *Dialogic approaches to TESOL: Where the ginkgo tree grows*. Mahwah, NJ: Lawrence Erlbaum.

Wong-Fillmore, L. (1976). *The second time around: Cognitive and social strategies in second language acquisition*. Unpublished doctoral dissertation, Stanford University, Stanford, CA.

Wong-Fillmore, L. (1985). When does teacher talk work as input? In S. Gass & C. Madden (Eds.), *Input in second language acquisition* (pp. 17–50). Rowley, MA: Newbury House.

Wright, A., Betteridge, D., & Buckby, M. (1984). *Games for language learning*. Cambridge, England: Cambridge University Press.

Wright, A., Betteridge, D., & Buckby, M. (2006). *Games for language learning* (3rd ed.). Cambridge, England: Cambridge University Press.

Wright, A., & Maley, A. (1997). *Creating stories with children*. New York: Oxford University Press.

Yamashita, J. (2007). The relationship of reading attitudes between L1 and L2: An investigation of adult EFL Learners in Japan. *TESOL Quarterly, 41*(1), 81–105.

Yang, R. L. (1993). A study of the communicative anxiety and self-esteem of Chinese students in relation to their oral and listening proficiency in English (Doctoral dissertation, University of Georgia). *Dissertation Abstracts International, 54*, 49–68.

Yep, G. (2000). Encounters with the "other": Personal notes for a reconceptualization of intercultural communication competence. *CATESOL Journal, 12*(1), 117–144.

Yongqi Gu, P. (2003). Fine brush and freehand: The vocabulary-learning art of two successful Chinese EFL learners. *TESOL Quarterly, 37*(1), 73–104.

Yorio, C. (1980). The teacher's attitude toward the students' output in the second language classroom. *CATESOL Occasional Papers*, No. 6 (pp. 1–8).

Yoshihara, K. (1993). Keys to effective peer response. *CATESOL Journal, 1*, 17–37.

Young, D. (1991). Creating a low-anxiety classroom environment: What does language anxiety research suggest? *Modern Language Journal, 75*, 426–438.

Yuan, F., & Ellis, R. (2003). The effects of pretask planning and on-line planning on fluency, complexity, and accuracy in L2 monologic oral production. *Applied Linguistics, 24*, 1–27.

Zacarian, D. (2007). Mascot or member? *Essential Teacher, 4*(3), 9–10.

Zamel, V. (1985). Responding to student writing. *TESOL Quarterly, 19*(1), 79–101.

Zamel, V. (1992). Writing one's way into reading. *TESOL Quarterly, 26*(3), 463–485.

Zamel, V. (1997). Toward a model of transculturation. *TESOL Quarterly, 31*(2), 341–352.

Zehr, M. (2005). Two-way language immersion grows in popularity. *Education Week, 24*(23), 6–8.

Zhao, Y. (2003). Recent developments in technology and language learning: A literature review and meta-analysis. *CALICO Journal, 21*(1), 7–27.

Zimmerman, C. B., & Schmitt, N. (2005). Lexical questions to guide the teaching and learning of words. *CATESOL Journal, 17*(1), 164–170.

Zuengler, J., & Miller, E. R., (2006). Cognitive and sociocultural perspectives: Two parallel SLA worlds? *TESOL Quarterly, 40*(1), 35–58.

INDEX

NOTES

NOTES